Research Strategies in Psychotherapy
by Edward S. Bordin

The Volunteer Subject
by Robert Rosenthal and Ralph L. Rosnow

Innovations in Client-Centered Therapy
by David A. Wexler and Laura North Rice

The Rorschach: A Comprehensive System, in two volumes
by John E. Exner, Jr.

Theory and Practice in Behavior Therapy
by Aubrey J. Yates

Principles of Psychotherapy
by Irving B. Weiner

Psychoactive Drugs and Social Judgment: Theory and Research
edited by Kenneth Hammond and C. R. B. Joyce

Clinical Methods in Psychology
edited by Irving B. Weiner

Human Resources for Troubled Children
by Werner I. Halpern and Stanley Kissel

Hyperactivity
by Dorothea M. Ross and Sheila A. Ross

Heroin Addiction: Theory, Research and Treatment
by Jerome J. Platt and Christina Labate

Children's Rights and the Mental Health Profession
edited by Gerald P. Koocher

The Role of the Father in Child Development
edited by Michael E. Lamb

Handbook of Behavioral Assessment
edited by Anthony R. Ciminero, Karen S. Calhoun, and Henry E. Adams

Counseling and Psychotherapy: A Behavioral Approach
by E. Lakin Phillips

Dimensions of Personality
edited by Harvey London and John E. Exner, Jr.

The Mental Health Industry: A Cultural Phenomenon
by Peter A. Magaro, Robert Gripp, David McDowell, and Ivan W. Miller III

Nonverbal Communication: The State of the Art
by Robert G. Harper, Arthur N. Wiens, and Joseph D. Matarazzo

Alcoholism and Treatment
by David J. Armor, J. Michael Polich, and Harriet B. Stambul

A Biodevelopmental Approach to Clinical Child Psychology: Cognitive Controls and
Cognitive Control Theory
by Sebastiano Santostefano

Handbook of Infant Development
edited by Joy D. Osofsky

Understanding the Rape Victim: A Synthesis of Research Findings
by Sedelle Katz and Mary Ann Mazur

Childhood Pathology and Later Adjustment: The Question of Prediction
by Loretta K. Cass and Carolyn B. Thomas

Intelligent Testing with the WISC-R
by Alan S. Kaufman

Adaptation in Schizophrenia: The Theory of Segmental Set
by David Shakow

Rational-Emotive Therapy with Children and Adolescents

THEORY, TREATMENT STRATEGIES, PREVENTATIVE METHODS

MICHAEL E. BERNARD
MARIE R. JOYCE
University of Melbourne

A WILEY-INTERSCIENCE PUBLICATION
JOHN WILEY & SONS
New York • Chichester • Brisbane • Toronto • Singapore

Material on pp. 384–386, 395, and 428 was reprinted and material on pp. 388–389, 392–392, 409–411 was adapted from *Help Yourself to a Healthier You*, by Ann Vernon. (Published in 1980 by University Press of America, Inc. Reprinted by permission.)

Library of Congress Cataloging in Publication Data:

Bernard, Michael Edwin, 1950–
  Rational-emotive therapy with children and adolescents.

  (Wiley series on personality processes)
  Includes bibliographical references and indexes.
    1. Rational-emotive psychotherapy. 2. Child psycho-
therapy. 3. Adolescent psychotherapy. I. Joyce, Marie R.
(Marie Rose), 1939–   . II. Title. III. Series.
[DNLM: 1. Psychotherapy—In infancy and childhood.
2. Psychotherapy—In adolescence. 3. Mental disorders—
In infancy and childhood. 4. Mental disorders—In
adolescence. WS 350.2 B521r]

RJ505.R33B347   1983   618.92'8914   83-23442
ISBN 0-471-87543-0

Printed in the United States of America

10 9 8 7 6 5 4 3

To my father, Fred Bernard, for his many years of continuous love and support.

M.E.B.

To my husband, Gerry Joyce, I express my warmest thanks for his encouragement, generosity, and tolerance over a long period of time. I appreciate, too, the acceptance with which Paul, Sarah, Catherine, Damian, and Justine put up with their mother's preoccupations, and I thank them for their loving assistance.

M.R.J.

"That before coming here, everything that went wrong I used to blame it on myself, I used to say I was no good at anything, and why don't I just kill myself. I didn't know the meaning of Rational or ERational thoughts—they have slowly changed the way I think, so I don't get upset as I used to. I used to think of my bad points but now I also think of my good points, so now I don't go off my rocker, I am lucky to be able to think Rational thoughts."

(From a 14-year-old boy referred for low self-esteem and underachievement.)

Foreword

Of the more than one hundred books on rational-emotive therapy (RET) and cognitive-behavior therapy (CBT) that I have read during the past several years, this one by Michael Bernard and Marie Joyce is one of the very best. In fact, in some important respects it is *the* best of a fairly good lot of competing volumes; and I am delighted to write this foreword and to heartily recommend it to what I sincerely hope will be a host of eager readers.

In what ways is *Rational-Emotive Therapy with Children and Adolescents* outstanding? In several:

First, although it largely applies RET to therapists, educators, and other professionals working with youngsters, it gives a comprehensive outline of the theory and practice of this special kind of psychotherapy that makes it crystal clear to anyone who truly wants to understand what it is—and is not. Its incisive (and highly accurate) exposition of RET serves to nicely bring its assets, as well as its limitations, to the attention of virtually any interested professional or lay person. To read this book carefully and *not* get an excellent understanding of what RET is all about will take real talent!

Second, therapists of all kinds—including those who deal with adults and aging individuals as well as those who specialize in helping children and adolescents—will find it a most useful tract because it contains very detailed descriptions of most of the major RET and CBT methods, some of which are now unduly neglected by busy practitioners.

Third, therapists (and educators) who see children and adolescents will find it to be a pioneering text that includes more practical details of RET and CBT methods for use with this population than any other book I know. I feel sure that when readers use the present volume in conjunction with the companion anthology that I have edited with Michael Bernard, *Rational-Emotive Approaches to the Problems of Childhood* (New York: Plenum Press, 1983) they will not miss any of the RET and CBT theory and practice that is important to working with young people.

Fourth, this book by Bernard and Joyce not only covers RET and CBT methodology but puts it into a general psychological framework and interrelates it with other important work that throws light on the psychology of children and on the treatment of their problem thoughts, feelings, and behaviors. Though primarily oriented toward RET, it is engagingly catholic (and ecumenical!) in its approach. The authors, while taking off from much of my own work, have minds of their own, and present their differences as well as their concurrences with my own brand of RET.

Fifth, following the scientific position that RET espouses, this book is undogmatic, realistic, and carefully rooted in two kinds of empiricism: (1) a considerable amount of clinical data, and (2) findings based on controlled experimentation. Its theories, which are intensively and extensively exposited here, are clearly tied to solid data bases.

Do I have any important reservations about this book? Damned few! It's very comprehensiveness, however, and its inclusion of literally scores of techniques and materials that therapists can use leads me to present one caveat about the manner in which some therapists use available methods. On the one hand, they safely stick with a few techniques they have used over the years and sadly neglect newer and potentially useful methods. But on the other hand, they cavalierly use virtually all the scores of techniques at their disposal and fail to see that some of them (e.g., paradoxical intention) have limited value and had better be only occasionally used with a few selected clients. I hope that the readers of this book will use the many techniques it presents selectively and experimentally, to determine which are most effective with which clients more of the time. RET, as Bernard and Joyce accurately show, strives for efficient as well as effective therapy. And, taking a number of ideas from the hundreds that are presented in this volume, I hope that the therapists and educators who read this book will use them in a discriminating, efficient manner.

ALBERT ELLIS, PH.D.

Institute for Rational-Emotive Therapy
New York, New York
February 1984

Series Preface

This series of books is addressed to behavioral scientists interested in the nature of human personality. Its scope should prove pertinent to personality theorists and researchers as well as to clinicians concerned with applying an understanding of personality processes to the amelioration of emotional difficulties in living. To this end, the series provides a scholarly integration of theoretical formulations, empirical data, and practical recommendations.

Six major aspects of studying and learning about human personality can be designated: personality theory, personality structure and dynamics, personality development, personality assessment, personality change, and personality adjustment. In exploring these aspects of personality, the books in the series discuss a number of distinct but related subject areas: the nature and implications of various theories of personality; personality, characteristics that account for consistencies and variations in human behavior; the emergence of personality processes in children and adolescents; the use of interviewing and testing procedures to evaluate individual differences in personality; efforts to modify personality styles through psychotherapy, counseling, behavior therapy, and other methods of influence; and patterns of abnormal personality functioning that impair individual competence.

IRVING B. WEINER

University of Denver
Denver, Colorado

Preface

This book is the result of almost four years of planning and writing. Initially, our intention was to put together some practical educational materials which could be used in teaching the principles of rational thinking and emotive problem-solving skills to school-age children. We had been conducting rational-emotive counseling groups in the upper primary and lower secondary levels and believed we had assembled and developed a good collection of activities, methods, and techniques. After Dr. Bernard visited the Institute for Rational-Emotive Therapy in late 1979, it became apparent that there was a need for someone to review and consolidate what had been written in the Rational-Emotive Therapy (RET) literature concerning how RET could be used with younger populations to both prevent and remediate psychological problems. We decided to take on this task and, as a consequence, wrote this book in addition to carrying out our initial idea for making available RET preventative and counseling materials (Appendix 1).

We have put together this book with a number of ideas in mind. First, we wanted to present as comprehensive a picture as possible of the "state of the art" of RET with children and adolescents. We have reviewed, we believe, just about all major published work over the past 25 years which pertains to the topic of this book. We have also obtained a large number of unpublished master's and doctoral dissertations. A lot of what we read was fascinating and we felt should receive the light of day. We therefore have elected to provide direct excerpts from primary RET sources in an effort to convey the potential of RET as well as the creative ways in which it has been used over the past two decades with younger populations.

We also wanted to make this book practical so that it could be employed by mental health practitioners who either are working or are being trained to work with school-age children. We have spent a number of years applying RET in school settings. In our writing we have combined what we have learned about how RET should be employed with children, their parents, and teachers with what other RET practitioners have had to say. We are hopeful that our attempt to integrate our personal perspectives and experiences with those of others "works."

The organization of this book reflects our strong belief that the teaching of any form of therapy or counseling needs to be embedded in a context of sound psychological theory and practice. In this sense, this book is more than a "how to do it" cookbook approach to RET. A brief overview of chapters will illustrate this bias. Chapter 1 presents an overview of the American Psychological Association's DSM-III classification scheme of childhood psychopathology and in addition details current attempts at prevention and treatment of the problems of childhood. A cognitive conception of psychological maladjustment precedes an introduction to using RET with children and adolescents.

In order to fully appreciate how RET can be utilized with younger populations, we believe it is necessary to understand the general theoretical foundations of RET as well as how RET is applied with adults. In Chapter 2 we present the philosophy of RET and the rational-emotive theory of personality and human behavior. RET assessment and intervention procedures initially developed with adults—some of which have been modified for use with children and adolescents—are presented in Chapter 3.

In considering the emotional and behavioral problems of children from a cognitive perspective, RET recognizes the uniqueness of childhood. Chapter 4 discusses the importance of taking into account the cognitive-affective developmental status of children as well as their home (and school) environment in understanding the disturbed cognitions (e.g., irrational ideas) and cognitive processes (e.g., faulty reasoning) we observe in children with problems. The specific faulty cognitions and cognitive processes which underlie different emotional disorders (e.g., anger, anxiety, low self-esteem, and depression) and behavioral problems (e.g., underachievement, stealing) of children are outlined in great detail in Chapter 5.

Before we present practical guidelines (with plentiful case illustrations) for assessing children (Chapter 6), teaching them the basic ideas and skills of RET (Chapter 7), and applying other cognitive therapies (self-instructional training, interpersonal cognitive problem solving, stress inoculation, cognitive-behavioral social skill training, attributional training), along with RET to both prevent and resolve problems of childhood (Chapter 8), we discuss in the first part of Chapter 6 key ethical concerns in deciding whether to intervene or not and why RET is an ethically sound practice to employ with younger populations. In addition to discussing general perspectives on child assessment (cognitive-behavioral approaches, multidimensional child assessment, developmental considerations), we spend some time in discussing and supporting the use of methodological behaviorism. Throughout our book, we emphasize the need to validate empirically the clinical utility of RET with children and adolescents through the use of tightly controlled strong inference experimental studies. As is the case with any therapy we can think of (with the exception of behavior modification), RET scientific investigation has lagged behind its practice. Although we think it important to present a variety of child-oriented RET procedures that we and others have used successfully, we recognize that the utility of some of these have not been empirically demonstrated. We strongly recommend that RET practitioners keep one foot squarely planted in methodological behaviorism.

Over the years, RET has been employed by parents and educators in an attempt to prevent or minimize the problems of children. Chapter 9 describes how RET conceptualizes the role of parents and, to a lesser extent, teachers in childhood maladjustment. Methods for helping parents overcome their own emotional difficulties, acquire helpful child-rearing philosophies and practices, and aid their children who manifest emotional distress are presented. A discussion of the causes and effects of teacher stress concludes the chapter.

When applied in educational settings, RET is frequently referred to as Rational-Emotive Education (REE). Over the years an impressive collection of activities have been described which can be employed to introduce REE in the classroom as a part of a school's affective education program. The aim of these REE programs is prevention of psychological difficulties and the promotion of mental health. These same materials are also employed with groups of children and adolescents who have been referred for a specific problem (e.g., low self-esteem).

Appendix 1 presents three sets of education materials which can be employed as a part of rational-emotive education and rational-emotive group counseling for children five to seven years old, eight to twelve years old, and thirteen years plus. Scales of irrationality which have been used with school-age children are presented in Appendix 2.

In writing this book, we have tried to avoid the use of sexist terminology and the exclusive use of masculine pronouns. We have also made extensive use of words such as "should," "needs," and "must," which, when conveying absolutistic and imperative qualities and meanings, had better be avoided. We found it quite cumbersome to eradicate them from our writing as some RET practitioners have done. We feel confident that the reader will consider their meanings as relative and conditional.

We have used chapters from this book at the university level with students in clinical psychology, counseling, psychology, and school psychology training programs. We believe this book can be used as a basic book in mental health professional training programs. It will be of value to research scientists who are studying childhood maladjustment and psychopathology. Anyone who is working with children and adolescents will, hopefully, find our book contains useful insights as well as practical methods and techniques for solving problems.

For those readers who have extensive background in RET and who want to quickly get to the essence of how RET is employed with younger populations, we suggest you begin with Chapter 5. Such readers may also wish to spend some initial time acquainting themselves with the rational-emotive education and group counseling material presented in Appendix 1.

This book would not have been possible without the financial, secretarial and administrative support provided by the Department of Education, University of Melbourne (with thanks to the chairman, Morris Williams). The University of Melbourne's Office of Research and Graduate Studies provided generous support which enabled the first author to visit the Institute for Rational-Emotive Therapy in New York City, establish a good working relationship with Albert Ellis (the founder of RET), become an Associate Fellow of the Institute, and an approved supervisor of RET therapists in training. Acknowledgments are extended to Frank Naylor, Department of Education, the University of Melbourne, for his review of Chapter 2, and to Frank Hooper, Department of Family Studies, University of Wisconsin, for his comments on Chapter 4. Leslie Posen provided valuable assistance in the final, hectic months of manuscript preparation.

MICHAEL E. BERNARD
MARIE R. JOYCE

Victoria, Australia
February 1984

Contents

CHAPTER 1

Enhancing Psychological Adjustment
in the Childhood Years

The wonderful adaptability of modern-day children is somewhat surprising and heartening given the ever-changing and often times turbulent world that they have to learn how to deal with. Children of today have an especially heavy burden to carry. They, of course, develop within themselves as people. That is, children grow from a dependent state of relatively undifferentiated natural reflex through progressive stages of self-differentiation and self-direction. This growth process is painful and difficult. The move away from familial security to personal autonomy requires an almost antigravitational effort on the part of the child. The striving for and joy of independence is counterbalanced by the happiness and serenity of security and dependence. Recently, this struggle with personal growth has been joined by another interpersonal struggle. Many children no longer have the benefits of a fairly predictable, stable, and secure family world to fit into. They must integrate a continuously changing picture of themselves with a world characterized more and more by conflict, competition, and change.

Our own individual developmental crises and stages of growing up tend to be long forgotten as we progressively master new tasks of life. When we observe children on a daily basis, however, we can observe the expression of the myriad personal conflicts they experience. The developmental milestones and crises that children surmount are profound. In the years before children begin school, they learn to control pleasure seeking and aggressive impulses and to conform to the demands of parental authority. They begin to acquire the cooperative and sharing skills that are necessary for effective functioning in a family. Children's growing sense of vulnerability acquired through knowledge of self and the world brings with it fears and anxieties (Macfarlane, Allen, & Honzik, 1954). These most children successfully overcome. Problems of sleeping, eating, and toilet training are also overcome. They establish a sense of trust with their immediate environment, begin to develop autonomous functioning, and to initiate self-directed activities.

As children enter school, they learn to readjust their egocentric view of the world through gaining self-perception and objectivity. They further learn to delay their demands and needs, tolerate frustration, and enter the world of others. Children begin to appreciate the value of work and take pride in personal accomplishment. They develop effective relating skills with peers and adults. They cope with the potentially pernicious effects of academic rating, competition, and evaluation that goes along with the onset of formal schooling. They learn to live with the anxiety of living up to parental expectations, tolerate the difficulties of school-related failure, and develop the capacity of reflectivity and concentration (Stone & Church, 1979).

In adolescence, the central crisis is that of finding an identity—who one is and the meaning of existence. The adolescents' identity emerges from a coordination or match between how they view themselves and how others see them. By and large, adolescents come to terms with their increased sexual and aggressive drives and develop new ways of relating to parents and peers (A. Freud, 1969). They begin to acquire a stable set of personal values and begin the formation of an occupational identity. Youngsters do survive the almost fanatical peer group pressures of the adolescent subculture. Many develop realistic appraisals of their aptitudes, interests, and a positive sense of self-worth. By the end of secondary school, many adolescents have learned conflict—resolution strategies that enable them to handle life problems with realism and levelheadedness. They have conquered numerous hurdles and have put up with innumerable life frustrations. They are less anxious and fearful than they have ever before been. They have learned to be more tolerant and not to exaggerate the significance of events. They generally feel less angry and hostile, their behavior is more temperate and appropriate.

The adaptability of children is all the more impressive and remarkable considering the external social stresses of modern day living. One out of three marriages ends in divorce. Fifteen percent of white children under eighteen and over 50% of black children live with only one parent. There has been a dramatic increase in the use of alcohol by parents. An estimated 15–20% of adolescents are subjected to child abuse and neglect. There has also been increasing mobility of the American family with over 50% of all families having relocated during the schooling of their child. Large-scale desegregation and integration have increased community-wide stress (from American School Counselor Association, 1979).

So when the United States President's Commission on Mental Health (1978) reports that between 5–15% of the school-age population is in need of some form of mental health care, it is surprising in some ways that the figure is not higher. It is some small comfort that between 85%–95% of children are estimated to be reasonably well-adjusted emotionally and socially.

It is the unfortunate case that a relatively small percentage but an extremely large number of school-age children today demonstrate a variety of forms of emotional maladjustment and behavioral disturbances. Some children growing up have not been successful in attaining the degree of personal and social integration and maturity that enables them to cope with the stresses of their changing familial, social, educational, and vocational worlds.

As a background to our introduction to how Rational-Emotive Therapy (RET) is employed with children and youth, we present a brief overview of childhood maladjustment, detail current attempts at both prevention and treatment of childhood emotional and behavioral difficulties, and discuss a cognitive model of maladjustment.

CHILDHOOD MALADJUSTMENT

We have, indeed, left the "dark ages" in terms of not only recognizing, but also studying and treating the psychological problems of children and adolescents. Up through the 1930s very little professional attention—with the exception of mental retardation—was directed toward disorders of the childhood period. The interaction of developments over the past 50 years in the mental hygiene movement, child guidance clinics, mental retardation, and psychometric measurement has resulted in the specialization of the field of childhood psychopathology (Knopf, 1979). The study of childhood psychopathology involves the examination of abnormal behaviors

> that persistently deviate from cultural and developmental norms in either extremes of frequency and intensity, and that are evidenced by impairment in one or more of the following areas of human functioning: intellectual and cognitive, emotional expression and control, and interpersonal relationships. [Knopf, 1979, p. 32]

Classification of Childhood Psychopathology

There has been increasing interest over the past fifteen years in developing classification schemes or taxonomies for describing childhood psychopathology. Three of the more advanced schemes for classifying "psychopathological syndromes" of childhood (constellation of behaviors that coexist) were put out in 1966 by the Group for the Advancement of Psychiatry (GAP), in 1969 by the World Health Organization (International Classification of Diseases, ICD-9) (Rutter, et al.), and in 1980 by the American Psychiatric Association (Diagnostic and Statistical Manual of Mental Disorders, DSM-III).

By way of demonstrating how mental disorders of childhood have been organized in a taxonomic system of classification, we shall briefly consider the DSM-III which is the most recent revision of a manual of mental disorders which was first published by the American Psychiatric Association in 1951. It should be kept in mind that RET does *not* employ DSM-III or any other nosological system. DSM-III is being presented to make the reader aware of a scheme that is useful as well as being widely used for classification of and communication about child disorders. DSM III seeks to provide a comprehensive system for the classification of the range of mental disorders observed in children and adults. The authors of DSM-III have conceptualized mental disorders as

> a clinically significant behavioral or psychological syndrome or pattern that occurs in an individual and that is typically associated with either a painful

symptom (distress) or impairment in one or more areas of functioning (disability). In addition, there is an inference that there is a behavioral, psychological or biological dysfunction, and that the disturbance is not in the relationship between the individual and society. [p. 6]

There are a number of innovative features in the latest revision, including a more inclusive set of categories of mental disorders as well as extensive detailing of mental disorders of childhood. The classification system consists of 17 major categories of mental disorders. These categories are operationally defined in terms of specific behaviors that are necessary for justifying a specific diagnosis. Additionally, DSM-III has adopted a multiaxial framework which permits diagnosis across the following five separate axes:

Axis I	Clinical syndromes; conditions not attributable to a mental disorder that are a focus of attention or treatment
Axis II	Personality disorders; specific developmental disorders
Axis III	Physical disorders and conditions
Axis IV	Severity of psychosocial stress
Axis V	Highest level of adaptive functioning past year

The major categories and subclasses of mental disorders in DSM-III that delimit mental disorders in infants, children, and adolescents are presented in Table 1.1. While these disorders are specific to persons under the age of 18, other categories of mental disorders that are not specific to childhood or adolescence (e.g., organic mental disorders, affective disorders, personality disorders) may also be employed in the diagnosis of childhood psychopathology.

The two major categories that are of interest to persons who are involved in counseling and therapy with school-age children are Categories II Behavioral (overt) and III Emotional. Summary descriptions of these categories and subclasses are presented in Table 1.2. A close examination of Table 1.2 will reveal to the reader the essential features of important emotional and behavioral disorders of the childhood period. There are, of course, many other ways of describing and categorizing behaviors that are subsumed within these disorders.

The DSM-III, GAP, and ICD-9 have been largely, though not exclusively, extrapolated from adult pathological disorders (Achenbach & Edelbrock, 1983). The identification of childhood syndromes has been largely through clinical observation. Arguing for a childhood classification scheme that is based on actual behavioral patterns of children rather than constructs derived from adult disorders, researchers have directed their attention toward reliable descriptions of children's behavior based on empirically derived syndromes. Recently, the use of multivariate analyses of parent, teacher, and mental health rating scales

TABLE 1.1. Summary of DSM-III Classes of Mental Disorders Usually First Evident in Infancy, Childhood, or Adolescence

I. Mental Retardation

Mild
Moderate
Severe
Profound
Unspecified

II. Behavioral (Overt)

Attention Deficit Disorders
  with Hyperactivity
  without Hyperactivity
  Residual Type
Conduct Disorder
  Undersocialized, Aggressive
  Undersocialized, Nonaggressive
  Socialized, Aggressive
  Socialized, Nonaggressive
  Atypical Conduct Disorder

III. Emotional

Anxiety Disorders of Childhood or Adolescence
  Separation Anxiety Disorder
  Avoidant Disorder of Childhood or Adolescence
  Overanxious Disorder
Other Disorders of Infancy, Childhood, or Adolescence
  Reactive Attachment Disorder of Infancy
  Schizoid Disorder of Childhood or Adolescence
  Elective Mutism
  Oppositional Disorder
  Identity Disorder

IV. Physical

Eating Disorders
  Anorexia Nervosa
  Bilimia
  Pica
  Rumination Disorder of Infancy
  Atypical Eating Disorder
Stereotyped Movement Disorders
  Transient Tic Disorder
  Chronic Motor Tic Disorder
  Tourett's Disorder
  Atypical Tic Disorder
  Atypical Stereotyped Movement Disorder
Other Disorders With Physical Manifestations
  Stuttering
  Functional Enuresis

(Continued)

TABLE 1.1   *(Continued)*

Functional Encopresis
Sleepwalking Disorder
Sleep Terror Disorder

V.   *Developmental*

Pervasive Developmental Disorders
   Infantile Autism
   Full Syndrome Present
   Residual State
Childhood Onset Pervasive Developmental Disorders
   Full Syndrome Present
   Residual State
   Atypical Pervasive Developmental Disorder
Specific Developmental Disorders
   Developmental Reading Disorder
   Developmental Arithmetic Disorder
   Developmental Language Disorder
   Developmental Articulation Disorder
   Mixed Specific Developmental Disorder
   Atypical Specific Developmental Disorder

Source: Diagnostic and statistical manual of mental disorders.
American Psychiatric Association, 1980.

TABLE 1.2.   **Summary Description of DSM-III's Categories of Behavioral and Emotional Childhood Disorders**

II.   Behavioral (overt)

A.   Attention Deficit Disorder (The essential features are signs of developmentally inappropriate inattention and impulsivity.)
   1.   With hyperactivity. The child displays, for his or her mental and chronological age, signs of developmentally inappropriate inattention, impulsivity, and hyperactivity. The signs must be reported in the child's environment, such as by parents and teachers.
   2.   Without hyperactivity. The criteria for the disorder are the same as those for Attention Deficity Disorder with hyperactivity except that the individual never had signs of hyperactivity.
B.   Conduct Disorder (The essential feature is a repetitive and persistent pattern of conduct in which either the basic rights of others or major age-appropriate societal norms are violated.)
   1.   Undersocialized, aggressive. A repetitive and persistent pattern of aggressive conduct physical violence, thefts) in which the basic rights of others are violated. Failure to establish a normal degree of affection, empathy, or bond with others.
   2.   Undersocialized, nonaggressive. A repetitive and persistent pattern of nonaggressive conduct (violation of important rules, running away, lying) in which either the basic rights of others or major age-appropriate societal norms or rules are violated. Failure to establish a normal degree of affection, empathy, or bond with others.
   3.   Socialized, aggressive. A repetitive and persistent pattern of aggressive conduct in which the basic rights of others are violated. Evidence of social attachment to others.
   4.   Socialized, nonaggressive. A repetitive and persistent pattern of nonaggressive conduct in which either the basic rights of others or major age-appropriate societal norms or rules are violated. Evidence of social attachment to others.

(Continued)

TABLE 1.2   *(Continued)*

III. Emotional

A.   Anxiety Disorders of Childhood or Adolescence (This subclass includes three disorders in which anxiety is the predominant clinical feature. In the first two categories, the anxiety is focused on specific situations. In the third, the anxiety is generalized to a variety of situations.)

    1.   Separation anxiety disorder. Excessive anxiety concerning separation from those to whom the child is attached as manifested by: unrealistic worry about possible harm befalling major attachment figures or fears that they will leave and not return; unrealistic worry that an untoward calamitous event will separate child from a major attachment figure; persistent reluctance or refusal to go to school in order to stay with major attachment figures at home; persistent reluctance or refusal to go to sleep without being next to a major attachment figure or to go to sleep away from home; persistent avoidance of being alone in the house and emotional upset if unable to follow the major attachment figure around the home; repeated nightmares involving the theme of separation; complaints of physical symptoms on school days; signs of excessive stress upon separation, or when anticipating separation, from major attachment figures; social withdrawal, apathy, sadness, or difficulty concentrating on work or play when not with a major attachment figure.

    2.   Avoidant disorder of childhood or adolescence. Persistent and excessive shrinking from contact with strangers. Desire for affection and acceptance. Avoidant behavior becomes sufficiently severe to interfere with social functioning in peer relationships.

    3.   Overanxious disorder. The predominant disturbance is generalized and persistent anxiety or worry (not related to concern about separation), as manifested by: unrealistic worry about future events; preoccupation with the appropriateness of the individual's behavior in the past; overconcern about competence in a variety of areas; excessive need for reassurance about a variety of worries; somatic complaints for which no physical basis can be established; marked self-consciousness or susceptibility to embarrassment or humiliation; marked feelings of tension or inability to relax.

B.   Other Disorders of Infancy, Childhood or Adolescence

    1.   Reactive attachment disorder of infancy. Age of onset before eight months. Lack of the type of care that ordinarily leads to the development of affectional bonds to others. Lack of developmentally appropriate signs of social responsivity. Weight loss or failure to gain appropriate amount of weight unexplainable by any physical disorder. Behavioral signs include: weak cry, excessive sleep, lack of interest in environment, hypomotility, poor muscle tone, weak rooting and grasping in response to feeding attempts.

    2.   Schizoid disorder of childhood or adolescence. No close friend of similar age other than a relative or a similarly isolated child. No apparent interest in making friends. No pleasure from usual peer interaction. General avoidance of nonfamilial social contacts, especially with peers. No interest in activities that involve other children.

    3.   Elective mutism. Continuous refusal to talk in almost all social situations, including at school. Ability to comprehend spoken language and to speak.

    4.   Oppositional disorder. A pattern of disobedient, negativisitic, and provocative opposition to authority figures as manifested by violation of minor rules, temper tantrums, argumentativeness, provocative behavior, and stubborness. No violation of the basic rights of others or of major age-appropriate societal norms or rules.

    5.   Identity disorder. Severe subjective distress regarding uncertainty about a variety of issues relating to identity including long-term goals, career choice, friendship patterns, sexual orientation and behavior, religious identification, moral value system, and group loyalties. Impairment in social or occupational (including academic) functioning.

Source: Diagnostic and statistical manual of mental disorders. American Psychiatric Association, 1980.

of the behavior of children has yielded factors that encompass the range of childhood pathological disorders. Popular rating scales and checklists used in research studies include the Louisville Behavior Checklists (Miller, 1967), Child Behavior Checklists (Achenbach, 1978; Achenbach & Edelbrock, 1979), Peterson Problem Checklist (Peterson, 1961), Devereux Child Behavior Rating Scale (Spivack & Levine, 1964), Pittsburgh Adjustment Survey Scale (Ross, Lacey & Parton, 1965), Kohn Symptom Checklist and Social Competence Scale (Kohn & Rosman, 1972), Behavior Problem Checklist (Quay & Peterson, Note 1), Teacher Rating Form (Clarfield, 1974), and the School Behavior Checklist (Miller, 1972).

Achenbach and Edelbrock (1978) have conducted an extensive review and analysis of empirical research of childhood disorders. Some of the studies they reviewed yielded a broad band of encompassing childhood syndromes. Four broadband syndromes include overcontrolled (inhibited, shy-anxious, internalizing), undercontrolled (aggressive, externalizing, acting out, conduct disorder), pathological detachment, and learning problems. Other studies have yielded a more narrow band of differentiated syndromes, including academic disability, aggressive, anxious, delinquent, depressed, hyperactive, immature, obsessive-compulsive, schizoid, sexual problems, sleep problems, social withdrawal, somatic complaints, and uncommunicative.

Achenbach and Edelbrock (1983) have presented the results of an extensive factor analysis of the Child Behavior Checklist. Table 1.3 presents a listing of derived syndromes for boys and girls across different age groups which are somewhat similar to those presented in DSM-III. It will be observed that the syndromes are different for boys and girls and that they change as children grow older. Additionally, the syndromes have been listed under broadband factors labeled as internalizing and externalizing. The results of all factor-analytic studies indicate the dimension of internalizing−externalizing appears to be a basic structure of childhood emotional disorders.

In delimiting dimensions of psychopathology in adolescents, Miller (1980) describes four dimensions which he subsumes under a broadband externalizing factor and four under an internalizing factor. According to Miller, the externalizing factor encompasses these four major spheres of social behavior:

1. Demands that personal needs take precedence over the needs of others (narcissism).
2. The use of violence to obtain need satisfaction.
3. Defiance or noncompliance with social and legal norms.
4. Defiance of or noncompliance with formal educational or intellectual demands. [p. 170]

The internalizing dimension encompasses the following four areas of social behavior:

1. Withdrawal from and a reluctance to participate in or extract pleasure from interpersonal relationships.

2. Development of maladaptive internal, behavioral, and somatic mechanisms for coping with stress and interpersonal relationships.
3. Submissiveness to the dominance of others and a reluctance to assert self to achieve need satisfaction.
4. Development of extreme and bizarre behaviors with an apparent indifference to the effect of this behavior on others. [p. 170]

The dimension of adolescent turmoil is represented in both the internalizing and externalizing factor.

This brief review of classification schemes of childhood psychopathology has hopefully served a number of purposes. It indicates that disorders of childhood can be differentiated from one another. The review also sensitizes mental health workers to different categorical views of disorders in children that they may not have previously been exposed to and that are being used extensively in the diagnosis of childhood disorders. The review also alerts practitioners that there are groups of somewhat diverse behaviors that appear to occur together and that can be usefully related under a broader hypothetical construct for the

TABLE 1.3. Psychopathological Syndromes in Boys and Girls across Age

Group	Internalizing Syndrome		Mixed Syndromes		Externalizing Syndromes	
Boys aged 4–5	1.	Social withdrawal	1.	Sex problems	1.	Delinquent
	2.	Depressed			2.	Aggressive
	3.	Immature			3.	Schizoid
	4.	Somatic complaints				
Boys aged 6–11	1.	Schizoid or anxious	1.	Social withdrawal	1.	Delinquent
	2.	Depressed			2.	Aggressive
	3.	Uncommunicative			3.	Hyperactive
	4.	Obsessive–compulsive				
	5.	Somatic complaints				
Boys aged 12–16	1.	Somatic complaints	1.	Hostile withdrawal	1.	Hyperactive
	2.	Schizoid			2.	Aggressive
	3.	Uncommunicative			3.	Delinquent
	4.	Immature				
	5.	Obsessive–compulsive				
Girls aged 4–5	1.	Somatic complaints	1.	Obese	1.	Aggressive
	2.	Depressed			2.	Sex problems
	3.	Schizoid or anxious			3.	Obese
	4.	Social withdrawal				
Girls aged 6–11	1.	Depressed			1.	Cruel
	2.	Social withdrawal			2.	Aggressive
	3.	Somatic complaints			3.	Delinquent
	4.	Schizoid–obsessive			4.	Sex problems
					5.	Hyperactive
Girls aged 12–16	1.	Anxious–obsessive	1.	Immature	1.	Cruel
	2.	Somatic complaints	2.	Hyperactive	2.	Aggressive
	3.	Schizoid			3.	Delinquent
	4.	Depressed withdrawal				

Source: Achenbach and Edelbrock (1983).

purposes of communication with other professionals, guiding treatment programs in a global fashion, and putting themselves in touch with a body of detailed experimental and clinical data that may be relevant (Evans & Nelson, 1977).

We do not wish to enter into arguments concerning the reliability and validity of childhood classification schemes, nor the pros and cons of labeling. It is our personal view that such schemes can be useful when employed as global assessment devices for the purposes of descriptive data-gathering, administration (e.g., placement), communication and classification and not to guide the selection and formulation of a treatment program. We also agree with Rutter and Schaffer (1980) that disorders rather than individuals should be classified.

We have also presented the aforementioned taxonomies because it has been our experience that many university and college training programs, especially in the areas of counseling and school psychology, do not expose prospective practitioners to categorical approaches to the study of childhood psychopathology. For those interested in this area, we recommend the texts of Erikson (1978), Kessler (1966), Knopf (1979), and Achenbach (1981). Behavioral classification schemes are presented and discussed by Adams, Doster and Calhoun (1977) and Phillips, Draguns, and Bartlett (1975).

Prevention and Treatment

Since the middle 1960s there has been increasing interest shown by mental health practitioners in developing preventative delivery systems and child treatment programs to meet the needs of maladjusted children and youth. Attempts were made to identify familial, educational, and other factors that contributed to the abnormal developmental and learning patterns observed in children with learning, socioemotional, and behavioral problems. A search for factors that put children "at risk" was the concern of professionals who dealt with primary prevention. Developmental, learning, psychoanalytic, and neural—psychological theories were extended downward in an attempt to understand the origins of childhood psychopathology. At the same time, the late 1960s saw the counseling profession and related disciplines turn their attention to developing educationally based preventative and treatment programs for primary and elementary school-age children (see Muro & Dinkmeyer, 1977).

School-Based Affective Education Programs

Psychologists, educators, and other mental health professionals have become increasingly concerned with the socioemotional development of children and have attempted to increase the number of children and youth who receive some form of preventative care by introducing educational courses into the schools. Curriculum developments in this area have been variously designated as affective education (Alschuler, 1969), emotional education (Ellis, 1971a), confluent education (Brown, 1971), values clarification (Raths, Harmin, & Simon, 1966) and human relations training (Weinstein & Fantini, 1970).

These approaches have in common the facilitation of social and emotional growth and the enhancement of self-esteem. Most focus on the feelings of students about themselves and encourage the expression by students of thoughts, feelings and experiences. They encourage the discovery of the individual's unique qualities, and the acceptance and appreciation of self. Concomitant with an emphasis on the individual's self, these programs have the objectives of improving the individual's skill in interpersonal relationships, emphasize active listening, and helping students become aware of the feelings of others (empathy). They generally foster an attitude of toleration of other people's individual differences, the development of a flexible outlook on life, and the building of a personal value system. All programs appear to have as final endpoints the acquisition of communication skills, of problem solving and decision making abilities, a responsible attitude for dealing with life's difficulties, and the capacity to act appropriately. Affective education seeks to promote school learning by insuring as much as possible the development of healthy attitudes toward oneself and others. It also encourages self-direction through teaching students to both identify and reach their own previously defined goals.

An underlying assumption of affective education programs is that if all children and adolescents are exposed to experiences that are designed to promote their socioemotional growth, then many potential problems can either be minimized or eliminated. The advocates of affective education do not, however, wish to do away with specialist support.

There appear to be three main ways in which affective education programs can be introduced within schools. First, is through *congruent courses* where specific principles and aspects of psychological and emotional growth are taught in a separate curriculum. Popular curriculum kits and approaches employed in congruent courses are *Developing Understanding of Self and Others* (Dinkmeyer, 1970), *Dimensions of Personality* (Limbacher, 1969), *Methods in Human Development* (Bessell & Palomares, 1970), *Toward Affective Development* (Dupont, Gardner & Brody, 1974), and *Magic Circle* (Palomares, 1972). Collections of resources, activities and references for affective education include Chase (1975), Thayer and Beeler (1975), Thayer (1976), Treffinger, Borgers, Render, and Hoffman (1976), and Valett (1974).

Confluent education is an innovative way of integrating cognitive and affective learning experiences and outcomes within the mainstream curriculum and classroom (Brown, 1971, 1975). Brown has described confluent education as

the putting together of the affective and the cognitive through conscious teaching acts (in) an attempt to make the educational process and its product, the student, more human. Along with other characteristics, being more human means exhibiting more intelligent behavior; that is, the use of the marvellously unique human mind in a context of reality where feelings influence the mind and the mind feelings, but where these feelings, too, arise from the same reality context. [1975, p. 101].

Brown and his colleagues at the Laboratory for Confluent Education at the University of California at Santa Barbara have modified a variety of traditional cognitively-oriented subject curricula by incorporating personalized and affective elements.

The *contextual approach* for implementing affective education involves modifying the climate of the classroom so that teacher−student encounters might stimulate psychological adjustment. Numerous teacher inservice and training courses are designed around principles of humanistic psychology (Rogers, 1961, 1969) and provide for the acquisition of affective interpersonal and communication skills (Gordon, 1974; Ivey & Gluckstern, 1974) as well as conflict−resolution strategies (Dreikurs & Cassel, 1972).

Within recent times, both local school districts and university-affiliated training institutes have become involved in the development of affective education programs. Some of the more important developers include the Association for Supervision and Curriculum Development, Esalen Institute, Ford Foundation, Human Development Training Institute, Institute for Rational-Emotive Therapy, Outward Bound, University of California at Berkeley and Santa Barbara, and the University of Massachusetts' Center for Humanistic Education.

An examination of the goals and objectives of affective education will reveal the strong influence of theories of humanistic and individual psychology (Adler, 1958) as well as developmental (Dinkmeyer & Caldwell, 1970) and client-centered counseling (Rogers, 1969). Other systems of psychotherapy and psychology that play an important role or have a strong influence upon the development of school programs concerned with the affective domain include psychoanalytic theory (Bettelheim, 1950), transactional analysis (Berne, 1964; Freed, 1971, 1973; Harris, 1967), gestalt therapy (Lederman, 1973; Perls, 1969), reality therapy (Glaser, 1969), and rational-emotive psychotherapy (Ellis, 1962).

Counseling and Therapy with School-Age Children

The treatment of children with emotional and behavioral problems continues to evolve partly in response to the difficulties encountered when employing a one to one child−practitioner approach as well as the lack of success of any one therapy in resolving the range of common problems of the childhood years. There has been a decreased interest in the fostering of specialty fields such as counseling and clinical and school psychology. A prescriptive approach is becoming favored by many child practitioners and applied researchers who have found that certain disorders are more responsive to certain techniques than others. As such, the training requirements of practitioners have broadened to encompass a fuller exposure to different therapies and techniques. These diverse approaches have been combined in professional practice in what has been referred to as "technical eclecticism" (Garfield & Kurtz, 1976; Lazarus, 1976). A very significant new trend in child therapy has been the training of caretakers or mediators of children such as parents and teachers to intervene directly with children (Tharp & Wetzel, 1969). There has been a tremendous increase in parent and teacher effectiveness training groups. Finally, there has also developed an interest in preventative and educational models of child treatment.

Gradually, schools have begun to assume a greater involvement in both the prevention and remediation of childhood problems. The advent of "developmental counseling" and "affective education" has been the response of counselor educators to the call for primary prevention of the mental health problems of childhood. Along with this response has been the move toward early identification of children at risk as well as the advent of direct guidance and counseling for elementary school-age children.

A review of texts that deal with child therapy and counseling (e.g., Keat, 1974; Muro & Dinkmeyer, 1977; Schaefer & Millman, 1978; Poppen & Thompson, 1974; Thompson & Poppen, 1974; Hansen, Warner, & Smith, 1980) as well as journals in the areas of school counseling and psychology, child clinical psychology and psychiatry reveals a full range of approaches, methods and techniques that are employed with children and adolescents.

We present a listing of 14 of the most common therapeutic and counseling approaches that are employed in helping children with emotional and behavioral problems (see Table 1.4). We have identified the important proponents of each approach and present a brief summary description of the methods and goals of each. These approaches derive from the fields of counseling, psychology and psychiatry. Each approach has its roots in one of the three major world views of humans: psychoanalytic, humanistic, and behavioral. The only exceptions to this is, perhaps, multimodal therapy which, given its eclectic orientation, does not appear to flow from any one model and psychopharmacological which derives from a neuropsychiatric model. Keat (1974) has indicated that each approach can be distinguished from another in terms of therapeutic focus (behavior, client—therapist relationship, appraisal and understanding, emphasis on personalizing and humanizing) and main function (providing for an action orientation, basis of counseling, and understanding of client). They can also be differentiated on the basis of whether cognitions, emotions, or behaviors constitute the major focus of therapeutic change.

As we indicated earlier, there has been considerable fertilization across the different professional disciplines concerned with children. It appears, with the exception of psychoanalysis, factors that determine which approach a professional will employ depend not so much on role identity as it does on the orientation of the practitioner's training program, number of years of pre-professional training, and locale of service delivery (school, community mental health center, private practice).

We have presented this summary as relevant background and to reinforce our view that there is no evidence to our knowledge that suggests that any one of the approaches has demonstrated unequivocal effectiveness in resolving the problems of childhood. We believe that each of these approaches provides unique ways of conceptualizing, describing, and communicating about prob-

TABLE 1.4. Therapeutic/Counseling Approaches Employed with School-Age Children

Approach	Founders/Leaders	Methods	Goals
Behavioral	Bandura, Eysenck, Wolpe, Pavlov, Skinner	Counterconditioning, modeling, operant conditioning, functional analysis, successive approximation, small sequential steps, self-management training.	Decrease maladaptive behavior, increase and maintain appropriate behavior, acquisition of new behavior.
Client-centered	Rogers	Empathy, congruence, genuineness, unconditional positive regard, active listening, transference relationship, insight.	Clarification of life plans and tasks, increase in life focus and self-awareness, improvement in overall functioning and interpersonal relationships.
Cognitive	Beck, Ellis, Meichenbaum	Analysis and modification of maladaptive cognitions and beliefs underlying emotional distress and behavioral disorders, verbal persuasion and other behavioral methods, stress inoculation emotive imagery.	Change in client's appraisal of self and world, development of coping skills.
Developmental	Dinkmeyer, Havighurst	Highly collaborative client–therapist relationship emphasizing client-centered approaches, self-examination, problem solving and decision making techniques.	Development of human potential and ability to plan, responsibility, maturity in social relationships.
Existential	Frankl, May, Moustakas	Verbal persuasion, paradoxical intention, deflection, insight through inward searching moving from self-awareness to decision making.	Help client find meaning in life, client's realization of potential through elimination of constraints, openness.
Gestalt	Perls	Confrontation with here and now, therapist confrontation and encounter with client, interpretation of body language, awareness expanding and self-discovery exercises differentiating reality from fantasy, empty chair technique.	Help client move from environmental to self-support, increase ability to use one's senses and personal responsibility, full personality integration, cultivate individuality, be fully present.
Individualistic	Adler, Driekurs	Development of good client–therapist relationship, data gathering by therapist about client's role in family and self-perception of purposes of behavior, interpretation, active reconstruction and redirection of client by therapist.	Change client's self-concept, correct perceptions of client, help client recognize mistakes in living, change in life goals.

Therapy	Theorists	Techniques	Goals
Multimodal	Keats, Lazarus	Pragmatic technical eclecticism including anxiety management training, imagery, cognitive, drug, and interpersonal treatments, assertion training, biblio- and audiotherapy, operant conditioning, desensitization, modeling, gestalt techniques.	Improvement in client's life functioning through changes in behavior, affect, sensations, imagery, cognitions, interpersonal relationships, drugs and diet.
Perceptual	Snygg, Combs	Accurate empathy, self-disclosure, facilitating process of furthering client's perceptions.	Change or reorganization of client's self-concept, and in turn perception of world.
Play Therapy	Axline, A. Freud, S. Freud, Klein	Free play situation where child acts out fantasies and conflicts, use of a variety of toys that provide for creative and aggressive activities, development of close therapist–child therapeutic relationship.	Diagnosis of areas and the degree of child's problems, understanding of child's fantasies, thoughts and feelings about him/herself and others, catharsis, reality testing by child, communication of human values, social learning.
Psychoanalytic	Axline, Erikson, S. Freud	Free association, interpretation, use of transference relationship, parapraxis, play therapy, dream analysis, insight.	Reduction in anxiety, ego construction, insight.
Psychopharmacological	Employed by many child therapists since early 1940s	Variety of psychostimulants, antipsychotics and tricyclics.	Removal of physiological cause of maladaptive behavior, changing psychological state of client to facilitate use of other therapies, increase child's functional capacity.
Reality Therapy	Glasser	Warm client–therapist relationship, verbally active focusing on present behavior, help client to make own value judgments, make realistic plans to enhance self-worth and make commitments.	Helping client make better choices and fulfill needs within constraints of reality.
Transactional Analysis	Berne, Freed	Teaching parent–child–adult model, analysis of verbal interactions and recurrent life plans, role play.	Help client to understand self, to strengthen functioning of child's adult state and to become more aware of life's options.

lems of living and adjustment. It would seem that until the relative clinical utility of these approaches has been demonstrated, it would be professionally unsound to dismiss any one of them on the basis of philosophic disagreement and bigotry. We also do not believe that we have sufficient information to judge the merits of an eclectic versus a theoretically consistent approach to the assessment and treatment of disorders of childhood. Given our background, training and experience, we feel that RET, with its emphasis on cognitive, emotive, and behavioral techniques, provides us with sufficient understanding and expertise to resolve many of the problems we encounter when working with school-age children.

A COGNITIVE VIEW OF MALADJUSTMENT

The assessment and treatment of emotional and behavioral problems of adults and, more recently, children, is being strongly influenced by the advent of a cognitive view of psychological adjustment and psychopathology (Beck, 1970a, 1976; Ellis, 1962; Kazdin, 1978; Mahoney, 1974, 1977; Mahoney & Arnkoff, 1978; Meichenbaum, 1977; Murray & Jacobson, 1978). The cognitive model is in an early stage of development and, unlike the older psychoanalytic, humanistic, and behavioral models, its theoretical parameters remain largely unarticulated. A reading of recent cognitive theorizing suggests little agreement and, at times, discussion concerning general issues such as the cognitive "world view" of the human organism (cosmology, epistemology), the cognitive view of human learning and development (continuous versus discontinuous, environmental versus teleological), and the range and definition of theoretical concepts and principles that are considered legitimate to be subsumed within the cognitive view (cognitive structure, cognition, inner dialogue). This ambiguity and state of uncertainty appears to stem from a variety of sources, a primary one being that the cognitive view as applied in clinical practice has evolved in a rather piecemeal and *ad hoc* fashion, borrowing and amalgamating concepts from cognitive, developmental, social and behavioral psychology, cognitively-oriented personality theory, investigations of cognitive processes in human learning research, and from cognitively and semantically-oriented psychotherapies, including behavior modification. Another related problem is that within the past ten years, an integration of behavior theory and cognitively-oriented psychotherapy has been instigated.

Historical Influences

We have identified [with the help of Mahoney (1974), Kazdin (1979), Kendall & Hollon (1979a), and others] a number of streams of influence which have directly or indirectly given life to the cognitive view. Research dealing with classical and operant conditioning has revealed the influence of cognitive factors (expectations concerning the relationship between unconditioned stimuli and conditioned responses; awareness of reinforcement contingencies) in explaining differences between animal and human learning as well as intra- and interindividual differences in human learning (Kazdin, 1978; Murray & Jacobson, 1978). Another domain of empirical work that suggests the importance of cognition in learning and psychological adjustment is the study of emotions. Findings from this area indicate that cognitive appraisals and covert self-verbalizations play a major mediational role between environmental events and emotional and behavioral responses (Murray, 1964; Lazarus, 1966), and that physiological arousal and autonomic functioning can be influenced by cognitive factors (Schacter, 1966). Thought management programs ("Day by day, in every way, I'm getting better and better") are historical predecessors (Coué, 1922; Carnegie, 1948; Peale, 1960) to cognitive restructuring and self-instructional training which are subsumed under the cognitive model. Certain personality theorists (Kelly, 1955; Rotter, 1954; Mischel, 1973) have advanced a phenomenological viewpoint which accords a major role to the individual's consciousness and higher mental functioning (cognitions, conceptualizations, constructions) in determining behavior. Cognitive psychology has yielded theories of learning which emphasize cognitive activity and cognitive structuring as primary learning processes (Lewin, 1935; Tolman, 1935). Miller, Galanter, and Pribram (1960) were particularly instrumental in articulating a cognitively-based computer model which accounts for human thoughts, feelings, and behaviors. This computer model serves as a precursor to a cognitive model of human psychological adjustment and disturbance. In the computer model, human beings are viewed as active processors of experience, "rather than a passive or functionally vacuous composite of stimulus—response linkages" (Mahoney, 1974, p. 128). According to this model, the human organism's behavior is a function of different types of information processing (attention, encoding, storage, retrieval). Murray and Jacobson (1978) describe the model as follows:

> Based on a computer analog, the new model stresses the flow of information through stages of perception, encoding, short-term memory, long-term storage, retrieval, and outputs of various kinds. Learning consists not just of linking stimuli and responses, but of placing the information provided by the antecedent or consequent stimulus in a hierarchically organized network. Man is viewed as a complex organism capable of impressive adaptation. He is in a continuous reciprocal relationship with his environment, a relationship which might be analogized as a cybernetic feedback loop. Behavior changes are influenced by the current physiological state of the organism, his past learning history, the existing environmental situation, and a variety of interdependent cognitive processes. [p. 145]

The Cognitive Model

Michael J. Mahoney has played a major role in attempting to articulate a cognitive-behavioral model (he refers to it as a *cognitive learning* model) of psychological adjustment. The difficulties in bringing the cognitive and behavioral approaches together have been attested to by Mahoney and Arnkoff (1978) when they write, "At the present time, the cognitive learning perspective continues to be a relatively diversified amalgam of principles that have yet to be formalized into a monolithic system or model" (p. 692). Mahoney and Arnkoff (1978) discuss three commonalities shared by proponents of different cognitive-behavioral procedures.

1.   Humans develop adaptive and maladaptive behavior and affective patterns through cognitive processes (selective attention, symbolic coding, etc.).

2.   These cognitive *processes* can be functionally activated by *procedures* that are generally isomorphic with those of the human learning laboratory (although there may be other procedures which activate the cognitive processes as well).

3.   The resultant task of the therapist is that of a diagnostician–educator who assesses maladaptive cognitive processes and subsequently arranges learning experiences that will alter cognitions and the behavior and affect patterns with which they correlate. [p. 692]

We believe that the first commonality is basically a cognitive conception of human behavior. The second and third points involve the use of behavioral principles and methods to influence cognitive activity. This is a position we are in accord with and which we outline below. We have resisted the temptation to describe the model by the hybrid cognitive-behavioral term and, instead, prefer to use the term *cognitive* to emphasize the importance of central mediating processes, and cognitive-symbolic processes, and of the person's cognitive-phenomenological view in human adjustment and disturbance.

We wish to differentiate between two types of mediational models which have been employed to account for symbolic factors and private events in psychological adjustment. The *covert conditioning* model

imposes the theory and language of conditioning on private experience. Thoughts, images, memories, and sensations are described as covert stimuli, covert responses, or covert consequences. The skull becomes a rather crowded Skinner box in which such conventional principles as reinforcement, punishment, and extinction are said to describe the function and patterning of private experience. The inferred mediators in the covert conditioning model are often discussed as if they were faded representations or approximations of publicly observable events. [Mahoney, 1974, p. 66]

A major assumption of this model is that principles of learning can be equally applied to describe the operation of both overt and covert events (e.g., Cautela, 1967; Homme, 1965; Ullman, 1970). While this model is regarded as a developmental link bridging cognitive and behavioral theory and therapy (e.g., systematic desensitization, thought-stopping, coverant control, covert conditioning therapies), we believe it is based more on a behavioral than a cognitive view of psychological disturbance. While we in no way wish to minimize the historical and clinical importance of the covert conditioning model and related therapies, our interest in this book is in describing rational-emotive theory and therapy which has its roots in a cognitive model of human disturbance that is far more complex than the covert conditioning model. It is to this model we now turn.

A central assumption of this cognitive model is that perception, representation, interpretation, and appraisal of external events influence in an idiosyncratic fashion the psychological adjustment of the human organism. The role of central mediation and cognitive-representational processes is seen as paramount in understanding psychological adjustment. The human organism is viewed as interpreting reality, assimilating new information into a preexisting structure of knowledge, and accommodating to the acquisition of new knowledge. Through the operation of cognitive factors such as expectations, attributions, interpretations, beliefs, selective attention, and different logical reasoning processes, the individual interacts with the world in a personal, idiosyncratic and largely self-determined way. Feelings and behaviors depend upon the content of thoughts and images. The analysis of cognition leads to an understanding of the origins of different feelings and behaviors. Cognitive deficits and errors are central to the understanding and treatment of psychological disorders. Therapy is directed toward cognitive modifications (Marzillier, 1980). This view differs greatly from both the psychoanalytic model which attributes psychological disorders to early childhood experience and unconscious forces of which the individual is largely unaware and the behavioral model which attributes dysfunctional emotional states and behavioral maladjustment to unfortunate pairings of conditioned and unconditioned stimuli. While differing in terms of where they locate the origins and causes of disorders (within person versus environment), both models share the theoretical premise that individuals have little control over their psychological adjustment. These two models have spawned many of the approaches used in the treatment of psychological problems of childhood presented in Table 1.4.

An important philosophical assumption underlying the cognitive model is that of *interactionism* and *reciprocal determinism* which emphasizes the complex and continuous causal interaction between individuals and their environment (Bandura, 1969, 1977; Thoresen & Mahoney, 1974). Unlike orthodox psychoanalytic and classic behaviorist views, the cognitive perspective places individuals at the center of their universe, and accords them a large amount of responsibility for creating their own emotional disturbances and for determining their destiny (Ellis, 1973a). In contrast to nonmediational and covert-conditioning perspectives, the cognitive-learning model views the organism as active:

> One of the cardinal characteristics of the cognitive learning perspective is its view of man as an active element in his own growth and development. He is both a controlled and controlling organism, a product and producer of environmental forces. The unending sequence of his experience is not passively etched on a *tabula rasa*. The "raw data" of experience are selectively filtered, transformed, categorized, and stored. [Mahoney, 1974, p. 146]

Cognitive versus Behavioral Models

In discussing the advent of a cognitive-behavioral treatment of psychological maladjustment, Kendall and Hollon (1979a) have written:

> Cognitive behavioral interventions are the offspring of bidirectional movements that have been directed and dictated by both empirical and pragmatic necessities. The bidirectional movements involve behavior therapists' increasing concern with mediational therapeutic approaches and cognitive therapists growing recognition of methodological behaviorism. [p. 2]

While there are definite therapeutic benefits which have accrued when cognitive and behavioral approaches have been combined (recently referred to as cognitive behavior therapy, CBT), we believe that the attempts to articulate a comprehensive cognitive-behavioral model may continue to be frustrated by irreconcilable theoretical and epistemological assumptions underlying the cognitive and behavioral views. It is beyond the scope of this chapter to present a thorough discussion of the problems which arise in attempting to articulate a unified and all-embracing cognitive-behavior model of psychological maladjustment. While different cognitive-behavioral approaches (RET, covert conditioning) share certain practices in common, the practices derive from different psychological theories which are themselves derived from logically independent and incompatible metaphysical and metatheoretical models.

By way of example, it seems to us that behaviorally-oriented CBT approaches are based on a mediational stimulus-organism-response *mechanistic model* which requires that all behavior, whether internal or external, has the same logical status (Fodor, 1965). At a metatheoretical level, humans are viewed as *reactive* organisms, essentially at rest, with activity resulting from external or peripheral influences (Reese & Overton, 1970). The epistemological position associated with behaviorally-oriented CBT theories is *naive realism* (a copy theory of knowledge where the learner plays no active role in knowledge acquisition). Psychological functions such as thinking, willing, wishing, and perceiving are viewed as "complex phenomena that are reducible to more simple phenomena governed by efficient causes (and history)" (Reese & Overton, 1970, p. 131). As the correspondence between internal and external behavior is direct and continuous, changes in cognition (brought about by therapy) ought to be revealed in immediate and, to some degree, situationally bound changes in behavior. The validation of behaviorally-oriented CBT approaches occurs when these changes are observed to occur.

Cognitively-oriented CBT approaches appear based on an *organismic model* which accepts behavior and cognition (contents and processes) as fundamentally different. The cosmology associated with this model is traceable to Leibnitz, who emphasized that humans are inherently and spontaneously active (Reese & Overton, 1970). Change is brought about through natural differentiation and individuation of the organism, rather than through an interaction of environmental forces and learning history. The epistemological position associated with the active organismic model is one of *constructivism*. (The learner actively participates in the construction of reality.) This constructionist position accords individuals major responsibility for their psychological states.

Adherents to this position are concerned with the structures of knowledge which mediate behavior, since what the organism knows (and, therefore, feels and acts) can be best understood in terms of analyzing available structure. In terms of pyschological theory and experimentation, the focus is much more on the role structures play in influencing a wide range of behavior. Within this model, the range of hypothetical cognitive constructs which account for human knowledge and, therefore, behavior vary greatly in degree of abstractness (automatic thoughts, beliefs) as they do not have to be tied directly to discrete and observable behavior. The validity of this approach involves documenting how changes in cognition and fundamental cognitive structures results in widespread changes in behavior. The documentation of maintenance and generalization is crucial in demonstrating the validity and utility of postulated underlying cognitive structures and processes.

We raise these issues to sensitize those who are attempting to define a unified theory and philosophy of CBT that such an enterprise *may not* be possible. We believe that a psychological model of maladjustment will have to be primarily cognitive or behavioral, and not both. We therefore choose to embrace a cognitive model which employs behavioral methodologies to test its theoretical propositions and principles. A more thorough consideration of a cognitive view of maladjustment will be presented in Chapters 2 and 5.

Cognitive Therapies

In their review of cognitive-behavior approaches in psychotherapy (see Table 1.5), Mahoney and Arnkoff (1978) enumerate three distinct classes of interventions which help to define the field of CBT. *Cognitive restructuring approaches* are oriented toward teaching clients more adaptive thought patterns which lead to decreases in emotional overarousal and/or acquisition of practical coping skills for dealing with problematic tasks and situations. Principle cognitive restructuring therapies include rational-emotive therapy (Ellis, 1962), self-instruction training (Meichenbaum, 1974), and cognitive therapy (Beck, 1970a, 1976). *Coping skills therapies* subsume a variety of procedures which are designed to teach clients how to cope with stress. The more popular of these include covert modeling (Cautela, 1971; Kazdin, 1973), coping skills training (Goldfried, 1971), and stress inoculation (Meichenbaum, 1975a, Novaco, 1978). The third major division of CBT includes *problem solving therapies* which are oriented toward teaching the individual how to go about solving interpersonal difficulties which often lead to a variety of emotional disorders. Chief among these are Spivack and Shure's (1974) interpersonal cognitive problem solving, D'Zurilla and Goldfried's (1971) behavioral problem solving, and Mahoney's (1974) personal science.

TABLE 1.5.   Contemporary Cognitive-Behavioral Interventions

Cognitive Restructuring	Coping Skills Therapies	Problem Solving Therapies
Rational-Emotive Therapy (Ellis, 1962)	Covert Modeling (Cautela 1971; Kazdin, 1973)	Behavioral problem solving (D'Zurilla & Goldfried, 1971)
Self-instruction (Meichenbaum, 1974)	Coping Skills Training (Goldfried, 1971)	Problem solving therapy (Spivak & Shure, 1974; Spivak, Platt & Shure, 1976)
Cognitive Therapy (Beck, 1970, 1976)	Anxiety management (Suinn & Richardson, 1971) Stress inoculation (Meichenbaum, 1975)	Personal science (Mahoney, 1974, 1977b)

Source: Mahoney and Arnkoff (1978, p. 703).

A number of different cognitively oriented techniques are being increasingly applied to the problems of children and youth. We have identified the following five techniques which are being employed or which hold promise for resolving childhood emotional and behavioral problems: self-instructional training, stress inoculation, cognitive-behavioral social skill training, interpersonal cognitive problem solving, and attributional retraining. The theoretical background to these approaches, as well as a review of how they may be employed, will be presented in Chapter 8.

Some Terminological Distinctions

Therapies which are grouped under the cognitive model are based on the general theoretical premise that cognitions underly emotional and behavioral disturbance (Marzillier, 1980). There is some confusion in the literature concerning the meanings of cognition. Marzillier (1980) indicates three ways in which cognition is employed. *Cognitive events* (cognitive behaviors) refer to thoughts and images occurring in the individual's stream of consciousness. We do not believe, however, that these events are always immediately accessible to the individual's awareness (see Chapter 2). *Cognitive processes* include ways in which external stimuli are appraised and transformed. Perhaps the most elusive of all the meanings of cognition is that of *cognitive structure*. Meichenbaum's (1977) humorous comment attests to the status cognitive structure occupies as a hypothetical construct: "Cognitive structure seems to be the cognitive psychologist's Rorschach card or Linus blanket—he can see anything he wants in it and it gives him a sense of security" (p. 212). Marzillier (1980) offers the following perspective concerning cognitive structures.

These are constructs used to account for more general, long-standing cognitive characteristics such as beliefs and attitudes. Kovacs and Beck (1978, p. 526) have termed such structures "schemata," which they have described variously as "relatively enduring aspects of a person's cognitive organization," "organized representation of prior experience," and "systems for classifying stimuli." These structures form the rules and principles that regularize and govern an individual's interpretation of events and his behavior, and describe more fundamental and deep-seated cognitive aspects. A similar view of cognitive structure is provided by Meichenbaum (1977) who writes of "that organizing aspect of thinking that seems to monitor and direct the strategy, route, and choice of thoughts." (p. 213), [p. 252]

Another conception of cognition which we believe to be very important for considering the role of cognition in human emotion and behavior is that of *inner-speech* (also called inner dialogue, private dialogue, private speech, automatic thoughts, covert self-instructions, covert self-verbalizations, covert self-statements, self-talk, self-referenced speech).

> The one thing psychologists can count on is that their subjects of clients will talk, if only to themselves; and not infrequently, whether relevant or irrelevant, the things people say to themselves determine the rest of the things they do. [Farber, 1963, p. 196]

We consider inner-speech as speech for oneself. As we indicate in the last section of Chapter 2, inner-speech has an idiosyncratic syntactic and semantic system which is really only intelligible to the individual (except when one is getting ready to communicate to another or is rehearsing a speech). Inner-speech may also vary in the degree to which the individual is aware of what it is he is saying to himself. We believe inner-speech serves two distinct functions. When people are using their inner-speech to think about, plan, and carry out a course of action, we can say that inner-speech is serving an *instrumental and cognitive self-guiding function*. Meichenbaum and Asarnow (1979) provide an example of a self-instructional dialogue which was designed to increase reading comprehension in poor readers and which illustrates the cognitive self-guiding function of inner speech.

> Well, I've learned three big things to keep in mind before I read a story and while I read it. One is to ask myself what the main idea of the story is. What is the story about? A second is to learn important details of the story as I go along. The order of the main events or their sequence is an especially important detail. A third is to know how the character feels and why. So get the main idea. Watch sequences. And learn how the characters feel and why. [p. 17]

When people talk to themselves about how they are feeling about what they are planning and/or doing, we designate inner-speech as serving an *affective function*. The following excerpt from a discussion with a depressed 12-year-old girl reveals the affect dimension of inner-speech: "It is my fault daddy left home; I should have been a better girl; I am a bad girl; everything is so icky." We have observed that these two functions or dimensions of inner-speech often run in parallel. As people describe to themselves a plan of action, they also wonder how they will perform. They engage in certain feeling self-statements which revolve around their expectations of success and how their performance will reflect on others and their own opinion of themselves. Meichenbaum (1977) indicates that inner-speech exerts both an influence on on-going behavior as well as influences cognitive structure. To maximize maintenance and generalization, the focus of therapy should be on insuring that changes in a client's inner-speech produce enduring changes in cognitive structure.

Cognitions as the Cross-Walk of Therapeutic Change

There appears to be one overriding reason why the cognitive view has, perhaps, the greatest utility for conceptualizing and treating psychological maladjustment. Over the years, a number of scholars who have attempted to distill the essential core elements of all forms of psychotherapy have arrived at the conclusion that significant improvements in client functioning result from fundamental changes in the way the clients *view* themselves and their world. Many have indicated that therapeutic changes result from clients learning how to redirect and modify their self-talk. Frank (1961), in discussing therapeutic change, accords a major role to changes in clients' perceptions and assumptions. According to Strupp (1969), a client acquires a set of new beliefs as a result of traditional therapy. Murray and Jacobson (1978), in summarizing Strupp's work, indicate that the general lessons to be learned in therapy "amount to giving up immature beliefs and strategies in favor of more mature, realistic, and responsible patterns" (p. 65). Franks and Wilson (1973, 1975) conclude, after their reviews of aversion therapy, that classical and operant processes appear to operate through cognitive processes. Traditional psychotherapy uses indirect insight-oriented techniques to arrive at changes in clients' understandings. Bandura (1977) has argued that behavior modification procedures are effective primarily because of their influence upon symbolic processes. Cognitive therapies tackle emotional and behavioral problems through direct cognitive modifications.

RATIONAL-EMOTIVE THERAPY WITH CHILDREN AND ADOLESCENTS

Rational-emotive therapy was developed by Albert Ellis, a clinical psychologist and psychotherapist, during the year 1955. Ellis practiced orthodox psychoanalysis in New York City from the late 1940s through 1951, and psychoanalytically-oriented psychotherapy from 1952 to 1954. A reading of his early work during this time shows his disenchantment with the passive methods of classical psychoanalysis and Rogerian nondirective therapy, as well as his growing awareness that insight gained through psychoanalytic interpretation was in many instances insufficient to bring about emotional adjustment and behavioral change.

RET has evolved over the past 25 years to the point where today it is considered one of the most popular schools of psychotherapy (Garfield &

Kurtz, 1976; Smith, 1982) and represents an essential component of the cognitive-behavior therapy movement. Given the acceptance within psychotherapy and, in particular, behavior therapy of the role of cognition in the formation of emotions and behavior (Bandura, 1969; Franks, 1969), RET has had more than ever before a profound effect on the field of psychopathology and personality theory. Rational-emotive *zeitgeist* is disseminated primarily from the Institute for Rational-Emotive Therapy. (Ellis is the executive director of the Institute, which is located at 45 East 65th Street in New York City.)

History

The application of RET to parenting and to the treatment of children and adolescents was pioneered by Ellis in the mid-1950s (Ellis & Bernard, 1983a). It was not too long after he began to use RET with adults that Ellis could see how it could be utilized by a practitioner working with children and with the children's parents and teachers. Cognitive parenting techniques were included in his first book on RET, *How to Live with a "Neurotic"* (Ellis, 1957). He tape recorded a number of sessions with young children, and these tapes, which were widely circulated, encouraged many practitioners to use RET methods with younger clients (Ellis, 1959). In the late 1960s RET was promoted by a number of RET practitioners who demonstrated how it could be effectively employed with school-age children (Doress, 1967; Ellis, 1967; Ellis, Moseley & Wolfe, 1966; Glicken, 1967, 1968; Hauck, 1967; Lafferty, 1962; Lafferty, Dennell, & Rettlich, 1964; McGory, 1967; Wagner, 1966).

During the 1970s, a large number of articles, chapters, and manuals appeared that explained the use of RET with children and adolescents (Bedford, 1974; Brown, 1974, 1977, 1979; Daley, 1971; DiGiuseppe, 1975a; Edwards, 1977; Ellis, 1971a, 1971b, 1972a, 1972b, 1973b, 1973c, 1975a, 1975b, 1976b; Grieger, Anderson & Canino, 1979; Hauck, 1974, 1977a; Knaus, 1974, 1977; Knaus & McKeever, 1977; Kranzler, 1974; Maultsby, 1974, 1975; McMullin, Assafi & Chapman, 1978; Muirden, 1976; Protinsky, 1976; Rand, 1970; Rossi, 1977; Sachs, 1971; Shibbles, 1978; Tosi, 1974; Young, 1974a, 1974b, 1977). Because of the observed success of RET that was found in early clinical and experimental investigations, the Institute for Rational-Emotive Therapy in New York started The Living School in 1970, a small, private grade school where all the children were taught RET along with the usual elementary school curriculum. The school prospered for a number of years, in the course of which it was found that teachers (not therapists) could teach young children RET in the regular classroom and thereby help them and their parents to improve their emotional health and well-being.

A number of important publications on how RET can be used in school settings have appeared (Di Nubile & Wessler, 1974; Ellis, 1971a, 1971b, 1975a; Gerald & Eyman, 1981; Knaus, 1974; Sachs, 1971; Vernon, 1980; Wolfe, 1970). Perhaps the most influential of these is a 1974 publication by William Knaus, chief consulting psychologist to The Living School, entitled,

Rational-Emotive Education: A Manual for Elementary School Teachers. This manual contains lesson plans which details how teachers and other mental health professionals can introduce basic rational thinking concepts and skills to groups of younger children. This program has been used as the major independent treatment in research studies which have explored the use of RET in the form of Rational-Emotive Education (REE) in child-oriented group counseling and as a major component of school-based affective education programs. In order to have a greater influence on classroom practice, The Living School was transformed in 1975 into the Rational-Emotive Education Consultation Service. It provides: (1) inservice workshops for teachers and counselors; (2) consultation to schools, classes, and teachers wishing to implement a program of RET; and (3) materials and techniques for use in classrooms and/or school counseling settings (Waters, 1981).

The 1980s appear to hold great promise for RET being more fully incorporated into the practice of child counseling and therapy. Chapters have appeared which describe how RET can be systematically employed with children (DiGiuseppe, 1981; DiGiuseppe & Bernard, 1983; Hauck, 1980; Waters 1982a, 1982b), adolescents (Young, 1983), parents (Bard, 1980; Hauck, 1983; McInerney, 1983; Woulff, 1983), and teachers (Bernard, Joyce & Rosewarne, 1983). RET guidelines for treating childhood maladjustment (e.g., conduct disorders, fears, anxieties, phobias, low frustration tolerance, social withdrawal, impulsivity, underachievement, sexual problems) have appeared in *Rational Emotive Approaches to the Problems of Childhood* (Ellis & Bernard, 1983b). Indeed, as a reading of this material demonstrates, there is now a sophisticated as well as a systematic procedure for employing RET with children and youth.

Applications

RET is currently being used with both elementary and secondary level students in the United States and is being increasingly applied at the primary and secondary levels in Australia, England, and other countries in Western Europe. When RET is applied in a school setting, it has been variously referred to as rational counseling (Wagner, 1965), rational behavior therapy, rational self-counseling (Maultsby, 1971, 1975), rational emotive education (Ellis, 1971; Knaus, 1974), rational thinking (Cangelosi, Gressard & Mines, 1980), and rational-emotive counseling (Protinsky, 1976). During the past decade, RET has been applied in other "child-treatment" settings such as community mental health facilities, child guidance clinics, child psychiatric out-patient units attached to hospitals, social welfare agencies, and in private practice by a variety of practitioners including psychiatric social workers, counselors, child psychologists and child psychiatrists.

RET is being applied by different professionals concerned with and responsible for the mental health of the child. In a school context, RET is generally introduced by a practitioner (psychologist, counselor, social worker) to teachers, administrators, other special service personnel, and to parents on either a one to one or group basis. RET serves two general functions when introduced to these populations. It enables adults who interact with school-age children to solve their own personal problems in order that these problems do not interfere with the upbringing of children (Morris & Kanitz, 1975). Additionally, as a consequence of being exposed to principles of RET, child care personnel are in an ideal position to introduce RET to children at the time children actually experience emotional distress and exhibit over- or underreactions. Such involvement through modeling and other instructional devices helps children surmount personal crises, overcome disabling emotions and behavior and, over time, acquire RET coping strategies that enable them to exercise self-control and to independently solve their own future problems.

RET is also applied by a variety of the professionals directly to children. In schools, school and pastoral counselors, psychologists, principals, teachers, and social workers meet with children on an individual or group basis and employ RET and REE in preventative or developmental counseling, as well as in problem-oriented counseling interventions. In the case of a one to one practitioner–child contact, RET has been successfully employed with children and adolescents referred for problems of acting out, violently destructive and disruptive behavior, impulsivity, stealing, cheating, social withdrawal and depression (general unhappiness), public speaking, test taking and social anxieties, fear and phobias related to school, truancy, underachievement and learning disabilities, poor motivation and procrastination, parent–child and teacher–student discord, and a variety of other problems of childhood adjustment including sexual behavior, sleep disorders, and over- and undereating.

Teachers and parents seen by RET practitioners have reported significant and beneficial changes (Brown, 1977) in up to 85% of children, with academic improvement existing in virtually all of these cases (Glicken, 1967). We have employed RET with children who have ranged from five to 18 years of age and older. A school psychologist (Brown, 1977) has reported introducing RET in many schools in Florida and indicates that he has used it mostly with children in grades six through twelve. For counseling children in earlier grades, he suggests teaching teachers the principles of RET. A teacher (Daley, 1971) reported employing reason and RET principles with deprived preschool children. RET has been employed successfully with school-age children from both low SES (e.g., Block, 1978) and middle income families (e.g., Brody, 1974). Recently, RET has been utilized with emotionally disturbed children (Wasserman & Vogrin, 1979), hearing impaired adolescents (Giezhels, 1980), learning disabled students (Meyer, 1982; Staggs, 1979), intermediate special education students (Eluto, 1980), and maternally deprived adolescents living in a residential group home (Dye, 1980).

There are two purposes for which RET can be employed with groups of children. For children in grades three through twelve, RET has been employed with intact classes or small groups of students who have not been referred for any specific problems. In this context, RET is employed preventatively by any of a number of school personnel as developmental counseling or rational-emotive education as a means to further the socioemotional and personal growth of participating students. RET has also been used in group counseling by trained mental health practitioners to help solve problems that children may be currently experiencing. RET counseling groups may be composed of students who share heterogeneous as well as homogeneous problems. Materials such as those presented in Appendix 1 can be employed as a part of both rational-emotive education and rational-emotive group counseling.

There are a number of reasons why RET is suited for use in schools. One primary reason is that RET views its main purpose as educational and focuses on teaching students a model for helping themselves resolve their own problems. The techniques it employs in training are educational and include guided discovery, didactic presentation, homework assignments, structural role play, assertion training, behavioral rehearsal, shame attacking, risk taking and emotion evoking exercises, and a variety of other exercises, activities and methods that are compatible with the educational process. Ellis (1975a) has written:

> Rational-emotive therapy (RET) proves particularly applicable to the work of a school counselor, since it closely follows an educational rather than a medical or psychodynamic model of psychotherapy and counseling. It holds that humans become disturbed and malfunction mainly because of their erroneous and irrational beliefs, attitude values, and philosophies, and that perhaps the most elegant and efficient means of helping them solve their emotional problems lies in teaching and demonstrating to them specifically how they needlessly upset themselves and showing them how to dispute and surrender their self-defeating beliefs. [p. 236]

Another related advantage of employing RET in schools is that the approach RET takes in working with students is one that reinforces many of the goals of independence, responsibility, and self-reliance that are endemic to the whole purpose of education. In accordance with this position, Protinsky (1976) writes:

> In contrast to the medical model of psychopathology which views emotional disturbance as an illness that the therapist takes responsibility for curing, RET maintains that people are responsible for and have the ability to control their thoughts and, thereby, their emotions and behavior. The role of the therapist is largely educational, and the client takes a more active and responsible role in self-change. [p. 242]

Wagner (1966) has applied RET with children in the form of Rational Counseling. He advocates the superiority of this approach over any other technique employed by school psychologists and school counselors, and has enumerated distinct advantages.

1.   Rational counseling is easier to learn and to apply. Experience has shown that the average school psychologist, having familiarized himself with the litera-

ture and listened to a few representative tapes, can do a respectable job with this technique after a few trial runs.

2. School problems are often pressing and require swift intervention and solution. Questions of transfer, promotion, suspension, etc., are sometimes imperative, and the counselor is not permitted the luxury of the months of therapeutic contact usually required with analytic or client-centered techniques. Rational counseling permits immediate intervention and a direct attack on the present problem.

3. Rational counseling teaches the child to live in his environment. The non-blaming attitude which is the essence of this technique helps the child to accept teachers, parents and peers, and to make the best of an imperfect world.

4. The basic principles are easy to understand, apply and can be adapted to children of most ages and IQs. It gives the child something to work with and provides immediate environmental reinforcement. The child is not burdened with complicated theories and "dynamics" which he often cannot understand, but is given a direct explanation of why he is maladjusted and is shown, in simple terms, how to become adjusted.

5. Children, having lived in this culture for a shorter period of time than their parents are usually less indoctrinated than adults and make good subjects.

6. Rational counseling, being shorter than most other techniques, permits greater and more effective use of the counselor's limited time and does not necessarily require the cooperation of recalcitrant or hostile parents. Furthermore, should the counselor fail to help the student, it is unlikely that he will hurt him. Rational counseling makes no dangerous incursions into the unconscious; it militates against irrational and anti-social behavior, and it discourages ruminations, woolgathering and preoccupation with historical antecedents or "dynamics." [p. 28]

RET can be incorporated in schools in a variety of ways. Workshops and training sessions have introduced principles of RET to administrators, school psychologists and counselors, social workers, and teachers. Brown (1977) has observed that through RET, "teachers see the objective reality that students are only doing what they should be doing, given what they have learned" (p. 205). Brown has taught rational self-counseling in high school psychology classes as a new theory of personal psychology. His course has the goals of teaching RET theory to students, seeing if they see any value the theory may have for their own lives, and applying RSC in daily living. "Students like the idea they control their own emotions" (p. 205).

RET resource rooms have been set up in high schools where students can go when they feel overstressed and where students are required generally to read RET bibliotherapeutic material and/or conduct a rational self-analysis. Low achieving students enrolled in prevocational job training programs have attended RET groups as a part of their work study program. In these groups, they learn how to solve problems of frustration in relation to their job experience. We have worked with low achieving and low self-esteem students in the grades six through ten range, most of whom are enrolled in remedial reading classes. These groups are generally extremely successful, and the students express favorable opinions about the time they spend in the groups.

Edwards (1977), in seeking to reach the largest number of students as possible, employed the medium of the high school newspaper. "In my two years as a counselor, I opened my door (and a few eyes) with my 'Ideas from Edwards' columns. They were fun to read. More important, they said something. And they brought students in" (p. 10). We present an excerpt from one of his columns.

PLAYING THE FOOL
OR HOW TO OVERCOME MISTAKES WITH
A MINIMUM OF PAIN

"What a donkey I am. I'd better join that guy who takes donkies around to play basketball. I really screwed up this time. My God, I'm ruined."

Anybody out there recognize these lines? I am afraid many of us are guilt-ridden slobs at one time or another. The person talking in the introduction is saying some irrational things. He's taking a mistake and turning it into the sinking of the Titanic. . . . More important, he is making his original error much worse. He is mentally kicking himself down for a goof. Ask yourself this question, "Will it help?" . . . It is important to note that *he* has made himself the fool. Of course he goofed. Why deny it? And yes, it was discouraging, even painful. But what does degrading himself do about fixing the damage? Nothing! Actually, it is worse than nothing. It strengthens his feelings of Foolhood. (Foolhood is a pretty cool idea for a club. If you belong, you get your own trashcan to wear on your head.)

"Okay, wiseguy, what can it do to fix things?"

I'm glad you asked that question. I hope you ask it of yourself. The first thing to do is recognize the mistake for what it is. It is a sign of being human. To err is human, and so on. Next, put the failure in its proper light. It is a pain and may be very unfortunate. But don't take the big plunge off the Heights of irrationality just because you goofed. Think about how you did it. Can you do anything to set it straight? If so, do it. If not, learn from your mistake. Don't laugh it off and say, "I don't care," if you do care, but put it in its place. Go into the next situation armed with experience and knowledge. Maybe you won't make the mistake again or at least not so big a mistake. [Edwards, 1977, pp. 10–11]

Ellis (1975a) proposed that RET can be disseminated to students through the use of *dramatic presentations*.

School counselors can supervise the presentation of skits, plays, role-playing sessions, TV shows, movies and tapes presentations in the course of which children learn to differentiate between rational and irrational beliefs, and in which they see how the latter almost invariably lead to dysfunctional results. In a role-playing skit, for example, a counselor got four members of a class to deliberately give a hard time to a fifth player and to sabotage her in every way possible. She was not so much to resist their sabotage as to prevent her from reacting with depression or hostility. Then her responses got critiqued by the rest of the pupils. The whole class learned a series of appropriate and inappropriate responses to the kind of sabotaging to which, in her role, she had deliberately submitted. [pp. 240–241]

Research

We have spent a fair amount of time trying to learn what the research literature indicates concerning the relative effectiveness of RET and REE with school-age populations. After reviewing all available material—and much empirical work can be found only in unpublished doctoral dissertations—we can conclude that the full utility of RET with younger populations is yet to be determined. The state of experimental investigation of RET is yet to be fully refined.

Most of the controlled experimentation which looks at the application of RET and REE with younger populations has taken place since 1970. A limited number of case studies have been reported in the late 1960s and early 1970s that indicate that RET principles can be effective with children (Ellis, 1970; Ellis, Moseley & Wolfe, 1966; Glicken, 1968; Hauck, 1967; Knaus, 1974). Beginning with a study of Albert (1972) and continuing for the next ten years (e.g., Meyer, 1982), experiments which have explored the effectiveness of RET with children and youth have followed a similar format. The experimental question of concern is generally an open-ended one: "What is the effect of RET (or REE) on ("normal," younger–older, fourth grade–eighth grade, dull–normal–bright, anxious, low self-esteem, learning disabled, emotionally disturbed, hearing-impaired) children?" "Normal" subjects have tended to be randomly selected on the basis of availability and on a volunteer basis (e.g., Robbins, 1976; Ritchie, 1978). A few studies (e.g., Babbitts, 1979; Warren, 1978) have used cutoff scores on an anxiety screening test as a basis for subject selection. By and large, subjects who participated in treatment groups varied greatly in a host of personality and cognitive characteristics that were unrelated to treatment. Within the past five years, subjects have been selected from populations of children with special problems. Dependent measures appear to have been selected in the hope of catching some effect and include personality tests (Junior Eysenck Personality Questionnaire, Junior–Senior Highschool Personality Questionnaire, California Test of Personality), measures of anxiety (Spielberger State-Trait Anxiety Inventory for Children, the Audience Anxiety section of the Children's Audience Sensitivity Index, The Children's Manifest Anxiety Scale, The Social Avoidance and Distress Scale, "Guess Who" sociometric measure designed to measure teacher and student perception of interpersonally anxious students, Fear of Negative Evaluation Scale), measures of self-concept and self-esteem (Coopersmith Self-Esteem Inventory, Tennessee Self-Concept Scale), measures of irrational thinking (Children's Survey of Rational Beliefs, The Idea Inventory), measures of locus of control (Intellectual Achievement Questionnaire, Bialer–Cromwell Children's Locus of Control Scale, Rotter's Internal–External Locus of Control) and behavior rating scales (Devereux Elementary School Behavior Rating Scale, Behavior Observation Checklist).

In the main, independent treatments include a comparison of an experimental group which receives a package of REE methods and materials often derived from Knaus' (1974) REE curriculum materials with other mental health programs, attention–placebo, or no treatment control groups. There have been more recent attempts to isolate the effects of different components of RET, including Rational–Emotive Imagery (Warren, 1978) and behavioral rehearsal and written homework (Miller, 1978). Experimental groups tend to be conducted by practitioners who vary widely in experience (zero years to practicing therapists). Several studies (Brody, 1974; DiGiuseppe & Kassinove, 1976) utilized one practitioner for experimental and control groups which may have biased the results. Sample sizes of each treatment group tend to be unaccountably small (eight to twelve) with within-group subject variability being quite high. Treatment groups are relatively short-term, tending to meet once or twice weekly for between 10 and 15 sessions, and very few studies report follow-up data (for exceptions, see Brody, 1974; Robbins, 1976; Warren, 1978). Pre- and post-test change scores and post-test differences across groups are generally analyzed through an analysis of variance and analysis of covariance.

We present in Table 1.6 a limited summary of the studies we have been able to find. A few of the earlier results were taken directly from a review of RET and REE research (DiGiuseppe, Miller, & Trexler, 1979) that concluded:

> Studies indicate that elementary school children are capable of acquiring knowledge of rational emotive principles and that the modification of a child's self-verbalization or irrational self-statements can have a positive effect on emotional adjustment and behavior. [p. 225]

A few of the summary descriptions also were found in dissertation abstracts. While incomplete information was therefore used to complete Table 1.6, we believe it is important to give the reader as complete a picture as possible as to what has been done in the area. We have not included a half-dozen studies which we know about because of insufficient or nonexistent information.

It is very difficult to make generalizations concerning the findings of these studies. It is clear that studies suffer from a lack of assessment instruments to measure changes in emotions. Dependent behavioral measures have been too global, masking more specific changes in behaviors. The heterogeneous composition of experimental groups and the use of parametric statistics also serves to mask potential changes in individual subjects. Certain early studies (e.g., Albert, 1972; Knaus & Boker, 1975) suffered from a number of difficulties which limit their internal and external validity, including: (1) no pre-test was administered to assess initial differences; (2) an attention–placebo group was lacking to control for the "Hawthorne" effect; and (3) only self-report depen-

TABLE 1.6. Summary of Available RET and REE Studies with Children and Adolescents

Study	Subjects	Treatment Groups	Dependent Variables and Findings
Albert (1972)	Normal fifth-grade students	REE, Control	Anxiety: REE *> control
Katz (1974)	Normal fifth-grade students	REE, REE + Small Group Training (REEG), Mental Health Program (MH), MH + Small Group Training (MHG)	Self-esteem (teacher rating): REE, REEG > MH, MHG Self-concept (self-report): nsd* Locus of Control: nsd
Brody (1974)	Normal fifth-grade students	REE, Control	Self-esteem (post-test): nsd (follow-up): nsd Anxiety (post-test): REE > control (follow-up): nsd Tolerance for frustration (post-test): REE > control (follow-up): nsd
DiGiuseppe and Kassinove (1976)	Normal fourth- and eighth-grade students	REE, Mental Health Program (MH), Control	Neuroticism (fourth-grade): REE > MH, Control (eighth-grade): nsd Anxiety (fourth-grade): REE > MH, Control (eighth-grade): nsd Irrational Beliefs (fourth-grade): REE > MH, Control (eighth-grade): REE > MH, Control
Warren, Deffenbach and Broding (1976)	Normal fifth- and sixth-grade students	RET, Control	Anxiety: nsd Arithmetic Performance: nsd
Robbins (1976)	Normal fifth- and sixth-grade students	REE, Human Development Program (HD), Attention Placebo (AP), Control (two groups of each)	Self-concept (post-test): nsd (follow-up): nsd Locus of Control (post-test): nsd (follow-up): nsd Irrational Beliefs (post-test): nsd (follow-up): nsd REE Content Acquisition (post-test): REE > HD, AP, Control (follow-up): REE > HD, AP, Control

(Continued)

33

TABLE 1.6 (Continued)

Study	Subjects	Treatment Groups	Dependent Variables and Findings
			Growth of Awareness of Self, Self-confidence, Effectiveness, and Tolerance (teacher rating)
			(post-test): nsd
			(follow-up): nsd
			Treatment × Counselor Interaction
Miller (1978)	Normal elementary-school children	REE, REE + Behavioral Rehearsed (BR), REE + Behavioral Rehearsed + Written Homework (BRWH), Control	Neuroticism: BRWH > REE, BR > Control
			Irrational Beliefs
			(idea inventory): BRWH > REE, BR > Control
			hi IQ Ss > lo IQ Ss
			(CSRB): nsd; hi IQ = lo IQ
			Anxiety: BRWH = BR = REE > Control
Warren (1978)	"Anxious" students in grades 7, 8 and 9	RET, RET + Rational-Emotive Imagery (REI), Relationship-Oriented Counseling (ROC), Control	Anxiety (post-test): RET = REI = ROC > Control
			(follow-up): RET, REI > ROC, Control
			Irrational Beliefs (post-test): nsd
			(follow-up): RET, REI > ROC, Control
			General Concerns (post-test): nsd
			(follow-up): nsd
Ritchie (1978)	Normal fifth-grade students	REE, Control	Irrational Beliefs: REE > Control
			Locus of Control: nsd
			Assertiveness: nsd
Babbitts (1979)	"Anxious" 12–14 year olds	RET Speech Specific (RETSS), RET General Anxiety (RETGA), Discussion Placebo (DP), Control	Neuroticism: nsd
			Behavior Observation Checklist re: anxiety (teacher report): RETSS, RETGA, DP > Control
			Children's Audience Anxiety (self-report): RETSS > RETGA, DP, Control
			Teacher Observation of Anxiety Scale: RETSS = RETGA > DP, Control

Study	Sample	Treatment	Results
Bernard (1979a)	"Low self-esteem" students in grades 6 and 7	REE, Control	Self-esteem: REE > Control Irrational Beliefs: REE > Control Locus of Control: nsd Personal Adjustment: nsd REE Ss: lo IQ improved more than hi IQ in self-esteem; hi extraverted Ss decreased in personal inferiority; hi neurotic Ss increased in social maladjustment, decreased in family maladjustment
Briley (1980)	Normal students in grades 5, 7, 9, 11	Correlational Study: Sex × grade × race	Irrational Beliefs: 11 > 9 > 7 > 5 (more rational) black > white (more rational) Significant increase in irrationality of whites in grade 11, not for blacks Males vs. Females: ambiguous findings
Staggs (1979)	Learning disabled intermediate-grade students	Rational-Emotive Counseling (REC), REC + Self-talk (ST), Control	Personal Adjustment: ST > REC, Control (REC alone, negative effect) Social Adaptability: nsd Reading Achievement: nsd
Wasserman and Vogrin (1979)	Emotionally disturbed 8–13 year-old children	Correlational Study: irrational beliefs × age × time spent in REE treatment × IQ × overt behavior	Irrational Beliefs correlated with overt behavior for older Ss IQ, months in treatment not correlated with irrational beliefs, nor overt behavior
Eluto (1980)	Intermediate special education 12- and 13-year-old students	REE, Problem Solving Therapy (PST), Mental Health Program (MH)	Interpersonal Problem Solving Skills: PST > REE, MH Adjustment: nsd No treatment × IQ interactions
Giezhels (1980)	Hearing impaired high school children (upper and lower linguistic ability)	REE, Mental Health Curriculum (MHC), Attention Placebo (AP)	Irrational Beliefs: REE, MH > AP Self-esteem: nsd Anxiety: nsd IQ, age, type of hearing loss correlated with treatment effects
Dye (1981)	Adolescents living in orphanage	REE, Placebo Control (PC), Control	Self-concept: REE > PC, Control
Meyer (1982)	Learning disabled 8–13-year-old students	REE, Recreational-Education Program (REP), Control	Self-esteem: nsd Anxiety: RET > REP, Control

*>To be read: Treatment group leads to an improvement in the dependent measure relative to other groups.

**nsd: no significant differences.

dent measures were used (DiGiuseppe, Miller, & Trexler, 1979). The use of subject blocking variables, multivariate and multiple regression statistics, apriori tests of significance, and larger sample sizes would help to improve the sensitivity and power of experiments. In addition, the lack of replication studies makes the confirmation of valid findings difficult to make. With these reservations in mind, we offer the following *interpretation* of the findings.

There is little question that RET concepts and emotional problem solving skills can be acquired by children as young as ten. With instruction in all studies reported in Table 1.6 taking place in groups of children (roughly between six and ten in a group), it is clear that RET can be taught in the form of REE as a part of a normal curriculum. It also seems apparent that RET can be applied with children to reduce emotional problems of anxiety and low self-esteem. There has been no study to date which looks at the effects of RET on anger management. It is our hunch that those studies which failed to find significant effects employed practitioners who were inexperienced or met with the children for too short a time period. A very strong and consistent finding is that children of all ages can acquire the content of REE lessons and use such content to modify their beliefs as measured by the two available tests of irrationality in children. Changes in irrational beliefs of children have not generally resulted in concomitant large-scale changes in behavior such as increasing assertiveness or reducing aggression. Future studies will need to examine changes in specific behaviors (e.g., talking more to peers, increasing study time) in relation to changes in specific irrational beliefs (e.g., "It is horrible to be rejected"; "I can't stand homework").

In terms of bringing about cognitive change, there is a consistent finding which indicates that REE does not bring about changes in causal attributions from external to internal. As such, we recommend that future REE treatments more fully emphasize how emotional control and responsibility increase the potential for behavioral self-direction. Simply stated, "If you are feeling okay (not overly upset), you can do many different things you never thought possible if you set your mind to it (and with a little practice)." Or, said another simple way, "You can control your world as much as your world controls you."

We believe that the changes that are brought about by REE have up to date been limited to changes in specific emotions and behaviors. Large-scale changes, as measured by standardized personality measures, have generally not been found. This has been probably due to the relative inexperience of practitioners who conducted the studies—few experimenters we know of have received either formal training in RET at any of the Institutes for Rational-Emotive Therapy and Rational Living across the United States or intensive supervision in RET at their university or college—and to the limited time spent with children. It seems sensible to suggest that specific emotive-cognitive-behavioral change can be brought about by relatively inexperienced RET practitioners who see children for no more than 10 to 12 sessions. Master's and Ph.D.'s should probably be designed accordingly. More extensive change should only be attempted by "seasoned" RET practitioners who have longer periods of time available to them. This is especially the case when subjects are drawn from "nonnormal" populations. Common sense would dictate this.

We are a long way from knowing which components of RET and REE are the important ones. Recent studies suggest that the more methods you utilize the better. The use of rational-emotive imagery, behavioral rehearsal, and written homework is advisable. The optimum package of RET for school-age children needs to be determined before we "tease apart" active ingredients.

Because of a limited number of studies with equivocal and, at times, contradictory results, it is impossible to make any statements concerning whether the age, sex, race, and intelligence of young subjects/clients interacts with the effectiveness of RET. While such variables differentially correlate with the incidence of specific and overall irrational beliefs, little guidance can be provided concerning optimum client—treatment matches.

It has only been within the past few years that a limited number of studies have appeared in the area of special education. One study suggests that students with lower intelligence have some difficulty in acquiring basic rational-emotive principles in a short time period. Work with learning-disabled students suggests that REE group counseling can have positive effects. There appears great promise for the modification of a REE program for use with hearing-impaired populations. We encourage more work to be done in these areas.

Finally, we would like to make the observation that we are uncertain what these findings have to offer the practitioner who is referred a child with a specific set of unique problems. Group results mask individual responsivity, and it is the single case we are generally concerned with. It is our belief that these results can be used tentatively to generalize to the counseling of groups of children, not to the individual. We would like to encourage the use of time series single-case designs to study the effects of RET on a young client. The only study to our knowledge which has done so (Bernard, Kratochwill, Keefauver, 1983), which is described in Chapter 6, reveals how different RET and CBT methods need to be brought to bear at different times over the course of therapy as a client responds (or does not respond) to treatment.

We conclude this chapter by indicating that RET is an extremely important and viable counseling and therapeutic approach that is being used both preventatively or as a therapeutic intervention with both primary and secondary level children. RET is being used extensively in schools in group counseling situations as well as in a one to one client—therapist situation. It has been used with children who manifest different emotional and behavioral problems that are listed in classification schemes of childhood psychopathology. RET has also been used in developmental counseling and affective education programs not only to prevent or lessen the severity of emotional disturbance, but also as a means of facilitating the emotional adjustment and growth of children.

CHAPTER 2

Theoretical Foundations of RET

RET has over the past twenty-five years evolved largely through the creative efforts of Ellis (1957, 1958, 1962, 1970, 1971a, 1973a, 1974, 1977a, 1978a, 1979a, 1980a, 1980c, 1980d; 1984; Ellis & Grieger, 1977; Ellis & Harper, 1975; Ellis, Wolfe, & Moseley, 1966; Ellis & Whitley, 1979). It appears that one of the major catalysts for the reformulation of RET over the years has been Ellis' repeatedly expressed concern that for a therapy to prove effective clients had better not only feel and think better, but, equally importantly, *behave* in ways that maximize their own personal goal attainment and enjoyment. Ellis has adopted as a final goal for his therapy that clients function more effectively in their own environment—not just in the office of the practitioner. The main emotional and cognitive outcomes of RET have been described by Ellis (1973a) as follows:

> My main goals in treating any of my psychotherapy clients are simple and concrete; to leave the client, at the end of the psychotherapeutic process, with a minimum of anxiety (or self-blame) and of hostility (or blame of others and the world around him) and just as importantly, to give him a method of self-observation and self-assessment that will insure that, for the rest of his life, he will be minimally anxious and hostile. (p. 147)

RET derives from multiple philosophic and psychological theories (for reviews, see Ellis, 1962, 1973a; Dolliver, 1979). To understand fully the origins of the clinical application of RET we feel it is necessary to be aware of some of the more important psychological and philosophical concepts and assumptions which have influenced its development.

We wish to emphasize that it is not necessary to totally subscribe to RET philosophy to be an effective RET practitioner. RET practitioners do differ in the degree to which they endorse RET values and ethical positions. Whereas some support the existential–humanistic orientation of RET and the emphasis it places on self rather than social interest, pleasure seeking and the ethical relativity of person and interpersonal decision making, others disagree with RET's relativistic philosophical position which proposes that values and moral standards are determined by and are relative to one's goals and experiences and that there are no absolute standards in this area. We believe the position that RET adopts toward values, ethics, and beliefs can be viewed relativistically and not as some absolute standard for judging human adaptiveness and psychological functioning.

Some of the major points and distinctions made in this chapter may seem to pertain closely to the problems of adults. This is in a sense true in that most of RET theorizing pertains to understanding and explaining the dynamics of emotional disturbance and neurotic behavior in adults. Many (though by no means all) RET-oriented techniques and procedures that are employed with children derive from this literature. We therefore cover this literature in some detail in order to demonstrate the origins of child-oriented techniques and procedures as well as to provide an advance organizer for considering applications of RET with school-age children.

RATIONAL-EMOTIVE PHILOSOPHY

Rational-emotive philosophy deals with questions such as how we know what we know (epistemology), the role of logical thought and human reason in the acquisition of knowledge (dialectics), goals which individuals strive for (values), and the criteria and standards for deciding how to relate to others (ethics). (These issues have been identified by Walen, DiGiuseppe, & Wessler, 1980, as being central to RET philosophy.)

RET philosophy does share some commonalities with a modern day rationalist position though it shares nothing with the absolute orthodoxy of classical philosophic rationalism. In this regard, Ellis (1962) has made the following points:

1. Reason and logic do not contain or convey evidence or truth in their own right, but are valuable tools for the sifting of truth from falsehood.

2. Science is intrinsically empirical; and scientific knowledge must, at least in principle, be confirmable by some form of human experience.

3. Rationalism is a tenable philosophic position insofar as the term means opposition to all forms of supernaturalism, spiritualism, revelation, dogmatism, authoritarianism, and anti-scientism.

4. Although man cannot live by reason alone, he can considerably aid his existence and lessen his disturbance by thinking clearly, logically, consistently, and realistically. [pp. 123–124]

In its key tenets, the RET philosophical position exemplifies the traditions of logical positivism, a philosophical movement which has clarified the definition of the boundaries of science, and formulated criteria for evaluating data, methods and concepts. Attempts to derive an epistemology or an ethics from a logical positivist position have been open to criticism (see Kolakowski, 1972). A major philosophical difficulty encountered by so doing is that the basic principles of the epistemology cannot themselves by verified by the methods claimed to be the basis for all knowledge. Any therapy that goes beyond the workings of its own discipline and espouses tenets of another discipline (e.g., philosophy), is open to critical evaluation from within that field. That is to say, philosophical issues of a nonpsychological kind are involved. By way of further example, statements of "relativism" such as "all knowledge is relative" which are basic to RET philosophy are by definition also relative (i.e., not true in every case nor for every person). The problem here is closely linked with notions of "truth." Attempts by RET philosophers to do away with notions of "absolute truth" and restrict the use of "true" to "relatively true" have the difficulty that they appear to empty the word "true" of meaning. The problems that are apparent in the logical positivist position *may* affect the philosophical status of RET more than the therapeutic practice of RET. The utilization by RET of the scientific method, however, in its attempt to ameliorate psychological distress appears to be sound.

We shall now summarize various aspects of RET philosophy in a manner which is, hopefully, consistent with Ellis'. Our summary does not constitute an endorsement by both authors of all of RET's philosophical concepts and principles.

Epistemology and Dialectics

RET advances the proposition that knowledge we acquire is influenced largely by the interpretations we impose on our perceptions. This knowledge can be considered in RET theory as the assumptive world, personal philosophy and belief system of the individual. Ellis places this "constructivist" view in historical perspective when he cites Epictetus, the Roman stoic philosopher, who in the first century A.D. wrote that "humans are disturbed not by things but by the views they take of them." Knowledge and truth are not considered, then, to exist in any absolute and final form either in the mind of the beholder or in the surrounding world. As we have indicated RET rejects the notion that there are any "absolutes" (final truths, laws of universe for conduct) to be discovered by the individual and adopts a "relativistic" position. According to RET, ideas we believe to be true had better be viewed as hypotheses and assumptions capable of being disproved and disconfirmed. We realize as others have indicated that this epistemological position can be criticized on the ground that its relativistic emphasis makes it difficult to ascertain whether there is a "surrounding world" from which knowledge is constructed and that by asserting everything we know is constituted in some way by our knowing it, RET is obliged to provide criteria for knowledge and to indicate how we could test for it. These are not issues which have received extensive attention in the RET literature.

The reason that this epistemological position of relativism is so central to RET is that RET considers psychological disturbance to result from idiosyncratic interpretations, and appraisals which people form and which they strongly believe to be true about themselves and the world around them often work against their happiness and survival. The personal dysfunctional philosophies and belief systems of people are viewed by RET as the basic target of intervention. The assumptions and understandings which people have acquired from personal experience and contact with parents, teachers, and other cultural institutions are considered to be capable of being scrutinized and modified in therapy largely through teaching people the scientific method of being better investigators of reality and hypothesis testers. Ellis has proposed that the basis for more emotional disturbance can be traced to ideas that people tell themselves about how the world and themselves should be, which they rigidly refuse to give up in the face of contradictory evidence.

There are a number of ways in which people may misrepresent reality. At a basic input level, people may distort reality by, for example, focusing on only select aspects of the full range of data available in their perceptual field and by minimizing or maximizing the significance of certain of these aspects. Reality distortion results in people making *antiempirical* statements which may be a beginning ingredient or step to psychological upset. A frequently heard anti-empirical statement in both children and adults which when it is untrue may derive from an error in selective attention is "My friend does not like me."

As we will demonstrate in a variety of places in this book, the role of human reason and logic is viewed by cognitive approaches in general and RET in particular as playing an important role in determining the manner in which people acquire self-defeating personal philosophies and beliefs. Reason and logical thinking processes can be considered as mediators between environmental inputs and the acquisition of knowledge. An example of a faulty reasoning process is when people make conclusions when evidence is lacking or is actually contrary to the conclusion. People who base a conclusion such as "no one likes me" on insufficient evidence is making an arbitrary inference. People who conclude that because no one likes them they are, therefore, "no good" are making the logical error of arriving at an unjustified generalization made on the basis of insufficient data.

Erroneous conclusions about the world which lead to emotional and behavioral problems can derive from a reasoning process whereby a person employs an assumption, or premise, about the world which is not based on any supportable evidence nor is it supportable logically to arrive at an erroneous conclusion (Ellis refers to this as an irrational belief). This idiosyncratic and dysfunctional reasoning process can be illustrated as follows:

General promise (irrational belief):	I must be loved and approved of by my peers and when I am not, I am a failure.
Special case:	No one likes me.
Conclusion:	I am no good.

It seems to us that the tendency to engage in faulty reasoning and information processing is increased when people have acquired and strongly endorse irrational beliefs. For example, the tendency to equate one's self with one's success in social relationships (overgeneralization) is, according to RET, based upon one's belief that one must be loved and approved of by all.

Values

The philosophical system of values underlying RET is controversial. By defining goals and values of human existence based largely on self-interest, RET has made it difficult for some clients and practitioners who adhere strongly to certain beliefs to accept RET. This we feel is unfortunate in that as we have suggested one does not have to accept all philosophical aspects of RET theory to be an effective rational-emotive practitioner. Wessler and Wessler (1980, pp. 57—62) have summarized a number of values that make up RET philosophy. RET values the "fully functioning" person which they define in Rogerian terms of being open to experience, trusting in oneself, having an internal locus of evaluation, and being willing to be a process and to change rather than being a static product. Other aspects of human functioning in which RET endorses specific values include *responsibility and decision making* (taking responsibility for our decisions; accepting personal responsibility for our own behavior and emotional responses), *style of life* (risk taking, hardwork, pleasure and happiness seeking), and *ways of thinking and knowing* (scientific method, self- and other-acceptance). The goals of rational-emotive philosophy have been stated by Walen et al. (1980) as being to establish beliefs and habits that are congruent with (1) survival, (2) achieving satisfaction with living, (3) affiliating with others in a positive way, (4) achieving intimate involvement with a few others, and (5) development and maintaining a vital absorption in some personally fulfilling endeavor (pp. 11—12).

An extremely important RET value is *hedonism*. That is, proponents of RET generally share the view that since there is a limited span of human existence and there is no evidence for life after death, the goals of living should be to maximize both the short- and long-term pleasure that are available to us. The maximization of enjoyment and happiness is an important element of RET philosophy. RET practitioners employ what has been referred to as a *hedonic calculus* to determine the rationality of a person's life activities and beliefs. The hedonic calculus enables one to both consider and determine the relationship between short-term pleasures and long-term goals. RET advocates moderation by encouraging the individual to weigh the long-term consequences of immediate gratification. RET takes the position that when we judge the appropriateness of our emotions and behavior, we had better make them in terms of our short- and long-term goals. While RET emphasizes that such goals should be based on personal happiness and enjoyment, RET does not demand that they be based on personal pleasure seeking. RET has been successfully employed with people who have non humanistic and religious faiths and who value social and spiritual goals.

These explicit RET values and goals of living provide one set of criteria for judging the rationality and irrationality of thoughts, feelings, and behavior. In employing RET, clients examine their personal goals which may or may not coincide with the goals and values of RET. If their thinking causes them to become so emotionally distressed and behaviorally inept that they are unable to achieve their goals then, by definition, all three modes of expression can be viewed as being irrational and suitable for examination and change.

Ethical Humanism

Ellis and RET are decidedly humanistic (Ellis, 1973a). Perhaps the most humanistic tenet of RET is that the ultimate authority for human conduct is human reason and not the wisdom of supernatural deities nor their mortal representatives. Decisions about how we relate to others is based not on moral commandments of right or wrong but in terms of how our actions affect our own personal goals and affect our relationships with others. This stance says that our actions are to be based on situational requirements and conditions and not on any absolute guidelines.

Rational-humanistic philosophy can also be seen in how Ellis encourages people to experience as much of life as possible. RET stresses the creative potential of persons which oftentimes remains unexpressed because of self-imposed inhibitions. According to RET philosophy, people are happier and more fully alive and joyful when they are engaged in productive and stimulating pursuits. So whereas people can cope with stress and difficulties by avoiding problematic situations, such behavior would work against the individual's natural tendency for self-actualization, pleasure seeking, and enjoyment.

Another humanistic concept that plays an extremely important role in the practice of RET is that of *human worth* (Ellis, 1965, 1972c). Ellis advances the argument that much human disturbance is based on people rating themselves and others as good or bad. This kind of person evaluation is pernicious because many people spend their lives seeking and demanding assurances from others that they are worthwhile. As a consequence, they inevitably put themselves down when they rightly or wrongly perceive they have failed to receive the love and approval of significant others and to have achieved well. Self-downing is at the core of most human misery. When people down themselves they find it extremely difficult to think objectively and rationally in problematic situations. What Ellis stresses is that human beings are not rateable for there is no universally accepted guideline for judging the worth of people. We rate ourselves and others using arbitrary definitions of good and bad. Ellis rejects all notions of absolute good or bad and adopts the position that while it is appropriate for people to examine their own traits and behaviors, it is not proper to use their performances as a basis for rating themselves. This is an especially important message we teach parents for it is our experience that parents in condemning and blaming their children for misbehavior plant the idea that they are essentially bad. As a consequence, children live their lives fulfilling the externally-imposed definitions of their parents.

RATIONAL-EMOTIVE THEORY OF HUMAN BEHAVIOR AND BEHAVIOR CHANGE

In attempting to understand and explain personality, RET emphasizes a *trait* view of human personality. According to RET, people demonstrate deeply ingrained thinking patterns which exert their influence on and are observed in the predictable ways people react emotionally and behaviorally. The regularity and consistency of human behavior and emotion can best be understood by analyzing the characteristics of the cognitive structure (beliefs) and cognitive processes (perception, reasoning abilities) of the individual. Subscribing to a cognitive perspective, RET asserts that the phenomenological viewpoint of the individual will dictate the individual's emotions and behavior in a given situation. RET also accepts the *interactionist* view that while the individual's belief system determines the range of emotions and behaviors an individual is likely to experience, the expression of emotions and behaviors is largely determined by aspects of the stimulus situation. That is, while certain environments are problematic for the individual, others—because they manifest different antecedent discriminative elements and reinforcement contingencies—do not serve to occasion neurotic behavior.

According to Ellis, the cognitive apparatus of the individual is handicapped by a biological and hereditary propensity for irrationality which works against the attainment of a person's basic values, purposes, goals, and ideals. This propensity can be seen both in the tendency to misrepresent reality as well as in faulty reasoning processes. Faulty thinking processes are influenced by, and reciprocally influence, the belief system of the individual. These cognitive distortions and the belief system of people can be viewed as generalized personality traits which largely govern and explain the psychology of human emotion and behavior. Said another way, RET describes and explains the full range of human emotions and behavior in terms of a few stable and relatively enduring traits of personality.

Origins of Personality

Ellis (1979b) has written that the origins of personality are multivariate and extremely complex. In seeking to answer the question as to specific historical factors and causes which underlly disturbance, Ellis would reply that not only are they mostly impossible to ascertain, but they are in themselves relatively unimportant. Ellis rejects the psychoanalytic position that early childhood experience is critical in personality formation and is the central cause of later disturbance. Ellis maintains that early childhood experiences cannot exert an influence on present day behavior unless people continue to reindoctrinate themselves with the horribleness of the original event, and continue as a result of the experience to evaluate and interpret themselves or others in an exaggerated and absolutistic fashion. Ellis finds the "learning history" and "conditioning" theories of behavioral psychology inadequate to explain why individuals rigidly and paradoxically acquire and maintain a set of self- and other-perceptions and evaluations that work, in many instances, diametrically against the well-being of the person. Ellis also believes that while the self-actualizing theory of humanistic psychology explains reasonably well why people strive for goals and ideals, it does not at all deal with the tendencies of human beings to defeat their own goals through the operation of such propensities as low frustration tolerance, procrastination and the inability to delay gratification.

RET hypotheses that because there is no rationally adaptive nor observably apparent reason why so many people in so many cultures experience extreme distress and impairments in socioemotional and psychological functioning, there most probably is a biological basis to human disturbance. In fact, because of the absence of any discernible environmental learning factors that can account for the tendency of humans to feel disturbed, to think irrationally, become needlessly upset, and to upset themselves about being upset, Ellis (1979b) has stated that "probably 80% of the variance in human behavior rests largely on biological bases and 20% or so on specific environmental training" (p. 17). Although Ellis places a heavy emphasis on the hereditary influence on personality, he also indicates that people can if they work hard enough overcome, to a large extent, the neurotic-inducing tendencies of their cognitive apparatus.

The present authors take exception with Ellis on the amount of variance in human behavior he attributes to hereditary and biological factors. It is our observation that children acquire basic behavioral patterns through modeling, operant, and other social learning influences. We believe that irrational beliefs and the faulty ways in which information is processed are largely transmitted to children in the language and communication patterns of adults. Parenting styles have enormous influence on shaping the behavior and affectivity of children. As a result of differences in parenting styles (permissive−loving vs. authoritarian−cold), we believe children acquire different beliefs and evaluations of themselves and the surrounding world (Hauck, 1972). We also believe that teaching styles can strongly influence the cognitive characteristics of children. We therefore adopt more of a learning perspective toward human psychological disturbance.

In accounting for the development of personality, Ellis (1979b) has enumerated a variety of environmental as well as innate influences that account for current behavioral patterns and emotionality. These include:

1. Relationships with other people.

2. Specific teaching by others, including parents, teachers, clergyman, and peers.

3. Teaching by the mass media (books, newspapers, radio, TV, films, popular songs, and magazines).

4. Group influences (peers, social classes, community organizations and groups, political institutions, and religious organizations).

5.   Biological and innate desires and urges.

6.   Many kinds of reinforcers or rewards, such as money, success, physical pleasures, and inner feelings of satisfaction.

7.   Many kinds of penalizers, such as disapproval, poverty, material frustrations, physical pains, and inner feelings of anxiety and depression.

8.   Self-ratings, including rating oneself as a "good person" for doing one kind of act or having one kind of trait and as a "bad person" for doing another kind of act or for having another kind of trait.

9.   Self-observation—noting how one behaves and the usual consequences of that behavior.

10.   Modeling after others—particularly after outstanding people, real or imaginary.

11.   Identification with certain groups or individuals and consequent acceptance or imitation of their behavior.

12.   Formulation of goals, purposes, and ideals and attempts to achieve them.

13.   Magical or mystical notions, such as belief in perfection, utopia, in gods and devils, and in a heaven-centered or hell-centered afterlife.

14.   Gullibility and suggestibility to the teachings and persuasions of others and of the mass media.

15.   Yearning for freedom and individuality. [pp. 24–25].

Origins of Human Emotions and Behavior

When we consider from a RET perspective how personality is expressed in behavior and emotions, we are concretely examining how the individual's current interpretations and appraisals of the surrounding world determine behavioral and emotional consequences. These interpretations, evaluations, and underlying belief system are largely responsible for the creation and maintenance of human emotion and behavior. Ellis has indicated that the three modes of human expression (cognitions, emotions, and behaviors) are often inseparable and that all three interact and reciprocally influence one another. Certain writers in the cognitive-behavioral movement who have examined the issue of the relationship between thinking and emotions have argued that emotions are not always activated directly by cognitive processes (e.g., Zajonc, 1980). Their arguments are based on the notion that both philogenetically and ontogenetically affective reactions are primary as well as on brain research which suggests that emotions may be triggered by left-hemispheric, nonverbal processes (e.g., Davidson, 1978; Eschenroeder, in press). Indeed, Ellis (1962) recognizes three separate origins of emotions: (1) sensorimotor processes, (2) biological stimulation mediated through tissues of the autonomic nervous system (subcortical areas), and (3) cognitive or thinking processes. Nonetheless, it is clear from Ellis' writings that he considers cognition as playing the most dominant role in the creation and maintenance of human disturbances. By way of simple illustration, it would appear that for someone to *remain* extremely upset after experiencing a disturbing event, the person would have to continually think and ruminate about the upsetting event.

Ellis also argues as do other personality theorists (e.g., Kelly, 1955) that irrespective of therapy, change in a client has to be accompanied by a change in the client's own perception and cognitive views. Ellis believes that the role of cognition is so paramount that a "major change in a person's philosophy can help bring about highly important and lasting changes in both emotions and behavior" (1979c, p. 45).

The ABCs of RET

Ellis has elaborated an ABC theory of emotional disturbance which describes how a person becomes upset. RET starts with an emotional and behavioral consequence (C) and seeks to identify the activating event (A) that appears to have precipitated (C). While the commonly accepted viewpoint is that A caused C, RET steadfastly maintains that it is the individual's beliefs (B) which are evaluations about what happened at A that determined C. For example, take 11-year-old Paul, a sixth-grader, who screamed in anger and thumped down hard on his desk because his teacher failed to call on him when he had his hand raised. As we illustrate in Figure 2.1, the common misconception is that A, the activating event of being ignored, caused Paul to feel angry, to scream and bang his desk (C). However, if just at the moment Paul is being ignored and before he gets angry we could somehow get him to forget and erase completely from his mind the memory trace of being ignored, we would observe a boy who was neither angry nor screaming. According to RET, it is Paul's evaluations (B) about the incident that created or caused C.

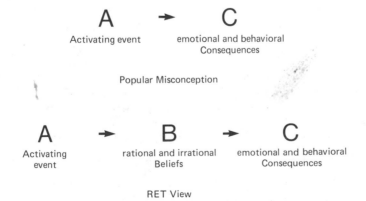

Figure 2.1. The ABC's of RET.

Ellis has extended his alphabetical notional symbol system for representing his theory by adding a DE link to his ABCs. Disputation (D) is one of the cornerstones of the RET method of therapeutic change and employs where possible the scientific method of challenging and questioning shaky or untenable hypotheses and imperative and absolutistic assumptions that individuals may hold about themselves, about others, and about the world (Ellis, 1979d). With younger and less intelligent clients, disputation may examine the rationality and sense of irrational self-statements ("How awful is it not to be called on?") where with more capable clients disputation of the beliefs themselves can occur ("Where is the evidence that you must succeed and get accepted by people?"). When clients begin to challenge their unsound assumptions and beliefs and to reformulate them into more empirically valid statements and when they really and strongly believe in their validity, they wind up with a new cognitive, emotive, and behavioral effect (E). When clients arrive at a new philosophic effect by giving up unsound beliefs, they begin to experience less severe emotional reactions, and to behave differently so as to be able, if they can, to improve and change the situation at A.

In the example of Paul, we can see that if Paul evaluated the activating event of being ignored rationally and sensibly, he would have said to himself something like "I don't like it when I'm not called on; I wish my teacher would pay more attention to me." He would have felt moderately annoyed, irritated and disgruntled, but he would not have thrown a temper tantrum and he would have in all likelihood tried to answer his teacher's next question. And if he stopped his evaluation of the situation with these rational self-statements, all would be fine. But people who are emotionally upset and whose behavior is dysfunctional follow-up their rational statements with irrational and absolute demands about how things should be. So when Paul said to himself that his teacher should not ignore him—that he can't stand being treated awfully and horribly and that his teacher is an awful person who deserves to be punished—he felt incredibly furious and irate and behaved in an aggressive fashion which no doubt would lead to unfavorable consequences for Paul in the future. The point to be made is that people literally *create* their own feelings. Events and situations cannot in themselves cause us to feel anything. Emotions are largely created in our heads by ourselves through the way we cognitively represent and evaluate reality. When our evaluations are based on irrational premises and beliefs, our emotions become distressful, our behavior maladaptive. The most elegant and direct route to the long-term alleviation of emotional disturbance and to the improvement in behavioral functioning is through the technique of logicoempirical disputation, where clients are helped to rid themselves of irrational and self-defeating beliefs. We will discuss "disputational techniques" in the next chapter.

Beliefs

Since the concepts of "belief" and "belief system" are central to RET theory, we shall spend some time discussing the variety of meanings attributed to this concept. We had better indicate that there is no consensus among RET therapists and theorists as to the exact meaning of *beliefs*. That is to say, people have used the term belief to refer to various characteristics and aspects of the thinking activity of the individual which are seen to "cause" or "create" dysfunctional emotional and behavioral consequences. The formulation which we will now present highlights some of the different ways the term belief has been employed and is, as far as we know, consistent with Ellis' current view. We recognize that other RET practitioners may, because they have studied with Ellis during an earlier time when his theory was defined differently than it is today or because they have reached their own understandings, take exception to our presentation.

Belief may be viewed as a very broad hypothetical construct that embraces at least three distinct subclasses of cognitive phenomena: (1) thoughts that an individual is thinking and is aware of at a given time about A, (2) thoughts about A that the individual is not immediately aware of, and (3) more abstract beliefs that the individual may hold in general (Bernard, 1981). Eschenroeder (in press) is in essential agreement with this analysis when he writers that the ABC scheme is a simplification of the complex processes of the perception, interpretation, and evaluation of events and the activation of emotional reactions and behavioral responses.

> The B-element of the ABC refers to rather different phenomena: (1) *thoughts* and *images*, which can be observed through introspection by the individual; (2) *unconscious processes*, which can be inferred post hoc from the individual's feelings and behavior ("unconscious verbalizations"); (3) the *belief system* underlying the persons thoughts, emotions, and behaviors.

The more abstract beliefs which people hold are unspoken and constitute the assumptive framework by which they evaluate, appraise, and form conclusions about what they observe to be happening to themselves, to others, and in the world around them. These abstract beliefs are not expressed in the self-talk of people but can be considered as relatively enduring cognitive structures which affect people's interpretations of reality and often, in so doing, guide subsequent behavior. They are inferred from the types of thought-statements clients are able to articulate both to themselves and to the practitioner as well as from their pattern of behavior. For example, people who strongly hold the belief that they desperately need others to depend and rely on will tend to interpret situations in terms of whether they offer particular sorts of personal security and will also search for environments and relationships which will satisfy this self-perceived desire.

Abstract beliefs can be differentiated on the basis of whether they reflect absolutistic and imperative (irrational) or relativistic and conditional qualities (rational). Those beliefs which lead to self-defeating emotional and behavioral consequences are almost always expressed as unqualified shoulds, oughts, musts, commands, and demands and are deemed "irrational." Ellis, who refers to these beliefs as a form of "musturbatory thinking," indicates that if people hold rigid views and beliefs about how they, others, and the world should or must be under all circumstances, then they are likely to experience some form of disturbance. Beliefs which are expressed not as commands but as preferences and which are viewed as conditional upon and relative to a set of circumstances are defined as "rational" and lead to more adaptive levels of emotionality and appropriate behavior. Compare the following irrational belief with the way it is re-stated as a rational belief.

Irrational belief: I must be loved and approved of by every significant person in my life.

Rational belief: It would be desirable and productive to concentrate on self-respect, on winning approval for practical purposes, and on loving instead of being loved.

Walen et al. (1980) have defined these somewhat elusive concepts of rational belief and irrational belief as follows:

1. *A rational belief is true.* The belief is consistent with reality in kind and degree; it can be supported by evidence; and it is empirically verifiable. It is logical, internally consistent, and consistent with realities.
2. *A rational belief is not absolutistic.* Instead, it is conditional or relativistic. A rational belief is usually stated as a desire, hope, want, wish, or preference, and thus reflects a desiring rather than a demanding philosophy.
3. *A rational belief results in moderate emotion.* Thus RBs lead to feelings which may range from mild to strong but which are not upsetting to the individual.
4. *A rational belief helps you attain your goals.* Thus, RBs are congruent with: satisfaction in living, minimizing intrapsychic conflict, minimizing conflict with the environment, enabling affiliation and involvement with others, and growth toward a vital absorption in some personally fulfilling endeavor. [pp. 72–73]

Irrational beliefs are defined in terms of a set of opposite characteristics.

1. *An irrational belief is not true.* It does not follow from reality; it may begin with an inaccurate premise and/or lead to inaccurate deductions; it is not supported by evidence; and it often represents an overgeneralization.
2. *An irrational belief is a command.* As such, it represents an absolutistic rather than probablistic philosophy and is expressed as demands (versus wishes), shoulds (versus preferences), and needs (versus wants).
3. *An irrational belief leads to disturbed emotions.* Apathy or anxiety may be debilitating at worst and non-productive at best.
4. *An irrational belief does not help you attain your goals.* When one is tied up in absolutes and shackled by upsetting emotions, one is hardly in the best position to work at the ongoing business in life of maximizing pleasure and minimizing discomfort. [pp. 73–74]

In terms of the ABC model, rational beliefs generally lead to moderate emotional consequences that enable clients to achieve their future goals by facilitating constructive behavior. We differ somewhat in our views from Walen's et al. insofar as we believe that occasionally rational beliefs may result in extreme levels of some emotions which are appropriate, such as extreme sadness and regret. Irrational beliefs lead to extremely stressful emotional consequences (intense anxiety, anger, depression) and behavioral reactions (aggression, withdrawal) which make it quite difficult for the individual to improve the situation.

The main irrational beliefs that people tend to hold and that very frequently "cause" or "create" dysfunctional emotional and behavioral consequences can be categorized under three major ones each, with many derivatives:

1. I must do well and win approval for my performances, or else I rate as a rotten person.
2. Others must treat me considerately and kindly in precisely the way I want them to treat me; if they don't society and the universe should severely blame, damn, and punish them for their inconsiderateness.
3. Conditions under which I live must get arranged so that I get practically everything I want comfortably, quickly, and easily, and get virtually nothing that I don't want. [Ellis, 1980b, pp. 5–7]

RET stresses there are three main forms of thinking that are "logical" derivatives of the basic irrational "must" which lead to psychological upset: (1) *Awfulizing* ("It is awful, or terrible, or horrible that I am not doing as I must"); (2) *I can't stand-it-itis* ("I can't stand, can't bear the things that are happening to me that must not happen!"); (3) *Worthlessness* ("I am a worthless person if I don't do as well and win as much approval as I must") (Ellis 1980b, p. 8). It is sometimes the case in the RET literature that these characteristic qualities of irrational thinking have been considered to be irrational beliefs (e.g., Mahoney, 1974). Sutton-Simon (1981) has indicated that "When irrational beliefs are identified by their characteristic qualities rather than their content, clinicians attempt to determine where clients have unknowingly attached absolutistic, evaluative, and demanding features to their assumptions about themselves and their world" (p. 66).

Irrational beliefs sometimes have been described as dysfunctional thinking processes in which disturbances in cognitive operations result in illogical and distorted thoughts (see Sutton-Simon, 1981, for further discussion). We prefer to confine the meaning of irrational beliefs to absolutistic and imperative personal philosophies rather than to faulty information processing and logical reasoning (e.g., selective abstraction, overgeneralization, arbitrary inference). While the latter are of great importance in understanding and assessing disturbance, we do not believe they have to be included within the rubric of "irrationality."

Abstract beliefs are often an expression of the values of people and as such play an important role in explaining (to therapist and client alike) the basic goals and purposes of their behavior. People come to value such things as love and approval from others as an achievement, and it is the degree to which these goals are valued which will influence the behavior and sense of well-being of people. Extreme valuations of, for example, security, would be likely to (but not always) lead to unhappiness and as such would constitute "irrationality."

Beliefs refer to our appraisals and evaluations of our interpretations of reality, rather than to the interpretations themselves. This distinction is a rather sticky one and is one which generates some disagreement among RET theorists. The basic notion here is that RET chooses to designate only certain aspects of cognitive content which deal with how the individual interprets reality as beliefs.

An examination of Wessler and Wessler's (1980) model of an emotional episode will, hopefully, make the distinction between an interpretation and appraisal more apparent. In their model, it can be seen that the antecedent event (A) can be conceptualized as involving cognitive content and can be subdivided into four steps. Step 1 is either an overt or covert stimulus which begins the emotional episode. The second step occurs at a psychological level and involves the activity of sensory neurons in providing information concerning our immediate external environment, our level of physiological arousal, and our cognitions which culminates in selective attention. Step 3 consists of how we perceive and represent symbolically reality and frequently, though not exclusively, this involves describing and defining the initial overt or covert stimulus. Wessler and Wessler indicate this description often involves verbal statements of the experienced stimulus ("I see a dog") and in referring to the work of Mahoney (1977) write that it is not environments that impinge upon us but our representations of environments. They define the fourth step, interpretation, as "the making of inferences about nonobservable aspects of the perceived stimulus (S^1) or about onself" (p. 6). An example of this would be when we assume that a person who walks by us without saying hello does not like us. According to Wessler and Wessler, interpretations may be a special case of a more general and enduring interpretation ("All people are not trustworthy; therefore this person is not trustworthy") or can be fairly specific ("This person is not trustworthy"). Step 5, appraisal, represents the crucial step in the emotional episode and is what Ellis appears to refer to with his idea of belief (B). The types of evaluations and appraisals people make of and the conclusions they draw from their interpretations of reality (positive, negative, or neutral) will determine the nature of their emotional response. Ellis indicates that while the initial interpretation of an event may trigger some degree of emotionality, it is the belief about the event, which as we have written, provides the basis of a "normal" or "neurotic" reaction. Step 6, affect, refers to autonomic arousal following a non-neutral appraisal while Step 7, action tendency, involves approach or avoidance behavior. The final step of the emotional episode involves the feedback that is received concerning the reinforcing consequences of the behavior and which affects future behavior. In distinguishing between interpretive cognitive content which belongs to part of the antecedent event from evaluative content which is subsumed as a part of the belief system, let us consider the statement: "I will never be any good at anything." This statement is not an irrational belief as it represents an over-generalization and misinterpretation of reality and, most importantly, lacks the imperative quality which underlies irrational beliefs. Underlying this statement is most generally the belief that "I must be perfect to be worthwhile" which constitutes the core irrational aspect.

Step			Event
A	1.	Reality	Stimulus (S)
	2.	Input and selection	S competes with other stimuli; awareness of S
	3.	Definition and description	What S is, S = S'; covert or overt verbal description of S'
	4.	Interpretation	Nonobservable aspects of S' or of observer
B	5.	Appraisal	Positive, negative, or neutral
C	6.	Affect	Arousal if positive or negative
	7.	Action tendency	Approach if positive; elimination of stimulus if negative: (a) avoidance, (b) destruction
	8.	Feedback	Reinforcing consequences of responses (Steps 6 and 7)

Figure 2.2   Model of an Emotional Episode (Wessler & Wessler, 1980, p. 5).

The term "assumption" within RET theory refers to both interpretations of reality which people make and which can be empirically tested as being true or false and to the appraisals and evaluations of those interpretations (beliefs) which can be examined as to their rationality and irrationality. The notion here is that what we assume to be true (what we think to ourselves) may refer to our interpretation or to our belief.

Irrationality in Psychopathology

We believe that if we could map out the different rational and irrational beliefs an individual holds, the degree of endorsement of these beliefs (weak–strong), and the degree to which the beliefs are taken literally, we would have a pretty good understanding of the personality of the person. The set of irrational beliefs of an individual can also be considered the core of psychopathology. Irrational philosophies often lead to phobias, obsessions, and psychosomatic disorders. The linkages of irrational beliefs to maladaptive behavior and emo-

tional disturbance can be further understood in terms of the following ways
RET regards psychopathology:

1. Any frequently repeated actions which tend to shorten the span of enjoyable living time, e.g., abusing the body so as to invite future pain and disability.
2. Any frequently repeated actions which generate immediate and unnecessary discomfort and pain, e.g., making oneself anxious when there is no real danger or exaggerating the magnitude of a real danger.
3. Failure to cultivate innate capacities for different satisfactions, thus resulting in a state of being marked by frequent periods of boredom, inertia, and dissatisfaction.
4. Preoccupation with short-range enjoyment which can only be obtained at the cost of longer-range satisfactions.
5. A pattern of avoidance of those opportunities to acquire knowledge (predictive power) which increases the individual's power to maximize future enjoyment. [Bard, 1980, pp. 23–24]

People who behave in such ways have one major characteristic in common.
They all "suffer from a state of mind marked by the absence and/or distortion
of reason. In short, psychopathology is essentially a condition of irrationality"
(Bard, 1980, p. 24).

Ellis (1962) has defined neurosis largely in terms of the individual believing
and rigidly holding on to fundamentally unsound assumptions and irrational
ideas.

> The individual comes to believe in unrealistic, impossible, often perfectionistic goals—especially the goals that he should be approved by everyone who is important to him, should do things perfectly, and should never be frustrated in any of his major desires. Then, in spite of considerable contradictory evidence, he refuses to surrender his original illogical beliefs. [p. 93]

Private Thought

We will end our review of the theoretical aspects of RET with discussion of the
nature of thought and how the characteristics and complexities of thought need
to be taken into account when practicing RET. In applying RET, one of the
main therapeutic tasks is for the practitioner to help clients discover the
irrational aspects of their thoughts. This stage is viewed as prerequisite to
helping clients change their philosophical outlook. The client with the help of
the practitioner may spend a great deal of time discovering and analyzing
rational and irrational thought-statements that activate emotional upset using
the ABC model. This step of identifying thoughts is critical, for if clients cannot
identify their irrational words, sentences, and beliefs, they would be unable to
see why it is they are upset, and, as a consequence, would be less likely to alter
their view of antecedent events. We take the position that when working with
young school-age children the process of identifying thoughts is not a natural or

easy one, nor is it a prerequisite skill that young people possess. Said another way, thoughts differ in terms of how accessible they are to client introspection and awareness. Especially when working with school-age children, careful introspection and reporting of internal experiences help to expand a person's awareness to encompass a continuous flow of images and thoughts (Beck, 1976).

A number of fundamental questions have been raised when the role of introspection and self-analysis in the practice of RET is examined.

> What is the relationship between thoughts a client is aware of and can verbalize and thoughts that a client is not aware of immediately? . . .

> How and why do thoughts that a client experiences but cannot immediately identify or verbalize to a practitioner activate emotional responses? . . .

> How can thoughts that a client may describe in compound, complex sentence form appear to occur in a fractional time period between an activating event and an emotional consequence? [Bernard, 1981, p. 128]

In addressing these questions, Bernard (1981) has proposed a model for representing thoughts that vary in client awareness and in therapeutic accessibility. The model derives from a variety of sources. Among the major influences is Fodor (1973), a psycholinguist, who postulates a "distinction between the internal codes in which our thinking is carried out and the linguistic systems in which we exchange the results of our computations" (p. 85). Vygotsky, a developmental psychologist, has written "internal speech is not the interior aspect of external speech. While in external speech thought is embodied in words, in inner speech, words die as they bring forth thoughts. Inner speech is to a large extent thinking in pure meaning" (p. 149). Arthur Staats (1964), a behavioral psychologist, has demonstrated experimentally that *single words* cannot only control and elicit numerous motor skills (push, pull, come, go), but also can elicit emotional responses (love, hate, anger, guilt), as well as, when presented contingently upon a behavior, can serve to either strengthen or weaken behavior (good, bad).

Other influences are from the area of cognitive psychology and cognitively-oriented psychotherapy where we have learned that memories of objects, individuals, or events that occasion emotional upset in a client may be stored in long-term memory in a form where it is not likely to be retrieved through directive verbal questioning. Tulving (1972) has distinguished between *semantic memory* where past events are represented in broad associative linguistic networks, and *episodic memory* where events are stored separately and are not part of the client's cognitive-linguistic structure. Goldfried (1979) illustrates the problems in assessing episodic memory when he writes that where "there are fewer associative cues to enable the individual to retrieve experiences stored in episodic memory, such events are less likely to be recalled and used as references for comprehension" (p. 143).

The inaccessibility of client thought has been illuminated by Beck (1976). Beck has reported that many of his clients were not fully aware of their unreported thoughts until he helped to focus on them. Beck labeled these ideations as *automatic thoughts* and described them in terms of the following five defining attributes:

1. They generally were not vague and unformulated, but were specific and *discrete*. They occurred in a kind of shorthand; that is, only the essential words in a sentence seemed to occur, as in a telegraphic style. . . .
2. They seemed to be relatively *autonomous* in that the patient made no effort to initiate them. . . .
3. The patient seemed to regard these automatic thoughts as plausible or reasonable. . . . The patients accepted their validity without question and without testing their reality or logic. . . .
4. . . . The content of automatic thoughts, particularly those that were repetitive and seemed to be most powerful, was *idiosyncratic*. . . .
5. These thoughts generally involved more distortion of reality than did other types of thinking. [pp. 36–37]

A model of private thought is presented in Figure 2.3. The outer ring of the circle represents thoughts that a client is immediately aware of. The form of these thoughts corresponds quite closely with the words and speech structures of the language system of the client. They are covert verbalizations that a therapist would understand if they were overtly verbalized. Thoughts may originate in this outer ring. That is, in a small proportion of the time that clients think, they are talking to themselves. This private talk corresponds with the speech of clients when they are talking to another person. A major proportion of thought, however, originates in the inner zone of concentric circles. This form of thinking occurs when clients have no immediate intention of communicating their thoughts to another person and is not engaging in mental rehearsal. The number of progressively smaller concentric circles suggests progressively lesser degrees of client conscious awareness. In addition, the progressively smaller areas encompassed by the circles indicate that thoughts may vary in temporal characteristics. The thoughts that a client generates in the outer concentric circles are more elaborated and correspond more closely with covert verbalizations and external speech. The small circles indicate a more abbreviated and elliptical form of thought. Thoughts originating in the outer concentric circles may occur over a longer time period than thoughts originating in the inner circles. It is, of course, possible that single word thoughts in an outer circle can occur in a brief time interval. The arrows indicate that thoughts that originate in the inner zones of private thought can be transformed by the client into covert verbalizations. This transformation may be motivated by their desire to communicate thoughts to someone else or by their desire to examine through a process of self-discovery thoughts that are occasioning certain feelings.

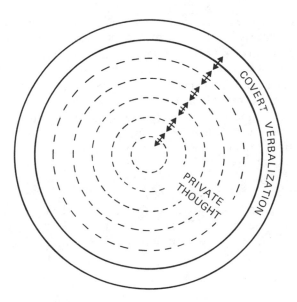

Figure 2.3.   A Model of Private Thought.

Conversely, covert verbalizations that have been internalized through therapeutic instruction may be transformed over time to private thought. This transformational process may be a critical stage to ensure maintenance and generalization of any learning experience. For example, Meichenbaum (1975b) was able to increase the creativity of college students by training them to covertly verbalize sets of previously modelled self-statements that were viewed as being compatible with creative behavior. In teaching a self-control technique, the question arises as to whether the trained students could continue to maintain increased creativity at the level of covert verbalization. As much of our learned behavior appears to occur habitually, rapidly, and almost automatically, it would appear that we may transform much of what we learn from others into private thought. The question then becomes whether the students in Meichenbaum's study would automatically transform the self-control technique into private thought. If they were not able to, maintenance and generalization would be doubtful. Meichenbaum (1977) has recognized the importance of this phase when teaching self-control techniques. He indicates that if enduring changes are to take place, modifications in internal dialogue must lead to concomitant changes in cognitive structure.

The implications of this theoretical model for RET practice is summarized in the following six points:

1. Many thoughts that contribute to emotional and behavioral disorders are not initially accessible to either a client or therapist.
2. Clients are not necessarily being resistant if they cannot communicate their thoughts.

3. Lack of introspective detail derives from inherent limitations in the way human beings represent experience to themselves in thought.

4. Clients may require systematic training and experiences to facilitate the process of discovering the ideational content of their private thoughts.

5. Rational-emotive techniques that are employed with adults may be too directive to insure sufficient levels of self-discovery in younger populations.

6. To facilitate the maintenance and generalization of client change, therapeutic instructions must be expressed in a form that is compatible with and that can be incorporated within the client's idiosyncratic language system and cognitive structure. [Bernard, 1981, p. 127]

We recognize that this chapter raises a number of issues concerning RET philosophy. It is our experience that the practice of RET is nondogmatic, does not rely heavily on the RET value system, and is eminently sensitive to individual differences in values, preferences, goals, and beliefs. We shall now discuss basic RET methods of assessment and intervention.

CHAPTER 3

The Practice of Rational-Emotive Therapy

The practice of RET derives from Ellis' theory of personality and human behavior. While the manner in which RET is practiced depends upon, among other things, the style and personality of the practitioner (active-directive-assertive vs. restrained-reflective-warm), the age and cognitive capacity of the client, and the type and severity of the problem, we believe that there are certain core therapeutic conditions that all RET practitioners share in common.

First and foremost, RET is a cognitive therapy. It teaches clients that they (not events or other people) make themselves disturbed. It seeks whenever and however possible to help clients rid themselves of mistaken cognitions that are largely causing them to become upset. RET is a present-oriented approach and works as quickly as possible to uncover self-defeating thoughts and underlying irrational assumptions and beliefs that are currently activating emotional upset. It does not spend a great deal of time examining historical antecedents and events. RET also employs a didactic educational approach. The rational-emotive practitioner functions largely as an instructor who demonstrates to the client through a variety of techniques (modeling, role play, verbal persuasion) the RET model of human emotions and behavior change, teaches skills for making accurate observations of reality, and strategies for drawing correct conclusions (scientific method). Being educational in orientation, RET expects clients to actively practice the skills acquired in therapy between sessions and generally includes a homework component.

RET practitioners unconditionally accept their clients irrespective of what problems they may demonstrate. This attitude accomplishes a number of things. It encourages in clients a greater acceptance of themselves, and therefore leads to a greater inclination on the part of clients to be open and non-defensive. It also focuses the therapeutic endeavor toward the solving of problems and the breaking of bad habits, rather than the curing of the client's mental "illness."

Ellis (1977b, 1980a) has distinguished between specialized or preferential and general or nonpreferential RET. General RET is very similar to other cognitive-behavioral therapies such as multimodal therapy (Lazarus, 1976) and cognitive therapy (Beck, 1976; Beck et al., 1979) and seeks through the use of a variety of cognitive, behavioral and emotive methods to resolve the present problems of a client. So, for example, when working with a teenager who has high test anxiety, general RET might give practice in the rehearsal of sets of task-oriented, anxiety reducing, coping self-statements (cognitive method). Through the use of rational-emotive imagery, RET would give the teenager experience in coping with anxiety through the imaginal rehearsal and role playing of problematic test situations (emotive technique). General RET might also get the teenager to self-monitor her own anxiety producing thoughts as well as to provide reward for herself for the amount of time she actively spent in preparing for the test (behavioral method). If the teenager demonstrated a reduction in test anxiety, RET would consider that a limited solution had been achieved. General RET, while achieving a solution to the problem, does not always result in a change in the client's fundamental disturbance creating philosophies. Ellis (1977b) indicates that specialized or preferential RET

> stresses (but never solely) the achievement of a profound cognitive or philosophic change in clients' basic assumptions, especially their absolutistic, demanding, musturbatory, irrational ways of viewing themselves, others, and the world. [p. 74]

So while specialized RET would try to modify the test-anxious teenager's antiempirical distortions of reality ("I can't pass, everyone will think I'm a jerk"), it would also show the teenager that even if she *never* passes a test, it would only be inconvenient, not "awful" or "horrible"; that she could accept herself even if she failed all tests; and there is no reason that she *must* be successful at any activity that she *wishes* to succeed at. Thus specialized RET, by teaching a more accepting, less absolutistic view toward oneself and others, better prepares the client to learn to not only resolve but where necessary accept other personal problems which will inevitably occur in the future. Whereas specialized RET is the more preferred mode, there are instances, especially when working with extremely strong-willed people as well as with younger children, where general cognitive-behavioral methods are the more appropriate.

We wish to emphasize again that while RET philosophy enumerates a variety of humanistic values and "self-oriented" goals for human living (survival, happiness, relating with others, intimacy, creative pursuits), it does not absolutistically impose them on clients. It is important that during assessment some time be spent discovering the particular values and goals of a client. This process may take some time as many clients come to therapy because of a confusion in their basic values. For example, helping clients to articulate and become aware of what they really want from life is sometimes sufficient to free them from emotional distress and enable them to behave more constructively.

Another important reason for clarifying clients' purposes and wishes is that the determination of what is and is not rational depends upon the goals of the individual and not the goals of RET philosophy. Rational as used in RET refers to people "(a) setting up or choosing for themselves certain basic values, purposes, goals, or ideas and then (b) using efficient, flexible, scientific, logical-empirical ways of attempting to achieve values and goals and to avoid contradictory or self-defeating results" (Ellis, 1979c, p. 40).

In this chapter we shall review the general methods of assessment and intervention which RET practitioners employ in working with clients. Specific applications and extensions of these methods with younger clients are reviewed in Chapters 6 and 7. We have isolated assessment from intervention methods, and we would like to indicate that in practice RET methods are combined across the course of treatment to suit the requirements of individual clients. That is to say, they are not used in an invariant "assessment−treatment" sequence as presented in this chapter. Assessment and treatment are integrated during the course of therapy as required, with the aim of helping clients to reappraise those aspects of their personal philosophies, belief systems, and self-talk which can be observed to interfere with the attainment of their personal goals and happiness. As we indicate later on, these aims translate when working with younger clients to enable them to acquire rational thinking skills, sets of rational self-statements, and to reduce the incidence of negative and self-defeating self-talk. RET frequently teaches clients a disputational strategy which enables them to monitor, identify, challenge, and change irrational self-statements and beliefs. This strategy is designed to aid clients in resolving current problems as well as unanticipated and novel problems which may occur subsequent to treatment.

ASSESSMENT

The manner in which RET defines the assessment process varies somewhat among RET theoreticians. We provide a view which we believe synthesizes the essential commonalities among practitioners. In so doing we have conceptualized RET assessment as containing two distinct parts: problem identification and problem analysis. In problem identification the goal of the assessor is to determine whether a problem exists, who owns the problem (parent, child), and to classify the variety of problems which the client presents as either practical or psychological ones or both. Such general designations determine the type of intervention the practitioner prescribes for a client and whether RET is an appropriate course of action. Problem analysis occurs when the practitioner examines the psychological problems of a client from a RET perspective and seeks to determine those aspects of the client's cognitive events, processes, and beliefs which are largely creating the disturbance.

RET recognizes that it is often the case that the designation of problems may change over the course of therapy. Different problems arise which may be more significant than those previously identified. RET practitioners keep an open mind to the overall goals of assessment, and continuously refine and redefine problems as new information is revealed.

Problem Identification

RET eschews traditional methods of psychodiagnosis including most objective and projective tests and rejects reliance upon any of the previously mentioned taxonomies of mental disorders described in Chapter 1. In contrast with traditional clinical practice, the rational-emotive therapist is not concerned with differential diagnosis. Grieger and Boyd (1980) indicate

> the (rational-emotive therapist) primarily focuses on uncovering clients' irrational beliefs or philosophies, understanding how these ideations uniquely contribute to the clients' problems and determining what to do to help clients resolve their problems. Only information directly relevant to treatment is gathered and DSM-II is left in the bathroom for more casual reading. [p. 33]

RET does employ a distinctive and functionally useful approach to assessment. A major distinction made during both RET assessment and treatment phases is between *practical* and *psychological* problems. Practical problems refer to the concerns of clients about outside, external, or environmental events. These problems typically involve the client having difficulty in managing, adapting to, or solving particular problems in their environment. Dealing with a difficult person at home, being poorly organized and not knowing what one wants to do with one's life are examples of practical problems that do not appear to constitute psychopathology and can be handled with guidance, advice, case management, or some form of environmental manipulation (Grieger & Boyd, 1980). Practical problems may be conceptualized as involving behavioral skill deficits where the client lacks specific interpersonal and problem solving skills and which may result from unrealistic environmental demands.

Psychological problems are dysfunctional emotional reactions such as undesirable levels of anxiety, anger, depression, and guilt and are frequently accompanied by maladaptive behavioral reactions such as aggression, withdrawal, and procrastination. Psychological problems are hypothesized to derive from irrational beliefs and generally are experienced as unpleasant emotions by the client. Neophyte RET practitioners frequently spend too much time analyzing and trying to treat practical problems and fail to help clients focus upon and solve their emotional and behavioral concerns. It is important to classify problems which clients present as either practical or psychological so as to be able to apply RET appropriately. It is, of course, frequently the case that clients have psychological problems about practical concerns and it is the practitioner's difficult task to understand the dynamics of the interplay between psychological and practical problems. Rational-emotive therapy is primarily useful in resolving psychological rather than practical problems. In discussing this distinction, Grieger and Boyd (1980, p. 36) make the following useful points:

1.   When clients bring vocational and environmental problems to the RET therapist, the therapist, where appropriate, either refers these clients to

an appropriate counselor specializing in these areas, or applies appropriate counseling and guidance methods.

2. In conceptualizing the entire problem area of clients, the RET therapist identifies the emotional-behavioral aspects and applies RET.

3. Most clients are able to successfully resolve or cope with practical concerns if they are free of psychological problems.

4. RET holds that relieving practical problems before emotional problems may rob clients of their motivation to solve emotional problems, leaving them more comfortable but still disturbed.

The importance of disentangling practical from psychological problems during problem identification is revealed in the following case. The first author recently saw a middle level executive of a fast growing business enterprise who requested help for "tension headaches." The initial interview revealed that Mr. Kendall's headaches were of recent origin beginning with the onset of increased demands which his senior executive made of him. Mr. Kendall indicated that he frequently experienced his headaches on the way to work in the car in the morning. When asked about his feelings at these times, he indicated he was very angry although occasionally he felt worried about being unable to get everything done at work. At the end of the first session both practical and psychological problems were apparent. Practical problems involved Mr. Kendall having too much to do at work, not being as efficient at work as he could be, not being able to delegate responsibility, and finding it difficult to communicate to his boss about what he considered to be excessive demands; and psychological problems included excessive anger and worry. In a case such as this, a number of therapeutic options were open such as helping Mr. Kendall be a more efficient and effective worker and communicator as well as teaching him to control his emotions through rational thinking and relaxation. And in such cases the practitioner is often seduced into the expedient solution of teaching practical problem-solving skills rather than focusing on helping the client acquire cognitive coping skills for dealing with demands and stress. By categorizing problems in this way, it is easier for practitioners to separate in their own minds the requirements of working on both types of problems and to make sure that sufficient time is available during therapy for the resolution of both. Too much time working on practical problems at the expense of psychological problems is regarded by RET practitioners as an extremely inelegant and palliative approach which has limited value for helping the client in dealing with and adapting to practical problems which have no ready made environmental—management solutions. In the case of Mr. Kendall, the therapist helped him to not only be more effective interpersonally and to work more efficiently (practical problem solving) but also to identify, dispute, and change irrational thoughts concerning his need to be perfect and approved of which lead to an eventual cessation of his headaches.

We have found no clear guidelines for deciding when specific emotional and behavioral problems are severe enough to warrant the judgment of psychopathology. It is not necessary for all psychological problems to be "abnormal" for RET to be considered an appropriate course of action. Indeed, many "mildly neurotic" problems are eminently treatable with RET. The judgment of "abnormality" or "deviance" is of greater significance when the client is young and is being referred for treatment by a parent or teacher. Then it becomes important for the practitioner to decide whether the referred problem of the young client is severe enough to justify intervention. This judgment is important in deciding whether the presenting problem is "owned" by the younger client or someone else.

We believe the following formula to be a useful one for determining the severity of psychological problems, especially in younger populations. In identifying emotional and behavioral problems, we examine the *frequency*, *intensity*, and *duration* of the response. The cross-situational pattern of response is also determined to estimate the magnitude of the problem. We also determine whether the dysfunctional emotions and behaviors are predictable and normal responses to a source of current stress or whether there is a long-standing history of problems in response to normal levels of environmental stress. Another important variable is the extent to which the emotions and behaviors are considered atypical for a particular age-group and for the client's cultural reference group. The answers to these questions enable the practitioner to arrive at a more secure opinion concerning the "pathological" nature of the psychological problems revealed during assessment.

Problem Assessment

The goal of a RET problem assessment is for the practitioner to identify the specific emotions and behaviors which are problematic and to become aware of the client's irrational thoughts and beliefs which underly the problems. RET usually begins its assessment of psychological problems by asking clients to describe their emotions and behaviors (Consequences) that are activated by a specific event or experience (A). Generally, clients will describe their problems in terms of feeling statements ("I'm unhappy, depressed, worried") rather than in terms of behavioral statements ("I seem to give up too easily"). The practitioner identifies emotional responses of the client which are causing the client greatest concern and pain, which are generally overreactions to a frustrating, painful, or obnoxious event and which, perhaps most importantly, lead to maladaptive and self-defeating behavioral responses. That is, the practitioner has the task of identifying those emotions which, because of their intensity, interfere with clients effectively solving their problems. The practitioner attempts to arrive at a consensus with clients as to appropriate labels for their feelings as well as to their intensity, frequency, and duration. Clients are often asked to rate the intensity of their feelings on a scale of 1 to 10 where 1 equals "feeling nothing" and 10 equals "couldn't feel anymore."

Not infrequently, rational-emotive practitioners find they have to provide clients with linguistic skills and conceptual schemes as a prerequisite to rational self-analysis. Clients have to be able to analyze their own feelings in terms of distinguishing one from another, degrees of intensity, and changes in intensity levels, before they can become fully competent in applying cognitive change procedures.

The practitioner may have to suggest labels to help clients describe their feelings. Where this is the case, we have found that we can pretty accurately judge and label the various feeling states of a client by examining the characteristics of the activating event. For example, we pretty well know that anger tends to be the dominant feeling when a person appraises another person's behavior or event as being a violation of some societal or personal rule or value. Anxiety flows from a person anticipating the negative consequences (catastrophe) of an event in the future. Performance (or anticipated performance) of an act that violates a personal standard of right–wrong will set the stage for guilt. By examining situations in which the emotions tend to occur the therapist can better understand (and empathize with) the emotional problems of the client. These relationships are defined and discussed more fully in Chapter 5. Walen et al. (1980) suggest the following three ways the experienced therapist can infer the presence of certain emotional states.

1. By using cues from the client's behavior.
2. By understanding typical emotional consequences to common life situations.
3. By deduction from rational-emotive theory so that from knowing a client's belief system one can infer a specific emotion. [p. 52]

Some clients put themselves down and feel badly about how they emotionally reacted to a situation. This phenomenon which has been labeled variously as "symptom stress," "disturbance about disturbance," "the problem about the problem" (Bard, 1980), and "secondary symptoms" (Grieger & Boyd, 1980) has to be assessed carefully, for if clients cannot accept the fact that they will from time to time emotionally overreact, the practitioner will usually find it extremely difficult to help them analyze and solve the original problem. This is because such people are so generally obsessed with the second order feelings of shame and worthlessness they have little motivation and energy left to examine the original problem.

The sixth-grade boy who explodes in anger when his teacher fails to call on him demonstrates secondary symptoms of anger which derive from his primary symptoms. His emotional outburst becomes for the boy a new activating event. He views his loss of control as being unforgivable and says to himself something like "I must never lose my temper. It is horrible and awful when I do. I can't bear even thinking about myself. I am totally hopeless." These irrational thoughts result in feelings of anger with himself, as well as shame, guilt, and depression.

It perhaps should be mentioned that not all negative emotional states require RET intervention. Indeed, many emotional reactions are appropriate and adaptive. It is only those reactions which are unduly excessive and painful, and which, most importantly, prevent the individual from constructive problem solving, that are of interest to the RET practitioner.

When clients describe their emotional reaction to an activating event the RET practitioner attempts to link the emotion with behavior. Emotions and behaviors (and cognitions) are closely interrelated. One can often be seen as an expression of the other and often occur at the same time. People who are depressed tend to withdraw while angry people tend to explode. Behavioral data gathering is extremely important. It is the only reliable and objective means whereby the therapist can determine the extent to which emotional distress results in behavioral malfunctioning. Behavioral data gathered during assessment provides a baseline for determining whether subsequent changes in the cognitions of clients result in (as RET hypothesizes) corresponding improvements in behavior. It has been our experience that certain children are able to change their philosophies toward life, but have a hard time "putting it into practice." If such is the case we are cued to employ stronger behavioral and emotive methods. A preferred RET solution necessitates changes in not only the cognitions and emotions of clients but, most importantly, clinically significant changes in baseline levels of the problematic behavior.

Rational-emotive practitioners do not dwell on the nature of clients' activating events. In problem assessment, RET practitioners have to be able to unscramble and pinpoint activating events so as to not only be able to anticipate, understand, and empathize with clients' feelings, but also so that they will be able to demonstrate to clients a number of basic RET insights. An important insight is that the dysfunctional emotions and behaviors of clients do not originate in some magical state but rather are occasioned by antecedent events. While this insight may seem obvious many clients seem surprisingly unaware that their behavior is closely linked with what is immediately happening in the world around them. As we suggested earlier, identifying antecedent events also enables the practitioner to help clients to identify and describe their feelings. The identification of activating events is also important as it represents an important element in teaching clients the ABCs of RET (see Chapter 2).

RET practitioners do vary in the extent to which they isolate antecedent events. Many practitioners believe that focusing on the As distracts both the practitioner and client alike from analyzing and changing fundamental assumptions and beliefs. These practitioners emphasize and spend most of their time uncovering the relationship between dysfunctional emotions (and behaviors) and irrational beliefs as a prerequisite to helping clients make shifts in their personal philosophies. They oftentimes do not employ the ABC model at all in the belief that it orients the focus of RET to the solution of specific problems rather than leading to fundamental changes in general irrational beliefs and assumptions.

Some rational-emotive practitioners who have been schooled in the traditions of behavioral assessment and methodology conduct a more thorough analysis of the total life environment in which the problematic emotions and behaviors of clients occur. In seeking to more fully understand both clients and their problems in context, the practitioner tries to determine which environments are problematic for the client (work, home, recreational). That is, where do the problems generally occur, with whom, and where do they not? Are there certain days of the week or hours of the day where the problems seem to be most acute? A more intensive analysis is made of the specific antecedent discriminative stimulus conditions within the problematic environment which, when perceived and interpreted by the person, lead to emotional and behavioral consequences. In addition, the environmental consequences and reinforcement contingency schedules for the client's problematic behavior are identified.

Some RET practitioners then conduct a psychosituational assessment of both environmental (antecedents, consequences) and internal problematic emotions (irrational beliefs) and conditions which surround psychological problems that may be useful data for solving practical problems. We take the interactionist position that although emotional and behavioral problems are largely governed by thinking disorders which can be considered to be fairly stable personality traits, the stimulus situation within which the people find themselves will as a result of reinforcement history, available role models, and other learning factors determine whether neurotic behavior is expressed. It is the case especially with mildly and moderately neurotic individuals that whereas they may experience extreme emotional distress and express maladaptive behaviors in certain situations, they demonstrate remarkably "normal" behavior once they remove themselves from the problematic environment. For persons interested in the theory and practice of psychosituational and behavioral analysis, we recommend the chapters and texts by Bergan (1977), Bijou and Peterson (1971), Ciminero, Calhoun and Adams (1977), Cone and Hawkins (1977a), Goldfried and Linehan (1977), Haynes (1978), Haynes and Wilson (1979), Hersen and Bellack (1976), Kanfer and Saslow (1969), Kazdin (1979), Keefe, Kopel, and Gordon (1978), Kratochwill (in press), Mash and Terdal (1976, 1981) O'Leary (1972), and Sulzer-Azaroff and Mayer (1977).

The assessment of the dysfunctional cognitions of a client is a challenging enterprise. This aspect of RET requires an extraordinary amount of therapeutic skill and interpretive insight on the part of the practitioner. There are two general objectives which RET practitioners pursue during this phase of problem assessment. First, they have to elicit from a client much introspective detail concerning the content of their thoughts so as to enable them to identify the full extent of client irrationality. Second, in listening to the client the practitioner has to be sufficiently conversant with the characteristics of dysfunctional thoughts to be able to weed through the mass of detail provided by the client and to identify, classify, and label them appropriately. That is to say, it is often the case that many of the thoughts a client verbalizes are really irrelevant to the problem at hand. Some clients spend too much time describing irrelevant details of the antecedent event and fail to zero in on the aspects of their thoughts which are causing their upset. Frequently, clients provide a plethora of negative but rational self-statements but are unable (for reasons to be discussed later in this chapter) to discover and articulate irrational thoughts. It is the responsibility of the RET practitioner to teach clients how to both tap into their intrapersonal communication system (self-talk) and to discriminate important cognitions from those that are unimportant.

We wish to indicate that unlike many traditional approaches to diagnosis and treatment, RET assessment procedures are interwoven with treatment throughout the course of therapy. The reasons for this are straightforward. When RET practitioners detect dysfunctional cognitions during assessment, in fairly short order they subject them to close scrutiny, help teach the client to recognize their irrational and antiempirical qualities, and substitute more rational and veridical content. This process is an iterative one and is conducted throughout the course of therapy as new problems arise.

There are a variety of different types of cognitions which well-rounded RET practitioners listen for and attempt to elicit. The distinctive contribution of RET to the field of cognitive-behavioral assessment is in alerting the practitioner to the importance of identifying the client's irrational thoughts and beliefs as well as emotions. The RET practitioner attempts to construct the personal belief systems of clients from what clients report they are thinking and saying to themselves.

While the major emphasis of this section will be on methods for detecting irrational thoughts and beliefs there are also other cognitive processes and content which are examined in the overall cognitive assessment of the client's psychological disturbance. Each of the major forms of cognitive-behavior therapy conceptualizes dysfunctional cognitions slightly differently from RET and as a consequence conceptualizes the targets of cognitive assessment differently. We shall briefly touch on these areas which can be employed along with the traditional RET approach.

The assessment of cognitions involves an examination of clients' perceptions and interpretations and appraisals of reality. There is impressive evidence that the act of perception is influenced by cognition. Over 80 years ago, Binet and Henri (1894, cited in Metalsky & Abramson, 1981) found that children's memories are influenced by their imaginations. Bartlett (1932) argued that the knowledge people bring with them selectively influences what they attend to and remember, while Metalsky and Abramson (1981) summarize the role of causal attributions in human learning research, remarking that "People's general beliefs or knowledge about the world constrain and select possible interpretations of events making interpretations more salient than others and some not possible at all" (p. 26).

One of the first tasks, then, in assessing cognitions is to determine the extent to which clients initially distort reality; that is, what is the discrepancy between the client's impressions and recollections of what happened and those that would be reported by several objective and disinterested observers. Mahoney

(1974) has identified four attentional cognitive processes which underly reality distortion:

1. *Selective inattention* involves the ignoring of performance relevant stimuli. . . .
2. *Misperception* occurs when impinging stimuli are attended to but inaccurately labelled. . . .
3. *Maladaptive focusing* occurs when the individual attends to external stimuli irrelevant or deleterious to performance. . . .
4. *Maladaptive self-arousal* involves the generation of private "stimuli" which are either irrelevant or detrimental to performance. [pp. 151–153]

Errors in cognitive or logical processing once information has been encoded is another target of RET inquiry. Cognitive distortions which occur when the individual draws incorrect conclusions and makes incorrect inferences on the basis of perceived reality which may or may not correspond with objective reality may also lead to psychological disturbance. Beck et al. (1979) have identified a number of systematic errors in thinking which are characteristic of depressed people and which appear to be present in other types of emotional and behavioral disorders:

1. *Arbitrary inference* (a response set) refers to the process of drawing a specific conclusion in the absence of evidence to support the conclusion or when the evidence is contrary to the conclusion.
2. *Selective abstraction* (a stimulus set) consists of focusing on a detail taken out of context, ignoring other more salient features of the situation and conceptualizing the whole experience on the basis of this fragment.
3. *Overgeneralization* (a response set) refers to the pattern of drawing a general rule or conclusion on the basis of one or more isolated incidents and applying the concept across the board to related and unrelated situations.
4. *Magnification and minimization* (a response set) are reflected in errors in evaluating the significance or magnitude of an event that are so gross as to constitute a distortion.
5. *Personalization* (a response set) refers to the patient's proclivity to relate external events to himself when there is no basis for making such a connection.
6. *Absolutistic, dichotomous thinking* (a response act) is manifested in the tendency to place all experience in one of two opposite categories; for example, flawless or defective, immaculate or filthy, saint or sinner. In describing himself, the patient selects the extreme negative categorization. [p. 14]

For a complete discussion of the role of these types of information processing errors in psychological disturbance, see Beck (1976) and Beck et al. (1979).
For clients who demonstrate behavioral problems in the area of interper-

sonal adjustment, RET practitioners frequently assess the extent to which these clients are equipped with appropriate verbal mediational strategies to guide and control their interpersonal behavior. Two major mediational strategies which Spivack, Platt, and Shure (1976) have found to correlate strongly with social problems in children and adolescents are the ability to generate a variety of possible ways of dealing with a problem situation (alternative thinking) and to think through the consequences of each alternative before acting (consequential thinking). Adults as well as younger clients frequently demonstrate verbal mediational deficits in this area and therefore it is an extremely important consideration for RET assessment. We present a more complete discussion of interpersonal cognitive problem solving in Chapter 8.

There is also increasing evidence that the manner in which people explain the causes of events in their lives and the extent to which they believe that they, rather than the world, are responsible for their own behavior influences both emotional and behavioral adjustment. The literature on causal attributions and locus of control (reviewed in more detail in Chapter 8) indicates the necessity in certain instances to listen during assessment for attributions clients make about both positive and negative events in their lives as well as the reasons they provide for their own successes and failures. For example, people who are depressed tend to take excessive responsibility for all that is wrong in their lives. These attributions often act as enduring "schema" which are often acquired very early in life and which maintain themselves in the face of quite often contradictory information.

RET practitioners have to try to get a sense of the self-talk of clients which occurs when the client is experiencing distress. The practitioner has to be alert to the variety of self-statements that the client may emit in problematic situations which are dysfunctional. So not only does the practitioner try to arrive at an idea of the way clients view reality, attention is also placed on the presence and absence of coping self-statements of clients. Simply stated, clients can either talk themselves into or out of problem situations and it is the task of the practitioner to diagnose dysfunctional self-statements, help the client reformulate self-defeating ones, and to educate the client with appropriate mediators when they are missing. As we indicated in Chapter 1, inner-speech performs both an instrumental and affective function and as such both aspects need to be examined during cognitive assessment. Both self-instructional training (Kendall, 1981; Meichenbaum, 1977) and stress inoculation training (Meichenbaum, 1977) emphasize the importance of providing clients with task and situationally appropriate sets of self-statements as well as statements to reduce debilitating levels of irrationality (see Chapter 8).

Ellis steadfastly maintains that while distortions of reality and faulty logic can lead to unpleasant emotional responses, it is the irrational beliefs that lie behind antiempirical self-statements that predispose the individual to reality distortion and illogical thinking. Lurking in the shadows of the lonely student's cognitive structure is the irrational philosophical belief that she must be liked by all her classmates, and if she isn't it is awful. The test-anxious student defines his self-worth in terms of his performances and implicitly believes that he *must* do well. According to Ellis, it is the evaluation and appraisal that individuals make of their subjective perceptions and interpretations of reality that determine the extent of emotional and behavioral upset. And when individuals demonstrate emotional and behavioral disturbance, it is the task of the RET practitioner to assess which irrational beliefs are operating.

There are literally hundreds of different irrational beliefs that underly human emotional upset. It is important during assessment to tap into the specific content of as many of the client's idiosyncratic beliefs as possible as a basis for understanding the client and because they represent the central therapeutic targets. It is again emphasized that from an RET perspective, emotional and behavioral problems are merely symptoms of underlying irrational philosophies.

It is impossible to list all possible irrational beliefs. Ellis (1977a) indicated that someday he may go to the trouble of listing the 259 major self-defeating beliefs he had up until then collected. Walen et al. (1980) indicate that all irrational beliefs appear to have central core irrational concepts that are revealed in one of four types of statements.

1. *Should statements*, reflecting the belief that there are universal musts.
2. *Awfulizing statements*, reflecting the belief that there are terrible and catastrophic things in the world.
3. *Need statements*, reflecting the belief that the client must have things to be happy.
4. *Human worth statements*, reflecting the belief that people can be rated. [p. 115–116]

In helping the client to identify irrational beliefs, the RET practitioner has to listen carefully to the client's verbalizations and be able to recognize statements that indicate he is rating himself or others ("I'm no good"; "She's a bitch"), is defining a want as a need ("I need to have her as a friend"), is making things worse than they really are by awfulizing ("I can't stand it when she doesn't say hello"; "It's terrible when by brother calls me stinky"), or is making absolutistic demands of himself, others, or of the world ("I have to get an A on the test"; "You shouldn't have done that"; "School should be a better place to live").

Ellis has identified a number of important irrational beliefs that are held by many individuals in our society who have emotional and behavioral problems. We have collected (and occasionally restated) these beliefs from the recent writings of Ellis (1977a), Ellis and Harper (1975), Bard (1980), and Walen et al. (1980).

1. I must be loved and approved of by every significant person in my life.
2. I am not worthwhile unless I am thoroughly competent, adequate, intelligent, and achieving at least most of the time in at least one major area.

3. Things must go the way I would like them to go because I need what I want; and life proves awful, terrible and horrible when I do not get what I prefer.

4. People (the world) must treat everyone in a fair and just manner; and if they act unfairly or unethically they amount to rotten people, deserve damnation and severe punishment.

5. Life should be entirely pleasant and enjoyable and thus any frustration, discomfort, and pain would be unbearable.

6. I desperately need others to rely and depend upon.

7. It is possible to measure human worth and to assign a global value rating to individual persons.

8. It is the past and all its bad experiences which continually ruin the present and which can never really be overcome.

9. Emotional disturbance comes almost completely from external pressure, and I have little ability to control my feelings.

10. One should be very upset over the problems and disturbances of other people.

11. When dangers of fearsome people or things exist in my world, I must continually preoccupy myself with and upset myself about them; in that way I will have the power to control or change them.

12. I must find correct and practically perfect solutions to my problems and other problems.

13. I must be able to control the attitudes and affections of other people.

14. It's easier to avoid than to face life's difficulties.

In assessing the irrational aspects of client thought, it is important for the practitioner to be on the lookout for one of the most self-defeating irrational beliefs—low frustration tolerance (LFT). There appear to be two types of LFT—one which leads to anger and hostility, the other to anxiety, procrastination or avoidance behavior. The older conceptualization of LFT focused on people's tendency to become angry when they are frustrated or thwarted. Ellis (1977c) makes the point that anger and hostility do not stem directly from frustration, but from people's inability to tolerate being frustrated (LFT):

> When you feel furious, your basic view consists of the idea that whatever frustrates you *should* and *ought* not to exist, that it not only proves unfair, but this unfairness, again, *must* not prevail, that you *can't stand* frustration, and those that unduly balk and block you amount to almost vermin who, once again, *should* not act the way they indubitably do. [p. 186]

In situations where people perceive that their basic needs have been blocked, we find that LFT sometimes leads to depression rather than anger. Ellis' (1979e, 1980b) newer view of LFT revolves around the irrational belief that people should be comfortable and without pain at all times. The inability to tolerate "discomfort anxiety" is revealed in a variety of maladaptive behavioral patterns which generally involve refusing to put in the effort that is required to accomplish some task. People who procrastinate find the effort that is required to do something in their best interests as "too painful" (giving up food, going to the library, doing therapeutic homework assignments) demonstrate LFT. Phrases which indicate discomfort anxiety include "I can't bear it," "I can't live with (or without) it," "I can't stand it," and "I can't tolerate it" (from Walen, et al., 1980, p. 138). Ellis (1978b) has defined discomfort anxiety as emotional hypertension that arises when people feel (1) that their life or comfort is threatened, (2) that they *must* not feel uncomfortable and *have* to feel at ease, and (3) that it is awful or catastrophic (rather than merely inconvenient or disadvantageous) when they don't get what they supposedly must.

Ellis (1977a) has developed a strategy that clients can use to *detect* their own irrational thoughts and beliefs. To detect irrational beliefs, Ellis suggests asking oneself the following four questions:

1. Look for your awfulizing. Ask yourself: "What do I think of as awful in connection with the antecedent event?"
2. Look for something you think you can't stand. Ask yourself: "What is it about the antecedent event do I think I can't bear?"
3. Look for your musturbating. Ask yourself: "What should or *must* I keep telling myself about in this situation?"
4. Look for your damning of yourself or others. Ask yourself: "In what manner do I damn or down anyone in connection with what went on at A?" (p.10)

In this manner, one can determine which of the four kinds of irrationalities one's disturbance stems from.

As we have indicated in Chapter 2, the meaning of the term "irrational belief" is somewhat unclear. It is important to recall that irrational beliefs are not to be equated with self-talk. They can be considered unspoken assumptions and unquestioned understandings which constitute what Beck has called the person's "personal paradigm" and which represent what the individual knows to be true. Irrational beliefs also vary in generality. The ones we have just listed are at the very highest level of generality. It is the task of the RET practitioner to translate the beliefs of a client in terms which relate to the life context of the client. This translation process results in a less general and more individualized expression of belief. For example, when working with certain teachers, Belief 12 may translate at a lower level to "I must be able to deal with all the problems of all my students" whereas Belief 13 translates to "I must have total control of my class at all times." These lower level or derived beliefs which again are assumed by the individual to be true and are generally unspoken are once removed from the self-talk of the person. Self-talk which corresponds with and, in a sense, flows from the above set of secondary beliefs would be, for Belief 12, "I am a failure because a student of mine dropped out of school." For Belief 13, the correlated thought would be something like "I cannot tolerate it when that student talks out of turn." It is at this level where covert verbalization leads to affects such as depression or sadness in the first instance and anger in the second.

In assessing the thoughts that a client verbalizes in therapy, it is useful to consider that some of the cognitions that activate emotional upset may be largely imaginal in nature. As RET uses emotive-imagery techniques, it is often revealing to ask clients to describe in as much detail as possible what it is they are "seeing" before becoming upset. Images often are activating events which occasion irrational thinking patterns. For example, one of the biggest problems of athletes in certain sports is the fear of physical contact. When the cognitions of these athletes are assessed as a prelude to rational-emotive imagery, pictures of horrific and painful consequences of bodily contact are frequently in evidence. These pictures serve as covert stimuli which occasion irrational and antiempirical self-statements such as "I will be destroyed and suffer excruciating pain the next time I collide with someone," and "I can't protect myself from injury at all times."

Sutton-Simon (1981) provides a thorough discussion of methods and strate- gies for assessing irrational beliefs. She indicates that there are several different definitions of irrational beliefs that have influenced the development of as- sessment strategies. The most common conception of irrational beliefs is Ellis' which refers to the content of specific "life rules" which underly psychological maladjustment. "Clinicians working with this conception of irrational beliefs attempt to assess them by identifying the particular content of beliefs outlined by Ellis" (p. 166). A second way of conceiving irrational beliefs is in terms of their characteristic qualities (Mahoney, 1974) where clients have unknowingly attached absolutistic, evaluative, and demanding features to their assumptions about themselves and their worlds (Sutton-Simon, 1981, p. 66). The dysfunc- tional thinking processes (dichotomous reasoning, arbitrary inference, catas- trophizing) that lead to irrational thoughts constitutes a third way of conceptu- alizing irrational beliefs. Each one of these conceptions may be the focus of a RET assessment.

There are three general procedures which Sutton-Simon (1981) enumerates as being employed during a RET assessment of irrational beliefs: *clinical interview*, *self-monitoring procedures*, and *psychometric procedures*. The most popular is the clinical interview where through direct questioning and imaginal role play, RET practitioners elicit descriptions of irrational thoughts and emotional reactions from which they infer certain irrational beliefs. During the clinical interview, the practitioners may also investigate the irrational qualities of underlying thoughts by tapping into the client's use of "should," "ought," and "must." A third goal of the interview may be to identify the faulty logic and reasoning behind irrational beliefs through examining the way in which the client forms hypotheses and draws conclusions and by uncovering "idiosyn- cratic definitions and unusual semantic networks" (Sutton-Simon, 1981, p. 71). A fourth interview approach focuses on aspects of the client's philosophical and religious systems which might be maladaptive. Self-monitoring procedures generally involve clients filling out a self-report form which elicits information concerning their thoughts and feelings during problematic situations (Ellis' *Rational Self-Help Form*; Maultsby's *Rational Self-Analysis*). These self-assessment forms are used primarily to monitor the progress of therapy and in planning future treatment. The use of psychometric instruments to assess irrational beliefs has been slow to develop due to definitional and scaling problems associated with belief systems. A number of tests have been devised which mostly assess the specific irrational beliefs outlined by Ellis: *Self-Rating Scale*, Bard, 1973; *Adult Irrational Ideas Inventory*, Fox and Davies, 1971; *Irrational Beliefs Test*, Jones, 1968; *Test of Irrational Ideas*, Laughridge, 1975; *Rational Beliefs Inventory*, Shockey and Whiteman, 1977.

With the advent of the cognitive-behavioral model, there has been increasing interest by practitioners in developing ways to systematically assess the full range of cognitions of clients. Additionally, cognitive-behavioral researchers have intensified efforts to develop psychometrically sound assessment instruments (Kendall & Wilcox 1979; Kendall & Hollon, 1981). We briefly review these elicitational approaches because they appear to hold great promise for extending the RET practitioner's assessment armamentarium.

Meichenbaum (1977) has discussed a *cognitive-functional* approach to assessment which involves the practitioner asking the question "In what psychological processes must the successfully achieving individual engage and in which of these is my client failing?" Meichenbaum's procedures involve identifying sequential psychological processes as they are revealed in the internal dialogue (self-statements) of the client that are necessary for successful task performance. He recommends that "the cognitive-behavior therapist attempt to discern the style and incidence of the client's cognitions (i.e., internal dialogue and images) and their relationship to the client's behavior and feeling" (pp. 248–249). The mapping out of task appropriate self-verbalizations enables the assessor to examine the extent to which the client's cognitions are compatible with efficient functioning. Through the manipulation of various aspects of the task or problematic environment, the practitioner is able to assess the full range of the client's capabilities and task and situationally-related deficits so that appropriate treatment strategies and goals may be identified. This functional aspect of Meichenbaum's approach is reminiscent of earlier forms of process-oriented "assess-down, teach-up" diagnostic teaching procedures.

Meichenbaum (1977) identifies five different ways his cognitive-functional assessment approach can be applied clinically. In a *clinical interview*, the practitioner elicits thoughts, images, and behaviors that the client experiences in difficult situations. The use of imagery is facilitative as clients are asked to run a movie through their heads so that they can reexperience the sequence of cognitions. Clients are sometimes encouraged to conduct a homework assignment to listen to themselves with a third ear so that they can become more aware of their thoughts. During the interview, the practitioner determines such things as the situational specificity–generality of dysfunctional beliefs and searches for common themes which may have occurred throughout the life of clients. *Behavioral tests* involve clients participating in either a role play or in vivo problematic experience. During these situations, clients are able to become more aware of their specific self-statements and images, changes in their frequency and intensity over time, and aspects of the problematic situation which occasion their occurrence. Meichenbaum recommends the use of videotapes of the behavioral assessment to enable the reconstruction by clients and practitioner of thoughts and feelings. A third way to elicit the internal dialogue of clients is to employ a *TAT-like approach* where clients are shown pictures related to target problems and are asked to both free associate and report specific thoughts, feelings, fantasies, and images. Meichenbaum nominates the use of *psychometric tests* which contain items that assess different types of cognitions (positive and negative self-statements, beliefs, attributions) which are related to the client's problems. *The assessment of cognition in groups* of clients with a common referral problem is another approach which enables the practitioner to identify cognitive deficits. "A shared exploration of the common set of self-statements and images is invaluable in having the clients come to appreciate the role thoughts play in their behavioral repertoire" (p. 258).

One of the leaders in the development of a psychometrically sound methodology for assessing cognition is Philip C. Kendall. He has encouraged cognitive-behavioral scientists and practitioners to keep one of their feet planted squarely in methodological behaviorism. He also indicated along with others (Bernard, 1981; Goldfried, 1979; Nisbett & Wilson, 1977) that cognitive content and processes are differentially accessible and self-reports of cognitive activity may not always be valid nor reliable. Kendall and Korgeski (1979) have reviewed different areas of cognitive assessment and identified three natural groupings.

> In-vivo thought sampling and self-statement inventories can be considered *methods* for assessing cognitive phenomena. Imagery ability, cognitive tempo, and to a lesser degree, attributional preference can be referred to as cognitive *styles* (individual differences), whereas beliefs, self-efficacy expectations, and actual self-statements are more appropriately thought of as cognitive *content*. [pp. 15–16]

They discuss a variety of methods for assessing cognitive content and style.

More recently, Kendall and Hollon (1981) have presented an imaginative review of four different methods for measuring self-statements: *Recording methods, endorsement methods, production methods, and sampling methods*. As we indicate throughout this book, self-statements are proposed by RET to play a major role in the creation of emotional and behavioral disorders. Kendall and Hollon indicate a number of reasons why self-statements should be examined: (1) to study the relationship of covert self-statements, or self-talk, to observable behavior and to experience and expression of emotions; (2) to investigate the role of self-statements in the development of various forms of psychopathology and the adaptive process of successful coping; (3) to confirm that a therapy which had been designed to alter cognitions actually produced positive change in the targeted conditions; and (4) to provide a manipulation check in studies that varied self-instructions (p. 91). We do not have the room to discuss each of the four methods in detail. A summary of the four methods is presented below:

1. Recording methods. Audiotape (or audio-videotape) recordings of subjects' speech have been employed in a number of studies as a method for assessing subjects' self-talk. Subjects' verbalizations can be recorded unobtrusively or following specific instructions. Once the recordings are made, the taped verbal behavior can then be transcribed and/or coded into categories (p. 91).
2. Endorsement methods. Inventories that contain a predetermined series of items (i.e., sample self-statements) have been employed to assess self-statements. For example, subjects perform a certain task and then complete the inventory by endorsing individual items to indicate whether they had experienced a particular thought and the frequency with which it had occurred (p. 95).
3. Production methods. This method of assessing self-statements requires that subjects retrospectively produce either thoughts that they had had during an immediately preceding interval or thoughts that were typical. The production method requires that subjects and/or judges read over the list of thoughts and categorize them along certain dimensions. The production method that has been most often employed is thought listing (p. 99).
4. Sampling methods. When sampling methods are applied to the assessment of self-statements, the research is seeking an on-the-spot measurement that requires the subject to provide a thought sample when cued by a sampling device. Much akin to behavioral time sampling procedures used to observe and code behaviors, thought sampling procedures attempt to get an accurate picture of subjects' self-statements by random sampling of thoughts at various times on different days. Thought sampling seeks a representative sample of subjects' self-statements (p. 102).

Problems in Detecting Irrational Beliefs

Not all of what clients report thinking about after they experience an activating event (and before emotional and behavioral consequences) are, of course, irrational thoughts. Remember that within the B of ABC is subsumed both rational and irrational evaluations held by the individual about the antecedent event A. As we have written, B may be viewed as a very broad hypothetical construct that embraces at least three distinct subclasses: (1) thoughts that an individual is thinking and aware of at a given point in time about A, (2) thoughts about A that the individual is not immediately aware of, and (3) more abstract rational and irrational beliefs that the individual may hold in general. The first two subclasses—thoughts that an individual may or may not be aware of—refer to internal, mental events that directly determine an emotional consequence. In other words, they represent the critical internal stimuli that activate a given emotional response. On the basis of the pattern of the client's verbalized thought-statements across time, persons, and situations, the practitioner begins to construct the client's general belief system. These beliefs are subsumed under the third subclass of B. A practitioner infers beliefs based on the pattern of the client's thought-statements. Such beliefs enable the practitioner to begin to establish regularity and consistency in client behavior, and, in a sense, to "understand" the client. They are not, however, activating verbal stimuli that influence emotional responses in any direct sense.

One of the more difficult aspects of RET assessment is discovering the maladaptive aspects of the client's cognitive apparatus. For while most clients are able to overtly verbalize rational thought-statements that lead to more mild and appropriate levels of emotional upset, the spontaneous production by a client of irrational words ("should," "awful," "must," "need") and irrational sentences ("I'm a failure," "I can't bear the pain") is less frequent.

So when the RET practitioner asks clients to report what it is they are thinking between the activating event and emotional and behavioral consequences, the practitioner may have to spend a great deal of time eliciting information. RET as practiced by Ellis tends to be very active and directive in actually confronting clients with what it is they almost have to be thinking if they are upset.

> The RET practitioner knows on theoretical grounds, even before he talks to the client, that this client most probably has some silly irrational ideas—particularly, that he holds some absolutistic shoulds and musts—otherwise he would very likely not be disturbed. And knowing this, the rational therapist looks for these irrationalities, often predicts them, and most often is able to discover them, to get the client to agree that they exist, and to show the client how to logical-empirically dispute and surrender them. [Ellis, 1977b p. 78]

While we agree with Ellis that the experienced RET practitioner often knows what clients are likely to be saying to themselves, we do not believe that inexperienced RET practitioners are "insightful" enough to be able to construct the client's underlying belief system from a relatively small sample of largely rational and descriptive thought-statements. Our experience is that many irrational thoughts lay away from immediate conscious awareness and that these thoughts are often at the core of the disturbance. We have the opinion that the idiosyncratic cognitive-linguistic identity of these thoughts are never really illuminated if RET questioning is too directive. There is value we feel in helping clients to discover their own thoughts. Our experience indicates that by giving clients major responsibility for identifying their thoughts, they acquire a cognitive strategy that they are able to employ outside of the practitioner's office after treatment has been terminated. Taking the additional time that is required for clients to discover the irrational core elements of their thoughts and beliefs may also (as we mentioned earlier) make it easier for them to incorporate RET concepts into their cognitive structure and to both generalize and maintain therapeutic gains over time. We recommend, therefore, when working with younger and less verbally-sophisticated populations, and especially in the earlier stages of RET assessment, that nondirective elicitational techniques be used. We do, of course, recognize that these same populations often require both intensive amounts of semantic education as well as concrete guidelines to follow before they can employ the ABC model.

Scattered throughout the RET literature are recommendations for how the practitioner can elicit in an interview irrational thought content which may appear to be "preconscious" at times and certainly is partially hidden from the client's immediate awareness. It is generally recommended that the practitioner educate clients to the difficulties in recognizing their own self-talk and that clients should be encouraged continually to focus in on their self-talk. Garcia (1977) makes the useful point that when clients externalize their self-talk, they frequently talk in "half-sentences." They often leave out the essential irrational aspect of their thoughts. For example, "I hate it when my brother tells me what to do" is a half-statement that omits the other half-statement "because no one should tell me what to do; it's awful when they do, and he's a butt-hole for doing so." This later half-sentence reflects an underlying value of right-wrong concerning another's behavior. Garcia indicates that "therapists should be looking for those unspoken values in order to get to the main universal concepts more efficiently" (p. 80).

We have found Walen's et al. (1980) guide for rational-emotive practitioners a good thesaurus for elicitational prompts. Hauck (1980) suggests the use of the words "why," "and," or "because" as a way of extending clients' self-analysis. Finally, the first author has described elsewhere (Bernard, 1981) several nondirectional methods for expanding clients' awareness of thought.

Using the model of private thought presented earlier in Chapter 2 and the view expressed by Vygotsky and Beck where private thought is viewed as abbreviated, elliptical, and embodied by complex subjective word agglutinations, an initial task of the rational-emotive practitioner is to direct clients in the expansion and transformation of their private thought. An assumption is made here that it may be only at the level of covert verbalizations that clients can actively challenge and dispute irrational thoughts. In a sense, covert verbalizations can be viewed as a bridging link between the objective world of experience and speech communication and the subjective, idiosyncratic world of private thought.

Understanding the problems of clients and establishing therapeutic goals is a difficult and problematic enterprise. In addition to the difficulties already alluded to, there are a number of practitioner and client stumbling blocks which may impede the diagnostic process. Grieger and Boyd (1980) describe the problems of practitioners as follows:

1. *Conceptual Confusions.* The practitioner has to be sufficiently conversant with RET theory to be able to accurately and exhaustively categorize and explain the bewildering array of information presented by the client.
2. *The Past History Trap.* Practitioners who spend too much time analyzing the past history of clients are generally wasting precious time and may be inadvertently teaching clients that the cause of their problems lie in their past.
3. *The Big Picture Trap.* Practitioners frequently attempt to understand the total client (past, present, and future) before starting treatment.
4. *The Myth of the Relationship.* Practitioners who overvalue the "psychotherapeutic relationship" may spend too much time nurturing it and insufficient time facilitating attitudes which facilitate client change.

Grieger and Boyd (1980) also discuss ways in which clients may undercut the therapy process, including "fear of disclosure, tendencies to distrust strangers, extreme upsettedness that interferes with efficient problem solving, and a rigid view of the environment as the source of one's problems (p. 78).

INTERVENTION

Just as there are a variety of different types of cognitions which are assessed during RET assessment, so too are there a number of distinct areas which are the focus of RET intervention. As we have indicated, preferred targets are the irrational thoughts, assumptions and beliefs of the client. RET employs a variety of cognitive, emotive, and behavioral procedures which are designed to help clients change their idiosyncratic and dysfunctional views of themselves and their surrounding world. RET considers an elegant therapeutic outcome is manifested when clients give up their absolutistic and imperative demands they make and adopt a more relativistic and conditional view.

RET practitioners attempt to produce change in both the irrational beliefs of clients as well as, where necessary and appropriate, other cognitive processes and contents. For example, RET practitioners help clients test their interpretations of reality for distortions, dispute with some clients their tendency to assume excessive responsibility for the misfortunes in their lives, teach other clients the dual strategies of alternative solution and consequential thinking, while others receive rehearsal in sets of rational self-statements which are designed either to enable them to cope with environmental stress or are seen to be necessary for effective interpersonal problem solving.

RET practitioners share in common with other cognitive-behavioral practitioners the view that cognitive modifications are the key to helping clients resolve their psychological problems. They assume that cognitions can with many clients of all ages and who manifest a variety of problems be directly modified with cognitive procedures. RET does not completely agree with Bandura's (1977) position that behavioral methods are the most effective ones (rather than cognitive methods) for influencing cognitive change. In fact, RET convincingly demonstrates that the dysfunctional cognitions of clients are eminently sensitive to change through verbal persuasion and other direct cognitive change procedures. RET does recognize that certain clients require the additional use of emotive and behavioral methods.

We shall not describe the characteristics of other cognitively oriented interventions and we refer the interested reader to primary sources for further details. We do discuss in Chapter 8, however, how other cognitive approaches can be integrated with preferential RET methods in working with school-age children.

The most important and distinctive RET intervention strategy is that of *disputation* (D). In disputation, clients through the use of cognitive, emotive and behavioral techniques, challenge and debate with themselves the different irrational beliefs and antiempirical statements they have detected during RET assessment. Disputation refers to any technique which demonstrates to clients "how their reasoning is faulty and why their beliefs are false" (Bard, 1980, p. 56). The aim of disputation is for clients to acquire a more flexible, sensible, and non-absolutistic view of themselves and their world. The outcome of disputation is the client achieving a new philosophy or *effect* (E). Disputation links the ABCs of RET assessment with therapeutic changes effected in the client. Disputation necessitates clients internalizing the following view of human disturbance.

1. If I am upset, I am largely responsible.
2. There is something about what I am saying to myself and how I am evaluating this situation that is causing me to be overly upset.
3. I had better be prepared to accept another point of view about what is going on.
4. And I had better be prepared to question my thoughts and beliefs about the world and not rigorously hold on to those (whatever they might be) that do not have any relationship with reality (and particularly with my goals).

When clients as a result of disputation learn to stop rating themselves and others, to view their wants and desires as important but not crucial for their personal survival, to accept the fallibility of themselves and others, to live with frustration without demanding that things be otherwise, and if they can learn to evaluate obnoxious and stressful events as being inconvenient and a hassle rather than a catastrophe and an intolerable horror, then their newly acquired philosophical effect makes it much easier for them to cope with their personal frustrations and failures. The new philosophy effected by RET disputation enables clients to be less disturbed when they fail to have their own way. The diminution of emotionality to more moderate levels enables clients to apply their personal resources to solve the problems of living. The outcome, then, of DE is a new cognitive viewpoint which frees individuals from the "tyranny of the shoulds" (Horney, 1945) and aids them in living more creatively, happily, and to realize their own personal goals and ideals.

The practice of disputation is, perhaps, the most difficult and most important aspect of RET intervention. The practice is most certainly developed from clinical experience and as a result of practitioners employing disputational strategies in resolving their own personal difficulties. The art of disputation is most graphically illustrated in Walen et al. (1980), and it is to this excellent book that we refer practitioners who want more specific details on disputational strategies and techniques. We now summarize the main disputational approaches that are employed with adults, some of which have been adapted for use with school-age children. (Specific RET intervention techniques that are employed with younger populations will be reviewed in Chapter 7.)

Cognitive Disputation

Cognitive disputation consists of a set of direct, verbally persuasive strategies for convincing clients of the irrationality of their beliefs. For practitioners to help clients verbally dispute irrational beliefs, it is, of course, necessary for them to have a firm understanding as to why certain concepts (must, awful, need, self-worth) and beliefs are irrational. We briefly present such a rationale.

We have previously noted that irrational beliefs seem to share one or more core irrational concepts. *Should statements* are irrational because they imply that somehow people have control over the way they think things should be, others should be, and the world should be. Clients prone to "shoulding on themselves" appear to strongly believe that the world revolves around them and that because it does, when they want something, they should get it. There is, however, no evidence that would support such a belief. Clients learn to accept that things are the way they are and that it is pointless to demand that they be otherwise. Ellis would say that any self-respecting Martian would laugh at the earthlings' propensities for insisting that the world *should* be the way they would *prefer* it to be and that the world is a rotten place when people are treated unfairly. This is not to say that people cannot have hopes, wants, and wishes, only that it is illogical to demand things one prefers.

Awfulizing statements are generally disputed on the basis of semantics. For when one says that something is awful, what they are really meaning is that some state of affairs is horrible, terrible, more than 100% awful, and in fact, the individual cannot bear or stand it any longer. When individuals "awfulize" or "catastrophize" they are engaging in reality distortion by magnifying the negativity of events out of all reasonable proportion. People tend to believe that a certain event is more awful than it is in any objective sense. They get so immersed in a problem that they foolishly exaggerate the awfulness of events ("Help! Someone scratched my new Rolls; I can't stand it! This must be the end!!"). Awfulizing is illogical because things cannot be more than 100% awful. So clients are taught to keep their awfulizing to a scale of one to a hundred. Clients are also helped to view their evaluations of events in relation to other possible events. So when youngsters state that it is 90−100% awful when their parents tell them to clean their rooms, we get them to greatly lower their evaluations and awfulizing of the event by asking them to rate other more serious events such as natural and physical calamities that might occur to them and members of their families. Ellis is also fond of disputing with clients their assertion that because things are so awful they can't stand it (Ellis refers to this as "I-can't-standitis"). Ellis lectures that we can stand anything (having nails banged into our fingers; being boiled in hot oil), although there are things we would find unpleasant and painful. The practitioner combats LFT by challenging the clients to prove they cannot stand anything.

Need statements are irrational because they imply that we must have things which in fact we do not need for survival. The first step in disputing need statements is to clarify the meaning of the word "need" and define it in terms of things we really require in life for survival. When clients state that they need something other than the essential requirements of life, they are assuming something that is not true. There is no evidence we know of that indicates we need such things as love, approval, certainty, success, and fidelity. While many of us value these as pleasurable and desirable and would define them as preferences, RET would insist that people can be happy and certainly survive without them. It is when we define wants as needs that we become upset because there are very few people who will always be able to find what they think they need (matching Rolls Royce touch-up paint). Disputation would involve among other things helping the client distinguish assumptions ("I need X") from facts ("I want X").

Self-worth statements as we indicated earlier are based on arbitrary definitions of "worth" and "worthless." When we say that someone is _____ (good, bad, strong, dependent, trustworthy) we are making an overgeneralization because in order for someone to be, for example, honest, they must never ever have misrepresented the truth as they knew it to be at the time. We feel this proposition would be very hard to substantiate. One of the most revealing RET insights is that people are not their behavior (adapted from Walen et al., 1980). An additional "ah-ha!" experience for many people occurs when they begin to believe that one person's opinion about themselves is merely opinion, not fact. When someone calls another "a bastard," this does not make it so (or as we said to someone recently, "Relax, you are not trash just because you read trashy novels."). Essential aspects of helping clients dispute their statements of self-worth is to teach them both the difference between facts and opinions as well as to recognize when they make overgeneralizations. They are taught not to confuse the whole of them with the part that is not working.

They are forcibly encouraged to give up self-rating which often has the effect on clients of stopping them from *demanding* perfectionism and superhumanness from others (Ellis, 1973).

When practitioners detect an irrational belief, they had better not only be able to explain why it is irrational but also help the client reformulate it into a new rational−philosophical effect. While with practice the irrational−rational conversion becomes easier, we have found it helpful when introducing RET to practitioners to provide a set of rationally restated beliefs. The list which follows is parallel to the set of important irrational beliefs we presented in the RET assessment section of this chapter. Some of the rational belief statements have been collated from other sources (Ellis, 1979b; Ellis & Harper, 1975; Walen et al., 1980).

1. It would be desirable and productive to concentrate on self-respect, on winning approval for practical purposes, and on loving instead of being loved.

2. It is more advisable to accept oneself as an imperfect creature with human limitations and fallibilities. It is better to do than to do well.

3. While I prefer things to go my way, there is nothing awful about not getting what I want.

4. The world is often unfair. People often behave stupidly and unethically and it would be better if they were helped to change their ways.

5. There's seldom gain without pain. I can tolerate discomfort although I might not like it.

6. While I enjoy the company of intimate others, I do not need anyone to help me get along in life; I can always rely on myself.

7. People are extremely complex. It is impossible to measure self-worth.

8. I can overcome the effects of past experience by reassessing my perceptions of the past, and reevaluating my interpretations of its influence.

9. I am largely responsible for my own emotional upsets. I can control my feelings by changing the way I view and evaluate events.

10. The only way I am going to be of any help to others is by remaining calm, making a judgment of the situation to see what I can do to help, and if nothing can be done, I will not surrender my personal peace to an impossible situation.

11. Worrying will not magically make things disappear. I will do my best to deal with potentially distressful events and when this proves impossible, I will accept the inevitable.

12. The world is an uncertain place to live. To fully enjoy life, I will have to make decisions and take risks without having any guarantees.

13. While I would like to have the affection and respect of others, there is no law of the universe that says that everyone must like me and follow what I say.

14. Problems seldom go away by sticking my head in the ground.

It is apparent when reading the RET literature that there are scores of cognitive disputational strategies that involve the use of different techniques of verbal expression such as philosophical persuasion, didactic presentations, Socratic dialogues, and vicarious experience (Walen et al., 1980). Perhaps, the most well-known cognitive disputational technique relies heavily on the use of *questioning* by the practitioner to force clients to prove or justify their beliefs. It is hoped that once clients see the illogicality of their beliefs, they will give them up. Walen et al. (1980) indicates that when practitioners detect irrational beliefs, they use questions to challenge their logical consistency ("Where is the evidence?" "What is the proof?" "Where is it written?"), semantic clarity ("How awful is it?" "How can doing that mean you're anything?"), and to determine whether the beliefs serve to further or hinder the attainment of the client's values ("By believing that, will you ever get what you want?"). Other popular cognitive disputational strategies described by Walen et al. (1980) include *didactic presentations* (mini-lectures, analogies, and parables), *humor* (exaggeration, paradoxical intention), and *vicarious modeling* (showing that others have learned to cope with a similar aversive event).

RET almost always includes cognitive homework assignments to assist clients in disputing their irrational beliefs. A form that is often employed as part of cognitive homework is the *Rational Self-Help Form* published by the Institute for Rational-Emotive Therapy. The form provides for practicing the ABC-DEs of RET during the week. Space is included on the form for clients to analyze their rational and irrational beliefs about an activating experience or event, describe their desirable and undesirable behavioral and emotional consequences, dispute or debate their irrational beliefs, and to describe the new cognitive, emotional and behavioral effects of disputing. Another formal cognitive method for practicing disputation is *Disputing Irrational Beliefs* (DIBs) which is published as a pamphlet. The technique involves the client selecting one major irrational idea and analyzing the belief by answering a series of disputational questions ("Can I rationally support this belief?" "What evidence exists for the truth and falseness of this belief?" "What are the worst possible and best things that could happen to me if I never achieve that which I think I must?"). RET employs *bibliotherapy* extensively to supplement therapy sessions and encourages clients to read basic RET self-help books, pamphlets, and other problem-related literature that will help clients relinquish their irrational beliefs. Another favorite RET cognitive technique is encouraging clients to use RET with others. Giving clients practice in disputing the irrationalities of others often helps them more effectively employ RET with themselves.

RET also employs *cognitive modeling* in which the practitioner demonstrates verbally the kinds of *rational self-statements* that a client might employ to combat emotional distress in a difficult situation. During therapy, clients are given extensive practice in overtly and then covertly rehearsing new rational self-statements. While the use of rational self-statements does not constitute a direct disputation of irrational beliefs, it can result through repetition and the use of *passionate self-statements* (see next section) in not only getting the clients to believe the specific content of the statements, but also—through the application by the client of the rational self-statements across a variety of problematic situations—induce a more general rational belief that would replace the old irrational one.

Emotional Disputation

Maultsby (1975, 1977a) has elaborated upon Ellis' ABC-DE model of therapeutic change. He has noted that it is sometimes the case that clients who demonstrate substantial cognitive changes have inordinate difficulties in changing their behavior. These clients apparently had not experienced significant emotional changes (developed the emotional muscle) that would allow and, in a sense, free them to behave more rationally. Maultsby (1977b) described this dilemma as being "how to get the gut to accept what the brain knows to be true" (p. 89). As a consequence of this therapeutic roadblock, Maultsby stresses the importance of emotional reeducation and has formulated a five-stage model of therapeutic change. Maultsby (1977a) has described the five stages (intellectual insight, converting practice, cognitive dissonance, emotional insight, personality trait formation) as follows:

> Intellectual insight means learning what you will have to practice to obtain the re-education you hope to achieve. Converting practice means converting your old involuntary emotional habits back to their original voluntary state. That's the only way the newly developing emotional habits can overcome the involuntary competition from the older emotional habits. To do converting practice, you must think, using your intellectual insights, and physically act them out. That activity puts you in the third stage of re-education, cognitive dissonance. As used in rational behavior therapy, cognitive dissonance means having new thoughts that are illogical for your old, not-yet-extinguished emotional feelings. Emotional insight means having learned to have new emotional feelings that are logical for your new way of thinking. Personality trait formation means you have converted your emotional insight into a relatively permanent involuntary emotional habit. [p. 54].

Maultsby has made a notable contribution to RET by emphasizing the importance of emotional change and by elaborating emotive techniques that speed up the emotional change process.

Emotive disputational strategies, while overlapping somewhat with behavioral and cognitive strategies, have in common the goal of evoking in the client emotions (desirable and undesirable) which the client can link up with the detection and cognitive disputation of irrational beliefs. Both in assessment and intervention, emotive methods can help the client "tune in" (and dispute) those irrational thoughts that precipitate high levels of emotionality. The notion here is that many emotional reactions have become so habitually expressed that they are strongly under the influence of environmental conditions. While we know that emotions derive largely from cognitions, certain techniques seek both to make the clients more aware of "preconscious" cognitions as well as to reestablish voluntary verbal control of emotions and behavior.

Emotive techniques may also serve to show clients the distressful feelings that constitute the essence of their disturbance are not as intolerable and awful as they might appear in the mind of the beholder. With certain clients, emotive methods are employed to show that they can stand being upset without falling apart. They can learn to live with the upsets without disturbing themselves because they are upset.

Rational-emotive imagery (REI) is a widely employed emotive-disputational strategy (Maultsby, 1975; Maultsby & Ellis, 1974). The use of imagery as a disputational strategy generally involves the practitioner asking clients to imagine themselves as vividly as possible in the problematic situation. There are a number of options that are available to the practitioner at this point. If they elect to employ *positive imagery*, clients are instructed to imagine themselves in the original situation but feeling better and behaving more adaptively. When clients indicate this image, they are asked to verbalize those statements they were making to themselves that enabled them to feel and behave differently. Clients generally report rational self-statements ("I didn't care as much; if I made it, I made it and if I didn't it wasn't the end of the world"). A variation of positive imagery is to have clients picture themselves thinking rational thoughts that they acquired as a result of employing the ABC-DE analysis and, at the same time, feeling more appropriate emotions. In *negative imagery*, clients are instructed to picture themselves in the situation and to try to feel as emotionally upset as they can. When clients report that they are feeling upset, they are requested by the practitioner to change the feeling from strong to moderate (e.g., anger to irritation). Most clients are able to shift their emotions and when asked how they did so indicate in a variety of verbal statements that they were no longer viewing the situation as seriously (catastrophizing) as before. Relaxation and hypnosis have been suggested as facilitating therapeutic adjuncts to be used with clients who are initially too upset to employ REI (Erikson, M.H., Rossi,E., & Rossi,S., 1976; Tosi & Reardon, 1976). REI is often employed as an emotive homework assignment. Clients are instructed to practice REI for a sustained period of time (e.g., 10 minutes) each day. Maultsby (1971) indicates that when REI is performed successfully, it results in the accomplishment by clients of three therapeutic outcomes.

1. They efficiently decondition themselves to the most important external stimuli which are usually eliciting the major parts of their undesirable emotional responses.
2. They create mental frames of reference for successfully behaving rationally, thereby increasing the probability of actually behaving in that rational manner in the future.
3. Regular REI efficiently enables patients to learn to "self-talk" (think) rationally as easily and as reflectively or "naturally" as they were irrationally doing prior to RBT (Rational Behavior Training). [p. 26]

Ellis (1979d) has indicated that "what we call 'emotions' or 'feelings' largely consist of, or at least are derived from quite vehement and dramatic self-verbalizations" (p. 85). To combat the effects of these verbalizations, Ellis proposes the use of *passionate self-statements* where clients are instructed to repeat in a highly vigorous and emotional manner sets of rational self-statements. By making clients passionately repeat these kinds of strong statements to themselves and to others, Ellis indicates that clients begin to believe in them.

Shame attacking exercises are generally employed with people who are emotionally upset because of what they perceive to be the shameful consequences of failure. They are afraid to engage in self-enhancing activities that often entail taking risks (test taking, giving speeches, making a date) because they view failure as a sign or reminder of their essential worthlessness. They view the consequences of failure as being personally unbearable. These people also tend to overestimate the likelihood and exaggerate the magnitude of future catastrophes and underestimate their own personal resources to cope with the future event. Shame attacking exercises which are given to clients for homework involve the client doing something "shameful" or "ridiculous" and to do them "without feeling ashamed and to even regard them as adventures" (Ellis, 1979d, p. 89). Some of the activities that Ellis has prescribed for clients with shameful feelings include walking a banana down the street on a red leash on a bright summer's day, wearing outlandish clothes, and walking into a drug store and loudly ordering three dozen condoms. Shame attacking exercises desensitize anxieties and provide people with evidence for disputing irrational beliefs.

Modeling and *role playing* are used as emotive as well as behavioral disputational strategies. In emotive modeling, therapists use the relationship with their clients to demonstrate the basics of RET. By unconditionally accepting clients, by being direct, open and genuine, and by accepting the responsibility for their own actions, the RET practitioner shows clients that it is possible to accept themselves without putting themselves down. Role playing is used as an emotive-deconditioning method. Clients are given practice in adaptive and assertive behaviors which because of the clients' anticipatory anxiety they were unable to perform. It provides clients with problem-simulated training so that when faced with troublesome situations they can, because of reduced anxiety and previously rehearsed verbalizations and behavior, act and feel more rationally.

Behavioral Disputation

RET employs a number of behavioral techniques (operant conditioning, role play, modeling, self-control procedures, assertion training, systematic desensitization, relaxation methods) which because of the close relationship among thoughts, feelings, and behavior often indirectly enable clients to adopt more rational views. These techniques often involve *in vivo retraining* and are based on the frequently validated clinical hypothesis that getting clients to expose themselves to situations they find initially very fearsome, anxiety provoking, and troublesome will over time enable the client to face and cope more effectively with the problematic environment.

The major behavioral disputational strategy involves the therapist giving clients behavioral homework assignments to perform in ways that challenge and refute their irrational beliefs. Shame attacking and risk taking exercises constitute exemplars of behavioral disputation. Other behavioral disputes as illustrated by Walen et al. (1980) include:

> If clients believe they cannot stand waiting for events they are asked to practise postponing gratifications. If they believe they cannot stand rejection, they are encouraged to seek it out. If they believe they need something, they are exhorted to do without. If they believe their worth is based on doing well, they are asked purposely to do poorly. [p. 106]

AN ABC-DE TRANSCRIPT

In the following transcript, different aspects of RET assessment and intervention are illuminated. Elements of preferential RET are employed with an older adolescent boy (C) by the first author (P).

Assessment of feeling and activating event:

C: Boy, am I down.
P: What are you feeling?
C: Don't know . . . sorta rotten . . . sick, like someone kicked me in the stomach.
P: Did someone?
C: Well, I did what we did last week. I went to the disco at my school last night. I went over my little speech that we did last week about how to ask Jane for a dance. I didn't feel as uptight 'cause I had something to say. And so I finally went over to Jane and before I could even ask her she walked away to dance with someone else. And she ignored me for the rest of the night.

Empathic reflection of feelings by practitioner:

P: Sounds like you feel depressed because Jane didn't dance with you and you really want her to like you. Is that about it?
C: Yeah.

Assessment of the ABC relationship:

P: Well, can you explain using the ABC method why you are still fairly upset?
C: Starting with C, I guess I am sorta depressed. And A was Jane dancing with this other guy.

Assessment of behavioral consequence:

P: Good, how did you react then?
C: That was it! I just gave up. Didn't dance, didn't talk to her. I just waited around outside until my dad picked me up.

Assessment of cognitions:

P: Okay, what about B? What is B again?
C: B are my thoughts . . . especially those . . . I can't remember. . . .
P: Irrational?
C: Right. Rational and irrational thoughts about A.
P: Okay, now what are you thinking about A? See if you can focus on some of the nutty things you might be saying.

(reflective pause)

C: Well, I sorta feel embarrassed. You know, she must not like me at all. She probably thinks I'm a jerk. I hate it when she did it. Makes me feel like a dill.
P: See if you can start your sentences with I'm thinking.
C: I'm thinking what a dill I am . . . and I'm thinking how much I want her.
P: How much?
C: More than anything.

Practitioner summarizes ABC assessment data:

P: Okay, that's great, Mark. You've done some good thought detection. You are feeling down and depressed not because you were rejected, but because you keep saying to yourself that you can't stand being rejected. You also are probably saying not only how much you want her, but that you'll die if you don't get her. And finally, as is your way, you are putting yourself down, down, down, down, down, lower and lower, to square zero, and even lower, because of what happened.
C: Uh-huh.

Practitioner guides client toward solving problem—The DE link:

P: Well, how does the good book say we can think our way out of misery?

C: I can see on your wall . . . that's right . . . D. I can challenge my thoughts.

P: Where shall you start?

C: Huh?

P: It seems to me that you can start to feel better by challenging and changing any one of three thoughts. That you are a dill because you have been rejected. That you need Jane to be happy. That you can't stand it when you are rejected. Shall I pick one?

C: Okay.

P: How about, and we've discussed this before, your tendency to put yourself down and rate yourself zero because of some personal failure?

C: I know I shouldn't do it. I know it's stupid to say I'm a dill because I do other things well.

P: Like?

C: I work well with my Dad's horses, and I'm pretty good at working with machines.

P: Good. So you can never be a dill. Ever! And when you catch yourself saying you're a dill or some other lousy thing, say to yourself something like "While I don't like it when I fail, it doesn't matter all that much; I do other things well."

C: It's nutty to put myself down for what I do wrong.

P: That's the message! Now how about nutty thought number two: That you must have the lovely, glamorous and scintillating Jane. Come on Tarzan, why must you have her?

C: Because she's beautiful and I want her.

P: I'm sure she is beautiful and that you do want her. But in your own mind you believe that you need her . . . for if you just wanted her without demanding that you have her, then you wouldn't be as upset when she rejected you. Do you see that?

C: I'm not sure.

To illustrate principle, practitioner employs an analogy:

P: Well, let's look at it another way. Suppose you woke up one morning and said to yourself "I really would like some chocolate ice cream. After school I'll go to my favorite shop where the chocolate is the best, the very best, and treat myself to a double." And suppose that when you arrived at the shop after school you were told that they were all out of chocolate. How would you feel?

C: I guess I could always get another flavor.

P: Right, you would feel disappointed momentarily, but you could either get another flavor or wait until the following day when they got some in. Now, suppose you woke up in the morning and said to yourself not only that you wanted your favorite creamy chocolate ice cream after school, but that you must have it, that not only will your day be ruined if you don't, but you would have a hard time functioning for the following week unless you had your favorite ice cream. What do you think you'd feel if you arrive at your ice cream haven and learned that they had just sold the last scoop of chocolate?

C: Pretty upset.

P: That's right. And you can see that if you say to yourself that you must have something that you think you'd like, like Jane or chocolate ice cream, and if you don't get it, you will tend to feel depressed. But if you stop musting—because you don't need Jane or ice cream to survive—then you will not get so down. I'm not saying that you shouldn't want or prefer certain things, but it doesn't help to exaggerate how much you want anything. Can you survive without Jane?

C: No.

Client is still experiencing some difficulties understanding the implication of the "need-want" distinction:

P: You mean without her you will shrivel up and die?

C: No.

P: So you can survive.

C: I really, really want her.

P: Good. That's terrific. Because by saying you really want something you can deal much better with not having it than if you say I need something. Can you stand being without her? Have you fallen down in a heap, eyes fallen out because she rejected you?

C: No.

P: So how awful is it when she rejects you?

C: I can see what you're saying. Things could be worse. I can live with the rejection. It is only when I think I can't that I feel real down.

P: You got it. And you've just successfully disputed irrational idea number 3 that you can't stand being rejected.

In this example, the practitioner elected not to examine what may have been one of the major contributing cognitive factors underlying the client's depression. The practitioner could have assessed Mark's initial subjective perception of Jane's behavior to determine whether in fact Jane really did reject him and whether she ignored him. In subsequent sessions, therapy is focused on the client's tendency to both selectively abstract data as well as blow things out of proportion. Referring back to the "internalizing−externalizing" dimension of psychopathology, we note that Mark appears to "internalize" as he largely punishes himself for his failures. "Externalizers" turn their frustrations outward and generally make it more difficult for other people than they do for themselves.

The first three chapters have provided the RET psychological and conceptual framework that is necessary to be able to apply RET with school-age children. It is hoped this review will enable RET practitioners to extend our understandings and skills as to how RET can be employed with younger populations. The following chapter presents a cognitive view of childhood psychopathology and, along with Chapter 5, how different RET theorists and practitioners have described psychological maladjustment in children and youth.

CHAPTER 4

Childhood Maladjustment

The distinctive contributions which Ellis and other RET theorists (e.g., DiGiuseppe, 1981; Ellis & Bernard, 1983a, b; Ellis, Moseley, & Wolfe, 1966; Hauck, 1974; Waters, 1982a, b) have made to the field of child psycho-psychology is in providing a detailed analysis of cognitive factors which occasion (and occur at the same time with) psychological problems. Rational-emotive theory holds that childhood maladjustment can best be understood from an examination of the thinking processes and thought content of the child who is manifesting a problem.

It is our view that a great deal of faulty thinking processes and irrational beliefs that underlly many psychological problems can be considered either characteristic of or a regression to earlier and more primitive stages of thinking. This principal of mental functioning has been articulated from a psychoanalytic perspective by Kessler (1966).

> For in general, abnormal psychological processes are drawn from psychological processes which are appropriate to younger ages. Abnormal behavior may appear as the inability to master the next higher level of learning, or as a regression to an earlier stage. [p. 18]

So whereas the older child has the potential for objective and rational thought, having acquired developmentally the capacity to think logically and reflectively (e.g., Kassinove et al., 1977), emotional distress and behavioral dysfunctions arise when more primitive thought processes and ideas are employed. It is not altogether clear why this regression to an earlier mental status should occur. Bleuler, writing in 1922 (as cited in Kessler, 1966), proposes a distinction between "directed or intelligent thought" and "undirected or autistic thought":

> It (autistic thought) has its own laws and these deviate from those of realistic logic. It is not often truths, but often the fulfillment of wishes; it does not operate with the experientially established associations of strict, realistic-logical thinking, but with incidental associations of ideas, vague analogies, and above all, *affective needs*. [1951, p. 439]

In a similar vein, Freud has distinguished between primary mental processes which operate according to the pleasure principle and secondary mental processes which operate according to the reality principle. Freud concluded that both principles operate side by side across the life span. Kessler (1966) indicates that emotional disturbance can be considered a product of primary processes. "A symptom originates from affective needs rather than logic, and it usually contains within it a kernel of irrational thinking" (p. 37).

A number of RET theorists (e.g., DiGiuseppe, 1983; Grieger & Boyd, 1983; Hauck, 1967) have emphasized the importance of the interaction between cognitive and environmental factors in childhood disorders. There are two environmental influences which have been considered in the RET literature. During the early and mid-1970s, Paul Hauck in particular indicated how different parenting styles, which he hypothesized to be maintained by different sets of irrational beliefs concerning children and child-rearing practices, can have a negative influence on both the attitudes and behavior of children. Second, as the behavioral approach has received greater acceptance by cognitivists (and vice versa), the effects of antecedent and consequent environmental conditions are being recognized as important in understanding how certain forms of child psychopathology are acquired and maintained.

In this chapter we will discuss cognitive–developmental as well as environmental factors which are, if you will, preconditions for or background to childhood maladjustment. We shall leave the detailed cognitive analysis of specific behavioral and emotional problems to Chapter 5. As a background to this consideration, we present a brief overview of different models and theories of psychopathology. Our discussion will mostly center on behavioral problems and emotional disorders and will not deal with the origins of mental retardation, physical disorders (e.g., anorexia nervosa, tics, stuttering) nor developmental disorders (e.g., infantile autism, reading disorders).

CONCEPTUAL MODELS OF PSYCHOPATHOLOGY

There are two major frames of reference for conceptualizing, understanding, and explaining abnormal behavior. Traditionally they have been referred to as the "medical model" and the "environmental model." Theories of psychopathology grouped within one or the other of these models differ largely in terms of whether they consider the course of abnormal behavior to be located within or outside the organism. (The organization and ideas presented in this section are synthesized from the major work of Knopf (1979) and we wish to recognize his contribution as such.)

The Medical Model

The *medical model* which has been borrowed from physical medicine attempts through the use of correlational research to demonstrate a relationship between genetic, biochemical, neurophysiological, or psychogenic pathological processes which occur within the organism and abnormal mental and behavioral symptoms. Knopf (1979) indicates four different models or views of abnormal behavior which have been developed by persons concerned with the relationship between irregularities in specific internal conditions (e.g., metabolic imbalance) and concomitant abnormalities in specific behavior patterns (e.g., hyperactivity). With the exception of psychoanalytic theory, the models to be described do not either conceptually nor empirically account for the full range of psychological disorders in children.

Many proponents of the *genetic model* take the position that heredity as expressed through genetic transmission, enzymatic content, or mutation effects provides the basic biological organization in which psychopathology may develop. Research conducted within the genetic model has found a positive relationship between genetic conditions and global disorders such as mental retardation and schizophrenia.

The *biochemical model* has involved research scientists searching for biochemical or psychotoxic agents responsible for producing mental illness. A number of agents have been studied such as bacteria, viruses, and aberrations in biochemical pathways (Knopf, 1979). Within the past 10 years, investigators have found systematic relationships between imbalances or disorders in the metabolism of brain chemicals responsible for transmitting neural communication and disorders such as childhood psychosis and hyperactivity.

Overlapping with the genetic and biochemical views of psychopathology is the *neurophysiological model* which assumes that the physical basis of all disordered behavior lies in defects of the brain. A wide variety of etiological agents have been studied (e.g., congenital anomolies, intrauterine disease) and correlational relationships have been found between anatomical and physiological dysfunctions related to the brain and abnormal behavior: brain lesions have been related to perceptual and memory deficits; electrical stimulation of the brain leads to seizures; electroencephalogram (EEG) recordings have been used to differentiate the central nervous system reactivity of persons with disordered behavior such as hyperactivity; cortical responses associated with the mental processes of attention, expectation, and motivation have been found to differ in children with learning disabilities and with psychotic children; peripheral measures of the autonomic system such as skin conductance has been found to reflect the underlying neural impairment of attention found in schizophrenia (Knopf, 1979).

Without doubt, the most influential and comprehensive view of psychological disorders is the *psychoanalytic model* developed by Sigmund Freud. It is obviously impossible to do justice to Freud's work in the space of a paragraph. Several psychoanalytic principles will, however, reveal why Freud's theory is subsumed within the medical model (Kessler, 1966):

1. Psychic determinism is the *sine qua non* of Freud's theory of personality development. Every thought, feeling, or action has a cause, and can be understood in terms of antecedent conditions. . . .
2. There is a continuity of principles governing "normal" and "abnormal" behavior alike. . . .

3. Psychoanalysis established the tremendous power of repressed thoughts and feelings. It should always be remembcred children have an unconscious storehouse of memories and feelings. . . .

4. Anxiety and the mechanisms of defense against it are a major cause of repression to unconsciousness and account for much of what seems irrational and unrealistic.

5. Unconscious memorics from the first five years of life exert a long-lasting influence. . . .

6. Sexual feelings and conflicts in early childhood are particular sources of difficulty. [pp. 9–10]

Freud's theory asserts that emotional disorders in children can be best understood as being an outward manifestation of intrapsychic conflict. The origin of intrapsychic conflict stems from the significance which the child attributes to events as they occur during different stages of the child's psychosexual development. States of indulgence or deprivation may result in the child becoming fixated at a given stage. Anxiety is a central component of psychoneurosis and is viewed as the painful emotional accompaniment of intrapsychic conflict. Through the deployment of defense mechanisms (e.g., repression, denial, projection), the ego attempts to reduce anxiety and tension. Neurotic behavior is considered as symptomatic of the attempts and efforts of the ego to dissipate anxiety. Intrapsychic conflict and anxiety, then, lead to disorders in children such as depression, social withdrawal, uncommunicative, obsessive, compulsive, somatic complaints, and a variety of antisocial behaviors. Freud has indicated that different disorders can be distinguished in terms of the primary defense mechanism which is used to deal with anxiety. (A brief description of these mechanisms is provided later on in this chapter).

There are other intrapsychic views concerning the origins of both personality and child psychopathology which arose in opposition to Freud's. Jung rejected Freud's emphasis on sex and aggression as the basis of psychic change and introduced concepts of the extroverted and introverted personality types as well as the collective unconscious to explain personality development (Knopf, 1979). Adler placed more emphasis on the social nature of the human organism and introduced the still popular concept "inferiority complex" to explain maladjustment. While the various proponents of the intrapsychic view differ in terms of the way they conceptualize internal conflicts, all would agree that the alleviation of neurotic symptoms resides in the treatment of the internal conflict.

The Environmental Model

In contrast to the medical model, the environmental model emphasizes the role of factors external to the individual as creating the conditions for abnormal behaviors. Simply stated, it is the environmental context of the individual which is "sick" and requires "curing" rather than the individual. The human organism is conceived as being reactive to a set of environmental influences rather than being active in influencing the surrounding world. Environmental models can be distinguished by the manner in which they conceptualize external factors which are seen to be the cause of both normal and abnormal behavior.

Sociological models consider society with its various cultural institutions as primary in shaping personality. Cultural, social, economic and communication variables are seen as instrumental in socializing people into becoming productive members of society. The theories of Durkheim, Mead, Merton and other philosophers and sociologists explain the manner in which children come to function in socially prescribed ways. Psychopathology (e.g., delinquency) is seen as occurring when certain social norms cease to serve the needs and interests of the individual. This phenomenon which results in a state of alienation has been described by Durkheim as *anomie* and "is characterized by anxiety, uncertainty, insecurity, lowered self-esteem, identity confusion, and a sense of impotence about acting in effective ways" (Knopf, 1979, p. 109).

A second major environmental approach can be labelled as the *humanistic model* and is exemplified by the existential and humanistic approaches of Abraham Maslow, and Carl Rogers. Theories subsumed within this model explain behavior in terms of the expression of inherent human needs, drives, and emotions. The individual is not motivated primarily through the operation of unconscious sexual and aggressive drives and intrapsychic conflict nor by reinforcement schedules. Rather, individuals are motivated by innate tendencies to become fully developed and self-actualized as well as by essentially psychological demands such as those enumerated by Maslow (e.g., safety, belongingness, self-esteem). Anxiety and neurotic behavior is brought about by the frustration of basic tendencies, human needs, and desires and if individuals are in situations where they are unable to continue their life-span process of self-discovery and growth, neurotic symptoms may arise (Knopf, 1979). A popular therapy which arises from the humanistic model is Roger's client-centered therapy.

Perhaps the next well-known environmentalist position is the *learning model* and associated learning theory. There are a variety of psychological theories which have attempted to explain human behavior in terms of principles of learning. There are also a number of major environmental influences which these theories propose as major determinants of abnormal human behavior. *Classical conditioning* theories (Pavlov, Wolpe) propose that certain maladaptive emotional reactions (e.g., anxiety) can be produced when the individual is exposed to objects or events that have aversive properties as a consequence of being associated with other environmental stimuli which the individual finds inherently aversive. Emotional problems are treated through modifying the aversive properties of the antecedent stimuli which occasioned their occurrence (e.g., systematic desensitization). *Operant theories* (Skinner) propose that abnormal behavior is best understood as a deficit in the individual's behavioral repertoire or as poorly learned response patterns. Through the systematic use of reinforcement principles the individual may acquire new skills and modify previously learned response patterns. *Social learning theories*

(Bandura, Rotter) also consider abnormal behavior as essentially reactive to reinforcement. The individual acquires expectancies (stimulus−response−consequences) about how to acquire reinforcement through either being directly reinforced or indirectly through *imitation* and *vicarious learning*. According to social learning theory, abnormal behavior results from the individual having (1) low expectations of success, (2) high expectations of failure, (3) inappropriate role models, (4) an inconsistent and impoverished reinforcement environment, (5) failed to discriminate stimuli which signal certain types of responses which will lead to reinforcement, and (6) acquired strong emotional reactions to certain environmental stimuli (Knopf, 1979). Therapy derived from the social learning perspective reeducates the individual using environmental modification methods which are thought to be responsible and necessary for learning to occur.

Social learning theory (Bandura, 1977; Mischel, 1973) has begun to conceptualize and delineate cognitive factors and mechanisms for explaining consistencies in the way the individual (mis)interprets and (mis)reacts to antecedent stimuli and subsequent reinforcement. At the same time, cognitive psychologists and semantic psychotherapists have begun to conceptualize abnormal behavior in adults employing cognitive constructs (e.g., Beck, 1976; Ellis, 1962; Mahoney, 1974; Meichenbaum, 1977; Raimey, 1975). The successful marriage of cognitive, social learning, and behavior theory in the treatment of adult disorders has led to an awareness of the importance of applying this perspective to the understanding and treatment of disorders in children and adolescents (e.g., Ellis & Bernard, 1983 a).

What follows is a cognitive perspective concerning factors which are important in considering childhood maladjustment. The perspective which is offered is one which strongly emphasizes the role of cognitive factors in childhood disorders. It also stresses the importance of environmental factors such as parental attitudes and behavior as well as situational factors (antecedent conditions, reinforcing consequences) which both lead to and maintain problematic emotions and behavior. The cognitive development of the child will be seen as important for understanding young clients for we believe there is a strong relationship between cognitive and affective development especially during the childhood years.

It is important to state that we have not attempted to provide a comprehensive review of all cognitive-developmental and cognitive-behavioral theorizing concerning childhood maladjustment. Rather, we have brought together points of view which we and other RET theorists believe contribute to an understanding of children and their problems.

A COGNITIVE PERSPECTIVE

We will not review the cognitive model of human behavior nor the RET perspective concerning personality development as we have already done so in the preceding chapters. A principle we would like to emphasize from that discussion is that of *interactionism*. We believe that emotional disorders and abnormal behavior in childhood can best be understood in terms of an interaction between "person" and "environmental variables." People demonstrate characteristic ways of thinking about and relating to their environment which exert an influence on their environment. Similarly, situations themselves modify the behavior and attitudes of people by both providing (or not providing) appropriate learning experiences and enrichment opportunities as well as rewarding and punishing consequences for behavior within certain contexts. We believe that there is an almost inexorable reciprocal relationship between abnormal behavior and a deviant environment such that abnormalities in either the person or the environment of the person tend to bring out abnormalities in the other. It would seem therefore necessary to determine how persons and environments interact and covary together in analyzing psychopathology.

A simple formula for explaining psychopathology would be that abnormal behavior is a function of the extent of dysfunction in both the person and the environment. By and large, the greater the dysfunction in both, the higher the probability of psychopathology. At the extreme we believe that highly destructive and deprived environments can produce abnormal behavior in a person who enters that environment with a "normal" cognitive-personality style and behavioral patterns, whereas it is possible that people who bring to a situation extremely deviant and maladaptive dispositions can often maintain their abnormal behaviors by modifying their otherwise healthy and "normal" environment.

Our cognitive conception of childhood maladjustment takes into account three major dimensions: cognitive-affective developmental status, psychological conditions, and environmental conditions. Our analysis is a preliminary one in that while we view these three influences as being central to any cognitive model of abnormal behavior and child psychopathology, we do not as yet fully understand the ways in which these three dimensions interact with one another.

Cognitive-Affective Developmental Status

As we have repeatedly emphasized, emotional and behavioral disorders of children and adolescents can be explained by the manner in which the young person interprets and evaluates experience. We believe that proponents of many different models of childhood psychopathology accept the principle that there is a reciprocal relationship between mental and emotional development. When children are very young the quality of their subjective emotional experience is very much limited by their capacity to think about and understand the meaning of experience. The cognitive limitations of the early childhood period can often result in children acquiring beliefs about themselves and their surrounding world which are untrue and irrational and which if not corrected can have an extremely deleterious effect on their future well-being. That is, children construct their own theories and arrive at their own conclusions based on inferences from what they have observed. The child's conception of the world is organized idiosyncratically and derives from the child's limited capacity to make observations and draw logical conclusions. The role of fantasy is extremely important in the child's construction of reality for the young child has difficulty in delineating the boundaries between reality and fantasy. An example of the influence of irrational beliefs can be seen in young children below the age of seven who may make the observation that "bad children get punished" and conclude that because they are frequently being punished they must be bad. By the age of seven, many children appear to have acquired a sense of their "goodness" and "badness" based on a faulty reasoning process and a primitive set of moral values which also derive from their limited reasoning capacities. If children believe they are "bad" whenever they are disciplined for misbehavior, then no doubt there will be a strong emotional component to their behavior. Moreover, a child's misbehavior is frequently prompted by feelings of worthlessness which accompany the child's self-concept.

In working with children, we are struck by the pervasive influence their ideas and beliefs have on their behavior. As we have indicated in Chapter 2, these beliefs are often implicit and frequently result from the child having formed a conclusion based on limited evidence and having used the conclusion as an "unquestioned" rule for guiding subsequent behavior. These rules (be they rational or irrational) which are formed early on become firmly fixed and represent part of the basic phenomenological framework of children providing the basis for self-evaluation, the demands they place on others, and the interpretations they make of the behavior of others. Children's capacity for rational and logical thought limit the types of ideas they acquire and frequently reinforce a variety of irrational beliefs which often take many years to overcome.

A cognitive analysis of maladjustment in adolescents frequently reveals beliefs about themselves, others, and the world as well as logical reasoning processes which appear to be either a holdover from or a regression to more immature levels of thinking and primitive belief systems. This awareness may help the cognitively-oriented practitioner to understand the problems of a younger client from a context different from the one which is frequently used; that is, a downward extension of an adult model of psychopathology. This perspective has the child psychologist and practitioner employing concepts which characterize earlier levels of thinking as basic units of analysis in seeking to understand a given disorder. Adopting a developmental perspective may provide the practitioner with additional wisdom to determine whether certain behaviors and thoughts of children are manifestations of broader psychological problems (e.g., anxiety and stress), or whether they can be interpreted as being symptomatic of a developmental phase in normal intellectual growth (Broughton, 1981). Moreover, it is not completely possible to determine the effects of an environmental event on a given child without knowing about the child's level of intellectual organization (Cowan, 1978). As RET and other forms of cognitive-behavior therapy have for many years been successful in treating a variety of childhood problems without formally taking into account the cognitive-affective developmental status of the individual, such knowledge while being important may not be necessarily a prerequisite for applying cognitive approaches with younger clients.

There can be little disagreement that Piaget's theory of intelligence and stage-related levels of cognitive development provides great insights into the characteristics of thought across the childhood period (e.g., Flavell, 1963; Piaget, 1952; Piaget & Inhelder, 1958). Piaget's theory deals mostly with the normal evolution of intellectual adaptation and while there have been a number of Piagetian studies which have examined the cognitive characteristics of psychotic and mentally retarded children, very little work concerning other childhood problems has come from the Genevan school. Piaget's major contribution in this area has been preserved in a monograph published in 1981 which presents a series of lectures delivered by Piaget at the Sorbonne during the 1953–1954 academic year that dealt with the relationship of intelligence and affectivity during child development. A few secondary works (Cowan, 1978; Rosen, 1977) have discussed the theoretical implications of Piaget's work for clinical practice though the emphasis has been on severe forms of psychopathology. What we shall do is to review aspects of Piaget's theory for the purpose of sensitizing the reader to the role of cognitive-developmental factors in emotional and behavioral adjustment and maladjustment. As any student of Piaget will attest, Piaget's conceptual system is an extremely difficult one to master. (We suggest the interested reader acquire any of the numerous basic texts which are available on Piaget's theory.)

Piaget's theory shares a number of common assumptions about RET beginning with its emphasis on *constructivism*. According to Piaget there are not facts independent of the observer; all statements about reality are interpretations or constructions which represent outcomes of the interaction between the figurative aspects of external stimuli (no inherent meaning) and operative conceptualizations (what the learner already knows) (Cowan, 1978).

A second interesting overlap between Piaget and Ellis is the faith they place in the scientific method of investigation and in the power of formal logical reasoning. According to Piaget, the most advanced level of intelligence is one which permits the individual to advance and systematically test propositions and hypotheses about the world by considering the full range of possible and potential outcomes. Piaget (1972) writes of the thought characteristics of the early adolescent period (14–15 year olds):

> The principle novelty of this period is the capacity to reason in terms of verbally stated hypotheses and no longer merely in terms of concrete objects and their manipulations. This is a decisive turning point, because to reason hypothetically and to deduce the consequences that the hypotheses necessarily imply is a formal reasoning process. [p. 3]

Ellis' therapy can be seen when practiced in its most elegant fashion (use of disputation, hedonic calculus) as an attempt to teach clients to apply principles of formal logic and reason to areas of their personal lives in which they are experiencing difficulty. A major difference, however, between RET and Piagetian theory is that Piaget postulates four levels of intelligence that each individual sequentially passes through, each defined by its own set of logical rules. So whereas Ellis might consider the logic employed by young children as unscientific, Piaget views these earlier forms of thought as "normal" and characteristic of the logic which operates at developmentally earlier levels of intelligence.

Piaget and Ellis appear in agreement concerning the importance of cognition in the experience and expression of emotions. Piaget has written that ". . . it is, in fact, only a romantic prejudice that makes us suppose that affective phenomena constitute immediate givens or innate and ready-made feelings similar to Rousseau's 'conscience' " (1954). He believes that emotions depend upon the individual's cognitive capacity to construct meaning from experience.

Piaget has proposed a conceptual model to describe the general cognitive organizational structure which regulates the child's conception of the world. This structure is what determines the developmental consistencies we observe in the child's acquisition of beliefs about the world. Piaget employs principles of formal logic to characterize the cognitive structure and operations which underly the ideas of children. Cowan (1978) describes the basic assumptions of Piaget's model as follows:

> It is assumed, then, that a general set of logic rules describes the cognitive organization underlying the specific content of children's reasoning. As we watch a child mature from birth to adulthood, we can see four major changes in these logical rules. . . . Each new set of rules integrates the one before into a more differentiated and flexible cognitive structure. And each new cognitive structure defines a new stage of intellectual development, with corresponding changes in the quality of the child's understanding of the world. [p. 17]

The different logical rules which characterize children's reasoning ability at different stages will be illustrated shortly in the context of a discussion of their influence on affective development.

During each stage of mental development the child acquires specific and consistent ways of categorizing incoming data, which Piaget refers to as *conceptual schemes*. The meaning of incoming stimuli and behavior is transformed by existing schemes through a process of *assimilation*. Assimilation provides meaning to environmental events whereas *accommodation* involves the newly incorporated information transforming existing cognitive schemes in order to cope with the new events. Piaget's *equilibration model* proposes that intelligence functions to adapt the human organism to the environment through modifying the environment to fit its needs (assimilation) and modifying itself in response to environmental demands (accommodation). As the young child learns more and more about the environment, new structures are created to meet the increasing demands of the external environment. The differentiation of cognitive schemes during a period of mental development result in a progressive reorganization of cognitive structure which culminates in a qualitatively advanced stage of mental development.

Piaget maintains that emotional and mental development can be seen as two sides of the same coin. This is because emotions provide the fuel for the intellectual machinery, the energetics of thought. Mental symbols for representing experience have both affective and cognitive meanings.

There are a number of meanings of "emotion" in the Piagetian literature. At one level, emotions become synonomous with energy, motivation, and arousal and can account for why we select certain goals and activities. At another level, emotions can be equated with "feeling states" (anger, love, worry) that are experienced by the individual.

Parallels between characteristics of cognition and emotion—motivation across different levels of development are as follows:

> Stable feelings about specific people do not arise until the fourth sensorimotor stage (at about six months of age) when the infant has constructed the scheme of the permanent object. This means, Piaget suggests, that there is necessarily a cognitive aspect of the infant's development of attachment. Later in the preoperational stage beginning at about two years of age and extending over the next five years, the development of symbolic representation and language leads to the formation of stable concepts. The structural underpinnings of these concepts also allows feelings to acquire stability over time. Still later, in the stage of concrete operations beginning at about seven years, the child's ability to construct classification hierarchies is accompanied by the emergence of a stable value hierarchy. This hierarchy represents the first emergence of what Piaget describes as the conservation of feelings. At the same time, we observe the beginning of a new level of moral judgment. [Cowan, 1981, p. xi]

Piaget proposes both affective and cognitive aspects to the general process of social development.

Piaget (1981) also indicates that we acquire conceptual schemes having to do with people. Rejecting the Freudian notions of transference phenomena, he proposes that interpersonal schemes

> make the subject react to people in more or less constant fashion in analogous situations even though the persons he is interacting with may vary. Schemes of this sort have their beginnings in the child's reactions to his parents and the schematization of the individual's affective and cognitive reactions make up his character. [Piaget, p. 51]

The implication of Piaget's hypothesis concerning social schemes is that consistencies in the way children and adolescents relate to family, peers, and teachers can be understood from an examination of their current social schemes. Their interpretations of situations determine feelings and not as Freud has theorized repressed childhood feelings. Once again we can see a similarity between Ellis and Piaget in their use of the concepts "beliefs" and "schemes."

Broadly speaking, there are two main principles of psychopathological functioning that derive from Piaget's theory. First, is *stage arrest* or *decalage* (unevenness in the emergence of logical operations) where children either fail to or are extremely slow in (delayed) progressing through age-appropriate stages and periods of cognitive development. Their psychopathological manifestations can be related to their tendency to employ cognitive operations that characterize earlier levels of thought. Second, *cognitive regression* occurs when older children who have at some time demonstrated concrete and perhaps formal level operational thought fall back on preoperational and concrete operational modes of thinking.

The four invariant stages of mental development which Piaget proposes are: sensorimotor (0−2 years), preoperational (2−7 years), concrete operational (7−11 years), and formal operational (11 years +). An examination of the irrational and magical thinking patterns of maladjusted children older than seven indicates the presence of elements of preoperational thinking. Five of the major characteristics of preoperational thought which reveal basic cognitive and logical-reasoning limitations are as follows:

1. The child is unable to reason logically and deductively. His/her judgments are dominated by his/her *perceptions* of events, objects and experiences.
2. The child can only attend to one perceptual dimension or attribute at a time (inability to *decenter*).
3. The child is *egocentric* and is conceptually unable to view events and experiences from any point of view but his/her own.
4. The child is unable to clearly differentiate between him/herself and the world; between the *subjective* realm of thoughts and feelings, and the realm of objective or physical reality.
5. Child's reasoning is *transductive*. Events are related alogically on the basis of spatial and temporal contiguities. [Harter, 1977, p. 421]

Children in this period demonstrate disturbances in their subjective perceptions and reasoning processes as they can only attend to one essential feature of a concrete situation while neglecting important others. They have not as yet developed the ability to direct, organize, and coordinate various viewpoints and dimensions into a single system that takes them all into account.

The implications of these cognitive constraints on the affective development of both the preoperational child and the older child who relies on preconcrete operational thought are extensive. Children's emotions at this stage derive from a cognitive structure that allows for subjective perceptions based on the egocentric perspective and needs of the child and only permits cognition based on one dimension of experience at a time. Children's feelings are dominated by evaluations of here and now perceptions. They cannot coordinate other information about themselves and the world that they may have learned and stored in memory. The lack of *reversibility* in thought does not permit them to maintain a constant appraisal of themselves and others when their view changes. If parents do something that the child considers bad, the child cannot at that moment conceive of his parents as good. Susan Harter (1977) in discussing the implications of Piaget's theory for employing play therapy with young children has generated some interesting hypotheses concerning the interrelationship between emotional and cognitive development. Writes Harter:

> The child cannot simultaneously acknowledge love and hate. He cannot conceptualize temporary feelings within the context of a larger emotional network, of an affective conceptual system, which at the time includes both positive *and* negative emotions. [p. 423]

Affective conservation where particular events do not transform the entire emotional system has not as yet been achieved.

According to Harter, the dominance of perception over rational and logical conception, and the relationship between cognitive limitations and emotional immaturity during this period, greatly influences the child's self-concept.

> Just as the preoperational child has difficulty focusing on more than one *perceptual* dimension at a time, the child also has difficulty focusing on more than one *emotional* dimension at a time. Thus, when the young child is faced with judgments based on such affective opposites as smart versus dumb or good versus bad his/her cognitive limitations make it difficult to view both as simultaneously operative. Rather the young child's thinking tends to focus on only one of these emotional dimensions, thereby leading to such all-or-none conclusions as "I feel like I am dumb" or "I'm completely bad." He/she simply lacks the conceptual capacity to entertain the other possibility simultaneously. [p. 422]

On an interpersonal level children who are unable to view things from another's perspective, who cannot conceive of anything beyond their own immediate experience and feelings, who are unable to simultaneously consider various aspects of reality such as the coordination required in means–ends thinking will likely exhibit behavior which would be considered dysfunctional if manifested by children at older ages. The lack of *simultaneous decentering* (viewing aspects of reality in isolation, sequentially in time, with no awareness of reciprocal interaction) has been hypothesized to underly problems in impulse control (Feffer, 1967). Those children who cannot modify their own anticipated behavior by first assessing how that behavior would be reacted to by others if carried out would be viewed if they were an adolescent as being antisocial (Rosen, 1977).

Other vestiges of egocentric thought that appear in later years include *animism* which involves endowing all things with potential life (dreams, monsters). Animism has been proposed to be at the basis of some phobias and fears and Anthony (1956) has commented that "Interpretations (of a fear) offering intellectual explanations arc not useful if the child's fear derives from animism." The concept of *imminent justice* where children believe that they could be punished at any moment for self-perceived immoral behavior carries over into later life and according to Piaget (1932) leads to generalized feelings of anxiety.

The cognitive limitations of preoperational children dictate the difficulties they experience in conceptualizing and dealing with their own personal and emotional realm. The transition from prelogical to concrete logical operations heralds the dawning of emotional stability and interpersonal awareness.

> For it is this particular transition, and the gradual development and solidification of logical operations during the concrete operational period, that seems intimately related to the child's comprehension and construction of a logical system of *emotional* concepts that define the affective spheres of his/her life. [Harter, 1977, p. 421]

This transition that occurs around the age of seven is best summarized as leading to increased flexibility, independence, and relativism (Fein, 1978). Flavell (1977) emphasizes the following four major cognitive developments that occur in this period of middle childhood.

1. *Inferred reality versus perceived appearances* (conservation). The child is less dominated by perceived appearances and forms judgments and draws conclusions about the physical environment on the basis of conflicting evidence from an unperceived reality.
2. *Decentration versus centration.* The child is able to attend to several aspects of his/her environment without being dominated by the more salient one. He/she no longer has difficulty in shifting attention from one dimension to another.
3. *Transformation versus unchanging states.* The child is now able to take into account the past as a basis for explaining the present as well as to anticipate potential and future events.
4. *Reversibility versus irreversibility.* Transformational sequences can be traced back to their point of origin to account for changes in their appearance. [p. 126]

Logic and objectivity progressively characterize children's thinking in this period and the ability to reason deductively emerges. An important acquisition is the capacity to think about concept classes in equivalent and hierarchical terms. The development of role and perspective taking appears and children begin to relate their behavior to the desires of others (decline of egocentrism). Overall, these children are able to increasingly subordinate immediate sense impressions to thought in organizing information about the environment. They can apply basic logical principles to the realm of concrete experience and events. Thinking begins to be organized into coordinated systems that the child can control.

The problem that can develop during this developmental process and which can be described as an *affective decalage* is that the "conceptualization of an emotional network of concepts may lag considerably behind the application of logical principles to the more physical, observable, or tangible realms of experience" (Harter, 1977). The notion here is that while children may apply logical reasoning to certain areas of their lives, these areas tend to be concrete and involve tangible and visual manipulations. By definition, the concrete-operational child cannot logically reason with abstract emotional concepts which do not exist in the child's sphere of perceived experience. Moreover, the reduction of egocentric thinking and the emergence of logical operations is brought about through cooperation and social communication with others. And whereas there appears to be ample opportunity for young children to receive feedback on their cognitive appraisals of their physical reality, such does not appear to be the case for their own personal and emotional reality. The verification of one's own point of view concerning likes and dislikes and overall affective reactions and perceptions appears to be a much less frequent occurrence. Rosen (1977) has indicated that primitive modes of egocentric thought remain longer in socially withdrawn and angry children who refuse to discuss or listen. Katan (1961, as quoted in Kessler, 1966) points out that while parents (and we include teachers) may encourage children to acquire the labels of objects and answer questions concerning things they can see and touch, they usually do not teach them to express their inner feelings. Katan provides the following marvelously insightful comment:

> The child perceives his feelings, and expresses some of them without words, by crying or laughing, by facial expressions or body motility. In the very early stages of development, however, these feelings are not usually given names. Often they are not understood by the parents, so the means of communication, like pointing, etc., that exists with regards to wishes directed toward the outer world is nonexistent for the expression of the child's feelings. . . . In my experience, feelings of pain or getting hurt are verbalized earlier than any other feelings; then follows the verbalizations of the feelings of fear, of being scared. Yet such feelings as sadness, excitement, happiness, and anger are often not verbalized for the child until a much later date. . . . If the child does not learn to name his feelings, a situation may arise in which there is a discrepancy between the strength of complexity of his feelings, on the one hand, and his modes of expression on the other. If the child could verbalize his feelings, he would learn to delay action, but the delaying function is lacking. [p. 30]

The final stage of formal operations has the potential for providing the adolescent with a sound basis for cognitive self-control, self-direction, and emotional well-being. The thinking of adolescents is qualitatively different from the thinking of children in the concrete−operational period, for with the acquisition of formal operations they have acquired the ability to think beyond the present and to free themselves from the prison of immediate reality.

> The adolescent is able to analyze his own thinking and construct theories. The adolescent is capable of reflective thinking, and this type of thinking makes it

possible for the adolescent to escape the concrete present toward the realm of the abstract and the possible. [Inhelder & Piaget, 1958, p. 342]

It is only after the age of 10 or 11 that children are capable of the complex symbolic reasoning processes that underly the scientific method of hypothesis testing. Consider the description of formal operations provided by Evans and McCandless (1978).

> Operational thought systems become integrated to form structures from which hypotheses can be generated and logical conclusions deduced purely symboli- cally. The ability to perform *combinatorial analysis* (combine in thought several rules, operations, or variables to solve problems) becomes apparent, as does the ability to formulate and execute symbolic plans of action. Logical forms can be examined apart from the content of a situation or statement, and potential relations among objects can be imagined. . . . [p. 280]

Formal operational thought structures enable the adolescent to engage in syllogistic reasoning, to detect logical incongruities in hypothetical contexts, to generate and consider alternatives for how things are done, to evaluate the quality and logic of their own thought (second order "reflective thinking"), and to reflect upon and evaluate themselves as people (Evans & McCandless, 1978).

The advent of formal operational thought in adolescents initially brings with it its own problems. Adolescents in their early teens begin to experience a form of egocentrism which frequently leads to a variety of emotional and behavioral problems. Piaget describes the naively idealistic aspects of adolescent ego- centrism.

> The indefinite extension of powers of thought made possible by the new instru- ments of propositional logic at first is conducive to a failure to distinguish between the ego's new and unpredicted capacities and the social or cosmic universe to which they are applied. In other words, the adolescent goes through a phase in which he attributes an unlimited power to his own thoughts so that the dream of a glorious future or of transforming the world through ideas (even if this idealism takes a materialistic form) seems to be not only fantasy but also an effective action which in itself modifies the empirical world. This is obviously a form of cognitive egocentrism. Although it differs sharply from the child's egocentrism (which is either sensori-motor or simply representational without introspective "reflec- tion") it results, nevertheless, from the same mechanism and appears as a func- tion of the new conditions created by the structuring of formal thought. [Inhelder & Piaget, 1958, pp. 345–346]

There are two major struggles that occur along with, and it would appear partly as, a result of the adolescent's increasing cognitive sophistication. As we indicated earlier, a central crisis of adolescence centers on the question of personal identity. Erikson has written most eloquently on the tendency of adolescents to question the kind of people they are and wish to be and the period of experimentation they go through in "shopping" around for roles, personal styles, and a career identity. Erikson indicates that it is important by the end of adolescence to have acquired a strong sense of identity and "self" if the transition from adolescence to adulthood is to be a smooth one. We are finding more and more in our clinical practice vestiges of unresolved adolescent crises in the attitudes of middle-aged adults.

The second struggle is on an interpersonal level between adolescents and their peer group and family. With an increase in social perspective taking, adolescents are extremely concerned about how others think about them. With the rapid physical and physiological changes, adolescents become extremely self-conscious and self-critical which frequently results in hostile overreaction to or withdrawal from social contact. They also enter into social relationships both as participant and observer.

> Each one (adolescent) appears to have several different tracks operating at the same time, a picture of him or herself as the focus of an imaginary audience, a feeling of being unique—an internal image of self as hero or heroine, hoping that others will see it. [Cowan, 1978, p. 292]

The social relationships of adolescents are frequently intense and fleeting accompanying their own changing needs and desires.

With the capacity for reflective and abstract thought comes a reexamination and redefinition of moral standards and judgments. Whereas, in the concrete operational stage, children evaluated unquestioningly their own actions (and the actions of others) in terms of concrete concepts of being "good" and "bad" and the degree to which actions serve to maintain authority and the social order, adolescents more freely examine the "rightness" and "wrongness" of rules and values to adopt those which correspond with their own abstract set of ethical principles (Kohlberg, 1969). Feelings toward parents, teachers and peers derive from a more abstract and differentiated value system. Adolescents begin to question and clash with others on the basis of their own personally constructed set of moral judgments. Generational conflicts result from adolescents questioning the values and practices of their parents and other significant authority figures. The strong feelings of adolescents and their parents concerning themselves (and criticism) as well as those heated emotions which accompany disagreements concerning matters of principles (rights to privacy, individual freedom) are all too well known to those of us involved in the upbringing of adolescents. The shifts in mood, personality style, and vascillation between conventional and experimental practices of adolescents places an incredible burden on those responsible for their welfare. Perhaps all that we can learn from the developmental patterns of adolescents is to expect the unexpected.

> If, as adults, we can use the notion of developmental progression to help us tolerate and appreciate some of the experimentation of young people as they

undertake the critical task of deciding who they will be, in what kind of world, perhaps we can provide an environment in which both generations can interact and grow. [Cowan, 1978, p. 294]

Our reading of the Piagetian literature suggests that adolescents and adults do not demonstrate formal operational thinking in all areas of functioning (e.g., Piaget, 1972). It seems most likely to be manifest in areas of personal expertise such as in an adolescent's stronger school subject or in an adult's area of vocational endeavor. So whereas we can expect Albert Ellis to be able to demonstrate formal operations in his professional work, we would not automatically expect that he would be able to do so in an area that he would know very little about and had little experience in such as planning scoring strategies for Australian Rules Football. By the same token, it is our experience that youngsters in their early adolescence do not routinely employ formal operational thought in thinking about and planning their social and personal lives. We would also expect a profound lag or decalage in the time that many adolescents are capable of employing formal level thought to resolve their own psychological problems. For those youngsters who are under the care of a RET practitioner it cannot be taken for granted that they are capable, in the short run, of understanding and employing fairly sophisticated and abstract disputational strategies. It may be that these youngsters are operating at the preoperational level in terms of the way they think about themselves, their emotions and behavior, people, events, and relations in their surrounding world.

The description of the thinking of children from a RET point of view is somewhat similar to the previously described Piagetian perspective although it concentrates more on explaining psychopathology. Consider the following RET perspectives concerning the self-defeating characteristics of childhood thought:

Emotional problems of children result from innate as well as acquired tendencies to think crookedly, to be grandiosely demanding, and to refuse to accept hassle-filled reality. [Ellis, 1971b, p. 3]

Tendencies toward short-range hedonism, oversuggestibility, grandiosity, over-vigilance, extremism, overgeneralization, wishful thinking, inertia, ineffective focusing, and discrimination difficulties . . . innate vulnerability to criticism, and damnation of others long after his original tormenter's barbs have ceased. [Ellis, 1973a, p. 33]

[Childhood neurosis] is an unrealistic, immature, and unusually self-immolating way of looking at oneself and the world. It is a perfectionistic or grandiose demand (rather than a reasonable enough preference) that things occur and people act in a certain way; it is *over*-concern about and an *over*-reactivity to the things that may or do happen in life; and it is usually a determined, pigheaded *refusal* to accept oneself and the world as they are and an asinine insistence that things *should*, or *ought*, or *must* be different from the way they are. . . . The true neurotic is a Jehovian or Hitlerian moralist who usually believes right is right and wrong is wrong and there are no two ways about it. [Ellis et al., 1966, pp. 19–20]

The point we wish to make is that many children and adolescents who have psychological problems hold on to and construct irrational beliefs and continue the tendency to think "crookedly." The inability to let go of their cognitive distortions is fundamental to their problems.

RET locates the *origins* of a great deal of psychopathology in children who are less than six because it is this group that has not as yet acquired the capacity for rational and logical thought. As Piaget indicates, children of less than six or seven appear to be extremely selective in what they attend to in their environment. Their perceptions are very much dominated by concrete and immediate stimulus salience. Their egocentrism and inability to decenter and view things from another perspective may make them appear extremely self-interested and antisocial in behavior. They also tend to see themselves and others in black and white and can only make good−bad evaluative judgments of people and events around them. The conclusions they make about the world around them and which help create their emotional and behavioral upsets are determined on the basis of arbitrary and imaginary associations and evidence that is only available in their own perceptual field. They tend to interpret the meaning of events when the evidence is lacking, they make outlandish overgeneralizations about themselves and others solely on the basis of a single event, and they tend to believe that everything they can observe happening around them is related to them. Young children's motivational system appears dominated by self-defined needs and pleasure seeking. Rather than saying to themselves they would like something, they carry on in a way that we infer they believe they must have certain things to be happy. Believing that the world revolves around them, many children make extraordinary demands upon others and believe that the world should always treat them fairly and justly and grant them their every wish when called upon. Children of this age are the greatest of awfulizers and their tendencies to think in all or none categories exacerbates mild frustration into catastrophic reactions. Children frequently appear to be born "people raters" for they are constantly making comparative judgments about themselves, their parents and peers. Unfortunately, because children are not able to logically and objectively evaluate themselves and their surroundings, they almost invariably accept the castigating attitudes of their parents, internalize them, and make them their own for the rest of their lives (Ellis, 1973a). One of the most pernicious attitudes that many children acquire early on is that of perfectionism and self-blame where they feel their self-worth depends upon the realization of unrealistically high standards and where they continuously put themselves down for mistake making and blundering.

According to RET most if not all children have low frustration tolerance. When their wills are thwarted they appear to experience large amounts of emotional stress and demonstrate LFT in a variety of maladaptive behaviors. As a result of both their inborn propensities as well as the reactions of significant others, children acquire different styles of and skills for handling frustration. We believe that the way children resolve frustration over the course of time is a tell-tale hallmark of their overall adjustment. What determines whether children are at risk for future emotional and behavioral problems is largely the product of how they cope with frustration. Bard (1980) appears to be in agreement in locating the origins of psychopathology in the irrationality of childhood thought.

> It is very clear that some children have much more difficulty overcoming the universal irrationality of early childhood than others do. It appears that all children believe the world *should* be the way they want it. Some give up that idea after a while; others do not. It appears that all children are born condemners; some get over a lot of that and some do not. It appears that all children are born catastrophizers; some get over it and some do not. [pp. 99–100]

While Ellis has shed most psychoanalytic concepts (id, ego, superego, unconscious) in conceptualizing human disturbance, he has retained the idea of *defense mechanisms* to explain how children ward off the powerful and debilitating effects of anxiety. Anxiety is an emotion that children learn how to avoid early on and continue to defend against as they grow older. Children are so afraid of losing the approval of their parents (who often rate them as little monsters for their misbehavior) and of failing in the eyes of others they evolve elaborate cover-ups. Children of the age of five and six have already learned to hide their own feelings and to reduce tensions and anxiety through what Freud originally called "classical ego defenses" (see Anna Freud's *The Ego and Mechanisms of Defense*, 1946). Some of the major defense mechanisms are briefly discussed.

Withdrawal, a popular defense mechanism of young children, involves children simply avoiding situations they find too threatening. *Denial* is a simple defense of refusing to admit that a situation or state of affairs exists. This refusal oftentimes involves denial of certain aspects of their wishes, feelings, fantasies, or behavior. *Repression* is an extreme form of denial which involves children erasing from their consciousness the anxiety producing feeling, memory, or fantasy. *Negation* stands somewhere between denial and repression and involves children expressing statements that reflect the opposite of what they actually believe or feel. They do not repress their thoughts but deny that they have them ("Don't think I'm unhappy because you're going away"). *Regression* is a return to an earlier form of behavior (thumb sucking, autogenital stimulation, dependency) as a way of coping with stress. *Reaction formation* involves the defending against feelings of fear and anxiety by displaying different and sometimes opposite feelings. Thoughts and wishes which if brought to fruition in behavior would lead to a child's censure and punishment are repressed, and further defended against by being replaced with acts and thoughts that counter the original anxiety producing impulse (Kessler, 1966). *Rationalization* is perhaps the most sophisticated defense maneuver and involves children making up plausible excuses to justify their own unacceptable thoughts or actions. They avoid having to acknowledge that they may have acted badly and thereby avoid anxiety producing consequences. *Compensation* involves children covering up an area of their lives where they perform poorly (i.e., academically) and exerting themselves in another area (i.e., athletics) where they do attain success. By throwing themselves into the latter self-enhancing activity, children oftentimes refuse to acknowledge that they have any deficiencies.

While we do not wish to overemphasize the role of defense mechanisms in children, one point we wish to stress is that children often do not admit their true feelings to others as well as themselves because of the personal psychological costs that these admissions would entail. The consequences of an over-reliance on these defensive maneuvers is that children avoid dealing with situations and people who occasion tension and anxiety. When children refuse to acknowledge their misdeeds and take responsibility for their misbehavior other people tend to reject them, which sets up what Ellis has called a "vicious cycle of maladjustment." Concerning defensive children, Ellis et al. (1966) have written:

> Defensiveness is almost always motivated by the philosophy that if the child has negative thoughts or behavior he is a complete no-good for having them and that therefore he'd better pretend to be a thoroughly different kind of individual. Although all kinds of neurotic behavior are self-defeating, defensive acts are especially so, since the non-defensive neurotic at least has a chance of seeing what it is he is doing and then can consciously work at his self-destructive thoughts and deeds. The defensive neurotic, on the other hand, has much less of a chance of *seeing* his true ideas and emotions and therefore almost certainly will not be able to work at changing them for the better. [pp. 55–56]

This discussion into cognitive-affective developmental characteristics of children has, hopefully, revealed ways in which psychological problems of school-age children can be viewed as resulting from dysfunctions, delays, and arrests in the cognitive-developmental process. We do not know exactly why people regress to earlier stages of cognitive functioning during periods of stress, nor do we really know why certain children seem to fixate at a given level of thought in dealing with their emotions. It does appear that the dysfunctional elements of preoperational and concrete operation thought characterize much of the thinking underlying childhood maladjustment.

It would be erroneous to conclude that because of the cognitive-developmental limitations of childhood thought previously mentioned that RET and other types of cognitive therapy are inappropriate for use with school-age children. On the contrary, many youngsters who employ immature forms of thinking are able, given time, the right amount of support and instruction, to become extremely skilled at employing therapeutic strategies aimed at changing their basic philosophical views. It is as if they have the *mediational potential* for thinking rationally and logically but suffer from a *production deficiency* where they do not use their "heads" to control and direct their emotions and behavior. Through skilled teaching, RET practitioners are able to help young clients be more objective, realistic, relativistic, and to use more advanced thought structures. For younger and less cognitively mature children, we tend to use more inductive, simple and direct cognitive-emotive and behavior change methods (e.g., telling a youngster exactly what to think and do in a problematic situation) which work extremely well. Elegant solutions have been achieved with extremely bright 10 and 11 years olds. The implications of cognitive-developmental constraints for employing RET with younger populations are discussed in Chapter 6.

Psychological Conditions

Psychological conditions can be conceived of as internal personality and cognitive variables which exert a direct and contemporaneous influence on the emotions and behavior of the individual. While they may vary in terms of the degree to which they are removed from observable data, they are considered as conditions which serve as the basis for mediation and self-control. As such they are in principle capable of being modified and are seen to have a controlling influence. An analysis of psychological conditions involves determining those conditions within the organism which are related to the manifestation of maladjustment.

It is possible to enumerate a variety of psychological concepts that can be employed to conceptualize internal conditions which influence emotions and behaviors. Those that are of most interest to us are those which are defined cognitively and which can be seen to have a direct link to emotions and behavior. It seems to us that there are at least five reasonably distinct psychological conditions which provide us with some understanding into the dysfunctional cognitive activity of the young person.

1. *Attention processes* refer to children's patterns of selective attention to certain aspects of both their external and internal worlds (Mahoney, 1974).

2. *Mediational processes* which are frequently but not always verbal range from the store of concepts the child has available for representing and understanding experience (Klausmeier, Ghatala & Frayer, 1974) to those processes which aid basic learning such as attention and memory (Kendler & Kendler, 1959). The covert verbalizations (Vygotsky, 1972) and images (Lazarus, 1973) of children which play an important role in controlling affective and instrumental responses can also be subsumed within this category

3. *Logical reasoning processes* characterize the manner in which children both interpret and draw generalizations and conclusions from personal observation, as well as employ premises, assumptions, and beliefs deductively to arrive at conclusions (Beck et al., 1979).

4. *Beliefs* are the understandings and assumptions children hold of themselves and of the world around them. There appear to us to be at least two different types of beliefs children evolve: (1) beliefs concerning

their individual needs, how others and themselves should behave, the manner in which they characterize the qualities of events and experience (e.g., "awfulize"), and the rules they apply and the conclusions they draw in judging the worth of themselves and others (Ellis & Grieger, 1977); and (2) beliefs children hold concerning the extent to which they view themselves as being the cause of events which occur in their lives (internal locus of control) or whether they consider outside environmental factors as responsible for their successes and fortunes (external locus of control) (Seligman, 1975).

5. *Cognitive strategies* are broad constructs which describe the capacity of children to generate plans and solutions to novel problems (Gagne, 1977) and can be seen, for example, in the variety of ways they employ the scientific method of problem solving (D'Zurilla & Goldfried, 1971) for dealing with impersonal and interpersonal problems (Spivack & Shure, 1974).

We believe that these five psychological conditions are broad enough to enable us to conceptualize different aspects of childhood maladjustment from a cognitive viewpoint. It is the case that the clinical and incremental utility of these conditions in practice has yet to be systematically assessed. However, in concretely describing different cognitive factors and content which underly different emotional and behavioral problems (see Chapter 5) it is our impression that our perspective is comprehensive enough to take each of the factors into account.

Environmental Conditions

This third category refers to those aspects of the immediate environment of children which provide stimulation and enrichment. Stimulation of different kinds and intensities is seen as facilitative of the cognitive-affective development of children. We believe that there are *critical periods* in the years of infancy and early childhood where the child requires both nurturance and proper intellectual and linguistic stimulation to grow emotionally and mentally. Moreover, there appear to be various points during the early development of children where they are especially vulnerable to improper stimulation (i.e., inadequate enrichment, desertion, exposure to conflict and criticism) which may serve to delay and inhibit development as well as promote dysfunctional cognitive thought processes and beliefs.

The environment of the child not only creates the conditions for normal cognitive-affective development, it also provides the basis for the child learning situation specific adaptive behavior as well as acquiring mediational control of emotions. An examination of *antecedent stimuli* and *reinforcing consequences* which surround children's emotional and behavioral reactions provides extensive insights in to the role the environment plays in either creating or maintaining maladjustment. Antecedent stimuli can be analyzed to determine why they are not occasioning adaptive behavior as is the density, quality, and consistency of the rewards and punishments which operate.

The delimitation of the importance of environmental conditions in childhood disorders is obviously not a distinctive contribution of RET. We would hope that any practitioner working with younger populations has a thorough grasp of behavioral principles. The distinctive role proponents of RET have played in describing environmental conditions is in their description of styles of parenting and child management which may have a deleterious influence on their children. It is our view that irrational parental beliefs often create inappropriate levels of emotionality which manifests itself in parent−child interaction. In this section, we present a general discussion of the role of parental styles and beliefs. (A more thorough analysis can be found in Chapters 6, 7, and 9).

We strongly believe that parents as role models and reinforcing−punishing agents may play a major part in preventing, minimizing, or exacerbating emotional and behavioral problems in their children. This is not to say that poor parenting is the only cause of psychological maladjustment in children. We frequently see children experiencing emotional strife who have parents who appear to be reasonably well-adjusted, who hold positive attitudes toward their child, and whose child-rearing practices appear to be sound. And we do not receive referrals for well-adjusted children whose parents, because of their problems, one would back at long odds to produce disturbed offspring. There appear to be temperamentally difficult children who, as a result of their frustrating behavior, literally create the conditions for their parents to drive themselves demented. We agree with Bard's (1980) comments:

> Some children seem especially prone to make themselves miserable about their parents' relatively minor imperfections. I emphasize this point at the onset to attack the myth that parents are always to blame and to alert practitioners to the fact that parent−child problems may be extremely complex. [p. 93]

Our view is that inappropriate parenting styles contribute to the creation of problems in children and can make things worse for children who are temperamentally difficult to raise to begin with.

We do not have room to document the impressive amount of evidence concerning the effects poorly adjusted parents have on their poorly adjusted children. To take but one area, schizophrenia, the thought patterns of adolescent schizophrenics have been characterized by idiosyncratic language concepts, concrete concepts, and cognitive processes that contain an abundance of logical flaws (Rosen, 1977). Research into the speech and language structures of their parents has indicated that flawed cognitive development may be supported by poor communication patterns within the family matrix (Trunnell, 1965). We also believe that irrational beliefs, emotional sensitivity and expressiveness, and faulty reasoning processes are modeled in parent−child communication and that children internalize these into their cognitive schemes through social modeling and language imitation.

Ellis (1962) has consistently maintained that the worst care parents can provide their children is that of blaming them for their mistake making and wrong doing. Such blaming encourages children to continue to blame themselves for their wrongs which inevitably leads to chronic feelings of anxiety, guilt, and low self-esteem for some children and hostility and bigotry in others. Writes Ellis (1973a):

> Parents or other early teachers usually help a child plummet down the toboggan slide toward disturbed feelings and behavior by doing two things when he does something that displeases them: (a) they tell him that he is wrong for acting in this displeasing manner; and (b) they strongly indicate to him that he is a worthless individual for being wrong, and that he therefore deserves to be severely punished for his wrongdoing. . . . For if they were really sensible about bringing up their children, they would obviously show their child that: (a) he is wrong when he engages in activities that displease them and other members of their social group, and that (b) he is still a highly worthwhile individual who will merely, if he wants to get along well in the community, eventually have to discipline himself and learn to be less wrong in the future. [pp. 229–230]

Paul Hauck (1972, 1977a, 1983) is the RET practitioner who has written most extensively regarding irrational parenting styles. Through his work with children and families he has identified the following erroneous parental beliefs concerning child management that are irrational not only because they are inaccurate and unempirically supportable, but because they also lead to destructive emotions and self-defeating behavior in themselves as well as their children (from Hauck, 1967). Most require no discussion as their irrationality is obvious.

1. Children must not question or disagree with their superiors.
2. A child and his behavior are the same.
3. Children can upset their superiors.
4. Punishment, guilt, and blame are effective methods of child management.
5. Children learn more from what their superiors say than from what they do.
6. Praise spoils a child.
7. Children must not be frustrated.
8. Heavy penalties work best if applied first.
9. A child must earn his parent's love.
10. Children should be calmed first, adults second. (pp. 15–36)

We present a brief discussion of three of the most common and devastating of these beliefs.

Children Must Not Question or Disagree with Their Superiors

The irrational notion here is that if parents demand that their children follow their advice unquestioningly, that not only may the advice lead to unfortunate consequences for the child, but it may also have the effect of causing the child to reject the advice thereby creating fuel for a power struggle. In addition, when children violate the rules which their parents demand that they must follow their parents become emotionally upset and hostile which, more often than not, makes the situation worse.

Children Must Not Be Frustrated

Children of parents who seek at all costs to prevent them from becoming frustrated often acquire what Hauck calls *frustration phobia*. RET contends that frustration is a natural life occurrence and rather than avoiding frustration, people in pursuit of their goals had better learn to live with and overcome frustration. If parents overprotect their children from unpleasantness, failure, and frustration, their children will not be prepared to cope with the frustrating aspects of daily living. As we have indicated earlier, low frustration tolerance leads to a variety of problematic emotions and behavior.

Children Should Be Calmed First, Adults Second

Parents oftentimes become extremely anxious and upset when they observe inappropriate behavior (lying, stealing, vandalism) and highly negative emotions (anger) in their child. They believe mistakenly that their upset and frustration are caused by their child's misbehavior and that in order for parents to be happy and relaxed their child had better settle down first. Most parents do not realize that when they get extremely upset their effectiveness in alleviating the problems of their children is greatly reduced, negated, and adds further wind to their child's sails. Moreover, during periods of upset parents tend to exercise poor judgment, such as prescribing unjust penalties and condemning and blaming their child for their misconduct.

Hauck indicates that the parental beliefs concerning their children produce different patterns of child rearing. *Unkind and firm* patterns ("unquestioning obedience toward authority combined with a kick in the ego," Hauck, 1977a) involves such parental behavior as the setting of rigid rules, never letting their child question their authority, focusing on the wrongdoing of their child, attacking the personality of their child, strictness, little praise, and consistency. As a consequence of unkind but firm parental behavior, children often regard themselves as worthless and inferior, and view everyone else as superior. They experience feelings of fear, anxiety, insecurity, and guilt and demonstrate avoidant, overly dependent, and submissive behavior.

Kind and not firm child-rearing practices involve the parent who while showing love and affection makes few demands and sets few limits. Parents who demonstrate this pattern appear to do so out of either not wanting to frustrate their child or out of guilt. When they do infrequently punish, they often use extreme levies which they later feel guilty about. Children of these parents may become "goofers" who are weak, egocentric, emotionally infantile and dependent, have low frustration tolerance, and shirk responsibility.

These kids being seldom frustrated set up their own rules, often get their way, and tend to be spoiled brats. They are the whiners of the world, the darlings of Mom and Dad who can't stand ice cream if it's older than a week, who get threatened and furious if you turn your back on them to talk to someone else, and who act like eternal babies. [Hauck, 1977a, p. 416]

People who are chronic rule breakers and who are in trouble with the law oftentimes have parents who are both *unkind and not firm*. Such parents harshly criticize their children for misbehavior and hardly ever praise them when they are "good." They believe their child is deliberately trying to misbehave and they denounce, scold, and blame for misbehavior. As a consequence, these children are expected to have the wisdom to be their own conscience and supervisor (Hauck, 1977a, p. 417). They become angry and frustrated for they are never able to please their parents. They act badly and test the limits to try to get their parents to show they care.

Kindness and firmness is the most desired and skilled form of parenting and needs to be applied consistently. According to Hauck, parents who raise their children in this fashion talk and reason with the child about objectionable behavior, focus on behavior and do not blame the child, set limits with clear consequences for rule violations, employ punishment that is related to rule learning not blame, occasionally frustrate their child when necessary, apply pressure to teach self-discipline, never punish out of anger, think well of their child, and frequently praise and show love.

RET theorists have recently begun to analyze parenting styles which are associated with different problems in children. For example, Grieger and Boyd (1983) have identified what they describe as "disturbed parenting styles" which appear to be closely associated with the development of childhood anxiety. We believe that these styles as described below can also lead to a wide variety of other emotional and behavioral problems in children.

1. *The criticism trap*. This is a style characterized by a high frequency of criticizing behaviors such as nagging, correcting, moralizing, reminding, blaming, ridiculing, and putting down their child. These parents appear to be angry, demanding and punitive and typically hold a variety of irrational beliefs described by Hauck (Nos. 1, 2, 4 and 6) and endorse the two additional beliefs: "Children *should* always and unequivocally do well and behave correctly" and "It is *horrible, terrible*, and *awful* when children do not do well, behave or question or disobey their parents." Children of these parents who are overly critical tend to have low self-esteem and are especially vulnerable to failure experiences.

2. *The perfectionism trap* is fallen into by parents who are very demanding of themselves and who believe that their children like themselves *must* do well and succeed in what they do, and

they equate their own self-worth and the value of their child in terms of the extent to which success is attained. The parents criticize or even reject their children frequently for doing poorly and communicate to their children that they are only valuable and lovable if they do well. Children of these parents tend both to be perfectionistic themselves and come to fear disapproval and failure. They frequently compulsively drive themselves to success or avoid risks by withdrawing.

3. *The scared rabbit trap* snares parents who are extremely fearful and who communicate and model these fears to their children. The beliefs these parents hold include: (1) "There are dangers about *everywhere* and one *must* be constantly on the alert lest something harmful takes you by surprise"; (2) "If something is painful or frustrating, it *must* be avoided at all costs"; (3) "Bad things that happen are *awful, horrible*, and *terrible*"; (4) "One *cannot stand it* when things go wrong"; (5) "One *has to get upset* when things go wrong"; and (6) "One *must* have a guarantee that things will go well."

4. and 5. *The false positive* and *guilt traps* in parents often lead to selfishness, low frustration, delinquency, and underachievement in children along with problems of anxiety. These parents spoil their child by excessively and indiscriminately lavishing attention and praise on them while attempting to remove all frustrations. These "unfirm" parents are motivated by beliefs such as: (1) "It is *awful* for my child to suffer, and I *must* therefore prevent it at all costs"; (2) "I *must* always do right by my child"; (3) "I *must* always be loved and approved of by my child"; and (4) "My *self-worth* is tied to how I do as a parent, so I had better not make any mistakes."

6. *The inconsistency trap* is revealed in parents who either have no consistent way of dealing with their child or who strongly criticize for mistakes without having set any guidelines or rules. These parents typically believe that: (1) "Whatever feels right is right"; and (2) "I'm too weak and helpless to know what is the right thing to do so I'll leave it up to the moment." Children of inconsistent parents have no way of predicting the behavior of their parents nor of knowing what the consequences of their behavior will be. Punishment and criticism is an ever present possibility. (pp. 220–222)

It is our experience that irrational beliefs of parents can influence their behavior in two ways. One is through their emotions. As an example, parents frequently get very upset when their child breaks a rule because they believe that: (1) "My child must be good all the time"; (2) "I find it awful or horrible when my child is not—I can't stand it"; and (3) "My child deserves punishment because he has made me so angry and for being such a bad child." The belief that children must never break a rule leads to extreme anger which produces intense and nonconstructive disciplinary action oftentimes accompanied by aggressive physical behavior.

Alternatively, we have observed parents who employ extremely inappropriate and counterproductive methods of child management simply because they believed that what they were doing was the correct thing to do and often it was the only way they could conceptualize relating to their children. Their maladaptive behavior was not associated with extreme emotional arousal but was directly motivated by their "unjustified" and outdated beliefs. For example, we have worked with several fathers who would administer physical consequences to their children whenever they caught them misbehaving. At these times, they were not particularly angry though they may have felt mildly irritated. These fathers held the simple belief that "children who break rules need to be punished severely to learn a lesson" and employed this rule as a basis for knowing what to do in problematic situations. Irrational beliefs of parents can therefore lead directly to behavior without the intervention of significant emotional arousal. The practitioner can help objectively dispute the rationality and adaptiveness of these beliefs without considering the emotional involvement. This is not to say of course that there are not more pervasive, absolutistic beliefs underlying these parenting beliefs which do occasion high degrees of emotionality such as, for example, "To be a perfect parent and a worthwhile person, my child must be totally obedient at all times." Both types of beliefs can exert an influence on parenting styles and behavior have to be considered in understanding the role of parental beliefs.

ABNORMAL PERSONALITY PATTERNS IN CHILDREN AND YOUTH

When we describe children or children's behavior as being immature, obsessive–compulsive, schizoid, hostile, depressed or cruel, we are, of course, making overgeneralizations because although children demonstrate certain consistencies in behavior that define psychopathological syndromes or hypothetical personality traits, they do not demonstrate these behaviors in all environments or in the same environment all of the time. We find the DSM-III distinction between personality and personality disorder as useful in thinking about this issue. Personality is defined as:

> Deeply ingrained patterns of behavior, which includes the way one relates to, perceives, and thinks about the environment and oneself. Personality traits are prominent aspects of personality, and do not imply pathology. Personality disorder implies inflexible and maladaptive patterns of sufficient severity to cause either significant impairment in adaptive functioning or subjective distress. [p. 366]

Caution must be exercised when describing and labeling personality profiles of children and adolescents as well as their emotional and behavioral problems so that we do not lose sight of the situational-specificity of maladjusted behavior. Antecedent stimulus conditions and consequent reinforcing events do largely determine the extent to which children express their personality in behavior. With these words of caution, we present two basic personality patterns or types which according to RET account for the expression of many different behavioral and emotional disorders.

Self-Depreciation ("The Internalizer")

RET is very much in accord with Adlerian psychology in its view that many childhood (and adult) disorders have at their roots an "inferiority complex." Many children are their own worst enemies in the way they evaluate their own reactions to failure and frustration. "Internalizers" appear to turn inward and punish themselves severely and incessantly for their self-perceived lack of success. Rather than turning outward (externalizing), they view, for example, their poor school performance as additional evidence of their worthlessness. They say things to themselves as "I should have done better; it's horrible having failed so miserably; I am so dumb." They attribute negative events to their own internal factors such as lack of ability. These children tend to be plagued by excessive feelings of worthlessness and anxiety and often express these feelings by being shy, inhibited, and withdrawing from social contact.

RET proposes two basic beliefs that underly self-depreciation. First, to be worthwhile it is a dire necessity to be loved and approved of. This belief leads some children to demand of themselves that others view them favorably. Their self-concept and level of self-esteem depends largely on other's statements to them and other's behaviors toward them.

> Feelings of worthlessness do not stem from the attitudes that an individual's parents take toward him but from his own tendency to take these attitudes too seriously, to internalize and perpetuate them through the years. [Ellis, 1973a, p. 34]

The second belief which leads to children making perfectionistic demands of themselves for success and achievement is that one must be thoroughly competent, adequate, and achieving in all possible respects to be worthwhile. Children who endorse this belief constantly compare themselves with others and blame and condemn themselves for failing. Ellis has indicated that if children feel they must do well, poor achievement (which occurs to almost all of us at one time or another) will result in low self-esteem and self-downing. There is a kind of "vicious cycle" which characterizes the emotive and behavior patterns of the internalizer. Fearing the consequences of social and academic failure leads to anxiety. To avoid anxiety, internalizers withdraw from competitive activities and become reclusive and listless. As a result of inactivity, they fail to develop the coping and academic skills which are necessary to achieve the success that is desired. The absence of these skills leads to heightened anxiety which maintains their noninvolvement.

Ellis (1973a) also notes that these children tend to be oversuspicious and supersensitive because they think others see themselves the way they see themselves. A self-fulfilling prophecy appears to operate because the worthless and inadequate view they believe others have of them leads them to behave poorly which in turn causes others to view them negatively.

Learned Grandiosity ("The Externalizer")

Children who demonstrate "grandiosity" are not difficult to pick on the playground. They are generally the loudest, the bossiest, the angriest, the most hostile, the ones on short fuses ready to explode, and who repeatedly ignore the rights of others. We infer "grandiosity" when youngsters demand that their needs take preference over all others, when they use violence to achieve their needs, and who oftentimes demonstrate little interest in formal educational tasks. Bard (1980) indicates that new and unexpected or dissonant inputs such as rapid changes in environments are difficult for these children and that they tend to feel anxious and where possible avoid participation.

"Externalizers" react to stress and failure in ways diametrically opposite to internalizers. When frustrated they turn outward, demanding that others should not behave in ways that interfere with their goals and blaming and damning others for behaving inappropriately. Not only do they hope, wish, and prefer that things be different, they demand that because a terrible, horrible, and awful situation exists which they cannot stand, others must change their behavior toward them. The RET notion is that to demand that things be the way we want them to be is grandiose.

Whereas Adler believed that the striving for superiority and power is based on the need for recognition and feelings of inadequacy, RET takes the position that children may be grandiose without having feelings of worthlessness. Children who internalize make unrealistic demands of themselves whereas children who externalize turn their demands on their environment.

> The young child strongly craves another child's toys and is furious that he cannot have them not necessarily because he thinks he is inferior and unimportant (which on other occasions he may also think) but simply because he is the kind of creature who has *low frustration tolerance*; who easily believes that he should have what he wants. [Ellis, 1973a, p. 117]

According to Bard (1980), there are two sources of grandiosity in children. Parents who are "overindulgent" in their child-rearing approach either because they wish to make life easy for their children or because they are covering up their negative feelings toward their children may inculcate their children into believing they can do and receive anything they so please. The other more pernicious and more difficult to treat source is simply the child's inborn propensity for grandiosity and a rigid mentality which may sometimes become obvious only as the child grows older.

CHILDREN AND ADOLESCENTS AT RISK

There appears to be two groups of different-age children who have the potential for experiencing maladjustment in later life. They are those children in the middle childhood years and those adolescents in the late adolescent period who fail to overcome the propensities for irrationality and cognitive distortion which are characteristic of earlier and more dysfunctional modes of thinking. There are children and adolescents who for very complex and oftentimes unknown reasons do not make the transition from emotional lability to emotional maturity, from irrationality to rationality. Youngsters who manifest the various kinds of emotional and behavioral problems we discuss in the next chapter are those who continue to perpetuate their neurotic producing views concerning self-rating and perfectionism, demandingness and low frustration tolerance, need-based immediate gratification, and awfulizing and exaggeration and who employ logical reasoning processes characteristic of an earlier stage of mental development.

Most older children (10–12) and older adolescents (15 plus) tend to make this transition though, of course, its expression is at a different level of cognitive-affective maturity. Children cease to evaluate themselves in an exaggerated and self-defeating way. They are less perfectionistic and can more objectively evaluate their performances without having negative judgments effect their feelings of self-worth. Their supersensitivity to disapproval and criticism from others so characteristic of younger children is greatly reduced. Adolescents give up making grandiose demands that just because things could be different, they should be different. Because they are less demanding and moderate their own needs, they are also more able to tolerate frustration, delay gratification, and work toward longer-range and self-enhancing goals. They also no longer regularly catastrophize about life's hassles. And as a consequence, they are less anxious and worried about and react more appropriately to things that may or may not happen.

We do not mean to imply by our discussion that all children under the age of seven or thereabouts demonstrate abnormal emotional and behavioral reactions. While the commonalities children share in the way they relate to their world (and, indeed, in the way they communicate with themselves) may be considered dysfunctional and irrational when observed in an older person, because of their high proportion of occurrence in these children they are not considered to be psychopathological. As a rule of thumb, to be considered epidemiologically abnormal, a problem or disorder must be statistically infrequent (less than 10%) within a given population (Sheppard, Oppenheim, & Mitchell, 1979). While we have painted the cognitive characteristics of children with one brush, we of course recognize that young children vary enormously in the way they think about themselves and their world. Individual differences in cognitive processing and in emotional and behavioral reactivity stem from many factors, cultural–familial environmental influences, and biohereditary factors. For example, in their classic work Chess, Thomas, and Birch (1965) have found that infants in their earliest days of life can be distinguished across a number of different temperamental characteristics including: activity level, regularity, adaptability, approach/withdrawal, physical sensitivity, intensity of reaction, distractability, positive or negative mood, and persistence. What we want to say is that although many of the thought patterns of children can be described as irrational, they do not, for the most part, either cause or lead to psychosocial maladjustment. Children learn to live with them and overcome them. However, a small proportion of children are maladjusted because of the severity, intensity, rigidity of their beliefs (i.e., demandingness), and the extent of their cognitive distortions of reality. Needless to say, there are a number of pre-seven year olds who demonstrate maladjustment in the form of social withdrawal, psychosomatic complaints, immaturity, depression, destructiveness, and aggression that can be traced to their distorted views of the world.

It is our belief that practitioners who work with children should have a background in child development so as to be able to consider the presenting problems of children in a life-span context. Much research indicates that emotional and behavioral problems of children change with age and we attribute much of this change to the increasing sophistication of the mental apparatus. In order for RET to be applied intelligently and flexibly with younger populations, the practitioner has to have an understanding of cognitive factors which influence childhood psychopathology. We believe it is important for the practitioner to be able to make good inferences about what it is young clients are thinking about when they demonstrate abnormal behavior and emotional reactions. We have also found it useful to understand the specific beliefs, assumptions, and reasons which underly and explain why a young person is distressed. In the chapter which follows, we present an analysis of common psychological problems of children and adolescents.

CHAPTER 5

A RET Analysis of Childhood Emotional and Behavioral Problems

The seeds of maladjustment in children and adolescents are the ideas, assumptions, and beliefs they have acquired as a result of the interaction of their developing cognitive-affective characteristics with social, cultural, and familial influences. It bears repeating that the child's conception of the world may often be quite discrepant with that of the RET practitioner. One of the most prevalent errors of judgment of practitioners who are inexperienced with children is their failure to recognize the importance of taking into account the distinctive and immature way children derive meaning from their world.

As we indicated in Chapter 4, most children and adolescents discard many of their irrational ideas as they grow older. Some, however, tenaciously hold on for dear life. And it is the group of children who have what appears to be an inborn propensity for reality distortion and irrational thinking who populate the offices of mental health practitioners.

Over the past 20 years, RET practitioners have written about their experiences in working with younger populations. More particularly, they have begun to identify common antiempirical assumptions, irrational ideas, and beliefs, which appear to underly a wide variety of problems in childhood (Bernard, 1984). This material we have found invaluable in our own work insofar as when assessing dysfunctional cognitions we are in a good position to know what to look for when we question a child concerning a specific problem.

It is important to indicate right from the beginning that the descriptions of the irrational underpinnings of childhood emotions and behavior have not been empirically validated and documented. The theory presented in this chapter derives from extensive clinical work conducted by ourselves and other RET therapists with children as well as the extensive clinical literature on the use of RET with adults. The ideas presented in this paper can be considered hypotheses to be tested by cognitively-oriented researchers who are becoming increasingly interested in childhood emotions. This paper does not review the research literature that is available on emotions in children, but rather describes what RET therapists consider the underlying irrationality to be in several types of emotional and behavioral problems in children.

The strategy which RET practitioners have employed in seeking to understand and interpret the emotional and behavioral problems of school-age children is one of *cognitive analysis*. The essential hypothesis testing cognitive-analytic question can be stated as follows: "In what irrational beliefs would a young person endorse and in which faulty reasoning processes would he or she engage in to feel and behave in this way?" The answer to this question provides us with some general insights into the cognitive origins (self-talk, irrational beliefs) that maintain a youngster's specific maladaptive emotions and behavior. A word of caution is in order. While the specific cognitive processes and self-verbalizations uncovered through one cognitive analysis may be sufficient to explain the problems of a given client, we do not hold that such an analysis is sufficient to explain the basis of the problems of all clients. These are empirical questions that remain to be answered in the future. We nonetheless believe that the results of cognitive analyses to be reported in this chapter provide the practitioner with tremendous insight and understanding as to why school-age children feel and behave as they do.

We had better indicate that the role of *images* in childhood maladjustment has not received much attention in the RET literature. For many years, images while recognized as important and potent covert stimuli, were accorded the status of covert activating events which in order to occasion an emotional reaction had to be cognitively appraised and interpreted. More recently, we are becoming more aware of the importance of a child's self-image, especially in the manifestation of particular emotional problems such as depression. We are hopeful that RET practitioners will begin to conceptualize and integrate the relationship among a child's maladaptive images, self-defeating verbalizations and beliefs, and specific childhood disorders.

What follows then is an account of the irrational thinking and thought processes that underlie much of the maladjustment which occurs in children and adolescents and which quite often persists into adulthood. The general irrational beliefs of childhood will precede a discussion of different childhood emotional and behavioral problems.

IRRATIONAL BELIEFS OF CHILDHOOD

In this section we detail some of the major irrational beliefs of children and adolescents. It will be seen that many are restatements or corollaries of those we presented in Chapter 3. The determination of whether a given belief will lead to one or more emotional and behavioral problems in children will depend upon, among other things: (1) the number of irrational beliefs the child holds, (2) the range of situations in which the child applies his ideas (school, home, peers, adults, work, play), (3) the strength of the child's belief, and (4) the extent to which the child tends to distort reality as observed in errors of inference about what has happened or what will happen.

There appears to be three major clusters of irrational beliefs in childhood. A detailed discussion of these beliefs can be found in Ellis, Moseley, and Wolfe (1966), Ellis (1973a), and Ellis and Bernard (1983 b).

There are two major beliefs which surround the child's developing sense of personal identity and self-worth: "It is a dire necessity for me to be loved by everyone for everything I do" and "I should be thoroughly competent, intelligent, and achieving in all possible respects." Children who hold these beliefs will doubtless experience feelings of inferiority, worthlessness, guilt, and anxiety, will tend to engage in excessive approval seeking behaviors, and will either work assiduously to avoid social and task situations where they believe they will fail or work compulsively to succeed in everything they do.

A second cluster of irrational beliefs which underlies a variety of problems include "I should always get what I want" and that "It is horrible when things are not the way I would like them to be." The "demandingness" observed in many children leads to feelings of anger, hostility, and jealousy, and can be revealed in antisocial behavior, underachievement, and aggression.

A third set of pernicious ideas of the childhood period surrounds Ellis' recent formulations concerning "discomfort anxiety." Children and adolescents who believe "I cannot stand feeling uncomfortable"; "It is horrible to be frustrated"; and that "Life should be easy and comfortable at all times" are at risk for a variety of emotional difficulties. Certain children escalate mild upsets into huge emotional disturbances because they are "sensation sensitive" and as a consequence find that they cannot stand even the mildest degree of emotional unpleasantness. Children who avoid schoolwork and domestic chores often find it impossible to tolerate or endure the initial feelings of discomfort they experience when confronted with a task.

These three clusters of general irrational ideas can be briefly summarized as follows:

1. I must do well and be approved of.
2. I must get what I want.
3. I must be comfortable and life should be fun.

Waters (1982a) has provided a more detailed list of the irrational beliefs of children as follows:

1. It's awful if others don't like me.

2. I'm bad if I make a mistake.

3. Everything should go my way; I should always get what I want.

4. Things should come easy to me.

5. The world should be fair and bad people must be punished.

6. I shouldn't show my feelings.

7. Adults should be perfect.

8. There's only one right answer.

9. I must win.

10. I shouldn't have to wait for anything. [p. 572]

For adolescents, the following irrational beliefs have been identified by Waters (1981):

1. It would be awful if peers didn't like me. It would be awful to be a social loser.

2. I shouldn't make mistakes, especially social mistakes.

3. It's my parents' fault I'm so miserable.

4. I can't help it, that's just the way I am and I guess I'll always be this way.

5. The world should be fair and just.

6. Its' awful when things do not go my way.

7. It's better to avoid challenges than to risk failure.

8. I must conform to my peers.

9. I can't stand to be criticized.

10. Others should always be responsible. [p. 6]

Many problems which children and adolescents experience can be related to these irrational ideas. As we indicate in Chapters 6 and 7, getting children to recognize and modify these beliefs through elegant or inelegant disputation will enable them to lessen their emotional distress and overcome personal difficulties.

EMOTIONAL PROBLEMS

RET does not consider that all children who emotionally over- or underreact to situations are prime candidates for the loony bin and therefore for RET. Obviously, most if not all children exhibit from time to time and from situation to situation emotional and behavioral reactions that do not serve their best interests. This is because others do not like to be around children who throw temper tantrums or who are sulking. Of course, emotional reactions can be used as primary offensive weapons in a child's power struggle with others and oftentimes, because of their aversiveness, act as negative reinforcers. Children turn on the tears, whines, or screams when they want something and turn them off when they get it. *RET identifies children who tend to consistently demonstrate inappropriate emotional reactions which occur with a high degree of intensity and which often last for long periods of time as in need of some form of help*.

As would be expected, RET adopts a cognitive model to explain the origins of emotional problems in children. The model identifies two sources of cognitive distortion which lead to emotional upset. The first type of cognitive errors occurs (according to Wessler & Wessler, 1980) at the interpretation stage where the child may distort reality through several illogical reasoning processes

such as arbitrary inference, overgeneralizing, selective abstraction, minimization, and magnification of what they experience (see Beck, 1976). This type of
error has been referred to as an error of inference (DiGiuseppe, 1981) insofar
as the child goes beyond the information present in his immediate sphere and
draws false conclusions or predictions. For example, a student who has trans-
ferred to a new school may at recess times sit alone and watch others playing
and think "No one wants to play with me. No one likes me." Such thoughts will
likely lead to feeling of anxiety or depression. If the student went on to say to
himself "It's awful not to be playing with my mates; there's something wrong
with me because no one wants to play with me," the student will likely feel
much worse because of his faulty appraisal of an interpretation. Faulty appraisals are the second type of cognitive distortion which exacerbates emotional
upset. Grieger and Boyd (1983) have suggested that faulty appraisals can be
considered errors of evaluation (i.e., irrational attitudes, ideas, or beliefs)
about what has occurred or will occur. As we have already mentioned, RET
maintains that the tendency to make errors of inference or faulty appraisals of
our interpretation is supported by the irrational beliefs a child holds. A child
who believes that everything should go his way is likely to misinterpret situations as being unfair and is equally likely to appraise the "unfairness" as
something truly awful.

RET is in general agreement with Beck's cognitive theory of emotional
disorders insofar as RET sees children who experience emotional problems as
those who either consistently misinterpret the meaning of neutral events or
who consistently blow mildly upsetting events out of proportion. In differenti-
ating between normal and healthy emotional reactions from those that are
abnormal and problematic, Beck (1976) has written:

> A significant difference between psychological disorders and normal emotional
> responses is that the ideational content of the disorders contains a consistent
> distortion of a reality situation. Whereas, the normal emotional response is
> based on a reasonable appraisal of the reality situation, the responses in psycho-
> logical disturbances are determined to a far greater degree by internal (that is,
> psychological) factors that compound the appraisal of reality. [p. 75] The spe-
> cific content of the interpretation of an event leads to a specific emotional
> response . . . Depending on the kind of interpretation a person makes, he will
> feel glad, sad, scared or angry. [p. 51]

The thoughts of children are in a constant state of flux and transition. The
private or connotative meaning of an event (concept) for a child may differ
dramatically not only from another child, but also from time A to time B. Other
psychological factors such as prevailing mood, motivation, expectations, and
attributions will influence the process by which a child *derives* and *constructs*
the meaning of an event. Andrea may feel angry at time A for being called on
because she has been picked on by other teachers during the day and may
interpret her teacher's behavior as being aggressive. Yet on another day the
very same teacher behavior may have occasioned her to feel anxiety because

she had not done her homework and feared the ridicule of her classmates. Her different thoughts on the two days will have caused her to experience different emotions. The conscious ideational content of the thoughts of children hold the secrets to their feelings. Children's misperceptions, misinterpretations, and irrational appraisals and beliefs constitute the core of their emotional problems. Those children who tend to go well beyond the objective reality situation and imbue the meaning of events with their own fantasies are especially at risk for a variety of childhood emotional problems. Most children as well as adults do not have the opportunity to check out, confirm, and disconfirm their private meanings, interpretations, and appraisals of events. One of the objectives of RET is to help children test the accuracy of their private conceptualizations of themselves and their world around them.

Beck (1976) has elaborated the concept of "personal domain" to explain why certain objects, events, and experiences may move one person to emotion and yet leave another person emotionless. We find his conception useful in thinking about why a child reacts emotionally to certain events and for predicting whether a child will have any emotional reaction at all. In discussing the personal domain of an individual, Beck (1976) writes that ". . . a person attaches special meanings to and is moved by, objects that he judges to be of particular relevance to him. The objects—tangible and intangible—in which he has such an involvement constitute his personal domain" (p. 54). Figure 5.1 illustrates the various components of the personal domain. At the center is the individual's view of himself which includes social, intellectual, and physical

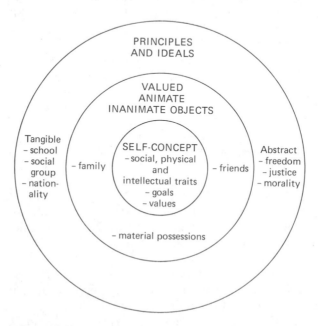

Figure 5.1. Personal Domain (adapted from Beck, 1976).

characteristics, as well as personal goals and values. Surrounding the self-concept are animate and inanimate objects that a person values such as friends, family, and material possessions. Finally, defined in the outer reaches of the domain are more abstract entities such as school, social group, and nationality as well as certain principles and ideals such as freedom, justice and morality. The model explains why people react emotionally to events far removed in time and space. It would appear that as children grow older, the differentiation and complexity of their personal domain becomes greater. For example, the issue of sexism and sex role stereotyping may not occasion any emotional reaction in children until they reach the middle or late adolescent years.

What we will now present is a RET cognitive analysis of a number of problematic emotions experienced by school-age children. In surveying the literature that deals with the cognitive basis of emotions, we have found some disagreements among theorists concerning their definitions of different emotions as well as in their specific analyses of the cognitive parameters of different emotions. We review some of these differences in order to provide the reader with a broad framework for conceptualizing childhood emotions.

The greatest amount of work in this area has been concerned with adult psychological disorders. Generally, we will review the work conducted with adults and then present a discussion of the cognitive analysis of emotion in children. Our reading of leading cognitive theorists is that there are similarities in the kinds of general reasoning processes and beliefs held by children and adults. We presume the differences especially in beliefs are greatest between younger children and older (but not senile) adults and that these differences become smaller as children become adolescents and adolescents become adults. In addition, as we have indicated earlier, emotional disorders of adults can be characterized by cognitive processes and views commonly found in the more immature and less logical stages of childhood thought. We stress, however, that the extent of the overlap between the irrational thinking processes of children and adults is a largely unexamined area of clinical inquiry.

Our own experience indicates that feelings which oftentimes are occasioned by the same activating event coexist in children. A student who gets rejected from a group of his peers may oscillate between the feelings of low self-esteem (for being rejected) and envy (for having to do without what his other friends have). As will be observed, there are a relatively small number of irrational beliefs and other cognitive distortions that underlie different emotions. In addition, there is some overlap among the different emotions (anger and jealousy, anxiety and fear).

Depression and Low Self-Esteem

Feelings of worthlessness, inadequacy, and inferiority are not exactly the same as their use in common parlance would have us believe. When someone says "I feel depressed" it may well be they are feeling inadequate because of some self-perceived rejection or failure. However, depression is a broader and more complicated state than is feeling badly about oneself. While depression does encompass an affective component that involves feelings of low self-esteem, it tends to be considered as a clinical syndrome that involves other areas of cognitive, behavioral, and emotive functioning. The multidimensional nature of depression which differentiates it from the simpler feeling of low self-esteem is revealed in the following definition by Burns and Beck (1978):

> Depression is a disorder of the entire psychobiological system including the emotions, thoughts, behaviors, and somatic functions. The emotional component is characterized by a blue mood involving feelings of sadness, anhedonia, guilt, irritability, and despair. The somatic symptoms include hypochondriasis, insomnia, or hypersomnia, weight gain or loss, constipation or diarrhea, fatigue, and decreased libido. The behavioral changes are characterized by passivity, lethargy, inactivity, social isolation, withdrawal from work, and avoidance of pleasurable activities. [p. 109]

We will first discuss low self-esteem which will lead to a general consideration of depression with specific attention directed toward childhood depression.

There is some confusion in the literature between *self-concept* and *self-esteem*. We view self-concept as the picture one holds of oneself. It is a general idea we have of our skills, abilities, and characteristics which we derive from personal experience. One's self-concept and one's personal identity can be conceived of as involving three general areas of self-appraisal (see Figure 5.2): social (skills in relating to people), intellectual (academic and cognitive abilities), and physical (characteristics of body). Self-concept is an idea, a cognition of oneself which does not involve any attitudinal or emotional judgments of what one sees. Self-esteem involves how individuals judge and evaluate the different aspects of their self-concept. Does the individual like or dislike, approve or disapprove of the things she sees in herself? The self-evaluations we make of our performances in our different roles (school, family, work, religion) across the three dimensions of our self-concept determine our feelings about ourselves. We tend to rate ourselves in terms of our performances in different activities. There are a number of standards we use in making these judgments. The criteria we employ to make our self-ratings involve our comparing our performance with our past performance, the performance of others around us, or some societally defined ideal. In these roles and for those activities we value and care about, we evaluate our behavior in terms of its success or failure on the basis of the previously mentioned criteria which in turn determines our feelings about ourselves. If we perform poorly, we feel badly about ourselves (low self-esteem). As the distance between the standards we set for ourselves and our performances becomes greater our self-esteem diminishes. The greater the "mismatch" between a person's ideal self and his or her self-concept, the greater the likelihood will be of low self-esteem. As Figure 5.2 indicates cognitive judgments of our success and failure experiences are a crucial element of our self-esteem. Our self-esteem can be considered a composite of all our self-evaluations and resultant feelings we have of ourselves.

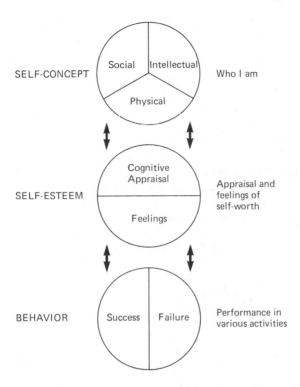

Figure 5.2. Relationships Among Self-Concept, Self-Esteem, and Behavior.

To feel badly when we perform poorly (fail, get rejected) is a normal human emotion. And even though RET views low self-esteem at the core of most human disturbance, not all people who play the game of ego rating are disturbed. Most people do not overly upset themselves when they fail to live up to some standard or goal they have set for themselves. And even when they put themselves down for failing, the resultant feelings of sadness and worthlessness do not last for very long and do not interfere with the individual's pursuit of goals. It is only those persons who frequently put themselves down and who experience prolonged and self-sabotaging periods of low self-esteem who are in need of support. In fact, prolonged periods of low self-esteem often lead to other behavioral and somatic effects which constitute a depressive disorder.

There are a number of dysfunctional cognitive processes and faulty beliefs that lead to feelings of worthlessness. The two main irrational beliefs appear to be "I must be loved and approved of by every significant person in my life and if I'm not its awful" and "I am not worthwhile unless I am thoroughly competent, adequate, achieving and attractive at all times." People who frequently experience low self-esteem tend to make the cognitive distortion of selective abstraction (they only view the negative aspects of their behavior), dichotomous thinking (they tend to see themselves in terms of bad and good), and overgeneralization (they view one instance of failure as proof of their basic inferiority). People with chronic low self-esteem often set overly ambitious and unrealistic performance standards for themselves. Perfectionism will almost inevitably lead to feelings of low self-esteem. This is frequently the case for depression prone children.

Young children frequently experience bad feelings about themselves. Because of their cognitive tendency to view themselves and others in all or none unidimensional dimensions, they are forever thinking to themselves they are bad because of some mistake and as a result temporarily feel lousy about themselves. When, however, their teacher smiles at them, or they get a spelling word correct, or make a good catch on the field, they are sublimely happy with themselves. There is a small percentage of children and adolescents who almost seem to search for failure, home in on it like a bee to honey, and sting themselves when they find what they are looking for. The "tunnel vision" of these children is similar to the compulsive, selective focusing witnessed in adult depressives. It is our view that it is only when low self-esteem becomes chronic should it be a sign that a child is at risk. As we shall indicate, chronic low self-esteem is one of the prime symptoms of learned helplessness and depression in children. The cognitive steps to low self-esteem are illustrated in the following example:

Antecedent event:	Mary is asked to spell a word and gives the wrong answer.
Rational thoughts:	"I failed to spell correctly and this is unpleasant. I hope this does not happen often. I had better study harder so I get it right the the next time."
Consequences:	Disappointment, mild shame and embarrassment. Better preparation.
Irrational thoughts:	"I failed to spell correctly and this is the worst thing that could ever happen to me; I am a hopeless failure."
Consequences:	Low self-esteem. Repeated failures.

By far the greatest amount of work into the cognitive dynamics of depression has been conducted by Aaron T. Beck and his associates (Beck, 1961, 1963, 1970b, 1972, 1976, 1979). His cognitive theory of depression is a radical departure from traditional views of depression which focus on the primary symptomology of the *affective* reaction in that it assumes feelings of sadness and loneliness that accompany depression are determined by the individual's interpretation of events rather than events themselves. In analyzing the thoughts of a variety of depressed adults, Beck (1976) concludes the common element to their depression is a "sense of loss." "They regard themselves as lacking some element or attribute that they consider essential for their happiness" (p 105). These lost elements could be failure at a job or in school, loss of a loved one, physical attractiveness, material possessions, health, and status. Beck also indicates that a depressed person tends to focus on hypothetical and pseudo losses. A person's sense of loss may also be the result of "unrealistically high goals and grandiose expectations" (p. 108).

Beck and Shaw (1977) have proposed the following three cognitive components (the "cognitive triad") as being central to understanding the development and maintenance of depression:

1. *A negative view of self.* The depressed individual shows a marked tendency to view himself as deficient, inadequate, or unworthy, and to attribute his unpleasant experiences to a physical, mental, or moral defect in himself. Furthermore, he regards himself as undesirable and worthless because of his presumed defect and tends to reject himself (and to believe others will reject him) because of it.

2. *A negative view of the world.* His interactions with the environment are interpreted as representing defeat, deprivation, or disparagement. He views the world as making exorbitant demands on him and presenting obstacles which interfere with the achievement of his life goals.

3. *A negative view of the future.* The future is seen from a negative perspective and revolves around a series of negative expectations. The depressed patient anticipates that his current problems and experiences will continue indefinitely and that he will increasingly burden significant others in his life. [p. 121]

Walen et al. (1980) indicates that the cognitive triad is similar to and overlaps with the following three irrational beliefs which RET suggests are major catalysts to depression.

1. A devout belief in one's personal inadequacy.

2. The "horror" of not having what one "needs."

3. And the "awfulness" of the ways things are. [p. 93]

Beck and Shaw (1977) and Hollon and Beck (1979) hypothesize that the manner in which adults process and distort information leads to them gradually acquiring negative views of themselves, the world, and their future. In reaction to an extremely stressful event or to a series of smaller events involving loss, failure and rejection, people begin to employ more primitive cognitive schemas for viewing themselves, the world, and the future. Their conceptualizations ". . . are framed in absolute rather than relative terms, are dichotomous rather than graduated, and are global rather than discriminative" (Beck & Shaw, 1977, p. 125). The thinking of adults who are depressed is dominated by arbitrary inference, overgeneralization, and magnification and results in an interpretation of life's experiences as follows:

The depressed patients tended to distort their experiences: they misinterpretated specific, irrelevant events in terms of personal failure, deprivation, or rejection; they tended to greatly exaggerate or over-generalize any event that bore any semblance of negative information about themselves: they also tended to per-severate in making indiscriminate, negative predictions of the future. [Beck & Shaw, 1977, p. 121]

Hauck (1971, 1973, 1977b) offers a cognitive view of depression that departs from Beck's on the issue of the cognitive triad and instead proposes his own three-factor theory of depression. Hauck argues that if people see the world according to Beck's triad, they need not be depressed at all. In fact, Hauck asserts, such a view may demonstrate good reality testing. (He cites the example of a victim of a concentration camp.) It is not the pessimism itself that causes the depression he argues, "but the additional act of blaming ourselves, or feeling sorry for others over the accurately and inaccurately assessed self, world, or future" (Hauck, 1977b, pp. 117–118). It is these three elements that account for Hauck's three-factor theory: self-blame, self-pity, and other pity.

According to Hauck (1971), underlying each factor are the following irrational beliefs that are the central causes of depression.

1. Self-blame: (a) "There are such things as bad and evil people in the world (he or she being one) and that they must be punished in order to assure the future avoidance of that heinous behavior"; (b) "one is not worthwhile unless he or she has achieved success or demonstrated generally acceptable intelligence and competence."

2. Self-pity: (a) "It is not merely sad, regrettable, and unfortunate when events do not pass as one hoped for, but that it is literally horrible, earth shaking and catastrophic"; (b) "that emotional pain is inflicted upon us from without rather than from within."

3. Pitying others: (a) "One should be upset over other people's disturbances and difficulties"; (b) "that it is vitally important to our existence what other people do, and that we should make great efforts to change them in the direction we would like them to be." [p. 33]

In contrasting the two views of depression of Beck and Hauck, the major theoretical difference appears to be the focus of cognitive distortion and faulty thinking. Beck emphasizes one's subjective perception of information whereas Hauck deals with one's evaluations and interpretations of those perceptions.

Ellis et al. (1966) indicate that there are two general activating events for depression: failure and being rejected by someone whose approval you definitely want to have. According to Ellis, feelings of rejection and failure do not produce depression; rather, depression derives from putting yourself down, blaming, punishing and, finally, pitying yourself for the failure or rejection. Rational thoughts after rejection and failure might be: "I don't like failing. I wish I had succeeded and been accepted by that person. How unfortunate for me to fail and get rejected." Irrational beliefs are revealed in the following declarative self-statements: "How awful to have failed and been rejected. I'll never get what I really want. This reveals me as a rotten person. How hopeless. I'll go on forever, never really getting what I most desire."

Wessler and Wessler (1980) synthesize the work of Beck, Ellis, and Hauck and indicate that depression involves the ideational components of self-pity, sclf-downing, helplessness, and hopelessness. They propose that depression can arise from guilt or shame, self-pity, and low frustration tolerance and associated discomfort anxiety. When guilty or shameful depression exists, the individual feels guilty or ashamed of something she has done and as a consequence feels helpless and hopeless about achieving self-worth. They are in accord with Beck's position that some forms of depression stem from self-pity that results from the loss of something or someone highly valued. The third form of depression they identify arises from the need for comfort and involves people who are unwilling to take the risks and experience the discomfort involved in removing themselves from problematic situations. They feel trapped and can see little they can do about it because of their unwillingness to "gain through pain."

There is increasing empirical evidence to suggest that depression in children and adults have some similarities, although there are a number of features that are thought to be unique to children (e.g., Frommer, 1968; Kovacs & Beck, 1977; Leon, Kendall, & Garber, 1980; Weinberg, Rutman, Sullivan, Penick, & Dietz, 1973). There is another point of view which suggests that childhood depression is quite distinct from the disorder in adults, and that depression in children is expressed in "masked symptoms" (behavioral equivalents) such as accident proneness, impulsivity, psychosomatic disturbance, and school avoidance (Blotsky & Kinsey, 1970; Cytryn & McKnew, 1972; Glaser, 1968; Malmquist, 1977; Toolan, 1962). Children who demonstrate a wide variety of the following behaviors with some degree of frequency may be diagnosed as depressed (from Lefkowitz & Burton, 1978): sadness, unhappiness, apprehension, weepiness, aggression, apathy, withdrawal, listlessness, self-deprecation, poor schoolwork, and some somatic complaints such as headaches and stomachaches. Lefkowitz and Tesiny (1980) characterize childhood depression as

> a state marked by a reduction in ebullience and in the capacity for pleasurable experience. Four areas of functioning may be involved: (a) affective, by manifestations of dysphoria, (b) cognitive, by manifestations of self-depreciation, (c) motivational, by decreased performance and withdrawal, and (d) vegetative, by fatigue, sleep problems, and loss of appetite. [p. 44]

Our view is that depression in children is extremely hard to assess due to the transitory developmental nature of many of the behaviors thought symptomatic of depression in normal children as well as the unavailability of psychometrically sound measurements.

We believe there is support for the notion that the cognitive views of depressed children and adults are similar. As we will indicate in our discussion of attributional styles and attributional retraining programs (Chapter 8), the cognitive attributions and beliefs that people hold concerning the causes of events in their lives influence their sense of helplessness, depression, and self-esteem. Research conducted mostly with college-age students indicates that people who attribute negative events in their lives to internal factors such as lack of ability are more likely to be high in depression and low in self-esteem (Metalsky & Abramson, 1981). It appears reasonable to assert that children who sense a lack of personal control over their environment for positive outcomes and who hold themselves responsible for negative outcomes (joint negative cognitive appraisals) would be prime candidates for depression. A number of studies (Diener & Dweck, 1978; Dweck, 1975; Dweck & Reppucci, 1973) have found that children who manifest chronic learned helplessness attribute their failures to their own stable and enduring characteristics.

Ellis (1973a) has provided his view on the cognitive basis of depression in children. He distinguishes between depression and displeasure and indicates:

> Depression, however, includes a much stronger feeling than that of displeasure: the feeling that the unpleasant event *should not* have existed, that it probably will *always* exist; and that it will lead to unbearable, horrible, results. [p. 118]

Ellis disagrees with Freud's notion that all depression consists in children (and adults) of anger turned inward and that all anger is depression turned outward. Occasionally (but not regularly) we get angry at ourselves for pitying ourselves and being depressed and turn our anger against others who have caused the events we believe we cannot tolerate.

Protinsky (1976) has conducted an ABC-DE analysis of depression with a schoolgirl who was referred to him for recent suicide attempts and feelings of depression. An excerpt from his analysis reveals some of the irrational beliefs that underly depression in adolescents. The activating event was the break up of her long-standing relationship with her boyfriend.

A: Her boyfriend breaks up with her.

B: "I must be loved by him in order to be worthwhile. I must be loved by him to experience life as pleasurable. Life is not worth living if I can't have him. I can't continue to live without him."

C: Depression, self-pity.

D: "It would be nice if I could have a relationship with him but no law says it must happen. Being deprived of that relationship will not kill me. I can find happiness with others. Even if no one ever cares for me again there are projects that are worthwhile that I can find pleasure in doing. Many people never get the love they crave but still manage to live happy lives. Because I am not loved by that one person does not mean that I am a worthless person."

E: Better functioning effects: "I can make it on my own. I am worthwhile. I can be happy in my present situation." [pp. 243–244]

Anxiety, Fear, and Phobia

There are a number of ways in which the related emotions of anxiety, fear, and phobia have been distinguished. There appears to be the greatest confusion between anxiety and fear. Hauck (1975) defines fear and distinguishes it from anxiety on the basis of the extent to which the emoting individual is conscious of the cause of the emotion. He argues that an individual who feels threatened in a situation without knowing exactly why and what it is she is afraid of is experiencing anxiety. Fear, on the other hand, is defined as a feeling of threat from a cause of which one is aware. Hauck makes the additional point that anxiety generally invites no clear cut evasive action whereas fear can be controlled simply by avoiding the feared stimulus. According to Hauck, the three most common fears are the fear of rejection, fear of failure, and the fear of being afraid.

Knaus (1974) indicates that anxiety and fear reactions are closely related and that with fear the source of the real or imagined danger appears more in focus. He proposes that anxiety stems from thoughts concerning an imminent threat that will result in "psychological disaster" and where the individual believes she is unlikely to cope.

Ellis et al. (1966) suggest that there are two major kinds of fears in children—fears of external things and events (animals, dark, moving objects) and fears of one's own basic inadequacies. The latter he redefines as anxiety. Specifically, Ellis differentiates the fear of being physically hurt from the fear of being socioemotionally hurt. He provides the following description of an anxious individual:

> He finds dangers when there are none; or he exaggerates them when they do exist; or he thinks the penalties and risks involved are much too great; or he keeps worrying, worrying about what may occur in the future, though there is less likelihood that the event he fears will actually occur, and still less that it will be truly catastrophic if and when it does. [p. 36]

According to Ellis (1973c), fear is a self-preserving emotion because it encourages the person to be cautious and vigilant toward the world around him. "Fear, in other words, is prophylactic, and includes the notions: (a) something or someone is dangerous to me; (b) therefore I'd better *do something* to protect myself against this dangerous thing or person" (p. 148). Anxiety differs from fear in that it includes the idea that because the person is basically incompetent and has experienced some difficulty coping with threats and dangers, he will *never* be able to cope with dangerous people or things, that he will *never* be able to come up with solutions to problems that entail dangerous aspects, and that he is *blameworthy* for being so incompetent. Whereas fear is based on an objective appraisal of a dangerous circumstance and leads to the individual trying to find effective solutions, anxiety, which is based on the individual's negative self-appraisal and self-perceived ineptness, leads to ineffective performance which in turn stimulates additional anxiety.

Ellis (1978b, 1979e, 1980c) has illuminated and separated two forms of anxiety that have origins in different irrational ideas. *Discomfort anxiety* (as we indicated in Chapter 3) stems from the idea that one must be comfortable and without pain at all times, that one cannot stand troublesome events, and that one cannot stand to feel distress. As a consequence of this irrational belief, people spend inordinate amounts of time worrying about and avoiding events and people because they anticipate feeling uncomfortable and miserable which they mistakenly believe they would not be able to tolerate. *Ego anxiety* results from the same irrational ideas concerning self-worth and the need for love and approval that underlie low self-esteem. The main difference is that ego anxiety stems from individuals *anticipating* events where they perform badly (commit a moral indiscretion) or poorly (failure and rejection), resulting in either others or themselves (or both) putting themselves down.

Beck (1976) adds another dimension when he argues that fear is not an emotion at all, but an ideation with anxiety as its emotional counterpart. "Fear is the appraisal of danger, anxiety is the unpleasant feeling state and physiological reaction that occurs when fear is provoked" (p. 138). The point here is that while a person may fear something in the sense of regarding it as a threat, the fear is not expressed as the emotion anxiety until the person is confronted with the feared stimulus either in vivo or imaginally.

In discussing the arousal of anxiety, Beck (1976) indicates that it stems from a two-step appraisal process. *Primary appraisal* occurs when the individual identifies a situation as threatening and assesses the probability, imminence, and degree of potential harm. *Secondary appraisal* involves the individual estimating his counter-harm resources, the ability to cope and neutralize the danger. The ratio of negative factors in primary appraisal to positive factors in secondary appraisal will determine the individual's perceived risk and the intensity of anxiety. Beck suggests that the threat the individual cognizes and which occasions anxiety can be real or "imaginary to the safety, health, or psychological state of any person within his personal domain" (p. 63) and can also represent a danger to some principle or ideal he values.

Wessler and Wessler (1980) emphasize that whereas feelings of guilt and shame derive from the individual already having done something stupid or wrong, anxiety relates to the anticipation of some dreaded event which has not as yet occurred. They indicate that future orientated self-statements that occasion anxiety often begin with "What if . . ." such and such would occur ("I did something wrong" or "I did something others would not like"), and continue with awfulizing and self-downing ("I can't stand the idea of doing something so bad, I would be the lowest form of life," or "It would be horrible and I would be totally worthless if I were to fail in the eyes of others").

Fears and anxieties are somewhat more distinguishable from phobias. For whereas fear is a relatively normal and healthy adaptive living emotional response to objects and events that may cause harm, phobias are irrational and disabling fears that are generally specific to one object or situation (Ross, 1980). Hauck (1975) indicates that a phobia is a combination of a fear and anxiety. "It occurs when you do not know what it is you are afraid of *but you think you know*. Furthermore, the object that you fear must symbolically represent the fear you actually have" (p. 22). Children who have a school phobia have a general idea what they fear (school, teachers, classmates, tests) but they cannot clearly articulate what it is they are specifically worried about. Their worry and uneasiness stems from a variety of sources at school which remain largely unclear in the mind of the child. Beck (1976) distinguishes phobia and anxiety by indicating that a phobia is more highly specific (tied to specific objects, places, people) than is anxiety and that a person with a specific phobia may avoid any feelings of anxiety through simply avoiding problematic situations. Anxiety, on the other hand, tends to be more diffuse, less related to one stimulus, and the person seems less able to rid herself of anxiety producing thoughts. Ellis (1973a) asserts that people who have a phobia cling to two major irrational beliefs: "(a) The world is much too difficult and dangerous a place to live in and *should* be made much easier, and (b) they cannot single-handedly cope with it and therefore they desperately and absolutely *need* the acceptance, love, and support of others in order to accept themselves and to perform even minimally well" (p. 218). In addition, they blame and condemn themselves for not being able to cope with their problems.

Traditionally, RET theorists have considered three major kinds of anxiety that are commonly observed in school-age children: interpersonal (fear of rejection), test, and speech anxiety (fear of failure). All three stem from the young person's cognitions which tend to catastrophize the personal consequences of failing at some activity. The younger client tends to overestimate the probability and personal cost of some undesirable event as well as underestimating her resources to cope with the perceived threat in an adaptive fashion (McFall & Wollersteim, 1979). Students who experience high levels of anxiety in competitive situations have at the core of their anxiety a poor self-concept and quite often low self-esteem. They view their performances as public (and private) signs of their self-worth. Hauck (1975) indicates that fear of rejection is more prevalent because children and adolescents are "often afraid to fail for the very reason they might be rejected if they do" (p. 16).

Students who obsessively ruminate about their performance have double trouble for not only do they experience the unpleasant and painful sensations associated with anxiety, their anxiety producing thoughts distract them from and interfere with effective task performance thereby increasing the likelihood of the impending doom they had been worrying about. Children and adolescents do make mountains out of molehills and talk themselves into believing that social rejection and academic failure would be horrible and awful. Hauck (1975) indicates that they think they are facing something the consequences of which would be shattering and tragic—life and death. Their inner dialogue runs something like "This is dreadful, I can't stand it. This is going to happen and it will be awful. I must think about the issue all day and tomorrow and worry over it at all times" (p. 27). Children who experience frequent episodes of anxiety subscribe to a number of self-defeating ideas including: (1) I must at all times be loved and win the approval of others. Unless others love and approve of me I am not a worthwhile person; (2) I must succeed at all times and if I fall short of my standard or if I fail that would be awful for it would prove I am a failure; (3) I cannot tolerate any sort of public embarrassment or humiliation; (4) It is impossible for me to face up and handle any situation successfully; and (5) I must worry and stew about the uncertainties of the future.

Children by nature are afraid and scared of many more things than are older adolescents and adults. We list in Table 5.1 a variety of children's fears that compose the Children's Fear Survey Schedule (Ryall & Dietiker, 1979) which can be administered to students between the ages of 4 and 12 years. Much research indicates that the content of children's fears change with age (e.g., Angelino, Dollins, & Mech, 1956; Jersild, 1960). Fears of young children are concerned with physical harm whereas older children show fears associated with psychological harm, including rejection and failure. Because of the range and intensity of fears of children, it is not always possible to recognize when fears become irrational and phobic. A fear can be viewed as being rational if a disinterested observer would label the situation as realistically dangerous. A fear can be labelled irrational if it is based on imaginary and fallacious assumptions or faulty reasoning. Children's fears, then, had better be assessed in terms of the reality of their perception of danger as well as the degree to which they exaggerate the awfulness of the feared event and underestimate their coping resources. The cognitive steps underlying irrational fears in children may be considered as follows:

Something is dangerous and will hurt me.
I must avoid being near it at all costs.
Being near it is awful; I can't even bear to think about it.
I can't cope.
I can't cope with the thought of being hurt.

It should be kept in mind that as children begin to be able to distinguish imagination from reality, a number of their fears begin to evaporate. Fears that persist after the age at which they would normally appear and which significantly impair the functioning of the child are of concern to the RET practitioner.

When children's fears become intense, persistent, and self-defeating they can be termed phobias. Their fears can either be of physical dangers of psychosocial stress. Thus one can talk of children who demonstrate abnormal distress, disability, and inhibition to physical and psychosocial danger as dog phobic, dental phobic (generally called dental anxiety), school phobic, test, speech, and social phobic (commonly referred to as anxieties). The RET view of childhood phobias is that children are more afraid of the consequences of

TABLE 5.1.   The Fears of Children

loud noises	death or dead people	being sick
bugs	closed-in places	mom shouting
fire	getting caught	going to the dentist
teachers	being in a fight	monsters
snakes	kidnappers	cats
being alone	grades on tests	shadows
spankings	the dark	sharks
strangers	big bullies	ghosts
dogs	getting a shot	being bawled out
to die	storms	poison
earthquakes	graveyards	seeing other kids fight
brothers	the principal	going to the doctor
spiders	lions and tigers	scary movies
to get hurt	dark, empty rooms	bears
haunted houses	guns	war
grades on report cards	dad	bad dreams

Source: Ryall and Dietiker, 1979.

confronting the feared stimulus than they are of the stimulus itself. Ellis et al. (1966) indicate that children who experience phobic reactions often have a general fearful attitude to their environment. They tend to be more afraid of physical dangers, of making mistakes, of being laughed at, and of being left alone. "Certain children are enormous catastrophizers who actually seek out conditions to worry and fret about" (p. 38). Some of their ideas which create phobias include: "I cannot stand being around scary things"; "I am unable to cope with things I am afraid of"; "I will be overwhelmed by scary things and that would be unbearable." In the case of school phobia, schools contain elements of physical and psychosocial danger. Children who exhibit school phobic reactions are oftentimes overstimulated by the number and severity of the physical dangers and social threats they imagine and anticipate, and they view themselves as largely incapable of coping with each and every one. The cognitions of these children are often those that create anxiety, including a sense that they are basically no good and that they cannot handle situations effectively.

In discussing childhood anxieties, fears, and phobias in children, Grieger and Boyd (1983) propose the following distinctions:

A *fear* is an apprehensive reaction to an external event or situation that is (1) objectively dangerous or (2) objectively safe but typically feared by a child of a given age and intelligence. The fear neither debilitates the child nor significantly interferes in his or her life. Therapeutic intervention in these instances, if necessary at all, would consist of reassuring the parents—and perhaps the child—that her or his fears are "normal."

A *phobia* is an apprehensive *overreaction* (including an obsessive avoidance) to some external event or situation that is neither developmentally appropriate nor objectively dangerous. It can also be an apprehensive *overreaction* to some external event that is truely aversive or dangerous. In both instances there is the belief that because the event is dangerous it is horrible to experience, and that one should be deathly afraid of it. With these beliefs the response is marked by its abnormal intensity, duration, and frequency. Social phobias and phobias to specific objects like dogs are examples.

An *anxiety* is an apprehensive overreaction to the possible consequences of some external event rather than the event itself. For example, the child dreading taking a test will usually be anxious about what will happen to him or her if the test is failed, such as being rejected by peers, feeling depressed, or scolded by parents. Most tragically, the dreaded consequence includes a strong, aversive feeling state (e.g., anxiety, depression, feeling of worthlessness) that the youngster believes to be too horrible to experience. [p. 213]

Grieger and Boyd have examined childhood anxieties in terms of Ellis' newer conceptions of ego and discomfort anxiety. Ego anxiety in children results from the belief that "she/he must do well and be approved for it or else she/he is worthless, bad, and an unworthy person whom no one could ever care for again" (Grieger & Boyd, 1983). Grieger and Boyd have identified four classes of problems which are related to *ego anxiety* in children.

Avoidance/withdrawal from people is reflected in such behaviors as shrinking from peers and strangers, dependency on family, labored communication, timidity, and lack of assertion and is manifested by generalized anxiety, self-doubt, feelings of inferiority, and secondary depression. Typical irrational ideas which underly social withdrawal include:

I must do well and be lovable in all respects or I will be rejected. Others not liking me makes me nothing.

If I do not do well and/or if I am not lovable, then I will be worthless. I must therefore avoid trying and getting noticed at all costs. So long as I can be left alone, and nothing is demanded of me, my worthlessness will not be obvious, and I won't feel worthless. [p. 224]

Attention seeking appears in three types of children (model child, cute and charming; class clown-show-off, pest; apparently shy, helpless child) and is affectively experienced as anxiety, self-doubt, feelings of insecurity, and a sense of pleasure when efforts pay off. Irrational ideas underlying approval seeking behaviors include:

I must be noticed at all costs or else I am lost and worthless.

I must be loved and approved of at all times or else I am worthless. [p. 224]

Avoidance/withdrawal from tasks is manifested both in expressions of concern about competence and/or difficulty of task, complaints about physical ailments, passivity in classroom, homework not completed or sloppily done, and procrastination as well as emotions such as generalized anxiety, worries about impending deadlines, feelings of inferiority, and self-doubt. Typical irrational ideas underlying task avoidance include:

I must do well and be approved for it or else I will be a terrible person whom no one could love.

Since I will be proven to be worthless for doing poorly, it is better to try nothing at all.

As long as I try nothing, my worthlessness will not be obvious and I won't feel worthless.

If others saw my inadequacy, they would reject me, and that would make me worthless. [p. 225]

A final ego anxiety related problem is that of perfectionism. Accompanying behavioral manifestations include compulsiveness, high achievement, and being over-driven. Emotionally, the child experiences a sense of pleasure when she is successful, generalized anxiety, heightened anxiety before performance, depression, guilt, self-downing when she fails, worries about deadlines, and obsessional self-doubts. Perfectionism producing irrational ideas are:

I must do well or else I will be rejected, lost and worthless. I must always do my best.

My performance at school and everywhere else must always be competent.

If I don't totally and always do well, then I am totally and always a failure. [p. 225]

Discomfort anxiety in children has a number of irrational beliefs and assumptions at its core, including the idea that "It is *horrible*, *terrible*, and *awful* when things go wrong or when something difficult or dangerous is confronted" (Grieger & Boyd, 1979). Discomfort anxiety may or may not begin with a child making a faulty inference about perceived reality.

The child who makes a faulty inference (e.g., "Because the neighbor kid was pushed down on the playground, I'll be hurt if I go to school") will be afraid; the child with only discomfort anxiety will be highly fearful; and children with both are usually terrified about many things, and their terror prompts them to continually create more faulty inferences and irrational evaluations. [Grieger & Boyd, 1983, p. 226]

Children who experience discomfort anxiety tend to exaggerate and awfulize about unpleasantness and they strongly believe and demand that things should always go the way they desire, quickly and easily.

Grieger and Boyd (1983) have detailed four childhood problems which are associated with discomfort anxiety. *School phobia* is manifested by a refusal to attend school, avoidance of children who attend school, clinging to mother, acute anxiety in the morning, nightmares and/or insomnia, psychosomatic symptoms, secondary ego anxiety, anger, and depression and derives from a number of irrational and antiempirical ideas, including:

> Because a neighbor child got hurt at school it means I will get hurt if I go, I might even be killed.

> Bad things might happen at school and I couldn't stand that. I must have protection.

> I must never leave mother and the comfort and security of home. It would be horrible to give them up even for a few hours; I couldn't survive.

> Because I'm nervous I'll make mistakes and the other children will not like me; this will show I'm no good.

> My feelings of anxiety are horrible and they will increase if I go to school; I'll completely fall apart and look foolish.

> They should not make me do what I don't want to do; they deserve to be punished.[p. 228]

A second common problem associated with discomfort anxiety involves *procrastination of schoolwork and home chores*. Behavioral manifestations of procrastination include forgetfulness, avoiding contact with requesting adults, feigning of ignorance, ineptitude, daudling, daydreaming, and incomplete work. Emotional reactions include diffuse anxiety, insecurity, inferiority, tiredness, laziness, psychosomatic symptoms, secondary anger, guilt about procrastination, and anxiety about adults' disapproval. Typical irrational ideas include:

> Life should be cozy and comfortable and I should get everything I want and nothing I don't want.

> When life is not this way it's horrible, awful, I can't stand the pain and fatigue of doing what I don't want to do.

> Because doing what I can't stand is so horrible I must find ways to put it off, somehow it will go away if I avoid it.

> Difficult tasks are impossible, work should be easy.

> I can't do difficult things, I'll fail if I try and show how inept and hopeless I am.

> They should not make me do these painful things, they are awful people.

> I am a bad person for not doing what I was told to do. [p. 228]

When children *obsessively worry about an event or activity* they tend to be preoccupied with preparation, lack spontaneity, are overly serious, irritable and experience intrusive thought. Emotions which frequently accompany obsessional worry include continual tension and anxiety, nausea and other psychosomatic symptoms, absence of laughter, controlled effect, acute anxiety before target event, and secondary anger. Underlying irrational ideas include:

This event may be terribly horrible and aversive, so painful it's beyond description.

I can't stand aversion and pain, it's more than I can bear.

I shouldn't have to bear discomfort; I am entitled to a happy life without discomfort.

I must be absolutely sure nothing will happen to cause me discomfort; I must use all my energies to plan and avoid potential pain; I must not relax until the danger is over.

People who cause me discomfort are bad and I hate them.

The world is rotten because it put me in this spot. [p. 229]

Childhood obesity, which is frequently a partial outcome of discomfort anxiety, can be characterized by continuous eating, timidity, nonassertion, overweight, lethargy, social withdrawal, and sedentary levels of activity. Emotionally obese children tend to be affectively constricted, insecure, low in self-esteem, nervous most of the time, irritable some of the time, experience outbursts of anger, shame over appearance, and guilt about eating habits. Characteristic irrational ideas which underly childhood obesity are:

I must have the approval of others and do well in my performance, otherwise I'm a worthless nothing (ego anxiety problem).

I can't stand the discomfort of anxiety, loneliness, and boredom; it is too painful, and it reminds me of how worthless and miserable I am.

I must have food to make me feel better, I need it to be less miserable.

Because of my fatness and eating I am a slob, I should be a better person than I am but there's nothing I can do, I can't stop eating.

Others have it easy and that's not fair, they shouldn't be happy if I can't, damn them. [p. 229]

Discomfort anxiety is often difficult to recognize because it often coexists with other emotional problems (e.g., anger, ego anxiety). Grieger and Boyd (1983) offer four diagnostic guidelines to help the practitioner identify discomfort anxiety.

1. Children often make a faulty inference or receive incorrect information which leads them to expect discomfort in an upcoming situation, then they awfulize about the anticipated discomfort and create discomfort anxiety. Look for these inferences and faulty premises.

2. Unwanted and discomforting situations and tasks are a realistic part of life, but youngsters (particularly pampered and sheltered children) are reknown

for exaggerating the pain involved, thereby creating a primary problem of discomfort anxiety. It is well to remember that low frustration tolerance is endemic to children and that a child can become very anxious about what seems to be an ordinary responsibility.

3.   Through various irrational thought processes children can create ego anxiety, anger, depression, and other forms of emotional distress, and these unpleasantries then become the antecedents for secondary discomfort anxiety. Children are frequently afraid of the pain in their own distressful emotions.

4.   Discomfort anxiety easily leads to other forms of emotional disturbance. Children can angrily damn others and the world for causing their discomfort, they can pity themselves into dipphoria, or adopt a hopeless and helpless attitude of depression. These emotions can mask a primary problem of discomfort anxiety. [pp. 226−227]

Anger

As with all other emotions, RET views anger and hostility as arising from anger-creating philosophies rather than directly from stressful or frustrating events. RET takes the position that although there is a large physiological component to anger, angry feelings become physiological only after they have become cognitively created. Frustration needs to be interpreted by the individual as being bad and as being a serious attack on his personal domain before it is reacted to negatively. According to Ellis et al. (1966), hostility does not stem from frustration but from our "childish, grandiose, unrealistic refusal to accept the fact that we are being frustrated" (p. 104). Ellis and Harper (1975) indicate that Miller and Dollard's (1950) frustration−aggression hypothesis stems from the irrational idea that you have to view things as awful, terrible, horrible, and catastrophic when you get seriously frustrated, treated unfairly, or rejected. Whereas many kinds of frustration do lead to feelings of anger, it is often the case that frustration may lead to other feelings such as self-pity, low self-esteem or even exhilaration ("I really like a challenge"), or to no feelings at all if the person elects not to view the frustration as all that awful or if the frustrating agent appears to be justified, nonarbitrary, or reasonable (Beck, 1976).

Ellis (1973d, 1975b, 1977c) draws an important distinction between anger that is healthy and unhealthy. Healthy anger is an emotion of moderate intensity (it does not overly upset the individual) which helps individuals attain goals, and is based on a nonabsolutistic view of self and others that is consistent with reality. Unhealthy anger is an extremely upsetting emotion which because of the turmoil it creates does not permit the attainment of personal goals and is based on a demanding, condemning, blaming and punishing philosophy which causes individuals to misinterpret and distort reality. Synonyms for healthy anger include the moderate emotions of irritation, disappointment, and displeasure where synonyms for unhealthy anger are rage, hate, and bitterness. The main RET idea is that when you are thwarted from obtaining what you desire or when someone else mistreats you or violates some personal rule or value that you feel strongly about, it is perfectly normal, rational, and appropriate to be moderately upset and irritated because such feelings will no doubt help motivate you to act constructively to change the situation so that you obtain what you want or so your rights are not violated in the future. However, if you become extremely angry and hostile after being frustrated it is quite likely that not only will you be unable to perform in a way that will rectify the situation, your behavior will most likely be viewed as provocative and aggressive and will tend to exacerbate the situation for the worse. Extreme anger results in effects that are not conducive to individual survival and general fitness. The short-term effects of raised blood pressure, increased heart rate, stomach upset, and perceptual confusion often lead to longer-term effects of stomach ulcers, high blood pressure, and heart attack (Ellis & Harper, 1975).

At this point it may be useful to distinguish between the emotion of *anger* and the physical act of *aggression*. It is not always the case that anger leads to aggressive and conduct disordered behavior. Many people who experience episodes of intense hostility and anger toward others have learned to control or hide their feelings. They may refrain from "hitting out" when they are upset because they have been firmly and consistently punished when younger for aggressive behavior or because they have been socialized away from the expression of anger. Equally, there are a significant number of children who demonstrate conduct disordered behavior (vandalism, stealing, bullying) who are not particularly upset at the time they are being destructive. They appear to behave impulsively without thinking and therefore may lack the cognitive means for creating the feeling of anger. These persons do not suffer from irrational beliefs but rather from the absence of appropriate verbal mediators for behavioral self-control. (We will discuss the characteristics of conduct disordered children shortly.)

There are a number of ways in which the cognitive view of the individual has been hypothesized to create anger. Knaus (1974) considers anger to be stimulated by a frustrated demand "that oneself, other people, or circumstances operate according to personal standards and values. This perfectionist insistence that others or oneself not make mistakes or act badly leads to thoughts and feelings of condemnation and intolerance" (p. 80). Bard (1980) proposes that anger and hostility "suggest an attitude of superiority in matters relating to how human beings should properly behave and a strong inclination to serve as judge, jury, and executioner of those who fail to meet the standards" (p. 56). Ellis (1975c) distinguishes two kinds of anger: personalized and impersonal. Personalized or autistic anger is revealed in the following sequence of self-statements: (1) "Because I dislike your behavior, you should not do it!"; (2) "Because you did that rotten act, you rate as a wholly rotten person"; and (3) "Because you flouted an absolute law of the universe by acting badly to me, you should get severely damned and punished." Impersonal anger on the other hand emphasizes consensual validation as the basis of judgment. The set of self-statements that typically underlie impersonal anger include: (1) "Because you acted badly to me and/or to others, everyone would agree you behaved unfairly. You shouldn't act that way!"; (2) "Because you acted so generally unfairly, you rate as a rotten person"; and (3) "Because you have essential rottenness, you deserve to get punished or damned." The three irrational core elements are the same in both kinds of anger: (1) a should or demand, (2) blame and condemnation, and (3) punishment.(Bernard, 1981b).

Ellis and Harper (1975) specify two basic irrational beliefs that create the conditions for anger. The first is the idea that when people act obnoxiously and unfairly, you should blame and condemn them and see them as bad, wicked, or rotten individuals. They describe the process of becoming angry in these cognitive steps: (1) "I do not like Joe's behavior"; and (2) "Because I do not like it, he shouldn't have acted that way." The second irrational idea that leads to anger is that one has to view things as awful, terrible, horrible, and cata- strophic when one gets seriously frustrated, treated unfairly, or rejected. Essentially one says "I don't like this situation. I can't stand it. It drives me crazy. It shouldn't exist this way. It simply has to change otherwise I can't possibly feel happy" (p. 126).

Beck (1976) views anger as occurring when individuals cognize an attack on their personal domain, including their values and moral codes. Other necessary conditions for the provocation of anger are: (1) the individual must take the infringement seriously and label it negatively; (2) the person must not consider the noxious situation as an immediate or continuing danger; and (3) the individual must focus primarily on the wrongfulness of the offence and the offender rather than any injury he may have sustained (Beck, 1976, p. 72). According to Beck's approach, the kinds of situations that lead to anger are intentional and unintentional direct attack and a real or hypothetical violation of laws, standards, or social mores. Examples of common situations that elicit anger in children are:

1. Intentional direct attack is usually instigated by other children. They may taunt, threaten, ignore or beat up a child who may then turn angry at them.

2. Unintentional direct attack is usually instigated by adults, particularly the teacher and the parent. The teacher often unintentionally hurts children by selective attention and rigid or biased marking. The parent constantly im- poses limitations on the child's behavior; for example, when, where, and with whom the child may go out, timing and duration of leisure activities, imposition of home duties and selective attention to siblings.

3. Violations of laws, standards, and social mores will increase as the child internalizes more and more of these standards and values. The younger child often demands material goods that are accepted as standard in his/her peer group. Concepts such as fairness and loyalty probably affect a whole range of a child's relationships even at an early age. Conflicts of values may often occur between the child's school and home environment, or between children themselves.

4. Hypothetical violations occur mainly for older children. A girl forming a friendship with another girl's boyfriend will soon be seen by many girls as stealing the boyfriend and as a threat to all their boyfriends too. [Andrews, 1980, p. 3]

Wessler and Wessler (1980) suggest that angry feelings result from low frustration tolerance and discomfort anxiety. Anger is one major emotional consequence of the irrational belief they indicate underlies LFT: "Life should be easy and go the way I want. If not, it's awful and I can't stand it." In accordance with Ellis and Beck, they believe that "anger derives from demandingness and awfulizing directed toward perceived frustration. We experience frustration when we do not get what we want; we experience anger when we do not get what we want *and* believe we *should have* and therefore it is *awful*" (p. 98). If people thwart themselves because of some inability or imperfection (procrastination), anger can be directed at themselves ("I should have worked harder!"). Otherwise, anger can be turned against others of the world depending upon where the individual appraises the source of frustration to be. They make an important distinction between feeling annoyed, which results from rationally preferring that other people not break personal rules and violate personal rights, and anger which stems from grandiosely demanding that others behave differently.

In relation to anger in children, a number of further comments can be made. Because younger children have difficulty controlling their anger once it starts, and because it seems to be triggered so easily especially in impulsive children, it sometimes appears that anger is under the control of external events and internal physiological rather than psychological processes. We believe this picture to be misleading and that underlying most unhealthy anger in neurologically intact children are a set of egocentric views concerning their importance. Discussing the anger creating view of a nine-year-old boy of average intelligence whom they were seeing, Ellis et al. (1966) write:

He believed that practically everyone in the world existed solely for the purpose of doing his bidding and making things easy for him and that when anyone acted otherwise, this person deserved instantly to be put in his place and made to feel miserable. [p. 101]

Ellis et al. (1966) also make the point that most children resent others for their undesired behavior and that this should not be viewed as a sign of abnormal aggression. There are, however, some children who are "not only angry when they are seriously frustrated, but they are also resentful when they are only mildly thwarted; or they are resentful out of all proportion to the frequency or degree of their frustration; or they find severe frustrations when there are actually few or none" (p. 47). Anger often serves to protect these children against their own feelings of worthlessness. "By being angry at others, one can demean them, then by comparison, make oneself feel enormously superior to others. Children compensate for inadequacy feelings and their relentless frustration by seeing others as miserable worms and themselves as would-be saviours" (p. 45).

An underlying irrational belief of children who have overly hostile reactions is that "Everything should be made exceptionally easy for me and that I should not have to put up with any kind of frustration." Angry children frequently have low frustration tolerance. Their demandingness derives from their rigidly held belief that things are unfair and should not exist. Consider Jeff who pushes in front of Jason and Mark to get into class first. Mark might think to himself: "I'm annoyed with Jeff for moving in front of me. I wish he wouldn't do it. I'm going to ask him to get back." Such rational thoughts would lead to irritation and the use of an adaptive problem solving skill. Jason, on the other extreme, might think to himself the nutty, irrational, unrealistic and anger-creating thoughts: "He can't get away with doing that. He has no right. The teacher will like him more than she'll like me and that's awful. He's really gone too far this time. I'ts not fair and I'm going to get him!" You can predict what Jason's ensuing emotions and behavior would be.

In his innovative approach to the understanding and treatment of conduct disorders, DiGiuseppe (1983) has described the cognitive origins of a variety of children's misbehavior, including teasing, temper tantrums, impulsivity, hitting, stealing, and verbal aggression. Behavioral excesses of children are not infrequently associated with the child experiencing disturbed emotions. According to DiGiuseppe, there are two main cognitive-emotive clusters which appear in children who manifest disorders in their conduct (demandingness– anger; "I can't stand-itis"– discomfort anxiety):

> Like adults, children usually get angry when they demand that the world be the way they want it to be, (Ellis, 1977). Significant others in the lives of children may very early treat them like they are special and should have unlimited rewards. These children are not hard to convince that they should always have their way. Their children's disturbance comes from the belief that since their parents believed that they should always have what they wanted, the rest of the world should do the same. . . . The second emotional-cognitive state which appears in children who manifest disorders in their conduct is discomfort anxiety and the corresponding irrational beliefs associated with low frustration tolerance. . . . These are, first, that any discomfort, pain, or onerity is terrible, awful, and intolerable; and second, that denial of a desire is unbearable and intolerable. [p. 117]

A third less frequently seen cognitive-affective cluster which underlies aggression in children is according to DiGiuseppe connected to the belief that they are worthless and will never be able to succeed in life.

> Some antisocial children behave aggressively because of a combination of depression and anger . . . These children are usually seen in residential centres for adolescents and usually have a history of parental abandonment or obvious and

sustained parental rejection. They have had a history of relaxed controls and thus failed to learn many appropriate behaviors and cognitive control skills similar to other children who misbehave. In addition, they condemn themselves for being unloveable. This group of children appears to experience no fear of negative consequences for their misbehavior and have no concern that they will negatively impact their life by misbehavior. There is an absence of hope and a sense of helplessness. All the bad things have already happened. For some, life is viewed as externally controlling and all the payoffs are negative, so they might as well do as they please. [p. 118]

Guilt

RET distinguishes between guilt and feelings of guilt (Bard, 1980). The former refers to someone having violated a societal standard of acceptable behavior which is defined as wrong because it interferes with a person pursuing and obtaining the long-term goals of social acceptance and survival in a community, getting along reasonably well with others, and forming and maintaining intimate relations with a few significant others. Guilt feelings stand somewhere between anger and anxiety and derive from people putting themselves down— blaming, condemning, and punishing themselves because of their having committed a wrong (Bard, 1980). Knaus (1974) provides the following definition of the affect guilt:

> An unpleasant cognitive-emotion stimulated by the belief that one has transgressed against one's own, or against normative codes of conduct, and has acted wrongly against another, and therefore deserving of blame. This awareness is followed by self-condemning thoughts, and frequently the belief that one is obligated to act justly and fairly under any and all circumstances. Related affects: anger, self-blame. Behavioral manifestations include attempting to undo the damage, contriteness, withdrawal, high-pitched agitated voice, subdued voice, apologetic language. Sometimes this reaction is followed by resentment. [p. 82]

Guilty feelings originate in guilty cognitions. Walen et al. (1980) indicate two cognitive steps to guilt. People believe they are doing, will do, or have done something wrong and condemn themselves for doing the wrong thing. The first step may be a correct interpretation or inference by the person based on a particular system of ethics and values which the RET practitioner will no doubt have a sense of from having conducted a RET assessment. The irrationality associated with the second element involves the concept of self-worth and self-rating which leads to dysfunctional emotional and behavioral reactions. The RET view is that it is certainly desirable for people to internalize a system of morality so that they both know what is adaptive behavior (self-helping and other accepting) and what is wrong (self-sabotaging and antisocial) so that they do the self- and socially approved thing. It is certainly not desirable and appropriate, however, to be *moralistic* and condemn and punish themselves and others for being mistaken and immoral.

Two emotional states related to guilt are shame and regret. Wessler and Wessler (1980) make the point that shame derives from others' evaluations of one's performance and self while guilt stems from an internal locus of evaluation. "Shame comes from receiving the disapproval of others; guilt, from receiving one's own disapproval. In both cases, the conclusion is 'I'm no good' " (p. 96). They indicate that a good way to determine if a person is feeling guilt or shame is to ask the question "How would you feel if I could guarantee that no one would ever know or think badly about your mistake, failure, or misdeed?" Shame would be the emotion if they indicate that they would feel okay. They summarize the ABC's of shame and guilt as follows:

A: Doing something that others disapprove of.

B: I need their approval. Because they think badly of me, that proves I'm worthless.

C: Shame.

A: Doing something I consider wrong.

B: I shouldn't do wrong things. Because I did, I'm no good.

C: Guilt. [p. 97]

Regret is a more rational-emotive reaction to having committed a wrong. Regret occurs when one is sorry, compassionate, and concerned for another person who has been disadvantaged or hurt by what one has done (Bard, 1980). Regret focuses more on the consequences of one's actions than on the culpability and rottenness of the perpetrator.

Guilt in children cannot be experienced as an emotion before the age of four or five because it is not until that age that children begin to internalize a socially accepted standard of behavior. Before that age, children's "good" behavior is motivated by a fear of punishment and a desire for reward rather than by guilt feelings associated with violations of social standards. When children younger than this age commit some impropriety, their ensuing feelings are not of guilt but rather fear stimulated by the anticipated consequences of discovery. Beginning around the fourth or fifth year, children begin to develop a rudimentary sense of "right" and "wrong" based on ethical principles and strongly adhere to the belief that wrongdoers (including themselves) must be punished and should repent for their "sins." Through an internalization of their parents' value system and "conscience structure" children begin to be aware of the importance of considering others. They "learn that their interests are best served by a spirit of cooperation and application of the golden rule 'Do unto others as you would be done by' " (Kessler, 1966, p. 58). Unfortunately, as children begin to internalize the values of their parents, they do not have the intellectual equipment to judge whether parental proscriptions of "dos" and "don'ts" serve their own best interests let alone the welfare of their parents. As a consequence, children acquire an abundance of moral commandments that they never have the opportunity to empirically test to determine whether they serve to enhance their well-being and the attainment of happiness and pleasure. By the time children are old enough to make such judgments their moral beliefs and values are so firmly entrenched in and serve to define their cognitive structures that they often operate at a preconscious level and often lead to self-defeating self- and other-appraisals. Simply stated, what their parents view as morally wrong may not "work" for their children. One problem for the children of parents who endorse a set of perfectionistic beliefs is that these parents oftentimes encourage their children's feelings of guilt by overreacting to and labeling their children's behavior as awful and criminal. "These children cannot escape the feeling of guilt no matter how exemplary their behavior" (Kessler, 1966, p. 59). Manifestations of guilt in children include remorse (self-hate), accident proneness, punishment seeking, depression, low self-esteem, and irrational fears. Common behavioral concomitants include lying, stealing, and physical violence.

The feelings of anger, anxiety, and guilt are sometimes experienced almost simultaneously by the child. One reason for this is that the child oftentimes tries to cover-up feelings through the use of such defense mechanisms as rationalization ("I couldn't help it, he started it"). The relationship of anger to guilt is that children come to despise and hate themselves for their morally corrupt thoughts and wishes as well as behavior. Anxiety and guilt tend to go together because children who feel continuously bad about themselves because of their sinful behavior begin to anticipate the punishment that awaits all sinners. Dangerous situations contain the seeds of imminent justice and the child never knows, as Jane Kessler cleverly observes, whether he will be the one to be eaten by the lion.

Two of the irrational beliefs underlying excessive guilt feelings in children appear to be "There are certain things that I do that are wrong and when I do them I am a bad and sinful person who deserves to be punished" and "I deserve whatever I get because I have done such a bad thing and I'm such a horrible person." Ellis et al. (1966) illustrate the cognitive psychology of guilt in children:

> Once, however, he performs an unmitigatedly heinous antisocial act he also knows that he may repeat a similar act anytime in the future; and this knowledge of his past and possible future immorality may keep him conceiving of himself as an arrant failure or sinner who is *hopelessly* immersed in failure (or iniquity) . . . He tends to denigrate himself morally, to feel that his entire being is worthless, and, therefore feels guilty or sinful. [pp. 40–41]

Jealousy

Jealousy is an emotion which most people seem to understand and which most people admit to having experienced at some time in their lives. It is also an emotion which has escaped the concentrated focus other emotions have received by cognitively-oriented theorists. Jealousy overlaps significantly with, appears to derive from as well as lead to, other feelings such as fear and anxiety, anger and rage, and worthlessness. Jealousy when used to describe the feelings of adults derives largely and commonly from a person suspecting the unfaithfulness of an intimate other, being apprehensive about the loss of another's exclusive attention, and being hostile toward and intolerant of the rival suspected of enjoying an advantage (adapted from Webster's New Collegiate Dictionary, 1977). A typical sequence of disturbed thoughts in adults that follows both real and imagined unfaithful acts and which create feelings of intense jealousy are as follows (from Hibbard, 1977): (1) "My spouse or lover might be intimate with someone else. I might be compared and might not be as good or as thoughtful. That would be awful!"; (2) "He or she might leave me. Others would find out. I would look foolish. I could not stand that!"; (3) "You upset me. My unhappiness is all your fault. You have no right to do that!"; and (4) "I should have tried harder. I'm a failure. I need someone to love me. I can't live without him." At various points in this sequence, the individual might show anxiety (because he or she is being compared to another person), embarrassment (because other people might find out), anger (because the person has no right to cause unhappiness), or low self-esteem and depression (because he or she feels unloved and unlovable).

The underlying irrational beliefs in the above sequence relate to the need for approval, to notions of self-worth, to the awfulness of being frustrated, to the false idea that human misery is externally caused, and to the irrational notion that one needs someone to depend and rely on. Feelings of inferiority and insecurity lead to errors of inference, selective abstraction, and other cognitive distortions that lead to jealousy. People who feel insecure rely on others to define their self-worth. Thus, if something causes an insecure person to question whether or not their spouse cares for them, a jealous reaction may develop (Hibbard, 1977). The general cognitive steps that lead to debilitating and irrational jealousy have been described by Butler (1980) as follows.

1. I need everybody's approval. To have this I must be better than everybody else.

2. If I'm not more successful, I will be compared and won't be as good. People won't like me. That would be horrible.

3. It's their fault that I'm unhappy. He has no right to be better than me.

4. I should have tried harder, I'm a failure. [p. 5]

Our alternate formulation of the cognitive steps that lead to jealousy is as follows (adapted from Butler, 1980; Walen et al., 1980):

1. I need your love and all your attention.
2. If you are with someone else, or not attending to me, it's not fair to me and is horrible for me.
3. I can't stand that situation. I hate you for doing this to me. I'll get back at you.

As would be expected, jealousy derives from different external sources in children than in adults and is expressed differently. The underlying belief system, however, appears similar. The feelings of jealousy and envy though different are often indistinguishable in children. Whereas jealousy stems from one's intolerance of a rival for possessing what one regards as being one's own possession or due, envy stresses a coveting of something which belongs to another or something (success, luck) which has come to another (adapted from Webster's Collegiate Dictionary, 1971). Envy is a painful awareness that someone else is enjoying an advantage and you would like to possess or experience the same advantage.

Ellis et al. (1966) indicate that one of the main causes of anger in children is jealousy and envy. "They see some child with more toys, more money, or more abilities than they possess. They become terribly frustrated because he has more and that makes themselves angry about their frustration" (p. 119). According to Ellis, jealousy stems from children believing they amount to very little as people because another child of whom they are jealous has certain things they want. Envy derives from children's belief that the world is horribly unfair for depriving them of its benefits.

We believe the general cognitive steps to jealousy in children are:

1. When I compare myself with you (on the basis of some measure of success such as size of present, winning a contest, number of friends), I do not seem very worthwhile and loved and that is awful ("I'm a failure," "I'm unlovable," "I should have tried harder").

2. Because you are more successful and loved than me (and because others can see this to be the case), I feel embarrassed, I might lose my friends, people will hate me, and that is intolerable.

3. You are to blame for all my problems. You have no right to do that. You are an ass and I hate you.

The first two steps lead to progressively greater amounts of anxiety and low self-esteem, whereas the third adds the affective component of anger. There appear two central irrational beliefs underlying jealousy and envy in children: (1) To be happy, I need other people to approve of me and to show their approval, and (2) I should not be deprived, disadvantaged, and do without.

The destructive effects of jealousy in children can be observed in severe instances of sibling rivalry. The irrational belief underlying sibling rivalry appears to be "I must be better than my sibling in all respects to show that I am not inferior." The variety of competitions that siblings play who endorse this belief are tests of each other's self-worth. Other deleterious effects of inter-sibling rivalry are that the siblings are constantly vying for the love and attention of their parents which serves to create a stressful and tense environment at home. They often develop profound hate for each other, sabotage each others' efforts, compulsively play games not for enjoyment but to take each other apart, and avoid areas of endeavor where the other sibling does very well and where he or she believes they cannot do better (Ellis et al., 1966).

BEHAVIORAL PROBLEMS

Emotions and behavior are often highly interrelated and reciprocally influence one another. Both stem largely from our perceptions, interpretations, and cognitive appraisals of antecedent and consequent events, from our evaluation and interpretation of the effectiveness, appropriateness, and quality of our ongoing behavior, and from our evaluations of the pleasantness and unpleasantness of the somatic sensations we call feelings and emotions. Emotions and behavior can be viewed as flowing together—emotions changing in the context of our ongoing behavior and our behavior being modified by the type and severity of accompanying emotional reactions. The following discussion reveals the commonalities in irrational beliefs and faulty reasoning that underlly emotions and behavior. Our intent is to describe some of the more common maladaptive behaviors in childhood from an RET perspective. We do not believe, however, that a child who infrequently demonstrates one of these problems is maladjusted. Other factors such as historical duration of problem, number, severity, and frequency of problems need to be assessed before a judgment of psychopathology or abnormality can be made.

It is possible for a person to demonstrate inappropriate behavior without the intervention of an emotional response. We tend to think of two types of dysfunctional cognitive chains: *cognitive-emotive* and *cognitive-behavioral*. Dysfunctional cognitive-emotive links involve the person upsetting himself through the advent of irrational ideas and faulty reasoning. RET is mostly concerned with the characteristics of cognitions which lead to emotional upset. Quite frequently, but not always, extreme emotionality will manifest itself in observable behavior. In these instances, we can trace the cognitive antecedents of maladaptive behavior to those faulty and distorted cognitions which underlie the primary emotional upset. In certain instances, a person's cognitions may lead directly to maladjusted behavior. Dysfunctional cognitive-behavioral links derive from a person *mistakenly thinking* that a given course of action will achieve certain goals, from *failing to think through* alternatives, consequences, and sequences of action which might be employed in a situation, and sometimes from *failing to think much at all*. Behavior which derives from ignorance of what to do in a situation, or from thinking what one is doing is adaptive when objectively it is counter-productive, is frequently not motivated by emotional upset. If we consider the two dimensions of inner speech described in Chapter 1, we can see that certain behaviors are produced and maintained by the instrumental dimension without an accompanying affective component. (Childhood behavioral problems—shyness, impulsivity—which arise from faulty cognitive-behavioral links will be discussed in Chapter 8.)

Lying

RET takes the position that dishonesty is not innately nor always morally wrong, that lying should not always be stamped out at all cost to the child, and that children who lie are not predestined to a life of crime in the streets. Lying may be considered wayward not simply because it is dishonest, but because it is usually self-defeating. There are a number of reasons that children lie. A common one that does not appear to be necessarily related to psychological maladjustment is the avoidance of punishment. Children oftentimes get punished for telling the truth. Parents' sense of outrage upon learning about their child's mistakes or poor behavior indirectly encourages lying. Parents who express negative reactions to their child abet dishonesty, for no one including children likes to admit mistakes that would cause others to damn them. It therefore appears perfectly normal for some lying to occur.

Lying becomes a problem when it is done as a way of avoiding the realities of life and as a way of bolstering one's "ego" in the eyes of others. Seldom does procrastination, escapism, or ego boosting enhance the accomplishment of one's goals in life. The boy who proudly announces to his father that he scored a goal will, when caught lying, lose rather than gain self-respect. When children lie to avoid having to do homework, more likely than not their chances for academic success which they indubitably crave are further compromised by the amount of work they have to do to catch up. So pathological lying is done as a way of avoiding the shame and frustration of some personal failure or shortcoming. As Ellis et al. (1966) have written, lying itself is not the issue, it is the *reason* for it that must be sought after, uprooted, and handled appropriately.

There appear to be three main irrational ideas underlying maladaptive lying in children. One is the idea that "I must behave perfectly and be totally achieving in all regards to be worthwhile." A second related idea is that "when I behave or achieve poorly I am blameworthy and deserve to be punished." These two beliefs lead children to lie in order to avoid feeling guilty, embarrassed, and worthless. The third major irrational belief underlying is that "Children cannot stand nor tolerate difficult or frustrating situations." Children who experience high amounts of discomfort anxiety related to accomplishing such tasks as homework and schoolwork, and doing chores around the house, frequently lie to hide their inability to deal with the frustration of hard work.

Tattling

Just as some kinds of lying are not all that unhealthy, it is sometimes the case that children who tell things about their peers to parents and teachers that their peers would not like them to tell do so for benign and innocent reasons. Tattling especially in combination with other problems is of concern when children do it to try to elevate themselves in the eyes of authority figures as well as when it's done as an expression of their moral outrage about the behavior of another.

Mary tattles on Susie and Janie because she moralistically feels that they have done the wrong thing, that she would never do anything similar, that they therefore deserve to be punished, and that she should be seen as the fair-haired girl of the neighbourhood for not doing what they did. [Ellis et al., 1966, p. 162]

Tattling stems from a child's feelings of hostility to and jealousy of others and is based on the irrational ideas that "Certain acts are awful and wicked and those who perform them should be severely punished" and "In order for children to be worthwhile, they must be approved of by their parents and teachers."

Cheating

There are any number of explanations as to why children cheat. RET's distinctive contribution is that it considers cheating—as it does most problems of maladjustment—a product of the child's irrational belief system. Children who cheat share similar views about life as those children who lie. Children who misrepresent things to others concerning what they have done and who cause others to accept as true things that are invalid often have profound senses of personal inadequacy. They seem to believe they are worthless unless their performance is up to a certain arbitrarily set standard. So children who cheat on examinations have little confidence in themselves and have the idea that they must do well in order to be approved of by their significant others. The philosophical value system and psychological roots of cheating in children which constitute invalid personal hypotheses are revealed in the following irrational beliefs (adapted from Ellis et al., 1966):

1. It is terrible and horrible for me to fail on an exam.
2. I would be a total idiot if I did fail.
3. I cannot risk the shame and embarrassment of failure and therefore I must do well on this test.
4. Because I have always cheated on tests and have somehow managed to pass, I will never be able to pass unless I continue to cheat.

At the same time, children who cheat (Ellis refers to them as "perennial goofers") often believe that because they find something hard (such as studying, cleaning a room, losing a game), they cannot tolerate the feelings that accompany frustration and therefore look for easy ways out.

Stealing

As is the case with other conduct problems, stealing is not always a sign of profound maladjustment. For when stealing is done for reasons of deprivation, absentmindedness, at an early age when children do not know what they are doing, or when it represents some kind of adaptive living skill within a subculture it may be considered more normal than abnormal. However, when it occurs persistently and when it results from a negative view of oneself and the world, then it represents a problem that prevents the young person from achieving important goals in life.

Stealing in its serious form is an outcome or symptom of a distorted view of life. In trying to understand stealing behavior, we ask what must children believe that would lead them to steal. Stealing can be viewed as compensating for underlying feelings of anger or inferiority that derive from two irrational beliefs. When stealing serves an ego boosting function, it stems from a child's belief that "I'm not getting what I need (love, approval, school success), I am worthless, and I'm going to take whatever I can to make me feel good." Children who feel that they are not getting enough love and approval from parents and others compensate for their feelings of inferiority by stealing. For children who feel "socially inferior," stealing may serve to impress and win over friends. In children who view themselves as "dummies" because of poor school performance, preoccupation with the interstices of stealing may bring welcome stimulation, entertainment, and diversion from the boring and ego deflating experiences associated with school. These children appear to demand that because things are going so horribly, they must have an immediate "hit," "fix," or "high" that they get from stealing. Children also steal because they are envious of others' advantages and irrationally believe that because they are not getting their fair share, the world is unfair and unjust. These children frequently described as "injustice collectors" steal out of a sense of feeling mistreated and of being deprived.

Bard (1980) identifies another irrational and antiempirical idea that may account for stealing: "I won't get caught, and even if I do, it's not such a big deal." Children who have a history of getting away with misconduct increasingly believe that their parent will always be there to rescue them and that they are immune from prosecution.

Bullying

Not all instances of physical violence in children are signs of an underlying distorted view or illogical reasoning. Up through the early secondary years, children are frequently getting into scrapes and expressing their opinions with their fists. While many adults find any expression of physical violence as being morally bad (especially in children) and a possible foreshadowing of dire things to come, RET takes the relativistic moral position that it is only when fighting significantly compromises the welfare of the combatants that it becomes a problem. Children who *constantly* threaten, intimidate, and employ vicious bullying tactics most likely have some underlying distorted view that had better be corrected.

Bullying often stems from the irrational idea that "To be approved of, loved and to feel worthwhile, I must be the strongest on my block." Children who endorse this idea often have chronic levels of low self-esteem, frequently perform poorly in school, and employ their physical prowess as a criteria for judging and establishing their self-worth. These children feel inferior in the company of their peers and to compensate for such feelings and to establish a place or self-definition in their group force and threaten others to act weakly (Ellis et al., 1966). Other children who equate their self-esteem with their capacity to intimidate others are often small physically, believe that muscle power rather than brain power is the key to success in school, and do not feel badly overall about themselves. This kind of macho nonsense permeates the subculture of males in our society. Some bullies believe that the only way they can prove they are men is through demonstrating to their peers and classmates through the use of physical force that they can make the world run their way. This kind of attitude is sometimes but certainly not always combined with a youngster's sense of inferiority. We frequently see children in the late primary and early secondary grades who are referred for fighting. A large percentage of these children are successful in their schoolwork, are reasonably attractive, and are not using their fighting to compensate for low self-esteem. These young-sters set extremely high standards for themselves (as do their parents) and grandiosely and continuously strive to be "king of the hill" in all areas of life. They perfectionistically believe that they must be the best at all academic, athletic, and social activities, and they must be seen as the strongest too. The distinction we are making is between children who terrorize others as a way of compensating for feelings of inadequacy and those children who feel reason-ably good about themselves and seek to feel even better by achieving ultimate control over others.

Vandalism

There are a number of causes of physical destructiveness in children. These had better be explored before a decision can be made concerning the seriousness of the act. Children may destroy property because they are not old enough to know better. Ellis et al. (1966) suggest that children may be curious about something and destroy it in the process of exploring its characteristics or they may be ignorant of societal attitudes toward the property rights of others and that it is not a good idea to have fun at the expense of destroying someone else's property. They also indicate that some kinds of petty vandalism occur because of peer group pressures and youngsters wanting either to show off or save face with their friends. In these instances, the causes of vandalism are not lodged in the philosophical views of the child and a course other than counseling or psychotherapy would be in order.

Children who destroy their environment because of the disturbed ways they think about themselves and deal with frustration require help. Ellis et al. (1966) list five pathological reasons why children engage in physically destruc-tive behavior.

1. They are hostile and want to wreak vengeance on other people and their possessions.

2. They feel weak and want to compensate for these feelings by showing how powerful they can be.

3. They are overly frustrated because they cannot compete in some aboveboard manner, so they sometimes resort to underhanded or sneaky kinds of destructiveness in order to "win."

4. They are terribly unhappy about something and find they can divert themselves from their unhappiness, at least temporarily, by being destructive.

5. They want to show off before others and can think of no better way of doing so than by breaking windows, ripping up furniture, or indulging in some form of sabotage. [p. 171]

As is the case with children who steal, destructive children often believe they are basically worthless and may demand that the world should not thwart them in any way. The adolescent who upon learning of a new dress restriction at school paints his principal's name across the walls of the bathroom is angry and destructive because he consistently over and over again tells himself that "They have no right to tell me how to dress; it is unfair and intolerable!" The student who consistently receives subpassing grades and who as a consequence views himself as a vegetable growing between the peas and corn, may as a result of frustration with himself commit various kinds of sabotage.

Exceptions to this view of vandalism may, however, be observed in the severely disordered aggressive and destructive behavior of the older "juvenile delinquent." There are certain youngsters whose destructive behavior does not appear motivated by feelings of anxiety, anger, and inferiority and who appear to enjoy a relatively normal mental status. Their behavior seems explicable by the belief that "destroying is enjoying" (Bard, 1980). While irrational ideas may have at one time led to their antisocial behavior, they do not appear to cause some of their current behavior. These adolescents would probably be classified as DSM-III as manifesting a *conduct disorder* (lying, stealing, fighting, underachievement, truancy, resisting authority, early and aggressive sexual behavior, excessive drinking, use of illicit drugs). As these youngsters reach 18 years of age their conduct disorder will often develop into and be classified as an *antisocial personality disorder*.

Underachievement

Underachievement is not necessarily the same thing as poor achievement for whereas the latter may be consistent with low academic aptitude of the student, the former refers to the discrepancy between high scholastic aptitude and low achievement. There are many youngsters in schools whose academic performance is poor because of the way they look upon and evaluate themselves and others' opinions of themselves. To paraphrase Ellis, an underachiever is a nonstupid person who behaves stupidly. Underachievers set unrealistically high expectations for personal achievement and place undue importance on the importance of others' opinions of them. Underachievers view their self-worth as equaling their academic performance and believe that other people will reject and condemn them if they do not perform as they think others expect them to do. Many of these children combat their fears of failure and rejection and feelings of worthlessness by not trying. Since they are convinced because of a low opinion of themselves that they cannot be totally successful (which they can never be even if they had high self-regard and superior ability), they put in only marginal effort at best. These children are often so totally obsessed with the idea that it would be awful to do poorly they are forever being distracted from their work.

The irrational beliefs that contribute to underachievement are similar to those that underly anxiety and low self-esteem. Some of the major ones and their corollaries are (from Ellis et al., 1966):

1. I must prove myself a thoroughly competent and adequate achiever or at least have a real skill in something important to me.
2. I must be totally successful and be the best in my school work or I am hopeless and worthless.
3. I must do well and win the approval of others for my performances or else I will rate as a rotten person.

Glicken (1968) indicates that one of the most frequently given reasons for a school referral being made to a counselor is underachievement. By attending closely to children's self-reports of their thoughts he has, as the following excerpt reveals, tapped into the underachievers' need for perfectionistic achievement, love, and approval as well as their extreme tendencies to awfulize:

> Very often the underachiever is a relatively bright child so brainwashed into perfectionistic thinking by his demanding parents that school becomes a nightmare of continual defeat. The underachiever often is convinced that unless he can do virtually everything well, he is really a terribly worthless person. If he fails to achieve competence in a subject quickly, he gives up. Effort, he irrationally maintains, might indicate that he really isn't a very competent person. After all, he might really try to master a subject and only get a B or a C, and that, he equally illogically declares, would be catastrophic, indicative of the fact that he really *is* the worthless, inadequate person he believes himself to be. Consequently, the defeatist attitude or belligerent facade is often an excellent coverup for his own fears (Glicken, 1967). Not trying but still passing gives him the excuse that had he *tried* harder, he would have done better. He easily lapses into lethargy, continues avoiding the issue, and is, to all practical outward appearances, poorly motivated. On the contrary, the underachiever in almost all instances is a terribly ambitious, power hungry, perfectionistic child. [p. 265]

Bard (1980) discusses the underlying beliefs underachievers hold with respect to themselves and their school performance. He indicates that many of these beliefs are in response to parental attitudes and behavior. One ubiquitous irrational idea is "If I can't be the best and get the best grades all the time, there is no use in doing anything." Bard indicates that this idea occurs in the children of parents who are not interested in anything but the best performance, who demand that their child be the best, and who impose unrealistically high standards. Other underachieving children may have built up perfectionistic rating scales as a result of self-perceived inadequacies in other areas (e.g., "Because I'm not as big and strong and fast, I'm not as good") (Bard, 1980). Parents who express little interest in the schoolwork of their children may provoke in their children the irrational notion that it does not make any difference how they do in school. Finally, Bard describes a group of parents who put down their children for less than perfect performance and as a consequence their children believe they are too dumb to do any better.

Recently, Bard and Fisher (1983) have identified five irrational beliefs (faulty assumptions) of adolescents which appear to underly underachievement which is *not* primarily related to other more perverse emotional disorders.

1. *Everything will turn out O.K. whether I work or not.* These authors indicate that this belief tends to be supported by parents who are overindulgent with their child, reward their child before rather than after effort or performance, are materialistic, and who have little interest in the school curriculum. Students who endorse this belief have a propensity for "dodging the bullet."

> Deadlines are extended; make up exams are arranged; homework assignments are negotiated and all the while the student manages to get along fairly well with the teachers. It is extremely important to realize that these "shenanigans" are not the product of any premeditated malice, nor do they represent any conspiracy. They are simply the skillful exercise of delay and avoidance tactics that are entirely justified at the moment . . . Our "happy-go-lucky" underachiever is not hostile. He may be dismayed by the pressure and exasperation of the persons who rag him. [p. 199]

2. *Everything should be entertaining and/or enjoyable with no unpleasantness whatsoever.* This belief tends to be extremely hard to rectify. Students who hold it often come from a well-to-do family, where the student is "doted" over, where the mother may compensate for father's strictness and anger which may lead to marital discord. There is frequently a very strong-willed and influential figure at home (father, grandparent) who controls the situation. The academic performance of these students tends to be uneven. If the student enjoys the subject or topic she will work, if not then schoolwork may cease.

3. *To do well in school would betray the relationships I have with my friends.* Bard and Fisher indicate that these students "Have been 'turned off' and alienated by the policies and practices of their parents and are ready to be 'turned on' by another set of principles, especially those which diverge from the family tradition." (p. 202) The parents of these students tend to be strict,

proper, and conservative. The students tend to hold blind allegiance to a peer group which unbeknownst to the student, may not mind if one of them succeeds academically.

4. *It is demeaning, dishonorable, and destructive of my personal integrity to cooperate with authority in any way.* The common features of families of these students are "parental helplessness" and an inability to enforce rules and procedures. Students tend to be antisocial and rebellious.

5. *Nothing I do at school will ever benefit me.* According to Bard and Fisher, families of students who are turned off to the value of school tend to be large, occupy lower socioeconomic levels, and have a resigned attitude toward their lot in life. The students are hard to identify because they may perform poorly from the very beginning of school.

We hope we have demonstrated in this chapter how a variety of childhood problems can be conceived of from a RET framework. We believe this information is necessary in order for the RET practitioner to be able to apply skills that are involved in conducting an RET assessment and intervention with school-age children. It is to these skills to which we now turn.

CHAPTER 6

RET Assessment of Younger Populations: Systematic and Practical Guidelines

In our review of the RET literature, we have discovered an impressive variety of techniques and activities for facilitating the use of RET with children and adolescents. Many of these have been described in *Rational Living*, a journal published by the Institute for Rational-Emotive Therapy, and as a consequence have not received widespread professional visibility and recognition. It is only since 1980 that the use of RET with children and adolescents has begun to be widely accepted by the mental health profession and written about (e.g., DeGiuseppe, 1981; Ellis & Bernard, 1983a; Waters, 1982b). This has been due in large part to the reputation RET has acquired as being primarily effective with verbally and cognitively mature older clients. It was felt by many that RET was too sophisticated and complex to be of any value for children given their cognitive-developmental limitations. It is the case that RET when practiced in its purest and most specialized form with its emphasis on the philosophical disputation of irrational beliefs is beyond the grasp of many children. Kendall and Fischler (1983) allow, however, that it is quite proper to utilize basic concepts of rational thinking with children if they are presented at an appropriate level of difficulty.

> As would be consistent with Piagetian theory (1926), abstract concepts, such as rational philosophies, may not be understood by children prior to the cognitive developmental stage of concrete, or even formal operations (which occurs in most children at approximately ages 7 and 11, respectively). Thus, the forceful confrontation of irrational beliefs which is often a highly useful technique with adult neurotics, may well be interpreted by the child as a scolding. Both the analysis of belief systems as to whether they are rational or irrational, as well as the effects these beliefs might have on their feelings and behaviors are likely to go "over" rather than "into" the heads of young children. This is not to say that rational versus irrational thinking may not be a worthwhile goal. Rather, it is important to recognize the child's limitations and modify the RET approach so that children can be taught rational thinking in an effort to prevent them from becoming irrational, disturbed adults as well as to attempt to ameliorate more immediate problems. (cf. Knaus, 1977). [pp. 180–181]

Our own experience with RET (and REE) indicates that children as young as five and six can be taught to think more rationally and as a consequence to solve their emotional problems. In response to the question "At what age can you start doing RET with kids?" Virginia Waters (1981) has written:

> One can model rational-emotive thinking skills for a child of any age and actually do RET with children as young as four years old. I tend to go along with Jerome Bruner's view that anything can be taught to anyone at any age, if presented properly. Although a therapist would not be likely to spend 45 minutes in rational debate with a five-year-old, RET can be successfully adapted to the requirements and cognitive developmental level of young children. Rational-Emotive therapists working with young clients are only limited by their own creativity in adapting RET to meet the level of understanding of their clients. [p. 1]

There is no question that the full utility of RET with younger populations (as is the case with almost any approach we can think of) is yet to be empirically determined. Despite the cognitive limitations of children, the Piagetian training literature does suggest that children are capable of being taught concepts and skills which according to Piaget's theory they should not be able to acquire and utilize as a consequence of their developmental level (see Beilin, 1971; Brainerd, 1978a, b). While the generalization and transfer of this knowledge to new and different problems does not appear to occur spontaneously, it appears to us that RET holds great promise for solving many specific psychological problems which are manifested by very young children. The reader may be interested in learning that Piagetian work suggests that the origins of formal reasoning are in evidence in young children (e.g. Siegler, Liebert, & Liebert, 1973). The extent to which RET can produce changes in the assumptive world of children so that they become more flexible in outlook and belief and able to solve future and novel problems which they may encounter is a moot question at this time.

In this chapter we shall initially present some general issues and concerns which have been raised in the child assessment and treatment literature which we believe are important for RET practitioners to be cognizant of if they wish to work with younger populations. This will be followed by a review of RET procedures for building rapport. A discussion will then follow of RET assessment techniques, activities, self-monitoring procedures, and psychometric instruments—some of which have been modified and distilled from those discussed in Chapter 3 while others have been developed exclusively for use with younger populations. A case illustration will complete this chapter.

As we have suggested earlier, it is important for the practitioner to assess the beliefs and emotions of the child's significant others to determine factors other than the child's thinking patterns, emotions, and behaviors which are maintaining and/or creating the problems. The discussion of details for integrating child assessment and intervention with that of parents is left to Chapter 9.

The focus of this chapter and the next which deals with intervention will be on RET approaches for assessing and resolving emotional problems of school-age children. Other cognitive approaches which can be used along with RET to deal with both emotional problems (stress inoculation, attributional training) and practical/behavioral difficulties (interpersonal cognitive problem solving, cognitive-behavioral social skill training, self-instructional training) are discussed in Chapter 8.

KEY CONCERNS

We take the position that when RET is applied with school-age children it should be done so in a way that both protects the rights and maximizes the well-being of the young client. This is the case when any form of assessment and intervention is being considered. The decision to employ RET is made after a number of issues have been considered and certain questions answered. While a discussion of these concerns would fill a separate volume, we present a number of perspectives which we believe are important for the RET practitioner to consider when working with children and youth.

To Intervene or Not to Intervene

The question which RET practitioners had better ask themselves when presented with a child who is referred for a specific problem is not "How can RET be most beneficial for this client (or for those who referred the client)?" Not all problems warrant intervention. Bard (1980) indicates that in working with clients of any age, the RET practitioner should initially determine what action can be of most benefit to the client.

> I believe that most practitioners can serve their clients in several different ways, and their initial responsibility is to determine as quickly as possible which service is most appropriate. [p. 3]

He enumerates three distinct services that are available to the RET practitioner.

1. *Direct Assistance.* Practitioner intervenes directly in the affairs of clients rather than working with or through them, i.e., transferring a student from Class A to Class B. . . .

2. *Advice.* Practitioner provides clients with information, i.e., community resources, names of people, so that they may resolve their own problem. Advice provides information or suggestions which may be aimed at something external to the client, i.e., a situation or set of circumstances which seem troublesome to the client. . . .

3. *Psychotherapy.* The practitioner provides information or suggestions which are aimed at something internal, i.e., the client's perceptions, interpretations, and emotional feelings. [pp. 3–4]

A great deal has been written in the child assessment literature concerning the importance of determining whether the problem for which the child has been referred actually exists or whether it represents more of a problem for the person making the referral. We believe this is a question the RET practitioner needs to consider before deciding upon the service which would be the most appropriate. We also take the position that when a problem has been identified, the RET practitioner should consider direct and simple solutions first before considering an RET intervention. We have found when working with school-age populations that many problems can be alleviated through environmental modification. A "rule of thumb" we employ is that children will experience the greatest amount of stress and manifest the greatest amount of maladjustment when there is a mismatch between their aptitudes, interests, and personality characteristics with the demands and expectations of their immediate environment (home, school). Simply stated another way, a child who receives little or no reinforcement in an environment may well withdraw or explode. We believe the "person–environment" match notion a useful one in searching for simple solutions. A model for matching a student's vocational and personality characteristics to a suitably reinforcing pre-vocational and work environment is outlined by Bernard and Naylor (1982).

We have found that a checklist prepared by Sulzer-Azaroff and Mayer (1977) that deals with practical issues to consider before instituting an applied behavior analysis program to be of use in deciding whether or not a RET intervention is an appropriate course of action. The checklist which is presented in Table 6.1 asks a number of relevant questions concerning whether or not a problem exists, whether or not direct and informal solutions have been attempted, and whether or not the proposed intervention has a sufficiently high priority and level of support to justify proceeding. RET (as is any counseling/ therapeutic approach) is difficult and time consuming to carry out. It requires the practitioner to exert a tremendous amount of mental and organizational energy (scheduling meetings, conducting sessions). So make sure that the situation requires RET intervention. And when it does, make sure it is employed as intelligently and conscientiously as possible.

Ethical Issues

Whenever psychological principles and techniques are systematically employed to modify the emotions, thoughts, and behaviors of individuals, a number of ethical concerns arise. The major concern is that potentially powerful techniques of thought and behavioral control will be employed to further goals that serve the best interests of social institutions rather than those of the individual. In discussing fears that arise from the specter of behavioral control, Kazdin (1980) illuminates the following three ethical issues which also appear to have direct bearing on the practice of RET:

1. The *purpose* for which behavior is to be controlled.
2. *Who* will decide the ultimate purpose and exert control?
3. Whether behavior control entails an abridgement of individual freedom.

TABLE 6.1.   Practical Considerations before Instituting an Applied Behavior-Analysis Program

1. Does a behavior problem exist?
   a. Have several people sought assistance for the problem? _____
   b. Does the person or group function very differently from the way that "typical" people or groups function? _____
   c. Have there been dramatic behavior changes? _____

2. Have direct or informal solutions been attempted?
   a. Physical examination? _____
   b. Changes in assignments and responsibilities? _____
   c. Changes in physical environment? _____
   d. Direct requests for behavior change? _____

Negative responses to any of these questions suggest that informal methods should be considered before instituting a systematic applied behavior-analysis program, but if answers are affirmative or not applicable, one is justified in proceeding.

3. Does the proposed behavior-analysis program have sufficiently high priority and level of support to justify proceeding?
   a. Is there adequate evidence that it is likely to succeed? _____
   b. Is the problem critical? _____
   c. Will the community support the program? _____
   d. Will the program receive administrative support? _____
   e. Does the behavior analyst have the competence to conduct the program successfully? _____
   f. Are there adequate funds, space, materials, and motivated personnel to conduct the program, or can reasonable substitutes be found? _____
   g. Are other community organizations unable to handle the problem adequately? _____

Affirmative responses to most of the items on this check list suggest that the most appropriate decision is to go ahead and begin selecting behavioral goals.

Source: Sulzer-Azaroff and Mayer, 1977.

These concerns are often raised informally when we discuss RET with different audiences. Our discussion and answers to these questions arise out of our own experience and practice with RET and does not necessarily reflect the position of Ellis nor other RET adherents. We do not believe that RET imposes a set of goals and values on clients. Through philosophical discussions and value clarification exercises the practitioner and client cooperatively arrive at an understanding as to those short- and long-term goals the client values and wishes to strive for. The extent and intensity to which the values of RET (see Chapter 2) are presented and discussed will depend upon the value orientation of the RET practitioner. When working directly with younger populations, we take extreme cognizance of the values which the parents of the youngster hold (as well as prevailing community and cultural attitudes and values). There are times when, in our opinion, the values held by a child as communicated through parents interfere with what appear to us to be the creative growth process and natural development of the child. These are value conflicts which require a great deal of tact and sensitivity to resolve. Occasionally, the first stage of RET practice with youngsters involves the use of materials and experiences to facilitate their self-awareness of their values as well as to encourage such awareness in their parents (Casteel & Stahl, 1975; Elder, 1972; Hawley, 1975; Howe & Howe, 1975; Raths, Harmin, & Simon, 1966; Simon, 1974; Simon, Kirschenbaum & Fuhrmann, 1972; Simon, Howe & Kirschenbaum, 1972). Once the values of a client are identified (and they are very often but certainly not always consistent with a RET value orientation), RET techniques are employed to teach clients a less absolutistic way of viewing both themselves and their world and to employ the ABC-DE problem solving model. The acquisition of a new philosophical outlook and self-control skills means that individuals can achieve the goals they value with minimal emotional upset and can prevent themselves from engaging in self-defeating behaviors which will sabotage their goals. As such, and this deals with the third of Kazdin's points, RET promotes rather than abridges individual freedom. It frees the individual from debilitating emotional distress and thereby encourages more adaptive behavior. The excising of self-defeating irrational beliefs and the "tyranny of the shoulds" leaves the individual free to explore life, experience self-enhancing activities, and to live more creatively and happily.

Walen et al. (1980) discuss two misconceptions of RET that appear to be based on ethical concerns. Some critics of RET have equated the term "rational" with "unemotional" and have expressed the concern that RET will lead people to become highly logical, objective, and emotionless. RET views emotions as extremely important motivational factors as well as essential qualities of human experience. As we have previously emphasized, RET strives for moderate levels of negative and self-defeating emotions rather than excessive emotion, or no emotion at all.

> "Rational" does not mean "unemotional"; rational-emotive theory does *not* say that all emotions are to be banned; rather, that it is not inevitable that one feels terribly upset or emotionally disturbed. Even when thinking rationally, the individual may experience discomforting negative emotions albeit to a more moderate degree. The distinction between the consequences of rational and irrational thinking is reflected in the *frequency*, *intensity*, and *duration* of the negative affect rather than its presence or absence. [Walen et al., 1980, p. 4]

Another ethical issue that is often raised is that RET, by teaching children that things are not all that bad or awful, encourages the preservation of the status quo. We believe that RET has just the opposite effect. By teaching a more tolerant and accepting view, RET encourages levelheadedness. If children are more able to control their dysfunctional emotional reactions, they are in a far superior position to take constructive action to change things. RET also teaches children to accept things as they are and not to get too bent out of shape if they cannot do anything about them. This accepting attitude is reflected in a saying of Reinhold Niebuhr which is frequently quoted by Ellis and other RET practitioners: "God grant me the serenity to accept the things I cannot change, the courage to change the things I can, and the wisdom to know the difference."

The goals of RET for children and youth are generally considered in terms of decreasing problematic emotions and behaviors as well as modifying thoughts, attitudes, values, and beliefs which interfere with happiness. There are a number of additional ethical considerations that the practitioner should keep in mind when approaching the matter of goal selection for this population. RET practitioners who operate in an ethically responsible manner had better select constructive rather than suppressive goals which provide both immediate and long-term benefits to the young person (Sulzer-Azaroff & Mayer, 1977). A RET intervention program should not only attempt to reduce problematic emotions and behavior, it should also incorporate goals of increasing adaptive behavior and pleasureable emotions. A primary means of accomplishing this end is through RET's extensive use of homework assignments and role play which frequently require young people to engage in novel activities and experiences. While this approach does not always meet the criteria for an elegant RET solution, we believe that increasing the behavioral (and emotive) repertoire of the child and adolescent will support and reinforce therapeutic and beneficial changes in the individual's belief system.

Sulzer-Azaroff and Mayer (1977) also make valuable suggestions for ensuring that the rights of students are protected during the selection and implementation of intervention strategies. They discuss a number of considerations, including (1) evidence of procedural effectiveness, (2) competency of therapist, (3) treatment and education should be conducted under the least restrictive conditions possible, (4) accountability, (5) flexible procedures so that they can be modified if the behavior is not getting better, and (6) informed consent and behavioral contracting (pp. 85–90). We believe these to be extremely important considerations which should indicate how the RET practitioner introduces RET with younger populations especially when it is done so in the school environment. We take up the issues of accountability and procedural flexibility in the next section.

GENERAL PERSPECTIVES ON CHILD ASSESSMENT

In this section we provide some up to date ideas concerning the goals and functions of child assessment which we believe all RET practitioners had better be aware of so that they can appreciate how RET assessment interrelates with other developments in the burgeoning field of cognitive-behavioral assessment. We highlight some of the unique features that are associated with the assessment of the emotional-behavioral problems of school-age children.

Methodological Behaviorism

We believe that assessment is a critical and integral part of RET practice. It is not an area that has received a lot of attention in the RET literature. By and large RET assessment is viewed as serving the function of revealing the underlying beliefs and thoughts which intervene between an activating event and dysfunctional emotional and behavioral consequences (the ABC method). While we consider this to be an essential role of RET assessment, we would like the role of RET assessment in the child—clinical and other areas to be considerably broadened. We believe that methodological behaviorism which underlies all forms of behavior therapy can be usefully integrated into the practice of RET and that behavioral methodology holds the greatest promise for providing further validation of the effectiveness of RET.

Kazdin (1978) has indicated the following five general characteristics which are common to behavioral assessment and treatment approaches:

1. A focus upon current rather than historical determinants of behavior.

2. An emphasis on overt behavioral changes as the main criterion by which treatment should be evaluated.

3. A specification of treatment in objective terms so as to make replication possible.

4. A reliance on basic research in psychology as a source of hypotheses about treatment and specific therapy techniques.

5. Specificity in defining, treating, and measuring the target problems in treatment. [p. 375]

These characteristics with some modifications and elaborations can be incorporated into RET practice with youngsters. We have, for example, begun to incorporate repeated measures of problem behaviors during RET assessment and treatment phases. We have defined the nature of the problem by specifying different dimensions of the problematic behavior such as its topography, intensity, and frequency. With this data we are able to formulate RET treatment objectives, which sometimes also include the specification of environmental conditions under which the targeted behavior is to occur as well as a criterion or standard for determining whether or not the treatment goal has been reached. By quantifying behaviorally the treatment goal, we are in a position to objectively determine if RET results in changes that are clinically and socially meaningful to the client and to the client's significant others. Repeated measures of the RET target behavior allows one to determine in a short period of time whether problematic behaviors are being influenced by the specific RET techniques being employed and whether or not additional and alternate RET techniques might be warranted.

We hope that RET practitioners will avail themselves of the increasingly sophisticated instrumentation in the behavior assessment area. It is impossible within this limited space to detail the impressive advances that have occurred in behavioral assessment over the past few years. There are now numerous books, chapters, journal articles, and journals (*Behavioral Assessment, Journal of Behavioral Assessment*) specifically devoted to the topic of behavioral assessment. (For a comprehensive review, see Cone and Hawkins, 1977b; Kratochwill, 1982.)

Cognitive-Behavioral Assessment

In response to the acceptance of methodological behaviorism by cognitive therapists and to the recognition by behavior therapists of the importance of cognitive events, practitioners have begun discussing the ticklish issue of cognitive-behavioral assessment. Kendall and Hollon (1981) indicate four specific aims of cognitive-behavioral assessment.

1. To study the relationships among covert phenomena and their relationship to patterns of behavior and expressions of emotion.

2. To study the role of covert processes in the development of distinct psychopathologies and the behavioral patterns associated with coping.

3. To confirm the effects of treatment.

4. To check studies where cognitive factors have either been manipulated or implicated in the effects of the manipulation. [pp. 3–4]

In a similar vein, Merluzzi, Glass, and Genest (1981), in their edited book which brings together current issues, methods, approaches and clinical practices in cognitive assessment, point to the role reliable and valid cognitive measures can play in documenting cognitive changes which occur in therapy, studying the role of cognitive factors in behavior change, and in understanding the process of psychotherapy. (A review of recent approaches to cognitive assessment has been presented in Chapter 3.) A summary of assessment approaches for cognitive-behavioral interventions with children is presented in Chapter 8 as well as in Kendall, Pellegrini, and Urbain (1981).

We therefore recommend that RET practitioners systematically assess the emotional and cognitive characteristics of a client, for not only is RET concerned with changes in overt behavior, it has historically been more concerned with changes in irrational ideas and emotions. RET practitioners should attempt to assess all three modes of human expressive functioning (cognitive, emotional, and behavioral) in order to pinpoint areas of dysfunction and then plan interventions around these areas. Again, we encourage frequent assessments over the course of intervention to monitor therapeutic progress. We emphasize, then, specificity in defining, treating, and measuring target cognitive, emotional, and behavioral problems. We also encourage practitioners to specify and define those aspects of their approach employed with a given young client and problem as objectively and precisely as possible so that they as well as others will be in a position to learn which aspects of RET are responsible for therapeutic change. We again express the opinion that RET assessment needs to be viewed as multipurpose. RET assessment can determine the nature of the problem so that specific RET techniques can be employed, examine the relationships among cognitions, behaviors and emotions, and confirm cognitive mechanisms hypothesized to underly therapeutic change.

A Multidimensional Approach

Child behavior therapists are moving away from a strict behavioral assessment model which mainly emphasizes the search for antecedents and consequences of operationally-defined target behaviors to "a more general problem solving strategy based upon ongoing functional analysis encompassing a greater range of independent and dependent variables" (Mash & Terdal, 1981, p. 7). As we indicated in Chapter 4, there is a greater need to take into account environmental variables (social, familial, cultural), psychological variables, and cognitive-developmental affective factors in understanding child behavior, especially for the purpose of selecting appropriate treatment strategies. RET assessment therefore had better place sufficient emphasis on examining children in terms of the variety of interacting social systems in which they participate, acknowledge the importance of operationally defining problem behaviors, and examine the role of both cognition and affect in influencing behavior. RET practitioners who work with children and adolescents have to broaden their search and scan assessment strategies beyond the ABCs of RET. We concur with Evans and Nelson's (1977) statement concerning child behavior assessment and believe it applies equally to RET.

> Behavior assessment of children can best be considered an exploratory strategy rather than a routine application of specific procedures. The elements of the strategy are complex, but they include an emphasis on the psychology of child development and an extension of the experimental method, although in practice the latter is often more reminiscent of Piage'ts *methode clinique* than a controlled experiment in the formal sense. [p. 610]

Evans and Nelson (1977) detail five common concerns of practitioners working with younger populations as follows:

1. The child's "problem" has been identified and presented by an adult and as a consequence the referral may bear little relationship to the child's own subjective feelings of distress.
2. As the child is under a great deal of social control, assessment needs to be made of the child's social–familial environment.
3. The strong social influence of the child's mediators (parents, teachers) needs to be assessed in planning an intervention program.
4. Behavioral assessment is inexorably linked with cognitive and intellectual assessment.
5. Behavioral assessment must take into account the constant changes observed in the developing child and the high rate of "spontaneous" improvement in common emotional and behavioral problems. [pp. 603–605]

The multidimensional nature of child assessment is being increasingly accepted. Mash & Terdal (1981) have written:

> This recognition that childhood behavior is embedded within normal develop-
> mental sequences and occurs within a context of social and situational influence,
> perceptions, and expectations on the part of significant adults as well as within the
> broader context of societal and cultural norms (Bronfenbrenner, 1977; Cochran &
> Brassard, 1979) necessitates a view of child behavior assessment as both unique
> and multi-dimensional, requiring consideration of the totality of the child's cur-
> rent life situation as well as significant developmental history (Ross, 1978). [p. 25]

The authors point to several generalizations which can be made based upon
this view, several of which are: (1) The assessment of childhood disorders
necessarily involves normative comparisons encompassing social judgments,
developmental deviation, and variation with respect to an appropriate reference group; (2) assessments of children invariably involve multiple targets,
including somatic and physiological states, overt behavior, cognitions and
affect; and (3) the pervasiveness of developmental change and situational
variation in children suggests the need to assess patterns of behavior over time
as well as more global situational consistencies (pp. 26–27).

Developmental Considerations

As we have discussed in Chapter 4, we are just beginning to take into account
the child's cognitive-developmental status in selecting appropriate cognitive-
behavioral procedures. The impetus in this area appears to be coming from
university child developmental researchers who have applied interests. Armed
with the knowledge that basic learning processes and abilities (e.g., attention,
memory, verbal mediation, cognitive strategy) appear to systematically develop in complexity over the childhood period (e.g., Flavell, 1982), these
scientist–practitioners have in the past few years begun to question the role of
different developmental characteristics in determining the efficacy of cognitive-
behavioral interventions (e.g., Cohen & Meyers, in press). The main work in
this area has been in determining whether children's level of cognitive development influences their capacity to profit from self-instructional training
(Meichenbaum, 1977) which is introduced at different levels of complexity
employing different teaching formats. For example, recent work by Schleser,
Meyers, and Cohen (1981) suggests that preoperational children may not have
achieved a sufficient level of metacognitive development to profit from verbal
self-instruction which employs directed discovery rather than direct expository
methods. The related research of Cohen and Meyers (in press) seems to
indicate that preoperational children would be unable to apply in a general way
cognitive self-guiding strategies. To our knowledge, there has been no systematic attempt in the RET literature to determine empirically the role of developmental variables.

There are several guidelines which we, as rational-emotive practitioners, employ in taking into account the child's cognitive status. We know from our review of Piaget that it is only when children are in the formal operational period that they are generally capable of the type of hypotheticodeductive reasoning we believe is a necessary prerequisite for disputational examination of fundamental irrational beliefs. We believe many children do not have the cognitive capacity to (1) recognize a *general* irrational belief (e.g., "The world should be fair and bad people should be punished") *when it is presented as a hypothetical proposition*, (2) rationally restate a belief (e.g., "The world is not a fair place to live and people who mistrust others can be helped to correct their ways"), (3) employ their rationally restated belief in all situations where they are treated unfairly, (4) spontaneously generate rational self-talk regarding others' behavior, (e.g., "It's okay to make mistakes"), and (5) employ rational self-talk to "cool" down emotions and guide behavior. We know from Piaget and others that children between the approximate ages of 7 and 11 (concrete operations) structure the world in an empirical and inductive manner. As a consequence, RET child practitioners employ very concrete examples and many teaching illustrations. The underlying logic of this approach is that the child in this period can be taught general attitudes and beliefs through extensive and intensive rational analysis of specific situations. For example, when working with aggressive and conduct disordered younger boys (7–11 years of age) we find that they frequently believe that people whom they perceive are "doing them in" deserve to be "done in" themselves. We have achieved good success in getting this population to change their beliefs by (1) discussing a specific situation (e.g., being unfairly treated in a math class by a teacher), (2) defining the concept of "fairness" and having them empirically analyze whether the current situation is unfair or not (this step frequently involves using puppets so that the child can view the situation from another's perspective), (3) discussing the concept of "mistake making" and explaining the different reasons why a math teacher may act unfairly and make mistakes, (4) providing a set of rational self-statements (e.g., "It's okay to make mistakes. No one's perfect; I can handle this situation, I don't have to get upset") which are modeled and role played, (5) discussing the concepts of "fairness" and "mistake making" in the context of other problematic situations (e.g., other teachers, parents, siblings, in class, at play, at home), (6) giving practice in applying the rational self-statements to novel situations, and (7) reinforcing the child (and getting him to self-reinforce) for using rational self-talk with the practitioner and in "real life" situations.

In working with young preoperational children (less than seven years), we are especially conscious of their difficulty in *readily* taking into account the perspective of others (egocentrism) as well as considering more than one relevant dimension. As children during this period rely heavily on perceptual analysis rather than conceptual inference (Morris & Cohen, 1982), we deemphasize extensive rational analysis of irrational concepts and instead, relying on the child's more advanced capacity for dealing with pictorial and imaginal representation, we employ a great deal of concrete and simple materials (pictures, diagrams, stories) which young children can more readily learn from (see Appendix A). At the same time, developmental work in verbal mediation (e.g., Flavell, Beach, & Chinsky, 1966) indicates that children between the ages of six and nine who fail to spontaneously produce relevant self-guiding verbal mediators may learn to do so from instruction. We therefore spend a great deal of time with younger children teaching them through a variety of different methods and techniques, first instructing them in acquiring rational self-talk and, second, in spontaneously uttering the self-talk.

In working with children (and to a somewhat lesser extent with adolescents) we remind ourselves that children especially at younger development levels are active learners and that knowledge acquisition is facilitated by "doing" as much as "seeing." Use of pictures ("the feeling thermometer," "the self-concept wheel," "thought bubbles") and stories may serve as imaginal mnemonic devices and enhance the experiential aspect of the learning episode which may also facilitate memory.

Cognitive-developmental research consistently indicates that while all children appear to demonstrate an invariant sequence in which they pass through Piaget's stages, the ages which Piaget proposes encompass each stage have proven to be only approximations and there are fairly wide individual differences with which children attain different stages. With this finding clearly in mind, we present a broad guideline for RET practitioners in considering the relationship between the age of the young client and selection of a RET intervention procedure (see Table 6.2). Whereas we employ instruction in rational self-statements with all ages, we generally do not cognitively dispute irrational concepts with children who are much less than seven years of age and do not dispute irrational beliefs with children much below the age of 11 or 12.

We also believe the work of a most important figure in educational psychology, David Ausubel (1968), has implications for the teaching of rational-emotive and other concepts to school-age children. Applying Ausubel's approach, it appears sensible to hypothesize that the extent to which rational self-statements, rational beliefs, and rational self-analysis are spontaneously utilized, maintained, and applied in different settings is dependent largely upon the extent to which rational concepts and principles are initially understood by the young learner. Ausubel describes this phenomena as "meaningful learning" and indicates that verbal and conceptual information will be learned most meaningfully when the learner is able to *subsume* and *relate* the new material into an existing set of meanings and understandings represented in the

TABLE 6.2.   **Relationship of Age of Child to RET Cognitive Change Procedures**

Procedure	Age Range
Disputation of Irrational Beliefs	11 years and above
Disputation of Irrational Concepts	7–11 years
Instruction in Rational Self-Statements	Less than 7 years

learner's "cognitive structure." If children do not have a context of knowledge within which they can relate new rational material, learning will be nonmeaningful and the attempted arbitrary integration of new ideas will result in rote learning and rapid forgetting (what Ausubel has called "obliterative subsumption"). Ausubel would counsel RET practitioners to insure that they provide when necessary adequate conceptual and linguistic background materials ("advance organizers") before introducing central RET concepts. In discussing the importance of having clients understand fully in their own terms the meaning of rational self-statements and beliefs, Bernard (1981a,) has written:

> If a client simply parrots to the therapist rational statements without accommodating their meanings to his/her own personal lexical and syntactic system, there will be little chance of the client spontaneously applying his/her newly acquired knowledge. It is therefore important in facilitating the process of contraction to ensure that the client uses words and sentences in disputing self-defeating beliefs that he/she will naturally use in independent thought. That is not to say that a therapist cannot teach a client a new verbal repertoire; it simply cautions the therapist that when teaching new words such as *rational*, *irrational*, as well as certain rational beliefs, that such words and beliefs be taught as concepts and principles. The meanings of the new words and beliefs must be clearly explained and illustrated. If the client is able to apply the newly acquired words and beliefs in describing the range of his/her behavior, then such words and beliefs will be more likely to be incorporated and spontaneously utilized in private thoughts. [p. 139]

RET practitioners had better ensure when working with young clients of all ages, that whatever they teach, they teach meaningfully.

It is also important that RET practitioners remain aware that the young clients they will see will vary widely in individual personality, and cognitive and learning capacities even though they may share similar presenting problems. Copeland (1981) in her review of the use of cognitive self-instructional techniques in the treatment of childhood disorders has listed the following subject characteristics as variables likely to influence treatment outcome: (1) age; (2) cognitive maturity; (3) language developmental level—as revealed in spontaneous use of verbal rehearsal; (4) attribution of personal causality; and (5) type and quality of therapist–child relationship. Practitioners then had better be guided by the individual response of each young client and be "tuned into" whether their approach is being "taken in." Frequent requests by the practitioner for client feedback (e.g., "Tell me in your own words what we have just been talking about") as well as close monitoring of client progress toward goals will ensure that sessions are profitable. It is most important that RET practitioners remain flexible and are willing and capable of changing their RET approach, methods, and techniques if after an appropriate time few changes are in evidence.

INITIAL STAGES IN THERAPY

There appears to be a consensus within the RET child orientated literature that the first stage of therapy with children (see Waters, 1982a) and adolescents (see Young, 1983) involves the *building of rapport*. This is because young clients are generally not in therapy because they want to be. For a young client to be open and self-disclose as well as to be motivated to change he or she needs to feel trust for and feel accepted by the practitioner. The second stage of RET therapy is assessment. There are two discernible phases of RET assessment. As we discussed in Chapter 3, *problem identification* involves an initial determination of whether in fact (1) a problem exists, (2) who owns the problem, (3) whether it is serious enough to warrant some form of intervention (e.g., guidance, therapy), and (4) whether RET is the most appropriate course of action. *Problem analysis* occurs after a problem has been identified and seeks to tie together the relationships among cognition, emotion, and behavior. In this section we review techniques to build rapport that have been discussed in the RET literature and we present methods and techniques for assessing a young client. It is important to bear in mind that there is considerable overlap across the different stages of RET therapy. For example, it is possible to assess a problem before a strong therapeutic relationship has been built.

Relationship Building

According to Ellis (1973a), RET is most effective when the practitioner employs an active–directive style. He also does not view a positive practitioner–client relationship as a crucial nor necessary factor in therapeutic change. In fact, RET practitioners frequently start disputing a new client's irrational ideas in the very first session (e.g., Wessler & Wessler, 1980). Other cognitive therapists suggest that cognitive restructuring procedures should be introduced with "tactful encouragement" (Mahoney, 1974), employing a "gentle directive" strategy (Goldfried & Goldfried, 1975), and can be introduced in a relaxed fashion by a therapist who employs a less active and more nondirective style (Walen et al., 1980). Recent writing which appears in the RET literature emphasizes not only that a good rapport between patient and therapist may be an extremely important element in facilitating therapeutic changes, but also other therapeutic styles can be successfully employed with RET (Eschenroeder, 1979). Walen et al., (1980) nominate the following list of characteristics adopted from Rogers (1951), Carkuff (1971), and Ellis (1962) as helping to build rapport: empathy, respect, warmth, genuineness, concreteness, confrontation, self-disclosure, the use of humor, and an active–directive style.

The relationship the RET practitioner builds with a young client is oftentimes a necessary precondition for change. We say oftentimes because in upwards of 15–20% of the children and adolescents we see, we are able to achieve positive and lasting results employing RET without actively working on establishing a high level of rapport. For the majority of young clients, however, there is a need to employ as many techniques as possible to establish a positive relationship. Many children who come to a RET practitioner for help oftentimes have a history of being in trouble and are suspicious of and distrust adults. If a youngster arrives with this attitude, it will be almost impossible to enlist his or her support and cooperation. We have not succeeded with a number of students over the years because we did not take the time to get to know them and did not attempt to build a rapport before commencing RET intervention. Walen et al. (1980) highlight the importance of the practitioner–young client relationship in terms of self-disclosure.

> For children and adolescents, self-disclosure may be particularly difficult. It is often not until late adolescence when close friendships or love bonds develop, that children begin sharing personal secrets. [p. 27]

When working with younger populations, they recommend patience, encouragement, gentle confrontation, and a generally slower pace of therapy.

We believe that three important practitioner–child relationship factors are positive regard, congruence or genuineness, and empathic understanding. Positive regard involves the practitioner unconditionally accepting the child without conditions or reservations. The child should feel she is positively regarded, accepted and respected by the practitioner regardless of behavior. Positive regard and acceptance can be communicated through the use of minimal verbal responses, nonjudgmental verbal messages, nonverbal attending, and through verbal sharing responses ("I enjoy talking with you") (Cormier & Cormier, 1979; Gordon, 1970). Genuineness means relating to the youngster in a real and honest fashion. Genuineness implies congruence as the practitioner's feelings should be "matched" with his verbal and nonverbal behaviors. Congruence then requires that RET practitioners be aware of their feelings about their young clients. Empathy involves both being able to understand the young person from her perspective as well as to be able to communicate that perception. Garcia (1977) indicates that empathy "is transmitting, verbally or nonverbally, to your client the understanding and acceptance you have of that person's emotions and the value he/she places on the presenting problem" (p. 74). Carkuff (1969a,b) and Egan (1975) describe two types of empathic responding. *Primary level empathy* involves the practitioner understanding what the youngster is saying explicitly and communicating empathic understanding at the same level of intensity expressed by the youngster's verbal and nonverbal behavior. In advanced empathy, the practitioner tries to understand what the youngster implies and leaves unstated, or the nature of the client's deficit (Cormier & Cormier, 1979). Carkuff employs a simple "fill in the blank" empathic technique for teaching how to respond effectively to students. We have modified it to accurately reflect not only a student's feeling and wants, but also thoughts.

You feel _____ because you are thinking _____ and you want _____ .

Ellis (1980d) suggests a type of advanced empathy which arises out of RET practice. He indicates that RET practitioners

> deeply sense what basic philosophies (and particularly self-sabotaging philosophy) lie behind clients' communications and significantly create or contribute to their disturbed feelings . . . It gives the client the feeling not only that they are being listened to and understood, but that their therapists understand some of their feelings *better* and more *helpfully* than they do themselves. [pp. ix-x]

Rossi (1977) discusses the importance of comprehending and responding appropriately to the developmental level of the child. He indicates that the attitude RET practitioners take toward their role with the child is a critical variable in determining the effectiveness of RET intervention. Rossi counsels that child practitioners should consider modeling their approach after someone who has proven success with interacting and communicating with children (television personalities such as Captain Kangaroo and Mr. Rogers) rather than after someone who has proved his or her effectiveness with adults.

> By clearly identifying a personal model to imitate, the therapist is opening the way to new forms of behavior. More likely than not, these new behaviors will be more relaxed, have more animated gestures, and include more smiling and laughing. If the model is envisioned and followed closely, it will also mean that the therapist avoids "baby talk" or "child language." It will mean using simple sentence structures and a basic vocabulary to communicate with the child. [p. 21]

Rossi illuminates the following ingredients and set of practitioner behaviors which make for a positive relationship with the child and which facilitate the RET therapy process: enthusiasm, liberal application of positive reinforcement which he calls praise, and a healthy amount of physical contact with the child. He indicates that the principle practitioner attitude should be "having fun" and advocates liberal use of the child's own personal materials (e.g., favorite records, comic books), games, and television as psychotherapeutic aids.

When employing rational counseling with young children, Wagner and Glicken (1966) have advised the use of a number of special techniques and gambits such as:

1. Employing the language level—or *patois*—of the child. Don't talk down to him, but avoid sophisticated or grown-up language.

2. Use humor liberally; e.g., it is perfectly sound to laugh good-naturedly about an obviously disturbed teacher so the child can learn not to take her seriously.

3. Emphasizing the self-defeating aspects of maladjustive behavior and de-emphasizing the moral, social, or disciplinary aspects.

4. Making liberal use of concrete examples.

5. Treating the child as an equal.

6. Using obvious internalized sentences as an ice-breaker; e.g., "Most boys your age tell themselves it's wrong to masturbate. Do you feel this way?"

7. Admitting that other people are often inefficient and disturbed, instead of rigidly insisting that adults are always right.

8. Emphasizing the need for homework and practice. It is useful to compare the development of rational thinking to a series of homework assignments which take time and effort but which pay off in the long run. [p. 30]

We would like to underline the importance of Wagner's fifth point. We have found over and over again that if the RET practitioner (as well as adults, teachers, and significant others) considers the child to be a "little adult" with rights and privileges, the child's relationship with adults will be maximized. Children and adolescents respond extremely well (all other things being equal) when they are treated with respect.

Glicken (1968) indicates that RET counselors need to convey their belief directly to the child that the child is responsible for and cabable of resolving many of his problems with minimal support from the practitioner.

The therapist functions essentially as an educator by teaching the child a new way of looking at himself and his world. In no way does he, as is so common in many forms of therapy, subtly encourage the child to improve by offering the child his love. The child is encouraged to improve for his *own* benefit, *not* the benefit of parents or therapist. [p. 264]

To facilitate rapport, Walen et al. (1980) indicate that it is important to dispel a child's misconceptions regarding the role of the RET practitioner and suggest providing the following kind of information: "I'm a psychologist. I help people solve different kinds of problems." They propose that this kind of introduction establishes a problem solving focus and ensures that the practitioner is not viewed by the child as a friend. Explanations about the role of the practitioner can be kept simple, brief, and straightforward.

In discussing her experiences with children who often are reluctant if not resistant consumers of psychotherapy, Waters (1982a) recommends the following orientation to build rapport:

Therapists may best achieve rapport if they appear friendly, but not overbearing, non-judgmented, and open to corrections from the child. . . . Although children do not generally come to therapy because they want to, the therapist can give the child a reason for staying in therapy. Most children have some aspects of their lives, be it friends, school, parents, or siblings, which they'd like to change. The therapist can point out how he or she can help the child change some of these troublesome things. It is also important from a RET perspective to point out to the child that your job isn't to force him to change into the perfect child that the adults in his life want him to be, but to learn to think more clearly, have better control over his feelings, accept himself more completely, and solve his own problems. . . .

It is also helpful to remember that children are not natural self-disclosers; that is, they don't naturally talk about their feelings, fears, mistakes and problems to anyone, much less a total stranger. Self-disclosure can be learned quite effectively if the therapist:

(1)   is a good model for self-disclosure:

(2)   accepts whatever the child says without putting him down; and

(3)   reinforces the child for disclosing. [pp. 573–574]

DiGiuseppe (1981) discusses ways in which self-disclosure can be nurtured after the child has learned the appropriate roles of the practitioner and acquired realistic expectations about therapy. He indicates that the roots of self-disclosure lie in rapport and trust and recommends the following three strategies:

1.   *Don't be all business.* If you initial expectations are too high, the child may find the sessions aversive and then just not talk to you. Allow the child some time to get acquainted with you through play and off-task conversation. Shaping can be used to develop the self disclosure and on-task conversation required in therapy.

2.   *Always be honest with the child.* Children are more cautious than adults, probably because they are more vulnerable. They appear to be sensitive to deception, which they use as a measure of a person's trustworthiness.

3.   *Go easily and carefully on the questions.* Children do not trust those who try to give them "the third degree." [p. 56]

Other useful suggestions for developing a relationship with a younger client include telling the child what information you as practitioner have, *not* beginning the relationship by asking questions, *not* asking what you already know, and *not* asking the same question more than once.

Adolescents also find it difficult to share their innermost feelings and thoughts with the practitioner. Whereas some young children can be very open and freely discuss their problems, adolescents as a rule tend to be more "defensive" and "resistant." Protinsky (1976) indicates two by-products of egocentric thinking in the early adolescent which may interfere with the attainment of the goals of RET assessment. The *imaginary audience* relates to the adolescents' tendency to believe that others are thinking about the same thing they are, namely, themselves. Thus when adolescents think poorly of themselves they believe others are being critical too. This tendency leads to a lack of self-disclosure and self-revelation. The *personal fable* refers to the adolescents' belief in the "uniqueness" of their feelings and thoughts. Protinsky indicates the belief that "this may apply to others but it certainly does not apply to me because I am different" prevents the adolescent from seriously considering rational principles of individual or group rational-emotive counseling.

It is easy for the inexperienced practitioner who demands quick results in therapy to come on too quickly with an adolescent client, thereby arousing distrust and driving the client away. Bedrosian (1981), in his article entitled "Cognitive Therapy Techniques with Adolescents," proposes that questioning of adolescents should be gentle and nonintrusive.

> When the patient balks at disclosing sensitive information, the therapist may respond by saying, "I know it's hard for you to talk about something, so I'm not going to push you. You might want to talk about this subject later on." Later in treatment, the teenager may well raise the issue spontaneously, particularly if the therapist has maintained an empathic, nonpunitive position. [p. 79]

Bedrosian also recommends that the practitioner's actions should communicate the following:

1. I can't necessarily condone your actions, so please don't ask me to.

2. I know I can't control your behavior and I don't intend to try.

3. I intend to separate my evaluation of you as a *person* from my reaction to some of your behaviors. [p. 78]

Such attitudes will, once rapport has been established, enable the practitioner to confront the target problems while minimizing unproductive reactions on the part of the client.

In working with adolescents, it is frequently the case that difficulties arise during the problem identification phase of RET assessment. As we have stated, adolescents are much more reluctant, vague, defensive, and hostile in sharing details of their problems with a stranger. In encouraging the adolescent to accept an open, problem focused and problem facing format, Young (1984) offers the following suggestions:

1. *Define the problem for the adolescent.* In many cases, young people who come to my attention are initially referred by parents, schools, or police. Usually to have some knowledge of their difficulties beforehand, a simple statement like "I understand you are here because you ran away from home," leads to a lively problem-focused discussion. . . .

2. *Simplifying the definition of a problem.* Many times a young client is afraid to reveal a problem because he thinks he has to tell his innermost secrets or that anyone with a problem is crazy. In order to overcome this obstacle, I will sometimes oversimplify, describing a problem that deserves counseling as hurt feelings, hassles with others, or doubts about the future. . . .

3. *Using a representative example from the life of another young person.* By discussing another teenager's problem, I am sometimes able to illustrate what I am looking for. . . .

4. *Offering a problem out of my own life.* This tactic is especially effective if it deals with criticism, rejection, and failure—all areas with which adolescents are frequently overly concerned. . . .

5. *Using visual aids.* I have found the most effective approach with the evasive or "problem-free" client is to use wall posters illustrating irrational ideas and their corollaries. I ask the young person to look at this list and see if he holds any of the ideas.

6. *Unraveling the problem with a rambling dialog.* . . . Some teenagers will come in for counseling, admit they have problems, but remain unable to pinpoint an issue. With this group I merely ask questions about school, family, friends, love life, and so on. Before long I usually perceive a problem that could use counseling assistance. [pp. 92–93]

From our experience we offer the following concrete suggestions for developing rapport with young clients.

1. Tell them your name.
2. Find out what they like to be called ("Tom," "Tommy," or "Thomas").
3. Show interest in their real life context—family, friends, hobbies, pet.
4. Find ways to set the relationship apart from other adult–child relationships. Sit beside the child, or adolescent, never behind a desk, or, for early sessions with very young children, choose a relaxed setting such as bean bags or the floor or the garden swings.
5. Guide the child as to what you expect. State the rules for the relationship. "This is not like other places. You can say anything you like. You can say just what you think and what you feel."
6. Early disclosure of feelings is helped by first suggesting to the child a general statement about children: "Children sometimes feel afraid about someone new" (or . . . "cross at *having* to do something"). "Do you think children feel this way?" "Maybe you feel this way right now?"
7. For an inhibited youngster, the practitioner may "read" the body language and tentatively put the feeling into words for the child. This can give the child confidence that the practitioner knows how he or she feels inside.
8. Show that you are a person who *listens* by not continuously interrupting, and by responding to what they have said.

Additional suggestions for very young children are as follows:

1. Use smiles and physical contact such as pats to put the child at ease.
2. "Tune in" to the child's preconceived ideas about treatment. Give the child a chance to ask the practitioner any questions on his or her mind. "You are probably wondering about me and what I do. . ." Answer the questions and explain your role in words the particular child can understand and using concepts relevant to that child's difficulties.

3. Use indirect means of eliciting information about the child. "Would you like to draw your family for me?" is preferable to "How many are there in your family?" and yields much more about the child and his family.

Further helpful suggestions for adolescents include the following:

1. Listen for the adolescents preconceived ideas about the practitioner and therapy.
2. As soon as possible, give the adolescent an idea of the time span (e.g., 6–8 sessions or 3 months) you think will be needed to work on the problem, and ask if he or she is willing to work with you for that time.
3. Where the adolescent is not self-referred, but sent by parent or teacher referral as is often the case in conduct disorders, it is especially important to establish rapport on a basis apart from authority–adult to child. Allowing the adolescent to call the practitioner by his or her first name can assist this, communicating that the relationship is one where two people are working together to solve a problem.
4. For practitioners in school settings, find opportunities to be around the client at other times than treatment sessions, e.g., sports, camps, concerts.
5. Inquire about what the adolescent is missing to attend treatment. He or she may be using the session to avoid something or may resent coming because of missing a favorite activity.

Assessment

There is no strong demarcation between RET assessment and treatment. Indeed, *RET assessment is an ongoing part of therapy*. This is due to the RET practice of continuously analyzing the cognitive, emotive, and behavioral characteristics of problems as they arise over the course of treatment, and concomitantly, subjecting dysfunctional cognitions, emotions, and behaviors to some form of disputational or other change procedure. With this in mind, we can discuss the way in which RET assessment of younger populations is conducted.

RET child and adolescent assessment is a problem solving enterprise. The purpose of the first few sessions is to identify, understand, and define the nature of the problem. Both children and their parents are interviewed to determine who owns the problem and whether a problem is present. That is to say, while children are the ones often referred by their parents or teachers to a practitioner, RET does not assume automatically that they (the children) own the problem. It is not infrequently the case that the main problem rests more with the referring parents or teachers, as their perceptions of the behavior of children may be distorted, they may be overly upsetting themselves about a relatively trivial problem, their expectations of child behavior may be unrealistic, or the way they react emotionally and behaviorally to the problem may unwittingly be causing and maintaining the problem. DiGiuseppe (1981) illustrates how teachers may be sole owners of a child's problem.

Mr. and Mrs. N. were an upwardly mobile family with rather permissive child-rearing practices. Their 5-year-old son, William, attended a special daycare program and nursery school. The school encouraged Mr. and Mrs. N. to seek help for William since he was "intolerable and constantly fighting with the other children." Mr. and Mrs. N. had no such problems with William at home. While their son frequently attempted to test the limits placed on him, he was well-behaved and intellectually precocious.

William was placed in a children's group in my office to observe his interactions with peers and to assess his ability to follow instructions by adults other than his parents. While the youngster was restless and somewhat uncooperative in the first session he quickly became accustomed to the group and the teacher. He presented no behavior problems after the second session. Contact with the school revealed an inexperienced first-year teacher who was easily frustrated when children acted out. More important, the teacher punished William in a most revealing way: He was sent to the program director's office for "special talks." William reported these experiences as more enjoyable than punitive, probably because there was more intellectual stimulation in the special talks than in the classroom. By helping the adults change their behavioral contingencies, William's inappropriate behavior in school was eliminated. [p. 55]

We discuss the interviewing and counseling of parents in Chapter 9.

In identifying the problem the practitioner is on the lookout for different types of problems. Hauck (1980, 1983) directs the practitioner to distinguish between *manipulative* (misbehavior) and *nonmanipulative* (neurotic) behavior.

Non-manipulative behavior is shown by children who would show their symptoms if they were alone on a desert island. The behavior has no ulterior purpose, it comes solely from within the interaction of the child with him or herself over some event in the person's life. Such behavior is not meant to impress, to control, or to influence anyone at all. It is simply a reaction to the irrational thoughts the child has expressed and because they are irrational, they have unfortunate consequences.

When a child develops a symptom and uses it for secondary gain, we call such behavior manipulative. Depression may now exist in order to get sympathy. Anger may gain in intensity because a child hopes to scare his parents into acquiescing to his desires. If he becomes nervous, perhaps his mother will let him stay home from school. Or, if a girl will not do her chores on time, or complete her homework, she may be doing this for revenge against a frustrating parent. I determine that behavior is manipulative if it seems goal directed. [Hauck, 1984, p. 33]

The choice of intervention will differ depending on whether the behavior appears to be manipulative or nonmanipulative. Children mainfesting non-manipulative behavior would be good candidates for RET. Their parents would be provided with rational arguments to help their child whenever he gets upset. As we will suggest in Chapter 9, when behavior appears to be primarily manipulative, much of the work of the practitioner is conducted with the parents in teaching them how to manage misbehavior more constructively. For a more thorough consideration of manipulative behavior, we refer the reader to the works of Rudolf Dreikurs.

In assessing children, Waters (1982a) distinguishes between emotional and practical problems. It appears to us that emotional problems can be equated with nonmanipulative behavior while practical problems show things in common with manipulative behavior. Practical problems involve the young client lacking appropriate behavior skills for dealing with problems he encounters in day to day living. For example, the child may lack appropriate skills for making friends. A child may lack skills in knowing how to handle specific situations such as being teased, being asked to do something he may not want to do, or getting the love and attention of parents. Practical problems result from maladaptive or nonexistent cognitive-behavioral links. Practical problems may not be accompanied by emotional problems which are defined in terms of inappropriate cognitive-emotive links. RET takes the position that when practical problems are accompanied by emotional problems, that emotional problem solving had better take place before or coincident with practical problem solving.

During problem identification, it is easy for young clients to believe that they are being blamed and accused of wrongdoing. To avoid the situation where the young client feels threatened, Bedrosian (1981) suggests the following approach:

> Now your parents (school counselor, etc.) are concerned about the way things have been going for you, and they feel there may be a problem that needs attention. You don't seem too happy about things either but you're not sure if you are the one who has the problem and I know you are not very pleased about coming in to see me. I can't read minds; all I can do is ask a lot of questions and try to find out what's going on with you, or with your family, and I'm not sure I can help or how. I'd like you to come back to see me two or three more times, so I can talk to you and maybe to your parents. We'll see how we get along and if there are any problems we can work on together. [p. 76]

Bedrosian's statement to the client includes the following useful points:

1. He or she does not necessarily accept the parent's (or the adolescent's) account of the problem.
2. The adolescent is not necessarily to blame for the problem.
3. He or she understands and accepts the adolescent's negative feelings about treatment.
4. He or she does not pretend to be omnipotent or clairvoyant, but can admit to being confused or making errors.
5. He or she wants the adolescent to feel comfortable about treatment and has no intention of force-feeding therapy to an unwilling individual.
6   He or she will try to gear treatment to the adolescent's needs.

The second phase of child assessment is instituted after it has been decided that the young client "owns" at least part of the problem. At this time, more analytical methods are employed to characterize not only emotional and behavioral strengths and weaknesses, but also the role of the client's cognitions. This second phase of assessment results in the determination and prioritizing of emotional, behavioral, and cognitive targets for change.

Most of the assessment information the practitioner collects from a young client is from a one to one interview. The practitioner at first seeks to ascertain the young client's perception of the problem and begins by helping the client define the nature of the problem and having the client describe when and where the problem occurs, its frequency, intensity, and duration, persons who are generally present when the problem occurs, what they are saying, doing, and feeling, and how they react after it occurs. The young client is asked to describe his behavior carefully so that the practitioner can get a measure of the degree of correspondence between his view and the view of others. The practitioner is concerned with behavioral overreactions (aggression) and underreactions (withdrawal).

The client is also asked to describe his feelings in the problematic situation, to indicate the variety of feelings experienced, and to rate his feelings in intensity from strong to weak. If the youngster has difficulty finding an appropriate label for the emotion, a list of possibilities and their definitions from which to choose is provided. (Exercises to develop an emotional vocabulary and to help children label their own feelings are provided in Appendix 1.) In the main, the practitioner is on the lookout for the three primary emotions of anger, anxiety (worry), depression (self-downing), and the related feelings of jealousy and guilt. (Distinctions among these emotional concepts have been presented in Chapter 5.) The practitioner will at this point have an initial idea of activating events (A) and emotional and behavioral consequences (C), is able to infer what a child is most probably feeling if he is behaving in a certain way, and what his behavior might be which accompanies specific emotional reactions. These inferences are also useful when the child does not provide full details of his feelings and behavior. It bears mentioning again that in certain cases maladaptive behavior such as aggression is not always preceded or accompanied by intense emotional overreactions such as 95% anger and that a certain emotion such as depression may not be immediately obvious in behavior.

It is sometimes useful to present to the young client the concepts of "emotional" and "practical" problems. An exerpt from an interview that Virginia Waters (1982b) conducted with a nine-year-old girl will illustrate how these concepts may be introduced.

Therapist: "I want to spend some time today talking about the different kinds of problems people can have. What different kinds of problems do you think people can have?"

Client: "Well, it depends on how old they are. If you're older, you can have problems with boys, and if you are younger, you can have problems with stopping bad habits, or at any age you can stop having bad habits. You can also have problems with natural things. Like mine when I'm afraid."

Therapist: "Do you think everybody has problems?"

Client: "Yes. At least one. It doesn't have to be big. Some can be small, some can be really bad. I think everyone has their own problems."

Therapist: "How would you define the word problem? Let's suppose someone from a foreign land came to this country and asked you what the world problem means. What would you say?"

Client: "Problem means different things. Things on your mind, things you're upset about, things that you want to do and can't, things you want to change."

Therapist: "Do you think feelings like anger and fear can sometimes be a problem to people?"

Client: "What do you mean?"

Therapist: "Practical problems would be things other than your feelings, which you don't like and want to change. Like the way someone treats you, or your behavior. Emotional problems would be feelings inside yourself which you don't like, interfere with getting what you want, and which you'd like to change. Like anxiety and anger."

Client: "I guess I understand. Practical problems would be things around me I want to change and things with me like habits, and feeling problems would be things inside me I want to change." [pp.25–27]

As we indicated in Chapter 3, clients may develop secondary symptoms of emotional disturbance when they upset themselves about the fact they are upset. Children are no different in this respect. It is therefore important during RET assessment of problematic emotions for the practitioner to consider whether the emotions which a young client may be discussing are primary or secondary. An example of secondary upset is provided by Grieger and Boyd (1980).

Seven year old Markie recently demonstrated a classic example of how one develops a problem about a problem. His mother stupidly allowed him to see the movie Jaws II, which contained a number of scary and vivid scenes of people being eaten by a shark. As she might have suspected, he found this very frightening and could not go to sleep that particular night. Putting this into RET language, he frightened himself by thinking fearful, awfulizing thoughts about this movie. This represented the first or original problem. As kids are wont to do, he came out of his bedroom several times telling how scared he was, until on the fourth occasion, he started crying. Interestingly enough, on this occasion, he told a completely new story about how stupid he was not using enough common sense to avoid going to that particular movie and for not "using his head" like his Dad regularly admonished him to do. In essence, he downed himself (1) for going to the movie, and (2) for getting so frightened. In doing this, he caused himself a guilt problem about his fright problem. [p. 51]

When practitioners begin to analyze the different cognitions which might be influencing the emotions of a client, they begin to listen for any indications of irrational self-talk, concepts, and beliefs which the client may be thinking during problematic situations. Generally, practitioners attempt to isolate the following types of cognitive distortions (from Grieger & Boyd, 1983): (1) errors of inference which refer to predictions or conclusions that falsely represent reality, and (2) errors of evaluation which involve affective judgment concerning the "goodness" or "badness" of the client's interpretations of reality from which are inferred the presence of irrational beliefs. Waters (1982a) suggests the following problem areas to assess: (1) Is the child distorting reality? (i.e., "Nobody likes me; they're all against me"); (2) Is the client evaluating situations in a self-defeating way? (i.e., "This situation shouldn't exist. It's awful!"); and (3) Does the client lack appropriate cognitions? (Lack of task appropriate verbal self-instructions.) We also probe, question and listen to hear if the client's self-talk aids or prevents the client from coping with stressful situations, whether the client thinks about different ways of handling situations in terms of possible positive and negative consequences, and whether the client attributes the cause of the problem to himself or to outside events which he has no control over. (In Chapter 8 we present more details as to how different aspects of the child's cognitive activity such as alternative and consequential thinking, causal attributions, and verbal self-instructions can be assessed.)

Direct questioning and a variety of less direct elicitational techniques are combined to get the client to verbalize and become aware of self-talk. General prompts include:

"What were you thinking when _____ happened?"

"What sorts of things were you saying to yourself when _____ ?"

"What name did you call your brother when he _____ ?"

"Tell me the first things which come into your mind when you think about _____ ."

"Picture yourself back in class, what did you think when _____ ?"

In her transcript of a counseling session with a fourth-grade girl, Waters (1982b) demonstrates how to identify irrational self-talk that creates emotional upset (anxiety), and reviews the relationship between thoughts and feelings.

Therapist: "Do you remember what your homework assignment was for this week?"

Client: "Yes, and I figured out half my problem."

Therapist: "I'd like to hear what you figured out."

Client: "Well, I give myself an overdose of what my real problem is. I didn't write it down because I remembered it. At first, I didn't think I'd be able to find out my thoughts and I said to myself, 'Oh no, what am I going to tell Virginia, I don't know.' So I slept at my Dad's house and although I usually don't get scared at my Dad's house, I thought, 'Maybe I can figure out the answer,' and I did."

Therapist: "Good, what did you figure out?"

Client: "I'm afraid I won't fall asleep and I don't know what I am going to do."

Therapist: "If you don't fall asleep?"

Client: "Yeah."

Therapist: "So what would happen if you were over at your friend's house and it's time to go to bed. Your friend gets into bed and falls right asleep. . . ."

Client: "And I'm mostly afraid if my friend falls asleep before me."

Therapist: "So you feel OK if you and your friend are both awake."

Client: "Yeah, as soon as she says, 'I want to go to sleep' I start getting worried and scared."

Therapist: "Then do you start thinking ahead and saying, 'What if' to yourself? (client nods) Like what if my friend falls asleep first? What if I can't fall asleep? What if I get scared? What if. . . ? What if. . . ? (client nods) Asking the question, 'what if' and not answering it is a sure way to make yourself feel anxious and scared."

Client: "Yeah, but I'm making it such a big thing. Really, not falling asleep is such a little thing. So what if I don't fall asleep?"

Therapist: "It sounds to me that what you are telling yourself about not falling asleep is making the problem. Are you saying, 'If I didn't fall asleep, it would be: TERRIBLE, HORRIBLE, I couldn't stand it?' "

Client: "Oh yes (enthusiastically), I'm saying that, but I don't know what causes the feeling. It just gives me an urge to cry."

Therapist: "Do you remember what we talked about when you were here a few years ago, about where feelings come from?"

Client: "I'm not sure."

Therapist: "Well, it has something to do with what goes on in your head."

Client: "Oh yes. We talked about feelings coming from what people think about."

Therapist: "That's right. So if you are thinking thoughts like, 'What if she falls asleep first, that would be awful. How horrible to be awake and alone at night.' What do you think you will be feeling?"

Client: "Scared and worried."

Therapist: "Yes. You probably would feel scared and worried and it would
               be those thoughts which would create those feelings." [pp. 11–13]

It is extremely difficult for some youngsters to become aware of and discuss their innermost thoughts, feelings, wishes and fantasies. Some of the reasons include the fact that this information is "hidden away" in their private thought (preconscious), that they have had little practice in discussing these matters with anyone, that they are afraid, hostile and embarrassed, and that some youngsters (especially boys) are taught it is not right ("masculine") to show and discuss feelings. Younger children find it much harder to introspect than older populations and the amount of cognitive material they provide is usually much smaller. With older children more didactic–expository teaching methods can be employed whereas younger children need slower paced and experiential learning activities. The use of pedagogical games and materials serves to build rapport, relax and disinhibit the young child. Do not expect to be inundated with an avalanche of thoughts from your young client. You won't be. Be prepared to be patient and to try as many elicitational techniques as seems appropriate.

RET Assessment Techniques and Activities

The assessment methods we list below have been developed to elicit from young clients their feelings and thoughts, to enable them to describe them orally in a manner which will facilitate and further their self-understanding, and to provide the practitioner with the young client's conceptual outlook and verbal–linguistic repertoire which provides the basis for cognitive restructuring. Some of the material presented can be used to not only assess the emotional and cognitive world of the child and adolescent, but also can be used in the initial stages of teaching the basic ABC's of RET.

Emotional (feeling) scales. These are aids for helping to determine the degree of emotional upset that children are experiencing. Children are given a 10-point scale such as the feeling thermometer (see Figure 6.1) and asked to describe how much of a particular emotion they are experiencing in a given situation. Clinical experience suggests that feelings of eight or higher represent overreactions and upset that are likely to lead to inappropriate behavior. These scales are useful in teaching children that their emotions can vary from strong to weak and thus may serve to expand the emotional repertoire and schema of children. They begin to realize that they have choices of alternate emotional responses to troublesome situations.

SUDS (Subjective Units of Discomfort Scale) (Wolpe, 1973). Children role play situations where they are asked to experience a certain degree of emotionality along a 10-point scale. Alternatively, children are asked to use the SUDS scale to help convey the idea of a continuum of emotions.

Emotional flashcards, emotional detective, and feeling charts (Waters, 1982a)

10 — Very very strong
9
8 — Pretty strong
7
6 — Medium
5
4 — Pretty weak
3
2
1 — Nothing happening

Figure 6.1.   The Feeling Thermometer (graphic design by Cartwright, 1977).

are activities which are especially good for increasing emotional awareness—an essential requisite for RET assessment. The practitioner and child can use *emotional flashcards* in a guessing game where each in turn "acts out the emotion on a chosen card and the other has to guess it, or each can take turns making up stories about each emotion. It is also possible to go through the emotional flash-cards and ask the child which emotions have been experienced that week" (Waters, 1982a). *Emotional detective* involves the practitioner asking the child to help investigate how either the child or different people handle their emotions and to report all evidence in the next session. *Feeling charts*, like the feeling thermometer, is a method for not only increasing the awareness of feelings but also for assessing feelings. Waters (1982a) indicates that children are asked to chart feelings according to various criteria and she provides the following example where a child is asked to chart his anger at a classmate.

Was your feeling

strong   — X — — — — — — — — — —   weak

helpful   — — — — — — — — X — — —   hurtful

pleasant   — — — — — — — X — — — —   unpleasant

long   — — — — — — X — — — — —   short

    Hand puppets can be very good vehicles for helping children gain sufficient "psychological" distance from themselves and, by so doing, gain some insight into not only what they are thinking and feeling in different situations, but also what others such as parents and teachers are thinking and feeling. For example, children who experience impulse control and anger management problems are often unwilling to provide introspective detail and seem totally unable to conceptualize the effects their anger has on others. By getting them to play "themselves" with the practitioner playing a significant other, these children seem more able to express their thoughts. By having them assume the role of others (parent, teacher, sibling), they seem to be able to more readily experience and therefore report on the effects of their behavior on others.

Thought bubbles can be employed both to convey the general idea that thoughts create feelings as well as can be used as an elicitational device for the unforthcoming child. For example, in a series of cartoons it is possible to illustrate a problem a child may be having (e.g., going to school, fighting with brother). Empty bubbles can appear over the child in each scene. Emotional expressions on the faces of the characters help dramatize the scenes and the child is asked to fill in the bubble with what he thinks the child in the scene is thinking (see Appendix 1). The thoughts are taken to be veridical facsimilies to those of the child.

The Talking, Feeling, and Doing Game (Gardner, 1973). This is a board game developed for children aged five to twelve who appear overly inhibited and uncooperative. It can be used in individual or group counseling. It can facilitate the expression of a youngster's thought and feelings. Poppen, Keat, and Maki (1975) describe the purpose of the game as follows (the cards may be modified to elicit different kinds of thoughts):

The Talking, Feeling, and Doing Game combines a variety of gaming procedures that make it enticing for children. The children roll dice and move a marker over the indicated number of spaces on the playing board. The child draws a color card corresponding to the color of the space landed upon. If the color is white, the child draws a "talking" card (e.g., "Of all the things you learn in school what do you like learning the least? Why?"). When the marker lands on a yellow space, the child takes a "feeling" card (e.g., "How do you feel when a person you are playing with starts to cheat?"). These feeling cards are probably the most meaningful ones, therapeutically. There are also blue "doing" cards (e.g., "Nod your head, clap your hands, and stamp your feet—all at the same time.") The game has therapeutic as well as diagnostic aspects. To an astute school counselor, the doing cards can be useful for informally determining strengths and weaknesses in the child's gross motor coordination, emotional development, and cognitive functioning. Each card can serve as a catalyst for interchange, but rewards also help maintain participation. After a card is drawn, the child still has the choice of whether or not to respond; but there is rarely a refusal. If the child decides to act, a reward or chip is given. The game involves competition; the player who accumulates the most tokens is the winner. Points are accumulated, for example, when one lands on a spinner space and must give three chips to the player on the right. Also, the player who finishes first receives a bonus of five tokens. Although competition is attractive for some children, others vote not to include competition in the game. For these children it appears that the noncompetitive phases of the game are in themselves rewarding enough. [p. 60]

The sentence completion technique (Elkin, 1984) can be employed to elicit a wide variety of cognitive-behavioral skills including coping self-statements, irrational beliefs, problem solving skills and emotional reactions. The practitioner develops a series of incomplete sentences that elicit relevant introspective information. Examples are:

When I arrive home from school, I often feel. . . .

When I can't do my homework, I think. . . .

The best way to get my brother to do something is to. . . .

The story-telling technique (Elkin, 1983) which appears to be very similar to Meichenbaum's (1977) *TAT-like approach* is an elicitational method which may be helpful where more direct techniques are not successful and it has the advantage of high interest in work with children. Like the Thematic Apperception Test, this method utilizes pictures of ambiguous social situations, selected for their relevance to target behaviors. The youngster is required to make up a story including the thoughts and feelings of the characters and what they can do about the situation. This can be a valuable source of information regarding the youngster's self-evaluations and attributions. Semistructured stories which illustrate certain themes may also be employed. Elkin (1983) suggests a variety of prompts which can be employed, including "What's going on in this picture?" "How will the little boy get out of the situation?" "What do you think he was thinking?"

Think-a-loud approaches (Genest & Turk, 1981) are beginning to be employed by rational-emotive practitioners (e.g., Elkin, 1983). To employ such an approach, the practitioner assigns the child a task to do and requests the child to think out loud at the same time. For example, a child who is having difficulty with his mathematics could be asked to work for 15 minutes on some relatively difficult problems. Aside from being able to examine more closely the child's mathematical algorithms, the practitioner can also get an idea of the affective quality of the child's self-talk such as "This is hopeless; I'm dumb, I'll never get this done!" Cognitive modeling of the technique by the practitioner is generally necessary in the initial stages.

Expansion—contraction (Bernard, 1981a) is a procedure which attempts to expand the abbreviated and elliptical private thought of young clients through the use of nondirective verbal prompts. The youngster is directed to describe in his own words the thoughts he experiences during a given problematic situation. As the youngster begins to describe his thoughts, the practitioner provides verbal instructions and questions such as "What do you mean when you say you thought that _____ ?" "Why do you think _____?" "What did you think after that?" "Describe to me the first thing that comes into your mind when you think about _____"; and "Who do you think would care if you did feel and do that?" These are some prompts that allow the young client to freely associate, construct, and transform his thoughts to a level of covert and then overt verbalization. Contraction refers to the need to insure that therapeutic instructions and ideas are expressed in a linguistic and conceptual form which can be meaningfully and nonarbitrarily incorporated by the young person.

Peeling the onion (Bernard, 1981a) can almost be viewed as a component of expansion–contraction and can be described as involving peeling away the layers of thought until one reaches the level of thought that is activating emotional upset. Bernard indicates that oftentimes hidden behind a facade of rational thought-statements are layers of thought not immediately accessible to the client. It is recommended that the practitioner not be dissuaded, fooled, or discouraged in searching for irrational thoughts and that it is important to keep focusing the youngster's attention on his thoughts through the use of verbal prompts. An example will illustrate this elicitational technique:

One day this therapist found a sixth-grade boy, whom he knew from a rational-emotive group counseling class that the boy attended, crying. When the boy, who was very bright, was asked what happened, he explained in between angry sobs that his Chinese teacher had thought he had not completed his homework. "I did do the homework! I did!" he screamed. He was reminded of his work in the counseling group and was asked to describe what he was thinking. Being very upset, he found it difficult to talk but managed to say, "I'm thinking she's a bitch, the worst teacher in the school." This therapist went away thinking that such thoughts, while being both rational and irrational, were insufficient to trigger the degree of upset that the boy was experiencing. Several days later this therapist met with the boy to see if any more irrational thoughts could be elicited. When he was reminded of the situation, the boy's anger quickly returned and he verbalized the similar thoughts as before. "Tell me more. What else is going on in your head?" "Nothing else," he replied. "Come on, Ian, why did you get so upset just because your teacher mistakenly thought you had forgotten your homework?" "It's not fair," he boomed. "It's just not fair." There it was. Hidden in one of the inner layers of his private thought was the concept of "fairness," which performed as the catalyst activating his anger. This discovery led to a fruitful discussion with the boy about different meanings and applications of "fair" and his belief that the world wasn't fair and that it should be. He was able to accept that there will be times in his life when he will be treated unfairly, that people aren't perfect, and that it was silly to upset himself because someone was acting out of ignorance. [Bernard, 1981a, pp. 139–140]

"And," "but" and "because" (Hauck, 1980) are extremely useful words which practitioners can use to help their young client to tune into and report automatic self-talk. If the child pauses at the end of what seems to be an incomplete sentence about what he is thinking, the practitioner coaxes and prods the client along with words such as "but," "and," "because," and other words.

Instant replay (Bedford, 1974, 1977) is a therapeutic technique developed for use with children and their parents. Bedford requests that each member of the family keep track of situations and events during the week that result in unpleasant emotions ("rough spots"). During the next meeting with the parents and child, each member of the family is requested to do a "rerun" or "instant replay" of the rough spot. Children and parents are asked to describe their feelings that each had in relation to the rough spot. The instant replay phase involves a more detailed description of the rough spots including time, setting, antecedent and consequent events. "I compare this to a television instant replay (and most people, particularly children know what these are). I usually have the child describe the situation first and then have the parents 'tell it like they say it' " (p. 183). Of particular interest is what Bedford calls *psychroscope* which is a method where family members are asked to tell their thoughts about the rough spot. The practitioner may ask such questions as: "What did you tell yourself about the rough spot?" and "How did you read that?"

Guided imagery (Meichenbaum, 1976) involves the practitioner asking the youngster to relax ("take a few deep breaths") and then to imagine as vividly as possible a problematic situation and to focus on feelings and self-talk. For example, if a male student is extremely anxious in situations where he is watched by others, such as working a mathematics problem on the blackboard, he is asked to imagine the scene paying attention to all details. He is asked to describe the scene and is encouraged to experience and communicate his feelings and thoughts associated with the setting. This procedure may be especially useful with youngsters who characteristically avoid problem situations as they prevent themselves from checking out their anxieties against reality, and they may be less "in touch" with the content of their painful feelings.

Anderson (1980) proposes that *guided fantasy* may lead to the uncovering of emotional blocks. Coming from a different orientation, he indicates that during fantasy experiences when children are encouraged to relax and let their feelings and thoughts surface naturally, "children have access to material that they are unaware of" (p. 44). He reports the following example of how fantasy helped a second-grade boy reconstruct an event and increase his awareness of his feelings and concerns:

> The counselor asked the boy to go over his morning in fantasy. He was instructed to imagine himself getting out of bed and doing everything he had done that morning. While describing his fantasy in the first person, he recreated his morning in his imagination. At one point his voice became tense, and he looked frightened. In response to a question about what he was afraid of, he related his fear of walking past a corner where some boys had once bullied him. The counselor used the fantasy activity to help the child become aware of feelings that were interfering with his normal functioning. Once the feelings were brought to the surface, they could be dealt with. Children are often unaware of the feelings, and self-perceptions that affect their behavior. Through fantasy, this material can be uncovered and discussed. [p. 44]

Children vary in their ability to sustain imagery. The following criteria have been suggested for selecting guided imagery as a therapeutic tool:

1. The client must be able to imagine a scene concretely, with sufficient detail, and evidence of touch, sound, smell, and sight sensations.

2. The scene should be imagined in a way that the client is a participant, not an observer.

3. The client should be able to switch a scene image on and off upon instruction.

4. The client should be able to hold a particular scene as instructed without drifting off or changing the scene (Marquis, Morgan & Piaget, 1973 as quoted in Cormier & Cormier, 1979, p. 10).

Labeling is a technique we use sparingly during the initial phases of the RET assessment interview. The technique is used when the youngster experiences difficulty in expressing thoughts in words. It is employed when the practitioner detects that the youngster has a private thought—social speech communication problem and not when the youngster is refusing for one reason or another to share thoughts. The technique involves the practitioner asking questions in which a potential covert self-statement is included. The questions usually begin with "Are you thinking . . . ?" and the remainder of the sentence is filled in with a thought which would if the youngster were thinking it produce the dysfunctional emotion and behavior being examined. "Are you thinking it's awful that your father walked into your room without knocking?" "Are you thinking your friend should know better than to borrow your favorite record without asking?" "Are you thinking you're dumb because you stutter?" "Are you thinking that you need to be the best player in your team?" If the youngster indicates that he is thinking "something like that," then the practitioner has started the youngster on the road to conceptualizing his problems from a RET perspective. This technique also often results in the youngster who has difficulty in putting his thoughts into words employing another language system in thinking. He may begin to think about himself using different RET concepts. Hopefully, the new language of description which is provided by the practitioner becomes integrated within, as well as expands, the youngster's inner dialogue and idiosyncratic patterns of thinking. This is another reason why RET assessment and interventions processes are considered to be intertwined and interdependent. We encourage the practitioner to fully explore and expand the natural and spontaneous innermost thoughts of the youngster before employing this technique.

Self-monitoring procedures have not been widely employed in the RET assessment of younger populations. We have adapted Ellis' *Rational Self-Help Form* for use with school-age children (see Table 6.3). We call this *HTFR form*. The first part of this form may be used during RET assessment as homework. The youngster is asked to record an unpleasant experience as soon after it

TABLE 6.3. The Happening Thought-Feeling-Reaction (HTFR) Form

1. Happening or situation (Write down an unpleasant experience.)

    _____

    _____

    _____

2. Your thoughts about the situation (Write down as many as you can think of.)

    _____

    _____

    _____

3. Your feelings (Write down as many as you can. Use your feeling thermometer.)

    _____ 1 2 3 4 5 6 7 8 9 10

    _____ 1 2 3 4 5 6 7 8 9 10

    _____ 1 2 3 4 5 6 7 8 9 10

    _____ 1 2 3 4 5 6 7 8 9 10
               nothing   medium   very,
               happened   very strong

4. Your reactions (Write down what you did. Examples: stir someone, ask someone for help, do nothing at all.)

    _____

    _____

    _____

5. Identify your irrational thoughts (Look at your list of thoughts and write them down.)

    _____

    _____

    _____

6. Change irrational thoughts to rational thoughts (Rewrite them.)

    _____

    _____

    _____

7. Your new feelings (Write down how you felt after you changed your thoughts.)

    _____ 1 2 3 4 5 6 7 8 9 10

    _____ 1 2 3 4 5 6 7 8 9 10

    _____ 1 2 3 4 5 6 7 8 9 10

8. Your new reactions (Write down if you behaved any differently after your thoughts and feelings changed.)

    _____

    _____

    _____

occurs as possible (step one). He is asked to write down as many thoughts about the experience as possible (step two). At step three he is instructed to list the different feelings he experienced and to rate each one on a continuum of intensity from 1 to 10 (the "feeling thermometer"). The different reactions of the youngster to the unpleasant situation are recorded in step four. The youngster may also be asked during the following session to indicate which of his thoughts are rational and irrational and to indicate his reactions. "Instant replay" and "expansion" techniques are employed to facilitate the youngster's detection of thoughts he may have had during and after the experience. The latter part of the HTFR Form is employed during RET intervention.

An informal assessment procedure we have developed we have called the *thought detection self-report form*. This elicitational technique asks the young person to indicate how often he thinks different rational and irrational thoughts (from "I never think like this" to "I frequently think like this"). The thoughts that are listed are provided by the practitioner and vary depending upon whether or not the practitioner wishes to conduct a broadly focused or problem specific assessment. An example of a broadly focused *thought detection self-report form (Trait)* is presented in Table 6.4. A "state" version of the *thought detection self-report form* involves the youngster answering questions concerning the different things he is thinking about himself and other people and situations *at this very moment*. Practitioners can develop their own alternatives depending upon the presenting problem.

Another informal self-report procedure we call the *analogue survey of cognitions, affect, and behaviors* involves a type of analogue assessment (see Table 6.5). The client reads a short vignette of a potentially upsetting experience which he is asked to imagine. The situation can occur at school or at home, may involve failure, rejection, conflict, and frustration and may be focused on the youngster interacting with another peer (classmate, sibling) or adult (parent, teacher). There are three assessment scales which focus on thoughts, feelings, and behaviors. An examination of the relationships between rational

TABLE 6.4. **Example of a Thought Detection Self-Report Form (Trait)**

Directions: Place a mark (x) in the space which indicates how often you generally think this kind of thought.

	Never	Sometimes	Very Frequently
1. That boy is an idiot.	_____	_____	_____
2. I wish I did better in maths class.	_____	_____	_____
3. I'm no good.	_____	_____	_____
4. I can't stand it when my teacher doesn't call on me when I raise my hand in class.	_____	_____	_____
5. I don't like doing the dishes.	_____	_____	_____
6. I am finding it impossible to do my homework.	_____	_____	_____

TABLE 6.5.   An Example of the Analogue Survey of Cognitions, Affects, and Behaviors

Directions: On this page is an event or situation that could happen at home or at school. Imagine you are part of what is happening. Circle the numbers that are closest to how you would think, feel and behave.

> Your parents have just returned home from a parent–teacher interview. They tell you they are terribly disappointed with the report they were given.

I would think:	Strongly Disagree	Disagree	Agree	Strongly Agree
1. I wish I had worked harder.	1	2	3	4
2. I'm a total idiot.	1	2	3	4
3. I don't like disappointing my parents.	1	2	3	4
4. Everything is my fault.	1	2	3	4
5. I will work harder next time.	1	2	3	4
6. It's the worst possible thing that could happen.	1	2	3	4

I would feel:	Very Little	A Medium Amount	A Lot	The Most
1. Angry	1	2	3	4
2. Depressed (very unhappy)	1	2	3	4
3. Afraid	1	2	3	4
4. Nervous (sick in the stomach)	1	2	3	4
5. Worthless (inferior)	1	2	3	4
6. Guilty	1	2	3	4

I would behave by:	Very Unlikely	Unlikely	Likely	Very Likely
1. Kick or punch something.	1	2	3	4
2. Ask them for help so I can improve my next report.	1	2	3	4
3. Do nothing at all.	1	2	3	4
4. Explain to my parents why my report was so bad.	1	2	3	4
5. Cry and run to my room.	1	2	3	4
6. Scream at my parents.	1	2	3	4

and irrational thoughts and emotional–behavior reactions is possible. The practitioner is able to tailor specific vignettes to focus on problem areas of the individual youngster. While we are moving to standardizing this instrument, at present we use it informally during our interview with the youngster.

As we have indicated, behavioral self-monitoring procedures can be employed along with RET. After a problem has been operationally defined, we may ask the youngster to monitor the frequency of occurrence of problem behaviors (e.g., verbal and physical fights, contacts with members of the opposite sex, questions asked in class, time spent helping around the house).

An illustration of how behavioral self-monitoring procedures can be employed along with traditional RET procedures is provided later in this chapter.

There are three rational belief scales that we are aware of which have been developed for use with school-age children (see Appendix 2). Knaus (1974) presents the *children's survey of rational beliefs* (form B and form C) for children between the ages of 7 and 12. These two inventories have a multiple choice format and contain questions which assess a variety of aspects of the child's belief system. *The idea inventory* was developed by Howard Kassinove and Richard Crisci and is designed to examine the extent to which children agree to disagree with certain irrational ideas and manifest maladaptive emotional reactions (Kassinove, Crisci, & Tiegerman, 1977). The essential difficulty with these scales is the relative absence of reliability, validity, and normative data. A recent study (Briley, 1980) indicates a high correlation between the idea inventory and the children's survey of rational concepts (form C). These scales can be useful for gathering informal data concerning a youngster's irrational concepts and beliefs although they are used more for research purposes than in clinical practice. They should be considered as supplements to the clinical interview and should rarely be used as formal diagnostic measures.

THE INITIAL INTERVIEW

At this point it may be useful to list and summarize some of the issues to consider in conducting the initial interview.

1. *Decide who shall attend the initial interview.*   Usually we attempt to see the parents and the child during the first session. Other members of the family and teachers may also be invited. However, we generally find that we just have time to obtain the information we are after with the immediate family. Other significant persons can be interviewed later either in person or by telephone.

2. *Length of interview.*   We generally require a full 50 minutes to begin to get a handle on the problem. We usually see the parents first and separately for about the initial 15–20 minutes. The final 10 to 15 minutes is used to meet with the parents to report your initial findings. Their child may or may not be invited to sit in. This will depend upon the nature of the problem and the age of the child.

3. *Collect referral information.*   In examining and appraising the behavior of concern, it is very useful to have the parents send you beforehand or bring in the cumulative school records of the young person. Frequently, if it is a school-based problem, you may ask the parents to request the child's teachers at the school to write a brief confidential report on what they know about the problem and its causes. Any records or medical reports the parents can provide, including any

information provided by another mental health specialist who may have seen the child, is extremely valuable. The more concrete evidence there is of a history of difficulties makes it easier to confirm and verify a current problem. Reports from others of a problem besides the parents makes it a little easier to rule out the possibility that the child's problems are an unrealistic construction of the parents. Test scores (IQ, language, achievement) allows one to determine the extent of under-achievement and what is a reasonable academic expectation to hold for the child.

4. *Explain the role of the practitioner.*   Many RET practitioners prefer to inculcate in their clients an attitude of collaboration so that both practitioner and client can assume joint responsibility for solving the problem generally. RET practitioners choose not to be seen as holding ultimate answers to happiness. The role of the practitioner is to help clients help themselves through hard work.

5. *Problem identification.*   As indicated previously, the practitioner has to determine, before beginning therapy, whether in his or her opinion a problem exists and if it does who owns it. Concrete descriptions of problems are critical. To facilitate this, we frequently ask the inter-viewee to describe the problem as if it were being seen through the eye of the practitioner. During this phase, it is extremely important to allow clients to talk without many interruptions. Questions are impor-tant, however, especially when the client rambles. Discussion should be geared to current problems and if the practitioner finds parents or child providing details that are seemingly irrelevant he or she should politely but forcefully guide the interviewee to stay on the topic.

6. *Problem Analysis.*   Once a problem has been identified, it is some-times very possible—especially if the practitioner is experienced in working with the problem—to conduct a brief probe into the ABCs of the problem. That is, for example, if underachievement has been identified, it sometimes takes little time to sort out which irrational beliefs are held by the client (and parents).

7. *Achieve a consensus.*   After meeting with all parties, it is important for you, the practitioner, to attempt to arrive at an initial agreement as to what appears to be the problem. Periodically, the practitioner is in a position of having to forcefully disagree that there is a problem. During the last part of the interview a summary is made of the different viewpoints, agreements and disagreements and are pointed out and discussed, a list of problems is identified, and goals of treatment are agreed upon. Specifically, the amount of change in client emotions and behaviors is ascertained. It should be kept in mind that this list of problems will often be clarified, added to, and reduced over the course of therapy.

8. *Select a target for change.* Once a list of problems has been identified, there is a discussion as to which problem will be tackled initially. Giving the child a choice sometimes is useful in motivating him or her to change. Obviously, more severe (school phobia) and potentially harmful (fighting) behaviors may take precedent over other less immediate ones.

9. *Sensitize clients to RET framework.* If time permits, it is sometimes useful to describe the cognitive orientation and underlying logic of the RET approach. The notion that we upset ourselves and that we can learn to control our emotions through rethinking problems often has immediate appeal. Clients frequently want to know what to expect in therapy and a brief outline of the different stages, goals, and strategies gives hope, direction, and most importantly, sensitizes the client to their role and a framework which is necessary for them to internalize. Goal and value clarification exercises may be employed.

10. *Assign homework.* It is often a good idea to get both children and their parents to make some sort of observation of themselves and each other before seeing them again. For example, all parties could keep track of the number of fights that occurred during the week. Each could self-report on their feelings at these times (on a scale of one to ten), what they did, and under what circumstances. Self-observation not infrequently has the effect of diminishing emotional reactivity. Be sure to have some sort of standardized self and other observation forms available which are easy to relate to any problems which you may uncover during an initial interview. Other homework assignments can include recommended reading which you believe will be of value to clients. The references of this book provide material which can be made available to clients. Also, you may wish to gather additional test material and therefore request that the parents and/or child be tested by you or someone else before the next treatment session.

11. *Schedule next appointment.* Initially, we tend to see clients on a weekly basis until we see some improvement. It is important to negotiate a convenient time to meet the following week for all parties so that appointments are not missed. An explanation as to your reasons for needing future sessions can be provided.

A CASE STUDY

We should like to illustrate different aspects of RET assessment procedures by describing a recent referral. (A complete description of this case is reported by Bernard, Kratochwill, & Keefauver, 1983). A 17-year-old female, Anna (the "client"), was enrolled in the eleventh grade at a large private school. Help was requested from the first author to stop her from pulling out her hair. Chronic hair pulling (trichotillomania) is an extremely rare and complex obsessive–compulsive disorder. Demographic data indicate a disproportionate incidence of the disorder among females. Sexual dysfunctions, severe anxiety reactions, eyebrow pulling, and interpersonal problems may accompany trichotillomania in older adolescents and adults.

The client, who was above average in weight, was the oldest of three children, the others being a boy, age 14, and a sister, age 9. Her mother and father were born in Italy and have been living in Melbourne since the client was three years of age. Both parents were self-employed as owners of a small grocery store.

An interview with the client's mother indicated that the client had been pulling her hair since she was 12 years of age. While the mother reported no traumatic event that was associated with that period of time, the mother (and client) reported an increase in academic demands at that time. During the tenth grade the client wore a wig to cover bald spots on both sides of her head. The interview with the client's mother revealed a positive mother–child relationship. While the father was not available for an interview, the mother indicated the father had a high level of expectation of his daughter to succeed in school. The client's tutor reported that to her knowledge the client did not pull her hair in school. An examination of the client's cumulative school record revealed a very mediocre secondary level performance with the client receiving a "bare pass" in English the previous year.

It was determined that the client was in need of some direct form of intervention and a clinical interview was conducted. The client reported that she wanted the help of the psychologist to stop her from pulling out her hair (the problematic behavior). She indicated that she controlled her impulses to pull her hair in school and that it was only at home (problematic situation) while she was in her room studying alone (antecedent condition) that she pulled out her hair. She revealed that during these times she felt extremely worried, anxious and depressed (problematic emotions). Using several cognitive assessment procedures (guided imagery, expansion–contraction), it was determined that she endorsed the following irrational beliefs (problematic cognitions): (1) I am not worthwhile unless I am competent at school; (2) I must be approved by my father; (3) I must continually worry about the uncertainties of my future; (4) it is awful when my performance in school is not what I demand it should be. The client engaged in the following sorts of self-defeating verbal self-statements: "I can't do homework; I am a failure; my father would be sad and that would be awful; I should know how to do that" (problematic cognitions). While the client reported that she had other concerns involving her weight, dating, the relationship between her father and mother, she indicated that she really only wanted help to stop her hair pulling. As such, RET assessment and treatment were focused exclusively on her hair pulling.

As the client was referred for a behavioral problem (hair pulling) and since it was clear that a reduction in hair pulling was the main object of interest, behavioral self-monitoring was instituted. Self-monitoring was also initiated so that the practitioner could get weekly feedback on the effectiveness of his proposed RET intervention. This seemed like an especially good idea since there was no research (nor personal experience) which indicated that RET had proven effective in treating trichotillomania. The client was asked to record both the number of hairs she pulled out while studying and the total amount of time she spent in her room studying. She was provided with the following recording instruments: a self-monitoring form that enabled her to record the number of hairs she pulled out during her evening study sessions as well as the amount of time she spent in her room studying, and a stop watch to measure study time. A ratio of the number of individual hairs the client pulled out per minute of study time was used as the basic assessment unit of analysis. The rationale for employing a ratio was twofold. First, hair pulling was linked to the amount of time the client studied. Second, this measure enabled a more stable rate of baseline and treatment measurements to be achieved.

The client self-monitored her hair pulling and study time for two weeks on each night of the week with the exceptions of Friday and Saturday when she reported she did not study and did not pull her hair. Table 6.6 and Figure 6.2 present a tabular and visual−graphical analysis of the data she collected during the baseline assessment (A). To make sense out of this information, we should indicate that RET intervention was instituted at the beginning of the third week and lasted for 12 weeks. During the third, fourth and fifth weeks of the experiment (RET B), principles and techniques of RET were explained and reviewed with a heavy emphasis on disputation training. At the sixth session (baseline A) no discussion of RET was conducted and the client was requested to continue to monitor her own behavior. RET treatment was continued during

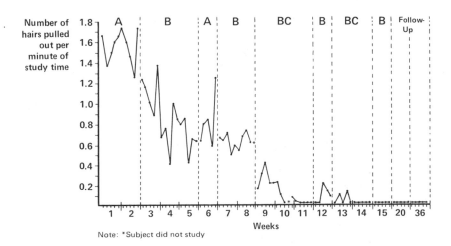

Note: *Subject did not study

Figure 6.2.   The number of hairs pulled out per minute of study time over baseline, treatment, and follow-up phases. Missing data (*) reflect times when the client did not study. (from Bernard, Kratochwill, & Keefauver, 1983).

TABLE 6.6. The number of hairs pulled during each study session, the amount of time studied, and the ratio of hairs pulled per minute of study.

Week		Monday No. of Hairs	Monday Time (min.)	Monday Ratio	Tuesday No. of Hairs	Tuesday Time (min.)	Tuesday Ratio	Wednesday No. of Hairs	Wednesday Time (min.)	Wednesday Ratio	Thursday No. of Hairs	Thursday Time (min.)	Thursday Ratio	Sunday No. of Hairs	Sunday Time (min.)	Sunday Ratio	Average for week No. of Hairs	Average for week Time (min.)	Average for week Ratio
1	baseline (A)	128	77	1.67	110	80	1.37	75	50	1.50	64	40	1.00	116	70	1.66	98.60	63.40	1.56
2	baseline (A)	151	87	1.74	120	75	1.60	70	48	1.46	45	36	1.26	142	85	1.67	105.60	66.20	1.55
3	RET (B)	118	96	1.23	99	84	1.18	82	80	1.03	52	60	.87	42	30	1.40	78.60	70.00	1.14
4	RET (B)	69	103	.67	53	68	.78	11	25	.44	45	44	1.02	111	130	.85	57.80	74.00	.75
5	RET (B)	100	125	.80	83	94	.88	45	110	.41	39	60	.65	55	88	.63	64.40	95.40	.67
6	baseline (A)	56	84	.67	50	63	.80	49	58	.85	47	81	.58	62	50	1.24	52.80	67.20	.83
7	RET (B)	94	140	.67	14	22	.64	81	112	.72	40	80	.50	11	18	.59	48.00	74.40	.62
8	RET (B)	30	55	.54	20	30	.68	74	101	.73	39	63	.62	did not study			40.72	62.20	.64
9	RET+SIT (BC)	25	150	.17	40	130	.31	25	60	.42	20	90	.22	18	80	.22	25.60	102.00	.27
10	RET+SIT (BC)	34	136	.25	7	68	.10	0	45	.00	did not study			10	128	.08	12.75	94.25	.11
11	RET+SIT (BC)	2	96	.02	0	54	.00	0	68	.00	0	110	.00	0	79	.00	.40	81.60	.00
12	RET (B)	0	20	.00	0	75	.00	12	54	.22	5	38	.13	12	117	.10	5.80	60.80	.09
13	RET+SIT (BC)	0	114	.00	5	54	.10	0	20	.00	12	85	.14	0	133	.00	3.40	81.20	.05
14	RET+SIT (BC)	0	73	.00	0	122	.00	0	20	.00	0	45	.00	0	84	.00	.00	68.80	.00
15	baseline (A)	0	118	.00	0	57	.00	0	89	.00	0	48	.00	0	110	.00	.00	84.40	.00
20	follow-up	0	78	.00	0	96	.00	0	100	.00	0	25	.00	0	33	.00	.00	66.40	.00
36	follow-up	did not study			0	48	.00	0	45	.00	0	40	.00	0	63	.00	.00	51.50	.00

the seventh and eighth sessions. As a visual analysis of the data during treatment revealed relatively few changes in the frequency of hair pulling during weeks 4–8, it was decided to introduce self-instructional training (SIT) in addition to disputational RET treatment techniques. Sessions 9–11 (BC) were devoted to a continuation of RET as well as including SIT. Session 12 dealt exclusively with RET with no practice in SIT. Sessions 13 and 14 continued RET treatment and reintroduced SIT. During session 15(baseline A), all treatment was discontinued and the client was requested to continue data collection procedures. Five weeks (week 20) and 21 weeks (week 35) after the termination of treatment, the practitioner met with the client who was asked to reinstate self-monitoring procedures.

A careful reading of the data in Table 6.6 demonstrates the immense utility of employing a behavioral self-recording procedure. A close examination of the variability of hair pulling indicates a systematic pattern. On Sunday and Monday evenings when the client indicated she was most worried about work and had the most homework to do, her ratio of hair pulling per minute of study was generally greater than on other midweek days. This relation led to the confirmation of the hypothesis that hair pulling was related to stress associated with school and homework and reinforced the need to teach the client cognitive coping strategies to manage her stress. RET, in combination with SIT, led to a rapid reduction in hair pulling by the twelfth week of therapy.

CHAPTER 7

RET Intervention with Younger Populations: Systematic and Practical Guidelines

It is quite interesting to note that up until this time there has been only one other book, *Rational-Emotive Approaches to the Problems of Childhood* (Ellis & Bernard, 1983b) which demonstrates how RET and other allied cognitive-behavioral approaches can be utilized to help resolve the emotional problems of children and adolescents. While there has been a fair amount of work which discusses and illustrates how cognitive approaches can be employed to modify childhood *behavioral problems* such as aggression and hyperactivity (e.g., Kendall & Hollon, 1979b), scant attention has been paid in the cognitive literature to *emotional problem solving*. As a rule, child oriented cognitive-behavior theorists and therapists act as though emotions play little or no role in child behavior problems and it is almost as if these scientists and practitioners have forgotten that emotions exist!

In this chapter we will describe the third and fourth stages of RET therapy: *skill acquisition* and *practice and application*. After relationship building and problem assessment have been undertaken, the practitioner begins to teach the basics of emotional and practical problem solving which includes helping the young client to become aware of self-talk, teaching the ABCs of RET, and illustrating the basic principles of cognitive change (skill acquisition). Once the basic skills of RET have been introduced, the practitioner shifts attention to helping the client practice and apply these skills in as wide a variety of situations as possible.

The decision as to which rational-emotive intervention procedure to employ depends upon a host of factors, including the extent of the emotional and practical problems uncovered during assessment, the "cognitive-maturity" of the young client, the willingness of the client to change, whether parents and teachers are willing to (and capable of) participating in a change program, time available for intervention, etc. For example, Claudio, aged 10, was referred for being aggressive, hyperactive, and for a negative approach to his school. Claudio's father, an unemployed machinist, drank a great deal and spoke little English while his mother, a part-time house cleaner, appeared extremely depressed as a consequence of the continued family arguments, her long working hours, and her family's poor economic circumstances. After several frustrated attempts at family intervention, it became clear that the father was not interested in changing so that his son might improve and his mother appeared a "poor risk" for successful family counseling. Claudio was willing to see the practitioner and, with the help of his teachers, a cognitive-behavioral program was implemented. His teachers set up a school-based response cost token system where Claudio was rewarded and punished for appropriate/inappropriate academic/social behaviors (response cost procedures appear more effective with children with impulse-control disorders). At the same time, a cognitive program was instituted with the goals of encouraging Claudio to: (1) interpret specific situations at school more accurately through an empirical analysis of his conclusions and predictions; (2) acquire more rational language concepts for interpreting and describing experiences; (3) develop a more rational picture of his self-concept; and (4) through the use of verbal self-instructions to aid his approach to his school work. As this illustration demonstrates, there are no "cookbook" approaches to applying RET with school-age children. For RET practitioners to be successful, they had better be sensitive to the unique characteristics of each case and be prepared to vary their approach accordingly.

THE BASICS OF INTERVENTION

Goals

RET is largely geared to teaching an attitude of emotional responsibility, that is, each of us has the capacity to change how we feel. Through the teaching of skills of rational self-analysis and critical thinking, RET instructs people how to become better solvers of their own emotional problems. The main goal of emotional problem solving is to teach children and adolescents how to change inappropriate to appropriate feelings. As Waters (1982a) indicates:

> Appropriate feelings are generated by rational beliefs, are an appropriate response to the situation, facilitate goal achievement, and are usually moderate as opposed to extreme reactions; whereas inappropriate feelings are generated by irrational beliefs, are an inappropriate response to the situation, impede goal achievement, and are usually extreme reactions. [p.572]

Examples of inappropriate and unhelpful emotions are when children feel very angry, enraged, hostile, depressed, and anxious while more appropriate feelings would be irritation, annoyance, disappointment, sadness, apprehensiveness and concern.

For younger children, the goals of RET can be expressed as follows: (Waters, 1981):

1. Correctly identify emotions.

2. Develop an emotional vocabulary.

3. Distinguish between helpful and hurtful feelings.

4. Differentiate between feelings and thoughts.

5. Tune into self-talk.

6. Make the connection between self-talk and feelings.

7. Learn rational coping statements. [p. 1]

For older children and adolescents, a more complex set of goals may be pursued in addition to the ones already listed (from Young, 1984):

1. Teach the ABC's
2. Dispute "awfulizing."
3. Dispute "shoulds, oughts, and musts" (personal imperatives).
4. Challenge "I can't stand itis" (low frustration tolerance).
5. Teach self-acceptance.
6. Correct misperceptions of reality.

We would again like to emphasize that RET does not lead to young clients becoming passive automatons who conform to the sometimes pernicious social influence of parents and teachers. One basic objective of RET is to teach young people to live as comfortably as possible in situations which cannot be significantly changed. We shall illustrate how a young client can be taught different ways to solve problems which up until the present, he or she either has done nothing about or dealt with in a nonproductive way.

An Overview of Intervention Strategies

There are two aspects of cognitive activity which can lead to emotional and behavioral disturbance and which are corrected through RET. *Distorted interpretations and perceptions of reality* are brought about by errors of logical inference and reasoning (arbitrary inference, selective abstraction, overgeneralization, magnification and minimization, personalization, and absolutistic/dichotomous reasoning), and can lead to moderately maladaptive levels of emotional arousal. Misinterpretations can be frequently retained by people as invalid assumptions about themselves and their world. A second and, from a RET point of view, major aspect of dysfunctional cognitive activity are the evaluations and appraisals the individuals make of their misinterpretations. These *evaluations of interpretations* which can be rational or irrational are seen to be the main source of emotional disturbance since rational appraisals of a distorted perception of reality will generally not lead to extreme and unproductive levels of emotional arousal.

An example provided by DiGiuseppe and Bernard (1983) will illustrate the differences between faulty inferences which lead to misinterpretations and self-defeating appraisals of distortions of reality.

> George, a ten year old, moved to a new neighbourhood and has not met new friends. He is sitting quietly in the neighbourhood playground while the other children are running about. He feels frightened and his associated action potential (behavior) is withdrawal. He sits alone leaning up against a wall reading a book. As he sees the other children coming, George thinks, "They'll never like me, they'll think I'm not very good at their games and they won't play with me, no matter what I do." George has drawn these inferences about the other children's behavior. In fact they are predictions about what might happen, but which never actually have. Inferences alone are not sufficient to arouse fear. Some children, although not George, might be perfectly happy to sit by themselves and read books, but George appraises the situation quite negatively and catastrophizes "It's awful that I don't have anyone to play with, I must be a jerk if they won't play with me." [pp. 48−49]

RET practitioners decide on the basis of the age of and goals for a young client whether they wish to target the client's interpretation of reality ("They'll never like me") for change, which Ellis would consider a limited solution, or whether the evaluative assumptions and beliefs ("It's awful . . . I must be a jerk . . .") are challenged. Once again, teaching clients to accept life as it comes without exaggerating its unpleasantness is a preferred goal of treatment.

There are a few basic strategies which RET practitioners typically employ to modify dysfunctional interpretations and appraisals and to teach rational thinking skills. *Empirical analysis* involves the practitioner and young client working collaboratively to design a simple experiment to test the client's interpretation of reality (Ellis, 1977b; DiGiuseppe, 1981). In arriving at an *empirical solution*, the "truth" of the client's inference is tested by having the client collect data which the client and the practitioner agree would be suffi-cient to either confirm or reject the client's assumption. In George's case, George and the practitioner could define those reactions of other children which would indicate that George was liked and those which would suggest dislike. George could then test his prediction that "No one will like me and play with me" by initiating a limited number of contacts with the children in the neighborhood he would like to know to see if, in fact, there was any evidence to support his self-defeating interpretative conclusions that he would be rejected. If little or no evidence was collected which supported George's conclusion, then his anxiety would, hopefully, decrease to a point where he would feel free and more relaxed to pursue other contacts. The practitioner could point to the fact that George's thinking was untrue and could help him to restate his ideas more objectively.

A second basic cognitive approach for changing cognitions is what Ellis calls *philosophical disputation* and is, as we indicated in Chapter 3, the core and distinctive RET intervention. Disputation can occur at a number of levels of abstraction (DiGiuseppe & Bernard, 1983). The client can be taught to question the specific appraisals of particular interpretations by examining the irrational content (and concepts) contained in the appraisal. This limited form of disputation is appropriate for children who are not able to discuss irrational concepts and beliefs in the abstract. George might be able to rationally re-evaluate his appraisal of social rejection by disputing concepts of "awful" and "jerk" in the context of the presenting problem, whereas discussion of concepts such as "exaggeration" and "self-acceptance" as they apply in the general case might be well beyond his grasp. If George was 12 or older, he might be a better candidate for a more general consideration and application of philosophical disputation to the irrational concepts and beliefs which underly his negative appraisals.

Both empirical analysis and philosophical disputation at whatever level they are applied constitute the basic components of *rational thinking* skills taught in RET. There are two other general approaches which RET practitioners frequently employ. *Rational self-statements* (De Voge, 1974; DiGiuseppe, 1975) are provided by the practitioner to the client for rehearsal and subsequent utilization in situations which tend to occasion in the client inappropriate levels of affectivity. The contents of the self-statement incorporate rational concepts and help the client overcome whatever emotions are interfering with behavior. We will demonstrate how rational self-statements can be employed with young clients as a part of *stress inoculation* in Chapter 8. George might be instructed through modeling to covertly verbalize self-statements which would compete with his social anxiety: "Just relax, George, just go up and introduce yourself. Don't worry, you can cope with whatever happens; be brave."

Another cognitive procedure which is being increasingly employed by RET practitioners with younger clients is rational-emotive imagery (REI). As described in Chapter 3, RET involves asking the young client to recreate as vividly as possible in his mind a mental picture of a situation in which he experiences an extreme emotional reaction. When the feeling is as strong as possible, the client is asked to try to change the feeling from being extreme (eight, nine or ten on the feeling thermometer) to a more moderate level (four, five, or six). For example, from extreme anxiety to moderate worry and concern. When the client is able to do this, it is pointed out that the way the emotional change took place is through a change in thoughts. RET can be employed both during *skill building* and *practice and application* phases of RET.

In addition to these four cognitive approaches RET practitioners, in helping young clients to solve practical problems which are not emotional (not knowing what to do in a situation, being overly aggressive), teach *practical problem solving skills*. Practical problem solving may vary from helping younger children to think about different alternatives (and their consequences) for handling a *specific* problem, to a broader set of cognitive strategies for thinking about and solving problems in general (Spivack & Shure, 1974; see Chapter 8).

Because George is only 10, emphasis would be placed on encouraging and where necessary teaching friendship-making skills which he could use to solve his problem.

SKILL ACQUISITION

We shall now describe in some detail the flow of rational-emotive intervention commencing with the decision, made by the practitioner as a consequence of RET assessment, that the young client "has" a problem. It is at this point that the different cognitions, emotions, and behaviors which are to be changed are listed and goals for initial, intermediate, and final sessions are tentatively formed. It is in fact the case that from this point onwards assessment and intervention are interwoven. As the young client begins to internalize at whatever level of complexity the ABCs of RET and as the therapeutic relationship develops, the quality of introspective detail provided improves and the specific identity of automatic cognitions and irrational beliefs becomes clearer. Thus, the specific goals for a young client will necessarily alter in response to new information uncovered during intervention. As new problems arise the practitioner continues to assess, as a prelude to intervention, the relationships among cognitions, feelings, and behaviors.

In the discussion which follows we illustrate how the RET goals which we have just described for both children and adolescents are accomplished. The practitioner will be guided as to the level at which RET shall be introduced by the variety of mediating factors we have already enumerated.

Basic Insights for the Younger Client

Before the practitioner begins the teaching of emotional and problem solving skills, it is most important to make young clients aware that not only are changes in their emotions and behaviors possible, but also that change is desirable (DiGiuseppe, 1981). Many children can only conceive of one way of dealing with and feeling in a situation and some find it illuminating to learn both the possibility of alternative courses of action and emotional change.

Many children have few words for emotions and a narrow vocabulary may limit their ability to conceptualize a situation. DiGiuseppe (1981) has recounted:

> Recently, while discussing a child's depressed reaction to the withdrawal of some of her privileges, I made the suggestion that she could have thought or felt differently about the situation than she did. The child responded, "What's the matter with you? Do you want me to be happy about it?" The child only conceptualized happy or sad as possible reactions. Frequently children's schema of emotional reactions are dichotomous and are limited to happy-sad or happy-mad constructs. It will be impossible to convince a child to change his or her automatic thoughts if the child believes the therapist wants him or her to be pleased with a situation that is obviously negative. [pp. 58-59]

We agree with DiGiuseppe that one of the first steps in cognitive therapy with children is to provide them with a schema that incorporates a continuum of responses and feelings and contains a vocabulary for these reactions.

In introducing the idea that one does not have to always feel the same way, and that feelings can vary in intensity from weak (a little) to strong (the most), we find it instructive to have younger children place their hands and arms close together to indicate feeling a little upset and to spread their arms as wide as possible to express extreme upset.

Discussing the negative consequences of present behavior in relation to the positive consequences (or less negative consequences) which may derive from different alternatives sometimes provides young clients with a "way out" of a chronic problem situation which they have been looking for desperately. Grieger and Boyd (1983) illustrate how a diagram (Jeff's mad thermometer) can be employed to emphasize the relationship between varying levels of upset and positive and negative consequences. In conjunction with such an activity, it is frequently helpful to explain to the client, as Virginia Waters suggests, that being very upset is like being in an "emotional" fog and that until one calms down, one will not be able to see how best to solve a given problem.

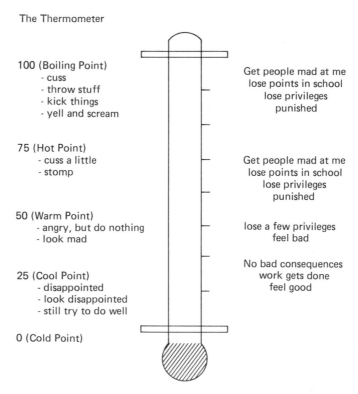

The Thermometer

100 (Boiling Point)
- cuss
- throw stuff
- kick things
- yell and scream

Get people mad at me
lose points in school
lose privileges
punished

75 (Hot Point)
- cuss a little
- stomp

Get people mad at me
lose points in school
lose privileges
punished

50 (Warm Point)
- angry, but do nothing
- look mad

lose a few privileges
feel bad

No bad consequences
work gets done
feel good

25 (Cool Point)
- disappointed
- look disappointed
- still try to do well

0 (Cold Point)

Figure 7.1.   Jeff's Mad Thermometer (from Grieger & Boyd, 1983).

For example, Craig a 13 year old, became very angry when he was told by the bus driver that he had to sit in his seat rather than on the arms of the seat.

THERAPIST: Well, how angry from 1 to 10 did you feel on the bus yesterday when the driver turned around and told you to sit down?

CLIENT: Almost 10 (arms stretched out wide).

THERAPIST: And do you always feel that angry when he tells you to sit down?

CLIENT: Yes.

THERAPIST: And yesterday you got off the bus, cursed the driver, and took the train home?

CLIENT: Uh-huh.

THERAPIST: Do you ever feel anything differently when he picks on you?

CLIENT: No.

THERAPIST: What do you think will happen if you continue to get angry at the driver?

CLIENT: I won't be able to use the bus.

THERAPIST: Is that a good thing or a bad thing?

CLIENT: Bad.

THERAPIST: Well, I will show you how you can make yourself less angry— let's say from a 9 to a 6—and, hopefully, by feeling less angry, you'll be able to keep on riding the bus.

Teaching the ABCs of RET

After a young client is made aware of the possibility and desirability of change, the next step is frequently teaching the basic RET insights concerning thoughts, feelings, and behavior. Before the young client is actually instructed in the ABCs, however, it is most important that she possess some understanding of emotions. Children of all ages vary a great deal in their ability to understand and express emotions. It is often the case that a young client is unable at first to express what she is feeling let alone identify what others are feeling. The practitioner had better make sure that the young client has a good grasp of emotional concepts and is able to express them before proceeding.

A good way to increase emotional awareness is to have a young client list all the feelings she knows as a way of assessing her emotional vocabulary. The client can then be encouraged to express both verbally and nonverbally the different feelings she may have experienced in different situations and, if possible, to provide her thoughts and self-talk at these times. Waters (1982a) has suggested a number of techniques for expanding emotional insight. She suggests that flashcards with an emotion on each can be used in a variety of ways.

The therapist and child can play a guessing game where each in turn acts out the emotion on a chosen card and the other has to guess it, or each can take turns making up stories about each emotion. It is possible to go through the emotion-al flashcards and ask the child which emotions have been experienced that week. [p. 575]

Waters also suggests that the young client can play an *emotional detective* and observe how different people handle different feelings. (Other activities for expanding emotional awareness and understanding appear in Appendix 1.)

For older children and adolescents who demonstrate sufficient levels of emotional awareness, it is possible to begin quite quickly to teach them, by employing a variety of strategies, methods, and techniques, the basic RET insight that thoughts and not people or events, cause people to feel (and behave) as they do. Corollary principles and insights include that feelings come from thoughts, that different thoughts lead to different feelings, that pleasant/unpleasant thoughts lead to pleasant/unpleasant feelings, and that if you get too upset about something, it is very difficult to do anything to improve the situation.

In illustrating these basic RET principles, the practitioner may begin by asking the youngster a question. The practitioner may ask the youngster to think about why children of similar characteristics react so differently to the same situation. If a situation event or happening *causes* our emotions then they should have the same feeling in the same situation. A concrete example would be if it snows some youngsters are happy, some are angry, and some are scared. "Why," the young client is asked, "do they feel differently?" Some youngsters come up with the answer that they must be thinking or imagining different things. "Correct!" you say (or you provide the answer if the youngster cannot) and you explain that the happy ones are probably thinking about missing school, the angry ones are thinking that their parents will force them to wear boots and gloves, and the ones who are worried are scared their school bus might slide off the road. Another way of illustrating this principle is to discuss how our feelings about something or someone can change if our thoughts change. Knaus (1974) provides the example of a youngster who gets angry when a stranger bumps or pushes her but who upon observing that the stranger was blind feels sad and guilty. The practitioner asks the young person to provide some of the thoughts that might lead to anger versus those that might lead to sadness or guilt. The practitioner provides these if the youngster has difficulty doing so. Children may require many concrete experiences and illustrations before they grasp the essentials of the ABCs. Finally, S. R. Harris (1976) provides the following illustration of how to teach groups of children that the same event occasions different feelings in different children:

> Ask children to rate on a continuum from −5 (very negative) to +5 (very positive) how they felt about such things as big dogs, eating spinach, and thunder and lightning. We found a wide variation in the emotional responses (point C) to the same event (point A). For example, one or two children had intense negative feelings about big dogs, some felt positive and others felt less intense or neutral.

The children shared their thoughts about big dogs such as "I really like to see big dogs, I feel excited by them!" or "I don't like to see them, I'm scared of big dogs!" Through discussions we helped them understand that what they were thinking about affected how they felt about events in their lives. [p. 118]

In teaching the basis of the ABC model, it is often useful to use a chart to illustrate the relationship between activating events, thoughts (self-talk), and consequences. We frequently use a happening–thoughts–feelings–behaviors chart such as the one below to teach the basic RET insight that when (1) something happens to you, (2) you think about what happened, (3) the thoughts you have lead to a feeling, and (4) the feeling will affect how you react.

What happened	What were you thinking?	What were you feeling?	What did you do?

(Material presented in the next section of this chapter and in Appendix A can be used to provide additional instruction in this area.)

While it is generally believed that both the practitioner and client have to share "a similar cognitive view of psychological problems and speak in a common cognitively based language" (Sutton–Simon, 1981, p. 68), occasionally it is quite possible—especially when working with very young children—to assess and modify self-statements without discussing with the client the underlying rationale. For example, the first author has worked with Richard, a boy in third grade, who was frequently seen crying after school when his mother was late in picking him up. After determining that there were no extenuating circumstances at home and that Richard had no major problems besides worrying from time to time about the standard of his work, it was decided that a limited RET contact might provide a solution. Richard was seen for two brief ten-minute sessions across a one-week period. During the first session, Richard was asked to describe his thoughts while he was waiting for his mother. He replied to the effect that "What if Mum forgets again, I'll be left all by myself, all alone." It seemed clear without probing for underlying beliefs that the self-statements concerning being forgotten and alone were greatly contributing to his feelings of worry. Richard was told that one way of feeling better was to say to himself while he was waiting for his mother: "It doesn't matter if I have to wait a little; I won't be forgotten for long, someone will pick me up; I can cope." Richard practiced saying this dialogue aloud to himself and was told to repeat it if he had to wait after school. During the following week, the several teachers on duty reported that Richard did not cry even though his mother was late twice. Richard said he was less worried and when asked why, he replied; "I said to myself, I can cope and that Mum will be here soon." Two months later, Richard was seen again and indicated that he was no longer worried about being left for a while after school. No attempt was made to teach Richard the relationship of thoughts and feelings. Children of Richard's age and younger are often quite willing to learn to change their thoughts as they are willing to change their clothes for a class in physical education.

As a prerequisite to teaching young clients how to challenge and dispute irrational beliefs, it is sometimes necessary that the concepts of "rational" and "irrational" are formally taught. In working with younger clients and, especially children, Waters (1982a) substitutes the term "helpful" and "hurtful" or "productive" and "unproductive" beliefs. Her explanation of these terms is as follows:

> Rational beliefs follow from reality, are self-enhancing, are apt to lead to achieve-ment of goals, and result in appropriate emotions; whereas irrational beliefs do not follow from reality, are self-defeating, usually block one from achieving goals, and result in inappropriate feelings. [p. 572]

There are a number of instructional techniques the present authors employ when teaching these concepts (see Bernard, 1975b; Bernard, 1977). We usually present a definition of each concept (definitions adapted from Knaus, 1974).

Rational thought: A sensible and logical idea that seems to be true.

Irrational thought: An unreasonable or absurd idea that seems to be false.

We then provide examples and non-examples of rational and irrational thoughts. The youngster is provided with instructional worksheets where he is given practice examples to classify (see Table 7.1). Verbal prompts, explanations,

TABLE 7.1.   Instructional Exercises to Teach the Concepts Rational and Irrational.

Directions: Place a mark (x) if you think the thought is rational or irrational. (Remember: Is the thought sensible and true, or is it absurd and false?)

	Rational	Irrational
1. Nobody in the world will ever be my friend.	_____	_____
2. I would be happier at school if I were better at my work.	_____	_____
3. I never do anything right.	_____	_____
4. If I am this bad at my work I will never be good at anything.	_____	_____
5. Everybody hates me.	_____	_____
6. I wish I had more friends at school.	_____	_____
7. I can't stand doing homework.	_____	_____
8. I wish I could play football as well as John can.	_____	_____

and feedback are provided. When the youngster demonstrates that he can discriminate between rational and irrational thoughts, he is guided to apply these intellectual skills in analyzing the characteristics of his own thoughts.

In working with older children and adolescents, it is desirable to teach them a "disputation" or "challenging" strategy for deciding if their thoughts are rational or irrational. We define challenge as "To question yourself to see if your thought is rational or irrational" and teach that "To find out if a thought is rational or irrational, ask yourself 'Is there enough evidence for me to say the thought is true?'" If there is, the thought is rational, if not, the thought is irrational. This strategy is used in teaching the basics of empirical analysis and philosophical disputation. Waters (1982a) suggests that children can learn to challenge their irrational beliefs by asking themselves and answering the following series of questions:

1. Is this belief based on fact, opinion, inference or assumption? Where is the evidence that this is really so?

2. Is it really awful? Is it true I couldn't stand it? Is it the worst that it could be?

3. Is this belief getting me what I want?

4. Why shouldn't it be so? Do I always have to get what I want?

5. Where is the evidence that this makes me worthless? How can this make me worthless or less than human? [p. 576]

(Activities and techniques for teaching the meanings of fact, opinion, inference, and assumption are provided in Appendix 1.)

Once the young client has been taught the difference between rational and irrational, it is sometimes instructive to demonstrate through the use of examples from the practitioner's and the client's life the consequences of rational and irrational thinking. Waters (1982b) suggests the "What if" game to explore the consequences of "demandingness" and "awfulizing."

What if you were to demand that you should always get your way? (1) What would you feel? (2) What would you do? (3) How would others respond to you? (4) Would you be more likely to get your way than if you didn't make this demand? On the other hand, what would happen if you thought that you would like to get your way all the time, but couldn't stand it when you didn't get your way? (1) How would you feel? (2) What would you do? (3) How might others respond to you? [p. 20]

Emotional Problem Solving

In this section we detail a number of the basic cognitive change procedures used in RET.

Rational Self-Statements

With younger children, the most common change procedure used to resolve emotional difficulties is rational self-instruction. This approach is a relatively straightforward one to employ. The practitioner (sometimes with the help of the young client) draws up a set of helpful self-statements which the client can substitute for the more upsetting self-talk used in a problematic situation. Waters (1982b) in her transcript we have referred to previously illustrates the elicitation of helpful and hurtful self-talk as a prelude to teaching her fourth-grade client the use of rational self-statements to combat her fear of sleeping over at a friend's house.

Therapist: "Let's work on that right now. There are certain things you can say to yourself to create that scared feeling. Let's make a list of those hurtful thoughts that create that ache all over, that lump in your throat and that 'crying' feeling. Once we identify those hurtful things then we can make a list of helpful things you can say to yourself, so you can comfort yourself and make yourself feel better."

(Therapist gets out paper and pencil and writes down "Hurtful Thoughts.")

Therapist: "Let's first make a list of the hurtful things you can say to yourself to create that scared feeling. If we can identify them then we can inoculate you against them. Let's suppose you are at your friend's house. What would some of those hurtful thoughts be?"

Client: "Well, I usually feel worse if I've forgotten my stuffed animal, Snoopy, because he comforts me."

Therapist: "So one might be: 'It's awful, I forgot my Snoopy' " (writing it down).

Client: "Yeah."

Therapist: "It would be awful if everyone fell asleep before I did."

Client: "Yeah and it would be awful if my friend's parents went out and left me alone, or it would be awful if I call my mother to say goodnight and she wasn't home; and I can't think of anything else. Those are the main things."

Therapist: "Now what we are going to do is come up with comforting, helpful things you can say to yourself to make yourself feel better when you are sleeping at your friend's."

(Therapist writes "Helpful Thoughts" on paper.)

Client: "I guess I could hug my Snoopy and pretend he's comforting me."

Therapist: "What would you pretend to have Snoopy say to you to comfort you?"

Client: "Well, I'd probably have him say that I'm really safe and nothing scary can happen, and I'd probably fall asleep soon and feel better."

Therapist: "What would be making you feel better?"

Client: "My comforting thoughts I guess."

Therapist: "Right. And now what I'd like to do is give you a chance to practice saying those helpful, comforting things to yourself, so when you are at a friend's house it will be easier for you to use what you've just learned to feel better."

Client: "I don't think I'm going to be able to do that unless I'm actually at a friend's house."

Therapist: "You can practice ahead of time, and that way you'll be in a much better position to stop the hurtful thoughts and say the comforting thoughts when the time comes."

Client: "You know, I think I was thinking ahead too much and saying too many 'What if's' to myself."

Therapist: "Yes, 'what if' is a good thing to ask yourself if you want to worry and scare yourself, because 'what if's' create lots of uncertainty. An important thing to remember about 'what if's' is that if you ask 'what if' be sure you answer the question. For instance, if you ask, 'What if she falls asleep first?' you can answer that by saying, 'Well if my friend falls asleep first that's too bad, I'll just try and relax and stay calm until I fall asleep too. So that's not so bad.'" [p. 12–13]

The practitioner explains to the young client that by saying these new things when she starts to feel upset she will feel better and be happier. The "helpful self-talk" is typically modeled by the practitioner and then rehearsed aloud and silently by the young client who is asked to imagine that they are in the "troublesome" situation. It is most important for the practitioner to positively reinforce the young client during the time the rational self-statements are being learned as well as when the client in subsequent sessions reports that an attempt was made and/or success was achieved in employing the statements outside the practitioner's office. The young client is also encouraged to provide "self-reinforcement" in the form of an imaginary "pat on the back." A few examples will illustrate applications of *rational self-statements*.

Kanfer, Karoly and Newman (1975) employed the following rational self-statements with 6 and 7 year olds who were afraid of the dark:

Example A: "I am a brave boy (girl). I can take care of myself in the dark."

Example B: "The dark is a fun place to be. There are many good things in the dark."

They found that rational self-statements (Example A) which emphasize the child's competence to deal with the stress inducing experience of exposure to the dark resulted in the longest tolerance times.

DiGiuseppe (1981) reported the use of self-instructional training with a six year old who was reported by her mother as deeply depressed about her parents' divorce.

Paula's father visited the child every Sunday. When the visits ended Paula cried about missing her dad. Also she cried frequently during the week, often giving the same reason. Coping statements were devised to help Paula ward off depression and crying. If she felt near tears Paula was instructed to say, "My daddy loves me and I'll see him next week." Using dolls and puppets the therapist played scenes where a father and daughter said goodbye and went away from each other. At each separation the child puppet used the coping statement and followed the appropriate behavior of no crying. Paula was then asked to take the role of the child character and use the coping statements in similar scenes. After only two sessions, Paula's crying after her father's visit stopped completely and had not re-occurred at the three-month follow up. [pp. 61–62]

In this case, it can be seen that while rational self-statements can work effectively to moderate emotional upset in a specific situation, one would not expect them to transfer across emotions or problem situations.

Bernard, Kratochwill, and Keefauver (1983), as we reported in Chapter 6, combined the use of rational self-instruction with philosophic disputation to bring about a reduction in the hair pulling of a 17-year-old girl. As the data presented at the end of Chapter 6 indicate, disputational training aimed at changing beliefs was in the short run insufficient to totally eliminate hair pulling. Visual analysis of the data reveals only moderate changes in the frequency of hair pulling during weeks 4 through 8. At this point, the practitioner cognitively modelled a set of self-instructions which took the form of a problem solving dialogue employed in self-instructional training (see next chapter). An example of the self-statements which the client progressively internalized is as follows:

PROBLEM DEFINITION: "What am I supposed to do?"

PROBLEM APPROACH: "I'm going to build a protective bubble around me so that nothing worries me until I get my homework done."

FOCUSING OF ATTENTION: "I'd better pay attention to my assignment. What is the next thing I have to do?"

COPING STATEMENTS: "Oh, I'm starting to get worried about school . . . and I just pulled out a hair. I know if I just relax and focus on my work that I won't worry.

SELF-REINFORCEMENT: "Hey, that's great. I finished that bit of work. I didn't worry. And I didn't pull my hair. I knew I could do it!"

The introduction of these self-statements led to a rapid cessation of hair pulling. It was impossible to determine the relative effects of disputational training and self-instructional training in this study.

A case study reported by DiGiuseppe and Bernard (1983) will indicate how RET in the form of rational self-statements can be used with very young and relatively unintelligent children.

Greg was a nine year old child who was referred by his parents for temper tantrums, pouting and non-cooperative behavior. Greg had a family history of extreme non-contingent reward. During most of his life, his parents had pampered him and he was allowed to do what he pleased. While this behavior was cute when he was younger, with maturity it came more unacceptable. Greg's parents attempted to have him follow rules and to behave appropriately. They punished him whenever Greg did not complete chores or age-appropriate behaviors. Greg believed that this meant a change in their affections and that they no longer cared for him. He also thought that it was terribly unfair that he should have to do such mundane things as clean his room and put his dirty clothes in the hamper. These things were just too difficult. Greg was a non-verbal child with low average intelligence and had difficulty following many of the disputing strategies. However, he was able to role play these situations with the therapist. During these role plays, the therapist modeled verbal self instructions such as "My parents care for me, they are only trying to do their job and help me grow up," "I don't have to feel upset about these things, I can do them." Through practicing these self statements and receiving reinforcement for appropriate behavior, Greg slowly learned to stop pouting and this provided the impetus for more mature, independent behaviors. [p. 74]

Empirical Analysis

A second more complex solution for solving the emotional problems of young clients is achieved when the practitioner changes the inferences children make of their distortion of reality (DiGiuseppe & Bernard, 1983). While *not* tackling the client's irrational appraisals of distortions of reality, the empirical solution frequently results in a moderation of affect and an improvement in behavior, and is easier to teach young clients than is philosophical disputation. The practitioner is hereby warned, however, that empirical analysis taxes intellectual and creative resources. It is at first a difficult approach to master.

If one wishes to use this approach with children, it is most important that the young client is taught the basic concepts such as discriminating between facts, opinions, inferences, and assumptions and the insight that what they are thinking and the ideas which they hold and others such as parents and teachers may not be true. DiGiuseppe (1981) provides some suggestions for teaching the child the importance of empirically testing ideas.

This can be done by telling about ideas that people believed in the past but that we now know are different. For example, people once believed that the earth was flat and that the sun revolved around our planet, but through theory building and testing we know differently. [pp. 62–63]

The degree to which empirical analysis can be used depends partly on whether children can acquire these concepts and on the generality of the idea being empirically analyzed. The more concrete the idea, the easier it is to achieve an empirical solution. A recent referral will illustrate the use of empirical analysis.

Craig, an extremely bright 13 year old (IQ 130+), was seen over an extended period by the first author to help him control his excessive worrying.
In Craig's case, excessive worry led to Craig working too hard at school, getting tired, and eventually falling prey to periodic anxiety related physical illnesses.

In spending many weekly sessions with Craig, it appeared that Craig held the idea that for him to achieve his goal at school of receiving very good grades, he must always put in 100% effort in his homework. He seemed to accept this idea unquestioningly and interpreted all school assignments as requiring a total effort. Over weeks and weeks, little success was seen in getting Craig to cut some corners in his schoolwork when he found himself getting tired. Craig relentlessly pushed himself to the limit when objectively there was no reason why he had to push himself to the extreme. That is, it appeared highly probable that Craig could attain his goals with less of an effort. Rather than continuing to dispute with Craig his self-defined perfectionistic demand to be successful at his schoolwork, it was decided that an empirical analysis of Craig's untested ideas concerning the amount of effort required for success should be put to the test.

The cognitive-analytic question the first author put to himself to set the stage for empirical analysis was "What does Craig probably think about the importance of studying hard?" which was answered by "To achieve good grades in school, I must work as hard as I possibly can." Craig readily agreed that this was something "I probably do believe" although he had not considered it before. It was explained to Craig that it was quite possible that this belief (1) was what may be forcing him to work so hard, (2) may or may not be true, and (3) could be examined to see if it was true through conducting an experiment. Craig took up the challenge and agreed that if his idea was proved to be false he would restate it. The hypothesis that both the practitioner and Craig agreed to put to this test was: "I must put in high effort to obtain satisfactory grades." The experiment involved decreasing his effort in studying for a history exam. Craig agreed to review the material only once and not to over-prepare. The hypothesis would be rejected if he obtained 85 or higher and rejected with a mark lower than 85. Two weeks later Craig reported he received a grade of 89 and was quite happy with the result. With no help from the practitioner, he concluded that he would put in less effort to get good grades and he would try to put his new idea into practice.

happy with the result. With no help from the practitioner, he concluded that he would put in less effort to get good grades and he would try to put his new idea into practice.
This episode was somewhat of a breakthrough in that up until that time Craig could not control the amount of time he worked due to his fear of failure. When he realized that less work meant more fun and equally good grades he was able to relax his approach to his studying. As will be evident in the first author's remarks to Craig during their final session of the school year (which are presented at the end of this chapter), the empirical analysis led to a satisfactory but limited solution to Craig's anxiety related problems.

DiGiuseppe (1981) described the case of Paul, a 10 year old, who displayed a variety of antisocial behaviors such as temper tantrums, and specifically, yelling at his parents. A behavioral analysis revealed that Paul generally argued whenever his parents disagreed on an issue, even if the difference of opinion did not result in a fight. A cognitive assessment indicated Paul endorsed two antiempirical ideas: (1) that disagreement leads to divorce; and (2) that he could not survive if his parents separated. DiGiuseppe elected to work on the first troublesome idea as the second one is an exceedingly difficult one to dispute with children.

> I asked Paul to set up an experiment to test his hypothesis that disagreement leads to divorce. He was willing to do so and we designed a questionnaire for this purpose. Paul polled his teacher and principal, several store-keepers, a police officer, and others about whether they decided to divorce every time they argued with their spouses. Paul found that disagreements were common in marriage and rarely resulted in divorce. His symptoms ceased. [p. 64]

Bard and Fisher (personal communication) demonstrate how the faulty inference of an adolescent, "Everything will turn out okay," can be corrected through the combined use of an empirical analysis and behavioral methods.

> Dale T., for example, a 17 year old senior with high intelligence, had managed to con his parents and teachers, avoiding academic work and achieving marginal grades throughout high school. His mother blamed and nagged him. His father, a successful businessman, had given him various "incentives" to get better grades and the most recent was a car. Charming, pleasant, Dale had attended therapy sessions assuring the therapist that he would do much better academically, was much better motivated since his father gave him a car, could overcome his "laziness," etc. Obviously, everything would turn out O.K. except the work was not forthcoming and his academic achievement remained marginal. The parents were involved directly and committed themselves to the incentive program, stop nagging, resist being conned and to stick with this approach. The school counselor in turn worked with Dale's teachers to accept only conformity to rules, deadlines and assignments. Dale became less cheery and chatty, getting down to business with some distress and many complaints. He was directed to discuss goals and shown that his underachievement of the past three years was the direct result of his erroneously believing that everything would turn out O.K. whether or not he worked. He painfully started working and discovered that he was poorly prepared to enter college. He was able to define some academic and vocational goals meaningful to him, had been accepted into a college program and was able to minimize avoidance and manipulation, as his pleasure ticket through the remainder of his senior year. In giving up his belief that everything would turn out O.K. without work, he was able to see that with work, effort and planning many of his goals could be achieved.

In this example, we can see how faulty inferences about the relationship between effort and achievement lead an adolescent to inaccurately interpret the consequences of his behavior. It can be clearly seen in this example that faulty assumptions can lead to self-defeating behavior without the mediation of strong emotional arousal. While Dale in fact may experience low frustration tolerance because of his belief that "Life should be fun at all times," no doubt his other assumption that everything will be all right prevented him from even approaching school tasks which might occasion discomfort anxiety.

Another example by DiGiuseppe and Bernard (1983) will indicate how young children can be taught to change inferences concerning the meaning of events in their lives.

> Sara was a nine year old girl who was particularly depressed because of the infrequency with which she saw her father. Her parents had been divorced for 6 years and her mother and father still continued to argue. Sara had a large number of siblings all of whom were much older than her and experienced a great deal of animosity towards the father. The father reacted by avoiding them. Our discussions revealed that Sara believed that since her father did not love or care for her mother or her siblings, he could not really care for her. Empirical disputing of this inference tested out quite the opposite. While the father made little attempt to see the siblings and continued to argue with the mother whenever he came to visit Sara, he came to visit Sara quite regularly. While dad was not the most demonstrative person, he was much more dedicated to this child than to any of his others and spent considerable amount of time visiting her, calling her, taking her places. Sara's upset was caused first by her inference that her father's behavior towards other members of the family indicated that he felt the same way towards her and the appraisal that if he did not care for her that would be catastrophic. Sara was quite unwilling even to discuss this last possibility. Challenging the idea that it wouldn't be terrible if a father didn't care for her led to silence and withdrawal. However, the empirical solution here got her quite interested in collecting data to verify her inferences. She was pleased with the results. This strategy was acceptable because of the therapist's inference that the father really did care for Sara. If the empirical disputing had not led in the direction it did, a more elegant approach would have been necessary. But here it was acceptable to limit ourselves with the empirical solution. [pp. 73–74]

A final word needs to be made concerning the use of empirical analysis. It is the case as DiGiuseppe (1981) indicates that children are sometimes faced with unchangeable, aversive events such as parents not caring. It would be a misdirected and inappropriate use of the strategy if a practitioner attempted to convince a child through "rigging" an experiment that a parent loved and cared for him when all evidence pointed to the contrary. As DiGiuseppe has insightedfully observed, such "conning" teaches the child a warped sense of values and distorted meanings for the concepts of "love" and "caring" which might lead to negative and unintended interpersonal effects for the child later in life. When it appears that the young client is being brought up in an uncaring environment, a suggested course of action (apart from working directly with the parents where possible) is to teach the young child that he may be happy with the rest of his life even though things at home may not be what he would desire them to be.

Disputation

The most widely used strategy for modifying irrational thinking is *disputation* (challenging). Challenging is used whenever and in whatever form possible to examine and change the variety of irrational concepts and beliefs which underlie emotional and behavioral problems of school-age children. Once the ABCs of RET have been taught, disputational techniques are employed to dissuade a young client from irrational thinking. Most of the work with young clients have employed cognitive methods for challenging irrationality and it is to these we now turn.

As we have indicated in Chapter 5, there are a number of basic irrational concepts (e.g., "demandingness," "awfulizing," "self-downing") which interact to define the different irrational beliefs of the childhood period. These concepts operate in various combinations to produce the different problems we discussed earlier. The major role of disputation is to teach the client how to challenge these concepts and to reformulate them into rational counterparts. For older and more cognitively mature adolescents, it is possible to employ the RET preferential techniques of philosophical disputation of general and abstract irrational beliefs to bring about elegant solutions. With those young clients who are unable to handle the degree of abstraction required to achieve a preferential solution, it is suggested that the practitioner help the client examine the irrational concepts contained in their faulty appraisal of specific activating events about which they are upsetting themselves.

Howard Young (1974a, 1983) has made significant contributions in demonstrating how philosophical disputation can be employed with adolescents. While his "down to earth" approach takes into account the difficulties of working with adolescents, he still manages to employ cognitive disputation effectively and relies heavily on "semantic clarity" to help teenagers rethink their problems.

Young (1983) indicates that while he sometimes teaches adolescents the ABC model, introducing it verbally and using cartoon drawing or illustration, he does not spend a great deal of time on presenting the formula. He prefers to tackle the irrational concepts which underlie adolescent thinking rather than having them understand the logic of RET theory. We now refer to Young's and others' methods and techniques for changing irrational thinking.

When the practitioner discovers evidence of "shoulds," "oughts," and "musts" together with the tendency for adolescents to treat their wants as desires ("I must have my way because it is deserved, earned, right, fair, just, etc."), Young suggests attempting to help his teenage clients to understand that using such absolutistic thinking results in both emotional and interpersonal difficulties. He suggests the following tactics:

1. Using "must" in place of "should." Teenagers use the word "should" so frequently and indiscriminately that sometimes just getting them to change the word to "must" gets the imperative quality across. Once this is established, they can begin to learn how to live without absolutes.

2. Using "gotta" in place of "should." "I should get an A" makes sense to a lot of teenagers, but "I gotta get an A" often encourages them to see the error of their ways.

3. Changing "should" to "no right." Another method of getting across the absolutistic meaning of "should" especially with angry teenagers, is to exchange "He shouldn't do that" for "He's got no right to do that." The irrationality of "He's got no right" is often easy for some teenagers to understand.

4. Using the want–need concept. Another way of getting teenagers to recognize and challenge absolutes is to teach them the difference between wanting and needing. I have found some of the most resistant and stubborn young people, especially those involved in behavioral excesses, are capable of understanding the critical distinction between desires and necessities and of using this insight productively.

5. Teaching "should" equals unbreakable law. I sometimes get somewhere with young clients who have difficulty understanding the absolutistic meaning of "shoulds" and "musts" by suggesting they are upset because their self-proclaimed laws have been broken. "Debbie's Commandments have been violated," or "It was Tom's turn to be God, and he got upset because someone broke one of His rules," are examples of this approach. Once the adolescents understand what it means to be unrealistically demanding, I proceed to show them they do not run the universe, so they would better expect things to go wrong. [pp. 95–96]

In the following therapy concept, Walen et al. (1980) illustrate how to distinguish wants from needs. The client is a seven-year-old girl who is having trouble making friends at school.

Therapist: Do you need to play with them?

Client: What does "need" mean?

Therapist: A need means this: what are some of the things that you need? You need water. What happens if you don't have water?

Client: You die.

Therapist: That's right. What happens if you don't have food?

Client: Die.

Therapist: That's right. Can we say that you need food?

Client: Yeah.

Therapist: And water?

Client: Yeah.

Therapist: And air?

Client: Yeah.

Therapist: That's right. Do you *need* television?

Client: No.

Therapist: But sometimes you say you need to watch TV, don't you?

Client: Yeah, 'cause I like to.

Therapist: Yeah, you like to and you want to, but that's not a need is it?

Client: No.

Therapist: No it's not. Do you need candy canes and ice cream?

Client: No.

Therapist: You don't need them, but you want them, don't you?

Client: Yeah.

Therapist: But you don't need them, do you?

Client: No.

Therapist: Do you see the difference between a *want* and a *need*? What's the difference? You try to explain it to me.

Client: A need is what you need to help you to live.

Therapist: A need is something you've got to have to live.

Client: And a want is that you want to have it.

Therapist: That's right. You'd *like* to have it, it's enjoyable. Now what about: Lisa wants the kids in school to like her. Is that a want or a need?

Client: A want.

Therapist: It's a want, right?

Client: Right.

Therapist: So we talked a little bit about wants and needs. Now what happens if you tell yourself "Oh I *need* to have so-and-so play with me in school—I need to have her like me." How do you think you're going to feel if she doesn't like you?

Client: Sad.

Therapist: Sad. Like sad a whole lot or sad a little bit?

Client: A lot.

Therapist: A lot. How about if you said, "I need to have Kate like me and *need* to be her friend."

Client: I *want* to be her friend.

Therapist: "I want to be her friend." Oh, but isn't there a difference? If you said, "I need to be her friend" and she wasn't, how would you feel?

Client: And she wouldn't?

Therapist: And she wouldn't. And you said, "I gotta have her friendship—
             I need it to live!—and she won't be my friend."

Client: Sad.

Therapist: You'd be very sad. So what if you said to yourself instead, "I would
             like to have Kate like me. I want to be her friend, but if she's not
             gonna be my friend, I can live without it." Would you be sad a little
             bit or sad a lot?

Client: Sad a little. [pp. 137–139]

The second irrational concept which is subject to disputation is that of
"awfulizing." The tendency to blow things out of proportion, to make mountains out of molehills, is characteristic of the thinking of people of all ages. In
making adolescent clients aware that they are "awfulizing," and that more
sensible and levelheaded thinking is required, Young (1984) suggests the
following:

1. Substituting the words disaster, catastrophe, or tragedy for awful, terrible, or
    horrible. The words awful, terrible, or horrible are so much a part of the
    average adolescent's working vocabulary that I have found it difficult to
    convince the adolescent that the meaning behind such words is the cause of
    his suffering. The emotionally distressed adolescent who insists his problem is
    awful is asked, "Was it a disaster?" or "Was it really a tragedy?" These words
    have a more precise meaning and can be subjected to question and reason
    more easily than "awful."

2. Using the phrase "end of the world" to show the client he or she is "awfuliz-
    ing." Again I find that asking, "Would it be the end of the world?" usually
    elicits an eye-rolling "Of course not" from most adolescents and permits the
    next question "Then exactly what would it be." The answer, almost always in
    the realm of realistic disadvantage, begins to persuade the client to correct his
    or her exaggerated evaluation of the problem.

3. Using the phrase "a fate worse than death." Once more the use of a familiar
    but obviously magnified term sometimes helps adolescents to begin to under-
    stand that their excessive, disturbing feelings come from exaggerated, unreal-
    istic ideas in their minds.

4. Asking, "Could it be any worse?" Often young clients exaggerate, consider-
    ing a situation totally bad. Encouraging them to conjure something that could
    make their problem even worse sometimes enables them to see that it is
    highly unlikely that any disadvantage (especially their own) is one-hundred-
    percent bad. This tactic can sometimes be used in a humorous way by adding
    all kinds of ridiculous dimensions to the problem situation. I find this ap-
    proach helps clients realize that problems are not always as bad as they think
    they are; by viewing situations in less exaggerated and more realistic terms,
    they learn to feel much less distressed.

5. Asking, "What's the worst that could actually happen?" I show anxiety-
    ridden teenagers they are catastrophizing their complaints by encouraging

them to focus on the most realistic but worst outcome they can imagine. This forces them to stay away from possibilities and to concentrate on actualities. In essence, they are learning to deal with the hassle and not the horror of the problem. [p. 95]

In working with young clients, it is frequently useful in helping them place a problem in perspective to employ a device called a catastrophe list developed by DiGiuseppe and Waters. This technique, which can be employed with clients of all ages, has been described by Walen et al. (1980) as follows:

On a blackboard or large sheet of paper, have the children list all the catastrophes they can think of (given the recent spate of catastrophic films and TV shows, this is easily accomplished). After listing towering infernos, tidal waves, invasions from outer space, earthquakes and atomic blasts, the therapist "remembers" one more, the child's complaint (e.g., "Tommy sat in my seat"). It will probably not be necessary to point out that one item does not belong on the list. [p. 126]

An irrational concept which is related to "awfulizing" and which leads to a variety of behavioral effects (underachievement, drug addiction) associated with low frustration tolerance and discomfort anxiety is what we previously referred to as "I can't stand-it-itis." In working with adolescents who strongly believe that they cannot withstand any inconvenience or discomfort, Young (1983) recommends the following anecdote.

1. Substituting "unbearable" for "can't stand." Often I can help a young client realize how pernicious the "can't stand" concept is by equating it with the term "unbearable." Hearing things put this way, many teenagers conclude, "Well, it's not *that* bad. I mean I can *bear* it."

2. Explaining "difficult" versus "impossible." Often the "can't stand" concept can be better understood by investigating whether a particular problem situation is impossible or is merely difficult to tolerate. Even some of the most resistant teenagers, grasping this point, can realize that just because something is a pain in the neck does not mean it cannot be lived with.

3. Substituting "won't" for "can't." Frequently, when I hear the word "can't," I quickly substitute "won't." This is an effective way of showing that the situation is governed by one's attitude, which is under the individual's control. It is the attitude, not the situation, that is overwhelming.

4. Suggesting to the client that he or she *is* tolerating the conflict in question. In spite of his complaints and protests, I remind him, he *is* enduring the problem. This tactic is especially useful with clients experiencing long-running problems with parents, teachers, or siblings. For example, the teenager who threatens to quit school in his senior year because he claims he can no longer stomach the bullshit is advised that he is, in fact, stomaching things. He may be miserable but he has, nevertheless, been putting up with school for twelve years, and this qualifies him as an outstanding stomacher of bullshit!

5. Explaining that a genuine "can't stand" situation would either end the client's life or render her unconscious. I frequently suggest that if her problem were truly impossible to bear, it would either cost her life or she would likely pass out from the overwhelming agony involved. Up to that point, I suggest, the client is standing the adversity or discomfort; she may not like it, but she is standing it. [p. 96–97]

(The transcript presented at the end of Chapter 3 illustrates a variety of ways for disputing "awfulizing" and "I can't-stand-it-itis.")

Another major irrational concept underlying much child and adolescent irrational thinking which may be directly disputed is that of "self-downing" ("I'm bad if I make a mistake"; "I shouldn't make social mistakes"). This is an especially difficult concept to teach as many children may not have achieved sufficient cognitive maturity to preserve a positive concept of self in the face of negative and contradictory evidence. Moreover, adolescents frequently judge themselves solely on the basis of peer opinion (Young, 1983). As low self-esteem may underly a variety of behavioral and emotional problems (discussed in Chapter 5), it is most important that the RET practitioner spends when possible several sessions teaching the young clients the basic notion that it makes little sense to judge how "good" or "bad" they are on the basis of a small aspect of their behavior. Doing so can only lead to unhappiness and self-defeating behavior. RET practitioners go to great lengths to provide young clients with a multidimensional cognitive scheme for viewing their "selfs." Basic ideas we utilize in teaching the principle of "self-acceptance" are:

1. Every person is complex, not simple.
2. I am complex, not simple.
3. Every person is made up of many positive and negative qualities.
4. I am made up of many positive and negative qualities.
5. A person is not all good or bad because of some of his or her characteristics.
6. I am not all good or all bad.
7. When I only focus on the negative characteristics of a person, I feel worse about the person.
8. When I only focus on my negative qualities, I feel worse about myself.
9. Focusing *only* on my negative qualities is irrational. I have other positive qualities.
10. When I think negative, irrational thoughts about myself, I get more upset with myself than if I think negative rational thoughts.

The most elegant solution to self-downing is if the client accepts the basic RET principle that human beings are not rateable (as we discussed in Chapter 2) insofar as there is no commonly agreed upon and exhaustive definition of "good" and "bad" people. We generally do not attempt this solution with younger clients as its level of abstraction is too far removed from their life context and day to day concerns. Instead, we opt to teach youngsters not to use negative qualities that they and others perceive in themselves as sole criteria for deciding whether they are "okay" or "not okay." In as persuasive and forceful a way as possible we try to change their attitude toward and beliefs about their mistake making and imperfections and to get them to adopt a self-concept which incorporates the good as well as the bad. For example, we frequently use a *self-concept wheel* to illustrate a number of these basic ideas (Knaus, 1974). The client is invited to insert a range of their positive and negative personal characteristics, traits, and behaviors in the smaller circles which appear inside the self-concept wheel (see Appendix 1). The "positives" are used to dispute with the client the belief that he is bad because he may do things badly or breaks rules. Challenging feelings of inferiority is the central task in helping young clients overcome feelings of frustration, anger, guilt, and jealousy as well as solving problems of procrastination, short-term behavior (sensation seeking), stealing, and physical violence.

Young (1983) demonstrates his creative application of RET by suggesting the following ways of combating "self-downing":

1. Using a visual aid. I draw a circle and label it "self." Next I draw a series of smaller circles inside the "self" circle. These represent the various traits, characteristics, and performances of the individual client. I try to demonstrate that rating one trait or feature as bad does not make all the other circles bad. In essence, I try to show adolescents they are a collection of qualities, some good and some bad, none of which equal the whole self.

2. Using an analogy. Although many examples can illustrate the illogicality of overgeneralizing from act to personhood, I have found that the flat tire example works best with teenagers. I ask if they would junk a whole car because it had a flat tire. The key word is junk. Once the client picks up on this word-image, I use it thereafter when they overgeneralize about mistakes or criticism. "There you go again," I tell them, "junking yourself because you did such and such."

3. Helping the client understand that although one is responsible for what one does, one is not the same as one does. This is sometimes tricky for adolescents to understand. They frequently argue that if they do something bad, they too are bad. I counter by suggesting, "If you went around mooing like a cow, would that make you a cow?" I usually receive a negative answer. Then I say, "But you are the one doing it. How come it doesn't turn you into a cow?" A few more examples like this one, and clients usually begin to separate what they do from who they are.

4. Explaining the difference between a person-with-less and less-of-a-person. Young clients suffering from feelings of shame, embarrassment, or inferiority have usually fallen victim to downing or degrading themselves. To the client who gets criticized or makes mistakes I point out that such problems only prove he is a person with less of what he wants (success or approval) rather than less of a person. Sometimes I illustrate this principle by taking something

from him (a shoe, a watch, etc.) and then asking, "What are you now? Are you less of a person or just a person with less of what you want?"

5.   Showing that blaming oneself is like being punished twice for the same crime. With those adolescents who damn themselves and feel excessively guilty, I usually try to illustrate that mistakes and failings have built-in penalties. Whenever we err, I point out, we not only disappoint ourselves and fail to live up to our own standards, but we likely endure some kind of adverse consequence. Through examples I help clients to see that just living with the disappointments or consequences of their actions is punishment enough. Adding to it by damning oneself only adds insult to injury and makes matters worse than they need be. [pp. 97–98]

The following excerpt from a conversation with a 17-year-old girl illustrates how the girl's jealousy of her friend can be treated by teaching the client a more self-accepting view.

THERAPIST: You seem pretty upset. What are your feelings right now?

CLIENT: Well, I don't really know. It's not right, that's all.

THERAPIST: What do you mean "It's not right? What's not right?"

CLIENT: Just because the others suck up to the teacher, they never get into trouble or have to repeat their homework. They get all the good things. The teacher likes them and I'm a nothing!

THERAPIST: Well, Jane, I can see there's some things there that are upsetting you. But as we've discussed previously, it is your thoughts about the situation that are causing this; that are making you feel worthless and jealous of your friends.

CLIENT: So what if I'm jealous. What does that change?

THERAPIST: It can change your feelings because it's your thoughts about the situation that control your emotions. Now, who said the teacher had to like you as much or more than the others? Is there anything that says a teacher isn't human and can't like some people more than others? Is it absolutely 100% "awful" that the teacher doesn't like you?

CLIENT: No, but. . . .

THERAPIST: And even if your teacher doesn't think highly of you and your friends are better off, that might not be fun, but it's not the end of the world. It doesn't mean you're less of a person or less worthy. You do other things well and you can learn to accept yourself for what you are.

CLIENT: That's true but it doesn't make things any easier for me.

THERAPIST: If you continue to think irrationally then it won't get any easier for you. If you're going to judge yourself on how much someone likes you and how much better off your friends are than you, then you'll waste so much energy being upset that you won't be able to do anything about changing your situation. Look at this objectively and you'll feel less upset.

CLIENT: I guess you're right. It's not so bad that this teacher doesn't like me. Other people like me. And my friends aren't always better off than me— and it wouldn't matter if they were!

THERAPIST: Why wouldn't it matter?

CLIENT: Because I'm not a worthless person just because somebody has more than me, or because somebody doesn't attend to me when I want them to.

THERAPIST: That's right. It doesn't matter how much attention and approval you get, it's not going to matter if you don't like yourself. And things aren't going to be the way you want at times, so you try to change them, or accept their existence.

CLIENT: Okay, I understand. Let me continue. It would be nice to do better, and if I try to get my homework done, I might have a more pleasant time in that class. And it would be better for me to concentrate on liking myself more instead of trying to get the teacher's attention. How's that for changing my irrational thoughts?

There are a number of irrational beliefs of school-age children which contain the component of "mistake making" (e.g., "I'm bad if I make a mistake"; "Adults should be perfect"; "I shouldn't make mistakes, especially social mistakes"). It is frequently the case that a young client believes that other people who are in positions of authority (parents, teachers) should never make mistakes (act unfairly). In getting the client to give up the demand for perfection in others, it is sometimes necessary to educate the client on the nature of and reasons underlying mistake making. Some of the ideas which we include in a mini-lecture are:

1. Everyone will always make mistakes.
2. No one is perfect.
3. Mistakes do not change a person's good qualities.
4. A person is not the same as his performance.
5. People are not bad because they make mistakes.
6. People who make mistakes do not deserve to be blamed and punished.
7. The reasons why people make mistakes are: (a) lack of skill, (b) carelessness or poor judgment, (c) not having enough information, unsound assumptions, (d) tired or ill, (e) different opinion, and (f) irrationality (adapted from Knaus, 1974).

The rational attitude which is hopefully adopted by the young client after discussion is that there is no point in overly upsetting oneself to the point where one's behavior compromises one's goals simply because someone is making a mistake such as not treating one fairly. An example of rational self-statements which we have employed with a client who unduly upsets himself about his teacher's behavior is:

"Oh well, there is my teacher acting stupidly again. I wish he was fairer. I'm irritated that he does not believe me when I tell him I've left my homework at home. He's probably having a bad day. No point in getting too angry."

For children and adolescents who put themselves down or get angry when they make mistakes, the following type of dialogue can be employed:

"I can't quite get the hang of this. No point in getting too upset. I'll stay calm and try my best; mistakes are what learning is all about."

Another irrational concept which permeates childhood irrationality is that of "fairness" ("Parents should be fair"; "Schools and teachers should be fair at all times"). "Fairness" can be discussed at two levels. At the interpretation stage, it is often possible to have the young client examine his judgment of fairness to determine whether others would agree that his judgment of "unfairness" is an objective and sound one. For example, Robert, age 12, was referred for general aggressiveness and underachievement. During the period he was seen by the first author, he was suspended for three days because he refused to report to the principal's office after school to serve a detention he was given earlier in the day for fighting. Robert thought it was unfair that the principal gave him a detention when it really was not his fault that he got into the fight. The following discussion took place:

THERAPIST: What happened?
CLIENT: I got into trouble for fighting.
THERAPIST: Describe to me what went on.
CLIENT: I was wrestling with a friend. Had him in a headlock. Some other kid came up and was going to jump on my back. I swung around and hit him.
THERAPIST: And then what happened?
CLIENT: I was told to see the principal but I didn't go.
THERAPIST: Why not?
CLIENT: It wasn't my fault.
THERAPIST: How come?
CLIENT: He shouldn't have bothered us. We were playing by ourselves and he should have stayed away.
THERAPIST: But you struck the first blow?
CLIENT: (nods) If I didn't he would have jumped on me and hurt me.
THERAPIST: You sure?
CLIENT: Un-huh.
THERAPIST: Look Robert. I'm on your side right?

CLIENT: Un-huh.

THERAPIST: How do you know that?

CLIENT: You want to help me.

THERAPIST: That's right. Now I'm going to disagree with you that what happened was unfair but remember, I'm on your side. O.K.?

CLIENT: Yes.

THERAPIST: Well, first of all, it sounds to me that you started it. You hit the other boy first?

CLIENT: Un-huh.

THERAPIST: What is the school rule for fighting?

CLIENT: You're not supposed to.

THERAPIST: What happens if you get caught?

CLIENT: Probably put on the "D" [detention] list.

THERAPIST: Well then, was it fair for you to be given a detention by the principal?

CLIENT: No.

THERAPIST: Why?

CLIENT: Because I didn't start it.

THERAPIST: As the school rule is "no fighting" and it doesn't matter who starts it, I think it was fair that you were given a detention because you broke the law. Just imagine you're driving a car and exceeding the speed limit because you're thinking about something else and your mind isn't on the job. It's a bright sunny day and the road is free of much traffic. All of a sudden a policeman stops you and begins to give you a ticket for speeding. You say to him that it's not fair to get a ticket because you didn't mean to speed. He gives you one anyway. Who's fair in that situation?

CLIENT: The policeman.

THERAPIST: Why?

CLIENT: Because I was speeding.

THERAPIST: And what would happen if you didn't pay the ticket?

CLIENT: Go to jail?

THERAPIST: Well you might have to pay even a bigger fine just like you had to serve a three-day suspension for not reporting for detention. Do you see that?

CLIENT: Yes.

THERAPIST: Now when you are in school, you have to obey the laws as well and you can't just say it's unfair because you didn't mean to. If you break a rule even if it wasn't totally your fault, it's fair to have to pay a ticket. Do you agree?

CLIENT: I guess.

THERAPIST: So in the future, try and think ahead and remember that if you break a rule, you'll have to pay the price.

The preferential solution which was not attempted with Robert was to work on the appraisal of "unfairness." The practitioner may use the previously described techniques for disputing "awfulizing" and for "can't-stand-it-itis" in helping the client place the problem of unfairness on a continuum and emphasizing that unfairness is a hassle and not a horror. In disputing the "demandingness" which often is an associated approach with ideas about "fairness," the practitioner can simply teach that the world is an unfair place and that one had better not be surprised by or expect anything other than "unfairness" from time to time. Clients are encouraged to remain calm in the face of "unfairness" so that they are in a position to change things when possible and accept those things one cannot change. DiGiuseppe and Bernard (1983) illustrate how RET can be used to change a young client's appraisal of one particular "unfair" activating event.

> Thomas was a 13 year old student with a history of behavioral and academic problems. Thomas reported that his teacher had a great dislike for him and she *had* become quite disgusted with him. As therapy progressed, Thomas made changes and behaved more appropriately in school. He became less angry, and less disruptive. However, empirical disputing of his thoughts that the teacher did not like him appeared to be accurate. Given the way he had been behaving it was hard to blame her. When Thomas would make some improvements or behaved well, she frequently did not acknowledge them or still accused him of behaving inappropriately. Thomas became angry at this point with the action potential of giving up and acting badly again. His irrational beliefs leading to this anger were somewhat along the lines that "people should be fair." My attempts to dispute this idea with Thomas got nowhere. He believed people should be fair. After all how would the world survive if people couldn't be trusted. Fairness was necessary for social life, so he said. Rather than trying to convince him that unfairness was a fact of life, which it was, and that there were probably millions of unfair people out there, we focused on a more narrow set of beliefs. That is, that this particular teacher had to be fair. We discussed: particular reasons why she could be unfair; how we could not change her even though we thought most people should be fair; to have an ordered world we could not demand that she be fair and there is no way we could force her to be so. While Thomas was not willing to accept the fact that unfairness would survive in the universe, he was willing to concede that this particular individual would remain unfair and that he could tolerate that little degree of unfairness. Thus, while we did not reach an elegant solution in changing his appraisal to a wide span of stimuli, we did teach him to appraise this particular stimuli in a much different way. His anger was reduced and he continued to make behavioral gains throughout the school year. [p. 73]

There is one other irrational idea which we uncover daily in working with children and adolescents which is that hard work and unpleasantness is something to be avoided at all times. The inability to tolerate the feelings associated with anxiety, frustration, anger, etc., is revealed across many irrational beliefs of the childhood period ("Things should come easily to me"; "I shouldn't have to wait for anything"; "Everything should be entertaining and/or enjoyable with no unpleasantness whatsoever"). We have indicated in Chapter 5 how people appear to have different tolerance levels for dealing with frustration and stress and how these propensities underlie many different disorders. Low frustration tolerance is one of the most difficult tendencies to overcome. While it is relatively easy to dispute the irrational beliefs which underlie it, it is, perhaps, the most difficult area clients have in putting thoughts into action. The instinct for pleasure seeking and pain avoidance seems to far outweigh the pull of rationality.

In disputing ideas which underlie low frustration tolerance, it is most important that the practitioner combines cognitive and behavioral methods. A brief case examination will illustrate this approach.

Darren, age 12, was seen over a three-month period for underachievement. Darren's main problem appeared to be an inability to settle down and start work and a tendency to tire and give up too quickly. A reasonably bright seventh grader, Darren's grades were generally in the C range. It became fairly apparent talking with Darren that he had developed the bad habit of avoiding work whenever he began to think about doing his homework. Homework related thoughts such as "This is going to be hard work, I'll be missing out on my favorite television show; I really can't be bothered with all of this" led to mild feelings of discomfort anxiety which Darren escalated into intense unpleasantness and arousal by labelling his initial anxiety as being extremely painful and intolerable. By this stage, Darren looked for any way out. In helping Darren overcome his discomfort anxiety, the following rationale was used: "There is no question that hard work can be unpleasant. However, as you will probably agree, one of the hardest parts of hard work is getting started. Getting started is like getting over a hump, or a mental obstacle. Once you get over the obstacle, you'll be fine. Now, what we can do today and for the next weeks is to help you develop mental skills so you can get over your mental hump in the road with as little fuss as possible. There are two basic mental skills you will need to learn. First is to improve your concentration so you do not distract yourself with thoughts which divert you from your goal. Second, you will have to learn to accept that you will sometimes feel uncomfortable and that that's okay—a fact of life. What we hope to do is to get you into condition so that you will be less distracted and troubled by your feelings when you are preparing to study." Stress inoculation (see next chapter) and RET were combined to help Darren prepare for and deal with feelings of anxiety and to acquire a more rational way of looking at and describing different aspects of emotional reactions vis a vis the time he spent studying. Darren was also asked to monitor the amount of time he spent studying each night which was graphed on a weekly basis and provided the basis for goal setting. He was shown how in his case it was better to start with easier subjects for homework rather than the more difficult ones as his school study guide suggested. His teachers were informed of the program and agreed to make extra efforts to praise Darren's efforts. Overall, an attempt was made to get Darren to trade the immediate payoffs of work avoidance for the delayed satisfaction of teacher approval of improved grades. Without receiving any help or support at home from his mother (Darren's father had left home), Darren achieved a solid B performance for his final term's work and the query as to whether Darren should repeat grade 7 was answered in the negative.

Rational-Emotive Imagery (REI)

REI is a procedure for learning how to change emotions through changing cognitions. It has been described by Ellis as an *emotive disputational* procedure as its focus is initially more on emotional than cognitive change. Our experience with younger clients is that it is a procedure that is more effective and less threatening when employed after the client has achieved some intellectual insight into the ABCs of RET and, as a consequence, some coping skills. If early on in therapy a young client is asked to imagine a scene which evokes extremely painful sensations, the client may lose trust in the practitioner and, as has happened, terminate therapy. So it is important to make sure that the client is prepared for a potentially upsetting experience. Maultsby has indicated, and we agree, that REI is especially good for clients who seem to have accepted the RET viewpoint but who lack the emotional muscle to put it into practice.

We present a portion of Virginia Waters' (1982b) transcript to illustrate how REI can be combined with rational self-statements to produce emotional change in a young client.

Therapist: "Now let's imagine a scene. First I'll play you and you can play the part of your friend. We'll pretend it's bedtime and I'll show you how you can say the comforting things to yourself to feel calmer. Then I'll give you a chance to practice."

Client: "OK."

Therapist: "You begin and tell me it's time to go to bed and I'll take it from there."

Client: "Well, it's time to go to bed. Good night."

Therapist: "Well, it's time to go to bed. I'm beginning to get that uncomfortable feeling, but it's not *too* uncomfortable. Now let's see what can I say to myself to make myself feel better. I'm very safe here. My friend is next to me and her parents are in the next room. I don't have to make myself feel uncomfortable by thinking those scarey thoughts and 'what ifs' to myself. I'll have Snoopy talk to me and see what he has to say. I even feel comfortable lying here. I know I can see my mother tomorrow and she'll be fine and my father is fine and I feel pretty comfortable and I think I'm falling asleep." (snore)

Client: (enthusiastically) "And there's nothing to worry about if you sit down and think about it."

Therapist:	"That's right. There's absolutely nothing to worry about right now."
Client:	"And I'm going to see my mother the next day. I'm only here for six hours, just for the night."
Therapist:	"That's right. Do you want to try it?"
Client:	"I don't think I could say all those things."
Therapist:	"That's OK. You don't have to do it just like I did. Just say what comes into your mind and then if you need some help we can write it down for you. OK?"
Client:	"Alright."
Therapist:	"Oh, it's time to go to bed!"
Client:	"Oh no! OK . . . Well, what do I have to worry about? Nothing! I have all my stuffed animals here. I have things to comfort me. I'm going to see my mother tomorrow. There's nothing to worry about. So I'll try and fall asleep before I say all those what if's to myself. So I'll just try and fall asleep and if anything happens, my friend's parents are right there, and my friend is right next to me. So the worst thing would be if I woke her and that's not so bad. And I'm only here for a little while and for one night I can afford not to sleep at my own house. This is for real, not pretend. I feel better right now. Even if I were going to spend the night here tonight with you, I would feel alright."
Therapist:	"Did you notice a difference in how you felt, saying the comforting things to yourself?"
Client:	"Yes. Very much even now."
Therapist:	"Good, and if you practice thinking these comforting things, you'll be able to do it better and better each time." [p. 17–19]

Practical Problem Solving

Practical problem solving can be employed both for practical and emotional problems though it's primarily designed to resolve the former. Children frequently are in trouble, or are less than happy, because they do not have the skills to handle a situation. If someone teases them, they may not know of any other way to handle the situation than to fight. They may not be particularly upset at the time. Many children would like to have more friends but do not know how to get them. These socially withdrawn children may or may not experience debilitating levels of interpersonal anxiety which prevent them from meeting others. RET assesses deficits in the practical skills of young clients which may be of concern and creating some distress in the client and in others.

When emotional problems accompany practical ones, practical problem solving may function as a form of *behavioral disputation*. For example, a young client might say to herself "I will never be able to complete all my homework; I'm hopeless," and feel depressed. By teaching her practical skills for thinking about how to be better organized and more efficient and by forcing her to force herself to actually complete various amounts of homework, her newly acquired behavioral skills provide evidence for rejecting her self-defeating belief and lead to a reduction in emotional stress.

In teaching practical skills, RET tries where possible to provide instruction in both how to *think about* a practical problem as well as how to go about solving it. While RET practitioners sometimes have to simply tell the client how best to handle a situation without going into what he should be thinking and saying, most practical problems involve the use of rational self-statements or more general cognition strategies (e.g., consequential and means−end thinking) combined with rehearsal of behavioral skills.

A number of RET practitioners (e.g., DiGiuseppe & Bernard, 1983; Waters, 1982a, 1982b) have arrived at a practical problem solving format which can be readily employed even with very young children, and includes the following steps (from Waters, 1982a):

1. Define the problem in concrete, behavioral terms.

2. Generate as many alternative solutions as you can without evaluating them. Remember, quantity is more important than quality; the more solutions the better.

3. Go back and evaluate each alternative solution, giving both positive and negative consequences and eliminating absurd solutions.

4. Choose one or two of the best solutions and plan your procedures step by step.

5. Put your plan into action and evaluate results. [p. 576]

An illustration of the first two steps of this approach is contained in the following transcript (from Waters, 1982b):

Therapist: "The other kind of problem people can have is a practical problem, and that has to do with wanting to change something in your life other than hurtful feelings, like. . . ."

Client: "I already did that."

Therapist: "What did you do?"

Client: "I changed my behavior and I listen more to my mother. That was a problem I changed."

Therapist: "Good. Yes, I'll bet you have already solved some practical problems."

Client: "I did it and didn't know it."

Therapist: "I'd like you to choose something else in your life which is a problem you would like to solve, and I'll show you a good way to go about solving it."

Client: "I'd like to change not seeing my friend P so much."

Therapist: "OK, that's a really good problem to work on, but let me check something with you before we begin. How do you feel about not seeing P as much as you would like?"

Client: "Not good. Sad, I guess. I'd like to see her more. I love her and want to see her more."

Therapist: "Feeling sad is certainly unpleasant, but it is OK to feel sad if you aren't getting what you want. Do you ever feel angry and depressed about it?"

Client: "Well, sometimes I used to but not now."

Therapist: "Because when people feel hurtful feelings, like anger and depression, they create like an emotional or feeling fog, which clogs their brains and makes it very hard for them to see clearly and think clearly about how to solve the problem. I think that feeling sad is appropriate and won't get in the way of you solving this problem. What do you think?"

Client: "I think if I was feeling really upset and crying over it, I'd be too hurt to think. I don't feel that way now."

Therapist: "OK, let's begin." (Pulls out problem solving sheet, goes over instructions once.) "The first step is to state the problem."

Client: "Not seeing P enough."

Therapist: "OK." (Therapist records.) "The second step is to come up with as many ideas as you can, as to how to see her more often. And while we're getting the ideas down, we aren't going to say whether they are good or bad, we're just going to get as many ideas as we can."

Client: "Well, my mother seeing her mother more often. Can I write it? (Client records alternatives and then goes through the list, noting which are possible.)

Alternatives

*1. My mother seeing her mother more often.

*2. I could join the Y with her.

3. Take other activities together.

*4. Ask her mother to bring her over more often.

*5. Ask my mother to bring me to her house more often.

*6. Meet somewhere between our two houses.

*7.   Get a taxi to take us to each other's houses.

8.   My grandfather could drive me over there.

9.   Ride a bicycle over to P's house.

*10.   Go to the Beauty Parlour together.

* Possible

Therapist: "Wow! There are seven possibilities here. That's quite good. We could probably go on like this, if we had time, and come up with even more alternatives."

Client: "Gee. There're a lot more things I could do than I realized. What's the next step?"

Therapist: "What the next step is, is to look at each of these possible alternatives and think of something positive and something negative that would happen for each one."

Client: "Like in the first one something positive would be that our mothers are friends and would like to see more of each other, which means my friend and I would see more of each other too, and something negative would be that they might not have the time to see more of each other."

Therapist: "Right. That's good thinking. For homework you could take this list home and think about a positive and negative for each of the possibilities and we'll continue with this next week."

Client: "OK. I may write them down so I won't forget." [pp. 30–34]

In the next chapter we provide extensive illustration as to how cognitive procedures can be used to teach practical problem solving skills.

PRACTICE AND APPLICATION

The final stage of RET involves helping the young client apply rational thinking skills outside the practitioner's office in real life situations. While the task of teaching the basics of RET can usually be accomplished, it is quite another thing to see young clients spontaneously applying RET. RET stresses therefore "the importance of practicing the skills in a variety of settings and of specific homework assignments. . ." (Waters, 1982a). Sounding a pessimistic note, Young (1983) indicates:

Problem solving, the basic goal of RET, is usually accomplished by persuading clients to put knowledge in therapy into practice in concrete situations. This usually requires conscious effort and hard work, traits that unfortunately are not high on the list of adolescent virtues. Young people are notoriously reluctant to apply themselves to any task that does not promise immediate results. It is important, therefore, not to harbour unrealistic expectations about counseling adolescents. Clinical experience has shown that teenagers usually do not undergo sweeping or dramatic personality changes, living happily ever after as a result of their therapy endeavours. Most come in for relatively few interviews; if these clients are handled skillfully along the lines I have suggested, they generally make moderate improvement. [p. 99]

The main way RET accomplishes the goals of the final stage of therapy is through *homework*. Once the young client accepts the possibility and desirability of change, the practitioner has sufficient leverage to "request" that the client "does one or two things between sessions." An example of such a request is as follows:

That was good work today Steven. You really did some good thinking. For next week, there are a few things I'd like you to practice which we discussed today. First, don't make mountains out of molehills. If something bad happens like your sisters refusing to play with you, remember to say to yourself the things we've written down to take home with you, (e.g., "It isn't that bad, I don't have to get angry"). Second, on this piece of paper, I want you to keep track of how many times you get angry. Write down how angry you were on a scale of 1–10, what was happening and what you did. And remember, pat yourself on the back when you control your temper.

Children and adolescents are used to being told by people at school to do certain things at home. While we avoid using the word "homework," we do communicate an attitude right from the beginning that it is expected that they will be doing work outside the sessions themselves.

Homework

This final phase is really the most taxing on the personal resources of the practitioners. It is at this time that some young clients begin to realize that the practitioner who up until then they had perceived as someone understanding and friendly was going to ask them to do things that they frequently do not want to do oftentimes because whatever it is involves hard work. This puts the practitioner into the same role as the client's parents and teachers. The point at which the practitioner starts to request the youngster to change sometimes breaks the relationship. The client may quickly reinterpret the value he or she places on, and the trust placed in, the practitioner. By being aware of this, the practitioner may dispute with the young client the idea "Because he is telling me to do something I don't want to do, he's no good" and that "It's unfair for him to ask me to do so."

Another point to keep in mind is that clients who tend to complete their school homework will tend to do what you ask them to do while those who have a history of not handing in homework at school will tend not to follow through with you. Remember, the problems you face in getting a client cooperating with you will be the same as those faced by the young client's parents and teachers. Therefore, make sure you prepare both the client, parents, teachers, and yourself before you assign homework. If you know that the young client is not likely to do what you ask, either do not ask or make sure that the client is, because of the relationship he or she has developed with you, prepared to change past behavior. Not infrequently we set up a token reinforcement system with younger clients to ensure appropriate levels of motivation. Communication and cooperation with parents is obviously essential.

There are numerous ways in which the young client may practice and apply skills acquired during sessions. Waters (1982a) indicates the following as typical homework assignments: (1) monitoring feelings; (2) making a list of personal demands; (3) REI; (4) practicing changing feelings and thoughts in a real situation; (5) taking a responsible risk; and (6) reinforcing self with positive self-talk.

Young (1983) recommends the following tactics to help teenagers learn what therapy is about, what to expect from their efforts, and how to put insight into action:

1. Explain psychological and emotional problems as habits. Sometimes I can encourage effort by adolescents through labeling their problems as habits. . . . What I usually do is ask in each session about progress. When a reported lack of improvement can be traced to a client's failure to put into practice what we have been discussing, I suggest that the client's problem, no matter how complicated or painful, is merely a habit. After some explaining and clarifying, I point out the client can expect improvement if he puts in the necessary work to change the habit. . . .

2. Checking out the client's expectations about therapy. Often adolescents have the wrong idea what to expect from counseling. Unless these misconceptions are corrected, clients will likely lose faith in therapy because it will not give them what they want. . . .

3. Writing out an A.B.C. homework for them. Although I am frequently successful in helping adolescents understand why their thinking is irrational, I find it difficult to get them to practice challenging and correcting their irrational ideas outside of therapy sessions. . . . For this reason, I try to outline their problems on a blackboard, or sheet of paper, using the A.B.C. model. At each session, I try to take the client through the model, and I also suggest he take my writing efforts home with him and look at them if the problem comes up during the week. . . .

4. Sticking to accepted insights. Once a particular insight has been presented, understood, and accepted by a teenager, I strongly suggest that this information be repeated without significant change. In other words, stick to what seems to impress the client as the cognitive source of his distress and use the same words, analogies, visual examples, and the like to reinforce the message. . . .

5. Tell the adolescent what to think. I have found, despite heroic efforts, some adolescents are not going to learn how to reason things out according to prescribed RET dogma. In such cases I simply give them the correct sentences to think. . . .

6. Arranging homework assignments. I usually try to design some kind of appropriate homework assignment for the client between sessions. . . . For instance, I might help a shy adolescent understand the cognitive sources of his shyness, but I also want to get him to do something assertive, such as going to a party, asking a girl out, or maybe saying no to someone he usually accommodates with a yes. I have found that young people are more likely to accept the ideas of rational thinking after they have tried them out in emotionally provoking experiences. [pp. 99–101]

We have found some of the following activities useful for reinforcing some of the RET ideas taught in sessions. We sometimes ask the young client to fill out a happening-thought-feeling-behaving diagram such as the one presented in Appendix 1. The youngster is asked to write down the thoughts he has in a problematic situation, his feelings on a 1–10 point scale, his reactions, and whether his thought was rational or irrational. If the thought was irrational, there is space for a new rationally restated thought to be written, as well as for a rating of new feelings and a description of a new reaction. This information is then used as a focus of attention for the following session.

We also frequently design materials to emphasize certain RET concepts. Two examples are provided in Tables 7.2 and 7.3. In Table 7.2 a young client is asked to describe certain positive and negative qualities about himself in an effort to expand his self-concept. In Table 7.3, a young client is given practice in applying his knowledge about why people make mistakes. These types of tables are useful instructional devices for hard to teach material and are easy to develop.

It will be seen from these examples that much of RET homework emphasizes not only cognition but also the emotive and behavioral dimensions of human experience. It endeavors to link up cognitive with emotional and behavioral change through the use of experiential and imaginal exercises.

Another technique we have found valuable for promoting a thorough understanding and application of RET techniques is that of *rational role reversal* (Kassinove & DiGiuseppe, 1975). After the young client understands rational ideas which underlie his problem, the practitioner assumes the role of the young client and the young client takes the role of the rational practitioner who explains to the "young client" the causes of his problem. "The therapist asks clarifying questions and raises cogent points that allow the client to forcefully rehearse rational thinking" (Grieger & Boyd, 1980, p. 180).

A technique related to rational role reversal which an older child may employ successfully is called *rational proselytizing* (Bard, 1973). We have seen this technique employed by young clients who report to us that they have

TABLE 7.2. My Characteristics

Positive Things About Me

Things I do:
1.
2.
3.
4.
5.

Things I do for other people:
1.
2.
3.
4.
5.

Things I feel:
1.
2.
3.
4.
5.

Personal things:
1.
2.
3.
4.
5.

Negative Things About Me (Sometimes I. . . .)

Things I don't do:
1.
2.
3.
4.
5.

Things I don't do for other people:
1.
2.
3.
4.
5.

Things I feel:
1.
2.
3.
4.
5.

explained ideas to their parents in order to help them understand what they are doing in the sessions with the practitioner. This frequently helps speed up the rate at which the younger client acquires the basis of RET as well as can have the effect of improving the client's relationship with her family. Parents begin to see that their child is making an honest attempt to change.

TABLE 7.3. Mistake Making

Causes of Mistakes	1.	Lack of skill
	2.	Carelessness or poor judgment
	3.	Not studying or poor students
	4.	Not having enough information, unsound assumption
	5.	Tired or ill
	6	Different opinion

Directions: Fill in the chart

Mistake	Cause	Your Thoughts about Mistake Maker
1. A baby spills milk on the beautiful carpet		
2. Mr. Smith doesn't see a stop sign and crashes into another car. Both drivers are hurt		
3. Ian fails an important exam		
4. Mary thought Damian was an interesting boy. She went on a date with him and spent a boring evening		
5. Mrs. Dow yells at Doug for not handing in his homework on time. Doug's father forgot to return it to Doug after he read it		

Other cognitive and behavioral activities we employ as homework include:

1. Practice of behaviors role played and rehearsed with the practitioner such as verbal assertion and extinction.
2. Writing down upsetting thoughts young clients have during the week.
3. Trying out of alternatives generated during practical problem solving.
4. Asking other people to write down positive things about the young client. This is especially useful for negative clients.

The final stage of therapy is completed when the practitioner assesses that the goals of therapy have been achieved. Waters (1982a) suggests that RET practitioners ask the following questions:

Is this child able to resolve emotional upsets?

Is this child able to solve practical problems?

Does the child take responsibility for his own emotions?

Is the child and the parents satisfied with the progress? [p. 576]

We always inform parents and the child that should they wish to resume treatment in the future that we are always available. Some practitioners send out follow-up forms to parents six to eight weeks after treatment sessions have been terminated.

MIDDLE INTERVIEW SESSIONS

As we did in Chapter 6, we shall provide a brief listing of topics and content of intermediate interview sessions.

1. *Review and discuss presenting problems and problem analyses.*   Parents and children frequently bring up different problems from those they presented in initial sessions. It is important for the practitioner to be aware of how clients are currently viewing their problems. If clients continuously change their problems each week, it may well be that they themselves are not fully aware of their problem. Value clarification as well as cognitive and emotive awareness exercises may have to be employed at these times.

2. *Discuss homework.*   If clients have performed their homework activities, you know they are more likely to be with you and motivated to change. Data from homework concerning thoughts, feelings, and behaviors enable the practitioner to more fully unravel the dynamics of the problem. If homework is not completed, emphasis should be placed on the collaborative nature of the counseling relationship.

3. *Handling resistance to homework.*   It is not unusual during the early days of therapy for clients to fail to carry out homework assignments. Practitioners should not become overly discouraged for, as Nina Woulff, a RET therapist, has pointed out," . . . it is this very resistance which is the royal road to the irrational beliefs which are perpetuating the cycle of interactions around the symptom" (1983, p. 379). Frequently it takes parents a number of sessions before they are fully compliant with directives to be, for example, firmer and stricter. This may be because of emotional difficulties (e.g., guilt) which are supported by irrational beliefs ("a child must love his parent all the time"). It is up to the practitioner to identify and challenge irrational beliefs of parents and children which are interfering with progress.

4. *Decide upon form of treatment.*   As therapy unfolds, it is up to the practitioner to decide whether a particular problem warrants all members of the family being seen together or separately. DiGiuseppe (1983) suggests that if a child presents with manipulative behavior, parents and child should be seen separately. Some RET family practitioners employ a "mixed" form of treatment where the child is seen alone for

the first part of the session, then the parents, and all members of the family are seen for the remainder of the session.

5. *Reinforce clients' progress.* Liberal praise for effort, as well as any progress, *however small*, is important. Praise behavior, not the client.

6. *Elicit new problems.* It is useful to question clients as to whether there are any new problems they wish to discuss. New problems help to further define the philosophy, beliefs, lifestyle, and goals of clients.

7. *Communicate summary interpretation of clients' problems.* Be sure to check out that your inferences concerning the ABCs of a problem relate with the clients'. If the clients do not accept your analysis, you've got to see whether you've missed important data, or whether the clients are being resistant. In either case, the clients have to be won over to a cognitive viewpoint of their problems before RET can commence. (This is especially the case when cognitive disputational procedures are to be employed.)

8. *Select problem for session.* Younger clients—especially less verbal ones—will need to be guided in this selection process. Try to center your discussion around one problem instead of moving from one to another. Problems selected should be consistent with the different cognitive, emotive, and behavioral changes agreed to by the client (parents and/or child).

9. *Discuss RET goals and principles in terms of problem selected.* This step involves teaching basic insights and the ABCs of RET.

10. *Clients summarize in their own language what is to be changed and how it is to be changed.* Clients should have a pretty good idea of how their emotions, behaviors, and cognitions influence the attainment of their short- and long-term goals. With older children, adolescents, and parents the role of rational self-talk and disputational challenging should be recognized.

11. *Employ emotional and practical problem solving procedures.* These procedures are geared to the developmental level of young clients and include those described in the skill building section of this chapter.

12. *Repetition and rehearsal of procedures including those required for homework.* As we have emphasized, the practice of rational thinking and other emotive and behavioral skills are crucial if clients are to maintain skills in real life situations. Therefore, insure that sufficient time is provided during sessions for clients to practice basic cognitive change procedures. Also, it is very important that clients understand exactly what they need to do for homework (e.g., how to fill out a self-report form; carry out a behavioral assertiveness exercise).

13. *Schedule next appointment.* It is still a good idea to continue to see clients on a weekly basis (or more often if needed) to insure that progress is made by clients in solving their own emotional and practical problems.

LATER AND FINAL INTERVIEW SESSIONS

1. *Discuss homework and review previous weeks' progress and problems.*
   Homework becomes increasingly important as it reveals whether significant changes in clients are taking place. More and more time is spent in
   analyzing progress and setbacks in real life situations. Clients are asked
   to carefully recount significant success and failure experiences. Such
   feedback enables the practitioner to design new experiences which
   tackle the idiosyncratic responsivity of clients.

2. *Repeat, modify, or employ new cognitive-emotive-behavioral procedures.*   It may take many sessions for intractable problems to show
   improvement. For these problems, it is sometimes possible to introduce
   a number of different procedures across sessions (e.g., relaxation,
   assertive training, rational self-statements). In so doing, it becomes
   possible to determine which RET method works best and whether
   change takes place more quickly when cognitive, emotive, and/or behavioral changes are targeted.

3. *Assist clients to identify progress.*   During later sessions, it is important
   to point out to both parents and children the different ways in which you
   see them improving. Praise for individual efforts to change may work to
   create improved self-esteem and internal locus of control. Sometimes,
   parents are so enmeshed with the problems of their children that they
   fail to notice or appreciate significant changes which occur in their
   children. Children, too, overlook changes in their parents' behavior.

4. *Clients rehearse their approach to recurrence of problem.*   One simple
   but effective way to prepare clients for a recurrence of problems is to
   prepare them for the eventuality. Indicating to clients that it is possible
   old problems may arise from time to time and they now have the skills to
   deal with them helps to insure that they are not caught unawares when
   problems arise and, as a consequence, are better able to handle them.
   Clients are asked to imagine problems reoccurring and to describe how
   they can rationally think their way out of them.

5. *Discuss ways of maintaining and generalizing progress.*   As Ellis has
   written and lectured about for many years, change requires *continuous*
   hard work and some people take almost a lifetime to break self-defeating thought patterns. Therefore, stress to clients that for therapeutic
   progress to be maintained, it is important to continue to practice the
   rational reformulation of irrational concepts and beliefs so that their
   overall belief system is permanently modified. It is extremely educative
   for the practitioner to ask clients how they would deal with novel
   situations which the practitioner can anticipate would be upsetting. The
   answers of clients indicate when they are likely to generalize the gains
   they have shown in dealing with specific problems. Other questions to
   ask could include (a) How do you explain the changes which have

occurred? (b) How could you slip back into your old pattern? (c) Specifically, how would you have to think and react to each other in order to get back into the old rut? (Woulff, 1983)

6. *Arrange for subsequent contact if required.*   Our practice is to indicate to all clients that we are available in the future should they like to see us. This option enables some clients to face subsequent problems with more assurance, knowing they can be in contact with us if difficulties arise. We do not encourage a dependent relationship. Instead, we communicate an attitude of concern beyond the boundaries of counseling sessions.

CASE TRANSCRIPT

We end this chapter with an extended transcript of a final interview session with a 14-year-old boy, Craig, who had been referred to the first author. As we indicated earlier, the major problem of concern both to him and his parents were his frequent illnesses (swollen glands, sore throat, fever, weakness) which occurred every month or so and which kept him home three to five days. The outbreak of these bouts of illness appeared to be associated with stress of schooling and especially with homework and studying for tests. The client was extremely bright (IQ 130+). His main emotional difficulty was found to be "anxiety" associated with his "demandingness" and "perfectionistic" attitudes. In this last session, RET concepts were reviewed extensively so that the client could listen to them during the summer. (He tape recorded each session.) For this reason, the therapist tended to do a majority of the talking.

THERAPIST: What shall we talk about today? What sort of things are of concern that you would like to go over?

CLIENT: Uh, a relapse mainly. I need to concentrate more on not going overboard, so I don't keep studying too hard, too long, too much.

THERAPIST: Right. Well how do you know when you first of all might be studying too long, too hard? What's going to signal you to think positive thoughts? They are just not going to materialize all of a sudden; something has got to remind you to think positive thoughts and generally it's the problem as it starts to creep up, which in your case is what?

CLIENT: Um, I start feeling pretty worn out at say, 8:30, a quarter to nine, but because I still have a fair bit to go I keep going, because sometimes I usually don't get started till, say, 7:30.

THERAPIST: Uh-uh.

CLIENT: So.

THERAPIST: OK. Let's stop there just for a minute. Those are the body signals, we talked about those before.

CLIENT: Yes.

THERAPIST: Those are your signals to think first of all.

CLIENT: Yes.

THERAPIST: OK. Now you said positive thoughts and I would say yes, positive thoughts but they are also signals for you to think about not pushing yourself too hard. That is the first message, when you feel yourself getting tired you know I'm getting tired, I'm likely to get sick, therefore I had better start to plan. Either plan times where I can have more rest or plan to go to bed at an earlier time and just forget about the work that I won't get done.

CLIENT: Yes.

THERAPIST: So your physical symptoms of tiredness, fatigue, irritability, will be signals for you to start to think thoughts. OK, and for you those thoughts had better be I'd better think about relaxing and not pushing myself too hard, otherwise I am going to get sick. Does that make sense to you?

CLIENT: Yes.

THERAPIST: OK. Now I have a question for you. There are two ways to go about changing excessive worry and I still think you tend to excessively worry about your school performance. One way is to lower your standards for yourself, and the other one is to keep the standards but expect, not . . . no, not expect less, but if you don't achieve those standards not to hammer yourself unmercifully. What's in the long run, which one of these is a problem for you and which one holds perhaps a partial solution for reducing your worry?

CLIENT: Um, I think the second one would be a better idea for me to think about rather than having to lower my standards, because that really is what I don't want to do.

THERAPIST: Right. That second one is called, and it may now be an old friend of yours because I think it has come up before, demandingness. You demand that you achieve a high standard and when you don't you hammer yourself and that's what you worry about, you're worried about what happens if I don't live up to that high standard. This is what we talked about several weeks ago and your worry was somehow your value . . . as a person would somehow be diminished and then you said, I think we agreed that that was irrational, that that wasn't a sensible thing, and you agreed to it although you said "It hasn't really sunken in."

CLIENT: Yes.

THERAPIST: So that would be something for you in the long run to practice thinking about. The fact is even if you don't get your A's in English it doesn't make you a worthless person and to force yourself to believe that. You don't force yourself. You cling on to your old ideas while you give lip service to the new ones. To give up those old ideas you are going to have to force them out of your head. Every time you even think you might be thinking of them you must dispute them. You must say to yourself these are not true, Dr. Wise-one has told me this, I must believe him. So that's one idea that I think bears repetition and which in,the long run will prevent relapses, because I think you probably still fight and push yourself too hard. The reason you do that is because you desperately need to get to that level and you are afraid not to get there. I am saying to you over the long run take some chances and if you don't get there see what the effects are going to be. You don't really give yourself a chance to see yet. Do you understand what I am saying? You don't allow yourself to fail. You struggle and you push yourself so hard so you won't fail, and what I am saying to you is when the opportunity comes up like middle year, take that chance and if it is a question of your health or the difference between a B+ or an A− I would think your health would want to come first and also test your ego, test how strong a person you are to be able to sustain a less than perfect performance, because you are not going to be failing everything by and large, you just won't be doing as well as, because you set yourself a high standard don't you?

CLIENT: Yes, I do.

THERAPIST: OK. What does all that mean in your words? (laughs) Right, in ten words or less.

CLIENT: (Laughs) Um, I shouldn't set myself the high standards and expect to reach them. I'll rephrase that. I shouldn't set myself high standards and work and work so I get there and then get sick.

THERAPIST: Right, that's a good point.

CLIENT: So, I either lower my standards or keep the high standards and realize that maybe I won't get there if I don't force myself to work as hard.

THERAPIST: What do we call when you force yourself to reach that high standard? That's what you do with your friends when they don't achieve your standards for them, and the same thing you do with yourself. You demand, so we can change demands into preferences, so that when you feel that you are demanding of yourself the attainment of that high standard, you could dispute that demand by saying "I'd like it, I'd prefer it, but I won't demand it." Because if you demand it you will push yourself too hard, so that would be called changing a demand into a preference or to liking or to a wish or you know, it would be nice if that happened, but not I must you know. Does that make sense?

CLIENT: Yes.

THERAPIST: You can see how you apply that to your friends.

CLIENT: Yes.

THERAPIST: Right. Now you said to me last week you weren't, because you do some of the things they do, you weren't going to demand that they be perfect. That's changing your standards which is OK, but that's changing standards. Do you see that? You say I want . . . to be perfect because I realize I am imperfect, why should I expect that from them there is no point in that, so that is changing a standard which is OK, but the other thing which I don't think you successfully dealt with your friends is demanding, to stop demanding that they achieve any standard that you might set for them. You've lowered it, but what happens when they don't. We are all guilty of that, we feel very let down when people don't achieve minimal standards, right? I think we all could profit from just accepting people as they are and wishing they were different, but not demanding. Do you still think you've demanded a little in your own self?

CLIENT: Yes, probably.

THERAPIST: As you demanded of yourself.

CLIENT: Mm.

THERAPIST: I would think if there is one overriding belief and answer you hold about yourself and the world is that of demandingness. You demand that you be perfect or almost totally successful in your work, and you demand that your friends be, live up to whatever your standards are. Now you have changed your standards and that is half the solution. But why demand? What would be a healthier outlook toward friends, rather than demanding that they be the way you want them to be, what could you say to yourself?

CLIENT: So what, they're not doing what I expect of them, they are still good people.

THERAPIST: Right, but you do *care* that they are not living up to a certain standard, I mean because you hold those as important, so rather than saying they *must*, what would be a, they must what? Something you value in your friends.

CLIENT: They must be generous.

THERAPIST: Right, and suppose you catch one being selfish in a moment where you think they should be generous right, that's the point, that sort of problem. OK, then you could say rather they *must* be selfish and he is a no-good-nik because he is not, you could say I wish he wasn't as selfish at that moment as he is. I wish. Now what do you think the consequence of wishing he would be less selfish at that moment would be?

CLIENT: I wouldn't have the demand.

THERAPIST: Right. What would your emotions be then?

CLIENT: I wouldn't get worked up about it.

THERAPIST: As much.

CLIENT: As much.

THERAPIST: So, you would still be irritated, but you wouldn't be as worked up, and what happens when you get that worked up?

CLIENT: I get sick.

THERAPIST: Right. Well, how about with your friends? You would choose not to have them.

CLIENT: Yes.

THERAPIST: Remember you said you would like to have a few more friends, but because they'd let you down and you get depressed a little bit. But if you adopted a more accepting attitude toward your friends and people you meet, then when they do let you down you can accept it and you don't get so emotionally upset that you feel so hurt, therefore you avoid those sorts of encounters. Do you see the quality of that demanding attitude and how it influences your emotions and behaviors toward others? That same attitude characterizes your relationship with yourself. Let's deal with it again in your world of work, your schoolwork. How does demanding relate to your feelings and your behavior and what might you do to change the demandingness?

CLIENT: To change, I would say I wish that I could get an A− and B+ in these subjects, but I might not, so. . . .

THERAPIST: Right.

CLIENT: It's not going to make me any worse a person, it just means that instead of getting an A− I got B+ and maybe because of that I won't get sick.

THERAPIST: Right, and how about your emotions relative to demanding, if you said I wish I could get an A− rather than a B+ but it is not the end of the world, what do you think your level of depression would be?

CLIENT: It wouldn't be as high.

THERAPIST: As it would be if what?

CLIENT: If I'm thinking I demand that I get A− rather than a B+.

THERAPIST: Right. So in terms of your question to prevent relapse in the long run, I still would argue that you could do more thinking homework by rechanging your thoughts. When you're overly stressed you will tend to get sick. Part of that stress is your very high expectation of yourself. Other people would be less stressed because they wouldn't demand perfection like you do. So part of your stress is brought about by what you bring to the situation, so you can have a friend of yours in a similar situation as you are in exams and wanting to do well, but because he doesn't demand perfection he is going to have less stress than you. Some of your friends are less demanding, I would guess all your friends would be less demanding of themselves than you are.

CLIENT: Yes.

THERAPIST: And they don't react the same way as you do. Your only problem is you have got this little Achilles heel for getting sick. Otherwise you would just be a worrier and you know that's unplesant. Everyone lives with worry, but that worry is a stress reaction and that leads to you getting sick. I would say in terms of preventing relapse give some serious thought to demanding and first apply it to your friends and see how that works and as I said, you have changed your attitudes about what you expect of them but now try to change the demandingness and change your demands and preferences. Then force yourself to change your demands of yourself. If you can give up perfectionism and accept the fact that sometimes you will fail, then it doesn't mean you are worthless as you said, and that the world is going to come to an end, and it doesn't you know, I know (laughs) and I've failed enough times to prove it. There, then, you'll feel less stressed. It is only when you are scared of failing, scared of making a mistake, that everything is a stress, especially in school which you value a lot, so if you accept the fact that even in your schoolwork it's OK to fail, that in the long run it doesn't matter, then you can relax a little bit more and you won't get as sick. Because I value my work not as much as you do, no I almost think my standards for my work are probably almost as high as yours if not, well they couldn't be as crazy as yours (both laugh). I mean they are pretty high but I don't demand perfection. I have stress reactions. Do you have stress reactions? I have stress reactions but they are not as severe as yours, because I accept the fact that first of all if I fail I'll still live and others will accept me and that's a lesson that you'll learn, hopefully, through experience that when you fail at things that you can accept yourself and others can accept you. Because you are likeable. There's nothing wrong with you is there that I know of? I find you reasonably pleasant and intelligent; so you'll have your friends regardless if you fail once or twice. Remember you said if you failed your music exam or something you would get laughed at by your friends and you said that would cause you some embarrassment; they wouldn't hold that against you; that might show that you are human. So I still think you could do some more think work but I certainly think you've also progressed a long way in your thinking than when I first talked with you what would it be, six or eight weeks ago or something like that. Do you think you've had a chance to think through some of these ideas a bit further?

CLIENT: Yes.

THERAPIST: When I first saw you you had the basics didn't you, but I think now you have been hammered by me over and over so that it is starting to sink in.

CLIENT: Yes.

THERAPIST: Right. Now that you have recorded my wisdom and you can always take it with you, and for next year, you'll be here next year? I'm here for you, OK, so if you feel the urge to come in and repeat some of these things, rehearse them again, that would be OK, just to refresh your memory . . . Well my speech is done for today, is there anything else you would like to bring up?

CHAPTER 8

Allied Cognitive-Behavioral Approaches

There are a number of other major cognitive approaches which can be employed along with RET to resolve a variety of problems of childhood. Indeed, a major strength of cognitive therapies is the fertilization of concepts and techniques from different approaches in the practitioner's ongoing search for improving the effectiveness of interventions. The current trend in the practice of RET with children is toward the use of several cognitive procedures to deal with a given emotional or behavioral problem. We have identified five cognitive approaches which either have been used or have the potential for use with younger populations. As will be shown, there is significant overlap in aspects of each approach, insofar as each targets similar problem areas (faulty cognitions) and each uses didactic and verbally persuasive techniques. As our interest is in the prevention and treatment of childhood emotional and behavioral disturbances, the emphasis in this chapter will be on the training components of each of these approaches. It will become apparent to the reader that most of the procedures have evolved in an attempt to resolve particular childhood problems such as impulsivity, shyness, and aggression.

The five cognitive approaches to be discussed in this chapter are interpersonal cognitive problem solving (ICPS), self-instructional training, cognitive social skills training (CSST), stress inoculation training, and attribution retraining. We shall discuss the basics of these approaches and when possible we will indicate how they can be combined with RET methods to produce maximally effective interventions. It will be seen that the value of integration lies in the highlighting by these approaches of other relevant cognitive dimensions besides irrational beliefs which underlie maladaptive thinking and provide a target for change. A brief discussion of the theoretical origins of each approach will be presented along with a brief reference to research that has examined the effectiveness of the approach with younger populations. Different methods of assessment will be presented which will be followed by treatment techniques.

In grouping the above five approaches together and describing them as being *cognitive* in nature, we are underlining their use of *verbal mediation* in the form of cognitive skills, strategies, and self-instructions as a means of influencing feelings and behavior. The approaches involve the use of verbal mediation by a young client to (1) enhance the problem solving; (2) inhibit undesirable behavior and reduce disruptive emotions; (3) evaluate alternate plans of action in social settings; (4) change beliefs (e.g., about personal causation); and (5) increase social skills. It will be seen that many of these procedures have direct and concrete clinical applications, such as inhibiting impulsive behavior in hyperactive and aggressive children (Meichenbaum, 1977; Kendall & Finch, 1979), teaching social skills to isolated and withdrawn children (Halford, 1983), reducing aggressive behavior in young children (Bash & Camp, 1975; Camp & Bash, 1981), reducing learned helplessness and perceived lack of personal control in children with problems associated with chronic failure (Dweck, 1975), and the reduction of disruptive emotions such as extreme anxiety and anger (Greiger & Boyd, 1983).

While some of the approaches under discussion have common historical influences (e.g., cognitive psychology, semantic therapy and Russian psychology), it is important to state clearly that the five approaches do *not* derive from a single cognitive model; there is no one theory of cognition in which all the approaches can be subsumed. In later discussion of the origins of each approach, it will also be apparent that although they sometimes share common goals and frequently borrow elements of techniques from different approaches, they belong to different theoretical streams in cognitive psychology.

Further, while we are considering these methods as techniques which can be used in conjunction with RET, they are not synonomous with RET. As we indicated earlier, Ellis (1980a) contrasts "preferential" RET, which aims to alter the philosophy and belief system of the individual, with cognitive behavior therapeutic techniques, which change specific self-statements or teach verbal mediational strategies. Preferential RET involves more far-reaching changes in the individual's attitudes and thinking patterns, whereas CBT methods are generally more limited in focus and generally provide the individual with the cognitive means for coping in specific problem situations.

Each cognitive-behavioral approach provides the young client with verbal mediators which are hypothesized to either facilitate adaptive behavior for impersonal and interpersonal tasks or to occasion more adaptive levels of emotionality. Beyond this, analysis shows that differences rather than similarities among these approaches are predominant. We now summarize some of the differences, as these will be helpful to keep in mind as each approach is dealt with in detail. The following table (Table 8.1) classifies the approaches according to (1) the nature of their therapeutic target (whether it emphasizes a cognitive-behavioral link or a cognitive-emotional one), and (2) the type of cognitive strategy employed—whether a general cognitive strategy or specific cognitive skills are taught.

The terms "cognitive-behavioral" and "cognitive-emotional" strategies are virtually synonomous with what we have called in earlier chapters practical and emotional problem solving. The distinction is a useful one to keep in mind, as some childhood disorders such as implusivity, shyness and some conduct disorders, can be considered as practical problems, without necessarily having an emotional underpinning. (See Chapter 5 for a discussion of behavioral

Table 8. 1   Classification of Cognitive-Behavioral Approaches

Cognitive Interventions	Therapeutic Target	Strategy: General vs. Specific
Interpersonal cognitive problem solving	Cognitive-behavior	General
Cognitive social skills training	Cognitive-behavioral	Specific
Self-instructional training (concrete)	Cognitive-behavioral	Specific
Self-instructional training (conceptual)	Cognitive-behavioral	General
Stress inoculation	Cognitive-emotional	Specific
Attribution retraining	Cognitive-behavioral/emotional	Specific

problems without accompanying emotional difficulties.) In such cases, the practitioner attempts to help the client gain cognitive control over ongoing behavior. No attempt is made to explore the relationship between dysfunctional cognitions—be they excesses or deficits—and inappropriate levels of emotionality. For example, the practitioner may teach a socially isolated child what to say to herself as she engages in different prosocial behaviors; hence the term, cognitive-behavioral. Other cognitive approaches such as stress inoculation (along with RET) are oriented at analyzing and changing the relationship between a child's self-talk and thoughts and emotions. When these approaches are applied the concern is with teaching emotional problem solving skills and not with the teaching of adaptive behavior. While RET is cognitive-emotional in emphasis, a number of the cognitive approaches have primary applications to the practical and behavioral difficulties a child experiences.

We now turn our attention to each of the approaches. Our discussion will show the practitioner that not only is there a wide range of cognitive interventions to apply to childhood problems, but that a multitreatment approach is beginning to evolve effective combinations of interventions for specific childhood disorders. DiGiuseppe (1981) has illustrated how RET and other allied cognitive interventions with children may be combined in a clinical context. He describes a general cognitive approach to assessment and treatment which includes, besides irrational beliefs, such things as interpersonal cognitive problem solving skills, the extent to which a child distorts reality, and a functional cognitive analysis of specific self-instructions which a child may fail to provide for a given task.

INTERPERSONAL COGNITIVE PROBLEM SOLVING

Theoretical Background

This section will present the main features of the work on interpersonal cognitive problem solving (ICPS) carried out by Spivack, Platt, and Shure and their colleagues at the Hahnemann Medical College and Hospital in Philadelphia, Pennsylvania. Much of their work is most directly relevant to developmental counseling programs with primary prevention as their aim. This is especially the case where the prevention of aggressiveness in young children is a prime concern. Applications of ICPS are also beginning to be made in the clinical domain, where practitioners are utilizing the ICPS approach along with other methods in their one to one work with children (e.g., DiGiuseppe, 1983). From the practitioner's point of view it is important to keep in mind that the work of Spivack and Shure (1974) is geared to factors that affect *social adjustment*, which they define somewhat differently from emotional well-being

> A person might have to solve the problem of getting something he wants from someone else, or of dealing with an interpersonal difficulty. . . . How he thinks in such circumstances is relevant to his ability to handle everyday life problems - whether and how he thinks about the interpersonal situation, considers different things he might do and their implications for him as well as others, and sees outcomes relative to his own desires and feelings. [pp. 3−4]

Practitioners interested primarily in modifying feeling states such as intrapersonal difficulties, may at one glance believe that ICPS, with its emphasis on the interpersonal domain, has little to offer. However, our experience is that improvements in interpersonal skills can lead to a reduction in emotional stress as previously difficult situations will arise less often. Of further interest is the way in which the ICPS approach can be applied to the teaching of disputational skills and for practical problem solving.

Spivack, Platt, and Shure (1976) have carried out extensive work in the area of problem solving in interpersonal interactions. Their approach to both prevention and remediation in mental health is an educative one in which children and adolescents are taught general cognitive skills which can be employed in dealing with interpersonal problems. The ICPS approach has been described by Spivack and Shure (1974) in this way:

> The philosophy implicit in the program is that if one wishes to affect the behavior of people one must affect the specific (cognitive) abilities that mediate the behavior in question. The search has been, and still is, to discover the mediating cognitions intimately affecting social adjustment. [p. 131]

In their research into interpersonal cognitive problem solving, they have identified a number of cognitive skills or types of thinking which are thought to mediate social behavior and to be necessary for effective interpersonal problem solving.

1. *Sensitivity or perspective taking*, which is awareness that there are difficulties or 'problems' in human interactions and that other people may have different thoughts and feelings from one's own.

2. *Alternative solution thinking*, which is the generating of a variety of possible ways of dealing with a problematic situation. By implication, the greater the number of possible alternative solutions a person can evolve, the more likely he is to come up with the best possible solution.

3. *Means—end thinking*, which is the conceptualization of the step by step means needed to reach a specific objective. Knowing a solution is of little help if one cannot devise the way to reach it.

4. *Consequential thinking*, by which a person "thinks through" the likely consequences of each alternative for himself and for other people involved. An alternative which may initially look promising, may on reflection turn out to be undesirable or have uncertain consequences if carried out.

5. *Causal thinking*, which is the spontaneous linking of cause and effect. Awareness of connections between events and emotional states may be a prelude to identifying elements of the problem situation and generating solutions.

These cognitive processes are not thought to be personality traits or facets of general intelligence as measured by IQ, but rather skills which are learned over time within the limits set by developmental constraints and which are generally learned as a result of modeling by parents and other adults in real problem situations. Spivack, Platt, and Shure (1976) have researched the relationship between ICPS and general intelligence measures and claim to have demonstrated a relationship between ICPS and social adjustment not accounted for by general intelligence.

These cognitive skills have been derived from a theoretical analysis of the general kinds of thinking required for healthy social interaction. Their analysis focuses more on *how* a child should think (general thinking processes) rather than *what* a child should think (content) in solving a problem.

> A focus on the "right" answer or conclusion focuses attention on the content of thought—the end product itself—and suggests that the role of the helper is to teach or supply solutions. A focus upon generation of thought puts attention upon how a person is thinking out a problem, and the role of the helper is to extract such thought processes or act as a catalyst to and guide through problem-solving thinking. [Spivack, Platt, & Shure, 1976, p. 159]

This approach contrasts markedly with cognitive social skills training which teaches a young client in the tradition of task analysis the specific behaviors which are assessed to be missing as well as provides instruction in task specific self-statements geared to bring the newly acquired social skills under verbal control.

Research Findings

Spivack and Shure (1974) have linked ICPS skills to developmental factors and argue that different skills characterize thinking capabilities at different age levels. They have investigated age groups from early childhood to adulthood to discover whether such skills in fact emerge at different developmental levels and if so, which skills mediate social adjustment at that age. Their findings may alert the practitioner to possible cognitive deficiencies in children of different ages they are seeing in a one to one clinical setting. Because the findings concerning ICPS skills in relation to development are complex, we have summarized the major findings in Table 8.2 in order to emphasize which thinking skills appear to be of greatest importance for adjustment at different developmental levels. In this way the practitioner can more readily judge which cognitive abilities may be important to focus on for a child of a particular age.

Examination of Table 8.2 will show that for young children, aged four to five years, alternative solution thinking is the best predictor of good social adjustment. An important finding for this age group is that whereas children who show poor ability for both alternative solution thinking and consequential thinking are likely to be inhibited, those children low in alternative solution thinking only are more likely to be impulsive children. The practitioner may wish to note that although the problem behavior of impulsive children tends to attract more attention especially in the classroom situation, the behavior of inhibited children may reflect relatively greater cognitive deficits. In middle childhood, means–end thinking and alternative solution thinking are both important. The thinking of poorly adjusted children at this phase typically features physical or verbal force as the chief means to reach personal goals.

> The well-adjusted ten-year old is typically able to generate alternative solutions to a problem when he has to and, having selected one solution, spontaneously articulates for himself the sequence of steps needed to carry it out. [Spivack, Platt, & Shure, 1976, p. 77]

Findings on adolescence suggest a broad set of relationships between ICPS skills and adjustment. Perspective taking, alternative solution thinking, and means–end thinking are all prominent in well adjusted adolescents' thinking, while deficiencies in these skills are apparent in poorly adjusted groups. The inability to review the pros and cons of rule breaking before acting may differentiate implusive from normal adolescents (Spivack & Levine, 1963), although no such difference was found with institutionalized teenagers (Platt et al., 1974).

By adulthood it appears that the pattern of ICPS skills is different. Alternative solution thinking recedes in importance and the other skills assume prominence. Adulthood is the only phase in which a relationship between causal thinking and adjustment has been demonstrated (Platt & Spivack, 1973). An important finding regarding adults is the difference between the ability of poorly adjusted individuals who could *recognize* but not *generate* socially

Table 8.2.   Summary of Findings on ICPS skills at different development phases

	Early Childhood	Middle Childhood	Adolescence	Adulthood
1. Problem Sensitivity and Perspective Thinking	Not a mediator of adjustment, though some differences		Perspective taking is significant. Sparse evidence on problem sensitivity (Platt et al., 1974)	Perspective taking is significant and is highly related to (3) (Platt & Spivack, 1973)
2. Alternative Solution Thinking	Single most significant predictor of adjustment (Shure & Spivack, 1975)	Some evidence of improvements in (2) being related to improved adjustment (Spivack & Swift, 1966, 1967)	Problems in adjustment linked to poor ability to generate solutions. (Spivack & Levine, 1963) (Platt et al., 1974)	Differences measured but appears related to IQ
3. Means–End Thinking	Not assessed	Correlation between (3) and high and low levels of adjustment (Larcen, Spivack & Shure 1972)	Treatment and institution groups had poorer means–end cognition than normal adolescents (Spivack & Levine 1963) (Platt et al., 1974)	Good adjustment is associated with ability to *generate* means, not just recognize them (Platt & Spivack, 1972, 1973)
4. Consequential Thinking	Variations found but less significant than (2) *5 year olds stronger than 4 year olds (Shure & Spivack, 1975)	Measurable but no relationship found to behavior	No differences found in ability to conceptualize consequences. Normals more likely than impulsives to think out the pros and cons prior to decision making (Spivack & Levine, 1963)	Normals were more likely than psychiatric patients to consider pros and cons before decision making (Platt & Spivack, 1973)
5. Causal Thinking	Can be measured at this age, but not a mediator of adjustment	Measured, but slight data on adjustment (Muuss, 1960) (Larcen et al., 1972)	No difference found	Indication that spontaneous consideration of causes is possible determinant of adjustment (Platt & Spivack, 1973)

appropriate means to solve interpersonal problems, and the spontaneous problem solving thinking of normal adults. This emphasis by ICPS researchers on the spontaneous generation of thought about interpersonal problems is directly reflected in their open ended, semistructured style of assessment methods and training procedures to which we turn in the following sections.

It is important for practitioners to know that research by others has recently been undertaken and complex findings are emerging. For example, the relationship between ICPS skills and social behavior has not been found in one study to be a simple and direct one. Deluty (1981) has shown in a study of alternative solution thinking that fifth to seventh grade submissive girls gave mostly assertive alternatives to interpersonal conflict situations; that is, although their thinking showed adaptive problem solving, their behavior did not. A research group at the University of Rochester (Weissberg & Gesten, 1982), which has undertaken comprehensive research on ICPS skills training, has had mixed successes and failures. For example, a ICPS training program for third graders found a positive effect on the adjustment of suburban children but not of urban children (Weissberg et al., 1981). Other findings suggested the need to improve ICPS technology, including curriculum content and format, and instruction and supervision of trainers.

While ICPS skills have so far appeared largely unrelated to intelligence, the applicability of ICPS training to populations of different abilities may be variable. Hazel, Schumaker, and Sheldon-Wildgen (1980) have compared the effect of training in behavioral social skills and cognitive problem solving in three groups of adolescents—learning disabled youths, a nonlearning disabled group and court-adjudicated youths on probation. It was found that the learning disabled youths acquired the behavioral social skills as well as court-adjudicated and normal youths, but showed less gains after training in cognitive problem solving (alternative solution thinking) than the other two groups. Hopefully, further research will explore relationships between training effectiveness and variables such as demographic factors, type of cognitive deficit, and behavior disorder. By way of summarizing the current status of the ICPS approach, Little and Kendall (1979), in reviewing research work with delinquent populations, describe training in ICPS skills as "a promising adjunct to behavioral and/or traditional methods, and perhaps a viable alternative" (p. 89). We turn now to a consideration of the methods commonly used to assess ICPS skills.

Assessment

As the assessment methods developed by ICPS researchers are numerous, only the ones relevant to the particular ICPS skills significant for each age group will be mentioned here. These methods which are summarized in Table 8.3 represent the assessment procedures used in the studies presented in Table 8.2 (see previous section).

All of these assessment methods use questioning as their primary elicitational technique in combination with open ended responses, both of which are categorized by the tester into standard categories. Sometimes aids are used in assessment—stories or pictures are presented, or roles are played as when the tester's assistant pretends to be a mother with a problem and the child is asked what the "mother" can do to solve the problem.

As is clear from Table 8.3, the two most important ICPS assessment methods for use with very young children are the Preschool Interpersonal Problem Solving Test (PIPS test) and the What Happens Next Game (WHNG). The PIPS Test measures alternative solution thinking by presenting the child with problems, using pictures as an aid, and eliciting as many alternative solutions as possible for two sets of interpersonal problems—peer and authority problems. The WHNG is employed to assess consequential thinking in four and five year olds. Small wooden figures are used to present a situation to the child in order

Table 8.3. Assessment Methods for ICPS Skills Prominent at Each Phase

	Early Childhood	Middle Childhood	Adolescence	Adulthood
1. Problem Sensitivity and Perspective Taking			TAT method	TAT method
2. Alternative Solution Thinking	Preschool Interpersonal Problem Solving Test (PIPS)	Question and answer technique—giving solutions	As for middle childhood	
3. Means—End Thinking		Children's Means—End Problem Solving Test (Children's MEPS)	Means—End Problem Solving Test (MEPS)	MEPS
4. Consequential Thinking	What Happens Next Game (WHNG)			Story telling procedure
5. Causal Thinking				Story telling procedure

273

to elicit multiple consequences. In one example the stick figures and toys are used to represent one child grabbing a wanted toy from another child and a series of questions is asked such as "What might happen next?" "What might (Child A) say?" "What might (Child B) say?" "What might (Child A) do?" "What might (Child B) do?" For both the PIPS Test and the WHNG the overall number of solutions or consequences is scored as well as the number of categories used.

In middle childhood, the Children's Means End Problem Solving Test (Children's MEPS) is the main assessment technique. In this test the child is given the beginning and end to each of six hypothetical problems and asked to make up the middle: "Fill in the middle," "Tell what happens in between," or "Tell how the ending got to be that way." Butler and Meichenbaum (1981) contrast the MEPS and PIPS.

> ICPS assessment measures can be arranged along a continuum in terms of the degree of structure imposed by the nature of the test stimuli and the procedures for administration of the test. The MEPS and Children's MEPS Tests, for example, are essentially "projective" tests, presented as imaginative storytelling exercises with no attempt being made to induce a problem-solving "set" in the subject. The variable of interest is presumably the individual's *spontaneous* tendency to generate problem-solving thought. The PIPS Test is somewhat closer to a standardized interview, with more explicit problem-solving instructions ("What could A do to solve the problem?") followed by a number of standardized probes. In this sense, the two kinds of tests have a slightly different emphasis: the PIPS Test comes closer to a test of *ability*, whereas the format of MEPS and the Children's MEPS Tests is somewhat more oriented toward assessing *typical performance* (Wallace, 1966). This disparity in instructional "sets" makes the interpretation of findings across different measures of ICPS skills for different-age populations somewhat problematic. [p. 202–203]

The Means End Problem Solving Test which is used to assess means–end thinking in adolescents and adults presents the beginnings and endings of stories and asks the person to tell, for example, how to find a lost watch, how to meet and marry a person to whom one is attracted, how to successfully steal a diamond (Spivack, Platt, & Shure, 1976). Stories are scored for:

1. The number and kind of means;
2. Enumerations (different examples of basic means);
3. Obstacles to reaching the goal;
4. The passage of time.

Studies have shown that two main scores from the MEPS are useful—the number of relevant means and a relevancy score (ratio of relevant means to total means named).

Other assessment methods also use the presentation of stories or pictures as elicitational materials and follow-up with a set of standardized probes. For example, in assessing consequential thinking from middle childhood through to adulthood, the individual is given four stories about a person faced with temptation. The individual is asked to finish the story, telling what the person is thinking about before making up his mind, and what happens afterward.

The wide variety of assessment methods employed in ICPS studies have so far been used only in research rather than in working with young clients. In the clinical setting such approaches are not new to practitioners who are familiar with projective methods of assessment. However, the use of these methods to evaluate specific cognitive abilities is novel. Practitioners may wish to adapt these for clinical settings and evolve ways of eliciting problem solving thinking about real problems confronting their clients by assessing (1) what happened in past problematic situations, and (2) what skills the young client may need to acquire to improve future situations.

Training Procedures

The feature of ICPS training programs which sets it apart from other cognitive training procedures is the emphasis placed on the *generation* of thoughts by the individual. The child, adolescent, or adult is taught to generate solutions to interpersonal problems, an ability which goes beyond being able to recognize a good solution from a poor one. Consideration of ICPS training methods will give the practitioner a guide as to how such skills may be taught.

ICPS training programs for different age groups have focused on the particular kinds of thinking that promote good adjustment at that age level. For example, Spivack and Shure (1974) have published a fully scripted program to teach alternative solution and consequential thinking to four and five year olds, in small groups over nine to ten weeks, using games and guided dialogues. They present seven basic principles employed in the design of this training program.

1. To teach prerequisite language and thinking skills before teaching problem-solving strategies.

2. To teach new concepts in the context of familiar content.

3. To base program content on people and interpersonal relations rather than objects and impersonal thoughts.

4. To teach generally applicable concepts rather than correct grammar.

5. To teach the habit of seeking solutions and evaluating them on the basis of their potential consequences rather than the absolute merits of a particular solution to a problem.

6. To encourage the child to create his own ideas and offer them in the context of the problem.

7. To teach problem-solving skills not as ends in themselves but in relation to the adaptiveness of overt behavioral adjustment. [p. 29]

Following the work of Bereiter and Englemann (1966) on language development for children in the four to five age group, the first phase in Spivack and Shure's program is to teach *prerequisite language skills*. They have adapted a number of Bereiter and Englemann's curriculum concepts, placing emphasis on interpersonal relationships. They include the concepts "and," "or," "not," "same," and "different" as the basis for teaching alternative solution thinking, and "why" and "because" as a basis for consequential thinking. When these prerequisite concepts have been acquired, problem solving skills are taught by means of three main steps: (1) Alternative solutions are elicited by asking, for example, "That's one idea. Who can think of a new different idea?"; (2) Alternative consequences are elicited with such questions as "What might happen next? That's one thing that *might* happen. Who can think of something different that *might* happen?"; and (3) The pairing of solutions with their consequences, as when children are asked: "What might happen next if (one solution is given)? What might the girl/boy *say*? What might the girl/boy *do*? What might the girl/boy *feel*? Maybe it's a good idea (or, not a good idea)." The practitioner wishing to teach these skills in a one to one setting need not use an exact script but can nevertheless adhere to the fundamental principles and adapt the questioning technique to aspects of the individual child's setting.

A school program for third- and fourth-grade children (Spivack, Platt, & Shure, 1976) illustrates the teaching of *means—end thinking*. After training in alternative solution and consequential thinking, children work on exercises to help them generate the necessary steps in carrying out their solutions successfully. Step by step plans are elicited from the children for everyday interpersonal situations, such as obtaining parents' permission to go camping. The teacher asks "What is the first thing to do?" and probes with further questions to elicit each step in the plan. Role playing of the plan by the children helps to highlight gaps or inadequacies in the plan. An additional method involves using videotapes of children solving problems. These are stopped at different points to allow the children to generate "the next steps."

For children in the second to fourth grades, the work of a group at the University of Rochester is of special importance. Because of difficulties in maintaining intervention effects with this age group across time, Weissberg and Gesten (1982) have extended ICPS training so that in addition to teaching the basic skills their program integrates training more closely with everyday classroom situations and uses "a sequential SPS [social problem solving] process which youngsters learn to apply behaviorally." Six steps are initially acquired and practiced by the children.

Problem definition	1.	Say (how you feel and) exactly what the *problem* is.
Goal statement	2.	Decide on your *goal*.
Impulse delay	3.	*Stop and think* before you act.
Generation of Alternatives	4.	Think of as *many solutions* as you can.

Consideration of Consequences	5.	*Think ahead* to what might happen next.
Implementation	6.	When you have a really good solution, try it! [p. 59]

In addition, their program has teachers modeling interpersonal problem solving for resolving their own difficulties. Program leaders use the dialoguing method to help children find solutions to everyday squabbles; that is, teachers respond to the children "by reflecting their feelings, asking what alternatives (besides telling the teacher) might be tried, and prompting the anticipation of realistic consequences for each" (Weissberg & Gesten, 1982, p. 59). A role playing method is used also to teach problem solving. The following example used for role playing concerns a conflict over the use of a bike:

Sharon: (to herself) I have a problem. I'm upset because Jenny has been riding the bike for a long time. My goal is to get a turn. I could push her off the bike and grab it, but she might get hurt. . . I could tell on her, but she'd say I was a tattletale. . . . Maybe she'd let me have a turn if I asked her nicely. "Jenny, can I please ride the bike?"

Jenny: "No, I'm using it."

Sharon: (to herself) I have another solution that might work. "Jenny, I've been waiting a long time. Let me ride the bike for 10 minutes and then you can ride it again."

Jenny: "Okay." [Weissberg & Gesten, 1982, p. 59]

It may be of interest to note the modifications of the Spivack and Shure programs which Weissberg and Gesten found desirable concerning the length and number of sessions with their youngsters. Changes were made from 17, 35−50 minute lessons to 34, 20−30 minute lessons. They comment that "children's behavior seems to change less from early lessons in alternative solution and consequential thinking, and more from practising and living the full SPS sequential process" (Weissberg & Gesten, 1982, p. 61).

Other training procedures have been developed for adolescents and young adults as has one for mothers of young children, collectively entitled *Interpersonal Problem Solving Group Therapy* (Spivack, Platt, & Shure, 1976). The young adults program is therapeutic in focus and, in contrast to the developmental counseling approach for young children, is designed for populations in need of treatment such as young heroin offenders and psychiatric patients. The same principles used with younger children are applied with adolescents and young adults but in addition certain themes are stressed during the program:

(1) that problems are solvable; (2) that the focus of the program is on problems of an interpersonal nature; (3) that interpersonal problems are a common part of

everyday life for everybody; (4) that the group members should see the group as a place to bring immediate problems with which they are now faced and which they are attempting to solve; and (5) that the proper temporal focus of the group is to the present and the future, not the past. [Spivack, Platt & Shure, 1976, pp. 245–6]

When basic skills have been acquired, "a self interrogation/direction sequence" to use in a problem situation is provided for group discussion.

1.   Why do I feel this way?

2.   I'm going to take my time solving this problem and not rush into it.

3.   What can I do to solve this problem and make myself feel good? What else, what else?

4.   What will happen if I do the first thing I thought of? What else?

5.   What will happen if I do the second thing I thought of? What else?

6.   What is the thing to do that will lead to what I want to happen?

7.   Okay, now, that's what I'll do! [Spivack, Platt, & Shure, 1976, pp. 257–8]

Although this sequence clearly has features in common with verbal self-instruction to be discussed shortly, it is used in a markedly different way. It functions primarily as a stimulus for the individual's thinking, and it is not learned, rehearsed and reinforced as is the case in usual self-instructional training.

The program for young mothers, entitled *Problem-Solving Techniques in Childrearing*, readapts the program for young children for use with mothers, the goal being for mothers to learn ICPS skills and transmit them to their children. Below is an exercise to teach mothers how to teach integrated ICPS skills to their children in the context of everyday happenings.

FOR MOTHER to Think About:

Encouraging Child to Solve Interpersonal Problems

Purpose: To think about how to encourage the child to think through and solve problems for himself based on the skills he has learned from the training program. At this point, both mother and child will be developing a problem-solving style of thinking and communication.

Type of Problem: Child engaged in interpersonal conflict.

Specific Problem: Child initiates hurting or grabbing behavior.

Questions to Encourage Problem-Solving Communication

1.   Why (did you hit him)?

2.   (Hitting) is one thing you can do. How did that make (Judy) feel?

3.   What happened when you (hit Peter)? What did Peter do or say?

4. Can you think of another way to (repeat reasons child gave why he hit) so that won't happen?

5. (After child answers) That's a different idea. What might happen if you try that? [Spivack, Platt, & Shure, 1976, p. 210]

No evidence is available at present regarding what differences there might be for individual training by a practitioner compared with classroom group training. Since the methods evolved by ICPS workers are richly diversified and appear to hold promise, practitioners using a multitreatment approach are beginning to integrate ICPS training into their clinical procedures, and it is hoped that evaluations will soon become available for such settings.

We turn now to a discussion of self-instructional training which shares the cognitive-behavioral focus of ICPS, but differs from it by providing task oriented self-talk for the child in order to increase self-control and reduce inappropriate behavior.

SELF-INSTRUCTIONAL TRAINING

Theoretical Background

Self-instructional training has been devised for children who fail to talk to themselves sufficiently and who demonstrate uncontrolled or inappropriate behavior as a consequence. Sometimes called *verbal self-instruction* or *cognitive self-instruction*, it is based on the view that certain behavioral excesses or deficits reflect either a lack of appropriate verbal mediators (i.e., the failure to develop inner-speech for self-regulation), or reliance on maladaptive inner-speech, the consequences of which may be inappropriate levels of emotionality or maladaptive behavior. (The use of self-instructional training to modify emotional states will be dealt with later, in the section on stress inoculation).

Self-instructional training was developed initially by Meichenbaum and Goodman (1971) in an effort to teach impulsive children a reflective problem solving style to improve their academic performance. The nonreflective approach to school tasks of this group of impulsive children was found to be associated with a lack of verbal mediation and self-control. In self-instructional training, a client internalizes a set of self-statements which are assumed through a prior analysis to have the potential to produce or elicit the client's desired behavior. Such behavior may be in the repertoire of the client, but is not under sufficient verbal control. The idea is to link through instruction (repeated modeling, rehearsal, feedback, and reinforcement) a set of behaviors with a set of self-instructions so that in situations the client's internal self-talk in the form of self-instructions occasions his desired behavior. Self-instructional training has generally been designed to inhibit behavioral excesses and improve specific task performances.

There appear to be two major historical influences which underly the emergence of self-instructional training. First, Soviet psychology has for many years studied the complex relationships among language, thought, and human behavior (Luria, 1961, 1969; Vygotsky, 1962). Of particular relevance is the developmental model of Luria which describes the way in which inner-speech of a child acquires a self-guiding function over the child's motor behavior. The three stage model comprises (1) external control of the child by the adult's verbal instructions, (2) the child's control of himself by overt speech, and (3) self-control by abbreviated, internalized speech. Although this model was derived from studies of motor behavior, it has provided a stimulus for researchers engaged in modifying more complex functioning, including cognitive tempo, performance on academic tasks, and social behavior. A second stream of influence is child developmental research in the area of verbal learning and verbal behavior. Over the past 20 years, extensive cognitively oriented experimentation has explored the role of verbal mediation in children's problem solving. Meichenbaum (1977) has indicated three types of mediational deficiencies which may explain inadequacies in the problem solving approach of children.

1. Comprehension (of the task or social situation) (Bem, 1972)
2. Production of appropriate mediators (having them in one's repertoire) (Flavell, Beach, & Chinsky, 1966)
3. Mediation proper (the use of these mediators in a self-guiding function) (Reese, 1962).

In the assessment section below it will be seen how a *cognitive functional analysis* can be used to identify which mediational deficits a child may have so that self-instructions can be tailored to her individual needs. The steps in self-instructional training can be designed to remediate sequentially all three types of the previously described mediational deficiencies for those children who have generalized deficits. For example, children who respond nonreflectively in problem solving tasks are taught to slow down, plan a response and try the plan out systematically and carefully, and at the same time learn to deal with mistake making. The steps by which they developed these skills have been identified by Meichenbaum (1977) as (1) problem definition, (2) focusing attention and response guidance, (3) self-reinforcement, and (4) self-evaluative coping skills and error correcting options. The verbally directive modeling techniques a practitioner uses to teach a child verbal self-control parallels Luria's developmental model.

In summary, Meichenbaum and Asarnow (1979) have listed the specific ways in which self-instructions facilitate behavior.

> First, overt verbalizations may serve to organize information in the task or stimulus array and to assist the subject in generating alternatives regarding the solution. Second, verbalization may aid the subject in evaluating feedback by

providing verbal mediators to distinguish relevant and irrelevant dimensions. Active rehearsal of hypotheses should facilitate the subject's retention in short-term storage and thereby reduce the memory load of the task. Self-instructional rehearsal may also enhance a positive task orientation, reinforce and help maintain task-relevant behaviors, and provide ways of coping with failure and self-reinforcing success. [p. 19]

Research Findings

The flexibility of self-instructional training is apparent in the wide variety of ways in which it has already been applied. Applications include successful modification of children's impulsive behavior (Meichenbaum & Goodman, 1971; Kendall & Finch, 1976; Kendall & Finch, 1978), children's aggressive behavior (Camp & Bash, 1981), college students' creativity (Meichenbaum, 1975b), adult schizophrenics' speech (Meichenbaum & Cameron, 1973), the reading comprehension of learning disabled children (Meichenbaum & Asarnow, 1979), and as has been described in Chapter 6, its inclusion in clinical "packages" such as in the treatment of an obsessive–compulsive anxiety disorder (Bernard, Kratochwill, & Keefauver, 1983). Some important research findings in regard to the efficiency of self-instructional training will now be discussed.

In their work with impulsive children Meichenbaum and Goodman (1971) demonstrated that whereas modeling of self-verbalizations alone led to a slowing down by the therapist of children's problem solving performance, the combination of cognitive modeling and *self-rehearsal* in self-instructional training led to both a decrease in errors and an increase in response latency thus bringing about more accurate and more reflective responding. That is, when children were requested to actually repeat aloud the set of self-instructions that were first modeled by the therapist, their overall performance improved in comparison to when they only heard but did not themselves repeat the instructions.

In research on self-instructional training there has been a continuing search for the effective components of the "package," especially those factors which lead to maintenance and generalization of improved performance. Developments have occurred in several directions: the integration of self-instructional training with other methods (e.g., with ICPS as in the "Think Aloud" program), the modification of initial procedures (e.g., the addition of fading of instructions), and importantly the modification of the content of self-instructions from specific task-oriented mediators to more general cognitive strategies.

Where self-instructional training is employed in the remediation of cognitive deficit as in the work with impulsive children, research findings suggest it may be advisable to use it in conjunction with certain behavioral procedures. Kendall and Finch (1979) comment on the distracting effect of positive contingencies on impulsive children and review the evidence for the effectiveness of *response cost* with these children. Their work suggests that response cost may provide incentive to persist and therefore increase the time spent on a task by the child. Used alone, however, response cost does not provide problem solving strategies to improve performance level. Therefore, the combination of self-instructional training and response cost appears to be a promising one when working with impulsive children.

The level of generality at which self-instructional training should be introduced to produce maximum improvements and generalization is beginning to be examined. Kendall and Wilcox (1980) compared "conceptual" versus "concrete" self-instructional training with a group of non-self-controlled third to sixth graders. They evaluated the effectiveness of concrete, task specific instructions versus more global, abstract instructions, in combination with a response cost procedure. Examples of the contrasting concrete and conceptual instructions for a matching task are as follows (Kendall & Wilcox, 1980). (Four sessions were spent on psychoeducational tasks, followed by two sessions of training in interpersonal cooperation using school and home activities.)

Concrete Self-Instruction Training

PROBLEM DEFINITION: I'm to find the picture that doesn't match.

PROBLEM APPROACH: This one's a clock, this one's a clock.

FOCUSING OF ATTENTION: Look at the pictures.

SELF-REINFORCEMENT: The cup and saucer is different; (check answer sheet) I got it right. Good job!

COPING STATEMENT: Oh, it's not the clock that's different, it's the teacup. I can pick out the correct one next time.

LABELING A RESPONSE COST: (done, obviously, by a therapist) No, it's not the clock, it's the teacup. You lose one chip for picking the clock.

Conceptual Self-Instructional Training

PROBLEM DEFINITION: My first step is to make sure I know what I'm supposed to do.

PROBLEM APPROACH: Well, I should look at all the possibilities.

FOCUSING OF ATTENTION: I should think about only what I'm doing right now.   •

SELF-REINFORCEMENT: (checking the answer sheet) Hey, good job. I'm doing very well.

COPING STATEMENT: Well, if I make a mistake I can remember to think more carefully next time, and then I'll do better.

LABELING A RESPONSE COST: No, that's not the right answer. You lost one token for not taking your time and getting the correct answer. [p. 84]

Kendall and Wilcox found that "conceptual" instructions led to stronger gains, maintained better over time than the "concrete" instructions. The conceptual group showed slowing down of response rate, fewer errors, improved behavioral self-control, and decreased hyperactivity ratings. Weaker effects in the same direction were found for the "concrete" group.

A follow-up study by Kendall and Zupan (1981) doubled the number of treatment sessions (to 12) and compared "individual" versus "group" application of the treatment using the same measures as before. They questioned whether group settings, being largely the ones in which children exercise their cognitive strategies, provide more effective treatment settings than the one-to-one child−therapist method previously employed. While both groups showed greater gains than controls, immediate post-test improvements were greater for group than for individual training. At a two month follow-up assessment, individual gains were similar to group trained children.

In the Kendall and Wilcox (1980) and Kendall and Zupan (1981) studies, improvements in self-control and lowering of hyperactivity levels were subjected to normative comparisons in which impulsive children were compared with a random sample of children. It was found that the lengthier treatment of the Kendall and Zupan study brought the children's scores into the normative range of self-control and hyperactivity. Comparison of findings concerning the number of treatment sessions therefore suggests to the practitioner that an extended intervention is needed to produce clinically significant effects. The choice between group or individual training appears to be still an open question.

The distinction between "conceptual" versus "concrete" self-instructions can be thought of as teaching "how to think" versus "what to think." Age related differences have been described by Copeland (1981), who has suggested that young children need more explicit instructions (what to think) whereas older children (8−12 years of age) are more able to generate their own self-instructions and can benefit from more general concepts. As we have discussed in Chapter 6, Cohen and Meyers (in press) have found that the cognitive level of the child ("pre-operational" or "concrete operational" in Piagetian terms) interacts with the type and content of the training to promote different degrees of generalization. A procedure used by Cohen and Meyers involved "directed discovery" in which a semistructured dialogue was conducted between the experimenter and the child, leading the child to "discover" the self-instructions as a more active participant. Only concrete operational children benefitted significantly from this more abstract procedure. These findings would suggest to practitioners who are applying self-instructional training with young children that "what to think" instructions are more likely to be effective than a "how to think" approach.

A number of programs designed for younger children do, however, employ a "how to think" approach. A detailed discussion of one of these, the "Think Aloud" program of Camp and Bash (1981), will be presented at the end of the chapter.

Assessment

In many applications of self-instructional training, assessment has involved the identification of a child as a member of a behaviorally extreme group such as "impulsive" or "aggressive" by means of behavioral observations, test scores on a variety of "personality" measures, or teachers' ratings. In addition to these procedures, a practitioner applying self-instructional training with individual children may wish to carry out a more detailed analysis of a particular child's needs which usually involves establishing that a child is functioning with one or more cognitive deficits. Such assessment prior to self-instructional training is based on a *cognitive functional analysis* of task performance which

> "analyses sequential psychological processes . . . The cognitive functional assessor must be concerned with the psychological demands of a particular task and with the sequentially organized set of cognitive processes that are required for adequate performance. The assessor asks the question, 'In what psychological processes must the successfully achieving individual engage and in which of these is my client failing?' " [Meichenbaum, 1977, p. 236]

The results of the cognitive functional analysis lead directly to the intervention. For example, Cameron (1976) identified three essential components of a problem solving task: (1) comprehension and recall of the task instructions, (2) the formulation of a plan or strategy, and (3) implementation of the strategy. He assessed impulsive children for each component and in this way specified the nature of each child's deficit, enabling the content of the self-instructions to be tailored to remediation of that deficit.

DiGiuseppe (1981, p. 52) has integrated the cognitive functional analytic approach in the context of a comprehensive cognitive-behavioral assessment of children. He proposes the practitioner ask herself the following questions: (1) What thoughts are in the child's head as the target behavior is being performed? (2) What are the child's self-statements? (3) What images are present? (4) Does the child guide the behavior by language? DiGiuseppe also alerts practitioners to noting the absence of reported self-statements, which may be as important as the presence of inappropriate ones.

The self-control rating scale (Kendall & Wilcox, 1979) has been developed for use by teachers to assess groups of impulsive children. While the initial purpose of the SCRS was less of an assessment of screening device than an instrument that can be used to study the generalized effects of self-control training, this scale can be used to identify impulsive children as well as to measure intervention effects. Factorial analysis of the SCRS yielded one major factor which has been labeled cognitive-behavioral self-control. The scale comprises "self-control" items (e.g., "Does the child work for long range goals?"), "impulsive" items (e.g., "Does the child butt into games or activities even when he or she hasn't been invited?") and items descriptive of both (e.g., "If a task is at first too difficult for the child, will he or she get frustrated and quit, or first seek help with the problem?").

This brief review of assessment methods for self-instructional training reflects the fact that assessment has received less emphasis by those applying it than the training procedures themselves. It is reasonable to expect that developments in the field of cognitive assessment such as in vivo assessment (Hollon

& Kendall, 1981) may at a later date become integrated with the individual cognitive functional analysis of children preceding self-instructional training.

Training Procedures

In teaching a child self-instructions, the practitioner models self-statements for the child who rehearses them, first overtly and then covertly, while performing a training task. Self-reinforcement and self-talk to cope with failure are included in the instructions. Kendall's (1981) adaptation of Meichenbaum's original procedure exemplifies the steps in self-instructional training with children and shows the steps for the practitioner to employ in teaching self-instructions (see Table 8.4). The training goal is a more reflective approach to finding one's way out of complicated mazes. Practitioners are advised to design the content of self-instructions appropriate to a particular child's deficits and the type of task but to follow the same sequence of modeling, rehearsal and reinforcement to enable the child to internalize the instructions.

In devising self-instructions practitioners will find the following guidelines presented by Meichenbaum (1979) helpful in promoting effectiveness.

1. Using the child's own medium of play to initiate and model self-talk.

2. Using tasks that have a high "pull" for the use of sequential cognitive strategies.

3. Using peer teaching by having children cognitively model while performing for another child.

4. Moving through the program at the child's own rate and building up the package of self-statements to include self-talk of a problem-solving variety as well as coping and self-reinforcing elements.

5. Guarding against the child's using the self-statements in a mechanical non-involved fashion.

6. Including a therapist who is animated and responsive to the child.

7. Learning to use the self-instructional training with low intensity responses.

8. Supplementing the training with imagery practice such as the "turtle technique" (Schneider & Robin, 1976).

9. Supplementing the training with operant procedures such as a response cost system (Kendall & Finch, 1976; Nelson, 1976). [pp. 21–22]

In deciding upon the type and complexity of self-instructions to use to remediate a problem, it is well worth asking the following.

1. Is it a specific task performance 1 wish to improve?

2. Is it a more general problem solving strategy I wish to teach?

3. At what cognitive level is my young client functioning?

Table 8.4.   Content and Sequence of Self-Instructional Procedures with Impulsive Children

Content of self-instructions	Sequence of self-instructions
Problem definition: Let's see, what am I supposed to do?"	The therapist models task performance and talks out loud while the child observes.
Problem approach: "Well, I should look this over and try to figure out how to get to the center of the maze."	The child performs the task, instructing himself out loud.
Focusing of attention: "I'd better look ahead so I don't get trapped."	The therapist models task performance while whispering the self-instructions, followed by the child's performing the task, whispering to himself.
Coping statements: "Oh, that path isn't right. If I go that way, I'll get stuck. I'll just go back here and try another way."	The therapist performs the task using covert self-instructions, with pauses and behavioral signs of thinking (e.g., stroking beard or chin, raising eyes toward the ceiling).
Self-reinforcement: "Hey, not bad. I really did a good job."	The child performs the task using covert self-instructions.

Source: Kendall and Finch, 1979.

The answers to these questions will help the practitioner to decide whether self-instructional training is applicable, and if so, whether specific concrete instructional content or conceptual strategies are more appropriate. Further detailed diagnostic assessment takes the form of a cognitive functional analysis as discussed in the assessment section.

It is possible to combine aspects of RET with self-instructional training. Grieger and Boyd (1983) recommend self-instructional training as a means of teaching rational self-talk to anxious children. DiGiuseppe (1983) includes self-instruction as part of a comprehensive treatment program for children with conduct disorders. In our work with adolescents we have sometimes integrated RET and self-instructional training to teach *cognitive disputation*. Some young students who have just reached formal operations are, at their best, capable of disputation of their irrational beliefs. However, when they are emotionally upset, perhaps very depressed or overanxious, their level of thinking regresses and their ability to dispute their inner dialogue diminishes. Rehearsal of new self-statements is not always a useful approach with these clients because, as one student put it, without disputation "I know I don't believe them." For these clients, using self-instructions in the practice of disputation can be effective.

One example of how this can be done is set out below.

1. PROBLEM DEFINITION: "What is it I have to do when I feel myself getting upset?"
2. PROBLEM APPROACH: "I have to ask myself some questions and answer them."

3. FOCUSING OF ATTENTION: "I'll think carefully and slowly. What am I saying to myself about what's happening? Is my belief sensible? Is it true? Is there any evidence for it? What is a sensible, rational way to think about this?"

4. SELF-REINFORCEMENT: "There. I remembered to dispute my self-defeating thinking that time. Good. I feel better."

5. COPING STATEMENTS: "I remembered a bit late that time. I was already 9 on the Feeling Thermometer. But that just reminds me I have to work extra hard at my thinking. I'll begin sooner next time."

As this technique is aimed at helping the young client to implement in everyday situations what has been learned in sessions with the practitioner, teaching of the ABCs and principles of disputation must precede this procedure, so that challenges to thoughts and new rational beliefs can be integrated with the self-instructions.

COGNITIVE SOCIAL SKILLS TRAINING

Theoretical Background

We now discuss how cognitive-behavioral methods can be employed with children who are shy or socially withdrawn. Most social skills training has been behavioral in orientation and has aimed to (1) increase specific behaviors judged likely to promote positive interactions between a child and his peers, or between a child and adults, (2) increase positive social consequences for the child, and (3) avoid negative social consequences. A number of behavioral social skills programs have been designed for helping young children (Sapon-Shevin, 1980) and adolescents (Goldstein, Sprafkin, Gershaw & Klein, 1980). However, the training methods to be considered in this section go beyond behavioral programs and they also differ from interpersonal cognitive problem solving procedures in that they emphasize the acquisition of appropriate self-statements to mediate and facilitate the acquisition and generalization of social skills.

The social skills training programs of special interest to us in this section are those with a heavy emphasis on covert verbalizations. These interventions are designed for children and adolescents who are withdrawn, socially isolated, or socially aggressive. These youngsters generally have difficulty interacting with others and have few friends.

Research Findings

The application of cognitive-behavioral methods to the remediation of social isolation in children can be illustrated in several studies of cognitive social skills training. Gottman, Gonso, and Rasmussen (1974) used self-instructional training via film models to teach third grade socially isolated children improved social skills. After viewing the models and listening to the accompanying self-instructional narration, each child was asked to express the cognitions in his own words ("What you might actually think to yourself. . . "). Rehearsal according to self-instructional procedures then followed. The training program also included two further stages which provided training in assertiveness and communication skills. Greater behavioral changes were evident in the training group as a result of this multitreatment program than for the control group.

A study by Jabichuk and Smeriglio (1976) also used films to model for preschool children adaptive self-speech for use in social situations. The films showed a child engaged in isolated play, then joining other children and sharing social activities. The accompanying soundtrack expressed in words the child's feelings of isolation, then coping self-statements and self-reinforcement. The three treatments compared in this study were the films with a first person narrative, the films with a third person narrative, and the films without sound-track. Both self-talk treatments led to increased social responsiveness on behavioral measures, with the first person narrative showing greater effective-ness than the third person narrative. These effects were maintained at a three week follow-up.

In a third study, Combs and Lahey (1981) compared a cognitive social skills program with behavior modification for three young children and found the cognitive methods to be less effective. Two self-instructional sessions were given using imaginary play settings with dolls and toys. Measures of specific social behaviors were made in classroom settings. Some short term benefits were found—the children increased the frequency of peer contact but these gains were not maintained at a six week follow-up.

Different outcomes in these studies may be the result of a number of factors, such as variations in the cognitive methods used, differences among the chil-dren sampled, specificity of outcome measures, and variable length of follow-up phase. Although all of these studies emphasize adaptive self-speech, the specific content appears to be decided upon on the basis of theory rather than individual assessment of the children's thinking. The approach of Halford (1983) which will be presented below suggests the importance of tailoring the cognitive content to the individual child's needs. Prior assessment of the child's particu-lar maladaptive cognitions could therefore be important in devising a training program.

Another recent study which is relevant to cognitive social skill training programs is that of Cohen, Vinciguerra, Ross, and Kutner (1980) who have noted the difficulties experienced by researchers in trying to discriminate groups of socially accepted children from unaccepted children by means of behavioral observation. They argue that adult "norms" may be imposed in the area of social competence instead of discovering the standards children them-selves use to accept or reject their peers. Cohen et al. used observations, self-reports and individual interviews to assess 48 fifth graders. They found that the major difference between accepted and unaccepted children "appeared in the classroom setting with unaccepted children dispensing a greater percentage of negative behavior than accepted children" (1980, p. 4). Contrary to what might be expected, social interaction in the playground was found to be relatively structured when compared with the classroom, as most interaction took place within the structure of games. They conclude that to help children who are socially inadequate in play settings it is more advantageous to teach playskills than to give training in specific positive behaviors such as giving and receiving compliments.

Assessment

Assessment for cognitive social skills training involves both cognitive and behavioral aspects (see Table 8.5).

There are a variety of methods available for assessing social behavior, including sociometric and peer ratings, self reports, natural observations, parent/teacher observation scales, and role play tests. Sociometric methods elicit peer ratings in response to questions such as "Whom do you like the most?" and serve to identify children who experience a high rate of rejection.

Table 8.5. Major Components of a Cognitive-Behavioral Social Skills Training Program

ASSESSMENT
Identification of cognitive and behavioral skill deficits

in vivo naturalistic observation

role playing

parent/teacher observation scales

cognitive assessment procedures

self-report measures

TRAINING
Increase in prosocial and cognitive skills; decrease in identified deficits

providing instructions

presenting a model

rehearsal

feedback

practice

EVALUATION
Assessment of program effectiveness across time and situations

in vivo naturalistic observation

role playing

parent/teacher observation scales

cognitive assessment procedures

self-report measures

A method used with older children is asking them to rate each child on a 5-point continuum, thus overcoming some of the ethical difficulties associated with negative questions (Hymel & Asher, 1977). Cartledge and Milburn caution users of sociometric techniques with young children and suggest that several measures should be taken over a period of weeks to increase the reliability of assessment.

Self-reports of social behavior are not considered sufficiently reliable to be used on their own. Self-reports provide useful information about the individual but may prove misleading if used as the only guide to social adjustment. Observation of performance in the natural environment is a good way to supplement the above assessment methods. Reliability of assessment will be increased if only one or two behaviors are observed and a systematic way of recording their frequency is employed. Behavior checklists are supplementary methods which provide parents' and teachers' ratings of the child's social behavior in different settings. Two examples are the Quay Peterson Behavior Problem Checklist (Quay & Peterson, 1967) which focuses on clinically disturbed behavior, and the Devereux Elementary School Behavior Rating Scale (Spivack & Spotts, 1976; Spivack & Shure, 1976) which has items on specific classroom behaviors. Further assessment methods include role playing, the use of structured situations, and audio and videotape recording. Readers interested in a more detailed account of these techniques for assessing the behavioral aspects are referred to Cartledge and Milburn (1980).

Cognitive assessment procedures focus on the individual child's self-statements, especially with respect to social "failure," rejection or disapproval by others as these are of importance in designing the content of the new self-statements to be taught. As Cartledge and Milburn (1980) indicate " . . .the basic task in assessing a child's cognitions is to get the child to identify his self-statements, especially those that occur while he is engaged in some maladaptive self-statements" (p. 58). The child may, for example, engage in maladaptive self-statements when he is rejected, such as "I'm dumb"; "What's the use of trying." A single setback may be exaggerated unrealistically: "I'll never have any friends"; "Everyone hates me." Meichenbaum (1979) has suggested two approaches to assess these cognitions.

1. The use of self-report in conjunction with a videotape of the child's behavior. The child watches the videotape and says what he was thinking at the time.
2. An alternative approach uses imagery. The child is asked to "run a movie through your head"—to describe the thoughts and feelings he/she had at the time.

Many elicitational techniques rely on the child's ability to communicate thoughts. A self-report method of assisting a child who has poor ability to communicate is to make a list of negative self-statements which are introduced to the child as thoughts "other children in your situation often think." In this situation, the child is asked to indicate which ones he or she may often think. Halford (1983) uses such a thought listing method, and discusses the importance of identifying both positive and negative self-statements of the young client. Table 8.6 reproduces typical examples of both positive and negative self-statements.

The elicitation of positive statements allows assessment of cognitive strengths to be made, and knowledge of these may provide a starting point for change in the intervention phase.

Training Procedures

Cognitive social skills training programs combine the teaching of new adaptive self-statements with new social behavior skills, characteristically using model-

Table 8.6. Characteristics and representative examples of positive and negative self-statements used by children and youths in social interaction.

	Characteristic content	Example
Negative Self-statements	Overestimating likelihood of negative outcomes	"I always say something dumb."
		"Everybody will hate me."
	Underestimating likelihood of positive outcomes	"No one will want to talk to me."
	Catastrophization (exaggerating the importance of negative outcomes)	"I can't stand it when they rubbish me."
	Self-effacement	"I'm too stupid."
		"They don't really think I did it well."
	Anxiety inducing, goal irrelevant ideas	"Everybody's staring at me."
		"I never know what to say." "Hell, I feel nervous."
Positive self-statements	Realistic estimation of likelihood of outcomes	"It may work out, it might not."
		"He's probably looking for someone to talk to as well."
	Realistic assessment of the importance of outcomes	"I would rather he said 'yes', but I guess I can ask someone else if he says 'no.'"
	Goal relevant, self-instruction	"What do I have to do first?"
		"I'll never know if I don't try, I'll ask them."
	Coping self-instruction for negative feelings/outcomes	"I'm uptight—just take a deep breath and relax."
		"Damn! Still, I'll get by."

Source: Halford, 1983, p. 258.

ing, rehearsal, and feedback methods and, sometimes, self-instructions. In Table 8.5 the major components of a cognitive-behavioral social skills training program are listed. The focus of the program reflects concern with the importance of generalization from hypothetical training situations to real life problems. This is a twofold issue of planning for generalization within the training program and evaluating intervention effectiveness on criteria of everyday behavior as well as "test" performances.

A typical cognitive restructuring program for socially withdrawn school children integrates cognitive and behavioral components. The aims of such programs are:

1. To develop relevant cognitive-mediating self-controlling statements.
2. To enable the client to regulate her own anxiety and behavior.
3. To engender self-reinforcement.
4. To train the client in certain social skills necessary to assertive behavior.

The program, which is generally taught over 10 to 12 weekly sessions of one hour, may have three phases.

1. *Cognitive preparation*, in which the child learns the basic role of irrational beliefs in mediating excessive emotional arousal. (2 sessions)
2. *Cognitive restructuring*, in which the child applies the ideas she has learnt to herself and examines in detail her own self-statements in social situations. New rational beliefs are modeled by the therapist and rehearsed by the child. (4 sessions)
3. *Social skill shaping and strengthening*. With continuing use of self-instructions the client progresses through graded steps of challenging maladaptive beliefs and learning new self-statements, then matching those sequentially with nonverbal assertive behaviors (e.g., eye contact, relaxed posture, serious expression), verbal behaviors ("Keep my voice low and speak slowly"), what to say in nonthreatening situations, then in threatening situations, and finally integrating the cognitive restructuring with assertive behavior skills such as standing up to speak in front of the class. (6 sessions)

Halford (1983) indicates that research evidence shows limited generalization over time and across situations for much behaviorally oriented social skills training. He suggests a number of strategies to enhance generalization.

1. The use of "booster sessions." The young client returns to the practitioner for further training as new situations arise.
2. Increasing as far as is reasonable the variety of practical situations in which the child acquires and rehearses the self-statements.

3. Back up for the practitioner in real situations by parents and teachers prompting and reinforcing the use of self-statements, and encouraging continuing self-monitoring by the child after therapy is terminated.

4. If the child is capable of learning elegant RET principles, this increases therapeutic gains and aids generalization.

5. The crucial factor in determining the degree of generalization, is whether the training "works," i.e. do the new self-statements effectively "reduce negative affect, increase positive affect, facilitate the use of overt behaviors which are reinforced and reduce the frequency of use of negatively punished behaviors in the target situations."

If the newly acquired ways of thinking and behaving are appropriate they will most likely be reinforced by others around them. Failure to obtain generalization may reflect the need for basic revision of training content; that is, the self-statements may not be fully appropriate ones.

The three approaches considered so far—ICPS, self instructional training and cognitive social skills training—can be considered together as predominantly *cognitive-behavioral* in orientation; that is, the intervention is aimed primarily at behavior change, not emotional well-being. Affective changes may or may not accompany changes in behavior. The two remaining approaches, stress inoculation and attribution retraining, focus on the *cognitive-emotional* link and aim primarily at cognitive-emotional change. Improvements in performance or other behavioral changes are indirect benefits of these approaches.

STRESS INOCULATION

Theoretical Background

Of the five techniques reviewed in this chapter, stress inoculation, while behavioral in perspective, is probably the closest to RET. Both analyze the self-talk of the person about situations which occasion emotional distress, and both intervene to alter the person's thoughts through a process of cognitive restructuring. Stress inoculation was developed by Meichenbaum and Cameron (1973a) and has been used to help people cope with anxiety (Meichenbaum & Cameron, 1973a; Meichenbaum & Novaco, 1978), anger (Novaco, 1978, 1979), and pain (Turk, 1975). The focus of stress inoculation is on *intra*personal emotional reactions in contrast to ICPS and cognitive-behavioral social skills training which center on *inter*personal interactions. Stress inoculation is more closely bound up with the person's internal psychological functioning than with external social behaviors. Cormier and Cormier (1979) indicate the connection between RET and stress inoculation.

One of the major assumptions that RET cognitive restructuring and stress inoculation share is that a person's beliefs and thoughts can create emotional distress and maladaptive responding. Another shared assumption is that a person's cognitive system can be changed directly and that such change results in different, and presumably more appropriate consequences. [p. 361]

The name, stress inoculation, draws on concepts borrowed from engineering and medicine. As inoculation against disease by means of controlled exposure provides the person with greater resistance and a "built-in" means of coping when exposed to the disease, so stress inoculation is thought to enable the person to deal with situations and events which previously prompted incapacitating emotional reactions (e.g., anxiety, anger).

"Stress" in the psychological context is perceived as analogous to the condition of strain on a physical structure, as studied in engineering. Novaco (1978) makes a helpful distinction between "*stressors* as aversive events that exert demands for adaptation, *stress* as a hypothetical state denoting a condition of imbalance between demands and responses for coping, and *stress reactions* as the adverse health and behavioral consequences of exposure to environmental demands" (p. 137.)

Research Findings and Assessment

Stress inoculation, unlike other approaches in this chapter, was designed primarily for adults, and practitioners are only now beginning to apply the procedure with younger populations. Novaco (1978, 1979) has reviewed applications with adults which have demonstrated the reduction of extreme stress reactions such as anger and anxiety by means of cognitive regulation. It is hoped that, with increasing applications, research findings will become available to enable evaluation of the effectiveness of stress inoculation procedures with these younger populations.

Cognitive assessment methods presently available are those developed for self-instructional training (see earlier section in this chapter). In addition to cognitive functional analytic procedures, Novaco (1979) indicates the need to assess the emotional component in terms of:

1. frequency
2. intensity
3. duration
4. mode of expression
5. effects on performance, health and personal relationships.

In this way the particular cognitive-emotional link can be established between the maladaptive thoughts or beliefs and emotional overreactions by the child. What are the thoughts leading to her five times a day angry outbursts? What

beliefs are creating such anxiety that she worries every morning and is beginning to avoid school? Answers to questions like these via cognitive-emotional
assessment will determine the content of the cognitive training to follow.

Training Procedures

Stress inoculation training involves several phases and is generally taught
employing the self-instructional method (Meichenbaum & Cameron, 1973a).
First, an *educational phase* (termed "cognitive preparation") aims to enable
the client to understand both the physiological and mental aspects of his
emotional reactions, to establish a language of communication between therapist and client, and to facilitate agreement about the planned therapy. Diaries
or logs are often used in this phase to assess thoughts and to enable the client
and therapist to become aware of specific emotional reaction patterns. These
logs may form the basis for self-monitoring and therapy evaluation.

The *rehearsal or skill acquisition phase* follows in which coping skills specific
to the individual's problem are practiced. In stress inoculation coping is defined
cognitively and the client learns to monitor his self-defeating thoughts in such a
way that maladaptive thoughts and feelings become cues to use new adaptive
self-statements. Thoughts and feelings which previously led to disabling anxiety or other disturbing emotion now signal him to employ cognitive coping
statements. There are four steps in the skill acquisition phase—*preparing for a
stressor, confronting and handling a stressor, coping with the feeling of being
overwhelmed,* and *reinforcing self-statements*. Using these four steps, the client
learns to control negative thoughts, to relabel the arousal he is experiencing, to
deal with the emotion, and evaluate his efforts and reinforce himself. The
following examples (see Table 8.7) from Meichenbaum & Turk (1975) demonstrate the four steps within the rehearsal phase and illustrate how the same
training can be adapted to different stresses such as anxiety, anger, and pain.

New self-statements are rehearsed by the client with the help of therapist
modeling and reinforcement. They can be seen to include relabeling of negative reactions, substitution of positive statements concerning the person's
ability to cope, adaptive reactions to arousal, self-instructions to relax and
self-reinforcement. A number of "direct-action" ways of coping may be taught
at this point (Cormier & Cormier, 1979). Besides mental and phsyical relaxation, these can include escape routes, which are specific things the client learns
to do (such as counting to 20 or leaving the situation) in order to avoid being
quickly overwhelmed by the stressor or overreacting to it.

The third phase, *application training*, provides practice in the exercise of
newly acquired coping skills, in role rehearsal with the therapist, or artificially
induced stress situations.

While stress inoculation training programs reported in the literature have
been designed for adults, the problems to which they are applied are common
to young children and adolescents, (e.g., phobic reactions, disruptive anger
and anxiety). Simplified elements may prove applicable to children in middle

Table 8.7 Examples of Self Statements Rehearsed in Stress Inoculation Training

1. Preparing for a Stressor	Preparing for a Provocation	Preparing for the Painful Stressor
Meichenbaum and Cameron (1973)	Novaco (1974)	Turk (1975)
What is it you have to do?	What is it that you have to do?	What is it you have to do?
You can develop a plan to deal with it.	You can work out a plan to handle this.	You can develop a plan to deal with it.
Just think about what you can do about it. That's better than getting anxious.	You can manage this situation. You know how to regulate you anger.	Just think about what you have to do.
No negative self-statements; just think rationally.	If you find yourself getting upset, you'll know what to do.	Just think about what you can do about it.
Don't worry; worry won't help anything.	There won't be any need for an argument.	You have lots of different strategies you can call upon.
Maybe what you think is anxiety is eagerness to confront it.	Time for a few deep breaths of relaxation. Feel comfortable, relaxed and at ease.	
	This could be a testy situation, but you believe in yourself.	

2. Confronting and Handling a Stressor	Confronting the Provocation	Confronting and Handling the Pain
Meichenbaum and Cameron (1973)	Novaco (1974)	Turk (1975)
Just "psych" yourself up—you can meet this challenge	Stay calm. Just continue to relax.	You can meet the challenge
One step at a time; you can handle the situation	As long as you keep your cool, you're in control here.	One step at a time; you can handle the situation.
Don't think about fear; just think about what you have to do. Stay relevant.	Don't take it personally.	Just relax, breathe deeply and use one of the strategies.
This anxiety is what the doctor said you would feel. It's a reminder to use your coping exercises.	Don't get all bent out of shape; just think of what to do here.	Don't think about the pain, just what you have to do.
	You don't need to prove yourself.	This tenseness can be an ally, a cue to cope.
	There is no point in getting mad.	
	You're not going to let him get to you.	

This tenseness can be an ally, a cue to cope.

Relax; you're in control. Take a slow deep breath. Ah. Good.

3. Coping with the Feeling of Being Overwhelmed

Meichenbaum and Cameron (1973)

When fear comes, just pause.
Keep the focus on the present; what is it you have to do?
Label your fear from 0 to 10 and watch it change.
You should expect your fear to rise.
Don't try to eliminate fear totally; just keep it manageable.
You can convince yourself to do it. You can reason your fear away.
It will be over shortly.
It's not the worst thing that can happen.
Just think about something else.
Do something that will prevent you from thinking about fear.

Don't assume the worst or jump to conclusions. Look for the positives.
It's really a shame that this person is acting the way she is.
For a person to be that irritable, he must be awfully unhappy.
If you start to get mad, you'll just be banging your head against the wall. So you might as well just relax.
There's no need to doubt yourself. What he says doesn't matter.

Coping with Arousal and Agitation

Novaco (1974)

Your muscles are starting to feel tight. Time to relax and slow things down.
Getting upset won't help.
It's just not worth it to get so angry.
You'll let him make a fool of himself.
It's reasonable to get annoyed, but let's keep the lid on.
Time to take a deep breath.
Your anger is a signal of what you need to do. Time to talk to yourself.
You're not going to get pushed around, but you're not going haywire either.
Try a cooperative approach. Maybe you are both right.

Relax. You're in control; take a slow deep breath. Ah. Good.

This anxiety is what the trainer said you might feel. That's right; it's the reminder to use your coping skills.

Coping with Feelings at Critical Moments

Turk (1975)

When pain comes just pause; keep focusing on what you have to do.
What is it you have to do?
Don't try to eliminate the pain totally; just keep it manageable.
You were supposed to expect the pain to rise; just keep it under control.
Just remember, there are different strategies; they'll help you stay in control.
When the pain mounts you can switch to a different strategy; you're in control.

(Continued)

297

TABLE 8.7 *(Continued)*

Describe what is around you. That way you won't think about worrying.	He'd probably like you to get really angry. Well, you're not going to disappoint him.	
	You can't expect people to act the way you want them to.	
4. Reinforcing Self-statements	*Self-Reward*	*Reinforcing Self-Statements*
Meichenbaum and Cameron (1973)	Novaco (1974)	Turk (1975)
It worked; you did it.	It worked!	Good, you did it.
Wait until you tell your therapist about this.	That wasn't as hard as you thought.	You handled it pretty well.
It wasn't as bad as you expected.	You could have gotten more upset than it was worth.	You knew you could do it!
You made more out of the fear than it was worth.	Your ego can sure get you in trouble, but when you watch that ego stuff you're better off.	Wait until you tell the trainer about which procedures worked best.
Your damn ideas—that's the problem. When you control them, you control your fear.	You're doing better at this all the time.	
It's getting better each time you use the procedures.	You actually got through that without getting angry.	
You can be pleased with the progress you're making.	Guess you've been getting upset for too long when it wasn't even necessary.	
You did it!		

Source: Meichenbaum and Turk, 1975.

childhood, with simplified content suitable to their language skills and level of rational thought, while the full multiphased technique may be applicable to adolescents.

Cartledge and Milburn (1980) have illustrated how stress inoculation may be adapted for a child overreacting to corrective feedback.

Preparing for provocation
    If the teacher marks something wrong I can handle it.
    I know what to do if I get upset.
    Making a mistake is not so bad.
Impact on confrontation
    Keep calm.
    Think about the ones you got correct.
    It's silly to get angry about one problem.
    The teacher is really right to show me what I did wrong.
    Being corrected helps me learn.
Coping with arousal
    I'm beginning to breathe hard, relax
    Stop and think about all the good work you did today.
    Try to keep cool.
Reflection on provocation
    a. When conflict is unresolved:
    It partly worked.
    I can do better next time.
    This is hard to do but I'll keep trying.
    b. When conflict is resolved or coping is successful.
    I did a good job that time, I even smiled at the teacher.
    I can be a good student. The teacher likes me. [pp. 81−2]

Following Meichenbaum, they recommend such training be combined with relaxation and the use of imagery during rehearsal.

Another stress-inoculation program of interest is one devised by Segrave (1979) for an angry and aggressive child. Over 10 sessions, using the three phases of education, skill acquisition, and application, elements of relaxation and desensitization, cognitive coping, and social skills training, are introduced successively to build upon previous training. The following self-instructions illustrate the cognitive coping statements taught during the fourth session:

"This could be a rough situation but I know how to handle it. There's no point in getting mad. I just have to think of what I have to do. I'm becoming tense. I can feel my muscles getting tight. Relax, breathe deeply. Slow things down. Remember relaxation, it's a lot better than anger." [p. 11]

In the next session the child is taught a problem solving approach.

> You feel yourself getting tense and are about to hit someone. You could say to yourself "I can work out a plan to handle this, you don't need to prove yourself. Don't make more out of this than you have to. My anger is a signal of what I need to do. Time for problem solving. I actually got through that without getting angry.'"[p. 11]

Then, in more detail, the practitioner models for the child.

1. The generation of a problem solving orientation.

2. The definition of a problem.

3. The generation of alternative solutions.

4. The selection of a solution.

5. The verification of the solution:

> So I've been left out of the football team. My problem is how can I be a part of the team without fighting my way in. I guess there are a number of things I could do. I could ask John if I can play in his team or I could see Mr. Black the Sports Master or I could go and play cricket. I think I'll try asking John. That was an easier way than getting angry. [p. 11]

These programs show that stress-inoculation can be adapted for children's problems and can be successfully integrated with other intervention techniques where appropriate. Where stress-inoculation is being used within a RET framework, both the cognitive preparation phase and the rehearsal phase contain strong RET elements, for example understanding one's own role in triggering the maladaptive behavior by irrational self-statements; exploration of underlying beliefs; new rational self-statements rejecting the "awfulness" of the situation, and affirming one's ability to cope; and rational self-statements to cope with failure.

ATTRIBUTION RETRAINING

Theoretical Background

Attribution theory focuses on peoples' beliefs concerning the causes of events in their lives. Statements such as "It was my lucky day" and "My teacher must have favored me" reflect beliefs about the cause of a student's successful school performance and are different from statements such as "I got to the top because I worked extra hard" or "This is my special field—I'm good at maths." Individual differences in such beliefs have been the target of theoretical and research interests of workers in several different fields. Personality theorists (Bem, 1972; Weiner, 1974), social learning psychologists (Rotter, 1966) and cognitive theorists (Dweck, 1975) have all approached this area from their own vantage points and, while they may have used slightly different labels—"causal attribution," "locus of control," "personal causation"—the overlap is marked. As most of the research on attributional retraining has been carried out with children in the context of their orientation to success and failure and achievement motivation, it is a particularly apt field for inclusion in our search for effective interventions to remedy maladaptive functioning in school-age children.

The main theoretical developments will now be presented, including the origins of causal thinking and the effects of different attributional beliefs on the individual's feelings and behavior.

According to attribution theory the individual constructs causal beliefs from his assumptions, not necessarily tested in reality, about the workings of the environment and the individual's perceptions of his own competency, effectiveness, or passivity. The view that these beliefs influence the way the individual interacts with the environment and determine the degree of psychological adjustment is consistent with the cognitive model presented in Chapter 1.

In considering the importance of attributions in human behavior, Ellis (1979f) has written:

> Humans attribute motives, reasons and causes to other people and to external events and internal physical states; and they significantly influence their own emotions and behavior by these attributions, even when they base them on quite false or misleading perceptions and conceptions. A good deal of their emotional disturbance stems from misattributions; and we may often help them overcome such disturbance by helping them to understand and change their cognitive misattributions. [p. 114]

Researchers have found strong relationships between personality variables such as self-esteem, achievement motivation and learned helplessness, and different measures of attributional beliefs.

In their recent review of attribution theory, Metalsky and Abramson (1981) discuss the role of situational information and beliefs in the formation of attributions.

> Our perspective on the attribution process emphasizes that people draw upon situational information as well as generalized beliefs and motivations to resolve ambiguity about causes of events in their lives. Interestingly, generalized beliefs may take precedence over situational information in influencing people's causal inferences. Indeed, the processing of situational information may be guided by people's general beliefs. [p. 37]

The fact that people's beliefs may be mistaken and at odds with reality can lead to cognitive errors and maladaptive functioning. Metalsky and Abramson (1981) argue that two classes of people—those holding strong, undifferentiated generalized beliefs, and those who characteristically turn to detailed memories of past situations to resolve present ambiguities—are most likely to demonstrate these cognitive errors. A cognitive *error of insertion* occurs when a person inserts situational information or causal inferences into a causally ambiguous event. An *error of discounting* occurs when a person rejects causal inferences at odds with his beliefs in spite of compelling evidence.

Rotter (1966) has explored two dimensions of an individual's causal attributions which influence how these beliefs affect behavior: *stability* of the factors the individual has identified as causes, and the *internal versus external* origin of these factors. Stable causes are those which the individual believes persist over time. "Internal" attributions center on the individual's belief that his effort is largely responsible for his behavior, and that he has control over what happens to him. "External" attributions refer to extrinsic factors the person believes he has little control over such as luck.

Four combinations which emerge from these two dimensions have been conceptualized to explain how a student may view his success and failure experiences in school (Rotter, 1966).

1. Stable—internal (e.g., ability).
2. Unstable—internal (e.g., effort).
3. Stable—external (e.g., task difficulty).
4. Unstable—external (e.g., luck).

A student's tendency to attribute his performance to one or other of these different causes can strongly influence his expectancy of future success or failure as well as his self-esteem, feelings of power or helplessness, and achievement motivation. For example, if a student believes that task difficulty causes his level of performance, he may demonstrate an attitude of "learned helplessness" and feel unable to improve his performance. Such an attitude is often associated with feelings of depression in adolescent students who are experiencing failure. In our experience these students are often high in ability but experience feelings of worthlessness and inadequacy in the face of lowered school performance. They frequently hold the irrational belief that one must perform 100% well or it is not worth trying. If they cannot label their work "perfect" they label it "not good enough" and so, as motivation and output drop, they fall behind and feelings of depression increase.

While there have been a variety of references to the importance of attributions (and changing them) in psychological maladjustment in the clinical and educational literature (Ellis & Whiteley, 1979; Stipek & Weisz, 1981; Genshaft, 1982), there have been few published instances to our knowledge where practitioners have set out to change attributions as a means of improving performance or psychological adjustment.

Research Findings

In the area of attribution retraining anecdotal data has provided a source of hypotheses for more systematic studies. An important anecdotal report concerning the way a child's attributional thinking may hinder effective change was made by Meichenbaum (1977) when documenting the external orientation of some hyperactive children who attribute their good and poor behavior to their medication or lack of it. This belief is often taught and encouraged by other people close to the child such as parents, teachers, or peers who link the child's lack of controlled behavior to his failure to take medication. Meichenbaum (1977) provides the following comments of a 12-year-old boy:

> "I'll go in and take 'em and then during the afternoon she (the teacher) thinks I'm getting 'off,' you know, hyperactive, and she'll say, 'Bradley, did you forget to take you little trip to the office this morning?' and I'll say, 'No!' " [p. 50]

Such beliefs which reflect perceived lack of control over oneself may undermine the effectiveness of interventions such as self-control programs based on self-instructional training. Therefore attibution retraining has been proposed as a prelude to self-management training for children who characteristically rely on these beliefs (Meichenbaum, 1977; Bugental, Whalen, & Henker, 1977).

Rothbaum (1980), in a review of clinical syndromes, examines evidence for a connection between certain child-rearing practices and generalized expectations concerning control.

> Since very directive parenting is likely to lead to a suppression of children's self-directed activities and consequently, to failure to perceive contingencies between one's own actions and subsequent outcomes, it is likely to lead to expectations of uncontrollability. . . . [pp. 232–3]

Crandall (1973) provides evidence that children whose parents (mothers) take too much charge of them and who do not let them learn for themselves fail to develop an internal locus of control. Independent functioning leads to "more opportunity for the child to observe the effect of his own behavior, the contingency between his own actions and ensuing events, unmediated by maternal intervention" [p. 13]. In spite of the strong wording of Crandall's statement, Rothbaum emphasizes the correlational nature between parenting styles and a child's sense of personal causality.

Several systematic research studies (Dweck, 1975; Hanel, 1974; Woollacott, 1978) will be discussed in the section on training procedures as they exemplify methods used to change children's attributional thinking.

Assessment

Early work with attribution constructs examined the consistency with which the person held attributions across situations and time; that is, a trait status was accorded the construct. Continued research, however, indicated that a person's attributional thinking could vary with the situation. For example, different causal attributions may be made for success and for failure by the same individual who may assume control over success but ascribe failure to external factors (Crandall, 1965; Mischel, Zeiss, & Zeiss, 1974) and as such situation specific assessment is most important. A variety of methods have been developed for assessing children's attributions and they include structured and unstructured approaches. Structured tests for assessing children's attributions includes the Bialer—Cromwell Test of Locus of Control (Bialer, 1961), Crandall's The Intellectual Achievement Responsibility (IAR) Questionnaire (Crandall, 1965), and the Nowicki—Strickland Internal—External Scale for Children (Nowicki & Strickland, 1973). These tests have been used more often for research purposes than in clinical settings. An alternative analogue approach to the assessment of causal attributions involves the use of vignettes, in conjunction with either a choice of attribution (Kendall, Pellegrini, & Urbain, 1981) or open ended questions (Stephens & Delys, 1973). All of these assessment techniques have been used mainly in hypothesis-testing research, and the usefulness of the methods for individual assessment by the practitioner is less clear.

Training Procedures

In those programs designed to retrain attributional thinking, procedures used have been of two kinds: (1) contingent feedback in conjunction with manipulation of tasks and the environment, especially success and failure (Miller et al., 1975; Chapin & Dyck, 1976; Woollacott, 1978), and (2) self-instructional training (Hanel, 1974, cited by Meichenbaum, 1977). Studies on attribution training have largely examined short-term effects and it remains for future research to discover how long-term changes in attributions can best be established and maintained.

Dweck (1975) carried out a training study on the phenomenon of learned helplessness in children in relation to the effects of success and failure experiences. The children studied were all "externals"; that is, assessment showed that they attributed success and failure to extrinsic factors over which they had no control. The children who were given attribution feedback following experimental "failure" trials ("You should have tried harder") showed both improved performance on later "failure" items, and modification of their attributions.

A training study involving sixth grade Australian children (Woollacott, 1978) found evidence for "a functional match" between attributional style and evaluative feedback. The IAR was used to assess attributional thinking, and academic tasks were employed in the training and experimental testing. Woollacott found that for externals, the combination of contingent reinforcement and attribution for effort on success and failure during training led to greater improvement in performance on a later spelling task, than did contingent reinforcement alone. Internals, however, were severely disrupted when given attribution for effort on failure, but no contingent reinforcement. As well as a deterioration in their performance, these subjects showed subjective distress in contrast to the quality of performance of "external" subjects who showed enthusiasm and pleasure for the task and wrote more neatly and slowly.

Demonstration of changes in attribution by way of a check on the cognitive manipulation presumed to account for the measured behavioral changes has proved difficult in training studies (Dweck, 1975; Woollacott,1978). This may reflect the short-term nature of the training. It also underlines the need for (1) finer discriminations in assessing attributions (for example, distinguishing between various "internal" attributions such as effort and ability), and (2) a longer term training period geared to maintenance and generalization.

The procedures used for attribution retraining by Hanel (1974, cited in Meichenbaum, 1977) were more extensive and included cognitive modeling of evaluation skills and self-reinforcement. Hanel's subjects were a group of fourth grade poor achievers with a fear of failure who were taught by a self-instructional program to change their self-talk, and to problem solve and thus to alter their motivation and level of academic performance. The training procedure involved group training where "the experimenter cognitively modeled for the children how to set standards, plan actions, calculate effort output, monitor performance, evaluate performance outcome, weigh causal attributions and administer self reward." [Meichenbaum, 1977, p. 52]

It appears to us that while the importance of children's attributions is recognized in principle, clinical applications are not common. As attribution retraining is more limited in scope as an intervention than other cognitive-behavioral approaches discussed in this chapter, it is likely that developments in useful procedures, especially for long-term changes in attributions, will be made in the context of a multitreatment approach. For example, self-instructional training and attribution retraining could be combined to remediate learned helplessness, or RET and attribution retraining integrated in the treatment of depression.

THE "THINK ALOUD" PROGRAM FOR CHILDREN: INCREASING SOCIAL AND COGNITIVE SKILLS

The "Think Aloud" program of Camp and Bash (1981), a major contribution in the area of cognitive-behavioral interventions with young children, is commercially available from Research Press, 2612 North Mattis Avenue, Champaign, Illinois 61820. It is of particular interest to us as it combines and integrates a number of the approaches reviewed in this chapter. Think Aloud is conveniently presented in a loose leaf ring binder and includes three main sections. Section I introduces the general cognitive-behavioral approach of Camp and Bash, describes the origins of Think Aloud and makes recommendations for its use. Section II presents 23 lessons and directions for teaching them. Section III examines short-term and long-term research studies on Think Aloud and associated programs.

The Think Aloud program was originally designed to teach self-verbalization skills to young aggressive boys. However, Camp and Bash emphasize, as we do with out RET materials, that Think Aloud can be used in either a therapeutic–remedial way or as a preventative educational program. Think Aloud combines self-instructional training with elements of interpersonal cognitive problem solving (as developed by Spivack & Shure, 1976) to teach children at kindergarten and lower primary levels a "how to think" approach to impersonal and interpersonal problem solving. During training the children learn to ask and answer four questions as they "think aloud" while performing a task.

1. What is my problem? or, What am I supposed to do?
2. How can I do it? or, What is my plan?
3. Am I using my plan?
4. How did I do? [Camp & Bash, 1981, p. 17]

Cue cards similar to those of Palkes, Stewart, and Freedman (1972) were used by Camp and Bash to signal the child to think aloud (see Figure 8.1)

1 What is my problem?   2 How can I do it?

3 Am I using my plan?   4 How did I do?

Figure 8.1. Training Figures on Cue Cards (from Camp & Bash, 1981).

Instructional materials have been selected so that tasks are presented with increasing complexity: coloring, finding similarities and differences, mazes, classification, perceptual puzzles, and matrices. The children learn to answer the Think Aloud questions in their own way as appropriate to the task. The logic underlying the Think Aloud instructional approach is that with frequent practice children will acquire cognitive skills of planning action and using thought to guide performance. Cue cards are used to remind children to apply their self-talk in a variety of social settings and to help learn the skill of generating multiple solutions. When this is mastered, Think Aloud skills are applied to social problems and children learn to generate multiple solutions.

Figure 8.2. Social Cue Cards (from Camp & Bash, 1981).

The following example from Think Aloud demonstrates the manner in which children are taught to resolve potential conflict situations by means of their self-verbalization plan. This example comes from Lesson 16 in which children are practising generating consequences:

Teacher: (Show the "Picnic in the Park" picture. Point to mother who is holding a baby, and point to Susan, who is running toward her mother.)

"Mother told Susan that the family would go to the park to play together since mother and father work all week. Susan wants to play with her mother but mother is holding the baby. Your problem is to think of ways Susan could get her mother to play with her and to think of what might happen next if she uses the solutions. Let me hear you think out loud."

Children: (respond)

Teacher: (Elicit and verbally categorize up to five solutions, but ask for multiple consequences for only two solutions, one positive and one negative solution if possible. . . conclude with self-evaluation.)

Children: (self-evaluate) [Camp & Bash, 1981, p. 156]

Following practice in generating consequences childen are taught to *evaluate* possible solutions by asking

1. Is it safe?

2. Is it fair?

3. How does it make you and others feel?

4. Does it solve the problem? [p. 156]

Think Aloud has been tested on groups of children, revised, and retested. Limited long-term results have resulted both in the development of a follow-up unit, "the refresher course," as an aid to maintenance of intervention effects as well as in considering the use of parents to run the course instead of teachers. Think Aloud procedures appear to have a good deal in common with the "directed discovery" method which Cohen and Meyers (in press) found useful with concrete operational children. As the six to eight year olds for whom Think Aloud is recommended are likely to be, at most, transitional between preoperational and concrete operational thought and therefore still focusing largely on *content* rather than the form or process of the training, the efforts of Camp and Bash to maximize generalization by means of extending the length of the program, intensifying the training of teachers who carry out their training and possibly involving families, may be frustrated if Cohen and Meyers' results are well founded. Camp and Bash may need to modify their expectations of younger children and apply their extensive and highly systematic program with somewhat older childen or to focus more on teaching childen of this age what to think rather than how to think.

CLINICAL APPLICATIONS

In this section we demonstrate how different cognitive approaches can be applied and sometimes combined together to treat a variety of childhood disorders.

Social Withdrawal

Elizabeth, a 16-year-old schoolgirl, was referred to the second author (MRJ) because of withdrawal from the school situation. She was not attending classes but spending her time sitting in the school library, isolated from teachers and peers, and producing very little work. Elizabeth was a diabetic and had suffered frequent illnesses after which she found it difficult to return to school.

Assessment showed that Elizabeth experienced intense discomfort anxiety when frustration built up in her life. Main sources of frustration for her were having to put up with the regimentation of school life, getting behind in schoolwork due to illness, and not being able to get others, especially peers, to follow along with her wishes. She approached life with an irrational demandingness, expecting others to meet her "needs," and when they did not, she reacted with silent anger and discomfort anxiety and withdrawal from situations.

It was also apparent from the assessment that Elizabeth lacked consequential thinking skills, and was unaware of the effects of her demandingess and whining on other people. Elizabeth constantly blamed herself and others for her difficulties and spent a lot of time thinking how things and people "should" be different. She habitually rated herself, often poorly, saying "If I think I am not accepted I feel inadequate." An additional "I can't" attitude reflected her feeling of helplessness about her problems and was an important target for therapy.

Elizabeth was taught the ABC's of RET and gradually was able to use them independently. She had difficulty initially with disputational skills, so she practiced asking herself several questions about her thoughts and beliefs—"Is it sensible?" "Is it true?" "Is there any evidence for this?"

Elizabeth was also taught rational-emotive imagery by means of which she practiced (1) relaxation, (2) imagining herself in a situation which produced discomfort anxiety, (3) thinking rational thoughts, and (4) feeling comfortable. Situations for which she rehearsed this were: being criticized by a teacher and getting 55% on a test (she felt a failure when she scored 79% on a German language test!). Elizabeth found the imagery helpful and spontaneously applied it to other situations in which she experienced anxiety—going into shops and meeting people she knew in the street.

Another aspect of the intervention was introduced when a sound working relationship was well established between Elizabeth and the practitioner. Elizabeth was taught to translate "I can't" into "I won't." This served two purposes: (1) underlying rebelliousness and resentment were brought to the surface and dealt with by facing her feelings and linking them to irrational demandingness, and (2) it returned to Elizabeth the responsiblity for herself and her actions. In addition, consequential thinking skills were taught and applied by following through possible alternative actions and thoughts to their likely consequences both for her own emotional state and her interpersonal relationships. For example, ideas that were elicited included (1) if she continued to hold her irrational beliefs, the consequences she could expect were continuing unhappy feelings, (2) working at changing these would lead to improvement, and (3) holding onto irrational beliefs and demanding perfection of family and friends would very likely lead them to get fed up with her and be rejecting, angry or disinterested. Elizabeth was also given frequent attributional feedback concerning her efforts to change. These communications, which were made in a louder voice to give emphasis to them, and were repeated several times in slightly different ways, reduced her attitude of helplessness, so that when she felt anxiety coming on unexpectedly she was able to respond by trying disputation and imagery instead of shrinking away helplessly. This new confidence in her own efforts was particularly noticeable when, ahead of schedule in the treatment program, she began applying the techniques she had acquired to new situations.

Depression

Penny, a 14-year-old schoolgirl with a hearing loss, was referred to one of the authors (MRJ) because her school performance had fallen off and she seemed unhappy. Penny was depressed, had lost concentration in her work, and was very flat emotionally. Assessment showed that she was under pressure at home from a perfectionistic and demanding father, and that she pressured herself to compete with and equal the very high achievements of her four older brothers. Examples of her self-verbalizations include "I'm hopeless"; "I'll never be as good as Ian." Penny described herself as nervous, lonely when her brothers were not around, and felt her childhood had been ruined because she had not done the risky and difficult things her brothers had asked her to do (such as jumping from high places). Therefore she rated herself as "gutless"—"I feel I should have done things even if it killed me."

The main focus of therapy was in teaching her rational-emotive ways of challenging her irrational beliefs, and altering her causal attributions regarding her unhappiness. She acquired a new causal attribution belief: "It is possible to do something about my unhappy feelings and I am the one who can do something about them." In addition, she learned that factors under her control, namely the learning of disputational skills and encouraging herself to make an effort, were major influences over what would happen to her in the future and how she would feel. The main irrational beliefs she learned to dispute were "I must have my brothers' love and approval at all times" and "I must perform well in my schoolwork at all times or I am a failure."

Penny was taught to distinguish between herself and her performance and learned to stop rating herself globally. Homework exercises helped her to rehearse exactly what she would say to them when asked to do something she did not want to try (e.g., riding a surfboard in heavy surf). Other in session rehearsals of rational self-talk, for dealing with schoolwork "catastrophes" worse than she had feared or imagined, reduced her exaggerated evaluations of events such as getting poor marks. Humorous exaggerations by the practitioner helped her to put her perceptions into a new perspective.

After eight sessions she was feeling happier and doing her schoolwork without rating herself globally on her performance level. Changes in Penny reported by her mother included improved self-acceptance, new positive perceptions of her teachers, and improvements in the independence and organization of her schoolwork.

Conduct Disorder

Karen, a 13-year-old schoolgirl, was referred to one of the authors (MRJ) for frequent misbehavior in the classroom and in peer settings. She was the middle child in a family of three and was academically capable. Assessment of this girl and her family showed that her misbehavior, which was associated with poor parental control, tolerance of misbehavior, lack of discipline and verbal punitiveness, was related to deficits in social problem solving, especially alternative solution thinking and consequential thinking. Karen was unresponsive to discussion about feelings, but became involved in learning about short- and long-term goals. She wanted to do well at school and have many friends but also wanted to do what she felt like doing and avoid having to work hard. In class, for example, she would not start work, not complete assignments and she would frequently talk and insult the teachers. In the playground and locker room she would play "tricks" on her peers or retaliate strongly against any action she imagined was aimed at her. She threw squashed fruit onto another girl's head; she put glue into locker keyholes; she stapled several girls' hair plaits together. Such actions naturally got her into trouble with both peers and authority figures. Detentions from teachers and poor relationships with peers followed.

After weeks of trying to reach this child in fortnightly sessions with her parents, rapport was finally established when the therapist visited her school camp in the country for a day. Sessions with the parents were then separate and parents were taught behavior management skills. Karen was seen by herself and her list of long- and short-term goals was used as a basis for teaching consequential and alternative thinking skills. She nominated her two or three most important goals, and learned that one of the consequences of seeking her short-term goals was to interfere with attainment of long-term goals. For example, if she insisted on demanding extended TV watching time at home after school, the therapist would ask "What might happen with your schoolwork?" "How might that affect you and what you want?" "What different ways could you plan your afternoons?" Karen suggested doing homework first, or no TV, or some homework, then watch her favorite program, and them more homework. Thus, the emphasis was on teaching her to *generate* thought rather than to provide her with solutions.

After some weeks Karen demonstrated improved ability to find alternative solutions to problems and to act on them. She is presently showing signs of leadership in her peer group, is enjoying new popularity, and teachers report improved classroom behavior.

It is worth noting that though Karen's thinking showed several irrational beliefs, early in the treatment she did not respond well to work on emotional problem solving. When involved in social problem solving, however, she was willing to confront and challenge her most troublesome irrational beliefs, namely that it is horrible to *have* to do things decided for you by others, and it's not fair if you can't do things just the way you want to. As her consequential thinking skills developed, she could see that such beliefs were self-defeating, that they led to trouble with parents and teachers and did not help her to achieve her long-term goals.

CHAPTER 9

Parents and Teachers

While advocates of RET have consistently maintained that many children who manifest chronic dysfunctional emotional and behavioral patterns *may* have an inborn propensity for irrational thinking, faulty reasoning, and cognitive distortion, they have also argued strongly that the home and, to a lesser degree, the school environment determine the extent to which children experience emotional and behavioral problems. That is to say, the manner in which parents and teachers react to and communicate with a child who manifests signs of maladjustment can either help or hurt the child. Moreover, RET theorists also agree that "disturbed" parenting styles can create problems in relatively "normal" children.

Most of the work which examines the interactive nature of the child and the environment in the genesis and maintenance of problems has dealt with parent – child relationships. As such, this chapter will mostly center on the RET parent counseling and education literature. It will pick up central themes we introduced in Chapter 4 concerning parental influences on childhood maladjustment. It is also our own experience that when teachers experience high levels of emotional arousal (stress), the quality of their interactions with other teachers and students deteriorates. Teachers who manifest extreme anger, anxiety, and depression can only exert a negative influence on their students. The last part of this chapter will introduce the reader to the nature of teacher stress.

WORKING WITH PARENTS

The earliest work in this area is reported in the two now classic books written in the late 1960s entitled, *How to Raise an Emotionally Healthy, Happy Child* (Ellis, Moseley & Wolfe, 1966), and *The Rational Management of Children* (Hauck, 1967). The first of these books provides practical suggestions to parents as to how they can directly deal with specific problems of their children, while the second (as discussed in Chapter 4) relates different erroneous beliefs of child management to parenting styles which tend to create problems in children. Our review uncovered very few other significant pieces of work in this area until a limited edition of a manual entitled, *Cognitive Restructuring Training for Families* (McMullin, Assafi & Chapman) was issued in 1978. Since then a number of chapters have appeared which discuss RET parent counseling, including Bard's (1980) "Parent–Child Problems," Hauck's (1980) chapter on "Child Counseling," Hauck's (1983) "Working with Parents," DiGiuseppe's (1983) "Rational-Emotive Therapy and Conduct Disorders," Grieger and Boyd's (1983) chapter on childrens' anxieties, fears, and phobias, McInerney's (1983) "Working with the Parents and Teachers of Exceptional Children," and Woulff's (1983) "Involving the Family in the Treatment of the Child: A Model for Rational-Emotive Therapists." This material and our own clinical experience provides the basis for the sections which follow.

Rationale and Goals of RET Parent Counseling

Parents are not as a rule well prepared to deal with the variety of difficulties which arise in bringing up a child. This is especially the case when their child presents special and difficult problems. They generally have not taken classes in child care nor have they read extensively in the area. Their implicit theories of child development, personality formation, and child-rearing, which guide their handling of their children, are not infrequently misinformed, inaccurate, and self-defeating. Parents may unwittingly be contributing to their child's difficulties out of *ignorance*. They may simply be unaware of the importance of basic principles and methods of child management such as the importance of being consistent, providing adequate structure, reinforcing desired behavior and extinguishing inappropriate behavior, employing logical consequences for misbehavior, giving children choices, setting appropriate expectations for compliant behavior, not being overly critical, punitive, or blaming the child, etc. Nor do they often know what to do and say when their child is experiencing fear, anxiety, anger, sadness, underachievement, or shyness. We agree with DiGiuseppe (1983) who has written:

> Parents may fail to provide adequate structure for their children for no reason. They may be ignorant or disturbed. It is more parsimonious to assume ignorance until one has evidence for disturbance. Many therapists do the reverse. They act on the parental disturbance hypothesis before they have made a full assessment. I am usually amazed at the frequency with which I hear my peers blaming parents for the conduct of their children. I am somewhat disturbed by the elaborate hypothesis therapists devise to make the parents look sick for inadequate parenting. Such a therapeutic attitude can be a grave error which will either send therapy on needless tangents, or unnecessarily alienate the parents. Parental personality problems, marital problems, or transient emotional difficulties frequently interfere with parents' good judgment and result in poor child management. . . . A good working assumption is that most parents are well meaning and would like to do the best by their child. [p. 125]

We have indicated how irrational and erroneous beliefs of child-rearing can lead to characteristic ways parents relate to their children, which may create or exacerbate a variety of psychological problems. Overly permissive child-rearing practices which are based on a number of unfounded assumptions ("children should never be frustrated"; "I must always be loved and approved of by my child") can lead to self-indulgent, egocentric, demanding, easily frustrated children, with low self-esteem. Parents who are overly strict, blaming, and unaffectionate hold a variety of erroneous ideas ("Children should not disagree with their parents"; "Praise spoils a child"; "Children must do well and behave correctly all the time") which can lead to their children becoming anxious, tense, guilty, and depressed.

Emotional difficulties of parents can have at least two distinct destructive influences on their children. First, it is our clinical experience that children who are especially susceptible to harsh parental expressions, language, and unkind influence, and who are exposed to emotionally upset parents, are likely to manifest similar problems themselves. An example would be the "fearful" parent whose verbal and nonverbal behavior in the presence of their children communicates a set of beliefs to their children which may be directly internalized (e.g., "The world is a dangerous place to live"; "If something is painful or dangerous, it must be avoided at all times"). The "angry" parent who rants, raves, and hits out (at his child) at the slightest provocation models a number of irrational and pernicious attitudes, including "When all else fails, yelling and physical violence are acceptable forms of human conduct"; "I must always have what I want; it is awful when I don't; those that frustrate me are bad people who deserve whatever they get." A second problem occurs when parents react to their child's problem in an overly distressed fashion. There are a number of difficulties which arise at these times. The parents' emotions interfere with their effectively employing whatever child management techniques they have available. Their overreaction may be reinforcing or creating more of a problem such as occurs when parents continuously blame their child for misbehavior. Also, children will label themselves as having a problem and may develop emotional problems about what parents are upset about (Grieger & Boyd, 1983).

Another way of conceptualizing the role of parents in childhood maladjustment and therefore their involvement in RET counseling is in terms of organizational, structural, and relationship problems that exist within the family. Nina Woulff (1983), a rational-emotive family therapist (REFT), has articulated a model which describes the interaction of family members as central to understanding psychological problems in any one family member (adapted from Haley, 1976; Minuchin, 1974).

The REFT therapist conceptualizes well-functioning families as groups of people who are able to accomplish the task of aiding the personality and social development of their offspring. This difficult task is hampered when the system has unclear or inappropriate rules, boundaries, and/or hierarchy. In an effective family system the parents comprise a cooperative working team that operates as the "executive" unit of the system and the children are a subsystem of clearly secondary power and status. The tasks of the parental subsystem are to work cooperatively in socializing the children and to be able to modify rules and expectations as children grow older. The task of the sibling system is to offer its members the opportunity to learn how to negotiate, cooperate, share, compete and make friends with peers. [Woulff, 1983, pp. 369–370]

When a child is referred for therapy, the RET practitioner investigates the possibility of inappropriate boundaries and hierarchical incongruities in a family, revealed in such problems as when "a parent is relating to his child as a peer, a child is closely enmeshed with one parent while the other parent is relatively distant, an older child makes most of the decisions for a family, or all members of a family relate to each other as equals in status" (Woulff, 1983, p. 70). From this perspective, dysfunctional family structures and relationships are primarily created and maintained by each family member's irrational assumptions about themselves and each other.

Similar to trends in child counseling and therapy (which we discussed in Chapter 1), RET is increasingly viewing parents as having the greatest potential for effecting the significant changes in their children. Not only can parents, through changes in their attitudes, emotions, and behaviors, attempt to ameliorate conditions which brought about problems in their children because of the amount of time they spend with their children, they can also perform as more effective teachers and counselors than the practitioner. Teaching parents to be less upset about their children's problems and how to perform counseling with their children is a central rationale of Hauck (1983) for working with parents.

Education of the parents in regard to the nature of the emotional disturbance of the child is generally thought to be the primary reason why parents are brought into the therapeutic process. I, too, feel this is a most important reason. However, an even more important reason to deal with the parents is to make them more stable so that they can *then* work more effectively with the children. Some years ago when I wrote *The Rational Management of Children* (1967) I made this point then and I make it just as firmly today. The lesson I have learned is that when a parent is encountering an emotional problem with a child, it is not wise to put that emotional problem first so that the parent can then be calmed later. It is much wiser for the parents to exercise whatever cognitive strategies they can in order to calm themselves first over the child's behavior and then work toward calming the child. [p. 334]

Talking to parents about their children's nonmanipulative emotions calls upon the wisdom of giving them enough instruction to be a surrogate therapist while not overburdening them with depth and intricacy of therapy so that they become confused.

Waters (1981) offers her own perspective concerning the importance of parents in child counseling.

As you might also expect, the younger the child, the greater the parental involvement in the therapeutic process. Therapists may wish to have the parents present for all or part of the therapy sessions with the child. It is equally important for the parents to learn the basics of RET so that they can reinforce at home what the child is learning in therapy. Involving parents in therapy serves three additional functions: 1) it offers the therapist the opportunity to observe parent–child interaction, as well as the parents' irrational beliefs; 2) gives the parents the opportunity to observe the therapist modeling rational-emotive thinking skills; and 3) it decreases the likelihood that the parent will sabotage therapy. [p. 1]

In terms of our review and our own practice, we have distilled the following as goals of RET parent counseling and education. The actual goals we target will, of course, be guided by the results of our assessment of parental involvement in the problems of their children.

1. Teach parents ways of conceptualizing the goals of families and roles of family members as well as appropriate attitudes of child rearing.
2. Teach parents family relationship and child management skills which are necessary for them to accomplish the goals of families as well as to solve problems.
3. Teach parents the ABCs of emotions so that they can overcome their own problems and, as a consequence, are able to prevent them from being transmitted to their child.
4. Teach parents how to calm down so that they can deal with problems levelheadedly.
5. Teach parents the ABCs of childhood emotions so that they know what to teach their child who is having a problem.

Erroneous and Irrational Beliefs of Parents

We have described a number of ways in which parents can create and maintain problems in their children. RET views the erroneous and irrational beliefs of parents as being central to understanding, assessing, and treating parent–child problems. RET adopts the position that it is very difficult to motivate children to change unless parents are prepared where necessary to change. Moreover, as Woulff (1983) has observed, "it is highly unlikely that a child who has learned rational thinking with his individual therapist will continue to maintain this change when his parents and other family members still strongly reinforce the old irrational beliefs and consequent behavior."

In our review of the RET literature, we have encountered over 70 erroneous and irrational beliefs of parents. The way in which these beliefs are conceived of and expressed by different RET practitioners varies considerably. Referring to our discussion of the nature of beliefs presented in Chapter 2, the irrational beliefs of parents vary from being expressed in very *general* terms—"If you are not loved and approved of by important people in your life, you are worthless. Rejection is painful and almost devastating, and you cannot avoid being upset when rejected" (Hauck, 1983)—to those that deal with the *specific* role of parents—"I am to blame for all my child's problems; therefore, I am a lousy parent" (DiGiuseppe, 1983). Erroneous beliefs of parents generally refer to things parents believe to be true about parenting and children which are not true—"As a parent, I have the power to make my kids do whatever I want" (McMullin et al., 1978)—while irrational beliefs of parents—"Children should always and unequivocally do well and behave correctly" Grieger and Boyd, 1983)—reflect absolutistic and imperative qualities. Some beliefs are stated in such a way that it is difficult to classify them as erroneous, irrational, or both (e.g., "Children should be calmed first, adults second," Hauck, 1967). Erroneous parent beliefs are generally corrected by presenting objective facts, new information and knowledge, and anecdotal stories which help prove the erroneous belief to be untrue (referred to by some as practical or empirical disputation), while irrational parental beliefs are disputed in the usual way. It would appear that erroneous and irrational beliefs can both lead to emotional upset as well as inappropriate child-rearing practices. It is generally the case that irrational beliefs create emotional upset, while erroneous beliefs have a direct effect on the way parents discipline their children without necessarily the intervention of their emotions. For example, parents may "mishandle" a child in the form of lack of structure because they erroneously believe that "children should not be frustrated," and not because they irrationally believe that, "I must have the love and approval of my child at all times." Obviously, parents who endorse both beliefs would be more likely to be, because of their anxieties, lax in the area of discipline.

We also find that the same belief can lead to a variety of different emotions in parents. For example, the belief, "My child should always behave well," when combined with, "and when he doesn't, I'm a failure as a parent and a person," leads to depression, whereas when it is followed by, "and when he doesn't he's a no good little brat who deserves to be punished," generates feelings of anger. It is therefore difficult to determine the individual effects of erroneous and irrational beliefs without examining other beliefs parents subscribe to.

We shall now present a list of combined erroneous and irrational beliefs of parents. We shall indicate the constellation of beliefs which surround poor parenting styles, dysfunctional family relationships, and different emotions of parents. The beliefs we have uncovered in our work with parents will be referenced in the lists of beliefs.

Inappropriate Child-Rearing Practices

We have indicated in previous chapters the different emotional and behavioral problems "disturbed" parenting styles can bring about in children (see Chapter 4). In our clinical work, we observe parents who present three types of parenting styles which tend to be counterproductive: *overly strict and harsh*, *overly permissive and undemanding*, and *inconsistent*. We shall now present different beliefs which go along with each style. When parents manifest an emotional difficulty along with improper child management practice, an additional set of beliefs which occasion the emotional distress will also have to be recognized to fully understand the dynamics of the problem. We will refer to these beliefs shortly.

Beliefs which underlie an overly strict and harsh style of parenting.
1. Getting angry is an effective way to modify my child's behavior (Di-Giuseppe, 1983).
2. Anger helps get things done (McInerney, 1983).
3. A child and his behavior are the same (Hauck, 1967).
4. Since a child should do well, praise and reward are unnecessary and spoil the child (Grieger & Boyd, 1983).
5. Doing bad *must* be punished since punishment, blame, and guilt are effective methods of child management (Grieger & Boyd, 1983).
6. A parent is always correct or at least has the authority in a situation, and, therefore, children must never question or disagree with them (Grieger & Boyd, 1983).
7. As a parent, I have the power to make my kids do whatever I want (McMullin et al., 1978).
8. Kids are naturally undisciplined and behave like beasts. Parents must beat them into shape to make them civilized (McMullin et al., 1978).

Beliefs which underlie an overly permissive and undemanding style of parenting.
1. Children must not be frustrated (Hauck, 1967).
2. All punishment is wrong (DiGiuseppe, 1983).
3. Children should be free to express themselves (DiGiuseppe, 1983).

Beliefs which underlie inconsistent parenting.
1. Whatever feels right is right (Grieger & Boyd, 1983).
2. I'm too weak and helpless to know what is the right thing to do, so I'll leave it to the moment (Grieger & Boyd, 1983).

Dysfunctional Family Relationships and Structures.   It is important for the RET practitioner to be aware of the different beliefs which occur in families with certain structural dysfunctions. Woulff (1983) has found the following beliefs in families where boundaries among family members are enmeshed:

1. It is terrible to be different from other people in my family—I must not think, behave or feel differently than they.
2. It is awful to fight or be annoyed with someone in my family.
3. I must be able to change people in my family.
4. It would be horrible if a member of my family left—we all *need* each other.
5. The source and solution to my problems lie in other members of my family.
   [p. 375]

Emotional Disorders of Parents

We have discussed how parents who experience emotional upsets unrelated to or in reaction to their child's particular problems need to learn to overcome their problems so that they can more effectively help their children overcome theirs. What follows is an analysis of the beliefs of parents which underlie their own emotional difficulties. Once practitioners teach parents the origins of their own emotional difficulties, parents will be in a better position to help their children to think more rationally.

Beliefs which underlie general parental upset.
1.   My child can upset me (Bernard & Joyce).
2.   I have little ability to control my feelings when something at home upsets me (Bernard & Joyce).
3.   One has to get upset when things go wrong (Grieger & Boyd, 1983).
4.   My kids cause all my unhappiness. They must change for me to feel better (McMullin et al., 1978).
5.   I have little ability to control the unhappiness I am experiencing (Woulff, 1983).

Beliefs which underlie parental anger.
1.   There are bad and wicked people in the world, and the only way to make bad people into good people is by being very severe with them, beating them, telling them how worthless they are (Hauck, 1983).
2.   When you don't get what you think is right or what you deserve, you are experiencing a horrible and catastrophic event. The world should be fair and if you deserve justice you should get it (Hauck, 1983).
3.   Children should always and unequivocally do well (e.g., be motivated, achieve, etc.), and behave correctly (e.g., be kind, considerate, interested) (Grieger & Boyd, 1983).
4.   It is *horrible*, *terrible*, and *awful* when children do not do well, behave, or question or disobey their parents (Grieger & Boyd, 1983).
5.   My child must always behave the way I demand (Bernard & Joyce).
6.   My child must do what I say (DiGiuseppe, 1983).
7.   A child and his behavior are the same and thus children who act badly or err are bad (Grieger & Boyd, 1983).
8.   My child must be fair to me at all times (Bernard & Joyce).
9.   Life is unfair (McInerney, 1983).
10.   My spouse must always behave the way I demand (Bernard & Joyce).
11.   My child shouldn't be so difficult to help (Woulff, 1983).

Beliefs which underlie parental depression.

1. If you are not loved or approved of by important people in your life, you are worthless. Rejection is painful and almost devastating and you cannot avoid being upset when rejected (self-blame) (Hauck, 1983).

2. If you are not outstanding, gifted, and almost perfect in practically everything you do, you again are worthless. To make a mistake is not just a human quality, it is a disaster (self-blame) (Hauck, 1983).

3. When you don't get what you think is right or what you deserve, you are experiencing a horrible and catastrophic event. The world should be fair and if you deserve justice you should get it (self-pity) (Hauck, 1983).

4. We cannot only be pained by physical things but by psychological acts as well. Words can hurt, gestures are painful, and a host of behaviors, even though not affecting us physically, certainly have to hurt us emotionally (self-pity) (Hauck, 1983).

5. It is only natural and decent to become upset over other people's problems and misfortunes. Simply caring for people in a calm and undisturbed way is not sufficient to show you care for them. You have to become upset to the point where you are almost as disturbed as the people you are trying to help (other-pity) (Hauck, 1983).

6. When I don't perform as I think a good parent should (e.g., worry all the time, solve all my child's problems), I am a complete failure as a person (Bernard & Joyce).

7. If my child misbehaves frequently, it is awful and I am a failure as a parent (Bernard & Joyce).

8. If my parents think I'm a poor parent, I'm worthless (Bernard & Joyce).

9. My worth as a parent depends upon the performance of my child (Grieger & Boyd, 1983).

10. My self-worth as a person is tied up to how I do as a parent, so I had better not make mistakes (Grieger & Boyd, 1983).

11. I am worthless because my child has so many problems (Woulff, 1983).

12. I am a terrible parent for being so annoyed with my child who cannot help his/her problem (Woulff, 1983).

Beliefs which underlie parental ego anxiety.

1. I must have the love and approval of my child at all times (Bernard & Joyce).

2. My child must do well in everything (Bernard & Joyce).

3. It is horrible, terrible, and awful when children do not do well (Grieger & Boyd, 1983).

4. One must have a guarantee that things go well or else it is unstandable (Grieger & Boyd, 1983).
5. I must worry about my child at all times and help him overcome problems (Grieger & Boyd, 1983).
6. I must have the approval of my parents at all times (Bernard & Joyce).

Beliefs which underlie discomfort anxiety in parents.

1. Difficult issues in life are best handled if they are avoided as long as possible. This is the best way to get instant gratification and that benefit is always greater than the benefit you might get if you did not procrastinate and faced your problem immediately (Hauck, 1983).
2. If something is frustrating, it must be avoided at all costs (Grieger & Boyd, 1983).
3. I cannot stand it if something bad happens (Grieger & Boyd, 1983).
4. I cannot stand my child's behavior (DiGiuseppe, 1983).

Beliefs which underlie the fears of parents.

1. Dangers abound *everywhere* and one must be constantly on the alert lest something take you by surprise (Grieger & Boyd, 1983).
2. If something is painful, it must be avoided at all costs (Grieger & Boyd, 1983).
3. Bad things that happen are awful, terrible (Grieger & Boyd, 1983).
4. I cannot stand it if something painful happens (Grieger & Boyd, 1983).

Beliefs which underlie parental guilt.

1. Past or present adversity is so unpleasant and awful that my child cannot be expected to live normally; restitution for this adversity needs to follow (DiGiuseppe, 1983).
2. I am the sole cause of my child's problems (DiGiuseppe, 1983).
3. If I make a mistake it will always affect my child (McMullin et al., 1978).
4. I could have and should have done something to prevent my child's disability (McInerney, 1983).
5. I am totally responsible for virtually everything that happens to my child (McInerney, 1983).
6. My child is being punished for my own personal inadequacy (McInerney, 1983).
7. It is awful for my child to suffer and I *must* therefore prevent it at all cost (Grieger & Boyd, 1983).
8. I must always do right by my child (Grieger & Boyd, 1983).

Stages of Treatment

We find it useful to describe our work with parents employing the same four-stage flowchart we used to characterize our work with children and adolescents. As was the case in working with younger populations, there is considerable overlap between stages. For example, the building and maintenance of rapport with parents occurs across assessment and intervention stages. Similarly, assessment and intervention are interdependent and often take place together during a single session with parents.

Relationship Building

Our work with parents as well as that of others indicates how vitally important it is for the practitioner to cultivate a positive relationship with parents. While the establishment of a good relationship is not sufficient to bring about change, it is generally necessary for several reasons. Many parents, when meeting for the first time about "the problems of their child," do not recognize their own involvement in the problem. They do not have the expectation that they will have to talk about their own feelings and, if they do, many are unwilling to do so to a total stranger, even though he may represent himself to be a "helping" agent. Accepting the fact that they may "own" part of the problem is not especially pleasant for parents because it may represent an admission of failure. Many parents (especially mothers) equate their self-worth with their effectiveness as parents. Over the years, we have lost a number of parents who failed to return to therapy because we came on too strong too early. Dropout may also occur later on in the course of therapy if the practitioner is too argumentative and leads parents to believe they are being accused, attacked, or blamed. McInerney (1983) illustrates this when he discusses the use of disputation with the parents of handicapped children. We believe his points apply to the parents of all children.

> Clearly, simply trying to argue parents out of their feelings is short-sighted. Given appropriate attention to relationship issues and the establishment of a contract to proceed, RET with these parents is not significantly different from work with other types of parents. . . . Many parents of handicapped children are rather sensitive to what they see as criticism of themselves or their child. Disputation, therefore, is best done sensitively with attention to both content and timing of therapist disputes. Directed, socratic dialogue is ideal for this purpose. Initially, experiential and cognitive disputation of the "inelegant" but pragmatic variety in this context are most effective. At times, parents will misperceive disputation as 1) an attempt to get them to deny their strong emotions; 2) a dismissal or trivialization of the emotion (e.g., "How dare you say it's not awful! How would he know how hard it is!"); and/or, 3) disapproval of the person for having the distress in the first place. These misperceptions need to be listened for, particularly when disputation fails, and corrected either directly or through further dialogue. Sometimes these reactions once confirmed may indicate that some of the relationship issues previously mentioned could use maintenance efforts or that the therapeutic contract requires re-examination. [p. 391]

We are not saying that the practitioner has to wait a number of sessions before beginning treatment. Indeed, Hauck (1983) often proceeds with active therapy at the first visit.

> Whenever this is possible, in fact, I urge you to do the same. Parents are enormously relieved when they realize the counselor is taking over. . . . To delay these efforts as we did years ago only leaves the family on its limited resources for a week or more, during which time the suffering can get worse. [p. 338]

Our experience has been that highly emotional and defensive parents have to be won over to our position and that it takes a number of sessions before a collaborative working relationship with parents can be achieved.

Getting parents to self-disclose emotional problems, as well as take an active role in the counseling process, can be viewed in terms of "resistance." From a RET perspective, resistance derives from a number of irrational beliefs that are activated when parents are asked to participate in the change process.

> Resistance can occur at the beginning of family therapy when the therapist attempts to enlist the involvement of the parents and throughout the therapy when the therapist gives the family specific tasks. When parents resist becoming involved in therapy there are several irrational beliefs which commonly occur. Sometimes these beliefs are easy to uncover and the therapist can then challenge them directly. However, resistance by its very nature tends to be difficult to deal with directly and the reasons for initial resistance often are not disclosed until later in therapy. The therapist must then infer the underlying beliefs. [Woulff, 1983, p. 376]

Some of the beliefs of parents that contribute to resistance include:

1. When my child hears us discussing these problems he becomes more upset and we cannot bear when he is upset.

2. My child's problems are all my fault and responsibility and this proves I am a terrible person.

3. It is a sign of complete failure to have to come for help on family matters.

4. The therapist might ask us to talk about other problems we have and that would be disastrous. [Woulff, 1983, p. 377]

There are a number of useful suggestions contained in the literature to help build rapport with parents as well as overcome resistance. McInerney (1983) indicates that it is a good idea as a prelude to building a relationship to dispel parents' misconceptions about therapy such as viewing it as a treatment for sick or mentally ill people. He provides the following statement as an example of how to establish a "self-help" atmosphere in parents which may lead parents to be open in discussing their thoughts and feelings about their child. We again feel the statement has relevance for the parents of any child who manifests a problem.

Psychologists over the years have found that people don't do difficult jobs very well when they are very upset, angry, or depressed. Your job as a parent of a handicapped child is certainly a difficult one. You'd probably do it better if you learned some proven ways of how to better manage your own fears, resentments and guilty feelings in addition to learning how to stimulate and work with your child. In our work together, I'm going to help you learn to manage your emotions better so you can do a better job with your child. [p. 389]

DiGiuseppe (1983, p. 125) suggests that "a collaborative relationship with the parents designed to explore the causes of their child's problems and collectively investigate solutions is a good step in developing the rapport." The discussion of parental involvement in terms of the child's long-term interest appeals to parents' sense of responsibility and provides good motivational leverage.

Woulff (1983, p. 377) suggests stressing to parents their importance by telling them their involvement "is crucial because they are the most significant people in their child's life and that they, more than anyone else in the world, are best equipped to help their child." She also indicates that the practitioner state the goals of therapy in terms of freeing the child of problems and that the parents will play a major part in helping their child.

In the building of initial rapport, it is often helpful to reinforce verbal self-disclosure. Ways this can be accomplished include direct encouragement through specific discussion topics, personally modeling self-disclosure and reinforcing self-statements by active listening or an empathic restatement of the thoughts and feelings of parents (McInerney, 1983). Other suggestions for facilitating the development of initial rapport include (adapted from McInerney, 1983):

1. The practitioner through stating she has knowledge and expertise relevant to parents' concerns establishes herself as trustworthy and credible. . . .

2. The practitioner should accept the parents' thoughts and feelings unconditionally and as facts which may be reexamined later on. . . .

3. The practitioner should express genuine concern about the parent and child's progress without being dependent on this progress. . . .

4. "Trustworthiness" is enhanced when the practitioner directly intervenes in the child's environment in an effort to search for optimum services. [p. 390]

Finally, we offer a summary of characteristics and skills of RET practitioners which Woulff (1983) believes are necessary to conduct effective family therapy and which appear to help the building of a helpful practitioner—parent alliance.

Family therapists need to be directive and focused in leading sessions, to plan sessions, to challenge realities that family members accept, to be persistent in encouraging people to change, to focus on present methods of coping and problem-solving and not be sidetracked by the intricacies of past history, to be clearly goal-oriented, to creatively design homework assignments, and to make flexible use of self in order to engage and motivate family members. [p. 382]

Assessment

There are two aspects of parent assessment that RET practitioners need to be concerned about. *Problem identification* determines the types of problems that exist within the family and the service (advice, direct assistance, or psychotherapy) which will be most appropriate and helpful to the parents (and child). With respect to this phase of assessment, Bard (1980) makes the useful point that in all cases something is "amiss."

> Either the child is reacting poorly, or the parents are reacting poorly, or everyone is reacting poorly to whatever conditions exist. There are no other possibilities. If something weren't amiss, no problems would have been presented in the first place. Even if the problems are simply fictions of the mother's imagination, they might be resolved by providing her with the proper guidance to allay her anxiety. [p. 95]

In assessing the problem, Bard indicates there are a number of possibilities which need to be considered, including whether the child may be brain damaged, mildly retarded, extremely gifted, temperamentally difficult, or emotionally disturbed; whether the parents may be slightly overzealous with their only child, mildly retarded, or emotionally disturbed; whether teachers may be incompetent or emotionally disturbed; and whether the school psychologist may be incompetent (p. 94).

In seeking to identify parent problems, the practitioner answers a number of self-questions. Are the parents' child-rearing attitudes appropriate and their child management skills sufficient for them to solve their child's problems? Is the husband's relationship with his wife supportive enough and their relationship with their child sufficiently differentiated and strong to enable parents to provide appropriate control and guidance? Are the parents' emotional difficulties contributing to the child's problems? Do the parents overreact when their child misbehaves?

RET practitioners vary a great deal in terms of whether they examine the total family structure for dysfunctions as well as whether they concern themselves with all possible problems a parent might be experiencing. Coming from a more problem-focused viewpoint, DiGiuseppe (1983) has written:

> As I have indicated when parents do become upset, their upset interferes with child rearing. This may occur because they are (a) upset about the child, or (b) upset about outside issues such as their marriage, their work, or themselves. It does not appear necessary that parents resolve all of their personal or marital problems before they can learn to use effective child management strategies. Thus the parents need not be sent off to individual therapy to work on themselves

or their marriage before attempting to change the child. Neither does the entire family structure need to be changed. Rather, parents are asked to change their emotions in limited situations with their children, even if they do not wish to work on the other major issues in their life. [p. 127]

Benefits of a family relations approach have been summarized by Woulff (1983) to be as follows:

> In terms of dealing with child related problems, the family therapy approach can be very time efficient . . . Family members can reinforce their own learning by challenging each other's beliefs, and family therapy sessions can function as a live laboratory in which family members experiment with new interactions. . . . By working with the whole family, family members develop a much stronger belief in their ability to function competently and solve their own problems. It is arguable that a therapist who works solely with children inadvertently reinforces the parents' belief that the solution to their problems rests with an outside agent—the therapist—thereby discouraging the development of an internal locus of control. [p. 384]

The breadth and focus of the practitioner's questioning during the initial phase of assessment will be dictated by their particular orientation.

The second phase of RET assessment, *problem analysis*, involves a more detailed consideration of parental thinking patterns, child-rearing philosophies, and irrational beliefs which are leading to dysfunctional family relationships, emotional stress, and inappropriate behavior. The unraveling of the mental world of parents is a cornerstone of RET practice. Parents may resist this work and it is up to the practitioner to build the type of relationship with parents which will enable this to happen.

RET practitioners appear to agree that the best approach to employ with parents is a combined *cognitive-behavioral* one. If the practitioner determines that the child's problem is manipulative behavior (see Chapter 6), then she is going to concentrate on assessing the parental use of reinforcements and punishments; whereas if nonmanipulative, emotional problems or neurotic behavior is of central concern, more attention will be directed to assessing and changing dysfunctional cognitions of parents and child.

The assessment of parents takes place in a parent interview. Some RET practitioners choose to meet with parents and child together, believing it affords them an opportunity to observe first hand the communication patterns and power relationships in the family, how families work together to solve problems, and the discrepancies between how parents and children view and react to problems. Others prefer to interview parents and children separately, believing it removes the child from parental pressures and therefore provides a safe environment for change, gives the practitioner a chance to communicate to parents about the nature of the problem, gives the parents a safe forum to acknowledge their roles in the child's problems, and makes it easier for practitioners to talk to the child without alienating the parents (Grieger & Boyd,

1983). We generally see the parents of children with manipulative behavior separately from their children and see the family together if the child's problem is emotional.

Some of the important goals of parent assessment have been described by Grieger and Boyd (1983) to be: "(1) to gather relevant information about this child, his/her problems; (2) to gather information about the role the parents play in creating and/or maintaining the 'problem'; (3) to ferret out perceptual distortions, irrational attitudes, and maladaptive behaviors in the parents; and (4) to begin to educate the parents to a psychosituational and cognitive definition of the problem and its eventual alleviation." They outline important aspects of the parent interview as follows:

1. An explicit, behavioral detailing of the parents' concerns or complaints about the child, including their frequency, intensity, and duration. This serves to reconstruct vague, interpretative, and/or blaming perceptions with objective units that lend themselves to problem solving, to perception checking about their "awfulness," and to the diffusion of overt or covert anger and hostility.

2. An explication of the specific situations or circumstances in which the "problematic" behavior occurs. Particularly open to inquiry here are the expectations or rules (i.e., "shoulds") the parents have about the child's behavior in these situations.

3. An identification of the immediate consequences following the child's behavior, including specifically what the parents think, feel, and do when the child behaves as s/he does at these times. The interview is particularly attentive at this point to the attitudes and behaviors that may serve to promote inappropriate and inhibit appropriate child behavior; concurrently the interview is on the alert for evidences of the faulty parenting styles described previously as they impact the child in relation to the "problem" behavior and in a more general sense.

4. A definition of goals for the child, again stated as explicitly and behaviorally as possible. This helps the interviewer to set appropriate goals; equally as important, it provides another opportunity for both the clinician and parents to reflect on the appropriateness of the expectations for the child and the rules or demands in the parents' cognitive schema.

5. An exploration of the more general, on-going patterns of interaction between the parents and child, including the perceived ratio of positive vs. negative interaction, the kind and quality of both positive and negative interactions, the methods and frequency of punishments, and the kind and quality of communication. [p. 230]

There are a number of ways the parents' disturbed emotions, behaviors, and attitudes can be assessed. For some parents, simply asking them how they feel about their child's difficulties (and to a lesser extent their own problems) elicits sufficient data. However, parents are often very private about what they feel, and husbands and wives often protect each other by failing to disclose important information concerning how each of them relates to their child at home, as well as to each other. For these families, more indirect data gathering methods are required.

One way to gain insight into how parents think and feel about their child is to observe how the parents react to what their child says and does during a joint interview session. Verbal and nonverbal parent–child messages are not difficult to read. A second way is to examine assessment data and note characteristics of the situations in which the problem behavior occurs, as well as antecedent stimuli and consequences which surround the target behavior. Self-questions which can guide the practitioners' examination of the mass of assessment data include:

> Does the child behave inappropriately more when one person is around? Is the child's behavior related to the parent's own upsetness? Does the parent ever get angry when the target behavior occurs? How do both parents feel when their child does misbehave? What do they think when their child misbehaves? [DiGiuseppe, 1983, pp. 126–127]

Another useful way to assess the thoughts and emotions of parents toward their child and toward therapy is to examine their compliance with homework assignments. Failure to comply with practitioner directives may reveal the parents are so immobilized by feelings such as guilt, depression, anxiety or anger, they sabotage therapeutic effort at helping their child. Examples of questions which a practitioner might direct to parents who failed to successfully implement a behavioral management program at home are:

> "What stopped you from punishing Jack?" "How did you feel when Julie didn't have enough points to go skating?" "What stopped you from giving Kim her rewards when her homework was completed?" "What feelings do you have when those temper tantrums started?" "How do you feel when you notice that Dean had not done his chores?" "What kinds of feelings do you have about having to check up on Scott to make sure his homework is done?" [DiGiuseppe, 1983, p. 127]

For the practitioner who believes it is important to assess structural dysfunctions and family members and to identify the beliefs which are maintaining the problem and the malfunctioning structure, Woulff (1983) suggests that they could ask themselves the following questions:

1. Are the parents united in the way they attempt to solve the problem?

2. How may the attempted solutions be actually reinforcing the child's problem rather than solving it?

3. Does the child have an inordinate amount of power and influence in this family?

4. Do the parents behave assertively with their child?

5. Do family members have any practical problems which could be contributing to the presenting problem (i.e., lack of child management or negotiation skills, financial problems, communication problems with the school, physical or neurological handicaps, etc.)?

6. What irrational assumptions could be influencing the way each member of this family reacts to the problem and to each other?

7. How do family members irrationally blame themselves or others for the problem?

8. How do the child's beliefs maintain his symptoms? [p. 371]

She also suggests the following questions which could be asked to the family directly:

1. Do you (the parents) discuss this problem? What happens when you discuss it?

2. Specifically, what does each person do when the problems occur? What has been done in the past?

3. What does each family member think is the cause of the problem?

4. What does each family member think is needed in order to solve the problem?

5. What do these problems mean about the child (i.e., is he sick, bad, stupid, evil, etc.)?

6. What does each family member feel and think when the problems occur?

7. What is happening around you and what are you thinking about when you experience your problem (asked of child)?

8. What does each family member want from therapy? [p.372]

Assessment results in an overall identification of parent (and child) problems and often a description of the role each family member plays in the problem. Woulff (1983) provides the insight that it often is beneficial if the practitioner can help parents reformulate destructive explanations of and definitions for their child's difficulties into more constructive ones with positive connotations (e.g., from "overly sensitive, disturbed, suicidal adolescent" to "separation anxiety precipitated by approaching adolescence").

Additionally, once a tentative diagnosis is formulated and communicated to the parents, it is generally a good idea to arrive at a therapeutic contact with parents and their child which communicates (1) the goals of treatment, (2) the form and frequency of treatment, (3) the general expectations regarding the parents' active role, and (4) homework requirements.

Skill Building

The focus of RET work with parents is to teach them when necessary new child-rearing attitudes and emotional and practical problem solving skills which will enable them to overcome their own difficulties as well as those of their child.

There are a number of insights which are necessary for parents to acquire before the teaching of new attitudes and skills can begin. A basic idea to initially communicate to parents is "Our Thoughts Determine How We Raise Our Children" (McMullin et al., 1978). A teaching example will illustrate how this can be done.

> Imagine two sets of parents faced with the same problem. Both have a 10 year old who came home crying because a neighborhood boy had taken away his baseball bat. Family #1 became very angry and went to the other boy's parents demanding they return their son's bat. Family #2 told their son it was his bat and he would have to get it back by himself.
>
> The parents acted differently because they believed different things. Parents #1 thought, "It is our job as parents to solve our child's problems. If someone cheats or hurts him, we must correct the situation." Parents #2 thought, "Our son must learn to solve his own problems when he is mistreated. Parents shouldn't interfere; otherwise, the child will never learn to take care of himself." [p. 10]

This example demonstrates to parents that it is their beliefs and thoughts about what to do in a situation, rather than the problem itself, which influences their approach. The point to be made is that erroneous beliefs of parents can lead parents to behave incorrectly.

Another extremely important idea to get across to parents is that the way they (over)react emotionally and behave toward their child can frequently be hurting the child rather than helping. For example, parents of children who misbehave frequently discipline with anger. In order for them to modify the demands they make of their child which lead to them being angry, they have to first realize that their anger is not doing any good.

Parents also have to come to understand that no matter how poorly their children behave, they and not their children are responsible for how they feel. Once parents realize this, it is more possible for them to stop blaming their child for misfortunes and the unhappiness they may be experiencing.

We believe that parents need to be taught that change in themselves (and their children), while difficult, is eminently possible. By demonstrating how it is possible to modify self-defeating emotions and patterns of behavior through rational restructuring of new attitudes and beliefs, parents begin to see hope that changes in themselves and their children can be brought about.

The acquisition of these insights does not occur all at once. As we have indicated, some parents resist the idea that their best efforts are indeed having a negative effect on their child and that they have to change before their child will change. Once parents begin to accept these insights, intervention can take place.

If the practitioner determines that parents are too permissive, punitive, or inconsistent in the way they raise their children, it is important to dispel the erroneous parental beliefs which lie behind these practices. This process involves persuading and convincing parents that while they may think their way of raising a child is "what the good book says," "is how I was brought up by my parents," and "is how we do it in my country" it is not helping them accomplish their goal.

> It is (also) important to convince the parents of a philosophy of child-rearing which emphasizes the desirability to teach frustration tolerance, the importance of setting limits and the advantages of inculcating appropriate social skills in compliance with the demands of others. [DiGiuseppe, 1983, p. 126]

In discussing the relationship of inconsistency in parenting and lack of discipline in children, Bard (1980) suggests that practitioners advise parents to insure that there is consistency between what parents say in front of their child and what they do, for example, not screaming at the children because the children are screaming at each other. Such modeling reinforces bad habits in children. Another type of parental inconsistency which leads to children being poorly disciplined is when parents yield to their child's whining.

> Most parents frequently make the mistake of saying yes or no without thinking the matter through. Having said no, they are vulnerable to the question, "Why not?" because there isn't any good reason why not, and then they succumb to the pressure. The danger here is that if this happens frequently, then no comes to mean maybe and confuses the issue. The simplest solution is to develop restraint in responding to the child's requests; this allows time to think the matter through and arrive at a rational decision which will more likely hold up. [p. 97]

Correction of erroneous beliefs of parents which we have listed in a previous section may involve the practitioner presenting objective evidence through anecdotal stories, self-disclosure, and authoritative facts that refute the ideas of parents. Below are examples of a number of erroneous beliefs of parents that often lead to improper parenting styles and emotional distress and which have been restated as rational beliefs (McMullin, et al., 1978):

1. If I make a mistake, it will always affect my child.

   Counter Argument:
   1. Children often forget mistakes. They live in the present. What happened yesterday is not as important as what is happening today.

   2. Parents come in only one variety—fallible. Occasionally, we all act unjustly and mistakenly. No one is perfect.

   Realistic Belief: I will try to correct my mistakes. If I can't, I will take precautions so I am less likely to make them again. Dwelling on my mistakes or wallowing in self pity will not correct my errors, change me or help my relationship with my children. I will practice not exaggerating the damage my mistakes cause. [p. 12]

2. As a parent, I have the power to make my kids do whatever I want.

    Counter Argument:
    The super-parent belief frequently leads to a parent-child power struggle— a confrontation which the parent seldom wins. A teen-ager will go to great lengths to win a power struggle. We have known of cases where children have stolen, failed in school or chosen seedy companions to "get back" at their parents. Parents can't make children think, feel or act in approved ways. Parents must avoid power struggles.

    Realistic Belief: My children are going to do things I don't like, but which I can't prevent. If the consequences of their actions do not cause real physical danger, I must allow them to learn by making their own mistakes. I must not threaten my children when I have no power to enforce the threat. [p. 15]

3. My kids cause all my unhappiness. They must change for me to feel better.

    Counter Argument:
    Blaming our children for our own unhappiness is ridiculous—they cannot cause our feelings about ourselves. We can hurt them by forcing them to change when we are the ones who really need to change.

    Realistic Belief: I will realize that my unhappiness is always caused by my own beliefs, not by my child's behavior. [p. 19]

4. Kids are naturally undisciplined and behave like wild beasts. Parents must beat them into shape to make them civilized.

    Counter Argument:
    Punishment doesn't usually work. Psychologists like B. F. Skinner conclude, after extensive research, that rewarding children for good behavior works far better than punishing them for bad. Punishment stops a child's misbehavior only as long as the parent is present. In addition, the severely punished child often hates the parents and will try any method to fight the parent's control. We should use punishment rarely and only if the child's misbehavior is more damaging than the problems caused by the punishment.

    Rational Belief: Children, like adults, work more to gain rewards than to avoid punishment. Instead of looking for my children's mistakes, I will try to catch them being good. I will compliment and praise them whenever they behave well. When I use punishment, I will use the least amount possible. [p. 24]

5. It is my responsibility to solve all my children's problems.

    Counter Argument:
    1. The head nurse is the most damaging type of parent. His or her beliefs prevent children from learning that they are responsible for their own actions.

    2. As therapists we try to help our clients face reality and stop running away from their problems. Any parent who accepts children's excuses, allows them to ignore reality or permits children to blame their behavior on someone else can make their children feel temporarily good at the

price of their permanent happiness. Children must learn to resolve their own problems. Parents who constantly rescue them keep them from growing up while training them to be helpless.

Rational Belief: Although I feel hurt when my children get into trouble, I realize that they must learn the connection between a behavior and its consequences. Rescuing them will prevent them from coping with their own mistakes. [p. 27]

The RET literature contains numerous suggestions as to which child management skills parents may need to acquire to handle a child whose behavior is primarily a function of a poorly arranged reinforcement system. Hauck (1967, 1983) argues persuasively that parents are the primary clients when a child's behavior is being performed primarily to manipulate the parents.

To try to reason with the child that the behavior he or she is exhibiting is self-defeating may sometimes work in which case the parents do not have to be brought into the counseling process. However, imagine how difficult it is for a child not to continue a rewarding bit of behavior when the parents, ignorant of what he is doing, repeatedly reinforce his irritating actions. [1983, p. 354]

In helping parents to modify their handling of manipulative behavior, he advises practitioners to be well acquainted with Dreikurs' work which isolates four goals of child misbehavior (attention getting, power struggle, revenge, giving up—physical disability) and proposes the use of logical and natural consequences to correct misbehavior. Hauck (1983) also lists a number of insights which will help parents modify their parenting techniques.

1. Behavior exists because it is reinforced.
2. Parents are usually the people most frequently involved in rewarding the behaviors of their children.
3. When parents change their training methods children change their behavior.
4. Actions speak louder than words.
5. Guilt and other-pity prevent parents implementing the program. [pp. 355–359]

Other practical skills which may be taught to parents to improve family relationships and child-rearing practices include empathy listening, assertiveness, relaxation, behavior modification procedures (e.g., time out, token reinforcement, reinforcement, punishment), and how to teach social skills to their children. Practitioners should be familiar with the basics of these techniques.

A large part of parent work involves helping parents overcome their own emotional problems so that they can both effectively implement child management strategies as well as help their children think rationally about problems they may be having. (The main cognitive, emotive, and behavioral disputational methods which are employed to challenge and change the irrational beliefs of parents which create emotional disturbance have already been described in Chapter 3.) "The goal is a profound understanding of the illogic, lack of empirical support, and self-defeating and child-defeating nature of their basic beliefs, as well as an awareness of more plausible and constructive alternatives" (Grieger & Boyd, 1983, p. 235).

A brief case study will illustrate how RET assessment and treatment procedures can be used to help parents as well as their child. John, age 11, was referred to the first author (MEB) for fighting and disruptive classroom behavior. As is not uncommon, John's school reports indicated that he has a moderate reading difficulty. A group administered intelligence test (OTIS) revealed an IQ of 106.

When John's parents were initially interviewed, they indicated that he had a history of noncompliant behavior at home. When he was asked to do something, he would oftentimes get extremely angry and sometimes break something. John frequently fought both verbally and physically with his older brother, Andrew, though the intensity of the fights appeared moderate and the duration shortlived. John's father would become extremely angry with John when he refused to do what he was asked to do. His father would frequently slap or use a strap on John. John's mother would attempt to get John to help around the house by being excessively nice to him. As a consequence, John appeared to have things pretty much his way—though at some cost. Therapy with parents which was successful involved the father learning to control his temper largely by changing his belief that "My son must always obey me when I ask him to do something" and by teaching him to accept his son with all his imperfections. Both parents were taught to be more firm and assertive with John and the use of logical and natural consequences as a punishment procedure proved effective in increasing compliant behavior.

John was seen for 16 sessions. A problem analysis revealed a complex set of cognitive deficiencies. John appeared to break rules and get into fights (consequent behavior) when he interpreted a situation as being "unfair" (antecedent events). At these times his emotions were generally of anger and frequently registered above 8 on a 1 to 10 scale of intensity. John was quite open in discussing his thoughts and feelings. His expressive language was somewhat restricted leading to an inference of an inadequate self-control inner language system. Primary among his dysfunctional beliefs were (1) Everyone should be fair to me at all times, (2) I should always get what I want, (3) I'm not good if I break a rule or make a mistake, and (4) I must be comfortable at all times and I can't stand the discomfort I have when I have to work hard. This last belief resulted in undesirable levels of frustration tolerance and discomfort anxiety which because of John's pattern of work avoidance, led to a low level of educational achievement. When John was confronted with situations with his peers where he believed they wanted to "take the 'mickey' out of me," he could not think of any alternatives to his fighting. When he believed that a teacher was saying something or requesting something which he felt was unfair, his only response was to simply refuse to comply with his teacher's instruction. Moreover, when he became aroused, he failed to consider at that moment the range of negative consequences which would result from his misdeeds. At times when he became angry, his self-talk was highly provoking and he lacked appropriate self-statements for keeping his anger in check. Therapy was partially successful in helping John to give up his "demandingness" and was very successful in improving his self-esteem. He acquired the ability to control his temper by the use of coping self-statements and was only "caught" once for fighting during the remainder of the school year. During treatment he became more aware of the perspective of others, began to recognize when situations were fair and when they were not, and that the world did not always have to revolve around him. He began to accept the behavior of others, understood the notion that it is unfair to get angry with people who make mistakes, and was seen by both parents and teachers to be more cooperative.

We will discuss in more detail in the following section, which deals with parent education programs, how some parents find it extremely difficult to dispute general irrational beliefs and that it is sometimes easier to teach them to dispute irrational appraisals of specific upsetting events (i.e., son disobeys his father) and to rehearse rational self-statements that reduce emotional arousal ("It's not that bad; things could be worse").

The following are some practical suggestions that McInerney (1983) has found to be successful with parents of exceptional children and which we again feel apply to parents in general:

1. Use rational self-disclosure to model the disputation processes, particularly at initial stages.

2. When presenting the disputational process didactically (e.g., the ABC-D model), use relevant examples of practical value to the parents in themselves.

3. Use pragmatic, relevant although "inelegant" cognitive disputes before more abstract philosophic ones.

4. Build in generalization by providing the connection between the disputation process and the content from various practical problems. Use questions to encourage conclusions about generalizations and new applications.

5. Ask for feedback and listen for misperceptions. Be flexible and use all types of disputation, particularly when one approach is unsuccessful.

6. Do not hesitate to use the dissonance between expressed parental values (e.g., "It is important to stimulate my child") and self-defeating ones (e.g., "It should be easy") in disputation.

7. Be persistent, although a "hard sell" approach seems to be easily dismissed by many parents.

8. Use homework assignments as well as self-help oriented readings to augment disputation. [pp. 391–392]

We have listed a few additional ideas which may be useful for practitioners to have at their fingertips to help parents overcome their disabling feelings and for parents to know so that they can identify and understand the reasons for the emotional problems of their children.

Anger
1. Anger is a conversion of a desire into a demand (Hauck, 1983).
2. Anger can be compared to a child having a temper tantrum (Hauck, 1983).
3. When parents get angry, it brings them down to the level of a four year old (Hauck, 1983).
4. Do not discipline with anger because parents will put their child down and, as a consequence, their child may develop a spiteful reaction (Hauck, 1983).
5. Getting angry will not help parents or their children; anger is only temporarily effective at best (DiGiuseppe, 1983).
6. No law of the universe says that what parents wish to happen, must happen; children are children, ignorant, mischievous (DiGiuseppe, 1983).
7. Anger frequently generates more anger and resentment in others (Mc-Inerney, 1983).

Depression
1. (Self-blame) Never blame yourself or others for anything (Hauck, 1983).
2. (Self-blame) We behave badly or poorly because of deficiency, ignorance, disturbance; how can we hold others (or ourselves) blameworthy when they did not know how or were not able to do something properly? (Hauck, 1983)
3. (Self-blame) Never hate the child, only disapprove his actions (Hauck, 1983).
4. (Self-pity) Parents should not pity themselves so that it won't be copied by the child (Hauck, 1983).
5. (Self-pity) We are usually better off than we think; think of one's blessings; never pity oneself (Hauck, 1983).
6. (Self-pity) Parents who pity themselves may create guilt feelings in their child (Hauck, 1983).
7. (Self-pity) Parents make themselves miserable, not their children (Hauck, 1983).
8. (Other-pity) Parents who pity their children encourage them to be self-pitiers (Hauck, 1983).
9. (Other-pity) Children's hardships are usually never as bad as parents make them out; parents shouldn't blow them out of proportion (Hauck, 1983).

10. A person's performance as a parent does not determine her self-worth (Bernard & Joyce).

11. The performance of a child does not determine the value of a parent as a person (Bernard & Joyce).

Fear

1. What children are afraid of is really not as serious as they believe (Hauck, 1983).

2. It is possible to stand it even if bad things happen (Bernard & Joyce).

3. Fear in itself rarely prevents the feared event from happening (McInerney, 1983).

4. Fear interferes with parenting (McInerney, 1983).

Anxiety (Ego)

1. It is more important to do than to do well (Hauck, 1983).

2. Another person's opinion of you does not determine your self-worth (Bernard & Joyce).

3. Failure, rejection, or disappointment are not as awful as they seem; they do not signify "worthlessness" (Bernard & Joyce).

Anxiety (Discomfort)

1. It is easier to face a task than to avoid it (Hauck, 1983).

2. It is not a catastrophe to have an anxiety attack (Hauck, 1983).

3. Short-term tolerance of frustration may well lead to long-term gain (DiGiuseppe, 1983).

4. Parents have in the past overcome frustration with their child (DiGiuseppe, 1983).

Guilt

1. Parents are not the sole cause of their child's problems (DiGiuseppe, 1983).

2. Parents can never be so omnipotent to prevent bad things from happening (DiGiuseppe, 1983).

3. Children can overcome many of their adversities (DiGiuseppe, 1983).

4. Parents are not solely responsible for their child's behavior or personality (DiGiuseppe, 1983).

5. Children can tolerate frustration (Bernard & Joyce).

6. Children's misfortunes are not as great as parents may make them out to be (Bernard & Joyce).

Other suggestions for parents to help them deal with specific problems of their child are reviewed shortly.

Practice and Application

At the same time parents are acquiring basic RET insights, skills, attitudes, and the variety of practical skills just discussed, the practitioner is encouraging parents to implement their new knowledge and skills with their child in the home environment. Homework is the principle means by which parents are given the opportunity to apply and generalize skills and attitudes. Moreover, homework in the form of bibliotherapy serves as a means of reinforcing and extending basic skills and insights acquired during early treatment session.

Homework that is assigned during the week basically involves two things. First, parents learn to control their emotions in situations where they previously became overly upset and reacted poorly. Second, parents carry out self- or practitioner-generated behavioral strategies for improving relationships among family members and managing the difficulties family members may be experiencing. Woulff (1983) indicates that the overall goal of behavioral homework is to "reverse incongruent hierarchies and to eliminate the reinforcers which are maintaining the symptom." Additional recommendations are that homework tasks are kept as clear, simple, and inexpensive as possible.

During the time when parents are initially applying these skills at home, the practitioner takes the major role in prescribing assignments. Assignments are designed to overcome a specific and concrete behavior of concern. Toward the end of treatment, the focus of homework is broadened to encompass a wider range of family concerns. Parents are also encouraged to generate their own solutions to specific problems through a process of negotiating with each other (Woulff, 1983).

There are a small number of materials parents can read which indicate how parents can apply rational principles of child management. Hauck's (1967) book, *The Rational Management of Children* is probably the best known. Another book, *How to Raise an Emotionally Healthy, Happy Child* (Ellis et al., 1966), also provides parents with insights as to how to handle specific problems of childhood.

A series of pamphlets written by Virginia Waters illustrates the ways in which irrational parental beliefs and practices can contribute to problems in children. The underlying principle of these self-help pamphlets is that when parents exhibit irrational emotions and behavior, they are unlikely to be of much help in assisting their children overcome theirs. The titles of some of the pamphlets reflect this self-help orientation: "Accepting Yourself and Your Child" and "Building Frustration Tolerance in You and Your Child." The contents of these pamphlets show parents how different irrational emotional reactions can interfere with their effectiveness and suggest ways they and their children can overcome their problems. An additional pamphlet, "Rational Problem-Solving Skills," alerts parents to the importance of learning how to solve their own problems (via the ABC-DEs of RET) as well as how to help their children cope with theirs. Some of the important ideas which Waters discusses are presented in the following excerpts from her pamphlets.

From "Accepting Yourself and Your Child" (Waters, 1980a):

"Self-acceptance" is unconditional acceptance – acknowledging and accepting responsibility for one's *traits*, *qualities*, and *behaviors*—both good and bad—without evaluating one's *self* as good or bad. "Accepting others" does not mean having to like everything that another person does; it means distinguishing between disliking another person's *traits* or *behavior* and disliking or rejecting the whole *person*. Parents who accept themselves and their children accept and love their children regardless of how they behave—without blaming themselves or their children for the children's mistakes. [p. 1]

From "Teaching Children to Light Up Their Lives: The Power of Rational Thinking" (Waters, 1980a):

"If you pictured other people in response to the question "who lights up your life?", then you are in the unfortunate and precarious position of depending upon others for your happiness and growth.

Actually the warm, happy emotions you probably experienced as you pictured the people who light up your life didn't come from the people you pictured. Where then did these feelings come from? You created these positive feelings for yourself by thinking positive thoughts, just as you can create negative feelings when you evaluate situations and people negatively. Consequently, you have the power to light up your own lives by taking responsibility for the feelings you create and choosing to view situations and people more rationally. [p. 1]

From "Building Frustration Tolerance in You and Your Children" (Waters, 1980a):

All human beings experience some frustration every day. It is natural for obstacles to interfere with our plans and objectives. As stated previously, it is not the presence of the frustration which is upsetting, but our attitude toward the frustration which creates either helpful, appropriate feelings or hurtful, inappropriate feelings. Individuals who have LFT consider any block or obstacle in their path to be awful, horrible and terrible and consequently, they frequently upset themselves. They are so busy demanding that things go their way that they upset themselves to the point of being unable to cope well with the actual situation. [pp. 1–2]

From "The Anger Trap and How to Spring It" (Waters, 1980a):

Anger is a learned reaction to frustration which rarely serves any useful purpose, and usually has some quite undesirable consequences. Four beliefs commonly associated with creating anger [are as follows] "*Awfulizing*" means evaluating a situation as more than a hundred percent bad, or as the worst that could be. "*I can't standitis*" cry parents with low frustration tolerance who have convinced themselves that they cannot tolerate obnoxious situations and shouldn't have to.

"*Demanding*" that the world and everyone in it behave according to your dictates is another sure way of creating anger. A fourth way parents can anger themselves is by condemning a person for obnoxious traits and behaviors. [pp. 4–6, 10]

From "Fear Interferes" (Waters, 1980a):

Many parents find that they are almost always anxious and fearful when it comes to raising their children. Their minds are full of scary thoughts of everything that could be wrong with children. Parents try to do their best in caring for their children. But when they demand that they themselves be perfect, and that their children turn out to be flawless, their anxiety about failing can interfere with their goal of effective and efficient child-rearing. The following examples illustrate some self-defeating beliefs about children and parenting that are guaranteed to produce constant high anxiety.

1. I must be a perfect parent. If I'm not always calm, competent and correct in handling my children, they will turn out badly.

2. I must see to it that my child is never uncomfortable, hurt or in any danger.

3. It would be awful if my children didn't love me all the time.

4. It's awful if others disapprove of the way I parent.

5. If I'm not constantly anxious and fearful about the welfare of my children, I'm a bad parent. [pp. 2–6]

From "Rational Problem-Solving" (Waters, 1980a):

People upset themselves with their beliefs and evaluations of situations. It is possible to learn to think more rationally and create feelings that are helpful rather than hurtful. Thinking rationally is not only more pleasant emotionally—it also improves your ability to solve your practical problems. Parents who think rationally will be better able to resolve conflicts with their children, and can more effectively teach them to cope with their own feelings and problems. [p. 11]

Parents Working with Their Children

In this section we review additional ways parents can be of help to their child. Parents are of immense help to children who experience inevitable upsets associated with living. They provide comfort, security, and the love and affection which tell children that not only will everything be okay, but that they are okay. (We recognize the latter to be an irrationality.) They can provide guidance for children to solve practical problems. Parents who are familiar with the ABC theory of emotions are in an especially good position to educate their own children about how to rationally deal with unfair and unpleasant events so that they do not overly upset themselves. In general terms, parents who understand the irrational ideas which underly their child's problems can talk to their child about why she is feeling and acting the way she is. Such communications provide the child with a sense that she is understood by her parents and may be more willing to listen to their advice. For example, parents can constantly remind children that mistake making is a part of living and that they should not despair if they do not succeed at everything they do. If parents can educate children not to blow things out of proportion, they will go a long way to inoculate them against future psychological disturbances. Another important lesson which parents can teach children, through the use of rational persuasion and positive reinforcement, is how to tolerate discomfort and frustration associated with doing unpleasant tasks such as homework.

Another way parents can help their child is by reading to her stories which illustrate in terms the child can understand rational ways to think about herself and others. There is also material which older children can read themselves.

Direct Assistance

Ellis has discussed in his 1966 book on raising a happy child ways in which parents can help their child overcome specific problems associated with growing up. We thought it might be useful to summarize suggestions from his book which practitioners can offer parents as solutions to the major emotional problems of children.

Overcoming Fears

1. If it is known that a child has a strong tendency to become frightened by dogs, the dark, loud noises or anything else, a special effort may be made to keep him out of the range of these things.
2. The easily upsettable child should preferably be kept away from excessively fearful adults and older children.
3. If you, as a parent, happen to be imbued with a great many intense fears, train yourself to suppress as thoroughly as possible these fears when you are with your child.
4. Children who are reasonably fearful of external events can frequently be talked out of their fears (through repetition of rational explanations) if those who raise them will reason with them in a patient, kindly, and persistent manner.
5. Blaming the child or making fun of him for his fearfulness usually won't help him at all but will tend to do him more harm than good. He should clearly be shown that the fear is groundless and that other children do not have it but that he has a perfect right to be wrong and that he is not inferior because he cannot handle himself in this area.
6. Getting children to laugh through the use of humor at their own and others' fears may be of value if it is directed at the child's panic rather than at him.

7. It is frequently possible to help the child (through deconditioning) to become pleasantly familiar with a feared object.

8. Calmness in dealing with a child's fears is one of the prime requisites for helping him overcome them.

9. Don't be deceived by a child's clever evasions of admitting his fears. If a child claims that she is not particularly afraid of other children or animals but that she simply dislikes them, ask yourself whether she is using dislike as a cover-up for her fears.

10. If a child's parent has a fear, it is advisable that personal catastrophizing be eliminated.

Overcoming Anxieties and Low Self-Esteem

1. Fully accept the fact that a child has not had time to learn all the strange rules of the adult world; consequently, he is unusually fallible and must inevitably make innumerable mistakes that will bother parents. Children will outlive their childishness only if they are allowed to act it out, to learn by making mistakes, rather than being warned of the dire consequences.

2. Learn to tolerate normal inefficiencies (child tying shoelaces) as they will always exist, rather than getting angry. Displace the onus of mistakes and failures onto the task rather than the child.

3. Do not expect that an emotionally labile child will be problem free. Once a child feels that others do not like him and that it is horrible that they don't, he frequently resorts to testing procedures, deliberately acting badly to see whether his peers and elders will accept him.

4. Once you have ascertained that a child's behavior is poor, try to estimate what he is capable of doing and not doing, and judge him accordingly.

5. If you honestly believe a child's behavior is correctable, keep in mind that change can be a very slow process; be tolerant and patient.

6. Keep in mind that the main reason for anyone's anxiety is his dire need to be accepted, approved, or loved by all significant people in his life. Show your child by example that you do not need others' love and that neither does she. Let her see that you are not overly hurt by your child's ungracious, inconsiderate, and hostile attitudes.

7. Avoid the sorts of family tensions that are characterized by scraps between parents; such fighting denotes your own inability to handle the troubles that come your way.

8. While children who are anxious about what others think of them demand a lot of pampering and mollycoddling, it is also important to be firm and show them that their behavior is self-defeating (reinforce and punish accordingly).

9.   Be wary of overly good behavior of any youngster. Try to discover if he is terribly anxious about losing your and others' approbation; and, if so, get in a good counterattack on his anxiety creating attitude.

10.   Children who are anxious tend to become upset and put themselves down, become embarrassed, panicky, and anxious about being seen as anxious. Tell children that most people react to their worry in some overexcited or withdrawing fashion and that it is not terrible to reveal to others how afraid one is.

Overcoming Anger

1.   First and foremost, be calm yourself.

2.   Remove, if you can, unnecessary frustrations from the child.

3.   Make sure children are not over-tired.

4.   Do not condemn or punish a child for his hostility when he is unusually hostile.

5.   Try to keep in mind that the child's hostility is an expression of underlying attitudes and beliefs and that expressions of or symptoms of human behavior are themselves normal and even healthy. Show the child that his anger arises from the sane belief, "I don't like this thing that is happening to me," and the mistaken belief, "and therefore I can't stand it, and demand that it shouldn't happen!"

6.   At times it is wise to let a child get his anger out of his system.

7.   Show children that they are not bad, but their ideas are.

8.   When there is not time to get to the very bottom of your child's anger, or when it is too late to start interpreting and arguing him out of it, you can frequently use some kind of diversion as an effective means of calming him down.

9.   Try to be as fair as possible in your dealings with your children.

10.   One of the main causes of children's anger is jealousy or envy of others. Teach the child that (1) deprivation and disadvantage is inevitable, and (2) one can amount to something even without the benefits and advantages of others.

RET Literature for Children

There are now a variety of materials written specifically for use by parents with their children. Depending on the age of the child, the books and pamphlets can either be read to children by their parents or by children themselves. While these materials can be used preventatively with children who demonstrate no particular problems, their main design is as a therapeutic adjunct to be employed by parents to help their children learn to think more rationally about particular difficulties they may be experiencing.

Color Us Rational (Waters, 1979) contains many large pictures for children to color. People and animals who populate twelve different stories teach children the differences between rational and irrational ways of responding.

Homer the Homely Hound Dog (Garcia & Pellegrini, 1974) helps children understand and deal with fears of rejection through a reconsideration of the "ugly duckling" theme. This book can be used in the home or in school.

Instant Replay (Bedford, 1974) is a picture book for all children and shows them how to tolerate frustration, do rational problem solving, and improve communication. A parent and teacher manual is available.

The *Rational Counseling Primer* (Young, 1974b), which has sold over fifty thousand copies up to date, is primarily designed for adolescents. The ABCs of rational thinking are outlined and illustrated.

Virginia Waters (1980b) has written a series of stories for children that are designed to accompany the series of pamphlets she wrote for parents. The short stories are well written and deal with how children can overcome their anger, fears, and anxieties, increase their happiness and self-acceptance, and to solve problems.

PARENT EDUCATION PROGRAMS

Rationale

In addition to parent involvement in the rational-emotive remediation of specific emotional disturbances of their children (DiGiuseppe, 1983; Ellis, 1978c; Grieger & Boyd, 1983; Hauck, 1983; Woulff, 1983), parent participation has been recommended in a comprehensive RET approach to the special needs of particular populations, such as handicapped children (McInerney, 1983). Our emphasis on *prevention* as well as remediation in the field of mental health has led us to implement rational-emotive education programs for parents in school settings. Muro and Dinkmeyer (1977), though not working in an RET framework, have commented on the lack of planned programs available for helping parents and have recommended that counselors develop such programs. At present, our programs are provided for parents of young children (up to grade three), but it is hoped to extend them to the parents of older children as well.

After some years of conducting single lecture–discussion sessions for parents at the invitation of schools, kindergartens, and other organizations, it became apparent that not only were many parents keen to learn new child management skills but also, in many instances, parents were experiencing unpleasant degrees of emotional stress in dealing with the everyday difficulties of child-rearing, even though their difficulties were not at that time so severe as to require referral to a clinic. As the details of our program are described, it will be clear that three main characteristics typify these education groups: (1) regarding membership, parents do not have children in treatment for emotional or behavior disorders; (2) program emphasis is on the education of parents (and indirectly their children), and the prevention of severe disturbance; and (3) program goals center on emotional problem solving.

While data are not yet available on the effectiveness of these programs, an evaluation is ongoing, and it is hoped that the programs will enable us to evaluate the effects of our rational-emotive parent education on the reduction of parental stress and to improved adjustment in children.

One of the authors (MRJ) is currently running a series of parent education programs which consist of eight two-hour sessions which meet once a week. Parents are invited to attend the first session in the form of a lecture—discussion, in which the purpose and content of the program are explained. (Details of this session and later ones are set out below.) Continued attendance then depends on commitment to the remaining sessions, which is required before each parent is accepted into a smaller group. Group size is currently 15−20, but experience suggests a smaller group of 10−15 may be more desirable for the group to give sufficient time to each individual.

Expectations of Parents

Parents have come to the groups willing to participate and to learn. Most bring difficulties that arise repeatedly in their daily family contexts, and while being dissatisfied with how things frequently turn out (child misbehaving, parent upset), they do not know what alternatives to try. They have normally "tried" several different ways of reacting (punishing, ignoring, cajoling), but concern over continuing difficulty had led them to experience strong negative feelings such as anxiety, anger, or depression. Over a period of time, these negative emotions can become inappropriately persuasive in child−parent interactions and, while the parent is often aware of its inappropriateness ("I know I yell too much, I'm always yelling at him"; "I seem to get upset so easily. I know it doesn't help"), he or she less often knows what to do about it.

When parents come to the program they are expecting to learn new strategies for dealing with their children, but they are surprised to learn that there are strategies available for them to deal with their own problem feelings, independently of how their child is behaving. This relates directly to their common irrational belief that their children are causing them to feel upset. For most, the discovery of strategies for emotional problem solving comes as a relief because they have been experiencing stress in relation to their ongoing difficulties. Therefore, the programs we provide are *cognitive-behavioral* in orientation and teach both child management skills and emotional problem solving skills. Since many manuals and practical books are available to parents on child management, but little on emotional problem solving in child−parent interactions, we teach only basic behavioral principles and emphasize mostly cognitive skills for the parents to use themselves and to teach to their children.

Goals of Parent Education Programs

The main goals of rational-emotive parent education programs are as follows: (1) to teach parents basic child management skills; (2) to teach parents rational-emotive skills, or new rational ideas and beliefs about themselves and their children; (3) to teach parents emotional responsibility, that they are largely responsible for how they feel, and that they are able to acquire new ways of dealing with emotional and practical problems.

Special Considerations in Parent Education Groups

When parents attend a group in association with the school which their children are attending, they may perceive the group leader in an authority role such as that of teacher or principal. While teaching is part of the group leader's role in a parent education program, the leader may well wish to establish the parent–leader relationship on a different basis to avoid anxiety and hostility associated with authority figures, and to promote positive attitudes of honest involvement and self-acceptance throughout the group. Establishment of these positive attitudes can be assisted from the beginning by (1) a nonjudgmental, non-blaming attitude; (2) appropriate physical arrangement of the group such as sitting in a circle with no special chair for the leader; and (3) the use of first names, if the group wants this.

Once the group is established, the leader will exercise skill to maintain a balance between didactic teaching and discussion which offers the opportunity to work through the parents' own schemata.

One difficulty that arises in parent groups is when the group leader finds that in discussion parents express views to one another and describe child-rearing methods which are unsatisfactory for the child or parent. Unless the leader is able to work on the unsatisfactory aspects immediately with the group (e.g., pointing out long-term disadvantages), these parents may be modeling an approach for other parents which is not a useful one for them to learn.

There may be variation in the group as to what *level of cognitive change* can take place. A few parents have trouble going beyond the learning of *new rational self-statements* within the range of eight group sessions, while others progress to *empirical analysis* and learn to subject their interpretations to some sort of empirical checking by the group (see Chapter 7). Some parents are able to learn philosophical *disputational skills* and model them for group members and for their children at home. Those who proceed to philosophical disputation are more likely to practice and perform these skills by disputing irrational beliefs manifested in particular situations with their children ("What's so *awful* if my child has a tantrum in front of other parents? It's inconvenient, but doesn't make me a bad parent").

The irrational beliefs of parents, listed previously, reflect specific forms of more general irrational beliefs as they are manifested in the parent–child relationships. These beliefs contribute to the persistence of troublesome emotions in parents, and indirectly to the maintenance of poor behaviors in the child, and the learning through modeling of irrational attitudes by the child. Learning to recognize these irrational beliefs in operation in their own family contexts—learning to dispute them and replace them with rational beliefs—are important parts of the program curriculum, which is now outlined in sessional sequence.

Outline of Sessions

Session 1: Understanding Your Child

This is the large group lecture−discussion which precedes the formation of small groups. Basic behavioral principles of reinforcement and extinction are taught with numerous examples, and the "praise and ignore" approach described. The emphasis is on "how children learn" and therefore how they can change. Examples are then given which demonstrate that changing behavior is not the only focus in child-rearing. Many emotions are experienced by parents and children (e.g., in discipline situations), and these emotions themselves can be problematic. The ABCs of RET are introduced by dramatizing an example: parents are asked to close their eyes and think about a problem with their child that they would like to share with the whole group. They are told the lecturer will come and tap them on the shoulder if they are chosen. A number of parents are tapped, then they are asked to tell the group what feelings they experienced when they thought they were chosen. Feelings range among excitement, embarrassment, resentment, and fear. Parents are asked why did everyone not experience the same emotion? This experience provides a starting point for learning the ABCs.

Session 2: Emotional Stress in Bringing Up Children

From the second session on, the program is conducted in small groups. Parents are taught that stress comes from the "Beliefs," especially their irrational beliefs about poor behavior. The term "self-talk" is used; emotions are identified by name and listed as an emotional vocabulary; the feeling thermometer (see Appendix 1) is introduced, and parents practice rating their feelings from zero to ten. Discussion is encouraged about extreme degrees of negative feelings such as anger or worry, and how they interfere with attainment of goals and lead rather to an "emotional fog" which interferes with problem solving.

Session 3: Disciplining Children

Discipline methods that are kind but firm and not carried out in anger are stressed in session 3. If parents are able to calm themselves first, then children are likely to follow their example and calm themselves and accept the discipline. Irrational beliefs about blaming are examined and their negative consequences for parent and child are stressed. Parental anger over children's mistakes and naughtiness is analyzed by contrasting demands and needs with wants and wishes. The importance of having rules that are few, clear, and consistent is explained and the effectiveness of "quiet reprimands" briefly described, with examples. Guilt feelings about discipline often arise in this session and may not be dealt with satisfactorily until the next session on self-rating.

Session 4: Teaching Your Child Self-Acceptance

This is a key session in which the focus is on the self-defeating process of global self-rating, or rating of others. Almost all the parents rate themselves globally as parents, and rate their children at times as good and bad. Ways to avoid overgeneralizing and irrational self-downing are taught with many examples from everyday home life. The main ideas taught in this session include (1) that our self-worth does not depend on how well we perform (e.g., as a parent); (2) our children's self-worth does not depend on how well they behave or perform in school—*a child does not equal his behavior*; (3) globally rating ourselves is a self-defeating process, with negative consequences whether we rate ourselves "at the top" or "at the bottom."

Session 5: *"When Things are Going Badly": Coping in a Crisis*

Parents are next taught to identify words of exaggeration (e.g., "awful," "devastating," "horrible") and words expressing unrealistic demands ("should," "must," "demand") and helped to understand their consequences. This is partly done by contrasting alternative rational and irrational pathways a person might follow in a problem situation.

Irrational Pathway
A.   Event
        children are fighting
        grandparents are criticizing
        children are whining
        other parent is overreacting
B.   Irrational Self-Talk
        "I can't stand this."
        "They are upsetting me too much."
        "They must change."
        "This is terrible."
C.   Feelings and Behaviors
        upset, angry or depressed
        emotional fog
        yell, overreact
        goal not achieved

Rational Pathway
A.   Event
        children are fighting
        grandparents are criticizing
        children are whining
        other parent is overreacting
B.   Rational Self-Talk
        "This is unpleasant or uncomfortable."
        "I don't like this."
        "I'll work hard to change things here."
        "What can I do to alter the way things are going?"

C.   Feelings and Behavior
        somewhat annoyed or frustrated
        think out alternatives
        try one
        If it works:
           feel pleased
        If it does not work:
           negative feeling
        BUT: not so strong
                won't last as long

These contrasting sequences demonstrate to parents that irrational self-talk is likely to lead to excessive upset (eight to ten on the feeling thermometer), inappropriate behavior, and lack of clarity regarding one's goals. Rational self-talk, on the other hand, is associated with moderate feelings and problem solving, because the person is motivated to do something about an unpleasant or inconvenient situation.

Sessions 6 and 7: Children's Behavior Part I and Part II

These two sessions focus more on children and their disturbances, but the parents are now ready to discuss their children with positive attitudes; namely, a nonblaming, nonrating approach, and an ability to distinguish clearly the child's performance and their own emotional reactions. Parents are ready to learn the difference between emotional and practical problems. For example, does the difficulty arise because of what parents and child are feeling, or does the situation require parent or child to *do* something differently?

The particular childhood difficulties discussed in these sessions depend entirely on what group members wish to discuss. Bed wetting, thumb sucking, jealousy, sleep problems, eating problems, fighting, shyness, fears, and not wanting to go to school are common examples. These are discussed from practical and emotional aspects. In addition, common irrational beliefs of children (see Chapter 5) are studied by the parents, and methods for helping children learn rational beliefs are taught. A number of *ways in which parents can help children increase their frustration tolerance* are emphasized.

1.   By their own example of tolerating frustration calmly (e.g., remaining calm when the child does not comply with the parents' request).
2.   By recognizing the child's feelings when frustrated but *labeling the feelings moderately* and *providing a sensible evaluation of the event.* For example, "Oh, you've lost the game. I know you don't like that, but it's not really so horrible, is it? I know you can stand it. We all lose sometimes."
3.   By expressing our confidence in the child when he or she is faced with frustration. For example, "People aren't always fair. It's good you are learning to live with that."

Situations to watch out for here might be: someone doesn't like the child; the child doesn't get exactly what he or she wants; the child has to wait for something; someone is not fair to the child; the child does not win.

4. By praising the child when increased ability to wait for something, or tolerate frustration in other ways, is shown. For example, "I like the way you can wait for what you want."

Session 8: Review

In this session, a review is made of basic principles with the emphasis on how to apply them. Any aspects of the program that proved difficult for parents in the group can be gone over carefully. It is useful in this final session to take what were key situations for many in the group and work them through.

Practical Considerations for Parent Programs

While a complete account of the workings of the program are beyond the scope of this chapter, several practical considerations can be mentioned. At the beginning of the program, parents are assessed by means of the Jones Irrational Belief Scale (Jones, 1968), which is used to pick out the dominant irrational beliefs of parents in the group. In addition to this, ongoing assessment is carried out during group sessions (as we have described in Chapter 6) with individuals.

The emphasis in teaching program content is on concrete examples, especially those relevant to the particular members of the group. When a parent shares a difficulty with the group, this can provide the basis for teaching the concept of that session. When new ideas are introduced, parents are encouraged to apply them to their own contexts. Practical exercises, such as role playing and written tasks, are used frequently. Table 9.1 provides one example used in the teaching of the concept of global rating.

Homework is given between sessions and reviewed at the beginning of the following session. At the beginning of the small groups (Session 2), each parent is given a folder in which to keep program notes and summaries. A sheet is provided with the sessions listed, and a space beside each for recording the homework task for that week. Homework usually requires recording of self-talk early in the program, analyzing ABCs, and implementing practical ideas in later sessions. The second author has modeled the doing of homework by setting herself the task of writing a summary of each session's discussion and giving it out to the group the following week.

Certain everyday situations arose in discussion repeatedly and clearly occasion difficulties for so many families that they are worth listing: monitoring their children's homework, getting children ready for school on time, visiting grandparents, having grandparents visit the family, driving in the car with young children, having to discipline children when they misbehave in the presence of other adults, eating dinner together. These situations were discussed many times with different emphases at various stages of the program.

TABLE 9.1. Parent Program Exercise

Which of the following are examples of global rating?

1. Parent says: "You've knocked over your milk again! You
   naughty little boy."   Yes _____   No _____
2. Parent thinks: "My child is always misbehaving. I'll never be
   any good as a parent."   Yes _____   No _____
3. Parent thinks: "My child has spoken rudely again. I'd better
   work harder at teaching her the polite way to speak."   Yes _____   No _____
4. Father thinks: "Oh no! I've done it again . . . lost my temper!
   What a rotten father I am!"   Yes _____   No _____
5. Child says: "Bill took my football at lunch play. He's stupid."   Yes _____   No _____
6. "Why can't I stay up and watch TV? You're mean and
   horrible." (Child to parent.)   Yes _____   No _____
7. Parent says: "I don't like the way you are throwing things
   around in the house because its dangerous. You had better
   remember that that's not allowed."   Yes _____   No _____
8. (Children are fighting while grandparents are visiting.)
   Mother thinks: "Oh no! Things always go bad when Mom and
   Dad come over. They must think I'm a dreadful mother.
   They're probably right!"   Yes _____   No _____

Changes in the parents' evaluations of these difficulties and improved ways of
dealing with problems were evident as the program progressed.

WORKING WITH TEACHERS

There is very little in the RET literature which describes how RET can be used
by teachers to resolve their own emotional problems as well as those of their
students. An exception to this is a rather extensive literature on rational-
emotive education (REE) which consists of curriculum units and lessons which
teachers can introduce in their classrooms and which we review in Appendix 1.
Guidelines for how mental health practitioners can introduce principles of
RET directly with a teacher who may be upset about a student, and who may
have actually referred the student, do not exist.

Both of the present authors work in schools as psychologists. In discussing
our experiences with each other, we have found that although we have for years
used RET directly with children and their parents we rarely, up until recently,
even mention RET ideas to teachers or principals who were concerned about a
student. Most of our time with teachers is spent providing advice, guidance,
and general classroom management procedures for the solving of problems.
For teachers who work closely with a student who is experiencing emotional
difficulties, we make suggestions as to the types of ideas and attitudes a teacher
should try to convey to the student. It has been our experience that teachers are
especially sensitive to any suggestions made by us, however tactfully, that they
may be overreacting emotionally to a student and, as a consequence, may be

contributing to the problem. In the only article we have found which describes a RET approach to consultation provided by a school psychologist, S. G. Forman and B. D. Forman (1978) indicate that school personnel are sometimes apprehensive about asking for help.

> This may be stated as, "I shouldn't really need to talk to you." "I guess I'm not a very good teacher, guidance counselor, principal, etc., if I need to call you in." "No one else around here asks you for help." "I'm the only one around here that can't handle this by myself." Underlying these statements, the basic irrational assumption appears to be, "I'm a failure because I have the problem." [p. 401]

In helping to overcome this problem, Forman and Forman suggest the consultant should state the objective reality of the situation (other people ask for help; even if they don't it does not mean they are handling their problems successfully), indicate that needing help with a situation does not mean that one will never cope with a situation, and communicate an attitude of self-acceptance which says that even if the consultee does not solve the problem, he or she is not a failure as a person.

We have begun to introduce concepts of RET to the teachers in one of the schools we consult for. We believe the reason we have been able to do this is that we have conducted a fairly extensive inservice program in this school where the principles and practices of RET have been introduced. The course we present to school personnel is entitled, "A Stress Reduction Program for Teachers," and has as explicit goals: (1) to help participants develop an understanding of emotions and stress, (2) to decrease irrational beliefs associated with stress among participants, and (3) to provide participants with techniques to help themselves manage their own emotions and behavioral stress reactions more effectively (details of this program will follow). As a consequence of introducing this program, we are now able to discuss with teachers their concerns in a climate of openness and acceptance.

It is our strong recommendation that RET practitioners who work in schools and who will be consulting with teachers concerning the welfare of students conduct a RET program for teachers. This program will sensitize teachers to your perspective and will make subsequent encounters with individual teachers easier. Another reason for introducing RET to teachers is that it has been our experience that teachers often fail to comply with suggestions and directives concerning how to handle a problem with a student because they are so emotionally involved they are unable and, sometimes, unwilling to comply. We find that inservice programs such as those based on behavior modification neglect the critical role emotions play in teacher behavior. (We have been "guilty" of conducting these programs in the past.)

Teachers are also interested in learning about the thoughts and beliefs of students. Indeed, *teachers can be much more motivated to employ procedures we suggest if they can see how they relate to the psychology of the child.* For example, a common problem teachers encounter especially with very young students is "out of seat" and "off task" behavior. Teachers are more likely to consistently employ extinction and social reinforcement procedures when they can see they are designed not only to reduce certain objectionable behavior but also to modify the student's belief that "The only way I can get my teacher's attention is by being out of my seat."

We have also taught RET to teachers as a part of their teacher training program at the Department of Education, the University of Melbourne. We generally present an initial introduction to RET in 10 to 12 sessions of one and one-half to two hours which we organize along the following lines.

Session 1.   Rational-Emotive Therapy and Rational-Emotive Education
Session 2.   The ABCs of Emotion
Session 3.   Rational Self-Analysis
Session 4.   The Beliefs of Teachers I
Session 5.   The Beliefs of Teachers II
Session 6.   Overcoming Anxiety
Session 7.   Overcoming Depression
Session 8.   Overcoming Anger
Session 9.   The ABCs of Childhood Emotion and Behavior
Session 10.   The Beliefs of Children (and Adolescents)
Session 11.   Understanding Childhood Problems I
Session 12.   Understanding Childhood Problems II

For examples of course content and experiential activities, we refer readers to a recent chapter entitled, "Helping Teachers Cope With Stress: A Rational-Emotive Approach" (Bernard, Joyce, and Rosewarne, 1983).

The approach we adopt is to equate teacher stress with teacher emotional arousal. Unhealthy emotional (stress) reactions in teachers lead to behavioral patterns which interfere with the achievement of a teacher's short-term and long-term goals. In the discussion which follows, we present an overview of teacher stress, a discussion of the irrational beliefs of teachers which both interfere with teaching effectiveness and create undesirable levels of stress, and present disputational counters to these beliefs.

Teacher Stress

Stress is a very broad construct which can be viewed from a RET perspective in terms of three dimensions of human experience: cognition, emotion, and behavior. In terms of cognition, *stress can be seen as a function of an individual's interpretation of a situation as demanding or threatening, of the individual's expectation of being able to cope with the perceived demand or threat, and of the individual's appraisal of both the initial perception of a demand or threat as well as of the personal and interpersonal consequences of the demand or threat.* The intensity of a stress reaction can be explained in terms of the ratio between the magnitude of perceived demand or threat to perceived coping resources as well as in the strength of the individual's belief that failure to cope is intolerable and unacceptable. Self-defeating and emotion arousing appraisals derive from an individual's faulty belief system in general and specific irrational beliefs in particular. The individual's "philosophy of life" and the extent to which the individual rigidly and unconditionally imposes absolutistic demands (shoulds, oughts, musts) can be seen to be at the root of stress.

The interpretation of a situation as demanding may be based on *external circumstances* which can objectively be seen to require the individual to perform, act, and adapt in a certain way (e.g., work "demands"). Alternatively, "demands" may have a largely internal origin stemming from the individual's own self-perceived personal needs, standards, and expectations which translate into demands which the individual makes of him or herself, others, or the world. Perceived "threats" can be either physical or psychosocial. While we accept that certain stresses which involve physical deprivations and pain may directly lead to stress reactions, we believe that most psychosocial stress derives from the manner in which the individual interprets and appraises a situation.

There are two types of stress reactions which RET recognizes. First, there are reactions which arise from specific antecedent events. Second,. there is stress which is occasioned by nonspecific and general demands for high levels of work related and personal performance which severely "tax one's system."

Let us consider the stress reaction of anger as expressed in a teacher, Mr. Russell. Mr. Russell frequently gets extremely angry when students do not comply with his instructions. His anger is unhealthy because he tends to blow his wind into his students' sails by arguing and yelling. He has a reputation with the principal of not being able to control his class. Several complaints have been raised by parents, specifically, the number of times their children get sent out of the room. Mr. Russell's health can be described as "fragile." He experiences frequent tension headaches and has been taking more and more time off from school. The origins of his stress can be observed in the way he thought about Chris who continued to talk to his neighbors in class, even after Mr. Russell asked him not to do so. Mr. Russell interpreted Chris' noncompliance as follows: "Chris is deliberately disobeying me again. He's upsetting me as well as the rest of the class. This is unfair. If I don't shut him up, the rest of the class will think I'm weak. He's got no right to behave that way. I'll show him and everyone else who's boss." The external threat in this situation was having to confront Chris while the demand was to establish classroom control. Mr. Russell's appraisal of his interpretation was "Chris should behave properly and fairly at all times, and when he doesn't, I can't stand him and find him intolerable." This appraisal escalated the irritation he experienced as a consequence of his interpretation into extreme anger. Underlying his appraisal was an overall belief that his self-worth as a person can be defined by his teaching performance, that students who misbehave deserve to be blamed and condemned, that students control his emotions, and, most probably, that life should be pleasant and without frustration.

We do not mean to imply that all stress is unhealthy. We believe stress may motivate, arouse, and fuel the intellectual machinery. For tasks that demand extreme effort and persistence, there appears to be, as Clark Hull has hypothesized, a linear relationship between stress and performance. On the other hand, for interpersonal tasks which require spontaneous problem solving, interpersonal sensitivity, and flexibility (i.e., maintaining classroom discipline), we endorse the old Yerkes–Dobson inverted-U hypothesis which associates too little or too much arousal with poor performance, while optimal performance is associated with moderate levels of stress.

In our discussions with teachers in workshop settings and in direct consultation situations, we have identified a variety of situations which occasion teacher stress. In our teacher education programs, we emphasize the three major emotional stress reactions of anxiety, anger, and depression (self-downing) which generally arise from certain situations and not others. We list in Tables 9.2, 9.3 and 9.4 these different situations involving either teacher–student or teacher–staff interactions along with typical stress reactions reported by teachers. It had better be emphasized that whereas these situations are likely to occasion the specific emotion indicated, we find individual variation both in terms of which stresses a teacher is likely to react to as well as differences in emotional and behavioral reactions.

TABLE 9.2.   Situations at School Which Occasion Self-Downing

Teacher–Student Interactions

Student Stressors

Being compared by students to more successful students, a "sea of blank faces," students not responding to discipline, lack of enthusiasm, not being efficient in individualizing instruction, personal comments about teacher (e.g., "This is boring"), students not showing up to an elective.

Teacher Stress Reactions

Absenteeism, moodiness, lack of enthusiasm, lack of lesson planning, withdrawal of emotional support, not caring, "knocking" students or school, being late, letting class out early, withdrawal from staff, public crying.

Teacher–Staff Interactions

Staff Stressors

Public criticism thought by teacher to be correct, exclusion from social groups after school, being ignored, poor exam results of students made public, not being promoted, someone else selected to go on a conference, another program or teacher receiving greater support.

Teacher Stress Reactions

Withdrawal from contact, transfer, quitting, lack of enthusiasm, not caring about school activities, apathy and listlessness, taking days off.

TABLE 9.3. Situations at School Which Occasion Anger

Teacher−Student Interactions

Student Stressors

Not doing homework, disobeying teacher instructions, tattling, bullying, talking back, inappropriate talking in class, throwing objects, swearing, showing disrespect to each other, excessive noise, day dreaming, not understanding, lying, lack of trust of teacher.

Teacher Stress Reactions

Yelling, sarcasm, criticism, inconsistency, humiliation, unfair punishment, excessive and unfair homework, picking on students, putting students on "D" list, walking out, physical contact, throwing student out, calling up parents, talking negatively of student to others.

Teacher−Staff Interactions

Staff Stressors

Disruptions outside of class, not being treated professionally by other teachers, differences in the manner in which teachers relate to and teach students, equipment not being returned, students dribbling into class, unfair timetabling, authoritarian decision making, preferences in teaching load, public disagreement in disciplining a student, unfair share of duty, having "worst" students, slackness of administration in ordering material, special arrangements frustrated, cliquishness, lack of personal and professional cooperation, unfair teacher dismissals.

Teacher Stress Reactions

Yell at students, keep back after class, direct verbal aggression, back stabbing, poor morale, noncommunicative, not volunteering, withdrawal of support, plan another conflicting activity, turning others against teacher.

TABLE 9.4. Situations at School Which Occasion Anxiety

Teacher−Student Interactions

Student Stressors

Teacher anticipating: physical threat, walking into class unprepared, students not achieving objectives, disruptive classroom behavior, not being liked by students, students being angry and "turned off," students reactions to being given poor grades, whether they will be asked a question they cannot answer.

Teacher Stress Reactions

Procrastination, lack of concentration, failing to discipline, overpreparing, overcontrol of student behavior, being weak, not preparing, intolerant when students do not try.

Teacher−Staff Interactions

Staff Stressors

Teacher anticipating: poor exam results of students and others finding out, conflict situations and disagreement with staff, being judged negatively by staff, criticism by principal or other member of staff.

Teacher Stress

Apathy, lack of assertion, not sticking up for "rights," not speaking up, being overly polite, submissive, not doing what teacher really wants to do.

The Irrational Beliefs of Teachers

As in all stress, we find that teachers who experience most stress endorse a variety of irrational beliefs which relate to their role as teachers and their relationship to students, and which derive mostly from Ellis' original discussions of irrational beliefs. We have not the space to list the total number of irrational beliefs that underlie teachers' unhealthy emotional and behavioral responses to stressful situations. In Table 9.5 we present 45 of the major irrational beliefs which compose a *teacher idea inventory* we are developing for use in our work with groups of teachers.

These teachers' beliefs are derivations of general beliefs which were discussed in Chapters 2 and 3 and which have particular relevance for teachers. In teacher education, inservice and individual consultation settings, it is necessary to focus on and deal with teachers' irrational beliefs and thoughts about the problem situation, instead of providing them with direct solutions to the problem situation itself. Examples of effective disputational approaches for some of these irrational beliefs include the following:

1. Those irrational beliefs which indicate that teachers are worried about having constant approval from significant others such as other teachers or students could be challenged by such statements as:
    (a) The teacher has no way of knowing what everyone will think of him or her.
    (b) Excessive "approval seeking" leads to excessive worry and interferes with one's interpersonal effectiveness.
    (c) It is very likely that most other people aren't thinking bad things about him or her at all.
    (d) If someone does not approve of you, or has negative thoughts, there is no reason to get upset as it is impossible to please everyone all the time.
    (e) The teacher is irrationally equating his or her self-worth with someone's opinion of the teacher.
    (Adapted from Forman & Forman, 1978)
2. Those irrational beliefs which imply a "should" statement such as "To be an effective teacher I must have total control of my class at all times," "Children must behave appropriately at all times," and "It's awful when things do not go the way I demand they should," could be challenged by statements such as:
    (a) The statement that something should not be, when it obviously is, is an irrational thought.
    (b) Demanding that something should not exist when it obviously does exist, only causes one to be angry, upset, unhappy, depressed, etc.

TABLE 9.5. The Teacher Idea Inventory

	No Opinion	Strongly Disagree	Disagree	Agree	Strongly Agree
1. It is very important that other teachers approve of me.	0	1	2	3	4
2. I strive very hard to be a perfect teacher.	0	1	2	3	4
3. Students should behave properly at all times.	0	1	2	3	4
4. I get *extremely* upset when I see schools being unfair.	0	1	2	3	4
5. I find it very difficult to motivate myself to do unpleasant tasks at school.	0	1	2	3	4
6. I generally need someone's advice at school to help me overcome problems with students.	0	1	2	3	4
7. You can really judge the worth of students by their behavior.	0	1	2	3	4
8. Teachers are extremely limited in what they can achieve with a student who has been unsuccessful at school in the past.	0	1	2	3	4
9. Students can make me upset.	0	1	2	3	4
10. I can become very upset when I see a student having a personal problem.	0	1	2	3	4
11. I seem to worry a great deal about things that happen at school.	0	1	2	3	4
12. I work hard to find the perfect solution to problems I have at school.	0	1	2	3	4
13. I put off making decisions at school.	0	1	2	3	4
14. As a teacher I must have the power to be able to make my class do what I want.	0	1	2	3	4
15. Parents are frequently to blame for the problems of their children.	0	1	2	3	4
16. It is most important to me that students approve of me.	0	1	2	3	4
17. For me to feel worthwhile, I should know how to solve each problem I encounter with a student.	0	1	2	3	4
18. It is easier to avoid problems or difficulties which may arise during the course of the day than it is to confront them.	0	1	2	3	4
19. Teachers who are unfair to students are "unfit" and ought to be severely disciplined.	0	1	2	3	4
20. I feel quite uncomfortable when students are being unpleasant.	0	1	2	3	4
21. I often feel "unable" to solve problems and hassles at school on my own.	0	1	2	3	4
22. Deep down I believe that students who achieve poorly are somehow of less value than high achievers.	0	1	2	3	4

(Continued)

TABLE 9.5. *(Continued)*

	No Opinion	Strongly Disagree	Disagree	Agree	Strongly Agree
23. It is almost impossible for teachers to change the way they handle a problem.	0	1	2	3	4
24. I have little ability to control my feelings when something at school upsets me.	0	1	2	3	4
25. Parents should know how to raise their children better.	0	1	2	3	4
26. I worry a lot about how much others approve of me.	0	1	2	3	4
27. I frequently feel down when I don't handle a situation at school as well as I would like.	0	1	2	3	4
28. I get quite upset when other teachers do not act professionally.	0	1	2	3	4
29. Students who do wrong are blameworthy and deserve whatever they get.	0	1	2	3	4
30. Students should not be frustrated.	0	1	2	3	4
31. Before reaching a final decision at school about how to deal with a problem I generally consult someone else.	0	1	2	3	4
32. The worth of teachers can often be determined by their effectiveness with students.	0	1	2	3	4
33. Students' "misbehavior" is frequently caused by bad things which have happened in the past and which can never really be overcome.	0	1	2	3	4
34. I seem to worry a great deal about the difficulties I see students experiencing.	0	1	2	3	4
35. I get extremely upset with parents who should be taking more responsibility in the raising of their child.	0	1	2	3	4
36. I concern myself a great deal about how successful I'll be in the future.	0	1	2	3	4
37. It is possible to find perfect solutions to the problems of students.	0	1	2	3	4
38. When I have a conflict with a student, I tend to avoid discussing it in the hope that it will go away.	0	1	2	3	4
39. It is most important for me to have control of my students at all times.	0	1	2	3	4
40. I feel that by worrying about the future it will somehow do some good.	0	1	2	3	4
41. Hard work will eventually lead to the right answer.	0	1	2	3	4
42. I think to myself "how awful" it is when students are rude.	0	1	2	3	4
43. I should have the respect of my students at all times.	0	1	2	3	4
44. I can't tolerate it when I see a student being treated unfairly.	0	1	2	3	4
45. Other teachers can upset me.	0	1	2	3	4

(c) Being overly upset, angry or depressed does not help one to solve problems, and stops one from functioning effectively.

(d) If one does not like things the way they are, it is in one's best interest to calmly pursue one's goal of changing things or to accept things that cannot be changed.

(e) Exaggeration is self-defeating. It may be unfortunate or inconvenient if things are not the way one wants them to be, but it is only a catastrophe if one believes it to be so.

(f) When one turns my anger or frustrations into a catastrophe, one is less likely to focus on appropriate problem solving strategies because one spends too much time and energy awfulizing and feeling sorry for oneself or blaming others.

(g) If one wants students to change their behavior, it is best to arrange conditions so that they will learn to behave differently rather than just demanding that they behave differently.

(Adapted from Forman & Forman, 1978)

Forman & Forman (1978) suggest the following as examples of questions which teachers can ask to prevent themselves from getting angry and to encourage rational problem solving.

"Why *should* these kids behave this way?"

"Am I just sitting here demanding that things change without doing anything to change them?"

"What, specifically, do I want these kids to do?"

"Is it reasonable to try to get kids of this age to behave in this manner?"

"What are the possible reasons for their not behaving this way?"

"What will I do in order to teach them this new behavior?" [p. 405]

3. The irrational belief that school ought to be fair can be challenged by statements such as:

(a) Schools will be unfair from time to time and to insist that they shouldn't is unrealistic.

(b) Demanding that schools are fair leads one to become angry and at times give up.

(c) It is more healthy to accept that schools will be unfair and work to change those aspects which are unfair.

(d) A rational view would be "I would prefer school to be a fair place, but if it isn't it's not the end of the world."

4. Challenging the irrational belief that students should not be frustrated involves recognizing that:

(a) Frustration is a natural part of life and it is the responsibility of schools to teach students how to cope with it.

(b) Students who never fail may be ill prepared to cope with it when they leave school.

5. The irrational belief that people (students, teachers) who misbehave, do wrong, act unfairly, are blameworthy and deserve severe punishment can be disputed by discussing that:

(a) It is often the case that people misbehave out of ignorance. It would be better to educate at these times rather than punish.

(b) Severe punishment frequently does not teach a lesson and, oftentimes, only exacerbates the problem.

(c) To blame someone for their misdeeds presumes that the person had total control of themselves and the situation and were operating premeditatively. Such is not always the case.

(d) Assigning blame frequently leads to putting the whole person down. This irrational overgeneralization may create in students especially feelings of inferiority and worthlessness.

6. Teachers who avoid tasks and interpersonal situations at school which they find are unpleasant demonstrate "low frustration tolerance" and endorse the belief that "life should be entirely without discomfort and frustration at all times." The following points can be made:

(a) Life wasn't meant to be easy.

(b) By avoiding unpleasantness, teachers frequently diminish both their teaching effectiveness and the potential pleasures of overcoming hardships.

(c) "I-can't-stand-it-itis" which frequently underlies LFT can be disputed by pointing out that objectively teachers can stand just about anything.

(d) "Discomfort anxiety" comes from making hassles into horrors and from making mountains out of molehills.

7. Those teacher beliefs which involve having to rely on another to solve personal and interpersonal problems at school can be challenged by statements such as:

(a) While it appears sensible to consult an authority *at certain times*, total reliance on another prevents one from ever learning to function independently.

(b) "Needing" someone else's help is irrational because one can still make a decision if one had to.

(c) Excessively relying on others may lead others to view a teacher as "dependent" and may work against professional advancement.

8. Beliefs which equate a person's self-worth with teaching or academic performance are irrational and can be challenged by reminding teachers that:

(a) Students and teachers are complex. To judge them on a limited aspect of their behavior is an overgeneralization.

    (b)   Students who perform poorly in school may later on be extremely successful in life.

    (c)   Rating the worth of a teacher on the basis of teaching behavior may demean that teacher in the eyes of others and may lead to teaching ineffectiveness.

9.   Teachers who believe that the past of a student (or themselves) makes change impossible can be shown that:

    (a)   Students with a history of academic and/or behavior problems may bloom in the right school environment.

    (b)   Students can be taught to correct their ways.

    (c)   Motivation changes over time.

    (d)   Teachers can learn to employ alternative and more effective ways of dealing with problematic situations.

10   The irrational belief that the feelings of teachers are caused by other teachers, students, or the problem situation can be challenged by statements such as:

    (a)   Feelings are caused by thoughts. The problem itself does not make teachers upset.

    (b)   Teachers can control their emotional upset by changing their thoughts.

    (c)   Believing that others control one's feelings leads one to be more upset than when one takes emotional responsibility.

11.   Teachers who believe that it is "unbearable" for students to be treated unfairly or have problems can be shown that:

    (a)   Getting *too* involved and upset about a student often interferes with a teacher helping constructively.

    (b)   Teachers who become "too upset" about a student's problems frequently lose sight of their own goals.

    (c)   "Unfairness" and "unhappiness" are facts of life which had better, when necessary, be accepted.

12.   Challenging the belief that teachers must be in total control of their class at all times involves making the following points:

    (a)   One will never have total control and to insist will only be counter-productive.

    (b)   Total control and obedience is not *necessarily* a good pedagogic principle.

    (c)   Students are different; some will like and respect a teacher while others will not. To insist (rather than prefer) is irrational and self-defeating.

13.   The irrational belief that "I must find the perfect solution to all problems" can be challenged by statements such as:

    (a)   There is generally no perfect solution.

     (b)   It is best to work hard to find a "reasonable compromise."

     (c)   Striving to find a perfect solution can drive one crazy.

14.   Teachers who blame parents for the problems of their children can be shown that:

     (a)   "Blaming" is frequently a "cop out" which absolves one from doing anything about the problem.

     (b)   Parents frequently act out of ignorance in raising their children. Mistakes will happen. To demand otherwise and condemn does little to improve the situation and frequently turns the teacher against the parent.

     (c)   It is more helpful to the student to try to understand why the student is having a problem rather than to automatically assume the parents are at fault.

15.   Those irrational beliefs which imply that "I must be a perfect teacher and never make mistakes," or "I should know how to handle every problem with every child" can be challenged by statements such as:

     (a)   No one can be a perfect teacher.

     (b)   Everyone makes mistakes.

     (c)   Even if one makes a mistake, one will not be a failure.

     (d)   One has probably solved many problems successfully in the future—every teacher has done something right.

16.   The irrational belief that it is easier to avoid problems or difficulties which arise during the course of a teaching day than to confront them can be challenged by such statements as:

     (a)   It is usually harder to continue with the problem than to do anything about it.

     (b)   Wishing hard or complaining about the problem will not make it disappear.

     (c)   Things are not likely to change merely because one wants them to change.

     (d)   Usually some further action is required for things to change.

We are hopeful that in the near future that RET theorists and practitioners will give more attention to how principles and practices of RET can be more fully utilized with teachers. In Appendix 1, which follows, we present materials which RET practitioners can employ in introducing REE to teachers. Moreover, this material can be utilized in rational-emotive group counseling with school-age children.

APPENDIX 1

Rational Emotive Education and Rational Emotive Group Counseling Programs in Action

Preventative–Educational Programs

Group Counseling Intervention Programs

REE and REGC

REE and REGC in Action

Sessions for Younger Children (5–7 years)

Sessions for Children (8–12 years)

Sessions for Youth (13–17 years)

RET can be employed with groups of school-age children to both prevent psychological problems from occurring as well as to treat emotional and behavioral problems. As we indicate in this appendix, the RET programs that have been developed for both affective education and group counseling are very similar; that is, there is a core set of materials which can be used both preventatively and to resolve specific problems. These programs are based on the basic RET principles and practice outlined in earlier chapters. As the reader would expect, the breadth and depth of coverage of basic RET covered in these programs depend upon the cognitive capacity of the young person. We have elected to organize the materials into three levels: young children (aged 5–7), children (aged 8–12), and adolescents (aged 13+).

This appendix briefly reviews different kinds of group programs for children and youth. Preventative mental health programs will be briefly reviewed, and the nature of rational-emotive education will be elaborated. A discussion of group counseling intervention programs will provide the context for a consideration of rational-emotive group counseling. Similarities and differences between rational-emotive education and rational-emotive group counseling will be highlighted followed by a discussion of issues such as ways to set up groups, deciding who should participate, desirable characteristics of the group leader, and insights concerning ways to facilitate progress in the group. The final section of this appendix will present the actual materials and activities which can be used with children at various age levels.

PREVENTATIVE–EDUCATIONAL PROGRAMS

Rational-emotive education has partially emerged from and been influenced by the affective education movement. It also has been influenced by the use of RET with individuals and groups of youngsters who have been referred for problems of adjustment. (The focus and aims of school-based affective education programs have already been reviewed in Chapter 1.)

A major contribution within the field of affective education has been Dinkmeyer's theory of *developmental counseling* which focuses on the evolving child and seeks ways to enhance psychological growth through working on normal developmental problems. Making new friends, getting along with one's family, and coping with schoolwork are typical concerns. Decision making, problem solving and self-examination are employed in developmental counseling to achieve its goals. The child is perceived as progressing through nonspecific life stages, and no assumption is made about a need for adjustment or the presence of psychopathology. Developing understanding of self and others (DUSO) (Dinkmeyer, 1970) is one program exemplifying the ideas of developmental counseling and typifies its *preventative* and *educational* goals. Specific therapeutic aims are not part of developmental counseling.

Following the traditions and concerns of affective education, and particularly developmental counseling, RET has been applied with similar preventative and educational aims in the form of rational-emotive education (REE). We shall turn our attention to REE in the next section.

Before that a brief but important digression on terminology is necessary. The term *counseling* is used broadly and, at times, confusingly in the literature to refer to both therapeutic and preventative educational programs. It is our intention to make some distinctions between these interventions and we wish to restrict the term counseling to those programs which have *specifically therapeutic aims* (e.g., to alleviate depression or reduce anxiety). Counseling will not be used to refer to the preventative–educational programs of REE. Therapeutic applications of RET are called rational-emotive group counseling (REGC) and will be treated later in the introduction.

Rational-Emotive Education (REE)

The traditional concerns of workers in the field of affective education have been the teaching of problem solving skills to improve interpersonal relationships, increasing in self awareness and understanding, and enabling the child to cope more effectively with normal developmental tasks (e.g., by improved goal setting and decision making). REE, the application of RET in the sphere of emotional education, has grown out of these traditions and been developed in school contexts. As we have indicated, the Living School which was begun in 1969 by Albert Ellis in association with the Institute for Rational Living (now the Institute for Rational-Emotive Therapy), was the scene of the earliest REE programs. The work of Knaus (1974) and Gerald and Eyman (1981) emerged from pioneer programs there. Vernon (1980) has also published REE activities which she piloted at Malcolm Price Laboratory School at the University of Northern Iowa. The ideas contained in these programs have been implemented in schools in widespread areas of the United States. Since 1977, we have introduced REE programs into a number of primary and secondary schools in Melbourne, Australia.

The goal of REE is primarily to teach the basic principles of rational-emotive thinking: children are taught that our thoughts cause us to feel the way we do, and that changing those thoughts will change how we feel. REE also places stress on helping children to give up irrational demandingness, to avoid tyrannical "shoulds," "musts" and "oughts," and to accept themselves as imperfect human beings who sometimes succeed, sometimes fail and sometimes do stupid things. REE emphasizes *thinking skills* whereby children learn to evaluate their own thinking according to rational criteria, and they are therefore equipped to recognize their own irrational thoughts and beliefs when difficulties arise in the future. These objectives for children and youth in REE programs need modification, we believe, for young children (aged 5−7 years) whose cognitive capacities do not permit rational analysis or complex conceptual understanding. For these youngsters we modify our goal and emphasize *the teaching of rational self-statements*. A language is developed for awareness of feelings and expression of emotion; self-statements are taught as substitutes for the negative self-defeating self-talk in which many children engage.

While some of the children taking part in REE groups may have serious problems, many are simply grappling with normal developmental stresses which may be reflected in temporary maladaptive reactions or may be experienced as increased inner conflict and tension. For these children, extensive personality change is not required, but self-acceptance and understanding are increased by the interpersonal processes taking place in the group.

GROUP COUNSELING INTERVENTION PROGRAMS

There are many programs and methods which have been developed which have been employed with groups of children. These programs vary widely on such dimensions as insight−action, rational−affective, leader-centered, member-centered, and process−outcome. We now review these programs and indicate how their scope and objectives correspond with those of rational-emotive group counseling.

Group counseling methods have been applied to children at many age levels and with varying aims. For example, some programs have emphasized improvement in interpersonal relationships in middle and high school students (Cross, Myrich, & Wilkinson, 1977; Hutchins & Cole, 1977). Others have focused upon assertiveness training where students learn the difference between nonassertive, assertive and aggressive behavior and acquire strategies for choosing appropriate behavior (Rashbaum-Selig, 1976). Programs such as the ALPHA program (Sparks, 1978) and the Baldwin Structured Activity Model (Baldwin, 1976) aim to facilitate communication skills, self-understanding and the reduction of self-defeating behavior. Group counseling with younger children is frequently oriented to specific maladaptive behaviors such as fears, anxiety, aggression, and disruptive classroom behavior (Rhodes, 1973; Tidiwell & Bachus, 1977; Culbertson, 1974). Groups primarily concerned with the transmitting of information are designated *guidance* rather than *counseling* groups. They would include occupational guidance groups, and educational groups such as those providing orienting information to assist in transition phases, for example, from elementary to high school.

The emphasis in *group counseling as intervention* is on providing remediation for children who are manifesting specific problems of adjustment. Such interventions are closely tied to traditional psychotherapies and have specifiable therapeutic goals. To illuminate similarities and differences among the various counseling theories or approaches, Frey (1972) has proposed a two-dimensional conceptual model, based on the dimensions rational−affective and insight−action (see Figure A.1).

Approaches which emphasize insight focus strongly on the internal frame of reference of individuals, whereas the action oriented approaches aim primarily at overt behavior change. Rational counseling stresses cognitive reasoning processes in contrast to affective counseling in which the expression and understanding of feelings, inner motivations, and needs are primary. RET rates closer to the "rational" and "action" poles of Frey's model, with less

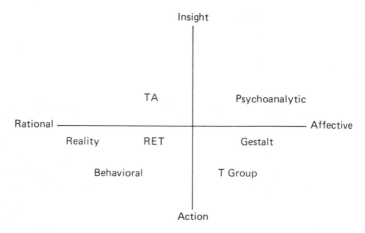

Figure A.1. Conceptual Model of the Relationships among Counseling Approaches (from Frey, 1972).

stress than some therapies on insight and affective processes. On the role of emotional ventilation in rational groups, Ellis (1962, p. 308) writes: "The final aim, as in all rational-emotive therapy, is to *change* the negative thoughts and feelings of the participants, rather than merely to offer them 'healthy' and gratifying expression."

An additional way of considering the differences among the various counseling approaches is to organize them according to types of outcome and styles of operation (see Figure A.2).

This model highlights RET as strongly *leader-centered* and as midway between aiming at *specific objectives* and focusing on the processes of group dynamics. The RET group leader is directive and brings a structured approach to problems raised. One of the primary aims of RET, the teaching of the ABCs of rational-emotive thinking, is achieved by didactic methods and group members learn to mould their contributions to rational concepts and structures. RET provides both a language for analyzing a problem as well as a set of *disputational skills* for altering the course of events (i.e. breaking the sequence of internal events which trouble the individual in the form of disturbing emotions such as depression, anxiety or guilt).

The characterization of how RET operates in a group counseling context can be summarized as follows:

1. It is strongly leader-directed.
2. It focuses on cognitive reasoning processes.
3. It is concerned with the individual's emotions—how they are experienced and expressed.
4. It looks for specific changes in thinking and behavior.

While Frey and Hansen were considering RET in the context of adult group therapy, this analysis is relevant to applications with groups of children and

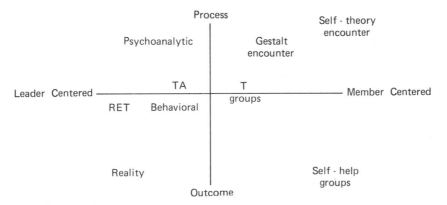

Figure A.2. Counseling Approaches according to Style of Operation and Type of Outcome (from Hansen, Warner, & Smith, 1980).

youth for REGC with children is largely a direct adaptation of RET with adult groups. For detailed accounts of RET groups with adults, the reader is referred to Wessler and Wessler (1980), Goodman and Maultsby (1978), and Hauck (1980).

Rational-Emotive Group Counseling (REGC)

REGC, like REE, employs an educational model to achieve its goals. We now turn our attention to elucidation of these goals and the methods of REGC. The *teaching of basic ideas*, which is done more directly than in many counseling methods, and the *modeling of rational attitudes* by the group leader are major strategies in REGC. Albert Ellis has described the *goals* of REGC with young clients in this way:

> They are continually taught, in the course of group counseling, that they can minimize their disturbances and achieve their maximum potential for growth and development by employing empirically based, rather than magical, hypotheses about themselves and the world, by seeing that nothing is aw(e)ful, sacred or all-important; by becoming thoroughly tolerant of all humans including themselves as well as others, and never damning or denigrating *people* for their reprehensible or ineffectual *acts*; by learning how to stop "proving" themselves with silly ego games, and instead start enjoying themselves; by becoming self-directing, not overly conforming individuals who still can be kind, considerate and loving and rationally (and self-interestedly) aware of and somewhat devoted to social interests. These are the specific goals of the rational-emotive group counseling process. [Ellis, 1973c, p. 83]

In adapting REGC and REE for younger age groups, we have modified these goals, so that the emphasis for younger children is on the learning of rational self-statements. Whereas the aim for older children is learning to challenge their irrational beliefs, the cognitive capacities of most seven year olds and younger preclude such complex reasoning. Both the challenging and disputing skills, and the judgment entailed in knowing when to employ these skills, are probably beyond the cognitive-developmental level of the five, six and seven year olds.

Our two guiding principles in designing and selecting activities for use with young clients have been the promotion of *internalization* and *consolidation* of rational thinking, to ensure that the children make the concepts their own, by integrating them with their own ideas and experiences, and by repeatedly applying these concepts in a variety of situations so that they will become part of a readily available repertoire of skills or habits for coping with situations and events which occasion disturbance. Homework activities are used frequently, especially with older children to help shape the desired thinking and behavior.

REGC has sometimes been used with special populations. For example, Knaus and McKeever (1977) have applied it with learning disabled children, and have demonstrated the useful strategy of "brainstorming" to find appropriate goals for their particular groups of children. This strategy could be fruitfully employed by practitioners with other special populations such as low achievers, children with low self-esteem, or aggressive children.

Rational-emotive group counseling programs in various contexts may take slightly different forms. One program we have run, for boys with low self-esteem and low reading achievement, was designed around a set of behavioral objectives which are now listed for each of the thirteen sessions (Bernard, 1979b).

  I. *Lesson One*
     A. *Objectives*
        1. Student will state the words that describe common feelings.
        2. Students will identify situations that occasion different feelings in themselves.
        3. Students will state the rule that feelings can vary in intensity from strong to weak.
        4. Students will demonstrate the rule by classifying their feelings on a continuum of intensity using the feeling thermometer.

        Pleasant feelings: happiness, joy, love, enthusiasm, excitement, curiosity, relaxation, confidence.

        Unpleasant feelings: anger, hate, sadness, depression, fear, guilt, worthlessness, loneliness, frustration, disappointment, anxiety, annoyance.
     B. *New Ideas*
        1. Different words describe different feelings.
        2. Feelings can vary in intensity from strong to weak.
 II. *Lesson Two*
     A. *Objectives*
        1. Students will state that thoughts cause feelings.
        2. Students will state that pleasant thoughts cause pleasant feelings and that unpleasant thoughts cause unpleasant feelings.
        3. Students will demonstrate by providing examples how their own pleasant thoughts cause them to feel pleasant and that their own unpleasant thoughts cause unpleasant feelings.
     B. *New Ideas*
        1. Thoughts cause feelings.
        2. Pleasant thoughts cause pleasant feelings. Unpleasant thoughts cause unpleasant feelings.
III. *Lesson Three*
     A. *Objectives*
        1. Student will identify which of his own thoughts lead to pleasant and unpleasant feelings.
        2. Student will apply the happening–thought–feeling–reaction diagram in analyzing himself.
        3. Students will state in own words that it is often difficult to

identify the thought that precedes a feeling because the thought may occur very quickly. The thought may be one word or a sentence fragment. Many times you do not hear yourself thinking the thought. Many times you may not realize that you have thought the thought.

    4.   Student will state that by changing your thoughts you change your feelings.

  B. *New Ideas*

    1.   Your feelings and behavior can be looked at in this way: HAPPENING + THOUGHT = FEELING—BEHAVIOR

       a.   Something happens to you.

       b.   You think about what happened.

       c.   The thought you have leads to a feeling.

       d.   Your feeling will affect how you behave.

    2.   By changing your thoughts you can change your feelings.

IV. *Lesson Four.*

  A. *Objectives*

    1.   Student will state in his own words the definition of rational thought, irrational thought, and challenge.

    2.   Student will state in his own words that to know whether a thought is rational or irrational, he must ask himself the question: "Is there enough evidence for me to say the thought is true?" If there is evidence, the thought is rational. If there is not enough evidence, the thought is irrational.

    3.   Student will identify examples and nonexamples of rational and irrational thoughts.

  B. *New Ideas*

    1.   Definition of new words:

       a.   Challenge: To question yourself to see if your thought is rational or irrational.

       b.   Rational thought: A sensible and logical idea that seems to be true.

       c.   Irrational thought: An unreasonable or absurd idea that is false.

       d.   How to find out if a thought is rational or irrational.

          Ask yourself "Is there enough evidence for me to say the thought is true?"   Yes or no.

          If YES, the thought is rational.

          If NO, the thought is irrational.

V. *Lesson Five*

  A. *Objectives*

    1.   Student will state in his own words that when he thinks irrational thoughts he feels more unhappy, worthless, angry and frustrated than if he thinks rational thoughts.

    2.   Student will quantify the frequency of their rational and irrational thoughts.

B. *New Ideas*
1. Thinking irrational thoughts makes you feel worse (unhappy, worthless, angry, and frustrated) than thinking rational thoughts.

VI. *Lesson Six*
  A. *Objectives*
1. Student will demonstrate rule "thinking irrational thoughts makes you feel more upset than thinking rational thoughts" by analyzing his own behavior.
2. Student will state that when we get too upset we can do nothing to help improve the situation.
3. Student will state that we can control how upset we are by changing our irrational thoughts to rational thoughts.
4. Student will demonstrate rule for identifying rational and irrational thoughts (Is the thought sensible and true, or absurd and false?) by analyzing his own thoughts.
5. Student will demonstrate rule for challenging and changing his irrational thoughts by restating them as rational thoughts.

  B. *New Ideas*
1. When I get too upset, I can do nothing to improve the situation.
2. I can control how upset I am by changing my irrational thoughts to rational thoughts.

VII. *Lesson Seven*
  A. *Objectives*
1. Student will state that each of us is complex, not simple.
2. Student will state that he is made up of many positive and negative characteristics.
3. Student will identify some of his positive and negative characteristics.
4. Student will state that he is not all good or all bad because of some of his characteristics.
5. Student will state that when he only focuses on his negative characteristics, he feels worse about himself.
6. Student will demonstrate by challenging the irrational thought that he is not what someone calls him, that he is made up of many characteristics.
7. Student will identify positive and negative characteristics of a teacher.
8. Student will state that a teacher is not all good or all bad because of some of the teacher's characteristics.
9. Student will state that when he only focuses on the negative characteristics of a teacher, he feels worse about the teacher.

  B. *New Ideas*
1. Every person is complex, not simple.
I am complex, not simple.

2. Every person is made up of many positive and negative characteristics.
    I am made up of many positive and negative characteristics.
3. A person is not all good or bad because of some of his or her characteristics.
    I am not all good or all bad.
4. When I only focus on the negative characteristics of a person, I feel worse about the person.
    When I focus on my negative characteristics, I feel worse about myself.

VIII. *Lesson Eight*
  A. *Objectives*
      1. Student will state that focusing only on the negative qualities of people (including himself) is irrational because people (including himself) have other positive qualities.
      2. Student will state that people (including himself) are not good or bad.
      3. Student will demonstrate rule for challenging and changing his negative irrational thoughts by restating them as negative rational thoughts.
      4. Student will state that when he thinks irrational, negative thoughts about people (including himself), he gets more upset than if he thinks negative, rational thoughts.
  B. *New Ideas*
      1. Focusing *only* on another person's negative qualities is irrational because people have other positive qualities. Focusing *only* on my negative qualities is irrational because I have other positive qualities.
      2. When I think negative, irrational thoughts about someone else, I get more upset with that person than if I think negative, rational thoughts.
      3. People are not good or bad.
          I am not good or bad.
      4. When I think negative, irrational thoughts about myself, I get more upset with myself than if I think negative, rational thoughts.

IX. *Lesson Nine*
  A. *Objectives*
      1. Student will state the definition of "fact" and "opinion."
      2. Student will state that people have different opinions.
      3. Student will state that not everyone *should* have the same opinion.
      4. Student will state that someone who disagrees with him is not bad or worthless.

       5. Student will state that when he disagrees with someone else (has a difference of opinion with), it doesn't make sense to get angry, upset, or behave stubbornly. .

  B. *New Ideas*

      1. A fact is a statement that is true.

      2. An opinion is someone's idea about something. It is neither true nor false.

      3. People have different opinions.

      4. Someone who disagrees with you is not bad or worthless.

      5. People who disagree with you do not deserve to be punished.

      6. When someone disagrees with you, it does not make sense to get overly upset, angry, or behave stubbornly.

X. *Lesson Ten*

  A. *Objectives*

      1. Student will state that just because he has an opinion about something doesn't make it true.

      2. Student will state the definitions of "belief," "sound assumption," and "unsound assumption."

      3. Student will state that some of the things he believes (his beliefs) are not true (are based on unsound assumptions).

      4. Student will classify examples of his own beliefs as being based on sound and unsound assumptions.

      5. Unsound assumptions lead to mistakes.

  B. *New Ideas*

      1. A belief: A conviction that something is true.

      2. Sound assumption: A belief likely to be true.

      3. Unsound assumption: Something that you believe to be true but which in reality is not.

      4. Some of my assumptions are unsound (untrue).

      5. When they are, I make mistakes.

XI. *Lesson Eleven*

  A. *Objectives*

      1. Student will state that everyone will always make mistakes.

      2. Student will state that no one is perfect.

      3. Student will state that mistakes do not change a person's good qualities.

      4. Student will state that a person is not the same as his performance.

      5. Student will state that people are not bad because they make mistakes.

      6. Student will state that people who make mistakes do not deserve to be blamed or punished. They require help to change.

      7. Student will state reasons why people make mistakes: (a)

lack of skills, (b) carelessness or poor judgment, (c) not studying, poor student, (d) not having enough information, unsound assumption, (e) tired or ill, (f) different opinion.
    8.   Student will state that it is irrational to rate people as good or bad.
  B. *New Ideas*
    1.   No one is perfect; everyone will make mistakes.
    2.   Mistakes do not change a person's good qualities.
    3.   A person is not the same as his performance.
    4.   People who make mistakes do not deserve to be blamed and punished. They require help to change.

XII. *Lesson Twelve*
  A. *Objectives*
    1.   Student will state the definitions of "want" and "need."
    2.   Student will identify examples of his own wants and needs.
    3.   Student will state the difference between a rational and irrational need.
    4.   Student will classify examples of his own rational and irrational needs.
    5.   Student will challenge irrational needs by restating them as rational wants.
    6.   Student will state that needs lead to making demands on another person.
    7.   Demands lead to anger and upset with another person.
  B. *New Ideas*
    1.   A need is something one has to have to survive.
    2.   An irrational need is a demand for something that you don't really need to survive.
    3.   A want is a wish for something you would like.
    4.   When I demand something that I do not need, I am being silly (irrational).

XIII. *Lesson Thirteen*
  A. *Objectives*
    1.   Student will practice challenging "awfulizing" and "catastrophizing."
  B. *New Ideas*
    1.   Situations and people are not as awful as I *think* they are.
    2.   Challenging awful thoughts improves the situation, and makes you feel less upset.

Over 13 weeks the boys complete lessons designed to teach these sequenced "new ideas" and they do practical homework exercises between sessions. Our experiences in these groups have taught us to use token reinforcement to maintain attendance and appropriate listening, and to reward children at the end of series. While adolescents participate better in discussion and show greater willingness to listen to each other, pre-adolescents respond with greater interest and involvement to activities presented as games with little similarity to school-work.

REE AND REGC

Contrasting features and common ground between REE and REGC have emerged in the preceding sections and will be summarized here. While REGC is initiated in response to existing problems in young clients and therefore has therapeutic aims, REE is preventative in purpose. The implementation of the sessions in a REGC group is specifically problem oriented according to group members' needs, while REE takes a general approach, anticipating experiences common to children at the various ages. Whereas REGC belongs with the traditional psychotherapies when its goals are considered, REE is in line with the traditions of affective education and developmental counseling.

The differences highlighted, while significant, cannot overshadow the important shared aspects: *the rational concept* to be taught is the same, the use of *groups* is the same, and the methods and techniques can be the same, because they both are designed to teach children rational thinking and to provide them with problem solving skills that persist beyond training.

Group Leader Characteristics

As modeling of rational attitudes is a major part of communicating clearly the ideas of rational thinking, it is desirable that "textbookish mastery" is avoided on the part of the leader, in favor of demonstrations of her own genuine attitudes (e.g. in handling of difficulties that arise during sessions) and beliefs. Albert Rossi (1977) discusses several ingredients of appropriate attitudes with children derived from his experience in rational-emotive therapy: enthusiasm, liberal use of positive reinforcement (especially praise), and a healthy amount of physical contact. He suggests one way enthusiasm is expressed with children is through movement. "(the leader) might do well to spend some of the time sitting, standing, walking and perhaps even lying on the floor. It might be that mere movement is one way to communicate enthusiasm to children" (Rossi, 1977, p. 23).

The giving and withholding of praise is an effective tool for the leader. Generous praise given irregularly (a variable ratio schedule) is recommended and can be communicated in a large variety of ways, including verbal praise, ("Good"; "Well done"; "I like the way you . . .") and nonverbal signs, such as smiles, nods and pats. Behavior to be rewarded could include:

1. Learning the concepts and skills of RET, particularly each small step towards the final goals (e.g. remembering a new idea, putting it into his/her own words, giving examples from his/her own experience).

2. Following the rules decided upon for the running of the group, (e.g. coming on time, doing the homework exercises).
3. Listening to other children.
4. Helping other children understand rational concepts.

Free and honest discussion by the children will be encouraged where the leader creates a *climate of acceptance*. This can be achieved by a nonjudgmental attitude by the leader, which would show itself, for example, in hearing a child out without interrupting, not criticizing the child, gently encouraging the child to think about new ideas he/she is being presented with, rather than imposing them in a heavy handed way.

From our own experience, we can make the following additional suggestions. Relate the new rational-emotive skills and knowledge learned by the youngsters to their "self-concept" ("You learned that well;" "You are making advances in this new kind of work"; "You are working hard and learning well"). Review the progress with them. They may not be necessarily aware of steps they have taken and need to be reminded of what has been achieved. Listen carefully to what children say as there are often indications as to what they are saying to themselves. Negative self-talk is manifested in statements such as, "I'm no good at . . ."; "Don't expect me to be able to . . ."; "I can never. . . ." A skillful RET practitioner will notice these and may be able to remind the youngsters of these in a later session when they are having difficulty relating RET ideas to their own experience. If children are especially anxious about making connections with their own experience, present the problems as though experienced by another child. Most children require "emotional distance" before they can discuss personal problems. Let youngsters know if you have a plan for your session. Younger children especially find security in a predictable routine. Where a session may feel long, if they know there are different parts to the session and can identify which step they are on, they can more readily anticipate the end. This can prevent negative questions such as "How long does this go on for?" Be alert to the "body language" of the youngsters. Negative feelings or withdrawal may be evident in the position and movement of their bodies before any verbal clues are evident. "Reading" the child's body language is another way of "listening" to the child and provides some useful clues to times when special encouragement or ventilation of feelings is needed. Some children with low self-esteem fail to attribute to themselves any responsibility for their success experiences. Rather, they regard external factors as totally causing events. It is helpful for these children to learn a new attitude, namely, that they can influence what happens to them *by their own efforts*. One way to engender this attitude is to make that attribution for them with comments like "You succeeded because you really tried" or "Good effort on your part—you did it!" Without this attitude, children will have difficulty in challenging their irrational thoughts. A moment's reflection will show that this attitude is implicit in RET (i.e., with effort and practice the child can learn to do something about his/her emotional upsets and behavioral problems).

Selecting Your Group: Assessment Methods and Criteria

Selection for your groups may be made by *informal* or *formal* means. Requests from teachers, parents, or the youngster constitute the main ways in which the young client's problems will come to the attention of the counselor. The kinds of childhood problems described by Peterson (1961) are all likely to be represented: conduct problems (e.g., fighting, attention seeking, disruptiveness), personality problems (e.g. anxiety, social withdrawal, feelings of inferiority) and "inadequacy−immaturity" problems (e.g. lack of interest, daydreaming).

Formal means for selecting group members include self-report and rating scale methods. The self-report method requires the young client to fill out a questionnaire or mark a checklist indicating, for example, his behavior and feelings in problem situations. Rating scales provide systematic information from others observing the child. The Quay−Peterson Behavior Problem Checklist (1975) and the Inferred Self-Concept Scale (McDaniel, 1973) are two examples of scales that can be readily administered by teachers or parents, as a basis for formal selection.

The advantages of formal methods are:

1. Ease of selection where large numbers of children are involved.
2. Inclusion of children not usually referred by teachers or parents as their difficulties do not constitute a problem for the adults.
3. Systematic preintervention information is obtained, which may be used as a basis for evaluating the program's effectiveness.

Regarding the *group's composition*, Muro and Dinkmeyer (1977) recommend that the group be heterogeneous in terms of behavior; that is, the leader can include active, withdrawn, and "model" children, if possible. More specifically, Muro and Dinkmeyer indicate that children who are likely to benefit from group counseling are compulsive children, "effeminate boys, restricted children, do gooders, children with specific fears and those with conduct problems." Exclusion from the group is desirable for those who have experienced a trauma such as a death or divorce, those who steal, those with sociopathic tendencies, and those experiencing severe sibling rivalry.

Group size of four to six members is appropriate for rational-emotive groups, though sometimes large groups such as school class groups use the sessions effectively in REE programs. A group which includes a number of aggressive children needs to be smaller than one in which there are a few withdrawn children.

Homogeneity is desirable in *age* composition of the group, with a range of no more than two years at elementary and high school ages. Groups usually meet once or twice a week, with short sessions (20−30 mins.) for young children, and longer sessions for children and youth (45 mins. to 1 hour).

REE AND REGC IN ACTION

What follows in the next three sections are lessons for various age groups for use by counselors or teachers. The first series of lessons are for young children approximately 5 to 7 years and are best used in a flexible way, the length and number of activities in a session being adapted to the needs of the particular children involved. The second series, for 8 to 12 year olds, is longer and more complex than the previous series, and it includes the concept of challenging and disputing. The third series, for 13 years and over, includes full disputation of irrational beliefs. As has already been stated, the lessons can be used as REE with a preventive educational focus, dealing with the children's normal developmental difficulties, or they can be applied in a REGC context, with focus on the specific problems of the children in the group.

Sessions for Younger Children (5–7 Years)

SESSION 1.   GETTING TO KNOW YOU

Notes for the Leader

A gentle introduction is essential for children to feel comfortable with the new tasks of sharing their self-talk and feelings with other group members. "Ice breakers" are therefore introduced at the beginning to enable interaction to begin in a "safe" context, and to move slowly into more personal areas.

Objectives

For each child

1.   to speak to the leader and to other group members about himself;
2.   to share his self-talk and feelings about favorite activities and disliked activities;
3.   to learn a concrete way of expressing the intensity of a feeling.

THE NAME GAME
(Materials: none)
Leader and children sit in a circle and take turns at saying their names. One child begins, telling the group his first name. The next child repeats the first child's name and adds his own. The third child says the first two names, plus his name. Continue around the group for as long as the children can do it. When a child forgets, begin the game again with that child. Repeat until names are fairly well known. (Useful variations include placing cards with each name in a box, and asking the children in turn to put each child's name card in front of each child, at the same time placing his hand gently on the other child's shoulder).

  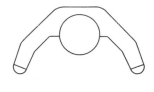

A little upset   Medium upset   A lot upset

Figure A.3.   Demonstrating Feelings.

My Favorites Game
(Materials: individual chalkboards and chalk, or paper and pencils)
Children and leader sit in a circle. The leader asks the children to make drawings and share their thoughts and feelings about them.

1. Draw your favorite animal.
    (Choose several children to name theirs and tell why they like them.) Ask "Is everyone's the same?" "Why?"
2. Draw your favorite food.
    (Choose several different children to name theirs and tell what they like about it.)
3. Draw a picture showing you doing your favorite activity. What do you like to do most?
    ('nvite sharing, with reasons.)
4. I'm going to tell you a sentence,
    "I like, least of all, having to . . . ."
    Think of what you like doing *least of all*.
    Draw a picture of yourself doing this.
    (Ask them to share: *How much* do you dislike having to do this?
    Show me with your arms.) (Demonstrate arms stretched wide apart for very intense feeling, or held closer together for milder feeling. See Figure A.3.) Give the children practice at using this method of describing how strong the feeling is by asking how group members feel about *others'* favorites. Ask child A how much does he like child B's favorite animal? "Show with your arms." Ask child C how much does he like child D's favorite activity? "Show with your arms."
    Ask: "How do you feel when you have to do it?"

SESSION 2.   WE ALL HAVE FEELINGS

Notes for the leader

Many children do not know appropriate words to describe their feelings. Use this activity to increase their knowledge of feeling words.

Objectives

For each child

1.   to learn new words which describe feelings.
2.   to connect feeling words with facial and bodily expressions in pictures.

FINDING FEELINGS
(Materials: large chalkboard; paper for large wall chart; paper strips for feeling words)

Ask the children to say all the feeling words they know. List them on the chalkboard. When the children peter out, tell them words from the list below and others you can think of that are appropriate.

happy	mad
sad	sorry
afraid	worried
excited	silly
upset	angry
cheerful	pleased
joyful	cross
glad	scared
lonely	down

Give each child some paper strips and ask him to write several of the feeling words in large letters, one to a strip. Each child then pastes his words onto the large wall chart "Our Feelings" for hanging in the classroom.

Invite children to choose a feeling and tell the group about one time when they felt that way. If "worried," "angry" and "down" are not chosen, ask someone to do them.

FUN WITH FEELINGS
(Materials: pictures from magazines and newspapers showing people expressing emotions)

Give each child (or allow free selection) several pictures (already cut out from magazines or newspapers) which show people expressing feelings in their faces or bodies. Ask each child in turn to demonstrate that expression for the group and *name* the feeling. Then the pictures can be pasted on the chart alongside the feeling word.

If children disagree about what the pictures show, discuss the difficulty of knowing exactly what another person is feeling just by looking at them.

STORY: I HAVE FEELINGS
(Materials: *I Have Feelings*, Terry Berger, Human Sciences Press, N.Y., 1971)

Read *I Have Feelings* to the children and discuss it with them. Did something in the book remind them of themselves? Ask them to tell what happened to them.

SESSION 3

Notes for the Leader

In this session the children are given practice in paying attention to ways in which people express feelings. They also practice expressing feelings to the group, and identify the subjective quality of the feelings.

Objectives

For each child

1.   to identify feelings expressed by other children.
2.   to mime expression of feelings to the group.
3.   to identify feelings as pleasant or unpleasant.

WHAT AM I FEELING?
(Materials: red stickers with pluses on them, for pleasant feelings; blue stick-
                     ers with minuses on them for unpleasant feelings)
    Each child may choose two feelings to mime. The group tries to guess what the feeling is. When they have guessed, the mimer is asked whether the feeling is pleasant or unpleasant ("A feeling you like to have?" or "A feeling you don't like to have?"). If it is pleasant he puts a red sticker beside that feeling word on the classroom wall chart (Session 2). If it is unpleasant he puts a blue sticker beside the word. The leader may mime some of the words also; the group continues to take turns until all words are mimed and labelled.

SESSION 4.   SHARING OUR FEELINGS AND SELF-TALK

Notes for the Leader

In this session the children are invited to talk about past situations in which they can remember experiencing particular feelings. Encourage the children to describe the situation and their feelings in some detail, including self-talk if they can. Highlight variations within the group, especially similar events connected with different feelings, and similar feelings connected with different events.

Objectives

For each child

1.   to learn that people feel and express their emotions differently.
2.   to share his own experiences of specific feelings, the events that occasioned them and self-talk associated with them.

FEEL WHEEL (adapted from Vernon 1980, p. 43)

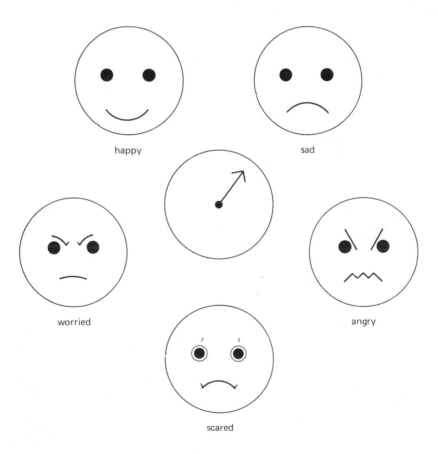

Feel Wheel

Figure A.4.   Feel Wheel (Adapted from *Help Yourself to a Healthier You*, By Ann Vernon. Published in 1980 by University Press of America, Inc. Reprinted by Permisison.)

(Materials: A "feel wheel," see Figure A.4)

Have the children take turns spinning the spinner, and when it lands, the child spinning is asked to share a time when he has experienced the emotion depicted by the picture. Then ask several other children to share their experiences with that *same* emotion. Before proceeding to another spinner, ask a question such as the following: "You are all sharing about the same feeling, but did the same thing happen to all of you?" (Emphasize in the discussion that different events are associated with the same feeling). If a child describes a situation already mentioned (e.g., going to the dentist) and associates it with a different feeling (e.g., scared) from another child (e.g., happy), discuss this with the children. Highlight the idea that the same event is associated with different feelings. If this comparison does not arise spontaneously, elicit feelings from other children about events another has described (e.g., "Have you ever been to a circus? How did/would you feel?" "Were you ever lost in a crowd?" "Were you ever given a puppy for a present?").

SESSION 5.   MISTAKES IN OUR THINKING

Notes for the Leader

In this session the children experience in a concrete way some consequences of erroneous assumptions; the story characters model problem solving by questioning assumptions, finding out more facts, and looking for a solution. An important idea to stress is that because they are thinking something does not necessarily make it true.

Objectives

1. To learn that people can make mistakes in their thinking about other people.
2. To learn that unpleasant feelings can come from mistakes in thinking.
3. To learn ways to change mistaken thinking.

I HATE YOU(from Vernon, 1980, p. 48)
(Materials: *The Hating Book*, Charlotte Zolotow, Harper & Row, N.Y., 1969)
(Synopsis—*The Hating Book*)

This is the story about a girl who hated her friend because her friend didn't ask her to help her do things, didn't choose her as a team member, and wouldn't walk home with her from school. The girl's mother kept telling her to ask the friend what was wrong—but she wouldn't do it. Finally she decided to talk with the friend, and the friend told her that when she had worn a new dress, someone had told her that the girl had said she looked like a freak. The girl said, "No I didn't—I said you looked neat." And so the misunderstanding was cleared up and they didn't hate each other any more.

Read the story to the group, then discuss:

1.   What do you think "hate" means?
2.   What were some of the things the friends were thinking about each other in the story? Were they true?
3.   What problems were caused by the friends thinking these things?
4.   What do you think would have happened if the girl had asked her friend why she was acting that way?
5.   If she hadn't had these ideas about why her friend was acting this way, would she have hated her?
6.   What have you learned about feelings after hearing this story?

SESSION 6

Notes for the Leader

This session aims to demonstrate in a rudimentary yet concrete way that thoughts lead to feelings. Encourage the children to discuss their suggestions and explore why "sensible thoughts" lead to more pleasant feelings, and why "not sensible thoughts" lead to less pleasant feelings. "Not sensible thoughts" are characterized by demandingness of others ("Mommy *must* let me have that new toy"), exaggerations ("It will be awful if I'm not invited to the birthday party"), overgeneralizations ("Nobody likes me") and they lead to unpleasant feelings. "Sensible thoughts" are realistic, express preferences rather than demands, appraise events in a way that helps us tolerate frustration and think clearly to solve problems, and sensible thoughts do not lead to distress and upsettedness but to milder (pleasant or unpleasant) feelings.

Objectives

For each child

1.   to link pleasant or neutral feelings with "sensible thoughts."
2.   to link unpleasant feelings with "not sensible thoughts."
3.   to learn new "sensible thoughts" for coping with frustrating situations.

MY THOUGHT FLOWER GARDEN (adapted from Brody, 1974)
(Materials: 4 green cardboard sheets; 4 brown cardboard strips glued to green cardboard sheets at intervals to allow slotting in between (see Figure A.5); 6–9 grey or black paper flowers (see Figure A.5) labelled as unpleasant feelings (sad, cross, upset, angry, unfriendly); 6–9 pale colored paper flowers, labelled as pleasant or neutral feelings (calm, O.K., friendly, ready to play)

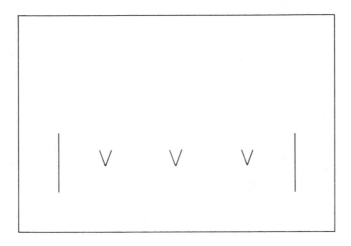

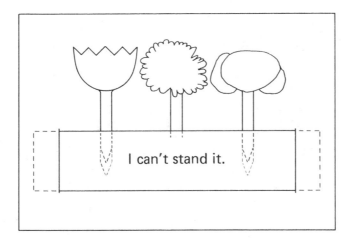

I can't stand it.

Figure A.5.   Thought Garden and Flowers (adapted from Brody, 1974).

Say to the children:

"Shut your eyes and pretend something has happened the way you didn't want it. Think of a story to tell the group about it." Ask one child to tell his story. When he has finished, show the group two flower gardens (green sheets) each with a thought "planted" in it: one with "I can't stand it" planted, the other with "This is disappointing—it would be nice if it were different," planted (see Figure A.5). Invite the storyteller to choose "flowers" from a box and insert two or three in each garden. Before he chooses, discuss with the group what kind of feeling flowers would grow in each of the two thought gardens: are they pleasant or unpleasant? Why? At the end the flowers can be

Figure A.6.   Thought Flower Gardens (adapted from Brody, 1974).

removed and another child tell his story and choose flowers; that is, repeat the above procedure with a number of children. Again ask them to close their eyes and ask them to imagine a story about how their friend stops playing with them in the middle of a game. Invite one child to tell his story. Present two more flower gardens with the thoughts: "It's not fair" and "I wish we were still playing, but my friend doesn't have to do what I want to do." Discuss these thoughts. Ask which is sensible and which not sensible. Why? Ask which would lead to pleasant feelings and which to unpleasant feelings. Invite the storyteller to place the flowers in the appropriate thought gardens (see Figure A.6).

I HAVE TO HAVE MY WAY (adapted from Vernon, 1980)
(Materials: none)

Read the following and discuss the questions:

Sid sat on the curb, waiting for the rest of the kids to come and play ball. When Sally came, she said she'd bat first. Sid stamped his foot on the ground and whined "I won't play if I can't be first." So they let him. The first ball that Sid hit was a foul; the next one was too. Sid yelled that the umpire was cheating and if he didn't get that counted as a run he'd quit. By this time the group said, "O.K., quit. The ump wasn't cheating." So as Sid walked away, he yelled, "You'll be *sorry*—I don't ever want to play with a bunch of cheaters again." And the group kept on playing happily without Sid.

1. What is a demand? (Explain if no one knows).
2. Do you think Sid made any? Examples.
3. What was the result of Sid's demanding?
4. What do you think he was saying to himself about this situation?
5. Do people have to have their own way?
6. Do you think demanding is a good thing?

I DON'T LIKE IT, BUT . . . ." (adapted from Vernon, 1980)
(Materials: none)

Ask children to think of several things that either their parents or their teachers have wanted them to do, but that they haven't wanted to. Have them share their ideas and list them. Then, using the list, discuss the following.

1. Once you actually do whatever it is that someone wants you to do, is it so bad?
2. Do you think that it is wrong to have to do something that you don't want to? Explain.
3. Do parents or teachers have to do things that they don't want to? Explain.
4. Do you think it's worth making a big deal over doing something you don't want to do?
5. What might be a good thing to "say to yourself" when you're asked to do something you don't especially want to do but know you have to do it? ("I don't like it but I can stand it" or "There are times when everyone does things they don't like to do").

SESSION 7. NAME CALLING

Notes for the Leader

Emphasize in the discussion that each person is made up of many different characteristics. No one is only *one* thing. If a person calls another a name, this does not *make* the other person that name.

Objectives

For each child

1. to name several of his characteristics;
2. to identify positive and negative characteristics in himself and others;
3. to learn that name calling does not cause the name to be true;
4. to learn that people *upset themselves* about name calling;
5. to increase tease tolerance.

STICKS AND STONES

(Materials: a circle of paper for each child prepared as "Myself Circle" (see Figure A.7); pencils; rulers; paper; scissors, sticking tape for stick puppet making; simple paper hats decorated with bright yellow suns, pasted or drawn on)

Part 1

Tell the children the saying "Sticks and stones can break my bones but words can never hurt me." Ask them if they think it is true. Why? Ask them to fill out their "Myself Circle" by completing each "I . . ." sentence or doing a drawing. Explain that the idea is to write down both "good" and "bad" things about themselves—things they like about themselves and things they may wish were different.

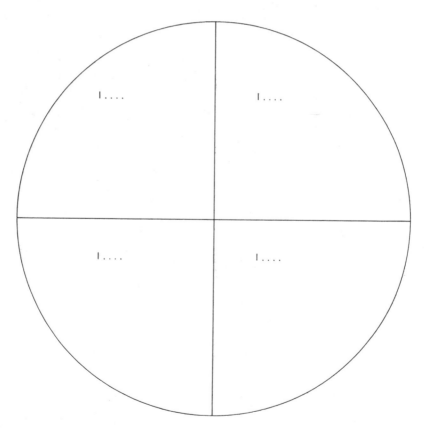

Figure A.7. Myself Circle.

Give them an example, saying: One child made his myself circle this way:

"I . . . help Mommy."
"I . . . fight with my sister."
"I . . . make friends at school."
"I . . . leave my room untidy."

Ask them to share their circles. If they have made drawings, ask them to explain them.
Discuss these questions:

Are there some things you like about yourself?
Are there some things you don't like about yourself?
Is anyone perfect?
When someone calls you a name, does that mean you *are* what that name says?
Use exaggeration and humor to explain this idea:
   "If someone calls you a spotted wombat, does that make you one?"
   "If someone calls you a purple rhinoceros, does that make you one?"
   "If some calls you 'stupid' or 'mean' does that make you 'stupid' or 'mean'? What could you think or say to yourself when you are called a name?"

Here are some things kids say to themselves when they are called names.

   "It doesn't matter. I don't care."
   "I won't worry about that. So what."
   "I don't like being called names but they don't hurt me."
   "I know I'm not a . . . ."
   "I know I'm not *always* a . . . ."
   "I know I'm not only a . . . ."
   "Being called a name is not the worst that can happen to me."

Part II

Use *puppet games* to practice appropriate rational self-statements. Each child makes a simple stick puppet of himself (a drawing of himself, cut out and stuck to the end of a ruler); pairs of children take turns to play the rest of the group. One puppet will be the "namer" and the other the "thinker." The children make the two puppets play and talk together until "namer" calls "thinker" a name. Then it is up to "thinker" to quietly say "Sticks and stones can break my bones but names will never hurt me." Then "namer" says "What are you thinking?" "Thinker" tries to remember a *sensible thought* (rational self-statement) and says it. If he cannot remember any, ask the group, or let "thinker" choose one from the list. If a child remembers a sensible thought, reinforce this by allowing him to wear one of the paper hats with yellow suns.

SESSION 8.   MISTAKE MAKING

Notes for the Leader

Ideas to emphasize include:

1.   Everyone makes mistakes sometimes.
2.   This does not mean they will always make mistakes.
3.   Mistakes are not bad; mistakes are mistakes. Assist the children to find "sensible thoughts" (rational self-statements) for times when they make mistakes.

Objectives

For each child

1.   to describe an event when he or she made a mistake, and the accompanying thoughts and feelings;
2.   to state some "sensible thoughts" for times when mistakes are made.

I GOOFED (adapted from Vernon, 1980, p. 3)

Discuss the idea of "goofing up" or making mistakes and about how everyone makes them. Then ask the children to close their eyes and think about a time when they made a mistake, then to draw a picture which represents that experience.

After pictures have been drawn and shared, use the following as discussion starters.

1.   Can you remember how you felt when you made this mistake?
2.   Did anything too terrible happen as a result of your mistake?
3.   Do you think it's O.K. to "goof up" once in a while?
4.   What can you learn by making mistakes?
5.   What are some "sensible thoughts" you could have if you've just made a mistake? (Make a list.)

Examples of "sensible thoughts":

> "I just made a mistake."
> "I made a mistake this time, but now I know how to do it."

"I wish I hadn't made that mistake—I'll try not to next time."
"Making a mistake doesn't make me worse than other people."
"Mistakes are not bad."
"I learn from my mistakes."

SESSION 9. SENSIBLE SELF-TALK

Notes for the Leader

Children need repeated practice to enable them to internalize the rational self-statements, building them into their own repertoire. Although this is a quiet session, children may wish to discuss their ideas as they make their posters.

Objectives

For each child

1. to internalize a rational self-statement;
2. to associate one "sensible thought" with his or her own experience.

SENSIBLE ME
(Materials: poster paper and magic markers or crayons for each child; box containing cut up list of "sensible thoughts" compiled from previous sessions; see Table A.1 for suggestions)

TABLE A.1. List of Sensible Thoughts

I can stand this.
I can try.
This is not so bad.
I made a mistake.
Things aren't always fair.
I feel disappointed.
I wish things were different.
Mistakes are not bad.
Making a mistake does not make me worse than other people.
I learn from my mistakes.
I won't worry about being called a name.
I know I'm not _____(name)_____ .
I know I'm not *always* _____(name)_____ .
I know I'm not *only* _____(name)_____ .
This is not the worst thing that can happen to me.
I feel sad.

Ask each child to select a "sensible thought" from the box. Allow them to spend a little time choosing one they really want to use. Ask each child to draw a poster picture called "Sensible Me," showing himself in a situation using that thought. Children can use "thought bubbles" like those used to show characters speaking and thinking in cartoon strips. Say: "Show yourself in a situation where that sensible thought could be used. Draw what is happening and show yourself with your thought in a thought bubble." Allow plenty of time for the children to think about their pictures, and invite sharing at the end.

Optional Activity

"Color Us Rational," Virginia Waters, N.Y.: Institute for Rational-Emotive Therapy, 1979.
(Materials: copies of the book as in the title above)
   Read the stories together in the group and provide time for coloring the pictures. Discussion of concepts can be encouraged during coloring activities.

SESSION 10.   BEHAVING WELL

Notes for the Leader

The purpose of this session is to extend the thought—feeling link to the thought—feeling—behavior links. In addition to the child's contributions, examples from everyday situations observed by the leader can be mentioned and discussed.

Objectives

For each child

1.   to learn that "sensible thoughts" lead to sensible ways of behaving;
2.   to learn that "not sensible thoughts" lead to not sensible ways of behaving.

WHICH IS BEST (adapted from Vernon, 1980, p. 131)
(Materials: none)
   Explain the concept of sensible and not sensible ways of handling situations—an example would be that if you can't do your reading assignment, it is sensible to tell the teacher that you don't understand but it is not sensible to tear up the paper and say that you're not going to do it. Then have the children share some examples of what they think are sensible and not sensible ways of responding to situations. Discuss the following questions.

1. Does it make the problem go away if you handle it not sensibly?
2. Are these situations really so bad after all?
3. Do you think that things should always go your way?
4. What is the best way to handle a situation?

FLIP THE COIN (adapted from Vernon, 1980 pp. 131–2)
(Materials: one coin and a set of two cards; see Table A.2)

Procedure: Reemphasize the material presented previously about sensible and not sensible beliefs. Divide the class into two groups, the "heads" and the "tails." Explain that you are going to flip a coin, and if you end up with "heads" the students on the "heads" team will draw a card, have you read it, and as a group talk about it and decide whether the situation described was handled sensibly or not sensibly. If "tails" is called, the "tails" team gets a chance. (There is no competition—the motivation comes from the flipping to see which team responds). After the activity, discuss the difference between sensible and not sensible beliefs, and ask students what they learned.

TABLE A.2.   Flip the Coin

Situations to be placed on cards.

1. You are in the grocery store. You see a five-year-old child pestering his parent(s) for a candy bar. They say no, and the child throws himself on the floor and screams.
2. You are asked by a friend to stay overnight. Your parent(s) say no, because it is a school night. You say O.K., and tell your friend you can't.
3. A friend says that he hates you, and you scream back "I hate you too."
4. Your parent(s) are going away on vacation. You want to go too, but they explain that they want to go alone. You scream and cry, and yell that they don't love you, and that you'll never speak to them again.
5. Your teacher asks you to stay in for recess because you didn't finish your work. You stay in and do it.
6. You are in the toy store. You ask your parent(s) for a ball. Your parent(s) say they can't afford it. You start to cry and say they're mean.
7. Your sister does better in gymnastics than you do. She always tells you that she's perfect. You tell her that you can do things too.
8. Your pet dies. You have had it ever since you remember. You cry, but then tell your parents that maybe someday you can get another one.
9. You are out for recess. Someone accidentally takes your coat that is by the fence. You think he stole it and you start running around telling everyone on the playground that Sam is a thief.
10. Your father forgot to pack your lunch so you have to eat hot lunch. You don't like the food, and when your teacher tells you to eat it, you start crying and say that you'll get sick if you eat it and if you have to, you'll never come back to this school.
11. A second grader calls you a name. It really hurts your feelings and you quietly tell this second grader not to do it again.
12. You didn't finish your work and the teacher says you have to stay after school. You just do it, even though you'd rather be outside playing.

Source: From *Help Yourself to a Healthier You*, by Ann Vernon. Published in 1980 by University Press of America, Inc. Reprinted by permission.

SESSION 11.   AWFULIZING

Notes for the Leader

The focus in this session is on exaggeration as a form of irrational self-talk. As in the previous session, the leader can contribute examples, especially any gleaned from observations of the group.

Objectives

For each child

1. to learn that exaggerations in difficult situations are not sensible and lead to more worry and upset, and less sensible ways of doing things.

EXAGGERATIONS (adapted from Vernon, 1980)
(Materials: none)
   Procedure: Discuss with students what it means to exaggerate and give some examples: "I saw a fight on my way to school vs. I've never seen such a terrible fight and I thought they would kill each other." Talk about the "fine line" that exists between reality and exaggeration, and then have students share some examples of exaggerations.
   Discuss the following:

1. Do you think any harm can come from blowing things out of proportion? Explain.
2. Is it helpful to exaggerate things?
3. What would be good to remember about exaggerating?

DISASTER (adapted from Vernon, 1980, p. 139)
(Materials: none)
   Review and reemphasize points from the previous session and have children give examples of times when they have exaggerated an incident and gotten terribly upset, when it could have been handled in a less disastrous manner.

1. Are things usually as bad as they seem at the time?
2. What do you think you could do to keep from exaggerating about these situations?

Sessions for Children (8–12 Years)

SESSION 1.   ICEBREAKER

Notes for the Leader

Introduce yourself to the group and group members to one another, and explain the purpose of the sessions to the children. Activities in this first session are designed to heighten awareness of feelings and to build trust between group members. It can be done in the group room, but feelings are heightened if it is done outside.

Objectives

For each child

1. to introduce himself, and to learn the goals and rules of the sessions.
2. to interact with other group members, by sharing thoughts and feelings in an emotion arousing activity.

THE BLIND WALK (adapted from P. Lehman , 1973)
(Materials: blindfolds for half the group)
This game is played in pairs, with one child of each pair being blindfolded and led around for some time by the other child. The children reverse roles so that each has a turn at walking "blind." When all pairs have finished, bring the group together to discuss the following questions.

How did you feel when blindfolded?
How did you feel not knowing where you were going?
What were you thinking during the walk?
Did everyone have the same thoughts and feelings?

SESSION 2.   KNOW YOUR FEELINGS

Notes for the Leader

Children may have a limited working vocabulary to describe their own experiences, thoughts, and feelings. In addition, most children lack conceptual skills for understanding that their experience of emotions may vary from strong to weak. The acquisition of an emotional vocabulary, and skills for discriminating different levels of emotional intensity, are viewed as prerequisites for acquiring rational thinking and problem solving skills. During this session children begin to see that situations occasion their feelings. The idea that thoughts cause feelings is not yet introduced. In preparation for that, emphasize in discussion the differences between the children's reactions, especially where a similar event has occasioned different feelings.

Objectives

1. To generate a repertoire of words which the children can use to label feelings.
2. To make links between feelings experienced by the individual and situations which occasion them.
3. To enable children to evaluate the intensity of feelings.

FINDING FEELINGS
(Materials: blackboard or poster paper)

Ask the children to name words that describe feelings and make a list which can be kept on the group room wall or notice board for use again in later sessions. The following are suggested for the list, and some may be contributed by the leader.

happy	joyful	sorry
sad	glad	ashamed
afraid	embarrassed	disappointed
excited	funny	frustrated
upset	lonely	confused
cheerful	mad	guilty
annoyed	nervous	O.K.
angry	curious	relaxed
worried	silly	envious
loving	worthless	weighed down
		jealous

FEELING THERMOMETER
(Materials: picture or model of the feeling thermometer; see Figure A.8)

Explain the comparison being made between degrees of heat and intensity of feeling. (A body thermometer tells "How hot are you?"—a feeling thermometer tells "How happy are you?" or "How angry are you?") Demonstrate

10	
9	— Very very strong
8	
7	— Pretty strong
6	
5	— Medium
4	
3	— Pretty weak
2	
1	— Nothing happening

Figure A.8. The Feeling Thermometer (Cartright, 1977).

the feeling thermometer with examples of weak, mild and intense feelings. Ask group members to explain it in their own words.

If a large cardboard model with a moving gauge is available, children could move the level up and down to indicate feeling intensities. This could be used in conjunction with activities to follow, e.g., the optional cartoon and story activities for this session.

MATCHING AND MIMING

(Materials: magazine or newspaper pictures of "people feeling")

Provide each child with several pictures showing people expressing feelings. Ask the child to guess what the feeling is (use the list), and classify it on the Feeling Thermometer. Then invite each child to mime several feelings and ask group members to take turns guessing the feeling and its temperature using the feeling thermometer.

Optional Activities

WORD MEANINGS

(Materials: My Cartoon, empty cartoon strips)

The purpose of this activity is for children to find the meanings for feeling words other group members are uncertain about.

Allot each child a feeling word (or allow him to choose). Give each child a strip of paper, prepared for a cartoon (see Figure A.9), and ask him to draw a cartoon telling a story or incident about the feeling. Invite each child to read his cartoon to the group.

A FEELING STORY

(Materials: sheets of paper with headings; see below)

Hand out sheets of paper headed "A story about the time I felt very . . . ." Give each child a feeling word to complete the title and ask him to write a story.

Afterwards, invite sharing of stories. Discuss.

If two people had the same or similar feelings to write about, did they have the same story?

Had anything like the story events actually happened to the children themselves?

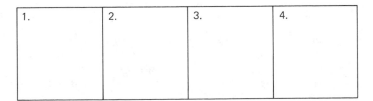

Figure A.9.   Cartoon Strip: "The time I felt *very* . . . ."

SESSION 3.   THINKING AND FEELING

Notes for the Leader

This session teaches the idea that thoughts cause our emotions. Begin with less personal content, and gradually help each individual child to relate the ideas to himself. Repeat ideas frequently. Ask members to explain the ideas in their own words. Partial links (thought−feeling) and (feeling−behavior) are being made in this session as groundwork for the happening−thought−feeling−behavior (HTFB) analysis to be presented in following sessions.

Objectives

For each child

1.   to learn that feelings are caused by thoughts;
2.   to learn that unpleasant thoughts cause unpleasant feelings;
3.   to learn that pleasant thoughts cause pleasant feelings.

BLINDFOLD AND IMAGINE (adapted from Wilson & London, 1977)
(Materials: blindfolds, paper and pencils)

   Ask all the children to wear blindfolds or close their eyes and imagine themselves on a crowded railway station platform. Have them imagine they receive a push from behind. Ask them to write down how they feel, without discussing it with each other (refer them to the feeling list). Then tell them to imagine that they discover the person who pushed them was a blind person who was trying to keep from falling. Ask them to write down again how they feel (e.g., sorry).

DRAW-A-FEELING GAME
(Materials: pencils and paper, a set of cards)

   This game is played in pairs. Each child draws a person who is feeling a *pleasant emotion* and a person who is feeling an *unpleasant emotion*. Underneath the pictures, the child writes a word to describe what the person is feeling. Children draw an empty "thought bubble" for each person drawing.

Mad	"I did not get invited to the party. I can't stand being left out like this."
Sad	"My best friend won't play with me. I'll never have any friends."
Happy	"Teacher says my math has improved. I'm doing well this term."
Excited	"I'll be getting my new bike tomorrow."
Worried	"Mum'll be mad when she knows I've lost my new school jumper!"

Figure A.10.   Cards for Draw-a-Feeling Game.

The children then exchange pictures with their partners and fill in the empty "thought bubbles."

A set of cards (see Figure A.10 for suggestions) can be used as prompts for those who need them. Each card has the name of either a pleasant or an unpleasant emotion on the front, and a thought for the thought bubble on the back.

Discuss with the whole group.

> What do you notice about the thoughts associated with pleasant feelings?
>
> What do you notice about the thoughts associated with unpleasant feelings?

THOUGHT GAME: TELL THE FEELING (adapted from Knaus, 1974)
(Materials: copies of sheet; see Figure A.11)

Distribute copies of sheet (Figure A.11) to the children. Read each item aloud and ask them to write down the feelings. Allow time and encourage them to write as much as possible.

---

1. Suppose that your mother bought you a new coat and told you to be careful and not to get the coat dirty. As you are walking down the street a car swerves near the curve and mud is splashed all over your coat. Write down how you would feel.
   If would feel

   Suppose that you saw that the driver was your mother's friend and that she had swerved to avoid hitting another child. She stopped and offered you a ride home and said that she would explain what happened to your mother. Write down how you would now feel.
   I would feel

2. Suppose that you are carrying a cardboard model of a toy you made for a class project through the park. You see a twenty cent piece near one of the park benches so you put the toy down and another child sits on it. How would you feel?
   I would feel

   Now suppose that you found out that the other child was blind and he could not see your cardboard model. How would you feel in this situation?
   I would feel

Figure A.11. Tell the Feeling

When you have finished the whole sheet, discuss their responses in the group. Highlight differences between individual answers. Ask why children expressed different feelings about the same event.

Highlight different thoughts leading to different feelings.

SESSION 4.   WHAT ARE YOU THINKING?

Notes for the Leader

The activities in this session are geared to teaching the relationships among thoughts, feelings, and behavior. The third objective below may be taught through direct discussion and comments, e.g., supportive remarks by the leader when individuals have difficulty finding thoughts. The elicitational prompts of "and . . ." "but . . ." "because . . ." can be used to help children expand their thoughts (Hauck, 1980) as well as the "peeling the onion" and "expansion−contraction" techniques mentioned earlier. It is not uncommon for children to have difficulty in verbalizing their feelings and especially their thoughts. If they do, other members of the group can be asked to suggest possibilities. The leader can provide further assistance by explaining the general cognitive content underlying the different emotions (as outlined in Chapter 5). A full description and explanation of the HTFB schema, used in the third activity, is provided in Chapter 7.

Objectives

For each child

1. to identify which of his own thoughts lead to pleasant and unpleasant feelings;
2. to learn the use of HTFB schema to analyze his own reactions;
3. to learn that it is often difficult to identify the thought that precedes a feeling because the thought may occur very quickly. It may be one word or a phrase.

EXPERIENTIAL SIMULATION
(Materials: none)

The leader presents one of the following situations (reading aloud) to each child and asks the child what he is *thinking* and *feeling*.

1. Role: English teacher (critical)
   "The essay you handed in is terrible. You had three weeks to do it and it appears you have worked on it for half an hour. Your spelling and punctuation are awful. I would expect this of a fourth grade student."

2. Role: Parent (angry)
   "I have asked you to do the dishes and clean your school shoes. You should know what to do without me always telling you. If you don't do it now, and I mean NOW, not only will you not be allowed to watch TV, but you won't be allowed out this weekend."

3. Role: School mate (whom student doesn't like) (teasing)
   "Boy, are you stupid. You only got 5 out of 50 on your math test. You are a real tomato. You remind me of a brick, real thick. I suppose that's the best you can do. If I were you, I wouldn't even get out of bed in the morning."

4. Role: School mate (bigger and stronger) (threatening)
   "You told the teacher that I was the one who wrote on the wall in the music room. You're coming with me right now and I'm going to smash your face in."

5. Role: Parent (stern)
   "As you probably know (name), your mother (father) and I haven't been too happy with your schoolwork. Until further notice, you are not permitted to play with your friends after school."

6. Role: Sports teacher (apologetic)
   "I know you have worked very hard this year to try to make the team. The competition has been very tough. I know your family really wanted you to make it. I am sorry but you weren't good enough. Maybe next year when you're a year older you might make it.

INSTANT REPLAY
(adapted from Bedford, 1977)
(Materials: none)
   Invite children in the group to:

1. tell about some "fun" events or experiences;
2. tell about some "unfun" events or experiences;
   (Choose one of the latter and label it a "Rough Spot". Rough spots are events that result in unpleasant emotions.)
3. give an *Instant Replay* (as on TV sporting program) on the Rough Spot, to include: Feelings: "I feel. . . ." (Focus on the body language involved.) Details of replay: setting, time, preliminaries, what happened, and result. Thoughts: What did you tell yourself about that Rough Spot?
4. search for options: have the child think of as many alternative plans he could have come up with at the time (when the Rough Spot happened). Other group members can contribute options and can help to highlight the part our interpretations play in emotions.

HTFB
(adapted from Knaus, 1974)
(Materials: work sheets as in Figure A.12 below)

	Happening	Thought	Feeling	Behavior
1.	Getting up in class and discussing an item reported in the news.			
2.	You have just been told you will be having a very important math test.			
3.	Your mother or father has just yelled at you for breaking an expensive vase (you didn't do it on purpose).			
4.	A schoolmate has just told you that he has lost your favorite pen.			

Figure A.12. HTFB.

Distribute the sheets to the children. Read each item aloud and ask them to fill out the sections in order. Discuss variations in the group when all items are completed.

SESSION 5.   BECOMING RATIONAL

Notes for the Leader

Discussion in this session will focus on some common irrational concepts, such as "should," "must," "awful," and "horrible." (For a detailed account of the irrationality of these concepts, including explication of the different types of "shoulds," the leader is referred to the relevant sections in Chapters 3 and 7.)

Present the New Ideas Card (see Figure A.13) and refer to it frequently as children gradually master the concepts. Emphasize each child putting the ideas

---

1. Definition of new words:

Challenge: To question yourself to see if your thought is rational or irrational.

Rational thought: A sensible idea that seems to be true.

Irrational thought: An unreasonable or absurd idea that is false.

2. To find out if a thought is rational or irrational, ask yourself: "Is there enough evidence for me to say the thought is true?" (Yes or No)

If Yes, the thought is rational.

If No, the thought is irrational.

Figure A.13.   New Ideas Card

into his own words. Be prepared to proceed slowly and carefully with these core concepts. Post the New Ideas Card on the group room board.

Rational thoughts can be recognized as true and sensible. Evidence can be found to demonstrate their credibility. Irrational thoughts have no basis in fact and are not sensible. No evidence can be found for them. A useful strategy to test for irrationality is to examine the thought to see if it contains irrational concepts such as should, must, awful, horrible.

Objectives

For each child

1. to give in his own words the definitions of *rational* thoughts, *irrational* thoughts and *challenge*;
2. to express in his own words that in order to know whether a thought is rational or irrational, he must ask himself the question: "Is there enough evidence for me to say the thought is true?" If there is evidence, the thought is rational. If there is not enough evidence, the thought is irrational.

THE FIRST STEP IN CHALLENGING

(Materials: New Ideas Card, see Figure A.13; blackboard; notes from previous session)

Discuss the Ideas Card. Ask the group to review the thoughts they listed in Session 4, and find one rational and one irrational thought. List these on the board. Point out the critical differences between rational and irrational thoughts (sensible and true vs. absurd and false).

SOME IDEAS ARE RATIONAL (SENSIBLE) AND SOME ARE IRRATIONAL (NOT SENSIBLE) (adapted from Kranzler, 1974)

(Materials: none)

Ask the students if they know what superstitions are. List them on the board. Example:

Superstitions

A black cat crossing your path brings bad luck.

Seven and eleven are lucky numbers.

A rabbit's foot can bring good luck.

Breaking a mirror brings seven year's bad luck.

Discuss why superstitious ideas are not sensible. Reinforce ideas approximating the notion that they are illogical or have no evidence to support them, or have no actual experience to back them up, except chance happenings (e.g., "I wore my rabbit's foot and then found a nickel. That proves . . . ").

Point out that there are other kinds of ideas besides superstitions that are not sensible or logical. Take the idea that "Everybody ought to go to college." Discuss how it doesn't make sense to go to college if your occupational goal does not require college; instead, it may require some other course of action (e.g., apprenticeship).

Have children report on other nonsensible ideas they have heard. Introduce the term "irrational idea." Tell them that irrational ideas include superstitions and other ideas that are not logical or sensible. Irrational ideas have no evidence to support them or are not based on objective experience. Tell them that in the next few lessons you will be discussing some commonly held irrational ideas or thoughts that people have that cause them to experience debilitative emotions—"to feel bad," "to be very upset," "to be very distressed." Tell them that when they can identify their own irrational beliefs and change them to rational beliefs, chances are that they will be less likely to experience strong, negative emotions.

CUES TO HELP CHALLENGING

(Materials: blackboard and chalk)

Ask the children: "Have you noticed any words that often occur in thinking that's not sensible?" Ask them to look back over items from previous activities, and, prompting them where necessary, devise lists such as those in Table A.3

Teach them that new words instead of the irrational (not sensible) ones can change their thinking. Make a new list. Include "rational" words such as wish, prefer, would like, can stand, can tolerate, unpleasant, unfortunate, hard to take.

AM I THINKING RATIONALLY?

(Materials: copies of "Am I Thinking Rationally?"; worksheet for each group member, see Figure A.14)

Ask the group to mark thoughts as rational or irrational. Discuss important criteria, especially on examples where they have difficulty.

TABLE A.3.   Cues to Help Challenging

Words of Exaggeration		Absolutes or Unrealistic Demands	
awful	horrible	must	should
terrible	bummed out	ought	got to
wiped out	devastating	need	insist
dreadful		have to	

Source: Gerald and Eyman, 1981, pp. 62–3.

Place a check ($\checkmark$) if you think the thought is rational or irrational. (Remember: is the thought sensible and true, or is it absurd and false.)

	Rational	Irrational
1. Nobody in the world will ever be my friend.	————	————
2. I would be happier at school if I were better at my work.	————	————
3. I never do anything right.	————	————
4. If I am this bad at work I will never be good at anything.	————	————
5. Everybody hates me.	————	————
6. I wish I had more friends at school.	————	————
7. I wish I could play football as well as John can.	————	————
8. I can't stand doing homework.	————	————

Figure A.14. Am I Thinking Rationally?

Optional Activity

THOUGHT POSTERS
(Materials: paper for posters; paints; magic markers or crayons)

Each child makes two posters—one showing rational thoughts, one showing irrational thoughts. Tell the children to write the thought in large letters on the paper and to decorate the poster colorfully to express their feelings. Help each child to identify several of their own thoughts to include, if possible. Or the posters might include pictures of themselves with many "thought clouds"; or lists of thoughts with pictures of people experiencing the consequences of rational and irrational thinking; or a number of thoughts, plus reminders to challenge, next to the irrational thoughts.

Some of the posters may be kept on the group board as reminders for later sessions. Others may be taken home and used in the children's own rooms.

SESSION 6. CHANGING OUR THOUGHTS: DISPUTING AND CHALLENGING

Notes for the Leader

Ideas to emphasize in this session are: "When I get too upset, it is difficult to improve the situation" and "I can control how upset I am by changing my irrational thoughts to rational thoughts." If your group finds it helpful, you may wish to put these ideas onto cards, for adding to the group room display.

Objectives

For each child

1. to practice changing irrational thoughts to rational thoughts;
2. to practice evaluating his own thoughts, and restating them;
3. to practice disputing the concepts of "terrible" and "awful."

MR. HEAD (adapted from Brody, 1974)
(Materials: bowl or paper bag with a drawing of a head; thought cards—one
        for each thought presented in Table A.4 and Figure A.15: Chal-
        lenge Wheel; paper and pencils)

Present Mr. Head, the bag containing rational (green border) and irrational (red border) thought cards. Explain that the head contains rational and irrational thoughts that they may think. Make sure each student picks one red and one green card.

Ask the children to write down each thought into an HFTB scheme (see leader's notes for Session 4), and to make up something for H, F, and B to suit the thought. The happening, feeling and behavior they write can come from their past experiences or can be something they imagine.

Invite the children to share what they have written.

Display the Challenge Wheel. Ask a number of children to read out the challenges. Each child is then asked to evaluate the thoughts they picked from Mr. Head. "Is the thought irrational?" If so, "Can you think of a rational thought, a challenge, to change that irrational thought?"

TABLE A.4.   Complete List of Mr. Head Thoughts

I can't stand it.
This is horrible.
If I make a mistake, it means I am a bad person.
It must mean that I am no good if that person does not like me.
That person is awful for not being the way I want him to be.
I don't like it, so how can I change it or make the best of it?
If people tease me, I don't have to take it so seriously.
Instead of needing to be *the* best, it is most important to me to try *my* best.
This is a difficult problem, but facing it and learning from it will help me
    overcome the problem.
This is really messed up, but it won't be awful unless I make it that way.
If I start to feel nervous or angry I can face it and accept it. I can be patient
    and not fight with myself.
I can have some control over the way I feel by controlling the way I think.
I don't like it, tough, so I don't like it.
It is horrible if I start to feel nervous or angry.
It would be nice if it was different.
Sticks and stones may break my bones, but names can never hurt me.
This is sure disappointing.
What's the worst that can happen? Is there anything I can do to help myself?
Nobody is perfect.
Mistakes can help me learn.
Blaming does not help. We all have a right to be wrong. Let's learn from it.
I don't like it, but that's the way things are now. Getting very upset about it
    won't help make it any better.
I might not be very happy about it, but I don't have to be very unhappy either.
Making mistakes is horrible.
It's no use trying any more. I give up.
I am no good.

Source: Brody, 1974.

Figure A.15.   Challenge Wheel (adapted from Brody, 1974).

Children may select a challenge from the Challenge Wheel, or make up one of their own. Children other than the one having the turn can also contribute ideas for challenges.

IT'S NOT SO TERRIBLE (adapted from Vernon, 1980)
(Materials: none)

As a group, make a list of real life catastrophes (e.g., "I lose both legs in a car accident"; "My whole house is burnt out") and ask each individual child to rate each one on a scale of 1−100. (100 is the most catastrophic.)

Discuss with the children the concept of people upsetting themselves because they tend to think too many things are terrible, when in reality, things may be bad, but not absolutely the end of the world. Ask the children to think of examples of situations which initially they thought were terrible but at a second thought they realized there were some good aspects too, or that the event wasn't 100% terrible. Then explain how to "challenge and dispute" beliefs about things which we think are terrible by asking "why" is it so terrible. In comparison with the real life catastrophes, how terrible is it, on a scale of 1−100? Use the following as an example.

Happening: "I'm going to move."

Thought: "It's awful—I'll never make friends and I hate to leave. I feel terrible. Life will never be the same."

Challenge or dispute: "Why is it so terrible? Is it the worst thing that could happen to me?"

Rational thought: "Well, I don't like it, but I know I can live through it—it'll be hard but not terrible. Compared with having nowhere to live (95), it's only about 20 on the scale of catastrophes."

Have children share some examples and events and practice disputing the "It's terrible" using the above model.

IDENTIFY AND DISPUTE (adapted from Vernon, 1980, p. 162)
(Materials: copies of the story, "Sally's Day")

Sally's Day

Sally got out of bed, late as usual, and started to get dressed. She looked through her closet and couldn't find a single thing to wear—everything looked so out of date she couldn't possibly be seen in it. Finally she pulled out an old dress and went down to breakfast. Eggs—how could anyone stand those? So she pushed the plate away and tried to find her books. Where are they? She figured her brother had hidden them. That creep . . . he shouldn't be so mean. So she just left without them and got to school five minutes late. The teacher said she'd have to stay five minutes after school, and once again Sally thought about what a mean teacher he was—what right did he have to make her stay? After her first class she went to gym. Oh no! Swimming today! Since Sally couldn't even backfloat, she figured everyone would laugh because she'd make such a fool of herself. But she got in the water anyway. Finally it was time for science. In science class, two girls and a boy started whispering and looking at her, and she just knew they were talking about her. How could they! Creeps! And so the day went . . . .

Distribute copies of the story and ask the children to underline irrational thoughts. Then have them pair up and write sequences for each underlined statement.

Debrief by discussing these questions:
What are Sally's irrational thoughts?

What is it that makes them irrational?

What are the disputes or challenges to each?

Do you find it difficult to think of the disputes?

Can you see any advantages in disputing?

STORY: FREDDIE FLOUNDER

(Materials: "Freddie Flounder," Virginia Waters, Institute for Rational Living
Pamphlet, N.Y., 1980b)

Read and discuss "Freddie Flounder" in the group. Ask the children to retell the story in their own words. Why was Freddie feeling so miserable? What did he do about it? Ask the children have they ever felt like Freddie. Invite them to tell about it. What could they have done about it?

SESSION 7.   THOUGHTS CAN MAKE YOU FEEL BAD

Notes for the Leader

As the children probe irrational thoughts associated with intense feelings they experience, some anxiety may be aroused. Communicate an attitude that everyone thinks irrationally sometimes. Contribute examples of your own (e.g., "My most embarrassing moment"). Be alert for irrational thinking about irrational thinking! It is not bad, awful, stupid or horrible to think irrational thoughts.

Objectives

For each child

1. to learn that thinking irrational thoughts make him or her feel more unhappy, worthless, angry and frustrated than if he or she thinks rational thoughts;
2. to examine the frequency of his or her irrational thoughts.

HOW AM I FEELING?

(Materials: copies of Figure A.8, feeling thermometer)

Review how to use the feeling thermometer (already used in Session 2) in this context. Read to the group the list of thoughts below and ask group members to imagine themselves thinking the thought and to write down their feelings. Then ask them to rate the feeling from 1 to 10, for example, someone might write "worried—8."

Thoughts
1. It would be awful if I didn't get good grades on my report card. (irrational thought)

2. It is unfair for me to have so much homework; I can't stand it. (irrational thought)
3. I think I can make the team, but I would be disappointed if I didn't make it. (rational thought)
4. Colin doesn't seem to like me. I wish he would . . . . (rational thought)

For an experiment, two thoughts that lead to pleasant feelings.

5. Getting a good mark on the important end of term maths test really is great. I'm feeling really terrific!
6. Ian invited me to his house this weekend. I'm looking forward to having a fun time.

Follow this with a discussion of their ratings, emphasizing the relationship between very unpleasant and pleasant feelings, and irrational and rational thoughts.

MY MOST EMBARRASSING MOMENT
(adapted from Wilson & London, 1977)
(Materials: blackboard)
   Ask each child to close his eyes for a few moments, and try to recall his most embarrassing moment.
   Invite them to share these moments: first it can be described as a story, then put into a HTFB schema on the blackboard.
   Ask them to rate the feelings from 1 to 10, using the feeling thermometer.
   Ask, "Were your thoughts like any of those discussed in 'How am I feeling?' For example, did you overgeneralize, exaggerate, self-down or make demands of yourself or other people?" If so, "What could you have thought to yourself to make you feel less embarrassed?"

MY USUAL THINKING
(Materials: copies of Figure A.16, "My Usual Thinking" worksheet)
   Give each child a copy of "My Usual Thinking." Explain the thought frequency scale. Read each of the eight thoughts and ask the children to indicate how often they think that "or similar" thoughts. Interpret for children the frequency of their irrational thoughts. Note that thought number 5 is rational and can be examined for contrast.

Optional Activity:

THOUGHT FLOWER-GARDEN (adapted from Brody, 1974)
   Ask the children to draw appropriate thought flower gardens (see Session 9, 5–7 years) showing their own irrational thoughts planted, and their unpleasant feelings as flowers.

Directions: Indicate how often you generally think this kind of thought.

1. That Steven is an idiot—real stupid.

1 2 3 4 5 6 7 8 9 10
I never think   I very
like this   frequently
think like this

2. I must do better in math class.

1 2 3 4 5 6 7 8 9 10
I never think   I very
like this   frequently
think like this

3. I'm no good.

1 2 3 4 5 6 7 8 9 10
I never think   I very
like this   frequently
think like this

4. I can't stand it when my teacher
doesn't call on me when I raise
my hand in class.

1 2 3 4 5 6 7 8 9 10
I never think   I very
like this   frequently
think like this

5. I do not like doing the dishes.

1 2 3 4 5 6 7 8 9 10
I never think   I very
like this   frequently
think like this

6. I am finding it impossible to do my
English assignment.

1 2 3 4 5 6 7 8 9 10
I never think   I very
like this   frequently
think like this

Figure A.16. My Usual Thinking

STORY: FLORA FARBER'S FEAR OF FAILURE
(Materials: "Flora Farber's Fear of Failure," Virginia Waters, Institute for
Rational Living Pamphlet, N.Y., 1980b)

Read the story together and discuss it. Ask the children about situations in which they are afraid of failing. Do they feel like Flora? What can they do about it? What did Flora do?

SESSION 8. WHO AM I?

Notes for the Leader

Assist the child if necessary in identifying his characteristics. Many children need help in identifying their positive characteristics, as the only feedback they receive is about their negative characteristics. Clarify the meanings of any words that are not understood, e.g., complex, simple.

Carry through what the children learned about challenging in previous sessions and apply it here to name calling. Demonstrate with the group how to use a challenge such as "I am not necessarily what someone calls me. I am made up of many characteristics."

Objectives

For all children

1.   to learn that each of us is complex, not simple;
2.   to identify some of their positive and negative characteristics;
3.   to learn that they are not totally good or totally bad because of some of their characteristics;
4.   to learn that overgeneralizing about themselves is irrational;
5.   to learn that when they only focus on their negative characteristics, they feel worse about themselves.

COMPLEX ME (adapted from Knaus, 1974)
(Materials: self-concept circles; pencils)
   Ask each child to fill in the self-concept circle (see Figure A.17). Help anyone who is having difficulty. Invite other group members to help also. Invite children to share their self-concepts. Discuss: Was it more difficult to find positive or negative characteristics? Why? Play a name calling game in

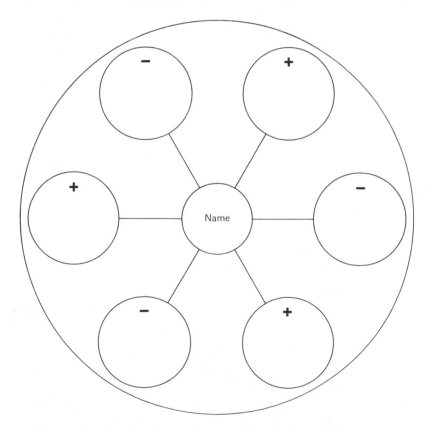

Figure A.17.   Complex Me = Self-concept Circle (adapted from Knaus, 1974).

pairs: Have each member of the pair call the other a name (with reference to their characteristics). The other member challenges the name aloud through reference to his positive and negative qualities, e.g., "Does one person's idea of me mean I am just what they think of me?" "If I have all these characteristics how can I be just . . . . ?" Help the children to introduce words like "sometimes," "occasionally," "rarely," "most of the time" when describing their qualities, as this helps them to focus on their complexity as individuals. Discuss that when they conclude they are a failure because they do something poorly or stupid because they sometimes behave stupidly, they are overgeneralizing— they are saying that their entire self if defined by only one of their characteristics, and forgetting that other characteristics of theirs are also important. Emphasize that to be stupid, they must do everything stupidly. Ask them to name some things they do not do stupidly. This can be illustrated and disputed by examining other positive aspects listed in the self-concept circle.

Optional Activity

Self-concept circles can be applied to another person, such as a teacher, a parent or a person the child has difficulty getting along with. The child can identify positive and negative qualities in that person, thus encouraging rational thoughts about others, as well as himself.

SELF-CONCEPT POEM (Katz, 1974)
(Materials: blackboard; paper; pencils)
    Explain to the children that they are going to write a poem, a special kind of poem:
Write on the blackboard

> "I can't
>
> But I
>
> I can't
>
> But I
>
> I can't . . . ."

Begin with an example of your own. Ask the children to complete their poems. Invite them to share.
    In discussion, focus on the complexity of each person, their strengths and weaknesses. What happens if we focus only on our weaknesses? How do we feel about ourselves? What happens if we focus only on our strengths. Highlight the difference between one's self and one's behavior.

STORY: HOMER THE HOMELY HOUND DOG
(Materials: *Homer the Homely Hound Dog*, E. J. Garcia & Nina Pellegrini,
            Institute for Rational Living, N.Y., 1974)
    Read "Homer the Homely Hound Dog" together in the group. Invite the children to express their feelings about it and share any experiences they may have in common with Homer. Ask them to retell the story in their own words.

SESSION 9.   NO ONE IS ALL GOOD OR BAD

Notes for the Leader

Individual group members will vary in the ease with which they apply these ideas. Some will be able to think about them clearly as they apply to the thinking of others but not their own thinking. For example, they will remember when others have focused only on their negative qualities. This is a good first step. The other two steps in understanding this session are: (1) thinking about how they themselves, at times, focus on only one characteristic of themselves, and (2) thinking about how they sometimes focus on only one characteristic in other people. As with earlier sessions, ask the children repeatedly to express the important ideas *in their own words*.

Objectives

For each child

1. to learn that focusing only on negative qualities in people (self and others) is irrational, because everybody has other positive qualities;
2. to learn that people are not totally good or totally bad;
3. to learn to challenge and change his or her negative irrational thoughts to negative rational thoughts;
4. to learn that thinking negative irrational thoughts leads to more upset than thinking negative rational thoughts.

This objective can be reached by following through the thought-feeling connection in discussion. For example, ask them to say how they *feel* (1) when they think a *negative irrational* thought, such as "I can't stand school—its horrible," and (2) when they think a *negative rational* thought such as "There are some things about school I don't like, and I'll be glad when I don't have to do them anymore!" Ask them to rate each feeling on the feeling thermometer (Figure A.8).

JUNKING YOURSELF
(Materials: none)

Teach the group Howard Young's "flat tire" example (Young, 1977): Ask, "Suppose you had a flat tire on your car, would you junk the whole car because it had a flat tire?"

Ask, "Who can explain how people 'junk' themselves?"

When anyone focuses only on some negative characteristic, they "junk" themselves. Ask the group for examples, and discuss why "junking ourselves" is irrational. Ask, "How do you feel when you junk yourself?"

CHALLENGE—A GAME TO DEMONSTRATE RATIONALITY
(adapted from Knaus, 1974)
(Materials: 36 playing cards—18 rational thoughts, 12 irrational thoughts (see
        Table A.5), 6 "challenges"; start and finish cards, Figure A.18;
        playing board reduced in size; and playing pieces)

Let four or five players take turns at playing the game. Shuffle the cards and let the players take one card each from the top of the pile. When a player reads his card, he must decide if the thought on the card is rational or irrational. If unsure, he may discuss it with other players or onlookers. Players with rational cards move ahead one space. Players with irrational cards must stay at the start position or return to start if they do not hold a challenge card which enables them to verbally challenge the irrational thought. Players with challenge cards may take either of the following risks: hold the card for future use with an

TABLE A.5.   Cards for Challenge—A Game to Demonstrate Rationality

Rational Thought Cards

 1. It is unpleasant wearing a school uniform.
 2. It is not much fun doing homework.
 3. I enjoy playing football.
 4. I dislike getting detentions.
 5. I wish I were better at school.
 6. I don't like sitting at a desk all day long.
 7. I do not like it when my parents do not listen to me.
 8. I feel excited when the bell goes for lunch.
 9. I don't like being yelled at.
10. If I don't pass my exams, I'll be disappointed.
11. I dislike exams.
12. I enjoy watching television.
13. I feel uncomfortable on very hot days at school.
14. Teachers sometimes shout too much.
15. I feel happy when I get good marks.
16. I would like a three-day weekend.
17. I like listening to music.
18. I dislike getting up at 7:00 in the morning.

Irrational Thought Cards

 1. Teachers are horrible.
 2. People who make mistakes ought to be shot.
 3. I can't stand school.
 4. Teachers make me feel angry.
 5. My parents are awful.
 6. No one will ever like me.
 7. School is unbearable.
 8. It is terrible to have to do homework.
 9. I can't stand exams.
10. I'm the worst person in the world.
11. Teachers make me sick.
12. I'll die if I don't get a good job.

Start Card: Hopelessly Irrational
Finish Card: Marvelously Rational

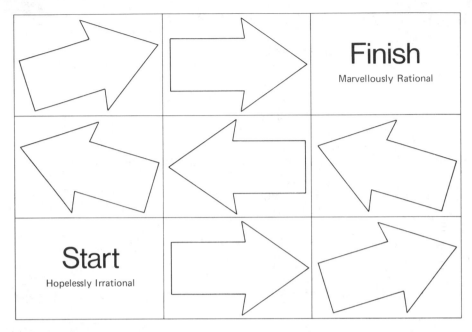

Figure A.18.   Playing Board for "Challenge" (adapted from Knaus, 1974).

irrational thought card, or trade the card with another player for his position on the board at any point in the game. The challenge cards enable the holder to move two spaces if he successfully challenges an irrational thought. Play continues until one player reaches the "marvellously rational" goal. At the completion of one or two games, invite discussion on the advantages of challenging. How can they remember to challenge in real situations?

Optional Activities

PUPPET PLAYS
(Materials: paper bags; magic markers)
   Ask the group to make simple paper bag puppet characters to tell some stories: the story of a problem (e.g., a fight, or someone feeling very miserable), *or* their own versions of fairy tales, *or* scenes from their favorite TV dramas.
   When they have acted out the stories ask, "Was there any irrational thinking in the story?" Ask them to retell the story using rational self-talk.

MUSIC ANALYSIS
(Materials: words from current popular songs, or tapes or records to play)
   Ask students to analyze the words of some popular songs, e.g., helplessness, worthlessness, absolute needs and demands may be in evidence.

SESSION 10   BEING A THOUGHT DETECTIVE

Notes for the Leader

The aim of this session is to teach the children that some of the things we think are true and some are false. Some thoughts that are not true can lead to feelings of upset and distress or anger if we often think them.

Objectives

For each child

1.   to learn to question his thinking;
2.   to learn that *thinking something does not make it true*.

ROLE PLAYING WITH MIND READER AND THOUGHT DETECTIVE (adapted from Miller, 1978)

(Materials: copies of two role playing scripts, Table A.6)

Have children take turns with the roles and read the scripts aloud. Discuss each one at the end.

TABLE A.6.

Role Playing Script I

NARRATOR: Today's case that we will attempt to solve is "Who Stole the Ten-Speed Bike." John received the Christmas present that he had always wanted . . . a new ten-speed bike. He went to visit a friend's house and he forgot to lock the bike up. When he went outside to go home, guess what he saw? No bike! That's right, the bike was gone and all that was there was a note saying, "Too bad sucker—you lose!"

JOHN: I can't believe that my bike was stolen. I feel crushed. I feel very, very, very upset . . . angry . . . depressed. Why did this happen to me? Poor me.

NARRATOR: John, you look really upset . . . what happened?

JOHN: My bike was stolen . . . my new favorite bike. I'm going to miss it. Not only did I lose the bike, but I'm going to lose my life when my parents find out. That will be the last bike I will ever see in my life.

NARRATOR: Is there any way I can help you?

JOHN: Nope . . . not this time. There is no way of you helping me other than getting me a new bike.

NARRATOR: Are you sure now? I can always call in the Thought Detectives and the bionic Mind Reader.

JOHN: There is nothing they can do either. What I could use is some real detectives, not some people who go around getting you to question your irrational thoughts. Believe me, how I'm feeling is how everyone would feel if they got their new bike stolen. Leave me alone . . . I'm too depressed to talk . . . I think I will end it all now.

NARRATOR: Listen, I can understand that you're upset and that most people would be *somewhat upset* and *saddened*. But you're feeling very upset and that's because of *your irrational thoughts*. I think I'm going to call in our Heroes again.

(Continued)

TABLE A.6 *(Continued)*

THOUGHT DETECTIVE #1:   Well, Well, what do we have here? Another person who *is getting himself upset by his irrational thoughts*.

THOUGHT DETECTIVE #2:   That's right . . . no matter what happens you still don't have to get upset about it. A situation, no matter how bad it is, can never get us upset. Only our thoughts can.

JOHN: Are you people for real? Somebody just stole my new bike and you're telling me that I don't have to get upset. What should I do, sing a song and thank the person who stole my bike?

THOUGHT DETECTIVE #1:   Nobody is saying that you can't feel *sad* or *annoyed* that your bike was stolen, but why get yourself so upset and depressed?

THOUGHT DETECTIVE #2:   That's right, it is *too bad* that your bike was stolen, but how is getting yourself so upset going to help? All it will do is get you more and more upset.

JOHN: Okay, you win . . . help me calm myself down.

THOUGHT DETECTIVE #1:   Great. John, what do you think you're telling yourself about the stolen bike? What do you *think your irrational thoughts are? Remember the irrational clue words*.

JOHN: Let me see, some of the irrational clue words are *awful*, *should*, *demand*, and *I can't stand it*. And I know that they are irrational because there is no evidence for them . . . they are silly words that do not make sense. I think I would like the Mind Reader to help me.

MIND READER: Thanks for asking for my help. Let's see if I can read your mind. Your irrational thoughts are:
1)   It's awful that my bike was stolen,
2)   It shouldn't have happened . . . why me?,
3)   I can't stand it, and
4)   When I tell my parents they will scream and yell and that will be terrible.

THOUGHT DETECTIVE #2:   You see, John, it's those irrational thoughts that are getting you *twice* as upset.

JOHN: Okay, *I know irrational thoughts are silly and untrue*. And *I know I always think them when I'm feeling upset*. But what I'm confused about is how to get myself less upset and how to change my irrational thoughts to rational thoughts.

THOUGHT DETECTIVE #1:   That's where we come in. As you remember we taught you how to be a thought detective. We said a thought detective *looks for the facts or evidence. He looks for clues to prove whether our thoughts are rational or irrational*.

THOUGHT DETECTIVE #2:   Now, John, *where is the evidence that it's awful that your bike was stolen? What does awful mean* and prove to us that it was awful.

JOHN: Well, it means the worst thing in the world that can happen . . . it means the end of the world. I don't think I can prove that my bike being lost is the worst thing in the world that can happen. I can think of a lot worse.

THOUGHT DETECTIVE #1:   Now, John, let's see if you can challenge the rest of your irrational ideas.

JOHN: I will try. *I thought that my bike shouldn't have been stolen and I should have been more careful*. Well, in the first place, *it's irrational because it means the world should be the way I, King John, demand it to be*. It's irrational because the world is far from the way I want it to be. *I also have no control over what others may do*.

THOUGHT DETECTIVE #1:   Terrific, John, but you left one irrational thought out. *Where is the evidence that you should have locked it up?*

JOHN: *There is none. If I should of, I would of . . . I guess what I mean is it would have been better if I locked my bike*. But *I'm not perfect* and instead of beating myself over the head about what I should have done, let's see what I could learn from this bad mistake.

(Continued)

MIND READER: That's right. We all don't do the things we *should. We are only human.* But if we get ourselves so upset about our mistakes, we never think about how we can handle things differently. *Putting ourselves down or thinking we are 100% dumb is irrational..*

JOHN: I think there is one more irrational thought that I have. *It will be awful and terrible when I tell my parents.* I think that by saying and believing that, it only scares me and gets me more upset. I know that it won't be awful and I may not like what my parents will say, but that's life, and *I can stand it.*

NARRATOR: How do you feel now?

JOHN: To be honest, I still feel sad and disappointed that my bike was stolen but not nearly as upset.

MIND READER: Well, John, rational thinking does not erase bad feelings or may not ever change the situation, but by thinking rational thoughts, you make things less bad and you get yourself less upset.

THOUGHT DETECTIVE #1: And when you're less upset, you think clearly. Now, what can you do to get your bike back?

JOHN: You know, I have been so upset that I didn't even think about it. Let's see, I can go to the police . . . look for it . . . get my friends to help me and offer a reward. You know, there might be hope that I may find it. Now I see what you mean. If I really believed that things were awful, I would just sit and be upset and have no hope. Even if I don't get my bike back, it's still not awful. I may not like it, but I don't like a lot of things and I'm still alive.

NARRATOR: John has learned that rational thinking may not get his bike back, but it can calm him down. Every time John gets upset in the future, he knows that it's because of his irrational thinking. The best way to change irrational thoughts to rational thoughts is by being a thought detective. If he questions, challenges, and looks for clue words, he can get himself less upset every time.

Role Playing Script II

NARRATOR: Today's crime that we attempt to solve is the "Case of the King of the World Who Thought That Life Was Awful." Chuckie worked on a special project really hard all week. He couldn't wait until he could show it to his father. But his father was busy when Chuckie tried to show him the project. Chuckie got so angry that he lost his temper and got punished.

CHUCKIE: Boy, that's unfair, I got punished. I feel really angry and upset. My father doesn't care about me. Nobody does.

NARRATOR: Chuckie, you seem upset. Would you like to figure out why you are so upset and angry.

CHUCKIE: I know why . . . my father doesn't care about me. Leave me alone . . . I'm mad.

NARRATOR: This looks like a really hard one. This is a job for the Thought Detectives and Mr. Mind Reader.

THOUGHT DETECTIVE #1: Chuckie, you look really mad. What happened?

CHUCKIE: How many times do I have to say it? My father didn't look at my project. Boy, you people are thick.

THOUGHT DETECTIVE #2: Well, Chuckie . . . believe it or not, that's not what's getting you so upset and angry. *A situation or a happening can never get you upset. You upset yourself by your thoughts about what happened.*

CHUCKIE: You're right, I don't believe you. How can my own thoughts get me upset? Are you saying I control my feelings by my thoughts?

THOUGHT DETECTIVE #1: That's right . . . you do control your feelings by your thoughts. In fact, it's your *irrational, silly thoughts* that get you upset. Everytime something happens, your thinking. . . .

CHUCKIE: I still don't believe you. I wasn't thinking anything. I just got angry.

(Continued)

TABLE A.6 *(Continued)*

THOUGHT DETECTIVE #2:   Well, we are going to prove to you that you were thinking irrational thoughts. In fact, we have somebody who is going to read your mind and tell you exactly what you were thinking.

CHUCKIE: This I would like to see.

MIND READER: Hello . . . I am the fantastic, super Mind Reader. I can read all minds. It's as easy as A, B, C.

CHUCKIE: Prove it.

MIND READER: Now, Chuckie, when your father said he didn't want to see your project, you were *thinking* how *terrible* and *awful* it is that he didn't look at your work.

CHUCKIE: It is terrible and awful.

THOUGHT DETECTIVE #1:   *Prove that to us . . . Where is the evidence that it's terrible, horrible, or awful?*

THOUGHT DETECTIVE #2:   The fact that your father didn't look at something you wanted him to doesn't make it awful. Is that the worst thing in the world that could ever happen to you? Because that's what awful means.

THOUGHT DETECTIVE #1:   *Awful means worse than bad.* Aren't you making it worse than it really is?

CHUCKIE: Well, I guess it's far from the worst thing in the world that could ever happen, but it is bad.

THOUGHT DETECTIVE #2:   That's right, it is bad. That thought is a *rational one. We can prove that it's bad, but we can't prove that it's awful.*

MIND READER: If you would have thought to yourself that "it's too bad that my father didn't look at my project, but it's not the end of the world," how do you think you would have felt?

CHUCKIE: A lot less upset. I see what you mean. *If I don't think that something is terrible, I won't feel like it's terrible.* I feel a lot better.

MIND READER: Wait a while. I know for a fact that there is more on your mind. In fact, I see more thoughts that I can read.

CHUCKIE: How do you know?

MIND READER: Easy, I am a super Mind Reader. But let me continue. You were also thinking that my father *should* look at my project and I CAN'T STAND IT, that he is not.

CHUCKIE: Well, shouldn't he?

THOUGHT DETECTIVE #1:   Now Chuckie, there you go again—thinking irrational thoughts. Do you know what "should" means?

THOUGHT DETECTIVE #2:   *Should is a demand.* It's like saying, "I, King Chuckie, demand that people always do what I think they should." Where is the evidence that anybody should do what ever you want them to do? Where is the evidence that you are King of the World?

CHUCKIE: *There is no evidence why people should do what I want them to do*, even if I want them to do it very badly. *I have no control over others*, they do what they want to do.

THOUGHT DETECTIVE #1:   Now, where is the *evidence* that *you* can't stand it when things do not go the way you want them to, you will be very upset. "I can't stand it" is a silly, irrational thought.

CHUCKIE: I would have liked my father to look at my project. I see what you are saying. If I would have thought rational thoughts like, "I wish my father would have looked at my project and it's too bad that he didn't," I wouldn't feel as upset.

MIND READER: You would have felt *disappointed*, but not angry. How do you feel now?

CHUCKIE: A lot less upset. I can really see *how my irrational thoughts can get me upset.* In fact, maybe now I can calmly tell my father how I feel.

(Continued)

MIND READER: That's the point. When you think irrationally, you become so upset you don't act sensibly and you end up in more trouble.

CHUCKIE: Boy, I feel a lot better even though I am not King of the World.

NARRATOR: Another case comes to a close. Chuckie now sees that demanding that things and people be his way will only get him angry and in more trouble. As soon as he stops demanding and "shoulding" and "musting" he will never get upset again.

Role Playing Script III

NARRATOR: Today's case that we will attempt to solve is the "Case of Why Does It Have To Be Me." Little Mary just got some bad news. As she came home from school her mother just informed her that her dentist just called and she has to wear braces. To make things worse, her eye doctor just called and she has to begin to wear glasses. To make things even worse, she just got a haircut and one side is shorter than the other. Mary is feeling *very* depressed, *very* angry, and *very* upset. She is afraid to go to school because she thinks the kids are going to make fun of her.

MARY: Poor me! All of the kids are going to laugh and tease me. I can just imagine the names that they are going to call me. They are going to think I look like a four-eyed tin can. What am I going to do?

NARRATOR: What's the matter, Mary? You seem upset. What could be getting you this upset?

MARY: My world is coming to an end. My rotten luck . . . I got a bad haircut, I'm going to have to wear braces and glasses. How am I ever going to face the kids in school? I think I will change my name or wear a paper bag over my head. Boy, am I depressed!

NARRATOR: Would you like to be less upset and not be as worried about what the other kids are going to say?

MARY: Nothing could make me feel better . . . my world is coming to an end!

NARRATOR: This looks like a job for our Super Heroes. the fantastic Thought Detectives and the six million dollar bionic Mind Reader.

MARY: No, don't bring anyone here. Do you think they will call me names?

THOUGHT DETECTIVE #1:   What seems to be the trouble here?

MARY: Look at me and please no names . . . don't laugh. The kids in school are going to do a job on me.

THOUGHT DETECTIVE #2:   Mary, you're still not telling us what's upsetting you. You're only telling us what may happen. *As you know, a happening can never, ever get us upset.*

MARY: Look, I'm going to be so embarrassed in school. I look like a four-eyed metal mouth. In fact, that's what the kids are going to call me.

THOUGHT DETECTIVE #1:   So let's suppose that does happen. What's still getting you *so* upset?

MARY: I know, I know. You caught me. *It's my irrational thoughts that are getting me so upset.* Well, if people can show me how I can un-upset myself by my thoughts, boy, will I feel grateful!

THOUGHT DETECTIVE #2:   It's as easy as ABC. Firstly, if I called you a pink elephant, would that get you upset?

MARY: No, of course not . . . that wouldn't bother me at all. I know I'm not a pink elephant.

THOUGHT DETECTIVE #1:   That's right, you wouldn't get upset because you would be thinking something like this: *Just because someone calls me a pink elephant, that doesn't make me one.* That, Mary, is a *rational thought.*

THOUGHT DETECTIVE #2:   Even if someone calls you a name that may be true, you still do not have to get yourself upset. *Remember, it's not the name or the name caller that gets you upset, it's your irrational thinking.*

MARY: I bet right now that you are going to call in the Mind Reader to read my mind. See, I paid attention in my health class.

(Continued)

TABLE A.6 *(Continued)*

MIND READER: Hello, Mary . . . I'm the six million dollar bionic Mind Reader. Watch me read your mind and watch me read everyone's mind. I will show everyone who gets upset when they are being teased exactly what *irrational thoughts they are thinking*. Mary, let's suppose I call you a four-eyed metal mouth, how would you feel?

MARY: Really mad, angry, and upset. I hate being teased.

MIND READER: You hate being teased because of your *irrational thoughts*. You see, every time someone teases you or calls you a name, you think that:
1)   It's awful that I'm being teased,
2)   I can't stand being teased,
3)   They shouldn't be teasing me, and
4)   The name that I am being called is true.

MARY: That's exactly what I am thinking. I know you people think that nothing is awful, but being teased really bothers me.

THOUGHT DETECTIVE #1:   Do you mean to tell us that just because someone calls you a name that you do not like . . . that's Awful? Do you remember what Awful and Terrible mean?

MARY: It means the worst thing in the world that could happen to me. It means 101% bad.

THOUGHT DETECTIVE #2:   Do you mean to tell us that someone calling you a name is like the worst thing in the world that can happen?

MARY: I know that it really is not Awful, but just bad. But I still do not like it when I'm being called a name.

MIND READER: That's right, you may not like it, *but you can stand it*. After all, can a name really hurt you? If you believe that it is Awful and you can't stand it when you are called names, how do you think you will feel?

MARY: Like it is Awful . . . I probably will feel angry and upset. I know those are *irrational feelings*.

THOUGHT DETECTIVE #1:   Well, Mary how do you think the person who calls you names wants you to feel?

MARY: He wants me to get myself upset and angry.

THOUGHT DETECTIVE #2:   That's right, so by your thinking *irrationally*, you act exactly the way he wants you to. *The more you act like you're upset when you're called names, the more likely it is that the person will tease you more*.

THOUGHT DETECTIVE #1:   After all, it's no fun teasing someone if they are not going to get upset.

MARY: Okay, I understand that names cannot get me upset because they are just words. But I still get angry and upset at the person who teases me. I think *I shouldn't be teased*.

THOUGHT DETECTIVE #2:   Mary, do you realize what you just said?

MARY: I said people SHOULDN'T tease me . . . it's not nice.

THOUGHT DETECTIVE #1:   Where is the EVIDENCE that they SHOULDN'T tease you? "Should" means that you are Queen of the World and you control what comes out of people's mouths. "Should" means that things be exactly the way you want them to be.

MARY: Well, I know I'm not the Queen of the World. I guess what I mean is that I would like them not to tease me, but I have no control over what they are going to do or how they act. Okay, now how is this going to help me tomorrow when I go to school with my glasses and braces?

THOUGHT DETECTIVE #2:   Well, if you think *rationally* when people call you names *you will stay pretty calm*. In fact, let's try it now. We will call you a name and you try to think rational thoughts to yourself.

NARRATOR: You have purple hair . . .

(Continued)

MARY: It's not Awful that I'm being teased . . . I don't like it, but I can stand it.

NARRATOR: You look like an overstuffed turkey . . .

MARY: Just because someone calls me a name, that doesn't make that name true.

NARRATOR: Your eyeballs look like snowballs and your neck looks like a giraffe's.

MARY: I wish that person would stop calling me names, but I can't control him. I wonder what his problem is.

NARRATOR: Hey, four-eyes . . . your mouth looks like a steel trap . . . .

Source: Miller, 1978.

ROLE PLAYING PROBLEMS (adapted from Miller, 1978)
(Materials: copies of role playing problems with rational alternatives, see Table A.7)

Three children role play at a time: one as a Narrator, one as Role Model (teacher, parent or friend), and one as the Rational Problem Solver. Narrator and Role Model each read their parts, and the Rational Problem Solver tries to respond aloud with rational self-talk. If he is unable to do this, give help from the rational alternative provided. Where only one rational response is given spontaneously, contribute the others.

TABLE A.7. General Rational Role Playing Problems

Objective: To get student to spontaneously behaviorally rehearse rational alternatives to problematic situations without the role playing script.

1. NARRATOR: "Jimmy went out to play with some of his friends. However, as soon as he arrived on the ball field, his friends began to tease him, and told him to get lost."

   ROLE MODEL FRIENDS: "We don't want to play with you . . . you're a jerk."

   RATIONAL ALTERNATIVES: (1) It's too bad my friends do not want to play with me; (2) Because my friends choose not to be with me, that doesn't make me a jerk; (3) It's not awful or terrible that my friends are rejecting me, I would like them to like me, but I don't need them to like me.

2. NARRATOR: "Sally was supposed to go to a birthday party right after school but her teacher made her stay after school to finish some class work."

   ROLE MODEL TEACHER: "Sally, you have to stay to finish your arithmetic."

   RATIONAL ALTERNATIVES: (1) It's too bad that I'm not going to go to the party, I may not like it, but that's the breaks; (2) It's not terrible that I'm not doing what I want; (3) It's not going to help by getting myself upset . . . I won't die if I don't go to the party; (4) I would prefer if my teacher was more reasonable.

3. NARRATOR: "Marc received an F on an exam in which all of his friends received an A."

   ROLE MODEL FRIEND: "Marc, what did you get on the test?"

   RATIONAL ALTERNATIVES: (1) It's unfortunate that I did not do as well as I wanted; (2) Failing the test does not make *me* a failure, it only makes me a FHB (fallible human being); (3) It's too bad I failed, I will try harder on the next exam . . . what's important is that I try; (4) Not everyone can be good at everything.

4. NARRATOR: "Arlette's father promised to get her a new ten-speed bike but changed his mind."

   ROLE MODEL FATHER: "Sorry, Arlette, the bike is much too expensive . . . no bike."

(Continued)

TABLE A.7 *(Continued)*

RATIONAL ALTERNATIVES: (1) So what if I didn't get the bike, nobody can get everything she wants; (2) I would have preferred having the bike, but I don't need it; (3) Perhaps someday I will get the bike, but if not, it's not awful—no kid ever died because she didn't get a bike.

5.   NARRATOR: "Jeffrey had football tryouts today and only two boys didn't make the team. Jeffrey was one of them. Now, he has to break the news to his father."

  ROLE MODEL FATHER: "Well, Champ, are you going to be another Joe Namath?"

  RATIONAL ALTERNATIVES: (1) Not everyone can make the team, I don't have to be on a team to feel like somebody; (2) I can always practice and try again next year . . . and if I don't make it next time, it's still not awful; (3) I would have liked to make the team, but I can still enjoy football, even if I'm not on the team.

6.   NARRATOR: "Tina was in class when her teacher called on her. She gave the wrong answer and all the students began to laugh."

  ROLE MODEL TEACHER: "Tina, what's wrong with you?"

  RATIONAL ALTERNATIVES: (1) No one is always right . . . everybody makes mistakes sometimes; (2) The world is not going to come to an end because my friends are laughing at me—I might not like it, but I can stand it; (3) It's okay to make mistakes, making mistakes is part of learning.

7.   NARRATOR: "Sue came home from school and went over to play with her dog, Frisky, but she couldn't find him. She goes upstairs and asks her mother where Frisky is."

  ROLE MODEL MOTHER: "Sue, Frisky is sick, we took him to the animal hospital."

  RATIONAL ALTERNATIVES: (1) If he dies, I will be upset, but dogs are like people and they have to die too . . . nobody can live forever; (2) It's too bad that Frisky is sick . . . I can only hope he will get better and if not I can learn to accept it.

8.   NARRATOR: "While Chuckie was watching his favorite Star Trek episode his father yelled to him to take the garbage out."

  ROLE MODEL FATHER: "Turn off that set and do your chores."

  RATIONAL ALTERNATIVES: (1) It would have been better if my father asked me later, but I have no control over that; (2) Maybe I can calmly ask him to wait, and if he won't it's not terrible that I won't be able to finish my program; (3) I may not like what my father just did, but that's life; (4) It's annoying that my father interrupted me but it's not the worst thing that could happen.

9.   NARRATOR: "Mary is having a big party, everyone is invited except Joey."

  ROLE MODEL FRIENDS: "Hey Joey! Are you going to Mary's party? It's going to be super—all the ice cream you could eat."

  RATIONAL ALTERNATIVES: (1) It's too bad that I wasn't invited; (2) It's a pain that not everyone likes me, but not everyone will.

10.   NARRATOR: "Danny and David mowed lawns all summer to save up money to buy a go-cart. Danny was in charge of the money but accidentally lost all of the money."

  ROLE MODEL DANNY: "Dave, I've got some bad news . . . Are you sitting down? I lost all the money."

  RATIONAL ALTERNATIVES: (1) It's not a disaster that Danny lost all the money, it's just too bad; (2) Blaming Danny for being a mistake maker and a fallible human being will not do anything; (3) Becoming upset over this will not accomplish a thing; (4) It's frustrating when things like this occur, but it's not the end of the world.

(Continued)

11.   NARRATOR: "It's Jenny's first day in school and she doesn't want to go because she is afraid that people will not like her. However, her mother talked her into going."

ROLE MODEL TEACHER: "Come over here, Jenny, I want to introduce you to the other children."

RATIONAL ALTERNATIVES: (1) Nothing so terrible will happen if I try to talk to another student; (2) If one person doesn't like me, it doesn't mean I'm an unlikeable person; (3) I hope they like me but I can't be liked by everyone.

Source: Miller, 1978.

SESSION 11.   MAKING ASSUMPTIONS

Notes for the Leader

Provide definitions of new concepts for the group.

> A *belief*: a conviction that something is true.
>
> *Sound assumption:* a belief likely to be true.
>
> *Unsound assumption:* something that you believe to be true but which in reality is not. Evidence you find will not support it.

Plenty of everyday examples will help to enliven this largely didactic session. Evolve definitions through discussion where possible. Ask children to repeat them *in their own words*.

Objectives

For each child

1.   to learn that having an opinion about something doesn't make it true;
2.   to learn that some of the things we believe (our beliefs) are not true (are based on unsound assumptions);
3.   to learn that unsound assumptions lead to mistakes.

OUR EVERYDAY ASSUMPTIONS (adapted from Knaus, 1974)
(Materials: none)

Ask the group why they think things like: people can fly to the moon (it's a fact that has been tested); going to college is good (this is an opinion based on preference or taste, but it is neither true or false, it depends on one's goals.) Introduce the notion that we also believe that some of our opinions are facts because we take them for granted or assume we're correct—even if our belief hasn't been tested.

In order to establish that we make assumptions all the time, and that some are sound and some are unsound, discuss the following. "Everyday we come to school, we *assume* that there is school that day, we assume that the school hasn't burnt down, we assume that the classroom will not collapse. Why do we take these things for granted? Why do you think we don't test out these guesses? Have any of you had a ceiling fall on you lately? Or the chairs you sat in collapse?" Ask the students to think about what everyday life would be like if they didn't take some things for granted or make sound assumptions about them. Establish that we make certain *sound* assumptions based on our first hand experience in the past.

Ask the children if they would be acting on a sound assumption by entering a room or building which had a sign outside warning that the building or the ceilings could collapse at any moment.

Ask the group if they have acted on either sound or unsound assumptions by crossing on the red light (unsound); thinking they were going to fail a subject because they had failed five out of six weekly tests and had not studied since (sound); thinking they were going to fail a subject because they had failed one out of six weekly tests (unsound); crossing the road on the green light (sound). Have students give reasons for their answers.

I SEE—I ASSUME (Vernon, 1980, p. 121)
(Materials: none)

Discuss with the children what an assumption is " . . . a statement which is taken for granted to be true, and in fact may be true, but needs to be checked out." Illustrate with an example such as: "I assume your eyesight is bad since you wear glasses." (The person could have poor eyesight, but could also just be wearing fashion glasses, so the assumption needs to be proven true before it is fact.) Next have the students pair up, facing each other. In each pair, person 1 says to person 2 "I see that you (have on red), therefore I assume you (like that color)." Then person 2 repeats the same procedure to person 1, with no response from either partner. After several rounds, have students discuss the assumptions with each other. As a class, have them react to the following.

1. What do you discover when you check out your assumptions to see whether there is evidence for them?
2. Are there times in real life where you make assumptions about things which in fact aren't true?
3. When this happens, what kinds of effects are there, if any?
4. Do you think assumptions are harmful or helpful? Explain.
5. If you were to make a general "rule" about assumptions, what would it be? (Check it out.)

THE HUDDLE GAME
(adapted from Knaus, 1974)
(Materials: a game such as a bean bag; envelope containing one Yes card and
          four No cards)

Select a child from the group. Provide him with an envelope containing one

Yes card and four or more No cards. Tell him that while he plays with the bean bag, you will select a child from the group who will ask to join you. When someone asks to join, go into a huddle (go out of sight) where the rest of the group cannot see you. Draw a card from the envelope and if it says Yes, the child can join. If No, he can't. If a new player joins the team explain to him the rules when you are out of the room selecting a card to see if another child can play. Play as long as time allows.

Ask the children what assumptions they made about why they were included or not included.

How did they feel if they were not included?

Were they *sound* or *unsound* assumptions?

Ask the group to help challenge irrational thoughts associated with unsound assumptions (e.g., being rejected).

What was the consequence of the unsound assumptions? (Mistakes and unhappiness.)

Sessions for Youth (13–17 Years)

SESSION 1.   ICEBREAKER

Notes for the Leader

Introduce yourself to the group and group members to each other. Explain the purpose of the group and how these young clients in particular come to be part of it.

The activity in this session provides for a significant input by each individual, and stresses interaction by individuals with as many group members as possible. It also places emphasis on listening to others from the beginning.

Objectives

For each member

1.   to initiate self-disclosure and "safe" facts and preferences;
2.   to develop a trusting attitude to others in the group as a basis for further self-disclosure.

GETTING TO KNOW YOU
(Materials: none)

The group forms into pairs, with if possible, someone they don't know. A talks to B about himself, telling for example, facts, likes and dislikes; then roles are reversed and B talks to A. The group comes together and listeners present what they can remember about their partners. New pairs are then formed and the process repeated, with each person telling the new partner facts and attitudes not already shared.

The activity can be repeated a number of times, depending on group interest and time available.

Optional Activity

THE BLIND WALK
(See Session 1, for 8–12 year olds)

SESSION 2.   FINDING FEELINGS

Notes for the Leader

Many group members are likely to have a limited vocabulary with which to discuss emotions. This session will enable them to extend their language, thus providing a basis for identification and evaluation of their own and others' emotions. While adolescents may have a reasonable vocabulary, they are often in the habit of stereotyping expressions of their emotional state using slang and sometimes inappropriate and exaggerated words.

We advise *the ongoing use of a large scrapbook* or notebook by each group member, so that he can write, draw, and keep notes from session to session. Members can be invited to copy stimulating ideas and drawings onto poster paper for the group room board. Exercises and homework activities can also be included in this book.

Objectives

For each member

1. to build up a shared language about common feelings, which can then be used in identifying feelings and talking about them.

DICTIONARY OF EMOTIONS
(Materials: blackboard; pens and paper; access to dictionary)
    Ask group members to write down as many "feeling" words as they can on their sheets of paper.
    Ask them to share what they have written. Make a group list on the board. Contribute from the list below, if necessary. Invite them to add words contributed by others to their own lists. (Distinguish between "physical" and "emotional" feelings, if this is a difficulty in discussion: a physical feeling is a reaction to something in the environment, e.g., hot, cold. An emotional feeling comes from our appraisal of outside events, i.e., from our inner thoughts and evaluations.)

Use words from Session 2 lists from 5–7 years and 8–12 years, plus those below.

disgusted	hateful	elated
doubtful	uptight	desperate
peaceful	low	satisfied
oppressed	sympathetic	insecure
interested	uneasy	discouraged
thrilled	resentful	proud
great	delighted	anxious
stubborn	bored	sorrowful
restless	amused	apprehensive
frightened	enthusiastic	hostile
grateful	surprised	depressed
puzzled	impatient	distraught
grief-stricken	hopeful	freaked out
grouchy	panicky	irritated
blue	confident	messed up
apathetic		

FEELING THERMOMETER

Introduce a picture or model of the feeling thermometer (see Figure A.8) and explain its use, as a way of describing feelings of varying intensity. Ask each member to think of two events they have experienced, one pleasant and one unpleasant. Ask them to name the feeling(s) occasioned by each event, and to use the feeling thermometer to describe the *intensity* of the feeling. Examples could be "going to hospital for an operation," fear–8, "being selected for the baseball team," happy–9.

MIMING OF OPPOSITES

(Materials: none)

Divide the group into pairs and let each pair of children select two words that are opposite, or nearly opposite, e.g., happy/sad, enthusiastic/apathetic, relaxed/worried. Each pair plans short, silent scenes to act out, illustrating each of the feelings. The group watches and tries to guess the pair of opposites being mimed. Group members record their guesses and also rate the feeling intensity from 1 to 10, using the feeling thermometer. At the end of each scene, the actors are asked the names of the feelings and their own ratings of feeling intensity. Invite the group to share their responses. In discussion, highlight any differences of judgment about the nature of the feeling and its intensity. Ask the group: How can we know what others are feeling? Is it wise to check? How can one do this?

SESSION 3.   EVENTS OCCASION FEELINGS BUT DO NOT CAUSE THEM

Notes for the Leader

During this session, group members will learn that a single event can occasion different feelings in individuals. Encourage discussion to probe the question of what causes the different feelings. Exploration of their feelings changing over time in response to the same event or object will highlight the same idea from a different angle.

Objectives

For each member

1.   to learn that events of themselves do not cause feelings;
2.   to observe that individuals react differently to the same event;
3.   to observe that their own feelings about things can change.

WHAT DO YOU FEEL? (adapted from Kranzler, 1974)
(Materials: workbooks, including the feeling thermometer)
   Develop a list of items responded to differently by young people in the age range of your group:

classical music	being watched while working
hot weather	darkness
big dogs	telling a joke in front of the class
eating peas	

Ask each group member to write down the predominant feeling the have when they imagine the above happening to them. Ask them to use the feeling thermometer to rate their feelings from 1 to 10.

   Discuss feelings associated with each item and highlight differences (e.g., that an event which occasioned worry and upset in one person, did not do so for another). Stress that any given item is not associated with only one feeling in the group.

FROM THE PAST
   Ask members to list in their workbooks two or three favorite toys from early childhood, and two or three favorite games from elementary school days. Ask them to rate their positive feelings toward these, using the feeling thermometer. Then ask them to write down and rate how they feel towards those toys and games now.

Optional Activity

BLINDFOLD AND IMAGINE
(see Session 3 for 8–12 year olds)
    Discuss: From all the above activities, what can we conclude about where
feelings from from?
    Emphasize that there is no one to one correspondence between an event and
a feeling; that individuals respond differently to the same event.

SESSION 4.   THOUGHTS CAUSE FEELINGS

Notes for the Leader

The critical connection of thought with feeling is made in this session. The link
between feeling and behavior is also made, in preparation for a full HTFB
analysis in the next session (see Session 4, 8–12 year sessions). Emphasize the
causal connection between quality of thoughts and quality of feelings. Some of
the ideas presented may hold anxiety provoking implications for some group
members. Having to take responsibility for one's feelings, rather than adopting
an "I can't help it" attitude is one such implication. Looking honestly at one's
thinking and doing away with self-pretence can also be anxiety provoking.
Difficulties in this session or refusal to accept the ideas may stem from such
anxieties. A gradual approach to the individual's own private world of thoughts
and feelings by initial discussion of the ideas in less personal contexts can be
valuable.

Objectives

For each member

1. to learn that thoughts cause feelings;
2. to learn that unpleasant thoughts cause unpleasant feelings;
3. to learn that pleasant thoughts cause pleasant feelings.

THOUGHT GAME: TELL THE FEELING
(See Session 3 for 8–12 year olds)

THOUGHT-FEELING GAME
    Each group member is asked to think of either a pleasant or an unpleasant
thought. Elicit feelings that accompany each thought, and write both thoughts
and feelings on the board.

Pleasant Thoughts	Feelings
1. I'm going sailing on Saturday.	excited
2. I have my favorite lunch today.	pleased
3. My team won yesterday.	proud

Unpleasant Thoughts	Feelings
1. The math test is tomorrow, I'll probably fail.	anxious
2. I'm not allowed to go to the rock concert with my friends.	angry
3. I'm not invited to that big party and what's more my friends didn't even notice I've been left out.	gloomy
	depressed

Emphasize the relationship between pleasant/unpleasant thoughts and pleasant/unpleasant feelings.

HAPPENINGS, THOUGHTS AND FEELINGS
(Materials: copies of Figure A.19)

Explain that the numbers below are the same as on the feeling thermometer.

Discuss their responses with emphasis on quality of thoughts and quality of feelings.

Ask them what they *might do* if they really experienced the thoughts and feelings in each example.

What is happening?

Happening	⟶	Thoughts
....		It's not fair. I hate him.
....		....

angry
Feeling   1   2   3   4   5   6   7   8   9   10

What are you thinking?

Happening	⟶	Thoughts
End of term exams coming and you have not studied.		....
		....

worry
Feeling   1   2   3   4   5   6   7   8   9   10

What are you feeling?

| Happening | ⟶ | Thoughts |
| You have just been laughed at by a member of the opposite sex. | | Am I hopeless, what's wrong with me. |

What are you feeling?
Feeling   1   2   3   4   5   6   7   8   9   10

Figure A.19.

SESSION 5.   MY OWN THOUGHTS

Notes for the Leader

Encourage the group members to examine their own thinking habits and identify thoughts they have frequently in association with pleasant and unpleasant feelings. Support discussion of difficulties experienced when they try to "find" their thoughts. The process may be modeled for them by sharing some of your own thoughts.

Objectives

For each member

1.   to explore which of his own thoughts lead to pleasant feelings;
2.   to explore which of his own thoughts lead to unpleasant feelings.

EXPERIENTIAL SIMULATION
(See Session 4 for 8–12 year olds)

INSTANT REPLAY
(See Session 4 for 8–12 year olds)

HTFB: HAPPENING–THOUGHT–FEELING–BEHAVIOR
(See Session 4 for 8–12 year olds)

SESSION 6.   THOUGHTS CAN BE RATIONAL OR IRRATIONAL

Notes for the Leader

Explain definitions of rational and irrational, according to the maturity of your group. Rational is sensible, a logical idea that seems to be true, backed up by experience.

Irrational is unreasonable, an absurd idea, one that is false, lacking in evidence, not based on experience, illogical, not sensible.

While helping group members to identify some of their own irrational and rational thoughts remember that the degree of self-understanding will vary among group members. Acceptance of their limited awareness will be especially important if the leader and other group members perceive their irrational thinking before they are aware of it themselves.

Objectives

For each member

1. to acquire the concepts of rational and irrational thoughts;
2. to identify some of his own rational and irrational thoughts.

PICK THE RATIONAL AND IRRATIONAL THOUGHT
(Materials: copies of Figure A.20)

   Distribute copies of the worksheet and ask each member to classify each thought as rational or irrational. Ask for important criteria which help them decide. Ask each member to try to make the example a nonexample by changing the wording of the thought. Help them with this if they cannot do it.

Directions: Place a check if you think the thought is rational or irrational.

	Thought	Rational	Irrational
1.	That Steven is an idiot—real stupid.	_____	_____
2.	I wish I did better in maths class.	_____	_____
3.	I'm no good.	_____	_____
4.	I can't stand it when my teacher doesn't call on me when I raise my hand in class.	_____	_____
5.	I do not like being told to do the dishes.	_____	_____
6.	I am finding it very difficult to complete my English assignment.	_____	_____

Figure A.20.   Pick the Rational and Irrational Thought

THOUGHT POSTERS
(Materials: poster paper; paints)

   In groups of two or three, group members are asked to plan and produce posters showing a person with two large "thought bubbles" (one expressing a rational thought, the other expressing an irrational thought) in response to *one* of the following.

   The person:
      is rejected by a friend;
      is not invited to a party;
      has just been told the exam is tomorrow when he thought it was two weeks away;
      has just been told the youth group trip he is going on will involve rock climbing and he is afraid of heights.

Post them on the group room wall to share the ideas and remind group members of the concepts.

SESSION 7. THOUGHTS CAN MAKE YOU FEEL BAD

Mr Head
It's Not So Terrible   }   (See Session 6 for 8–12 year olds)
Identify and Dispute

SESSION 8. THOUGHTS AND BELIEFS

Notes for the Leader

All of us say both rational and irrational things to ourselves from time to time. These thoughts stem from our *beliefs* (appraisals, evaluations) about ourselves, others around us, and about events that happen to us. Some of those beliefs are *irrational* and some are *rational*. Irrational beliefs lead to irrational thinking. In this session we begin to focus on some key words which can cue us to the presence of irrational beliefs. Should, must, and ought are examples of such words, and they signify irrational *demanding*. (See earlier chapters for a discussion of the irrational aspects of demandingness.)

Objectives

For each member

1.   to learn that irrational thinking stems from irrational beliefs;
2.   to learn that words can help us identify irrational beliefs, e.g., "should," "must," "ought" reflect irrational demanding;
3.   to explore the idea that irrational demanding may lead to anger, depression and anxiety.

A Person Called "Troubles" (adapted from Knaus, 1974)
(Materials: blackboard)
   Introduce on the blackboard the person called "Troubles" (see Figure A.21). Draw his sad/worried face and give him thought bubbles with the following thoughts.

1.   Nobody likes me.
2.   That's not fair!
3.   I mustn't fail my math.
4.   I'll have to win in that debate.
5.   This class is so boring! I can't stand it!

Figure A.21.   "Troubles" (from Knaus, 1974).

Ask the group to describe the way "Troubles" is likely to *feel* most of the time (unhappy, mad, depressed, miserable, angry).

Ask them what *beliefs* might underly these thoughts of "Troubles."

I must be liked by everyone.
Everyone should be fair to me.
I must succeed in everything I do.

Ask the group members whether they know anyone who thinks this way or has these beliefs.

Have they ever thought this way themselves?
How did they feel?
Ask, what could "Troubles" *do* if he wanted to be happier?

(Introduce the concept of changing beliefs by changing one's thinking: in readiness for the next session.)

YOUNG'S TECHNIQUE (adapted from Young, 1974a)
(Materials: HTFB sheets as in Figure A.12, blank except for "should," "ought," "must" in the T column)

Ask members to close their eyes and think of a time when they became very angry. Ask them to relive the scene for a few moments in their imagination.

Distribute the HTFB sheets and ask each member to write in the H, F and B. Then ask them to fill in the Ts around the "should," "ought" and "must." Other irrational concepts of "awfulizing" about what happened and "blaming/condemning" others for mistake making and wrong doing could also be emphasized.

Invite members to share their analyses and discuss them in the group. Ask, were the thoughts and beliefs rational or irrational? Why? What could they do to change the irrational ones?

Optional Activity

CALL ME RET-MAN AND HAVE A BALL
(Merrifield, C. & Merrifield, R., Institute for Rational Living, N.Y., 1979)
(Materials: copies of comic book as in title)

Groups members may read the comic individually and then discuss it in the group as a supplement to other activities for this session.

SESSION 9.   CHALLENGING AND DISPUTING

Notes for the Leader

Ideas to emphasize in this session include: we can avoid getting very upset by changing our thinking; we can change our thinking by challenging and disputing our irrational beliefs; we would do well to avoid "irrational beliefs about irrational beliefs"—it's not bad or terrible to hold an irrational belief; there is no law of the universe that says people must, ought or should be rational. But increasing our rationality gives us a better chance of fulfilling our own goals and avoiding self-defeating behavior.

Objectives

For each member

1.   to learn that challenging irrational beliefs can lead to changes in thinking and less upset feelings;
2.   to practice challenging and disputing some common irrational beliefs;
3.   to practice challenging and disputing some of his or her own irrational beliefs.

THINKING THROUGH THE CHALLENGE (adapted from Gerald & Eyman, 1981, pp. 64–65)
(Materials: a copy for each group member of questions 1 to 5 below, including example answers)
    Read (or express in your own words) the following instructions to the group: "Once you have decided, either by yourself or with the help of others, that some of your actions or emotions and the beliefs that produce them are irrational, here is a way to bring about some change. It is a technique for challenging and disputing any irrational belief, and it involves asking yourself a series of questions. As you ask yourself the questions, answer as honestly as you can, and use our examples to help you analyze your answers." Ask group members to look back over their written records from Session 6 (e.g., HTFB sheets) and earlier sessions, to pinpoint an irrational belief they would like to work on. When everyone has selected one, begin with question 1; the leader or group members in turn read each question and example. Pause after each one for the group to write answers. If a member experiences difficulties, the group can discuss it and help the individual. When each step has been completed by all the group, invite members to read out their answers for discussion. If a variety of irrational beliefs are exemplified more than one session may be needed to discuss each person's analysis thoroughly.

1.   *What is the irrational belief?* Define it. State it as you would say it to yourself.
     Example: If I don't make the school basketball team this term, it means I'm no good and I'll never be able to play team basketball again.
2.   *How much do you want to give up this belief—how willing are you to work at the challenging and disputing?* Answer on a scale of 1 (very little) to 10 (very much). The closer your honest answer is to 10 the better chance you will have of giving up this irrational belief.

3. *What proof is there to show that the belief is false (irrational)?*
   Examples:
   a. Even if you don't make the school team, it does not mean that you're no good (overall as a person) and it may or may not mean that you are not skilled in basketball.
   b. If you don't make the school team this year, you might make it another year.
   c. If you're not accepted in this particular situation, there is no good reason to generalize to all situations. You could become a valuable member of a team for a community center or a boy's or girl's club or a Y.
   d. Even if you're very poorly skilled in basketball, there is no reason that you can't play the game at your own pace and level and enjoy it. If you care about it, you probably can improve.
   e. There are many examples of people who have failed in some task or endeavor, only to go on to success in the same area at a later time. A number of professional basketball players did not get on their high school team.

4. *Does any evidence exist of the truth of this belief?*
   Example: No. Not making a school basketball team, especially if you worked hard at it, is very disappointing. That kind of rejection can lead to all kinds of negative feelings—but in no way does it prove you're no good. Because that implies you are never good in anything you do, never have been, and never will be and step 3 above shows this to be false.

5. *Can I rationally support this belief?* After you carefully progress from steps 1 to 4 above, your answer to this question will probably be NO!

SIX IRRATIONAL CHARACTERS (adapted from McMullin & Casey, 1975)
(Materials: reproduction of the characters in Figure A.22. These may be blackboard drawings or paper copies. Simple dressing up clothes or paper hats may be used in this activity, but are not essential)
Using the reproductions, introduce to the group the following six characters who each symbolize an irrational belief.

Monster ("It's dangerous")
Fairy Tale ("Things should be different")
I stink ("I'm no good")
You stink ("You're no good")
Doomsday ("It's horrible")
Namby Pamby ("I can't stand it")

For each situation described below, ask the group to select two or three characters appropriate for role playing the situation. Ask two or three mem-

FAIRY TALE

Fairy Tale — 'Things should be different!' These are thoughts that situations should be changed, when it's not in one's power to change them. For instance, 'People shouldn't be so selfish.' or 'I'd be a lot happier if it didn't rain so much.'

MONSTER

Monster — 'It's dangerous.' These thoughts tend to upset people by placing the label 'dangerous' on situations. Then they start responding to the label, instead of the situation! For instance, 'It's dangerous to be depressed.' or 'I've been anxious lately, and that's really dangerous.' What is the real danger?

I STINK

I Stink — 'I'm no good.' At best, these thoughts are gross overgeneralizations. They always end up making the person feel bad about himself. For instance, 'Since I can't cook, I can't do anything right.' or simply, 'I'll probably never have very many friends.'

YOU STINK

You Stink — 'He's no good.' These, too, are overgeneraliz-ations. Usually a person is not totally wrong; he has more than one side. But even if he is totally wrong, hating won't make him change his evil ways. Nor is it a very pleasant emotion to feel in any case. Here are some examples, 'I hate my son because he never does what I tell him.' or 'I hate my boss because he's too cheap!'

DOOMSDAY

Doomsday — 'It's terrible, horrible and catastrophic!' These are thoughts that grossly exaggerate and dwell on tragedy. It can easily reach a point where all we feel is pain and it is difficult to go on leading a normal life. For instance, 'My husband asking for a divorce is the worst thing that could happen to me.' or 'I cannot go on living now that my daughter has died.'

NAMBY PAMBY

Namby Pamby — 'I can't stand it!' These are thoughts that a person can't tolerate a situation when, in fact, he can. Usually, these thoughts produce so much anxiety that the person can't think of solutions to the problems he 'can't stand.' For instance, 'I can't stand my wife's snoring!' or 'I can't tolerate my job!' — when he has stood it for years.

Figure A.22. Six Irrational Characters (from McMullin & Casey, 1975).

bers to role play it with emphasis on expressing the irrational beliefs. Other group members write down the irrational beliefs and the whole group discusses them at the end and tries to come up with counters—summary ideas that challenge the irrational belief (e.g., This belief . . . "hurts me"; "does not accomplish my goals"; "is not true"; "gets me into trouble with people").

The following situations may be used, or any that are problematic for group members.

> Failed a test.
> Not been invited to a party.
> Turned down by a boy/girl.
> Caught out telling a lie.

EMPTY CHAIR (from Nardi, 1979)
(Materials: two chairs)

Invite a group member to tell about an upsetting event that has happened since the previous session. Invite him to sit in *one of two empty chairs* to tell what happened. One chair represents rational thinking and the other irrational thinking. Group members are asked to listen closely to the description of the event. They may ask questions about how the person was thinking or feeling. Whenever someone thinks he detects irrational thinking he asks the person in the chair to move to the other chair. When a suitable rational challenge can be expressed, the person may return to the rational chair.

Optional Activity

MR. HEAD (See Session 7 for 8–12 year olds. This activity may be useful for lower age groups in this range, i.e., 13 and 14 year olds.)

SESSION 10.   SOUND AND UNSOUND ASSUMPTIONS

OUR EVERYDAY ASSUMPTIONS
I SEE, I ASSUME   (See Session 11 for 8–12 year olds)
THE HUDDLE GAME

SESSION 11.   WANTS AND NEEDS

Notes for the Leader

You may wish to begin the session with a discussion of people's basic needs. Point out that people think and act as though they *need* more things than they actually do.

Objectives

For each member

1. to distinguish between wants and needs;
2. to practice challenging irrational needs and expressing them as rational wishes or preferences.

SURVIVAL
(Materials: none)
   Ask the group to imagine themselves and some others on a desert island. What do they need in order to survive?
   What does the *demanding* person assume about his needs? He assumes he needs more things than he actually does.

CHALLENGING IRRATIONAL NEEDS AND DEMANDS
(Materials: blackboard)
   List on the board the following *four irrational needs*.

1. Having your own way ("I must have my way and go out. I don't care what you say.")
2. Being successful ("I've failed English. I'm stupid.")
3. Being liked by all ("I'm feeling awful. He doesn't like me.")
4. Demand for comfort ("I can't stand it when I have to do homework.")

Discuss these and use the following questions to help them challenge.
   Does it have to be the way I want?
   What terrible consequence could follow if I don't get my way?
   Pairs can role play the opposite attitudes for each example (the rational and irrational) and then reverse their roles.

SESSION 12.   OVERGENERALIZING IS IRRATIONAL

Notes for the Leader

Overgeneralizing underlies much irrational thinking in relation to oneself ("I'm hopeless"; "I'm a failure"; "I'm the worst"; "I'll never be any good") and in relation to others ("He's always mean to me"; "You never let me have what I want"). Activities in this session help group members to see themselves and others as complex individuals, distinct from their performances (behavior).

Objectives

For each member

1. to learn that overgeneralizing is irrational;
2. to learn that focusing only on negative qualities of people (self and others) is irrational, because people also have positive qualities;
3. to learn that people are not "good" or "bad";
4. to learn to challenge and change her negative irrational thoughts and beliefs to negative *rational* thoughts and beliefs;
5. to learn that thinking negative irrational thoughts leads to more upset than thinking negative *rational* thoughts.

JUNKING YOURSELF
(See Session 9 for 8–12 year olds)

COMPLEX ME
(See Session 8 for 8–12 year olds)

OVERGENERALIZING IS IRRATIONAL (adapted by Kranzler, 1974)

1. Have students make a list of all the different things they can think of that they do well, e.g., play the piano, football, mathematics, etc. Then have them list one or two things that they think they do poorly, e.g., English essays, helping around the house, etc.

     Ask them, "Which are you, *a failure*, or a competent person?"

     Help them to conclude that they are neither, that they can never become more or less than a *person* who does some things well and some things poorly, and that when they conclude that they are a *failure* because they fail at some tasks, or a *fool* because they sometimes behave foolishly, or a *jerk* because they sometimes behave "jerkily," then they are overgeneralizing—they are saying that their entire self is defined by only one of their behaviors or characteristics. Thus, they can *never* be a dumb person, a shy person, or a mean person. Only a person who sometimes in the past has behaved "dumbly" (by someone's standard) or shyly or meanly, BUT who in the future could behave smartly, aggressively, or kindly if the conditions necessary for the occurrence of those acts existed.

2. Ask them to write down some things that they would very much like to do, things that they have tried to do, but have concluded that they can't. Discuss their lists. Discuss whether or not some items on their lists may be overgeneralizations, i.e., there are some things at which they have failed in the past, but who knows, if they were to continue to work at it they would succeed in the future. Ask them to substitute the phrase, "I won't . . ." whenever they say "I can't" to see if that isn't more rational.

3. Point out that overgeneralizing not only is irrational, but also can be used to upset oneself. If we believe that we will *never* be able to do something, or that we *can't* do something, or that we are a *stupid person*, then we tend to feel unhappy and fail to keep working hard to get what we want.

APPENDIX 2

Scales of Rational and Irrational Beliefs for Children and Adolescents

Children's Survey of Rational Beliefs: Form B, Ages 7–10

Children's Survey of Rational Beliefs: Form C, Ages 10–13

The Idea Inventory

There are two scales available for the assessment of the irrational beliefs of children. Knaus (1974) developed two forms of the Children's Survey of Rational Beliefs (Form B, ages 7–10; Form C, ages 10–13). While both these forms have been used extensively as dependent mesures by RET researchers in seeking to confirm the effects of rational-emotive interventions on school-age populations, it is unfortunately the case that no normative, reliability, and validity test data are available. In seeking to measure developmental trends in rational thinking, Kassinove, Crisci, and Tiegerman (1977) developed the Idea Inventory. This scale assesses the degree of endorsement of a number of irrational ideas and can be administered to students in grades four through twelve. Limited reliability and validity data are reported. In the Kassinove et al. study, results indicated irrationality decreased with age although the relation between individual irrational ideas and grade was variable. In investigating grade, race, and sex differences in rational thinking, Briley (1980) found a high correlation between the Idea Inventory and the Children's Survey of Rational Beliefs (Form C).

Both scales are easy to score. We have provided the "rational" answers to the Children's Survey of Rational Beliefs scales. The higher the score the more rational a child is deemed. There is no indication as to a cutoff score to determine whether a child is thinking rationally. The Idea Inventory measure 11 irrational items each of which is represented by 3 items. Each of the 33 items is stated as an irrational idea so that disagreement with each represents rational thinking. Total irrationality scores can vary from 33 (highly irrational) to 99 (highly rational). In addition, scores on each individual idea can be computed, ranging from 3 (less rational) to 9 (more rational). Correlations of the Idea Inventory with the neuroticism scale of the Junior Eysenck Personality Inventory ranged in the Kassinove et al. (1977) study from $-.35$ in Grade 4 to $-.64$ in Grade 11 (all grades combined, $-.55$).

Children's Survey of Rational Beliefs: Form B, Ages 7–10 (from Knaus, 1974)

Directions: Next to each question there are three possible answers. Pick out the answer you think is best for you. Write the letter on the answer sheet beside the number of the question.

1. When somebody calls your best friend or mother a bad name:
    a.   you have to fight
    b.   you have to tell him off
    c.   you can think before you act

2. If you can't answer the teacher's question:
    a.   you'll get a bad report card
    b.   you may be able to answer the next one
    c.   it shows that you can't learn

3. When you get mad at somebody:
    a.   it is because of what that person did
    b.   you think yourself into getting angry
    c.   it is because the person is no good

4. A child who throws a temper tantrum:
    a.   is a spoiled kid
    b.   always gets his own way
    c.   is acting immaturely

5. You feel upset because you believe the world should be perfect. You can handle this problem by:
    a.   trying to figure out why the world should be any different than it is
    b.   trying to force the world to be your way
    c.   telling yourself it doesn't matter how the world is

6. When you feel anxious (nervous) it is because:
    a.   somebody is going to punish you
    b.   you are thinking thoughts like "some awful thing is going to happen"
    c.   you are a bad person

7. If you can't learn your school lessons right away:
    a.   you'd better give up because you'll never learn right
    b.   the work is too hard to do
    c.   you'll need more time to practice

8. When somebody teases you, you:
    a.   can wonder what his problem is
    b.   think that people don't like you
    c.   think that he is stupid and no good

9. If a person is not acting his age, the first thing to do is try to:
    a.   show him he is acting silly
    b.   understand that not everybody acts their age at all times
    c.   pretend he doesn't exist

10. When you feel worried (anxious) you:
    a.   can't stand feeling that way
    b.   think there is nothing you can do about feeling that way
    c.   can ask what you are getting yourself anxious over

11. If you have trouble learning to read that means:
    a.   you must be pretty stupid
    b.   you won't learn anything well
    c.   you have to spend more time practicing

(Continued)

Children's Survey of Rational Beliefs *(Continued)*

12. The best way to get over your worries and troubles is:
    a. try to forget them
    b. complain to your friends
    c. question your troubling thoughts
13. When you do well in school
    a. you are a good person
    b. you know the subject
    c. you were lucky
14. Some people who easily become angry
    a. have a hard time liking themselves
    b. have many bad things happen to them
    c. can never stop being touchy people
15. A person who doesn't like himself
    a. doesn't think much of his positive qualities
    b. is not a very smart person
    c. is never liked by other people
16. If a person thought "It's too bad I didn't get what I wanted," he would likely feel:
    a. angry (mad)
    b. disappointed
    c. nervous (anxious)
17. Your feelings come from:
    a. how people behave toward you
    b. how you think about things which happen
    c. your heart and your stomach
18. A person who is angry or "mad"
    a. has been treated unfairly
    b. sees only one side of the story
    c. is a bad person

Children's Survey of Rational Beliefs: Form C, Age 10–13 (from Knaus, 1974)

Directions: Next to each question there are four possible answers. You are to pick out the answer that you believe is best for you. Write the letter on the answer sheet beside the number of the question.

1. A person who feels angry toward another person thinks:
    a. he can't stand the other person's behavior
    b. the other person has no right to act the way he does
    c. nobody is perfect and this person is no different
    d. all the above answers are correct
2. If a person says it is human to make a mistake and then feels awful when he makes a mistake, he:
    a. can't help feeling that way
    b. generally is a liar
    c. doesn't really believe it is right for him to make a mistake
    d. will always correct his mistakes

(Continued)

3. A person who is angry because the world is not perfect can help get rid of this feeling by:
    a.   trying to force the world to be the way he wants it
    b.   telling himself that it doesn't matter how the world is
    c.   questioning why the world must be the way he wants it to be
    d.   giving up and pretending not to care

4. If you see a person who is not acting his age, the first thing to do is:
    a.   try to change him by teasing him out of his behavior
    b.   ignore him completely
    c.   tell him to grow up and act his age
    d.   try to understand that not everybody can act their age

5. When a person hates herself when someone laughs at her:
    a.   she thinks she needs the other person to like her so that she can like herself
    b.   she has to believe the other person is unfair
    c.   her grades will start to drop at school
    d.   she will never get over feeling that way

6. A person who has trouble learning to read:
    a.   will probably have trouble learning everything
    b.   is stupid
    c.   will have to work harder at it than some of his other classmates
    d.   should give up because he is not going to do well

7. A person who feels annoyed when somebody teases him:
    a.   believes he doesn't like to be teased
    b.   believes it is unbearable when he is teased
    c.   believes the other person should be punished
    d.   always should go to the teacher for help

8. Any person who gets poorer grades in school than her friends:
    a.   is going to be ashamed
    b.   is not as good a person as they are
    c.   can still accept herself
    d.   will find that her friends will stop playing with her

9. What makes a person complex?
    a.   a person can have many different qualities like fairness and truthfulness
    b.   a person is capable of behaving in many different ways
    c.   a person is capable of thinking in different ways
    d.   all the above answers are correct

10. Which of the following is an example of a sensible (rational) belief?
    a.   I don't like it when somebody is treated unfairly
    b.   I can't stand it when I see somebody treated unfairly
    c.   people who treat others unfairly should always be punished
    d.   all the above answers are correct

11. How would a person feel who had the thought "It really is too bad that I failed the test"?
    a.   afraid
    b.   ashamed
    c.   disappointed
    d.   depressed

12. If asked what they think the world is like, different people would:
    a.   have the same opinion of the world
    b.   agree that the world is a great planet to live on
    c.   will all state that the world is a complicated place
    d.   will have different opinions

(Continued)

Children's Survey of Rational Beliefs (*Continued*)

13. Which situation can be frustrating?
     a.   you put a puzzle together and find some parts are missing
     b.   you are not able to do what you want
     c.   you can't find the meaning of an important word
     d.   all the above situations can be frustrating

14. A person who demands (insists) that things go his way, is most likely to feel:
     a.   angry when he doesn't get his way
     b.   good, because he is doing something to get his way
     c.   great annoyance when he doesn't get his way
     d.   both a and c are correct

15. A person's opinions are:
     a.   always based upon facts
     b.   ideas about something that could either be true or false
     c.   always incorrect
     d.   based upon unsound assumptions

16. People who spend most of their time thinking how awful everything is:
     a.   usually have bad things happen to them
     b.   are usually treated unfairly
     c.   are hopeful that their life will change if they complain enough
     d.   usually solve their problems by facing them

17. Standards or values are most helpful in:
     a.   determining what personal goals to work for
     b.   knowing what to blame or praise yourself for
     c.   knowing who is a good person and who is a bad person
     d.   none of the above answers is correct

18. The better method of changing unsound (irrational) upsetting thinking is:
     a.   say you are going to stop thinking unsoundly
     b.   question unsound (irrational) ideas
     c.   insist to yourself that you start thinking only sound rational thoughts
     d.   try to forget your upsetting thoughts

19. One thing we know about how people express feelings is:
     a.   people who have had the same experiences express their feelings in the same way
     b.   different people can express the same feeling in different ways
     c.   all ways of expressing feelings are appropriate
     d.   none of the above answers is correct

20. An example of an unsound assumption is:
     a.   day and night follow each other
     b.   the milk tasted sour
     c.   Ann doesn't like me because her grades are higher than mine
     d.   all the above answers are correct

21. You believe something because:
     a.   it is a fact
     b.   it is your opinion
     c.   answers a and b are both correct
     d.   answers a and b are both wrong

22. Most bullies have in common:
     a.   they really don't like themselves
     b.   they always have a lot of money
     c.   they never act fairly
     d.   both a and c are correct

(*Continued*)

23. A person who is angry:
    a. has been treated unfairly
    b. sees only one side to the story
    c. is a bad person
    d. all of the above answers are correct

24. Someone who thinks life is awful and will never get better probably feels:
    a. angry
    b. annoyed
    c. depressed
    d. uncaring

25. Human emotions are most likely to result from:
    a. the way your parents taught you how to feel
    b. how you think about things that happen
    c. how other people think about you
    d. none of the above answers is correct

26. Everbody is likely to feel the same way:
    a. at a birthday party
    b. when they do poorly in school
    c. when they forget their best friend's birthday
    d. none of the above answers is correct

27. Which of the following is not a feeling?
    a. sad
    b. itchy
    c. glad
    d. all are feelings

28. Which of the following is an example of unsound (irrational) thinking?
    a. I really don't like it when I can't play a game well
    b. it makes me sick to see her acting so silly
    c. it is too bad if I am not loved by everybody
    d. none of the above are unsound (irrational) thoughts

29. If a person treats you unfairly, it would be appropriate for you to feel:
    a. angry
    b. good, because you think you are better than they are
    c. annoyed or sad
    d. anxious or nervous

30. A person who tries to think rationally (sensibly):
    a. never is emotionally upset
    b. is friendly only with people who think sensibly
    c. easily solves all his problems
    d. is better able to accept his mistakes

31. If you can accept that a bully has problems:
    a. you have to put up with his behavior
    b. you can try to change the behavior you don't like
    c. you shouldn't be upset if he or she bothers you
    d. you must stay out of his or her way

32. A person can get into emotional troubles by expecting to be:
    a. happy and comfortable
    b. successful
    c. liked by everybody
    d. all the above answers are correct

(Continued)

Children's Survey of Rational Beliefs *(Continued)*

33. Some people create extra worries and troubles by:
    a. having two problems that are difficult to solve
    b. blaming themselves for having emotional troubles
    c. trying very hard and not succeeding
    d. none of the above answers is correct

34. What is a person who thinks sensibly (rationally) likely to recognize?
    a. if he is nervous he is making himself nervous
    b. if he is nervous, it is because of something that has just happened
    c. if he becomes nervous, he can't help it because he is a nervous person
    d. none of the above answers is correct

35. The best way to deal with worries and troubles is:
    a. forget them
    b. complain about them to your friends and get sympathy
    c. always solve them on your own
    d. none of the above solutions is very good

36. When you get a high score on a test, you:
    a. are a smart person
    b. know the subject well
    c. you will do well in the future
    d. were very lucky

37. A person who thinks rationally (sensibly):
    a. will sometimes feel ashamed
    b. will always be happy
    c. will be liked by everyone
    d. will always be successful in solving his problems

38. If you think you can't stand being frustrated, that means you:
    a. won't have any friends
    b. really don't like yourself
    c. will never get to do things your way
    d. will probably get less work done

Answer Key: Children's Survey of Rational Beliefs

Form B.

1. c	4. c	7. c	10. c	13. b	16. b
2. b	4. a	8. a	11. c	14. a	17. b
3. b	6. b	9. b	12. c	15. a	18. b

Form C

1. b	8. c	15. b	22. a	29. c	36. b
2. c	9. d	16. c	23. b	30. d	37. a
3. c	10. a	17. a	24. c	31. b	38. d
4. d	11. c	18. b	25. b	32. d	
5. a	12. d	19. b	26. d	33. b	
6. c	13. d	20. c	27. d	34. a	
7. a	14. d	21. c	28. b	35. d	

The Idea Inventory (from Kassinove, Crisci & Tiegerman, 1977)

Name: _____

Sex: Male _____ Female _____

Age: _____

Date: _____

People have different ideas. We are interested in hearing about your opinions and ideas regarding the following statements. Place an "X" through the number which best reflects your beliefs about each of the ideas.

$$1 = \text{Agree (A)}$$
$$2 = \text{Uncertain (U)}$$
$$3 = \text{Disagree (D)}$$

		A	U	D
1.	People need the love or approval of almost everyone they consider important.	1	2	3
2.	I feel like I'm a stupid person when I don't do as well as my friends.	1	2	3
3.	Criminals need to be severely punished for their sins.	1	2	3
4.	It's awful when things are not the way one wants them to be.	1	2	3
5.	People in my family sometimes make me very angry.	1	2	3
6.	I constantly worry about dangerous accidents occurring.	1	2	3
7.	It's easier to put off some responsibilities and difficulties rather than face them directly.	1	2	3
8.	I get upset when there is no one to help me think about difficult problems.	1	2	3
9.	It upsets me to recognize that some of my long held beliefs are almost unchangeable.	1	2	3
10.	One should be upset over other peoples' problems and difficulties.	1	2	3
11.	I'm afraid I won't find the one best way to deal with my superiors.	1	2	3
12.	I get upset when other people dislike my looks or criticize the style of clothing I wear.	1	2	3
13.	To be a worthwhile person, we should be thoroughly adequate, achieving and competent in almost all ways.	1	2	3
14.	Our enemies should be made to suffer and pay for their evil acts.	1	2	3
15.	I get upset and angry when my plans go wrong.	1	2	3
16.	Unhappiness is caused by people or events around us and we have almost no control over it.	1	2	3
17.	I frequently worry about getting a terrible disease.	1	2	3
18.	I get very anxious and try to stall when I must face a difficult task like giving someone very bad news.	1	2	3
19.	We need to be dependent on others and on someone stronger than ourself.	1	2	3
20.	I get depressed when I realize that I'll never be able to change some of my strong habits.	1	2	3
21.	I get very depressed when I hear that one of my acquaintances is seriously ill.	1	2	3
22.	It's awful when we can't find the right or perfect solution to our problems.	1	2	3
23.	When I walk into a party, I feel very bad if people don't come over and greet me.	1	2	3
24.	I feel inadequate and worthless when I fail at school or work.	1	2	3

(Continued)

The Idea Inventory *(Continued)*

		A	U	D
25.	People who are bad and wicked should be blamed and punished.	1	2	3
26.	I feel angry and rejected when my opinions and ideas are not accepted.	1	2	3
27.	I can't help but feel depressed and rejected when others let me down.	1	2	3
28.	When something is dangerous and causing great concern, we should constantly think about the possibility of its occurrence.	1	2	3
29.	Since I get very nervous, I avoid situations where I will have to make difficult decisions.	1	2	3
30.	I become anxious and need the help of others when I must face difficult responsibilities alone.	1	2	3
31.	Many events from our past so strongly affect us that it is impossible for us to change.	1	2	3
32.	I get overwhelmed with emotion when I see a severely retarded person.	1	2	3
33.	I worry that I won't find the right solution to my problems at school or work.	1	2	3

References

Achenbach, T. M. The child behavior profile: I. Boys aged 6–11. *Journal of Consulting and Clinical Psychology*, 1978, *46*, 478–488.

Achenbach, T. M. *Developmental psychopathology*, 2nd edition. New York: John Wiley, 1981.

Achenbach, T. M., & Edelbrock, C. S. The classification of child psychotherapy. *Psychological Bulletin*, 1978, *85*, 1275–1301.

Achenbach, T. M., & Edelbrock, C. S. The child behavior profile: II. Boys aged 12–16 and girls aged 6–11 and 12–16. *Journal of Consulting and Clinical Psychology*, 1979, *47*, 223–233.

Achenbach, T. M. & Edelbrock, C.S. Taxonomic issues in child psychopathology. T.H. Ollendick & M. Hersen (Eds.), *Handbood of child psychopathology*. New York: Plenum Press, 1983.

Adams, D. E., Doster, J. A., & Calhoun, K. S. A psychologically based response classification system. In A. R. Ciminero, K. S. Calhoun, and H. E. Adams (Eds.), *Handbook of behavioral assessment*. New York: Wiley, 1977.

Adler, A. *What life should mean to you*. New York: Capricorn, 1958.

Albert, S. *A study to determine the effectiveness of affective education with fifth grade students*. Unpublished master's thesis, Queens College, 1972.

Alschuler, A. Psychological education. *Humanistic Psychology*, 1969, *9*, 1–15.

American School Counselor Association Pamphlet. Organizing for action: *Ideas for mobilizing resources on behalf of elementary guidance*. Falls Church, Virginia: The American School Counselor Association, 1979.

Anderson, R. F. Using guided fantasy with children. *Elementary School Guidance and Counseling*, 1980, *15*, 39–47.

Andrews, J. S. *Overcoming anger*. Unpublished manuscript. University of Melbourne, Department of Education, 1980.

Angelino, H., Dollins, H. J., & Mech, E. V. Trends in the fears and worries of school children as related to socioeconomic status and age. *Journal of Genetic Psychology*, 1956, *89*, 263–276.

Anthony, E. J. The significance of Jean Piaget for child psychiatry. *British Journal of Medical Psychology*, 1956, *29*, 20–34.

Ausubel, D. P. *Educational psychology: A cognitive view*. New York: Holt, Rinehart and Winston, 1968.

Babbits, R. *Cognitive and automatic group procedures with special-anxious children*. Unpublished doctoral dissertation, Yeshiva University, 1979.

Baldwin, B. A. A structured activity model for personal exploration and discussion groups. *Journal of College Students Personnel*, 1976, *17*, 431–36.

Bandura, A. *Principles of behavior modification*. New York: Holt, Rinehart and Winston, 1969.

Bandura, A. *Social learning theory*. Englewood Cliffs, N.J.: Prentice-Hall, 1977.

Bard, J. A. Rational proselytizing. *Rational Living*, 1973, *8*, 13–15.

Bard, J. A. *Rational-emotive therapy in practice*. Champaign, Ill.: Research Press, 1980.

Bard, J. A., & Fisher, H. R. A rational-emotive approach to academic underachievement. In A. Ellis and M. E. Bernard (Eds.), *Rational-emotive approaches to the problems of childhood*. New York: Plenum Press, 1983.

Bartlett, F. *Remembering*. London: Cambridge University Press, 1932.

Bash, M. A., & Camp, B. W. *Think Aloud program: Group manual*. Unpublished manuscript, University of Colorado Medical School, 1975.

Beck, A. T. A systematic investigation of depression. *Comprehensive Psychiatry*, 1961, *2*, 163–170.

Beck, A. T. Thinking and depression. *Archives of General Psychiatry*, 1963, *9*, 324–333.

Beck, A. T. Cognitive therapy: Nature and relation to behavior therapy. *Behavior Therapy*, 1970a, *1*, 184–200.

Beck, A. T. The core problem in depression: The cognitive triad. In J. Masserman (Ed.), *Depression: Theories and therapies*. New York: Grune and Stratton, 1970b.

Beck, A. T. *Depression: Causes and treatment*. Philadelphia, Penn: University of Pennsylvania Press, 1972.

Beck, A. T. *Cognitive therapy and the emotional disorders*. New York: International Universities Press, 1976.

Beck, A. T., Rush, A. J., Shaw, B. F. & Emery, G. *Cognitive therapy of depression*. New York: Guilford Press, 1979.

Beck, A. T. & Shaw, B. F. Cognitive approaches to depression. In A. Ellis and R. Grieger (Eds.), *Handbook of rational-emotive therapy*. New York: Springer Publishing, 1977.

Bedford, S. *Instant replay*. New York: Institute for Rational Living, 1974.

Bedford, S. Instant replay: A method of counseling and talking to little (and other) people. In J. Wolfe and E. Brand (Eds.), *Twenty years of rational therapy*. New York: Institute for Rational Living, 1977.

Bedrosian, R. C. The application of cognitive therapy techniques with adolescents. In G. Emery, S. D. Hollon and R. C. Bedrosian (Eds.), *New directions in cognitive therapy*. New York: Guilford Press, 1981.

Beilin, H. Developmental stages and developmental processes. In D.R. Green (Ed.), *Measurement and Piaget*. New York: McGraw-Hill, 1971.

Bem, D. J. Self-perception theory. In L. Berkowitz (Ed.), *Advances in Experimental Social Psychology*, Vol. 6. New York: Academic Press, 1972.

Bereiter, R. C., & Englemann, S. *Teaching disadvantaged children in the preschool*. Englewood Cliffs, N.J.: Prentice-Hall, 1966.

Bergan, J. R. *Behavioral consultation*. New York: Charles E. Merrill, 1977.

Berger, T. *I have feelings*. New York: Human Sciences Press, 1971.

Bernard, M. E. The effects of advance organizers and within-text questions on the learning of a taxonomy of concepts. *Technical Report No. 357*. Wisconsin Research and Development Center for Cognitive Learning, 1975.

Bernard, M. E. The effects of advance organizer, sequence of instruction, and post-organizer on the learning and retention of a taxonomy of concepts. *The Australian Journal of Education*, 1977, *21*, 25–33.

Bernard, M. E. *Rational-emotive group counseling in a school setting*. Paper presented at the Amercian Educational Research Association's Annual Meeting, San Francisco, April, 1979a.

Bernard, M. E. *A manual for rational-emotive group counseling*. Unpublished manuscript, The University of Melbourne, Department of Education, 1979b.

Bernard, M. E. Private thought in rational-emotive psychotherapy. *Cognitive Therapy and Research*, 1981a, *5*, 125–142.

Bernard, M. E. *The psychology of presidential anger*. Unpublished manuscript. The University of Melbourne, Department of Education, 1981b.

Bernard, M. E. Childhood emotion and cognitive behavior therapy: A rational-emotive perspective. In P. C. Kendall (Ed.), *Advances in cognitive-behavioral research and therapy, Vol. III*. New York: Academic Press, 1984.

Bernard, M. E., Joyce, M. R., & Rosewarne, P. Helping teachers cope with stress. In A. Ellis & M. E. Bernard (Eds.), *Rational-emotive approaches to the problems of childhood*. New York: Plenum Press, 1983.

Bernard, M. E. Kratochwill, T. R., & Keefauver, L. W. The effects of rational-emotive-therapy and self-instructional training on chronic hair-pulling. *Cognitive Therapy and Research*, 1983, *7*, 273–280.

Bernard, M. E., & Naylor, F. D. Vocational guidance consultation in school settings. In T. R. Kratochwill (Ed.), *Advances in school psychology*, Vol 2. New Jersey: Lawrence Erlbaum, 1982.

Berne, E. *Games people play*. New York: Grove Press, 1964.

Bersoff, D. N. Silk purses into sows' ears: The decline of psychological testing and a suggestion for its redemption. *American Psychologist*, 1973, *28*, 892–899.

Bessell, H., & Palomares, V. *Methods in human development*. San Diego, Calif.: Human Development Institute, 1970.

Bettelheim, B. *Love is not always enough*. Glencoe, Ill.: Free Press, 1950.

Bialer, I. Conceptualization of success and failure in mentally retarded and normal children. *Journal of Personality*, 1961, *29*, 303–320.

Bijou, S. W., & Peterson, R. F. Functional analysis in the assessment of children. In P. McReynolds (Ed.), *Advances in psychological assessment*, Vol. 2. Palo Alto, California: Sciences and Behavior Books, 1971.

Binet, A., & Henri, V. La memoire des phrases (memoire des idees). *AnneePsychologuique*, 1894, *1*, 24–59.

Bleuler, E. Autistic-undisciplined thinking (1922). In D. Rapaport (Ed.), *Organization and pathology of thought*. New York: Columbia University Press, 1951.

Block, J. Effects of a rational-emotive mental health program on poorly achieving, disruptive high school students. *Journal of Counseling Psychology*, 1978, *25*, 61–65.

Blotsky, M. J., & Kinsey, L. R. Childhood depression. *Texas Medicine*, 1970, *66*, 64–69.

Bokor, S. *A study to determine the effects of a self-enhancement program in increasing self-concept in black, disadvantaged sixth-grade boys.* M. A. Thesis, Queens College, 1972.

Brainerd, C. J. *Piaget's theory of intelligence.* Englewood Cliffs, N.J.: Prentice-Hall, 1978b.

Brainerd, C. J. The stage question in cognitive-developmental theory. *The Behavioral and Brain Sciences*, 1978a, *2*, 173–213.

Briley, C. M. *Grade, race and sex differences in student's rational–irrational thinking: The rational–emotive model.* (Order No. 8000062) Ann Arbor, Mi.: University Microfilms International, 1980.

Brody, M. *The effect of the rational–emotive affective education approach on anxiety, frustration tolerance and self-esteem with fifth-grade students.* Ph. D. Thesis, Temple University, 1974.

Bronfenbrenner, U. Toward an experimental ecology of human development. *American Psychologist*, 1977, *32*, 513–531.

Broughton, J. M. The divided self in adolescence. *Human Development*, 1981, *24*, 13–32.

Brown, D. A. Rational success. *Art in Daily Living*, 1974, *3*, 7.

Brown, D. A. The fourth "R": A school psychologist takes RSC to school. In J. Wolfe and E. Brand (Eds.), *Twenty years of rational therapy.* New York: Institute for Rational Living, 1977.

Brown, D. A. Chad cannot be rotten. *Journal of School Health*, 1979, *19*, 503–504.

Brown, G. I. *Human teaching for human learning. An introduction to confluent education.* New York: Viking Press, 1971.

Brown, G. I. (Ed.), *The live classroom.* New York: The Viking Press, 1975.

Bugental, D., Whalen, C., & Henker, B. Causal attributions of hyperactive children and motivational assumptions of two behavior-change approaches: Evidence for an interactional position. *Child Development*, 1977, *48*, 874–884.

Burns, D., & Beck, A. T. Cognitive behavior modification of mood disorders. In J. P. Foreyt and D. Rathjen (Eds.), *Cognitive behavior therapy: Research and applications.* New York: Plenum Press, 1978.

Butler, J. *Overcoming jealousy.* Unpublished manuscript. The University of Melbourne, Department of Education, 1980.

Butler, L., & Meichenbaum, D. The assessment of interpersonal problem-solving skills. In P. C. Kendall and S. D. Hollon (Eds.), *Assessment strategies for cognitive-behavioral intervention.* Academic Press, 1981.

Cameron, R. *Conceptual tempo and children's problem-solving behavior: A developmental task analysis.* Unpublished doctoral dissertation, University of Waterloo, 1976.

Camp, B. W., & Bash, M. A. S. *Think Aloud. Increasing social and cognitive skills-a problem-solving program for children.* Champaign, Ill.: Research Press, 1981.

Cangelosi, A., Gressard, C. I., & Mines, R. A. The effects of a rational thinking group on self-concepts in adolescents. *The School Counselor*, 1980, *27*, 357–361.

Carkhuff, R. *Helping and human relations. Vol. 1: Selection and training.* New York: Holt, Rinehart and Winston, 1969a.

Carkhuff, R. *Helping and human relations. Vol. 2: Practice and reaseach*. New York: Holt, Rinehart and Winston, 1969b.

Carkhuff, R. *The development of human resources*. New York: Holt, Rinehart and Winston, 1971.

Carnegie, D. *How to stop worrying and start living*. New York: Simon & Schuster, 1948.

Cartledge, G., & Milburn, J. F. (Eds.), *Teaching social skills to children: Innovative approaches*. New York: Pergamon Press, 1980.

Cartwright, R. *The feeling thermometer*. Unpublished graphic design, Melbourne, Australia, 1977.

Casteel, J. D., & Stahl, R. S. *Value clarification in the classroom: A primer*. Pacific Palisades, CA: Goodyear, 1975.

Cautela, J. R. Covert sensitization. *Psychological Reports*, 1967, *20*, 459−468.

Cautela, J. R. Covert conditioning. In A. Jacobs and L. B. Sachs (Eds.), *The psychology of private events: Perspectives on covert response systems*. New York: Academic Press, 1971.

Chandler, M. Egocentrism and anti-social behavior: The assessment and training of social perspective skills. *Developmental Psychology*, 1973, *9*, 326−332.

Chase, L. *The other side of the report card: A how-to-do-it program for affective education*. Pacific Palisades, CA: Goodyear, 1975.

Chess, S., Thomas, A., & Birch, M. G. *Your child is a person*. New York: The Viking Press, 1965.

Ciminero, A. R., Calhoun, K. S., & Adams, H. E. *Handbook of behavioral assessment*. New York: John Wiley and Sons, 1977.

Clarfield, S. P. The identification of a teacher referral form for identifying early school maladjustment. *American Journal of Community Psychology*, 1974, *2*, 199−210.

Coates, T. J., & Thoresen, C. E. Teacher anxiety: A review with recommendations. *Review of Educational Research*, 1976, *46*, 159−184.

Cochran, M. M., & Brassard, J. A. Child development and personal social networks. *Child Development*, 1979, *50*, 601−616.

Cohen, E. A., Vinciguerra, P., Ross, R. & Kutner, R. *The assessment of social competence in children*. Paper presented at the 14th Annual Convention of the Association of Advancement of Behavior Therapy, New York, November, 1980.

Cohen, R., & Meyers, A. W. Cognitive development and self-instruction interventions. In B. Gholson and T. L. Rosenthal (Eds.), *Applications of cognitive development theory*. New York: Academic Press, in press.

Combs, M. L., & Lahey, B. B. A cognitive socials skills training program. *Behavior Modification*, 1981, *5*, 39−60.

Cone, J. D., & Hawkins, R. P. (Eds.), *Behavioral assessment: New directions in clinical psychology*. New York: Bruner−Mazel, 1977a.

Cone, J. D., & Hawkins, R. P. Current status and future directions in behavioral assessment. In J. D. Cone and R. P. Hawkins (Eds.), *Behavioral assessment: New directions in clinical psychology*. New York: Bruner-Mazel, 1977b.

Copeland, A. P. The relevance of subject variables in cognitive self-instructional programs for impulsive children. *Behavior Therapy*, 1981, *12*, 520−529.

Cormier, W. H., & Cormier, L. S. *Interviewing strategies for helpers: A guide to assessment, treatment and evaluation.* Monterey, CA: Brooks-Cole, 1979.

Coué, E. *The practice of autosuggestion.* New York: Doubleday, 1922.

Cowan, D. A. An introduction to J. Piaget's "Intelligence and affectivity: Their relationship during child development." In M. R. Rosenzwerg (Ed.), *Annual Reviews Monograph*, Palo Alto: Annual Reviews, Inc., 1981.

Cowan, D. A. *Piaget: With feeling.* New York: Holt, Rinehart and Wilson, 1978.

Crandall, C. J. *Differences in parental antecedents of internal—external control in children and in young adulthood.* Paper presented at the meetings of the American Psychological Association, Montreal, 1973.

Crandall, V. C., Kratovsky, N., & Crandall, V. G. Children's beliefs in their own control of reinforcement in intellectual—academic achievement situations. *Child Development*, 1965, *36*, 91−109.

Cross, G., Myrick, R., & Wilkinson, G. Communication lab: A developmental approach. *The School Counselor*, 1977, *24*, 186−91.

Culbertson, F. M. An effective, low-cost approach to the treatment of disruptive school children. *Psychology in the Schools*, 1974, *11*, 183−87.

Cytryn, L., & McKnew, D. H. Proposed classification of childhood depression. *American Journal of Psychiatry*, 1972, *129*, 149−155.

Daley, S. Using reason with deprived preschool children. *Rational Living*, 1971, *5*, 12−19.

Davidson, J. R. Specifying and patterning in biobehavioral systems. *American Psychologist*, 1978, *33*, 430−436.

Deluty, R. H. Alternative-thinking ability of aggressive, assertive, and submissive children. *Cognitive Therapy and Research*, 1981, *5*, 309−312.

De Voge, C. A behavioral approach to RET with children. *Rational Living*, 1974, *9*, 23−26.

Diagnostic and statistical manual of mental disorders. American Psychiatric Association. Washington, D. S., 1980.

Diener C. I., & Dweck, C. S. Analysis of learned helplessness: Continuous changes in performance, strategy and achievement cognitions following failure. *Journal of Personality and Social Psychology*, 1979, *37*, 621−634.

DiGiuseppe, R. A. The use of behavioral modification to establish rational self-statements in children. *Rational Living*, 1975, *10*, 18−20.

DiGiuseppe, R. A. Cognitive therapy with children. In G. Emery, S. D. Hollon and R. C. Bedrosian (Eds.), *New directions in cognitive therapy.* New York: Guilford Press, 1981.

DiGiuseppe, R. A. Rational emotive therapy and conduct disorders. In A. Ellis and M. E. Bernard (Eds.), *Rational-emotive approach to the problems of childhood.* New York: Plenum Press, 1983.

DiGiuseppe, R. A., & Bernard, M. E. Principles of assessment and methods of treatment with children. In A. Ellis and M. E. Bernard (Eds.) *Rational-emotive approaches to the problems of childhood.* New York: Plenum Press, 1983.

DiGiuseppe, R. A., & Kassinove, H. Effects of a rational-emotive school mental health program on children's emotional adjustment. *Journal of Community Psychology*, 1976, *4*, 382−387.

DiGiuseppe, R. A., Miller, N. J., & Trexler, L. D. A review of rational-emotive psychotherapy outcomes studies. In A. Ellis and J. M. Whiteley (Eds.), *Theoretical and empirical foundations of rational-emotive therapy*. Monterey, CA: Brooks/Cole, 1979.

Dinkmeyer, D. *Developing understanding of self and others (DUSO)*. Circle Pines, Minn: American Guidance Service, 1970.

Dinkmeyer, D., & Caldwell, E. *Developmental counseling and guidance*. New York: McGraw-Hill, 1970.

Di Nubile, L., & Wessler, R. Lessons from the living school. *Rational Living*, 1974, *9*, 29–32.

Dollard, J., & Miller, N. E. *Personality and psychotherapy*. New York: McGraw-Hill, 1950.

Dolliver, R. H. The relationship of rational-emotive therapy to other psychotherapies and personality theories. In A. Ellis and J. M. Whiteley (Eds.), *Theoretical and empirical foundations of rational-emotive therapy*. Monterey, Calif: Brooks/Cole Publishing Company, 1979.

Doress, I. The teacher as therapist. *Rational Living*, 1967, *2*, 27.

Dreikurs, R., & Cassel, P. *Discipline without tears*. New York: Hawthorn, 1972.

Dupont H., Gardner, O. S., & Brody, D. S. *Toward affective development*. Circle Pines, MN: American Guidance Service, 1974.

Dweck, C. The role of expectations and attributions in the alleviation of learned helplessness. *Journal of Personality and Social Psychology*, 1975, *31*, 674–685.

Dweck, C., & Reppucci, N. Learned helplessness and reinforcement responsibility in children. *Journal of Personality and Social Psychology*, 1973, *25*, 109–116.

Dye, S. O. *The influence of rational-emotive education on the self-concept of adolescents living in a residential group home*. Unpublished doctoral dissertation, University of Virginia, 1980.

D'Zurilla, T. J., & Goldfreid, M. R. Problem solving and behavior modification. *Journal of Abnormal Psychology*, 1971, *78*, 107–126.

Edwards, C. RET in high school. *Rational Living*, 1977, *12*, 10–12.

Egan, G. *The skilled helper: A model for systematic helping and interpersonal relating*. Monterey, Calif: Brooks/Cole, 1975.

Elder, C. A. *Making value judgements: Decisions for today*. Columbus: Merrill, 1972.

Elkin, A. Working with children in groups. In A. Ellis and M. E. Bernard (Eds.), *Rational-emotive approaches to the problems of childhood*. New York: Plenum Press, 1983.

Ellis, A. *How to live with a "neurotic"*. New York: Crown, 1957.

Ellis, A. Rational psychotherapy. *Journal of General Psychology*, 1958, *59*, 35–49.

Ellis, A. *Psychotherapy session with an eight-year-old female bedwetter*. Cassette recording. New York: Institute for Rational Living, 1959.

Ellis, A. *Reason and emotion in psychotherapy*. New York: Stuart, 1962.

Ellis, A. Showing clients they are not worthless. *Voices*, 1965, *1*, 74–77.

Ellis, A. Talking to adolescents about sex. *Rational Living*, 1967, *2*, 7–12.

Ellis, A. Rational-emotive therapy. In L. Hersher (Ed.), *Four psychotherapies*. New York: Appleton–Century–Crofts, 1970.

Ellis, A. An experiment in emotional education. *Educational Technology*, 1971a, *11*, 61–64.

Ellis, A. *Rational-emotive therapy and its application to emotional education*. New York: Institute for Rational Living, 1971b.

Ellis, A. *Growth through reason*. Palo Alto, Calif.: Science and Behavior, 1971c.

Ellis, A. The contribution of psychotherapy to school psychology. *School Psychology Digest*, 1972a, *1*, 6–9.

Ellis, A. Emotional education in the classroom: The living school. *Journal of Clinical Child Psychology*, 1972b, *1*, 19–22.

Ellis, A. Psychotherapy and the value of a human being. In J. W. Davis (Ed.), *Axidogical studies in honor of Robert S. Hartman*. Knoxville, Tenn.: University of Tennessee Press, 1972c.

Ellis, A. *Humanistic Psychotherapy: The rational-emotive approach*. New York: McGraw–Hill Paperbacks, 1973a.

Ellis, A. *A demonstration with an elementary school child*. Filmed psychotherapy session. Washington: American Personnel and Guidance Association, 1973b.

Ellis, A. Emotional education at the living school. In M. M. Ohlsen (Ed.), *Counseling children in groups: A forum*. New York: Holt, Rinehart and Winston, 1973c.

Ellis, A. *Healthy and unhealthy aggression*. Paper presented at the American Psychological Association 81st Annual Convention, Montreal, August 27, 1973d.

Ellis, A. Rational-emotive therapy. In A. Burton (Ed.), *Operational theories of personality*. New York: Bruner–Mazel, 1974.

Ellis, A. Rational-emotive therapy and the school counselor. *School Counselor*, 1975a, *22*, 236–242.

Ellis, A. *Raising an emotionally healthy, happy child*. Videotape. Austin, Texas: Audio Visual Resource Center, School of Social Work, University of Texas, 1975b.

Ellis, A. On the disvalue of "mature" anger. *Rational Living*, 1975c, *10*, 24–27.

Ellis, A. *Dealing with conflicts in parent–child relationships*. Videotape. Austin, Texas: Audio Visual Resource Center, School of Social Work, University of Texas, 1976.

Ellis, A. The basic clinical theory of rational-emotive therapy. In A. Ellis and R. Grieger (Eds.), *Handbook of rational-emotive therapy*. New York: Springer Publishing Company, 1977a.

Ellis, A. Rejoinder: Elegant and inelegant RET. *The Counseling Psychologist*, 1977b, *7*, 73–82.

Ellis, A. *How to live with-and-without anger*. New York: Readers Digest Press, 1977c.

Ellis, A. The rational-emotive approach to counseling. In A. M. Bucks (Ed.), *Theories of counseling*. New York: McGraw–Hill, 1978a.

Ellis, A. *Discomfort anxiety: A new cognitive-behavioral construct*. Cassette recording. New York: B. M. A. audiotapes, 1978b.

Ellis, A. Rational-emotive guidance. In E. L. Arnold (Ed.), *Helping parents help their children*. New York: Brunner/ Mazel, 1978c.

Ellis, A. Rational-emotive therapy. In A. Ellis and J. M. Whiteley (Eds.), *Theoretical and empirical foundations of rational-emotive therapy*. Monterey, Calif.: Brooks/ Cole Publishing, 1979a.

Ellis, A. Toward a new theory of personality. In A. Ellis and J. M. Whiteley (Eds.), *Theoretical and empirical foundations of rational-emotive therapy*. Monterey, Calif.: Brooks/Cole Publishing, 1979b.

Ellis, A. The theory of rational-emotive therapy. In A. Ellis and J. M. Whiteley (Eds.), *Theoretical and empirical foundations of rational-emotive* therapy. Monterey, Calif.: Brooks/Cole Publishing, 1979c.

Ellis. A. The practice of rational-emotive therapy. In A. Ellis and J. M. Whiteley (Eds.), *Theoretical and empirical foundations of rational-emotive therapy*. Monterey, Calif.: Brooks/Cole Publishing, 1979d.

Ellis, A. Discomfort and anxiety: A new cognitive-behavioral construct, Part I. *Rational Living*, 1979e, *14*, 3−7.

Ellis, A. Rational-emotive therapy: Research data that support the clinical and personality hypotheses of RET and other modes of cognitive-behavior therapy. In A. Ellis and J. M. Whiteley (Eds.), *Theoretical and empirical foundations of rational-emotive therapy*. Monterey, Calif.: Brooks/Cole Publishing, 1979f.

Ellis, A. Rational-emotive therapy and cognitive behavior therapy: Similarities and differences. *Cognitive Therapy and Resarch*, 1980a, 325−340.

Ellis, A. An overview of the clinical theory of rational-emotive therapy. In R. Grieger and J. Boyd (Eds.), *Rational-emotive therapy: A skills-based approach*. New York: Van Nostrand Reinhold, 1980b.

Ellis, A. Discomfort anxiety: A new cognitive behavioral construct. *Rational Living*, 1980c, *15*, 25−30.

Ellis, A. Foreword to S. R. Walen, R. DiGiuseppe and R. L. Wessler, *A practitioners guide to rational-emotive therapy*. New York: Oxford University Press, 1980d.

Ellis, A. *Rational-emotive therapy and cognitive behavior therapy*. New York: Springer, 1984.

Ellis, A., & Bernard, M. E. Rational-emotive approaches to the problems of childhood. In A. Ellis and M. E. Bernard (Eds.), *Rational-emotive approaches to the problems in childhood*. New York: Plenum Press, 1983a.

Ellis, A., & Bernard, M. E. (Eds.), *Rational-emotive approaches to the problems of childhood*. New York: Plenum Press, 1983b.

Ellis, A., & Grieger, R. *Handbook of rational-emotive therapy*. New York: Springer Publishing Company, 1977.

Ellis, A., & Harper, R. A. *A new guide to rational living*. North Hollywood, Cal.: Wilshire Book Company, 1975.

Ellis, A., Moseley, S. & Wolfe, J. L. *How to raise an emotionally healthy, happy child*. New York: Crown and Hollywood: Wilshire Books, 1966.

Ellis, A., & Whiteley, J. M. (Eds), *Theoretical and empirical foundations of rational-emotive therapy*. Monterey, Calif.: Brooks/Cole Publishing Company, 1979.

Eluto, M. E. *Effects of a rational-emotive education and problem-solving therapy on the adjustment of intermediate special education students*. Unpublished doctoral dissertation, Hofstra University, 1980.

Erikson, M. T. *Childhood psychopathology: Assessment, etiology and treatment*. Englewood Cliffs, N.J.: Prentice−Hall, 1978.

Erikson, M. H. Rossi, E., & Rossi, S. *Hypnotic realities*. New York: Irvington Press, 1976.

Eschenroeder, C. Different therapeutic styles in rational-emotive therapy. *Rational Living*, 1979, *14*, 3−7.

Eschenroeder, C. How rational is rational-emotive therapy. A critical appraisal of its theoretical foundations and therapeutic methods. *Cognitive Therapy and Research*, in press.

Evans, E. D., & McCandless, B. R. *Children and youth* (2nd edition). New York: Holt, Rinehart and Winston, 1978.

Evans, I. M., & Nelson, R. D. Assessment of child behavior problems. In A. R. Ciminero, K. S. Calhoun and H. E. Adams (Eds.), *Handbook of behavioral assessment*. New York: Wiley, 1977.

Farber, I. E. The things people say to themselves. *American Psychologist*, 1963, *18*, 185−197.

Feffer, M. H. Symptom expression as a form of primitive decentering. *Psychological Review*, 1967, *74*, 16−28.

Fein, G. *Child Development*. Englewood Cliffs, N.J.: Prentice−Hall, 1978.

Flavell, J. H. *Cognitive development*. Englewood Cliffs, N.J.: Prentice−Hall, 1977.

Flavell, J. H. *The developmental psychology of Jean Piaget*. New York: Van Nostrand, 1963.

Flavell, J. H. On cognitive development. *Child Development*, 1982, *53*, 1−10.

Flavell, J. H., Beach, D., & Chinsky, J. Spontaneous verbal rehearsal in a memory task as a function of age. *Child Development*, 1966, *37*, 283−299.

Fodor, J. A. Could meaning be an rm? *Journal of Verbal Learning and Verbal Behavior*, 1965, *4*, 73−81.

Fodor, J. A. Some reflections on L. S. Vygotsky's thought and language. *Cognition*, 1973, *1*, 83−95.

Forman, S. G., & Forman, B. D. A rational-emotive approach to consultation. *Psychology in the Schools*, 1978, *15*, 400−406.

Forman, S. G., & Forman, B. D. Rational-emotive staff development. *Psychology in the Schools*, 1980, *17*, 90−95.

Fox, E. E., & Davies, R. L. Test your personality. *Rational Living*, 1971, *5*, 23−25.

Frank, J. D. *Persuasion and healing*. Baltimore: John Hopkins Press, 1961.

Franks, C. M. *Behavior therapy and appraisal and status*. New York: McGraw−Hill, 1969.

Franks, C. M., & Wilson, G. T. (Eds.), *Annual review of behavior therapy: Therapy and practice*. New York: Brunner−Mazel, 1973.

Franks, C. M., & Wilson, G. T. (Eds.), *Annual review of behavior therapy: Therapy and practice*. New York: Brunner−Mazel, 1975.

Freed, A. *T. A. for kids*. Sacramento, Calif.: Jalmer Press, 1971.

Freed, A. *T. A. for tots and other prinzes*. Sacramento, Calif.: Jalmer Press, 1973.

Freud, A. Adolescence as a developmental disturbance. In G. Kaplan and S. Leborici (Eds.), *Adolescence: Psychological perspectives*. New York: Basic Books, 1969.

Freud, A. *The ego and mechanisms of defense* (translated by Cecil Baines). New York: International Universities Press, 1950. (Originally published, 1946).

Frey, D. H. Conceptualizing counseling theories: A content analysis of process and goal statements. *Counselor Education and Supervision*, 1972, *11*, 143–250.

Frommer, E. Depressive illness in children. *British Journal of Psychiatry*, 1968, *2*, 117–123.

Gagne, R. M. *The conditions of learning*, (3rd. ed.). New York: Holt, Rinehart and Winston, 1977.

Garcia, E. J. Working on the E in RET. In J. L. Wolfe and E. Brand (Eds.), *Twenty years of rational therapy*. New York: Institute for Rational Living, 1977.

Garcia, E. J., & Pellegrini, N. *Homer the homely hound dog*. New York: Institute for Rational Living, 1974.

Gardner, R. A. *The talking, feeling and doing game*. Cresskill, N.J.: Creative Therapeutics, 1973.

Garfield, S. L., & Kurtz, R. Clinical psychologists in the 1970's. *American Psychologist*, 1976, *31*, 1–9.

Genest, M., & Turk, D. C. Think-aloud approaches to cognitive assessment. In T. V. Merluzzi, C. R. Glass and M. Genest, *Cognitive assessment*. New York: Guilford Press, 1981.

Genshaft, J. L. The use of cognitive behavior therapy for reducing math anxiety. *School Psychological Review*, 1982, *11*, 32–34.

Gerald, M., & Eyman, W. *Thinking straight and talking sense*. New York: Institute for Rational Living, 1981.

Giezhels, J. S. *Effects of REE on a hearing-impaired high school population*. Unpublished doctoral dissertation, Hofstra University, 1980.

Glaser, K. Masked depression in children and adolescents. *Annual Progress in Child Psychiatry and Child Deviance*, 1968, *1*, 345–355.

Glasser, W. *Schools without failure*. New York: Harper and Row, 1969.

Glicken, M.D. Counseling children. Two methods. *Rational Living*, 1967, 1, 27–30.

Glicken, M.D. Rational counseling: A dynamic approach to children. *Elementary School Guidance and Counseling*, 1968, *2*, 261–267.

Goldfried, M. R. Systematic desensitization as training in self-control. *Journal of Consulting and Clinical Psychology*, 1971, *37*, 228–234.

Goldfried, M. R. Anxiety reduction through cognitive-behavioral intervention. In P. C. Kendall and S. D. Hollon (Eds.), *Cognitive-behavioral intervention: Theory, research and procedures*. New York: Academic Press, 1979.

Goldfried, M. R., & Goldfried, A. P. Cognitive change methods. In F. H. Kanfer and A. P. Goldstein (Eds.), *Helping people change*. New York: Pergamon Press, 1975.

Goldfried, M. R., & Linehan, M. M. Basic issues in behavioral assessment. In A. R. Ciminero, K. S. Calhoun and H. E. Adams (Eds.), *Handbook of behavioral assessment*. New York: John Wiley and Sons, 1977.

Goldstein, A. P., Sprafkin, R. P., Gershaw, N. J., & Klein, P. Social skills through structural learning. In G. Cartledge and J. F. Milburn (Eds.), *Teaching social skills to children: Innovative approaches*. New York: Pergamon Press, 1980.

Goodman, D. S., & Maultsby, M. C. *Emotional well-being through rational behavior training*. Springfield, Ill.: Charles C Thomas, 1978.

Gordon, T. *Parent effectiveness training*. New York: Wyden, 1970.

Gordon, T. *TET-teacher effectiveness training*. New York: Wyden, 1974.

Gottman, J., Gonso, J. & Rasmussen, B. *Social interaction, social competence and friendship in children*. Unpublished manuscript, Indiana University, 1974.

Grieger, R. M., Anderson, K., & Canino, F. Psychotherapeutic modes. In E. Ignas and R. Corsini (Eds.), *Alternative educational systems*. Itasca, Ill.: Peacock, 1979.

Grieger, R. M., & Boyd, J. D. Childhood anxieties, fears and phobias: A cognitive-behavioral psychosituational approach. In A. Ellis and M. E. Bernard (Eds.), *Rational-emotive approaches to problems of childhood*. New York: Plenum Press, 1983.

Grieger, R. M., & Boyd, J. D. *Rational-emotive therapy: A skills-based approach*. New York: Van Nostrand Reinhold, 1980.

Group for the Advancement of Psychiatry, Committee on Child Psychiatry: Psychopathological Disorders in Childhood: Theoretical Considerations and a Proposed Classification. GAP report No. 62, June, 1966.

Haley, J. *Problem-solving therapy*. San Francisco, Ca.: Jossey–Bass. 1976.

Halford, K. Teaching rational self-talk to help socially isolated children and youth. In A. Ellis and M. E. Bernard (Eds.), *Rational-emotive approaches to the problems of childhood*. New York: Plenum Press, 1983.

Hanel, J. *Der einfluss eines motivanderungsprogramms ave schullektung schwach misserfolgsmotivierter grundschyler der 4 klasse*. Psychol. Institut der Ruhr Universitat: Unpublished dissertation, 1974.

Hansen, J. C., Warner, R. W., & Smith, E. J. *Group counseling. Theory and process* (2nd edition). Chicago: Rand McNally, 1980.

Harris, S. R. Rational-emotive education and the human development program: A guidance study. *Elementary School Guidance and Counseling*, 1976, *11*, 113–123.

Harris, T. *I'm OK, you're OK*. New York: Harper and Row, 1967.

Harter, S. A cognitive-developmental approach to children's expression of conflicting feelings and a technique to facilitate such expression in play therapy. *Journal of Consulting and Clinical Psychology*, 1977, *45*, 417–432.

Hauck, P. A. *The rational management of children*. New York: Libra Publishers, 1967.

Hauck, P. A. An RET theory of depression. *Rational Living*, 1971, *6*, 32–35.

Hauck, P. A. *Reason in pastoral counseling*. Philadelphia: Westminster, 1972.

Hauck, P. A. *Overcoming frustration and anger*. Philadelphia, Penn.: The Westminster Press, 1974.

Hauck, P. A. *Overcoming depression*. Philadelphia, Penn.: The Westminster Press, 1975a.

Hauck, P. A. *Overcoming worry and fear*. Philadelphia, Penn.: The Westminster Press, 1975b.

Hauck, P. A. Irrational parenting styles. In A. Ellis and R. Grieger (Eds.), *Handbook of rational-emotive therapy*. New York: Springer Publishing, 1977a.

Hauck, P. A. A three-factored theory of depression. In J. L. Wolfe and E. Brand (Eds.), *Twenty years of rational therapy*. New York: Institute for Rational Living, 1977b.

Hauck, P. A. *Brief counseling with RET*. Philadelphia, Penn.: The Westminster Press, 1980.

Hauck, P. A. Working with parents. In A. Ellis and M. E. Bernard (Eds.), *Rational-emotive approaches to the problems of childhood*. New York: Plenum Press, 1983.

Hawley, R. C. *Value exploration through role playing*. New York: Hart, 1975.

Haynes, S. N. *Principles of behavioral assessment*. New York: Garden Press, 1978.

Haynes, S. N., & Wilson, C. C. *Behavioral assessment*. San Francisco, Calif.: Jossey–Bass Publishers, 1979.

Hazel, J. S., Schumaker, J. B., & Sheldon-Wildgen, J. *Application of a social skill and problem-solving group training program to learning disabled and non-learning disabled youth*. Paper presented at the 14th Annual Convention of the Association for Advancement of Behavior Therapy, New York, 1980.

Hersen, M., & Bellack, A. S. *Behavioral assessment: A practical handbook*. New York: Pergamon Press, 1976.

Hibbard, R. W. A rational approach to treating jealousy. In J. Wolfe and E. Brand (Eds.), *20 years of rational therapy*. New York: Institute for Rational Living, 1977.

Hollon, S. E., & Beck, A. T. Cognitive theory of depression. In P. Kendall and S. D. Hollon (Eds.), *Cognitive-behavioral interventions: Theory, research and procedures*. New York: Academic Press, 1979.

Hollon, S. D., & Kendall, P. D. In vivo assessment techniques for cognitive-behavioral processes. In P. Kendall and S. D. Hollon (Eds.), *Assessment strategies for Cognitive-behavioral interventions*. New York: Academic Press, 1981.

Homme, L. E. Perspectives in psychology: XXIV. Control of coverants, the operants of the mind. *Psychological Record*, 1965, *15*, 501–511.

Horney, K. *Our inner conflicts*. New York: Norton, 1945.

Horton, D. L., & Turnage, T. W. *Human Learning*. Englewood Cliffs, N.J.: Prentice–Hall, 1976.

Howe, L. W., & Howe, M. M. *Personalizing education: Values clarification and beyond*. New York: Hart, 1975.

Hutchins, D. E., & Cole, C. G. A model for improving middle school students interpersonal relationships. *The School Counselor*, 1977, *25*, 134–136.

Hymel, S., & Asher, S. *Assessment and training of isolated children's social skills*. National Institute of Child Health and Human Development (NIH), Bethesda, Md., March, 1977.

Inhelder, B., & Piaget, J. *The growth of logical thinking*. New York: Basic Books, 1958.

Ivey, A., & Gluckstern, N. *Basic attending skills: Participants manual*. Amhert, Mass.: A. Ivey, 1974.

Jabichuk, A., & Smeriglio, U. The influence of symbolic modeling on the social behavior of preschool children with low levels of social responsiveness. *Child Development*, 1976, *47*, 838–841.

Jersild, A. T. *Child psychology* (5th edition). Englewood Cliffs, N.J.: Prentice–Hall, 1960.

Jones, R. G. *A factoral measure of Ellis' irrational belief system with personality and maladjustment correlates*. Unpublished doctoral dissertation, Texas Technological College, 1968.

Kanfer, F. H., Karoly, P., & Newman, A. Reduction of children's fear of the dark by competence-related and situational thought-related verbal cues. *Journal of Consulting and Clinical Psychology*, 1975, *43*, 251–258.

Kanfer, F. H., & Saslow, G. Behavioral diagnosis. In C. Franks (Ed.), *Behavior therapy: Appraisal and status*. New York: McGraw–Hill, 1969.

Kassinove, H., Crisci, R., & Tiegerman, S. Developmental trends in rational thinking: Implications for rational-emotive school mental health programs. *Journal of Community Psychology*, 1977, *5*, 266–274.

Kassinove, H., & DiGuiseppe, R. A. Rational role reversal. *Rational Living*, 1975, *10*, 44–45.

Katan, A. Some thoughts about the role of verbalization in early childhood. In *The Psychoanalytic Study of the Child*, Vol. 15. New York: International Universities Press, 1961.

Katz, S. *The effects of emotional education on locus of control and self-concept*. Unpublished doctoral dissertation, Hofstra University, 1974.

Kazdin, A. E. *Behavior modification in applied settings*. Homewood, Ill.: The Dorsey Press, 1980.

Kazdin, A. E. Covert modeling and the reduction of avoidance behavior. *Journal of Abnormal Psychology*, 1973, *81*, 87–95.

Kazdin, A. E. *History of behavior modification*. Baltimore, Maryland: University Park Press, 1978.

Kazdin, A. E. Situational specificity: The two-edged sword of behavioral assessment. *Behavioral Assessment*, 1979, *1*, 57–75.

Keat, D. B. *Fundamentals of child counseling*. Boston: Houghton Mifflin, 1974.

Keat, D. B. *Multimodel therapy with children*. New York: Pergamon Press, 1979.

Keefe, F. J., Kopel, S. A. & Gordon, S. B. *A practical guide to behavioral assessment*. New York: Springer, 1978.

Kelly, G. *The psychology of personal constructs*. New York: Norton, 1955.

Kendall, P. C. Assessment and cognitive-behavioral interventions: Purposes, proposals and problems. In P. C. Kendall and S. D. Hollon (Eds.), *Assessment strategies for cognitive-behavioral interventions*. New York: Academic Press, 1981.

Kendall, P. C., & Finch, A. J. Jr. A cognitive-behavioral treatment for impulse control: A case study. *Journal of Consulting and Clinical Psychology*, 1976, *44*, 852–857.

Kendall, P. C., & Finch, A. J. Jr. A cognitive-behavioral treatment for implusivity: A group comparison study. *Journal of Consulting and Clinical Psychology*, 1978, *46*, 110–118.

Kendall, P. C., & Finch, A. J. Jr. Developing nonimpulsive behavior in children: Cognitive-behavioral strategies for self-control. In P. C. Kendall and S. D. Hollon (Eds.), *Cognitive-behavioral interventions: Theory, research and procedures*. New York: Academic Press, 1979.

Kendall, P. C., & Fischler, G. L. Teaching rational self-talk to impulsive children. In A. Ellis and M. E. Bernard (Eds.), *Rational-emotive approaches to the problems of childhood*. New York: Plenum Press, 1983.

Kendall, P. C., & Hollon, S. D. (Eds.), *Assessment strategies for cognitive-behavioral interventions*. New York: Academic Press, 1981.

Kendall, P. C., & Hollon, S. D. Cognitive-behavioral interventions: Overview and current status. In P. C. Kendall and S. D. Hollon (Eds.), *Cognitive-behavioral interventions: Theory, research and procedures*. New York: Academic Press, 1979a.

Kendall, P. C., & Hollon, S. D. (Eds.), *Cognitive-behavioral interventions: Theory, research and procedures*. New York: Academic Press, 1979b.

Kendall, P. C., & Korgeski, G. P. Assessment and cognitive-behavioral interventions. *Cognitive Therapy and Research*, 1979, *3*, 1–21.

Kendall, P. C., Pellegrini, D. S., & Urbain, E. S. Approaches to assessment for cognitive-behavioral interventions with children. In P. C. Kendall and S. D. Hollon (Eds.), *Assessment strategies for cognitive-behavioral interventions*. New York: Academic Press, 1981.

Kendall, P. C., & Wilcox, L. E. Self-control in children: Development of a rating scale. *Journal of Consulting and Clinical Psychology*, 1979, *47*, 1020–1030.

Kendall, P. C., & Wilcox, L. E. Cognitive-behavioral treatment for impulsivity: Concrete versus conceptual training in non-self-controlled problem children. *Journal of Consulting and Clinical Psychology*, 1980, *48*, 80–91.

Kendall, P. C., & Zupan, B. A. Individual versus group application of cognitive-behavioral self-control procedures with children. *Behavior Therapy*, 1981, *12*, 344–359.

Kendler, T. S., & Kendler, H. H. Reversal and nonreversal shifts in kindergarten. *Journal of Experimental Psychology*, 1959, *58*, 56–60.

Kessler, J. *Psychopathology of childhood*. Englewood Cliffs, N.J.: Prentice–Hall, 1966.

Klausmeier, H. J., Ghatala, E. S., & Frayer, D. A. *Conceptual learning and development*. New York: Academic Press, 1974.

Knaus, W. J. Rational-emotive education. In A. Ellis and R. Grieger (Eds.), *Handbook of rational-emotive therapy*. New York: Springer Publishing Co., 1977.

Knaus, W. J. *Rational emotive education: A manual for elementary school teachers*. New York: Institute for Rational Living, 1974.

Knaus, W. J., & Boker, S. The effect of rational-emotive education on anxiety and self-concpet. *Rational Living, 1975, 10*, 7–10.

Knaus, W. J., & Eyman, W. Progress in rational emotive education. *Rational Living*, 1974, *9*, 27–29.

Knaus, W. J., & McKeever, C. Rational-emotive education with learning disabled children. *Journal of Learning Disabilities*, 1977, *10*, 10–14.

Knopf, I. J. *Childhood psychopathology: A developmental approach*. Englewood Cliffs, N.J.: Prentice–Hall, 1979.

Kohlberg, L. Stage and sequence: The cognitive-developmental approach to socialization. In D. A. Goslin (Ed.), *Handbook of socialization theory and research*. Chicago: Rand McNally, 1969.

Kohn, M., & Rosman, B. L. A social competence scale and symptom checklist for the preschool child: Factor dimensions, their cross-instrument generality, and longitudinal persistence. *Developmental Psychology*, 1972, *6*, 430–444.

Kolakowski, L. *Positivist philosophy*. Hamondsworth: Penguin, 1972.

Kovacs, M., & Beck, A. T. An empirical clinical approach towards a definition of childhood depression. In J. G. Shutterbrandt and A. Raskin (Eds.), *Depression in childhood: Diagnosis, treatment and conceptual models*. New York: Raven Press, 1977.

Kovacs, M., & Beck, A. T. Maladaptive cognitive structures and depression. *American Journal of Psychiatry*, 1978, *135*, 525–533.

Kranzler, C. *Emotional education exercises for children*. Eugene, Oregon: Cascade Press, 1974.

Kratochwill, T. R. Advances in behavioral assessment. In C. R. Reynolds & T. B. Gutkin (Eds.), *The handbook of school psychology*. New York: John Wiley, 1982.

Lafferty, G., Dennell, A., & Rettlich, G. A creative school mental health program. *National Elementary Principal*, 1964, *43*, 28–35.

Lafferty, J. C. *Values that defeat learning. Proceedings of the eighth inter-institutional seminar in child development*. Dearborn, Michigan: Edison Institute, 1962.

Laughridge, S. Differential diagnosis with a test of irrational ideation. *Rational Living*, 1975, *10*, 21–23.

Larcen, S. E., Spivack, G., & Shure, M. *Problem-solving thinking and adjustment among dependent-neglected pre-adolescents*. Paper presented at Eastern Psychological Association, Boston, Massachusetts, 1972.

Lazarus, A. A. Multitudinal behavior therapy: Treating the "BASIC ID". *The Journal of Nervous and Mental Disease*, 1973, *156*, 404–410.

Lazarus, A. A. (Ed.), *Multimodal behavior therapy*. New York, Springer, 1976.

Lazarus, R. *Psychological stress and the coping process*. New York: McGraw-Hill, 1966.

Lederman, J. *Anger and the rocking chair*. New York: Viking, 1973.

Lefkowitz, M. M., & Burton, N. Childhood depression: A critique of the concept. *Psychological Bulletin*, 1978, *85*, 716–726.

Lefkowitz, M. M., & Tesiny, E. P. Assessment of childhood depression. *Journal of Consulting and Clinical Psychology*, 1980, *48*, 43–50.

Lehman, P. Practical applications of RET: Group techniques. *Rational Living*, 1973, *8*, 33–36.

Leon, G. R., Kendall, P. C., & Garber, J. Depression in children: Parents, teachers and child perspectives. *Journal of Abnormal Child Psychology*, 1980, *8*, 221–235.

Lewin, K. (Ed.), *A dynamic theory of personality*. New York: McGraw–Hill, 1935.

Limbacher, W. J. *Dimensions of personality*. Dayton, OH.: Geo. A. Plaum, 1969.

Little, V. L., & Kendall, P. C. Cognitive-behavioral interventions with delinquents: Problem solving, role-taking, and self-control. In P. C. Kendall and S. D. Hollon (Eds.), *Cognitive-Behavioral Interventions Theory Research and Procedures*. New York: Academic Press, 1979.

Luria, A. *The role of speech in the regulation of normal and abnormal behaviors*. New York: Liveright, 1961.

Luria, A. Speech and formation of mental processes. In M. Cole and I. Maltzman (Eds.), *A handbook of contemporary soviet psychology*. New York: Basic Books, 1969.

Macfarlane, J., Allen, L., & Honzik, M. P. *A developmental study of the behavior problems of normal children between twenty-one months and fourteen years*. Berkeley and Los Angeles, Calif.: University of California Press, 1954.

Mahoney, M. J. *Cognition and behavior modification*. Cambridge, Mass.: Ballinger, 1974.

Mahoney, M. J. Reflections on the cognitive learning trend in psychotherapy. *American Psychologist*, 1977, *32*, 5–13.

Mahoney, M. J., & Arnkoff, D. B. Cognitive and self-control therapies. In S. L. Garfield and A. E. Bergin (Eds.), *Handbook of psychotherapy and behavior change* (2nd ed.). New York: John Wiley, 1978.

Malmquist, C. P. Childhood depression: A clinical and behavioral perspective. In J. G. Schulterbrandt and A. Raskin (Eds.), *Depression in children: Diagnosis, treatment and conceptual models*. New York: Raven Press, 1977.

Marzillier, J. S. Cognitive therapy and behavioral practice. *Behavior Research and Therapy*, 1980, *18*, 249–258.

Mash, E., & Terdal, L. *Behavior therapy assessment: Diagnosis, design and evaluation*. New York: Springer, 1976.

Mash, E., & Terdal, L. *Behavioral assessment of childhood disorders*. New York: The Guilford Press, 1981.

Maultsby, M. C., Jr. Rational emotive imagery. *Rational Living*, 1971, *6*, 24–26.

Maultsby, M. C., Jr. The classroom as an emotional health center. *The Educational Magazine*, 1974, *31*, 8–11.

Maultsby, M. C., Jr. Rational behavior therapy for acting-out adolescents. *Social Casework*, 1975, *56*, 35–43.

Maultsby, M. C., Jr. Basic principles of intensive rational behavior therapy: Theories, goals, techniques and advantages. In J. L. Wolfe and E. Brand (Eds.), *Twenty years of rational therapy*. New York: Institute for Rational Living, 1977a.

Maultsby, M. C., Jr. The evolution of rational behavior therapy. In J. L. Wolfe and E. Brand (Eds.), *Twenty years of rational therapy*. New York: Institute for Rational Living, 1977b.

Maultsby, M. C., Jr., & Ellis, A. *Techniques for using rational-emotive imagery*. New York: Institute for Rational Living, 1974.

McDaniel, E. L. *Inferred self-concept scale*. Los Angeles, Ca.: Western Psychological Services, 1973.

McFall, M. E., & Wollersteim, J. P. Obsessive-compulsive neurosis: A cognitive-behavioral formulation and approach to treatment. *Cognitive Therapy and Research*, 1979, *3*, 333–348.

McGrory, J. Teaching introspection in the classroom. *Rational Living*, 1967, *2*, 23–24.

McInerney, J. Working with parents and teachers of exceptional children. In A. Ellis and M. E. Bernard (Eds.), *Rational-emotive approaches to the problems of childhood*. New York: Plenum Press, 1983.

McMullin, R. E., Assafi, I., & Chapman, S. *Cognitive restructuring training for families*. Lakewood, Colorado: Counseling Research Institute, 1978.

McMullin, R. E., & Casey, B. *Talking sense to yourself*. Lakewood, Colorado: Counseling Research Institute, 1975.

Meichenbaum, D. Self-instruction methods. In F. H. Kanfer and A. P. Goldstein (Eds.), *Helping people change*. New York: Pergamon Press, 1974.

Meichenbaum, D. A self-instructional approach to stress inoculation training. In I. Sarason and C. D. Spielberger (Eds.), *Stress and anxiety*, Vol. 2. New York: Wiley, 1975a.

Meichenbaum, D. Enhancing creativity by modifying what subjects say to themselves. *American Educational Research Journal*, 1975b, *12*, 129–145.

Meichenbaum, D. The cognitive-behavioral management of anxiety, anger and pain. In P. Davidson (Ed.), *Behavioral management of anxiety and depression and pain*. New York: Brunner–Mazel, 1976.

Meichenbaum, D. *Cognitive-behavior modification: An integrative approach*. New York: Plenum, 1977.

Meichenbaum, D. Teaching children self-control. In B. Lahey and A. Kazdin (Eds.), *Advances in child psychology*, Vol. 2. New York: Plenum, 1979.

Meichenbaum, D., & Asarnow, J. Cognitive-behavioral modification and metacognitive development: Implications for the classroom. In P. C. Kendall and S. D. Hollon (Eds.), *Cognitive-behavioral interventions: Theory, research and procedures*. New York: Academic Press, 1979.

Meichenbaum, D., & Cameron, R. *Stress inoculation: A skills training approach to anxiety management*. Unpublished manuscript, University of Waterloo, 1973a.

Meichenbaum, D., & Cameron, R. Training schizophrenics to talk to themselves: A means of developing attentional controls. *Behavior Therapy*, 1973b, *4*, 515–534.

Meichenbaum, D., & Goodman, J. Training implusive children to talk to themselves: A means of developing self-control. *Journal of Abnormal Psychology*, 1971, *77*, 115–126.

Meichenbaum, D., & Novaco, R. W. Stress inoculation: A preventative approach. In C. Spielberger and I. Sarason (Eds.), *Stress and anxiety*, Vol. 5. New York: Halstead Press, 1978.

Meichenbaum, D., & Turk, D. *The cognitive-behavioral management of anxiety, anger and pain*. Paper presented at the Seventh Banff International Conference on Behavior Modification, 1975.

Merluzzi, T. V., Glass, C. R., & Genest, M. (Eds.), *Cognitive assessment*. New York: The Guilford Press, 1981.

Merrifield, C., & Merrifield, R. *Call me RET-man and have a ball*. Institute for Rational Living, New York. 1979.

Metalsky, G. I., & Abramson, L. Y. Attributional styles: Toward a framework for conceptualization and assessment. In P. C. Kendall and S. D. Hollon (Eds.), *Assessment strategies for cognitive-behavioral interventions*. New York: Academic Press, 1981.

Meyer, D. J. *Effects of rational-emotive group therapy upon anxiety and self-esteem of learning-disabled children*. Unpublished doctoral dissertation, Andrews University, 1982.

Miller, G. A., Galanter, E., & Pribram, K. N. *Plans and the structure of behavior*. New York: Holt, Rinehart and Winston, 1960.

Miller, L. C. Louisville behavior checklist for males, 6–12 years of age. *Psychological Reports*, 1967, *21*, 885–896.

Miller, L. C. School behavior checklist: An inventory of deviant behavior for elementary school children. *Journal of Consulting and Clinical Psychology*, 1972, *38*, 134–144.

Miller, N. J. *Effects of behavioral rehearsal, written homework and level of intelligence on the efficacy of rational-emotive education in elementary school children*. Ph.D. dissertation, Hofstra University, 1978.

Miller, R., Brickman, P., & Bolen, D. Attribution versus persuasion as a means for modifying behavior. *Journal of Personality and Social Psychology*, 1975, *31*, 430–441.

Minuchin, S. *Families and family therapy*. Cambridge, Mass.: Harvard University Press, 1974.

Mischel, W. Toward a cognitive social learning reconceptualization of personality. *Psychological Review*, 1973, *80*, 252–283.

Mischel, W., Zeiss, R., & Zeiss, A. Internal–external control and persistence: Validation and implications of the Stanford Preschool Internal–External Scale. *Journal of Personality and Social Psychology*, 1974, *29*, 265–278.

Morris, C. W., & Cohen, R. Cognitive considerations in cognitive behavior modification. *School Psychological Review*, 1982, *11*, 14–20.

Morris, K. T., & Kanitz, H. M. *Rational emotive therapy*. Boston, Mass.: Houghton Mifflin, 1975.

Muirden, G. Violence is a school problem. *Associate News*, June 28, 1976, 12–13.

Muro, J. J., & Dinkmeyer, D. C. *Counseling in the elementary and middle schools*. Dubuque, Iowa: Wm. C. Brown, 1977.

Murray, E. J. *Motivation and emotion*. Englewood Cliffs, N.J.: Prentice–Hall, 1964.

Murray, E. J., & Jacobson, L. J. Cognition and learning in traditional and behavioral therapy. In S. L. Garfield and A. E. Bergin (Eds.), *Handbook of psychotherapy and behavior change* (2nd ed.). New York: John Wiley, 1978.

Muss, R. E. The relationship between "casual" orientation anxiety and insecurity in elementary school children. *Journal of Educational Psychology*, 1960, *51*, 122–129.

Nardi, T. J. The use of psychodrama in RET. *Rational Living*, 1979, *14*, 35–38.

Nardi, T. J. Irrational beliefs of an adopted child. *RET Work*, 1981, *1*, 2–4.

Nay, W. R. *Multimethod clinical assessment*, New York: Gardner, 1979.

Nelson, W. M. *Cognitive-behavior strategies in modifying an impulsive cognitive style*. Unpublished doctoral dissertation, Virginia Commonwealth University, 1976.

Nisbett, R., & Wilson, T. D. Telling more than we can know: Verbal reports on mental processes. *Psychological Review*, 1977, *84*, 231–259.

Novaco, R. W. *A treatment program for the management of anger through cognitive and relaxation control*. Unpublished doctoral dissertation, Indiana University, Bloomington, Indiana, 1974.

Novaco, R. W. Anger and coping with stress. In J. Foreyt and D. Rathjen (Eds.), *Cognitive behavior therapy: Therapy, research and practice*. New York: Plenum Press, 1978.

Novaco, R. W. The cognitive regulation of anger and stress. In P. C. Kendall and S. D. Hollon (Eds.), *Cognitive-behavior interventions: Theory, research and procedures*. New York: Academic Press, 1979.

Nowicki, S., Jr., & Strickland, B. R. A locus of control scale for children. *Journal of Consulting and Clinical Psychology*, 1973, *40*, 148−154.

O'Leary, K. D. The assessment of psychopathology in children. In H. C. Quay and J. S. Werry (Eds.), *Psychopathological disorders of childhood*. New York: Wiley, 1972.

Palkes, H., Stewart, M., & Freedman, J. Improvement in maze performance of hyperactive boys as a function of verbal training procedures. *Journal of Special Education*, 1972, *5*, 337−342.

Palomares, U. *Magic Circle*. La Mesa, CA: Human Development Training Institute, 1972.

Peale, N. V. *The power of positive thinking*. Englewood Cliffs, N.J.: Prentice−Hall, 1960.

Perls, F. *In and out of the garbage pail*. Lafayette, CA: Real People Press, 1969.

Peterson, D. R. Behavior problems of middle childhood. *Journal of Consulting Psychology*, 1961, *25*, 205−209.

Phillips, L., Draguns, J. G., & Bartlett, D. P. Classification of behavior disorders. In N. Hobbs (Ed.), *Issues in the classification of children* (Vol. 1). San Francisco, California: Jossey−Bass, 1975.

Piaget, J. *The moral judgement of the child* (Marjorie Gabain, translator). London: Kegan, Paul, Trench, Trubner and Co., 1932.

Piaget, J. *The origins of intelligence*. New York: Norton, 1952.

Piaget, J. Les relations entre l'intelligence en l'affectivite dans le developpement de l'enfant. *Bulletin Psychologique*, 1954, *7*, 143−150, 346−361, 522−535, 694−701.

Piaget, J. *The child's conception of the world*. New Jersey: Littlefield Adams, 1960 (originally published 1926).

Piaget, J. Intellectual evolution from adolescence to adulthood. *Human Development*, 1972, *15*, 1−12.

Piaget, J. Intelligence and affectivity: Their relationship during child development. In M. R. Rosenzwerg (Ed.), *Annual Reviews Monograph*, Palo Alto, CA: Annual Reviews Inc., 1981.

Piaget, J., & Inhelder, B. *The growth of logical thinking*. New York: Basic Books, 1958.

Platt, J. J., & Spivack, G. Problem-solving thinking of psychiatric patients. *Journal of Consulting and Clinical Psychology*, 1972, *39*, 148−151.

Platt, J. J., & Spivack, G. Studies in problem-solving thinking of psychiatric patients: Patient-control differences and factorial structure of problem-solving thinking. Paper presented at American Psychological Association, Montreal, 1973. *In Proceedings, 81st Annual Convention of the American Psychological Association*, 1973, *8*, 461−462.

Platt, J. J., Spivack, G., Altman, N., Altman, D., & Peizer, S. B. Adolescent problem-solving thinking. *Journal of Consulting and Clinical Psychology*, 1974, *42*, 787−793.

Poppen, W. A., Keat, D. B., & Maki, K. D. Idea exchange column. The talking, feeling and doing game. *Elementary School Guidance and Counseling*, 1975, *10*, 58−62.

Poppen, W. A., & Thompson, C. L. *School counseling: Theories and concepts*. Lincoln, Nebraska: Professional Educators, 1974.

Protinksy, H. Rational counseling with adolescents. *The School Counselor*, 1976, *23*, 240–246.

Quay, H. C., & Peterson, D. R. *Manual for the behavior problem checklist.* Unpublished manuscript, University of Illinois, 1967; Revised edition, University of Miami, 1975.

Raimey, V. *Misunderstandings of the self.* San Francisco: Jossey–Bass, 1975.

Rand, M. E. Rational-emotive approaches to academic underachievement. *Rational Living*, 1970, *4*, 16–18.

Rashbaum-Selig, M. Assertive training for young people. *The School Counselor*, 1976, *24*, 115–121.

Raths, L., Harmin, M., & Simon, S. B. *Values and teaching.* Colombus: Merrill, 1966.

Reese, H. W. Verbal mediation as a function of age. *Psychological Bulletin*, 1962, *59*, 502–509.

Reese, H. W., & Overton, W. F. Models of development and theories of development. In L. R. Goulet and P. B. Baltes (Eds.), *Life-span developmental psychology: Research and theory.* New York: Academic Press, 1970.

Rhodes, S. L. Short-term groups of latency-age children in a school setting. *International Journal of Group Psychotherapy*, 1973, *23*, 204–16.

Ritchie, B. C. The effect of rational emotive education on irrational beliefs, assertiveness and/or locus of control in fifth gade students. *Dissertation Abstracts International*, 1978, *39* (4B), 2069–2070.

Robbins, S. *REE and the human development program. A comparative outcome study.* Unpublished doctoral dissertation, 1976.

Rogers, C. R. *Client-centered therapy.* Cambridge, Mass.: Riversdale Press, 1951.

Rogers, C. R. *On becoming a person.* Boston: Houghton Mifflin, 1961.

Rogers, C. R. *Freedom to learn.* Colombus: Merrill, 1969.

Rosen, H. Pathway to Piaget: *A guide for clinicians, educators and developmentalists.* Cherry Hill, N.J.: Postgraduate International, 1977.

Ross, A. O. Behavior therapy with children. In S. L. Garfield and A. E. Begin (Eds.), *Handbook of psychotherapy and behavior change: An empirical analysis.* New York: John Wiley & Sons, 1978.

Ross, A. O. *Psychological disorders of children* (2nd edition). New York: McGraw–Hill, 1980.

Ross, A. O., Lacey, H. M., & Parton, D. A. The development of a behavior checklist for boys. *Child Development*, 1965, *36*, 1013–1027.

Ross, H. *Fears of children.* Chicago: S. R. A. Associates, 1978.

Rossi, A. S. RET with children: More than child's play. *Rational Living*, 1977, *12*, 21–24.

Rothbaum, F. Children's clinical syndromes and generalized expectations of control. *Advances in Child Development*, 1980, *15*, 207–246.

Rotter, J. B. Generalized expectations for internal versus external control of reinforcement. *Psychological Monographs*, 1966, *80* (1), 1–26.

Rotter, J. B. *Social learning and clinical psychology.* Englewood Cliffs, N.J.: Prentice–Hall, 1954.

Rutter, M., Lebovaci, S., Eisenberg, L., Snevnevskij, A. V., Sadoun, R., Brook, E., &

Lin, T. Y. A triaxical classification of mental disorders in childhood. *Journal of Child Psychology and Psychiatry*, 1969, *10*, 41–61.

Rutter, M. & Schaffer, D. DSM-III. A step forward or back in terms of the classification of child psychiatric disorders? *Journal of the American Academy of Child Psychiatry*, 1980, *19*, 371–394.

Ryall, M. R., & Dietiker, K. E. Reliability and clinical validity of the children's fear survey schedule. *Journal of Behavior Therapy and Experimental Psychiatry*, 1979, *10*, 303–309.

Sachs, N.J. Planned emotional education: The living school. *Art in Daily Living*, 1971, *1*, 8–13.

Sapon-Shevin, M. Teaching co-operation in early childhood settings. In G. Cartledge and J. F. Milburn (Eds.), *Teaching social skills to children. Innovative approaches.* New York: Pergamon Press, 1980.

Schacter, S. The interaction of cognitive and physiological determinants of emotional state. In C. Spielberger (Ed.), *Anxiety and behavior.* New York: Academic Press, 1966.

Schaefer, C. E., & Millman, H. L. *Therapies for children.* San Francisco, Calif.: Jossey–Bass, 1978.

Schleser, R., Meyers, A., & Cohen, R. Generalization of self-instructions: Effects of general versus specific content, active rehearsal and cognitive level. *Child Development*, 1981, *52*, 335–340.

Schneider, M., & Robin, A. The turtle technique: A method for the self-control of impulsive behavior. In J. Krumboltz and C. Thorensen (Eds.), *Counseling methods.* New York: Holt, Rinehart and Winston, 1976.

Segrave, J. Stress inoculation program for children. Unpublished manuscript. Department of Education, University of Melbourne, 1979.

Seligman, M. E. P. *Helplessness.* San Francisco: W. H. Freeman, 1975.

Sheppard, M., Oppenheim, B., & Mitchell, S. *Childhood behavior and mental health.* New York: Grune and Stratton, 1979.

Shibbles, W. Emotion: *A critical analysis for children.* Whitewater, Wisc.: Language Press, 1978.

Shockey, C., & Whiteman, V. Development of the rational behavior inventory: Initial validity and reliability. *Educational and Psychological Measurement*, 1977, *37*, 527–534.

Shure, M. B., & Spivack, G. Cognitive problem-solving skills, adjustment and social class. *Research and Evaluation Report #26.* Philadelphia. Department of Mental Health Sciences, Hahnemann Community Mental Health, 1970.

Shure, M. B. & Spivack, G. *A mental health program for pre-school and kindergarten children and a mental health program for mothers of young children: An interpersonal problem-solving approach towards social adjustment.* A comprehensive report of research and training. No. MH-20372. Washington D.C.: National Institute of Mental Health, Mental Retardation Center, 1976.

Siegler, R. S., Liebert, D. E., & Liebert, R. M. Inhelder and Piaget's pendulum problem: Teaching preadolescents to act as scientists. *Developmental Psychology*, 1975, *11*, 401–402.

Simon, S. B. *Meeting yourself half-way.* Niles, Ill. Argus Communications, 1974.

Simon, S. B., Howe, L., & Kirschenbaum, H. *Values clarification*. New York: Hart, 1972.

Simon, S. B., Kirschenbaum, H., & Fuhrmann, B. *An introduction to values clarification*. New York: Hart, 1972.

Smith, D. Trends in counseling and psychotherapy. *American Psychologist*, 1982, *37*, 802–809.

Sparks, D. G. Group goal setting. *The School Counselor*, 1978, *25*, 235–238.

Spivack, G. & Levine, M. *Self-regulation in acting-out and normal adolescents*. Report M-4531, National Institute for Health, Washington, D.C., 1963.

Spivack, G. & Levine, M. The Devereux child behavior rating scales: A study of symptom behaviors in latency age atypical children. *American Journal of Mental Deficiency*, 1964, *68*, 700–717.

Spivack, G., Platt, J., & Shure, M. *The problem-solving approach to adjustment*. San Francisco, CA: Jossey–Bass, 1976.

Spivack, G., & Shure, M.B. *Social adjustment of young children: A cognitive approach to solving real-life problems*. San Francisco, CA: Jossey–Bass, 1974.

Spivack, G., & Spotts, J. *Devereux child behavior rating scale manual*. Devon, PA: Devereux Foundation, 1976.

Spivack, G., & Swift, M. *Devereux elementary school behavior rating scale*. Devon, PA: Devereux Foundation, 1976.

Staats, A. W. Conditioned stimuli, conditioned reinforcers and word meaning. In A. W. Staats (Ed.), *Human Learning*. New York: Holt, Rinehart and Winston, 1964.

Staggs, A. M. *Group counseling of learning disabled children in the intermediate grades enrolled in the public school special education program: Training in cognitive behavior modification*. Unpublished doctoral dissertation, 1979.

Stephens, M. W., & Delys, P. A locus of control measure for preschool children. *Developmental Psychology*, 1973, *9*, 55–65.

Stipek, D. J., & Weisz, J. R. Perceived personal control and academic achievement. *Review of Educational Research*, 1981, *51*, 101–138.

Stone, L. L., & Church, J. *Childhood and adolescence* (4th Ed.). New York: Random House, 1979.

Strupp, N. N. Towards a specification of teaching and learning in psychotherapy. *Archives of General Psychiatry*, 1969, *21*, 203–212.

Suinn, R. M., & Richardson, F. Anxiety management training: A non-specific behavior therapy program for anxiety control. *Behavioral Therapy*, 1971, *2*, 498–510.

Sulzer-Azaroff, B., & Mayer, G. R. *Applying behavior-analysis procedures with children and youth*. New York: Holt, Rinehart and Winston, 1977.

Sutton-Simon, K. Assessing belief systems: Concepts and strategies. In P. C. Kendall and S. D. Hollon (Eds.), *Assessment strategies for cognitive-behavioral interventions*. New York: Academic Press, 1981.

Taylor, M. H. A rational-emotive workshop on overcoming study blocks. *Personnel and Guidance Journal*, 1975, *53*, 458–462.

Tharp, R. G., & Wetzel, R. J. *Behavior modification in the natural environment*. New York: Academic Press, 1969.

Thayer, L. (Ed.), *Affective education: Strategies for experiential learning*. La Jolla, Calif.: University Associates, 1976.

Thayer, L., & Beeler, K. D. *Activities and exercises for affective education*. Ypislanti, Mich.: Eastern Michigan University, 1975.

Thompson, C. L., & Poppen, W. A. *Guidance for the elementary school*. Springfield, Tenn: Robertson Country Board of Education, 1974.

Thoresen, C. E., & Mahoney, M. J. *Behavioral self-control*. New York: Holt, Rinehart and Winston, 1974.

Tidiwell, R., & Bachus, V. Group counseling for aggressive school children. *Elementary School Guidance and Counseling*, 1977, *12*, 2–7.

Tolman, E. C. Psychology versus immediate experience. *Philosophy and Science*, 1935, *2*, 356–380.

Toolan, J. M. Depression in children and adolescents. *American Journal of Orthopsychiatry*, 1962, *32*, 404–414.

Tosi, D. J. *Youth: Toward personal growth, a rational-emotive approach*. Columbus, Ohio: Charles E. Merrill, 1974.

Tosi, D. J., & Reardon, J. The treatment of guilt through rational stage directed imagery. *Rational Living*, 1976, *11*, 8–11.

Treffinger, D. J., Borgers, S. B., Render, G. F., & Hoffman, R. M. Encouraging affective development. A compendium of techniques and resources. *Gifted Children Quarterly*, 1976, *20*, 47–65.

Trunnell, T. Thought disturbances in schizophrenia: Replication study using Piaget's theories. *Archives General Psychiatry*, 1965, *13*, 1–18.

Tulving, E. Episodic and semantic memory. In E. Tulving and N. Donaldson (Eds.), *Organization of memory*. New York: Academic Press, 1972.

Turk, D. *Cognitive control of pain: A skills training approach for the treatment of pain*. Unpublished master's thesis, University of Waterloo, 1975.

Ullman, C. P. On cognitions and behavior therapy. *Behavior Therapy*, 1970, *1*, 201–204.

United States Commission on Mental Health. *Task panel reports submitted to the President's Commission on Mental Health, Vol II*. Washington, D.C.: U.S. Government Printing Office, 1978.

Valett, R. E. *Affective-humanistic education: Goals, programs and learning activities*. Belmont, CA: Fearon, 1974.

Vernon, A. *Help yourself to a healthier you*. Washington: University Press of America, 1980.

Vygotsky, L. S. *Thought and language*. New York: Wiley, 1962.

Wagner, E. E. Rational counseling with children. *School Psychologist*, 1965, *9*, 3–8.

Wagner, E. E. Counseling children. *Rational Living*, 1966, *1*, 26, 28.

Wagner, E. E. & Glicken, M. Counseling children: Two accounts. *Rational Living*, 1966, *1*, 26–30.

Walen, S. R., DiGuiseppe, R., & Wessler, R. L. *A practitioner's guide to rational-emotive therapy*. New York: Oxford University Press, 1980.

Wallace, J. An abilities conception of personality: Some implications for personality measurement. *American Psychologist*, 1966, *21*, 138–188.

Warren, L. R. *An evaluation of rational emotive imagery as a component of rational-emotive therapy in the treatment of interpersonal anxiety in junior high school students*. Unpublished doctoral dissertation. University of Oregon, 1978.

Warren, R., Deffenbach, J., & Broding, P. rational-emotive therapy and the reduction of test anxiety in elementary school students. *Rational Living*, 1976, *11*, 28–29.

Wasserman, T. H., & Vogrin, D. J. Relationship of endorsement of rational beliefs, age, months treatment and intelligence to overt behavior of emotionally disturbed children. *Psychological Reports*, 1979, *44*, 911–917.

Waters, V. *Color us rational*. New York: Institute for Rational Living, 1979.

Waters, V. Series of pamphlets for parents: *Accepting yourself and your child; Teaching children to light up their lives: The power of rational thinking; Building frustration tolerance in you and your child; The anger trap and how to spring it; Fear interferes; Rational problem-solving skills*. New York: Institute for Rational Living, 1980a.

Waters, V. Series of stories for children: *Cornelia Cardinal learns to cope; Fasha, Dasha and Sasha Squirrel; Flora Farber's fear of failure; Freddie Flounder; Maxwell's magnificent monster*. New York: Institute for Rational Living, 1980b.

Waters, V. The living school. *RETwork*, 1981, *1*, 1.

Waters, V. Therapies for children: Rational emotive therapy. In C. R. Reynolds and T. B. Gutkin (Eds.), *Handbook of school psychology*. New York: John Wiley and Sons, 1982a.

Waters, V. RET with a child client. Unpublished manuscript. 1982b.

Weinberg, W. A., Rutman, J., Sullivan, L., Penick, E. G., & Dietz, S. G. Depression in children referred to an educational diagnostic center: Diagnosis and treatment. *Journal of Pediatrics*, 1973, *83*, 1065–1072.

Weiner, B. (Ed.), *Achievement motivation and attribution theory*. Morristown, N.J.: General Learning Press, 1974.

Weinstein, G., & Fantini, M. D. *Toward humanistic education: A curriculum of affect*. New York: Praeger, 1970.

Weissberg, R. P., & Gesten, E. Considerations for developing effective school-based social problem-solving (SPS) training programs. *School Psychology Review*, 1982, *11*, 56–63.

Weissberg, R. P., Gesten, E., Rapkin, B. D., Cowen, E. L. Davidson, E., Flores de Apodaca, R. & McKim, B. J. Evaluation of a social-problem-solving training program for suburban and inner-city third-grade children. *Journal of Consulting and Clinical Psychology*. 1981, *49*, 251–261.

Wessler, R. A., & Wessler, R. L. *The principles and practice of rational-emotive therapy* San Francisco, Cal.: Jossey–Bass, 1980.

Wilson, S. B., & London T. Rational behavior education with young adults. *Rational Living*, 1977, *12*, 16–19.

Wolfe, J., & Staff. Emotional education in the classroom: The living school. *Rational Living*, 1970, *4*, 23–25.

Wolpe, J. *The practice of behavior therapy*. New York: Pergamon, 1973.

Woollacott, H. Causal attributions in children's academic performance. Unpublished master of arts thesis, The University of Melbourne, Australia, 1978.

Woulff, N. Involving the family in the treatment of the child: A model for rational-emotive therapists. In A. Ellis and M. E. Bernard (Eds.), *Rational-emotive approaches to the problems of childhood*. New York: Plenum Press, 1983.

Young, H. S. A framework for working with adolescents. *Rational Living*, 1974a, *9*, 2−7.

Young, H. S. *A rational counseling primer*. New York: Institute for Rational Living, 1974b.

Young, H. S. Counseling strategies with working class adolescents. In J. L. Wolfe and E. Brand (Eds.), *Twenty years of rational therapy*. New York: Institute for Rational Living, 1977.

Young, H. S. Principles of assessment and methods of treatment with adolescents: Special considerations. In A. Ellis and M. E. Bernard (Eds.), *Rational-emotive approaches to the problems of childhood*. New York: Plenum Press, 1983.

Zajonc, R. B. Feeling and thinking. *American Psychologist,* 1980, *35*, 151−175.

Zolotow, C. *The hating book*. N.Y.: Harper and Row, 1969.

Author Index

Subject Index